STRIVING AND FEELING
Interactions Among Goals, Affect, and Self-Regulation

Edited by

Leonard L. Martin
Abraham Tesser
University of Georgia

1996

LAWRENCE ERLBAUM ASSOCIATES, PUBLISHERS
Mahwah, New Jersey

The participants in the Goals and Affect conference at the University of Georgia were as follows:

1. Jefferson Singer
2. Keith Oatley
3. Duane Wegener
4. Paula Niedenthal
5. Robert Emmons
6. Peter Salovey
7. Abraham Tesser
8. Edward Hirt
9. Judith Harackiewicz
10. Richard Petty
11. Charles Carver
12. Ralph Erber
13. Timothy Strauman
14. Jamin Halberstadt
15. Hugh McDonald
16. Leonard Martin
17. Kristin Kling
18. Carol Sansone
19. Carolin Showers
20. William McIntosh

STRIVING AND FEELING
Interactions Among Goals, Affect,
and Self-Regulation

Copyright © 1996, by Lawrence Erlbaum Associates, Inc.

All rights reserved. No part of the book may be reproduced in any form, by photostat, microform, retrieval system, or any other means, without the prior written permission of the publisher.

Lawrence Erlbaum Associates, Inc., Publishers
10 Industrial Ave.
Mahwah, New Jersey 07430-2262

Library of Congress Cataloging in Publication Data

Striving and feeling : interactions among goals, affect, and self
  -regulation / edited by Leonard Martin, Abraham Tesser.
     p.   cm.
  Includes bibliographical references and index.
  ISBN 0-8058-1629-1 (cloth). — ISN 0-8058-2039-6 (pbk.)
  1. Goal (Psychology) 2. Motivation (Psychology) 3. Affect
(Psychology) I. Martin, Leonard L. II. Tesser, Abraham.
BF504.S77   1995
152.4—dc20   95-15793
                                                                    CIP

Books published by Lawrence Erlbaum Associates are printed on acid-free paper, and their bindings are chosen for strength and durability.

Printed in the United States of America

10 9 8 7 6 5 4 3 2 1

Contents

Preface   ix

1 Introduction
Leonard L. Martin and Abraham Tesser   1

PART I: AFFECTIVE AND BEHAVIORAL CONSEQUENCES OF GOALS

2 A Control-Process Perspective on the Origins of Affect
Charles S. Carver, John W. Lawrence, and Michael F. Scheier   11

3 When Does Goal Nonattainment Lead to Negative Emotional Reactions, and When Doesn't It?: The Role of Linking and Rumination
W. D. McIntosh   53

4 Goal Orientation and Emotional Well-Being: Linking Goals and Affect Through the Self
Robert A. Emmons and Heather A. Kaiser   79

5 The "What the Hell" Effect: Some Effects of Goal Proximity and Goal Framing on Performance
Winona Cochran and Abraham Tesser   99

PART II: AFFECTIVE CONSEQUENCES OF SELF-ORGANIZATION AND SELF-REGULATION

6 Cognitive Organization of Different Tenses of the Self Mediates Affect and Decision Making
Jamin B. Halberstadt, Paula M. Niedenthal, and Marc B. Setterlund — 123

7 The Organization of Self-Knowledge: Implications for Mood Regulation
Carolin J. Showers and Kristen C. Kling — 151

8 Self-Beliefs, Self-Evaluation, and Depression: A Perspective on Emotional Vulnerability
Timothy J. Strauman — 175

9 "I Don't Feel Like It": The Function of Interest in Self-Regulation
Carol Sansone and Judith M. Harackiewicz — 203

10 Motivated Memory: Self-Defining Memories, Goals, and Affect Regulation
Jefferson A. Singer and Peter Salovey — 229

11 The Self-Regulation of Moods
Ralph Erber — 251

PART III: HOW GOALS AND AFFECT INFLUENCE OTHER PROCESSES

2 Mood as Input: What We Think About How We Feel Determines How We Think
Leonard L. Martin and Peggy Stoner — 279

13 Processing Goals and the Affect–Performance Link: Mood as Main Effect or Mood as Input?
Edward R. Hirt, Hugh E. McDonald, and R. Jeffrey Melton — 303

14 Effects of Mood on Persuasion Processes: Enhancing, Reducing, and Biasing Scrutiny of Attitude-Relevant Information
Duane T. Wegener and Richard E. Petty — 329

15 The Communicative Theory of Emotions: Empirical Tests, Mental Models, and Implications for Social Interaction
Keith Oatley and Philip N. Johnson-Laird   363

Author Index   395

Subject Index   407

Preface

This book attempts to integrate two recent lines of research—one that explores the effects of goals on people's feelings and one that explores the role of goals in moderating the influence of people's feelings on their thoughts and behaviors. The general aim of the book is to bring together investigators who are operating from new, integrative perspectives, and who are giving us new ways to think about goals and affect.

A number of studies have shown that people in positive moods often use short-cuts in their cognitive processing, whereas people in negative moods process information more systematically. Recent studies have qualified these findings by showing that these effects depend not only on people's moods but also on their goals. When people are faced with a task in which they must process to some criterion of accuracy or confidence, for example (as in solving anagrams to demonstrate their intelligence), those in negative moods process more systematically than those in positive moods, replicating the initial research. When people perceive their task as a source of fun or enjoyment, however (as when they are solving anagrams for fun), then a reverse finding is obtained: those in positive moods process more systematically than those in negative moods.

At the same time that this work was proceeding, a separate line of work was demonstrating the importance of goals in determining the valence and intensity of people's moods. This work showed us, for example, that people feel better upon attaining their goals than upon not attaining them. This outcome is qualified, however, by the type of goal (want vs. ought), and by people's beliefs about the consequences of attaining a specific outcome (e.g., its relation to a higher order goal). If two people are overweight, for example, the one who thinks that the excess weight will lead him or her to be less popular will be more depressed than the one who does not believe this.

In short, the recent social psychological literature has presented us with two lines of research showing a relationship between goals and affective states and have presented us with a series of studies that suggest qualifications or extensions of the initial work. Although these two lines are clearly related, they have proceeded relatively independently of one another. The point of this book is to bring together in one place the prominent researchers in each of these leading-edge areas. It is our hope that a book that pulls this new work together will not only be interesting in its own right, but may also lend some coherence to what are currently separate (yet related) lines of work.

The book grew out of a conference organized by the authors and sponsored by Dr. William Prokasy, the Vice President for Academic Affairs at the University of Georgia. We would like to thank not only Dr. Prokasy but also the following for helping to make the conference a success: Dr. Joseph Allen, Ike Chang, Nicole Chen, Julie Cline, Jon Collins, Gilda Ivory, Sharron Thompson, and Dan Whitaker. Finally, we would like to thank Weaver D's Fine Foods ("Automatic!"), Spring House Barbecue, the Last Resort, Inoko Japanese Restaurant, the 40-Watt Club, The Go-Figures, and the Sony Jaminator for making the conference fun as well as intellectually stimulating.

1 Introduction

Leonard L. Martin
Abraham Tesser
University of Georgia

In Gordon Allport's (1985) classic definition, social psychology was described as the scientific investigation of people's thoughts, feelings, and behaviors as a function of the real, imagined, or implied presence of other people. A review of the field reveals that this definition has remained fairly accurate over the years. Of course, the field's central emphasis has fluctuated between thinking, feeling, and behavior. For example, the plethora of person memory studies in the 1980s led some people to describe that era as the decade of cognition. Based on a count of the number of current studies involving affect as a central component, one might be led to conclude that the 1990s is the decade of affect. We believe, however, that the current emphasis on affect has not come at the expense of either cognition or behavior. In fact, there are a number of researchers conducting integrative work on affect, cognition, and behavior, and some of these have contributed to this volume. More specifically, the volume reports on research examining the separate and interactive effects of goals and affect on people's thoughts, feelings, and behaviors.

The volume began as a conference organized by the editors and sponsored by the University of Georgia's vice president for academic affairs. For three days, the contributors and editors met in Athens, Georgia, to present data, discuss the implications of this data, and generally have a good time interacting. The chapters in this volume grew out of these presentations, discussions, and interactions.

The chapters are organized into three broad sections. Part 1 involves the affective and behavioral consequences of goals, Part 2 involves the affective consequences of self-organization and self-regulation, and Part 3 involves the role of affect in a number of processes (i.e., affect as an independent rather than a dependent variable).

In chapter 2, Carver, Lawrence, and Scheier describe a way in which their control theory of self-regulation can account for affect. According to control theory, people engage in a continual process of establishing goals and intentions, and adjusting current patterns of behavior so as to more closely match these values, using informational feedback as a guide to progress. Carver, Lawrence, and Scheier assume that affect is not influenced directly by a discrepancy between goals and current behavior. Rather, it is influenced by the perceived rate of discrepancy reduction (velocity) and by perceived changes in rate of discrepancy reduction (acceleration). This view of affect implies a mechanism within the organism that actively prevents the too-frequent occurrence of negative as well as positive feelings. The advantage of such a mechanism is that it allows people to balance their attention and effort between various strivings. Evidence consistent with this model is presented, and implications for goal setting and different types of emotions (elation–depression, relief–anxiety) are discussed.

McIntosh explores the processes by which some people become more heavily invested in goal pursuit than others and with what consequence. To do this, he considers differences in people's beliefs about goal attainment. Linkers are people who interpret nonattainment of lower order goals (e.g., ideal weight) as threats to the attainment of higher order goals (i.e., happiness). Nonlinkers do not make this interpretation. These differences in goal beliefs are discussed in terms of their implications for happiness, rumination, negative affect, depression, physical illness, and mood repair. McIntosh concludes with some suggestions as to how people might avoid negative emotional reactions to goal nonattainment and ends with a discussion of the relation between linking and other constructs.

Emmons and Kaiser suggest that irrespective of the content of one's goal pursuits, individual differences in goal setting and striving have important ramifications for a person's emotional life. Generally speaking, personal goal systems are precursors of life satisfaction and long-term positive and negative affective states. Their chapter addresses different types of individual differences in goal orientations, including level of specification, approach versus avoidance, conflicts between goals, and differentiation between goals. The effects of these different goal orientations are discussed primarily in terms of subjective well-being and reports of physical illness. Emmons and Kaiser conclude that goals capture affectively charged themes that are central to a person's life and that these goals emerge from and determine the nature of the person's transactions with the social world.

Cochran and Tesser address an interesting but perplexing breakdown in self-regulation known as the "what the hell?" effect. They ask why goal nonattainment sometimes leads people to engage in behaviors that lead them even further from attaining their goals. For example, after exceeding his or her desired calorie intake at lunch, a dieter may say "What the hell, I've already blown it for the day. I may just as well get the banana split for dessert." Cochran and Tesser review and discount several possible explanations of this effect. Then, they present a model that implicates the interaction of goal proximity and goal framing (i.e., avoidance vs. approach). They present evidence consistent with this model and discuss the implications of their work for the effectiveness of self-regulation more generally.

Part 2 begins with Halberstadt, Niedenthal, and Setterlund's exploration of the role of self-complexity in affective reactions. Halberstadt et al. suggest that people do not possess a single unitary mental representation of who they are. Rather, people have representations of who they are, who they have been, and who they could be and will be. In this chapter, the authors focus on people's conceptions of their future selves. The authors present evidence that the future self is distinct from other self-concepts, that people vary in their degree of future self-complexity, and that this complexity accounts for affective reactivity. Halberstadt, Niedenthal, and Setterlund also discuss the role of future self-complexity in performance and decisions relevant to future behavior and suggest other domains to which a future self-complexity analysis might be fruitfully applied.

Showers and Kling outline a theoretical framework that describes the relationships between specific self-regulatory goals and distinct types of self-concept organization. They suggest that the organization of self-information, and not just its content, can influence self-evaluation. The differences they explore are between compartmentalized and evaluatively integrated organization. Compartmentalized selves have positive and negative beliefs in distinct categories and are associated with extreme affective reactions. Integrated selves have positive and negative beliefs mixed within a single category and are associated with mild affective reactions. Showers and Kling further note that while organization can influence affective reactions, people's goals and affect can also influence the organization of their self-concepts. Finally, Showers and Kling discuss the advantages and disadvantages of each type of self-organization and indicate when each is likely to occur.

Strauman presents a theory of the relation between self-evaluation and vulnerability to negative mood states. According to the theory, people learn the emotional consequences of their behavior and the stimuli related to those consequences. This learning may involve the development of a representation of people's reactions to our behavior. These representations, in turn, operate as self-guides, possessing inherent emotional and motivational significance. As children develop the capacity for continuous, largely unintended self-evaluation, they may also experience affective states for reasons that are not necessarily accessible to awareness (i.e., automatic self-evaluations). Strauman's model depicts a general pathway to a final dysregulated state that could result in clinical depression. The role of biological factors, traumatic life events, and cognitive and personality development are also discussed.

Sansone and Harackiewicz explore the possibility that explanations of the form "I felt like it" or "I didn't feel like it" may, under some conditions, be legitimate explanations for behavior. More generally, they explore the mediating role of phenomenal experience in motivating performance. They note that most current approaches to behavior regulation are teleological in orientation. That is, most models hypothesize that people's motivation depends on and is defined in terms of the potential outcomes of their actions. Sansone and Harackiewicz suggest that in some conditions what an individual feels like doing may be the more vivid and compelling determinant of the individual's action. They suggest that the coordination and regulation of process-derived and outcome-derived motivation may be the essential task of self-regulation. The model they present represents a bridge between research on self-regulation and research on intrinsic motivation.

Singer and Salovey start with the observation that purely associationistic, mechanistic models cannot account for the mood-memory link. They suggest that conscious recruitment of memories may provide people with vital cognitive and affective information about the status of future events and desired events. A specific kind of memory, those they call self-defining, are particularly useful in this regard. Self-defining memories are those that are affectively intense, vivid, repetitive, linked to similar memories, and focus on an unresolved conflict in one's life. Singer and Salovey suggest that people come to know themselves and be known by others through the repetition of these memories. Individuals may retrieve memories selectively relevant to the attainment of desired goals as a means of self-encouragement in the pursuit of these goals. In short, self-defining memories may provide an affective "virtual reality" that makes meaningful the effect of goal attainment or nonattainment. Evidence consistent with this hypothesis is discussed.

Erber provides a theoretical and empirical account of the conditions that are likely to elicit attempts toward mood regulation and discusses the processes that are likely to be effective toward this end. He begins by assessing the widely held assumption that people always seek out and preserve good moods while at the same avoiding or repairing bad moods. His conclusion is that this assumption paints an oversimplified picture of people's mood regulation tendencies. Erber's suggestion for a more complete model involves the consideration of goals and social context, and this suggestion is spelled out in his social contingency model. According to this model, people modify their moods not just in response to what is positive but in response to perceptions of what is appropriate or fitting given the social constraints on their behavior and emotions. Evidence consistent with this view is discussed.

Part 3 begins with Martin and Stoner's exploration of the effects of moods on cognitive processing. They begin with the assumption that there are few, if any, effects that follow directly from the mere fact that one is experiencing a certain mood. They suggest, instead, that the effects of any given mood depend upon the context within which the mood is experienced. They present evidence for this so-called *mood as input* model and compare this model with others that assume that affective states give rise to specific predispositions (e.g., to process in a heuristic manner) that can then be overridden with effort (e.g., instructions to pay attention). A variety of phenomena (e.g., creativity, categorization, evaluation) are addressed and are interpreted in terms of the mood as input model.

Hirt, McDonald, and Melton investigate the manner in which mood influences processing and performance. They note that a perusal of the literature shows conflicting results that cannot be easily accommodated by the existing models. Next, they describe the view that moods have stable, predictable effects on processing and thus on performance. This is compared with the view that moods have no stable processing implications and that the effects of moods on performance depend on people's current processing goals. Hirt, McDonald, and Melton discuss a study that found support for both models and that also found support for direct as well as mediated effects of mood (i.e., task interest). Finally, the authors address some factors that might moderate these effects and suggest that the mood as main effect and the mood as input models can peacefully co-exist.

Wegener and Petty explore the way in which moods influence attitude change. They suggest that the currently diverse literature on mood effects in persuasion could be organized in terms of the goals message recipients have when they encounter persuasive appeals. Wegener and Petty begin with a description of the role of elaboration likelihood (i.e., the extent to which people are either motivated or able to think carefully about the substantive information in a persuasive communication) in determining the process by which attitude change takes place. Following this, they outline their hedonic contingency hypothesis that emphasizes the role of mood management in determining the effects of mood on persuasion. Evidence consistent with this hypothesis is discussed and its relation to other models is addressed. Wegener and Petty's general conclusion is that the effects of mood appear to be more flexible than previously described and demonstrated.

Oatley and Johnson-Laird discuss their theory of emotion. They present the original version of their theory, discuss some tests and criticisms of it, discuss the relation between this and other theories, and then present a revised version of the theory. They begin with the assumption that emotions are based on signals within the brain that reflect priorities of goals and that predispose people toward appropriate classes of action. Happiness, for example, encourages people to continue doing what they are doing, whereas sadness signals an interrupt. Their theory accounts for basic emotions, derived emotions, and mixed emotions. Oatley and Johnson-Laird also discuss the implications of their theory for attachment, psychopathology, vicarious emotions, and the interaction between emotion and intellectual performance.

As can be seen, each chapter reflects the specific research of its author(s). What may be less obvious from these summaries, however, is the extent to which the chapters address common themes. These themes include:

1. *The effects of intrinsic versus extrinsic goals.* Sometimes goal objects are sought as ends in themselves. Sometimes they are sought only as means to an end. These alternate motivations have important consequences for people's performance as well as for their affective reactions upon attaining or not attaining a goal. This issue is addressed by McIntosh; Emmons and Kaiser; Sansone and Harackiewicz; and Hirt, McDonald, and Melton.

2. *The different effects of approach versus avoidance goals.* In some cases, a person's goal is to obtain some desired object or outcome (e.g., to be in good physical shape). In other cases, a person's goal may be to avoid some undesired outcome (e.g., to be in poor physical shape). These orientations have different psychological antecedents as well as different performance and affective consequences. This issue is addressed by Carver, Lawrence, and Scheier; Emmons and Kaiser; Cochran and Tesser; and Singer and Salovey.

3. *The role of awareness in goal pursuit.* When a person says that he or she has a certain goal, what is the relation of this stated goal to the person's actual goal? Can people specify the goals that are guiding their behavior? This issue is addressed by McIntosh; Emmons and Kaiser; and Sansone and Harackiewicz.

4. *The role of awareness in affective states.* When a person's affective state influences that person's performance, what is it about the affect that is doing the influencing? Is it the phenomenal experience or is it some more direct (e.g., unconscious) signal in the brain? This issue is addressed by Carver, Lawrence, and Scheier; Hirt, McDonald, and Melton; Sansone and Harackiewicz; Martin and Stoner; and Oatley and Johnson-Laird.

5. *The meaning of affective states in relation to goal attainment.* To the extent that affective states communicate information to the person experiencing those states, how specific is this information? Do certain feelings stand in one-to-one relations with certain motivations or are the relations more mutable and context dependent? This issue is addressed by Carver,

Lawrence, and Scheier; McIntosh; Erber; Martin and Stoner; Hirt, McDonald, and Melton; and Wegener and Petty.

6. *Are people really motivated by hedonistic concerns?* Presumably, if given the chance, most people would chose to experience a positive affective state over a negative one. But how far can we take this assumption? Can it form the basis of our explanations of the effects of mood on processing, or does it leave out important factors? This issue is addressed by Carver, Lawrence, and Scheier; Sansone and Harackiewicz; Erber; Hirt, McDonald, and Melton; Martin and Stoner; and Wegener and Petty.

7. *How do people regulate their moods?* Given that people do not desire the mood they are currently experiencing, what can they do to change it? When are they likely to attempt to change their moods? These questions are addressed by Showers and Kling; Sansone and Harackiewicz; Singer and Salovey; Erber; and Wegener and Petty.

8. *What is the role of the self in affective experiences?* Why are some goals more important than others? Why do some people react more strongly to goal attainment and nonattainment than do others? The answer to both questions may have something to do with people's self-concepts. The role of the self in affective experience is discussed by Halberstadt, Niedenthal, and Setterlund; Showers and Kling; Strauman; and Singer and Salovey.

In summary, we feel that each of the chapters addresses the interactions among affect, cognition, and behavior, and that there is a great deal of connection between the conceptual issues addressed in each of the chapters. We hope that this integration both within and between chapters will allow readers to derive some new insights into affect, cognition, and behavior and that this may influence their own thinking and research.

REFERENCES

Allport, G. W. (1985). The historical background of social psychology. In G. Lindzey & E. Aronson (Ed.), *Handbook of social psychology* (3rd ed., Vol. 1, pp. 1–46). New York: Random House.

Affective and Behavioral Consequences of Goals

2 A Control-Process Perspective on the Origins of Affect

Charles S. Carver
John W. Lawrence
University of Miami

Michael F. Scheier
Carnegie Mellon University

We have been interested for some time in the logical principles that are reflected in human behavior (two of us for somewhat longer than the third). The phrase *human behavior* is a very broad one, perhaps too broad to be truly informative. We are most interested in behavior at the level of abstraction that is the focus of personality and social psychology (although we are also more concerned than some people are about the fact that abstract aspects of behavior must ultimately be translated into patterns of physical action). For example, how does the intention to take a trip, or to complete a writing project, or to develop a relationship find its way into behavior? How do people deal with unanticipated obstacles that they confront along the way? Our interest in the structure of behavior led us some years ago to a set of ideas we have continued to find useful in thinking about human behavior as a process of self-regulation (Carver & Scheier, 1981).

More recently we took up a different question: how to think about the experience of emotion. Whether too old to learn new tricks, or perhaps just obstinate, we approached this question with the same conceptual tools as we had been using already to think about action. In a way, the question we posed was simply an interesting puzzle: Can the ideas we were using be informative about the nature of affect? Some would regard it as pretty unlikely, as mechanistic as those ideas were. After all, feelings are supposed to be squishy irrational aspects of the human experience. We have joined the growing chorus that says, to the contrary, that feelings are perfectly rational (e.g., de Sousa, 1987; Frijda, 1986, 1988; Greenberg, Rice, &

Elliott, 1993; Oatley, 1992; Ortony, Clore, & Collins, 1988). It's just that it isn't always obvious what their origin is and why they are arising.

In the end, we did arrive at a model of the origin of feelings using these conceptual tools (Carver & Scheier, 1990a). It is a bootstrapped model. It was generated by exploring possibilities. It may not be right, but it does have what we think are some very interesting things to say. Some of its implications are straightforward, but others are quite counterintuitive. In this chapter we explore that model and some of those implications.

GOALS AND BEHAVIOR

We begin with a brief overview of the basic principles on which the shakier part of the edifice is built (for more detail see Carver & Scheier, 1990b; a broader treatment is in preparation—Carver & Scheier, 1995). We tacitly assume a great deal about cognitive processes, although we do not dwell on it here. We assume that people impose order on their experiences based on regularities encountered across time and events, resulting in schemas in memory. We assume further that memory includes knowledge used for perceiving, construing, and interpreting and also knowledge used as prescriptions for action.

In what follows, we will treat schemas that provide prescriptions for behavior as providing *goals* for behavior. Saying that someone has taken up a behavioral goal is in some sense equivalent to saying that the person wants to manifest in his or her actions a particular quality that is represented in a knowledge structure in his or her memory.

Goals

We believe that human behavior is fundamentally goal directed, even though there are times when, either as observers or as actors, we don't know exactly what the goal behind an action is. Goals provide the structure that defines people's lives. Moreover, goals can be dynamic—not simply end points to be attained but paths to be negotiated.

Goals can exist at several levels of abstraction. The attributes of behavioral knowledge can be extremely concrete (e.g., levels of muscle tension) or they can be abstract (e.g., the quality of grace or dignity in a person's bearing or in a person's handling of a situation). Goals can be restricted in scope and quickly attained (e.g., to pick up a pencil) or they can be elaborate and attained slowly (e.g., to acquire a solid reputation in one's work, to develop a sound relationship with a partner). Since most goals imply a need for physical movement, there presumably is a translation process by which abstract aspects of schemas are translated into concrete act qualities. Although very concrete aspects of behavioral schemas are of great interest to those who contribute to the literature of motor control (e.g., Adams, 1976; Kelso, 1982; Rosenbaum, 1987; Salmoni, Schmidt, & Walter, 1984; Schmidt, 1987, 1988), we focus here primarily on goals that are of higher levels of abstraction.

The idea that human behavior—indeed personality—can be analyzed in terms of goals has been very prominent in recent years. Here are a few examples of goal constructs and the theorists who have written about them (see also Pervin, 1989). Elliott and Dweck (1988), using the simple term *goal*, emphasized how different goals can underlie achievement efforts. Klinger (1975, 1977) has used the phrase *current concern* to denote goals with which a person is now engaged; Cantor and Kihlstrom (1987) called *life tasks* the dynamic goals that occupy people at various periods of their lives; Markus and Nurius (1986) pointed to *possible selves*, representations of desired and undesired qualities of the self, goals to be attained and to be avoided. Emmons (1986) held that personality can be described in terms of patterns of *personal strivings* that characterize the individual; Palys and Little (1983) used the term *personal projects*. The notion that goals are intrinsic to human action is also implicit in Higgins's (1987) concept of *self-guide* and Vallacher and Wegner's (1985) concept of *act identification*.

Although distinctions can be made among these concepts, in each case the central theme is that human behavior is defined in terms of the person's goals. Each places an emphasis on the idea that understanding a person means understanding the person's goals.

From Goals to Behavior

Goals are important, but they aren't enough by themselves. We have argued that goals have their influence on behavior through a process of feedback control (see, e.g., MacKay, 1963, 1966; Miller, Galanter, & Pribram, 1960; Powers, 1973). In a discrepancy reducing, or negative, feedback loop an existing condition is compared against a reference value (Fig. 2.1). If a discrepancy between the two is detected, an output function is engaged. The output creates an adjustment in the existing state of affairs, aimed at diminishing the discrepancy. If the adjustment is effective, subsequent perceptions will align more closely with the reference value. The overall function of the loop is to reduce (or keep reduced) sensed deviations from the comparison value.

We hold that these functions are implicit in human behavior. Behavioral information is taken as a guide, goal, reference point, or a standard of comparison (terms we use interchangeably here). People periodically check on their activities, states, or qualities (input function) and compare these perceptions against the reference values. If the perception or construal of

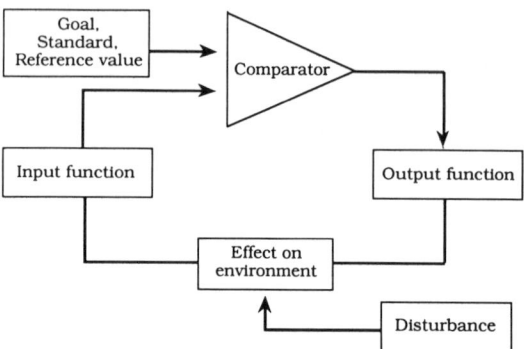

FIG. 2.1. The negative, or discrepancy-reducing, feedback loop.

behavior is discrepant with what the person intended to be doing, the result is typically a change in behavior, aimed at diminishing or removing the discrepancy (cf. Norman, 1981).

In the logic of the feedback loop, behavior is inherently purposive (even if the purposes underlying many acts are relatively trivial), undertaken in the service of creating perceptions of conformity to some reference value. Human life is viewed as a continual process of establishing goals and intentions, and of adjusting current patterns of behavior so as to more closely match these values, using informational feedback as a guide to progress.

Hierarchies in Self-Regulation

Although going farther than goals by themselves, the single feedback loop is inadequate to account for the elaboration and flexibility of human behavior. Complexity is added, however, by the idea that feedback systems can be interconnected—for example, ordered in a hierarchy. Powers (1973) argued that this sort of organization underlies the self-regulation of behavior in living organisms, and arguments of a similar form have also been made by other theorists focusing on very different aspects of behavior (e.g., Broadbent, 1977; Dawkins, 1976; Gallistel, 1980; Vallacher & Wegner, 1987). We find aspects of this argument interesting and have adopted this notion as a conceptual heuristic.

In a hierarchical organization of feedback systems, there are relatively superordinate feedback loops and relatively subordinate loops. The output function of the superordinate system consists of the resetting of reference values at the next lower level of abstraction. To put it differently, higher order systems *behave* by providing reference values to the systems just below them in the hierarchy.

The reference values that are being specified become more concrete and restricted as one moves from higher to lower levels of a hierarchy. Control at each lower level reflects regulation of some quality that contributes to the quality controlled at the next higher level. Each level within the hierarchy monitors input at a level of abstraction that is appropriate to its own functioning, and each level adjusts output so as to minimize discrepancies at that level. Powers (1973) argued that such a hierarchy underlies the physical execution of whatever action is taking place.

Our own interest is in the implications of the hierarchy at relatively high levels of abstraction (see Marken, 1986, and Rosenbaum, 1987, for evidence regarding the usefulness of similar notions at lower levels). At the highest level proposed by Powers are such values as the global sense of idealized self. Self is not the only reference value that occurs at this level, although it may be the most intuitive example of the type of standard that occurs here and may also be the most often used reference value at this level. Other possibilities include the idealized sense of a relationship (Read & Miller, 1989) or of a society.

Values at this level are very abstract. A reasonable question is what behavioral outputs are relevant to the attempt to self-regulate toward such a value. How does a person act so as to minimize discrepancies between these highly abstract values and behavior? Powers (1973) suggested that the behavioral output of this highest order system consists of providing reference values to the next lower level, which he termed the level of *principle* control. People act to "be" who they think they ought to be or want to be by using any of several guiding principles implied by the idealized self to which they aspire. The makeup of the idealized self to which the person aspires obviously will differ somewhat from person to person. Thus, the principles that will be specified as output will also vary.

Principles begin to provide form for behavior. They are aspects of behavior for which we have names (essentially trait labels) in everyday language—for example, honesty, responsibility, thrift, and expedience. They are still fairly abstract, however. Principles are not specifications of acts, but rather of qualities that can be manifest in acts of many types. People do not just go out and "do" honesty, or responsibility, or thrift, or expedience. Rather, people can manifest any one (or more) of these qualities in their behavior by doing any number of specific activities.

The specific activities, in which behavior finally becomes more recognizable as behavior, are termed *programs*. A program specifies a course of action but with many of the details left blank. The details are left unspecified because what is done at a particular point in the script depends on what circumstances are encountered at that point. Clearly, much of what people do in their day-to-day lives appears program-like in character. Going to the grocery store, cooking dinner, writing a report, taking a walk—all these are programs.

Programs are the sort of activities that most people take for granted as "behavior." Although they often are undertaken in order to attain relatively abstract goals, the programs themselves are sufficiently concrete and overt that they are easily recognizable as actions. It is very easy to describe the actions in a program. Executing them, however, is a more complex process than naming them. In the model proposed by Powers (1973), programs act by specifying yet more restricted qualities as reference values to lower level control structures.

Highly relevant to this line of thought is a body of work by Vallacher and Wegner (1985, 1987). This work appears to argue strongly for the viability of the notion of hierarchical organization, at least as applied to relatively high levels of control. Vallacher and Wegner noted that people can identify any given act in a variety of ways, some of which are concrete and some more abstract. Furthermore, the level of abstraction at which people identify their actions can have predictable influences on behavior. Research stemming from Vallacher and Wegner's theory is interesting in its own right, but the point we wish to make about their work at present is that it seems to bear out the usefulness of a hierarchical view of behavior. Furthermore, most of the behavioral qualities by which variations in act identification have been illustrated are easily assimilated to levels of control in the hierarchy proposed by Powers (1973).

Nor is this line of research the only one that fits with the notion that behavior is hierarchically organized. A great many theories are based on the idea that people are motivated by a desire to have high levels of self-esteem, and the further assumption that various aspects of behavior are sensitive to how best to maintain such a positive self-evaluation (see, e.g., Snyder, Higgins, & Stucky, 1983; Taylor & Brown, 1988; Steele, 1988; Tesser, 1980, 1986, 1988). Such theories would appear to represent hierarchical models in which one attains a fit between one's perceived self and desired self by making particular behavioral choices at a more concrete level.

Hierarchical Organization: Additional Points

There are several more points that can be made about the theme of hierarchical organization in behavior (for broader treatment see Carver & Scheier, 1995). First, this view holds that control of behavior occurs simultaneously at all levels below whatever level is functionally superordinate. That is, a person doesn't engage in a high-order action and then stop and wait for lower level activities to catch up. Nor does a person engage in low-level act qualities as preparation for attainment of high-level acts. Rather, the process of carrying out a high-level act *consists of* the carrying out of low-level acts (see also Vallacher & Wegner, 1985, 1987). Thus, if you're matching your behavior to the principle of kindness by doing a favor for a neighbor, the matching is being enhanced throughout the doing of the favor, not just when the favor is completed. In this view, exceedingly restricted and concrete acts (changes in muscle tension, changes in postural orientation) are intrinsically embedded in the creation of very abstract behavioral qualities (e.g., conveying a certain mood in a piece of art, being gracious to others, delivering a speech with style). Whenever a high level of control is engaged, so are all levels below it.

On the other hand, it is *not* necessarily the case that higher levels of the hierarchy are engaged at all times. There are many circumstances in which behavioral self-regulation appears not to be guided by the superordinate sense of self, but rather by reference values at the level of program control. To put it differently, moderately low levels of control are functionally superordinate when the person's current concern is at that lower level (cf. Klinger, 1975; Shallice, 1978; Vallacher & Wegner, 1985, 1987). This would appear to be the case, for example, when people engage in the "maintenance" activities of life—e.g., shopping for groceries, washing dishes, driving to work. During such actions people may lose sight of higher order goals, as they focus on the concrete realities of the situations confronting them (cf. Norman, 1981).

We have tended to assume that self-regulation at any level higher than the level that is functionally superordinate is suspended until attention is refocused on reference values at the higher level. This does not mean that actions taken while under low level control have no implications for higher level discrepancies. When behavior is being controlled at lower levels, discrepancies at higher levels can remain unchanged, they can be decreased, they can even be increased, depending on the consequences of the lower level activity in which the person is engaging. Effects on high-level discrepancies presumably would not be noted, however, until attention were redirected to the higher level. We should note that we are speculating here. It might well be that high-level values always influence behavior, with the influence simply being slighter and more subtle when these values are not focal in one's attention.

Thus far we've addressed behavior as having a single purpose at a time, but people often try to move toward a number of goals simultaneously. We mean more here than that lower order values are always being matched in the service of higher order values in any hierarchical system. Rather, we mean that multiple goals are often operative even within a given level of the hierarchy. In some cases the reference values are fully compatible with each other (e.g., being frugal while also being austere). In other cases the goals are more mutually exclusive (e.g., being frugal while also being a patron of the arts). Reducing discrepancies with respect to one of these values means enlarging discrepancies with respect to the other, resulting in conflict. Indeed, such conflict is a major source of dissatisfaction in life (Emmons, 1986; Van Hook & Higgins, 1988).

Although the hierarchy we are discussing is in some ways very simple, it has implications for several basic problems in thinking about behavior. For one thing, it is implicit in this approach that goals at any given level can often be achieved by a variety of means at lower levels. This flexibility in goal-attainment is particularly apparent as one examines the upper levels of the hierarchy where the goals are more abstract. A particular principle can usually be realized in many programs of action in many different behavioral domains. This flexibility in goal attainment permits the hierarchical view to address in a meaningful way the fact that people sometimes shift radically the way in which they attain a goal when the goal itself has not changed appreciably (cf. Wicklund & Gollwitzer, 1982).

Just as a given goal can be obtained through multiple pathways, so can a specific act be performed in the service of diverse goals. For example, you could buy someone a gift to make that person feel good, to repay a kindness, to put that person in your debt, or to fulfill your perceived holiday-season role. Indeed, a given act can be aimed at meeting goals at different levels of abstraction. For example, walking through a door and closing it behind you may be a mindless *sequence* of action, it may be a part of a *program* of choices (reflecting a decision to go somewhere other than the room you are in), or it may be a manifestation of a *principle* (choosing to leave a room where someone is behaving dishonorably).

Thus, a given physical act can have strikingly different meanings, depending on the purpose it is intended to serve. This is an important subtheme of the viewpoint under discussion: Behavior can be understood only by reference to the goals to which the behavior is addressed.

A final implication of the notion of hierarchical organization we wish to note concerns the fact that goals in behavior are not equivalent in their importance. The higher one goes into the hierarchy, the more fundamental to the overriding sense of self (or whatever value is at the superordinate level) are the qualities that are encountered. A related point is that the "importance" of reference values at low levels is at least partly a product of the degree to which their attainment contributes to success in the attempt to reduce discrepancies at higher levels.

Positive Feedback Loops

Thus far we've limited our discussion to negative feedback loops, discrepancy-reducing or discrepancy-negating loops (thus the label negative). Such a system has a positively valued reference value, a desired goal. The function of such a system is to shift present conditions to conform more closely to the goal. A positive feedback loop, in contrast, is a discrepancy-*amplifying* loop (see Carver & Scheier, 1981; DeAngelis, Post, & Travis, 1986; Ford, 1987; Maruyama, 1963). The reference value of this system is an undesired quality. Discrepancy amplifying loops attempt to move the currently perceived value as far away as possible from the reference value (see Fig. 2.2). Deviation amplifying loops are believed to be less common in naturally occurring systems than discrepancy reducing systems, because they are unstable. They do occur, but their action is typically bounded or constrained by negative feedback loops.

We have argued that such systems occur in behavior in situations when the motive behind an act is the desire to prevent a condition from existing. For example, the desire to avoid taking the position held by a negative reference group causes people to shift their attitudinal positions in a direction that opposes the position held by members of the negative reference group. Such a behavior would seem to reflect the action of a positive feedback loop (Carver & Scheier, 1981, pp. 157–165; see also Ogilvie, 1987). Such behavior is not usually aimless, however. When people try to actively avoid a position in this way, they typically do so by finding a position to move toward. Thus, the action of the positive loop is bounded by the effects of a negative loop (Fig. 2.3).

One more concrete illustration: Adolescents often wish to be unlike their parents. They may take great pains to amplify any differences they observe between themselves and their parents (a positive feedback loop). However, although there are infinite ways in which they can differ from their parents, what results is usually not an infinite variety of attempts to differ. Ordinarily what happens is that the adolescents find some position that deviates from their parents which can be taken as a positive value to approach. Thus, at the same time as they are enhancing discrepancies with

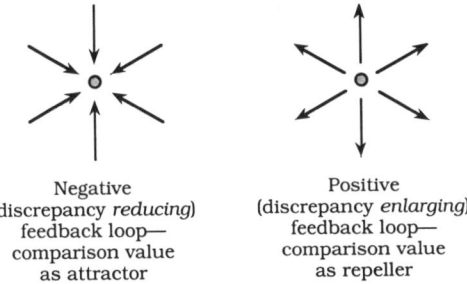

FIG. 2.2. Negative feedback loops cause sensed qualities to shift *toward* positively valenced reference points. Positive feedback loops cause sensed qualities to shift *away from* negatively valenced reference points (from Carver & Scheier, 1995).

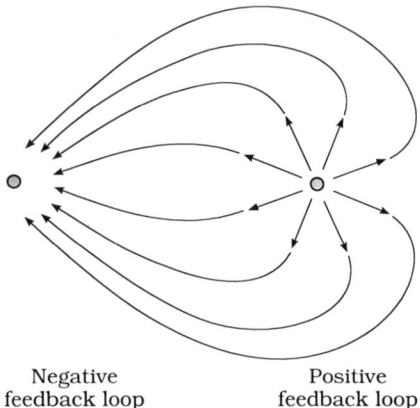

FIG. 2.3. Positive feedback systems are often bounded or constrained by negative feedback systems; one often avoids some undesired condition by moving toward a desired condition (from Carver & Scheier, 1995).

respect to their parents, they are approaching alternative values. In general, it appears to be more functional in life to have a value to move toward than to have only a value to avoid.

ORIGINS OF AFFECT

Thus far we have focused on the regulation of behavior and have said next to nothing about affect. In doing so, however, we have introduced the fundamental constructs that serve as building blocks for what will follow. In this section we consider the origins of affect, from the framework developed in the preceding section.

What causes affect? This question is a deceptively simple one. Some people would say that good feelings are generated by getting what you want and that bad feelings are generated either by failing to get what you want or by being exposed to punishing events. There is clearly a grain of truth to these observations, but we believe that they also miss something. For example, they fail to deal well with the fact that affect sometimes arises on the way to goals, rather than simply at goal attainment (or the failure of goal attainment). Nor do they deal well with the fact that negative affect sometimes occurs when goals are close, or even attained, and that positive affect sometimes occurs when goals are far away. Prompted in part by observations such as these, we proposed a different answer to the question (Carver & Scheier, 1990a). In order to address this answer, we must back up for a moment and reexamine our position on the self-regulation of behavior.

We characterized people's conscious self-regulation as a process of monitoring the results of their present actions and comparing the qualities that they perceive to the reference values that currently are salient, making adjustments as necessary to render discrepancies minimal. In what follows, we use the term *monitoring* to denote this feedback process. As just indicated, we see this monitoring loop as fundamental to the control of intentional behavior.

We suggest that there is also a second feedback process that builds on this one in a fashion that's orthogonal to the hierarchical organization involved in action. This second feedback process operates simultaneously with the monitoring function and in parallel to it whenever monitoring is going on. The second feedback system serves what we will term a *meta-monitoring* function.

Discrepancy Reduction and Rate of Reduction

In trying to describe this meta-monitoring function, an intuitive way to begin is to say that the meta loop is checking on how well the action loop is doing at reducing its behavioral discrepancies. More specifically, we propose that the perceptual input for the meta loop is a representation of the *rate of discrepancy reduction in the behavioral (monitoring) system over time*. What's important to the meta loop is not merely whether discrepancies are being reduced at the level of the action loop, but how *rapidly* they are being reduced. If they are diminishing rapidly, the action loop's rate of progress toward its goal (as perceived by the meta loop) is high. If they are being reduced slowly, the action loop's rate of progress is lower. If they are not being reduced at all, the action loop's progress is zero. Any time discrepancies are enlarging at the level of action monitoring, of course, the action loop's progress is inverse. (For convenience we use as equivalent phrases such as *progress of the action loop* and *rate of discrepancy reduction in the action loop*.)

Although it may be somewhat less intuitive than the preceding, we find an analogy useful in describing the functioning of these two systems (an analogy that may also have more literal implications). Because action implies change between states, consider behavior to be analogous to distance (construed as a vector, because perception of one's action incorporates both the difference between successive states and also the direction of the difference). If the monitoring loop deals with distance, and if the meta loop assesses the rate of progress of the monitoring loop, then the meta loop is dealing with the psychological equivalent of velocity (also directional). In mathematical terms, velocity is the first derivative of distance over time. To the extent that this physical analogy is meaningful, the perceptual input to the meta loop presumably is the first derivative over time of the input information used by the action loop.

We have argued that the meta-monitoring process functions as a feedback loop, in part because the same rate of progress can have different affective consequences under different circumstances. Thus we have suggested that the meta system involves more than the mere sensing of the rate of discrepancy reduction in the action loop. This sensing constitutes an input function, but no more. As in any feedback system, this input is compared against a reference value (cf. Frijda, 1986, 1988). In this case, the reference value is an acceptable or desired rate of behavioral discrepancy reduction. As in other feedback systems, the comparison process determines whether there is a discrepancy or deviation from the standard. If there is, an output function is engaged to reduce the discrepancy.

We suggest that the outcome of the comparison process that lies at the heart of this loop is manifest phenomenologically in two forms. The first is a hazy and nonverbal sense of expectancy regarding the eventual success or failure of the behavior. The second is affect, a feeling quality, a sense of positiveness or negativeness.

When sensed progress in the action loop conforms to an acceptable rate of progress, the meta-monitoring system accordingly registers no discrepancy (see Table 2.1, Example 1). Given an absence of discrepancy at the meta level, affect is neutral. When the action loop is making steady progress toward reducing its own discrepancy but its rate of discrepancy reduction is slower than the reference value being used by the meta system, a discrepancy exists for the meta loop (Table 2.1, Example 2). The result in this case should be a degree of doubt and negative affect, proportional to the size of this meta-level discrepancy. When the rate of discrepancy reduction in the action loop is higher than the meta loop's reference value (Table 2.1,

TABLE 2.1
Four Conditions of Behavior Over Time, How They Would Be Construed at the Level of the Action Loop, How They Would Be Construed at the Level of the Meta-Monitoring Loop, and the Affect That Theoretically Would Be Experienced

Behavioral Situation	Construal at Action Loop	Construal at Meta Loop	Affect
1. Progress toward goal, at a rate equal to the standard	Discrepancy reduction	No discrepancy	None
2. Progress toward goal, at a rate lower than the standard	Discrepancy reduction	Negative discrepancy	Negative
3. Progress toward goal, at a rate higher than the standard	Discrepancy reduction	Positive discrepancy	Positive
4. No progress toward goal	No discrepancy reduction	Negative discrepancy	Negative

Example 3), there is a positive discrepancy at the meta loop, an overshoot of the reference value that is reflected in confidence and in positive feelings.

It is obvious that the two systems under discussion (monitoring and meta-monitoring) are related to each other, but we have argued that only one of them has implications for affect. The first three examples in Table 2.1 all have two things in common: At present there is a discrepancy in the behavioral loop, and discrepancy reduction at the behavioral level is also taking place. These conditions, however, do not determine affect. Affect may be neutral, it may be positive, or it may even be negative (Examples 1–3), depending on the adequacy of the *rate* of discrepancy reduction. The fourth example in Table 2.1 shows a case in which our theory makes the same prediction as do theories based on the mere existence of discrepancies. That is, in a case where no movement is occurring toward the behavioral goal, there is a negative discrepancy both at the behavioral level and at the meta level.

It is important to note (and again somewhat counterintuitive) that in this model the size of the discrepancy confronted by the action loop at any given point does not play an important role in the perceptual input to the meta loop. A large discrepancy—even a *very* large discrepancy—perceived at the level of the action loop can be associated with perceptions of either abundant or insufficient progress. This same discrepancy thus can be associated with either favorable or unfavorable expectancies and with either positive or negative affect. What matters with respect to the meta system is solely whether or not the perceived *rate of progress* in the action system is adequate.

The same point can also be made of cases in which the behavioral discrepancy is relatively small. If the meta system senses that there is an abundant rate of change toward full discrepancy reduction, there should be positive affect and confidence. If it senses an inadequate rate of change, there should be negative affect and doubt.

Thus, ironically, it should be possible for a person who has a large discrepancy at the action loop to feel more positive affect than a person who has a small discrepancy at the action loop, if the first person is perceiving a more acceptable rate of progress than the second person. In terms of the physical analogy (and assuming comparable set points), the first person is more distant from the goal but is moving toward it with a higher velocity. Evidence that this can be so will be discussed momentarily.

Just as the monitoring of action apparently can take any of several levels in a hierarchy of behavioral control as superordinate, so should the meta system be able to function at any of several levels. It seems likely, however, that discrepancies noted by the meta system have more emotional impact when they concern a central element of self than when they bear only on a more peripheral goal (a program or a sequence of action). Sometimes a failure has a big impact on one's feelings, sometimes it does not (cf. Dweck & Elliott, 1983; Dweck & Leggett, 1988; Elliott & Dweck, 1988; Hyland, 1987; Srull & Wyer, 1986). The difference between these cases may be the level of abstraction at which the person is focusing. The consequences of meta-monitoring are more impactful at higher levels than at lower levels of the hierarchy (see also Frijda, 1988).

Evidence: Hsee and Abelson

At least a little evidence has begun to accumulate to support aspects of the arguments just made about the origin of affect in a rate or velocity function. Some of this evidence was reported in an article by Hsee and Abelson (1991), who came independently to the notion that a velocity function is important to affect. Hsee and Abelson set out to replicate previous findings that final outcome and distance traveled to the outcome influence level of satisfaction, and to examine the relationship between velocity and level of satisfaction. In one study, subjects read hypothetical descriptions of paired outcome scenarios and indicated which outcome they would find more satisfying. For example, to test the role of velocity in predicting satisfaction, subjects chose whether they would be more satisfied if their class standing had risen from the 30th percentile to the 70th over the past 6 weeks, or if it had done so over the past 3 weeks.

Each participant answered seven questions, which paired different outcome scenarios. The questions tested the role of final outcome, distance changed, velocity, and direction of change as influences on satisfaction. For purposes of the present discussion, the effect of velocity is of greatest interest (e.g., holding the amount of salary change constant and varying the time over which it changes). As Hsee and Abelson predicted, subjects preferred improving to a high final outcome compared to a constant high outcome; they preferred a fast velocity over a slow velocity; and they preferred a high velocity/short distance to a slower velocity/longer distance (this last preference demonstrated the robustness of the time element in predicting satisfaction). When the direction was negative (salaries got worse, indicating a downward velocity) subjects preferred a constant low salary to a salary that started high and fell to the low level; they preferred slow falls to fast falls; and they preferred large/slow falls to small/fast falls.

That study asked subjects to read about possible outcomes and imagine which of a pair they would find more satisfying. A second study was designed so that subjects would experience an outcome while it was actually changing in time, by watching hypothetical outcomes that changed in a graph form on a computer screen. The computer displayed a bar that moved vertically along a scale portraying changes in outcome (e.g., the price of a stock the subject had invested in). Unlike the first study, in which outcome scenarios were paired and the participant was to pick which would be more satisfying, this time subjects had a reference scenario that they were told had a degree of satisfaction of 5 on a 9-point scale. They were to make ratings of satisfaction in comparison to the reference scenario. In this study, distance changed was held constant while direction, final outcome, and velocity were varied.

Study 2 replicated the findings in Study 1. There was a significant final outcome effect. More importantly, there was a highly significant velocity effect. Subjects preferred a fast velocity when outcome was improving and a slow velocity when outcome was declining.

Evidence: Lawrence, Carver, and Scheier

The research of Hsee and Abelson is quite interesting. A potentially important limitation of that work, however, is that the outcomes were in all cases hypothetical. Although subjects were asked to imagine themselves experiencing the outcomes portrayed, the credibility of the findings depends in part on assuming that subjects were actually able to experience the outcomes as having personal relevance. It remained to be shown that velocity influences affective consequences while people are actually engaged in goal-related behavior. In part for this reason, we felt it desirable to conduct additional research on the matter.

The study we conducted (Lawrence, Carver, & Scheier, 1995) used a paradigm in which feedback of progress toward a desired goal could be manipulated plausibly over an extended period of time. The experiment was disguised as a study of social intuition, in which subjects made a long series of ambiguous judgments. The cover story was that the project was investigating people's ability to intuitively sense the meaning of words from obscure foreign languages (actually nonsense words). On each trial the subject would be shown a word and asked if this word meant the same thing as a comparison English word. As a way of engaging interest in the task, the cover story also emphasized how this intuitive skill could be very important in the broader social world.

The cover story also indicated that many factors influence performance on this task, including momentary mood fluctuations, how many people the subject typically interacts with on an average day, and so on. To control for these factors, assessments would be made periodically during the course of the session. Mood was assessed (on an 11-point scale ranging from "very positive mood" to "very negative mood") before the task began and at the end of the sixth block.

Each block of 10 judgments was followed by feedback regarding performance on that block (the conceptual equivalent of a stock price from the Hsee & Abelson, 1991, research). Subjects received one of five patterns of performance feedback (see Fig. 2.4), converging across blocks such that feedback on block 6 was identical for all subjects (50% correct). Subjects in

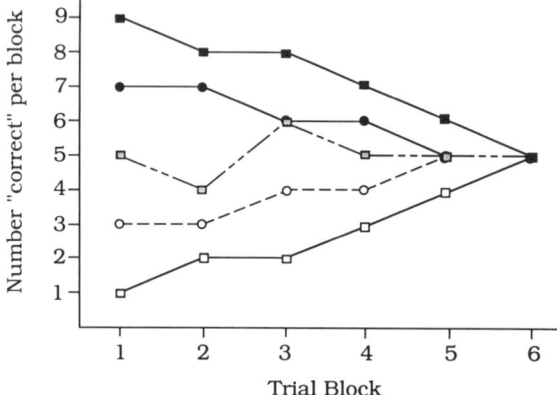

FIG. 2.4. Pattern of feedback across trial blocks given to subjects in each of five experimental conditions. Some subjects began with good performances and got worse; others began with poor performances and got better; a control condition consistently performed at an average rate (from Lawrence et al., 1995).

a neutral condition received a 50% score on the first and last block and 50% on average across all blocks. Two groups had positive changes in their performances (thus positive velocities), starting poorly and performing gradually better across blocks. One had a relatively large change (from 10% to 50%), the other a more moderate change (from 30% to 50%). The final two groups had negative changes (thus negative velocities), starting with good performances and performing gradually worse. Again, one change was large (from 90% to 50%), the other more moderate (from 70% to 50%). The five groups thus were experiencing five different velocities at the point where they all received feedback of 50% correct after block 6.

In contrast to velocity, operationalized as just described, distance to the goal can be considered in either of two ways. First, all subjects received a score of 50% on the final block. If one thinks of distance in terms of the adequacy of current performance, the five groups are at that moment equidistant from their goal. However, it is also possible to think of the task as a whole, in which case the performances prior to block 6 also influence distance from the goal. Considered from this angle, subjects who performed especially well on earlier trial blocks would have the smallest behavioral discrepancies after block 6 (thus far they were closest to the goal overall), those who performed especially poorly on earlier trial blocks would have the largest behavioral discrepancies after block 6 (thus far they were farthest from the goal overall).

It is of some interest that when viewed in this way, subjects in the conditions with positive velocities—whom we expect to have positive change in mood ratings—are precisely the subjects for whom discrepancy from the behavioral goal (doing well) is actually greatest at the end of block

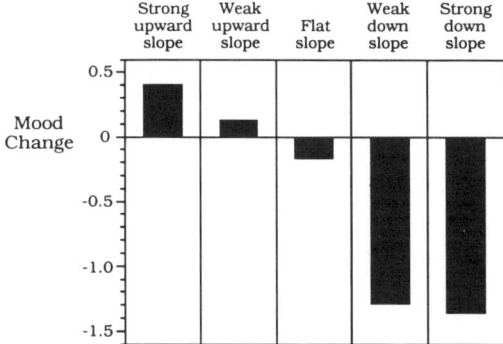

FIG. 2.5. Mood change from pretask to following trial block 6 (data from Lawrence et al., 1995).

6. If behavioral discrepancy is what matters, these subjects should be in the worst mood. Similarly, subjects in the conditions with negative velocities — whom we expect to have negative change in mood ratings — are the subjects for whom discrepancy from the behavioral goal is actually smallest at the end of block 6. If behavior discrepancy is what matters, these subjects should be in the best mood.

The results of the study favored the prediction based on velocity (see Fig. 2.5). Subjects whose performances improved across the six trial blocks reported shifts in mood to become more positive at the end of block 6 (change that was somewhat constrained by a ceiling effect); those whose performances decreased across the six blocks reported shifts in mood to become more negative. We reiterate that the subjects whose mood had become more negative were those with the *best* average or cumulative performances; those whose mood had become more positive were those with the *worst* average or cumulative performances. We also reemphasize that the final block of performance feedback was identical for each subject group (50% correct). This pattern appears to be very consistent with the analysis portrayed in Table 2.1, earlier in the chapter, in which affect is related to rate of discrepancy reduction rather than to discrepancy reduction per se.

CONCEPTUAL QUESTIONS WITHIN THE MODEL

The affect model presented in the preceding pages raises several sorts of issues and questions. Some pertain to the model itself, others pertain to the relation between the affect model and the model of behavior from which it evolved, yet others pertain to the relation between this model and other approaches to affect. In the remainder of the chapter we address some of these matters (for further discussion see Carver & Scheier, 1990a, 1995).

Is This Really a Feedback System?

Carver and Scheier's (1990a) statement on affect suggested that affect results from a comparison process in a feedback loop. It is important to recognize that the position taken there was not that affect is the controlled quality in this loop, but rather rate of progress. This has an important implication that is quite counterintuitive.

Positive feelings reflect a positive discrepancy. This is good in at least two senses: things are going better than they need to, and the experience feels good phenomenologically. To a system that has the goal of controlling sensed rate, however, a discrepancy in either direction is still a discrepancy, and discrepancies are to be reduced. If this is really a feedback loop whose goal is to control sensed rate, neither positive nor negative affect is a state that this system wants to see. Either quality of affect (either kind of deviation from the standard) would represent an "error" and lead to changes in output that would reduce it.

If the meta loop were truly a feedback system, it would follow that an overshoot of the reference value should lead to a self-corrective attempt to return to the reference value. To put it more concretely, this view argues that people who have exceeded the desired rate of progress are likely to slow their subsequent efforts. They are likely to *coast* for a while. The result of this in the person's phenomenology would be that the positive affect resulting from the overshoot is not sustained for long (see also Erber, chap. 4, this volume).

The existence of a natural tendency that has the effect of causing positive affect to be short-lived seems at first glance highly unlikely, even preposterous. A plausible basis for such a tendency may be seen, however, in the idea that behavior is hierarchically organized and involves multiple current concerns. People typically are working toward several goals more or less simultaneously, and many lower level efforts contribute to minimizing discrepancies at high levels. To the extent that movement toward goal attainment is more rapid than expected in one domain, it permits the person to shift attention and effort toward strivings in another domain, at no cost. To continue the unnecessarily rapid pace in the first domain might increase positive affect with respect to that activity, but by diverting efforts from other goals that action may create the potential for negative affect in other domains. Such an arrangement would be consistent with the idea that the organism is structured more to avoid negative events—which can have life-threatening consequences—than to attain positive events (Pratto & John, 1991; Taylor, 1991).

Although little systematic evidence bears on the idea that positive affect leads to coasting, casual observers of athletic contests often see such a pattern in the ebb and flow of games. When one team gets ahead, it's very common to see that team lose momentum. The mechanism behind such phenomena is unclear (and these informal observations are subject to the problem of not knowing which team creates the momentum shift, the one that's behind or the one that's ahead), but it would seem likely that loss of concentration is a contributor, consistent with our model.

Clearly this idea represents a speculation beyond any evidence now available. Indeed, this aspect of the model raises a number of questions that we can not readily answer. For example, sometimes people who are engaged in activities they are enjoying appear to take their positive affect as a sign to continue the activity, rather than as a sign that they've done better than they needed to do and can now turn to something else. The circumstances under which positive feelings cue one response versus the other (cf. Martin & Stoner, chap. 12, this volume) is an issue that deserves much further attention than it has yet received.

Meta-Level Standards Vary in Stringency

In considering the functioning of such a system, an important question is what reference value is used by the meta system. We assume this system can use widely varying standards. Sometimes the standard is very demanding, sometimes it is less so. Sometimes this value is imposed from outside (as when work has a deadline for completion), sometimes it is self-imposed (as when someone has a personal timetable for career development), sometimes it derives from social comparison (as when people are in competition with each other). Regardless of its origins, the reference value must be adopted by the behaving person as relevant to his or her experience in order for it to have affective consequences.

As an example in which the meta standard is both stringent and externally imposed, consider the requirements of degree programs in medical or law school. In such cases even continuous behavioral progress (continuous increments in mastery of required material) is adequate only if it occurs at or above the rate required by the degree program. Thus, as the person attempts to attain the action goal of becoming a doctor or lawyer, the reference value for meta-monitoring is a relatively stringent one. Although the reference value for rate of progress is externally imposed, most people entering this situation build the rate requirement into their understanding of the situation they are in; it is now their requirement as well.

How stringent a standard is used at the meta level for any given activity has straightforward implications for the person's emotional life. If the pace of progress used as a reference point is too high, it will rarely be matched, even if (to an outside observer) the person's rate of progress is extraordinarily high. In such a case, the person will experience negative affect often and positive affect rarely. If the pace of progress used as a reference point is low, the person's rate of behavioral discrepancy reduction will more frequently exceed it. In this case, the person will experience positive affect more often and negative affect more rarely.

Changing Meta Level Standards: An Opponent Process?

Not only do meta-level reference values differ across people and categories of behavior, but they can also shift as a result of time and experience (cf. Lord & Hanges, 1987). To put it differently, as people accumulate more experience in a given domain, adjustments can occur in the pacing that they expect and demand of their efforts.

Sometimes the adjustment in rate criterion is downward. For example, a researcher experiencing difficulty in his attempt to be as productive as his colleagues may gradually adopt less stringent standards of pacing. One consequence of this is a more favorable balance of positive to negative affect across time. In other cases the adjustment is upward. A person who gains work-related skills may undertake greater challenges, requiring quicker handling of each action unit. Upward adjustment has the side effect of decreasing the potential for positive affect and increasing the potential for negative affect.

The adjusting of meta-level reference values over the course of experience looks suspiciously like a self-corrective feedback process in its own right, as the person reacts to insufficient challenge by taking on a more demanding pace, and reacts to too much challenge by scaling back the criterion (see Fig. 2.6). If a feedback process is involved in changing standards at the meta level, it is far slower acting than are the feedback processes we have focused on thus far. Shifting the reference value downward is not usually the immediate response when the person has trouble keeping up with a demanding pace. First the person tries harder to keep up. Only more gradually, if the person cannot keep up, does the meta standard shift to accommodate. Similarly, an upward shift is not the immediate response when the person's rate of discrepancy reduction exceeds the standard. The more typical response is to coast for a while. Only when the overshoot is frequent does the standard shift to accommodate.

A possibility worth considering is that this shift of meta standard reflects the long-term consequences of what Solomon (1980) called an *opponent process*. Solomon proposed that two systems are always involved in regulating emotional reactions. One system (which he did not discuss in detail) creates the emotional response to the emotion-eliciting circumstance. The second system, of greater interest to him, opposes the first one (thus the name opponent process). It comes into play whenever the initial emotional response occurs and acts to dampen emotional reactions.

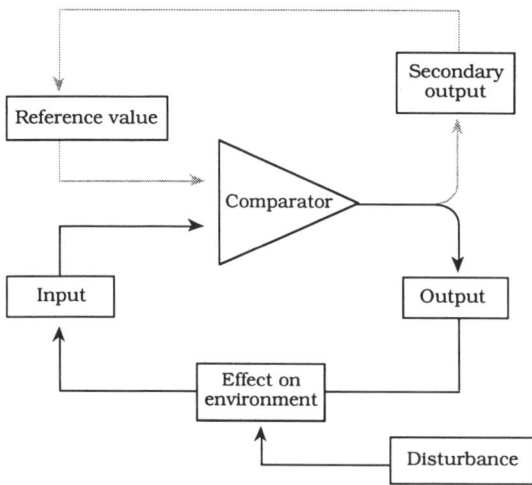

FIG. 2.6. A feedback loop (in this case, the postulated meta loop) acts to create change in the input function, to shift it toward the reference value. Sometimes an additional process is in place as well (gray lines), which works to adjust the reference value in the direction of the input. This additional process is presumed to be weaker or slower. Thus, the reference value is stable, relative to the input value. Such a loop would be similar to one manifestation of what Solomon (1980) termed an *opponent process* (from Carver & Scheier, 1995).

Indeed, the opponent process dampens emotional reactions in two senses. In the short term, it causes the affect that was evoked by a given event to return to neutral. In the longer term (after repeated experiences of similar events), the opponent process causes the event to produce a less intense manifestation of that same emotional response than it did at first. This latter effect—the reduction in the emotional reaction that takes place— seems comparable in some ways to the idea that the repeated experiences have led to a shift in meta standard (for a consideration of subtle differences between positions, see the broader discussion of this issue in Carver & Scheier, 1995).

The opponent process concept has many implications that go beyond the scope of this discussion, but some of its implications in this context are quite interesting. The idea that these changes are produced by a slow acting feedback system may help to account for why it can be so hard to shift meta standards voluntarily. That is, one can easily make a change in self-verbalization ("stop being so demanding of yourself—be more satisfied with what you're accomplishing"), but this sort of self-verbalization rarely takes effect immediately. If a true shift in meta standard relies on a slow acting feedback loop, that would account for why subjective experience tends to lag behind the self-instruction.

It is also of some interest that these patterns of shift in reference value (and the resultant effects on affect) imply a mechanism within the organism that functions in such a way as to actively prevent the too-frequent occurrence of positive feeling, as well as the too-frequent occurrence of negative feeling. That is, the (bidirectional) shifting of the rate criterion over time would tend to control pacing of behavior in such a way that affect continues to vary in both directions around neutral. As we suggested with respect to the functioning of the meta system, such an arrangement for changing meta-level standard would not result in maximization of pleasure and minimization of pain. Rather, the affective consequence would be that the person experiences more or less the same range of variation in his or her affective experience over extended periods of time. In effect, this would represent a continuous recalibration of the feeling system, across changes in the organism's situation.

Conflict and Mixed Feelings

Our discussion thus far has focused on the existence of one feeling at a time. Affect associated with goal-directed effort need not be purely positive or purely negative, however. It is entirely possible for a single event to produce more than one feeling quality.

It's not uncommon for an action to have implications for two (or more) distinct goals. The goals making up the hierarchy of a person's self-definition are not always perfectly compatible with each other, and occasionally two conflicting goals become salient at the same time (see Emmons, 1986; Van Hook & Higgins, 1988). For example, the goal of career advancement and the goal of spending a lot of time with one's young children may both be desirable, but the 24-hour day imposes limitations on the time available for trying to attain them. Sometimes the actions that permit progress toward one goal (working extra hours at the office) simultaneously interfere with progress toward the other goal (spending time with one's children). To the extent that both goals remain salient, the result is mixed feelings—positive feelings from the career advancement, negative feelings from the failure to spend as much time as desired with one's children.

Even the process of experiencing a particular emotion can arouse another emotion. For example, consider a person who has been taught that to feel pride over an accomplishment is not a good thing, because his happiness causes others to feel bad and inferior (not an unusual lesson in some cultures). Upon experiencing rapid movement toward some goal, this person experiences positive affect. Upon the realization that he is feeling happy and proud (and thus deviating from the cultural standard), he feels shamed. The result is mixed feelings.

Thus, a hierarchical model of goals suggests a very simple explanation for the existence of mixed feelings. People often have many goals at once. People who are making rapid progress on some of their current concerns and poor progress on others should experience positive feelings with respect to the former and negative feelings with respect to the latter. As a result, the experience of mixed outcomes must be common, even in the course of a single day.

We should perhaps note at this point that this way of talking assumes meta-monitoring with respect to more than one regulatory system at the same time. We assume that this does in fact happen—indeed, that meta-monitoring happens even with regard to goals that are more or less outside consciousness. It may be that one of the factors causing affect to seem so mysterious over the years is that we can have feelings, even strong feelings, without a clear grasp of their source. This would be expected to happen when for whatever reason, the goal relevant to those feelings is submerged away from current consciousness. This inaccessibility doesn't mean the goal isn't there, however, and it doesn't mean the person isn't trying to self-regulate with respect to it, even though not being aware of doing so.

Changes in Rate: Acceleration and Deceleration

The model presented here addresses various rates of progress toward action goals. It should be obvious, however, that the rate of progress can itself change. Change in rate at the action loop is subjectively manifest not merely as affect, but as *change* of affect. Increases in rate are reflected in shifts toward more positive feelings. The precise quality of the experience will depend, of course, on the initial and final rates. When the change is from a rate far below the meta standard to a rate closer to the standard but still below it, affect should change from more negative to less negative. If the change is instead to a value that exceeds the meta standard, affect should change from negative to positive.

In the same manner, downward changes in sensed rate at the action loop are also reflected in affective shifts. Again, the quality of the experience will depend on the initial and final rates. When the change is from a rate that exceeds the meta standard to a rate below the standard, the affective change should be from positive to negative. When the change is from just below the standard to far below the standard, the affective change should be from mildly negative to very negative.

Shifts in rate of progress at the action loop can be gradual or they can be abrupt. The more abrupt is an increase in the action loop's progress, the more the subjective experience incorporates a rush of exhilaration. This exhilaration can be seen as reflecting the contrast between the more negative feelings and the more positive feelings (cf. the description of *sentimentality* by Frijda, 1988, p. 350). In a complementary fashion, the more abrupt a slowing of the action loop's progress, the more the subjective experience should incorporate a kind of "de-exhilaration." This is the well known *sinking feeling* that reflects the contrast experienced when feelings suddenly shift in a negative direction. These experiences of abrupt shifts either upward or downward would seem to embody the characteristics of *surprise* (Carver & Scheier, 1995).

We suggested earlier that the quality of experience that the meta loop senses as its input is analogous to the physical quality of velocity. Let us carry this analogy one step further. What we are addressing now is not velocity, but change in velocity—acceleration. Acceleration is the second derivative of distance over time. Given that people apparently are equipped to sense experiences such as these, the analogy seems to suggest that some neural processor is computing a second derivative over time of the information input to the action loop.

In the same way that distance and velocity are independent of each other, both are, in principle, independent of acceleration. (An object moving at 20 feet per second can at that instant be accelerating, decelerating, or its velocity can be constant; the same is true of an object moving at 80 feet per second.) We have taken the position that the same independence exists on the other side of the analogy (Carver & Scheier, 1990a). We argued earlier that affect experienced is independent of the degree of discrepancy at the action level. In the same fashion, we have held that the rush or exhilaration associated with acceleration is itself independent of the size of the discrepancy at the action level and also independent of the rate of discrepancy reduction at the action level. The Carver–Scheier model holds, then, that this exhilaration is distinct from positivity-negativity.

This position gains indirect support from the fact that emotion theorists have always had difficulty dealing with the experience of surprise. Although many consider surprise an emotion (Izard, 1977; Tomkins, 1984), they often take great pains to distinguish it from other emotions. Further, there's evidence that people in general don't think of surprise in the same way they think of other subjective states that are more clearly viewed as emotions (Fehr & Russell, 1984; Shaver, Schwartz, Kirson, & O'Connor, 1987). There's also evidence that surprise in itself is neither positive nor negative (Izard, 1977, p. 283; Ortony et al., 1988, p. 32; Roseman, 1984, p. 31; Tesser, 1990); rather, its tone is a product of the experiences that are associated with it.

In contrast to this indirect support from the emotion literature, there's also evidence that our position on acceleration is incorrect, although the data in question are not without ambiguity. The evidence comes from a study recently published by Hsee, Salovey, and Abelson (1994, Experiment 2). In this study subjects watched a number they were told indicated the price of a stock they owned. The number changed repeatedly over a

45-second period that corresponded to the passing of 3 months. Subjects were asked to make a continuous record of their satisfaction with the stock, using a pointer on a 15-point scale. The stock price was varied between subjects in several patterns, with the key differences being shifts that established differences in acceleration toward the end of the 3-month period while maintaining equivalence of velocity during the final month.

Portions of the data appear to support the idea that satisfaction was responsive both to velocity and to acceleration. However, it's difficult to interpret the findings because of aspects of the procedures. In order to create acceleration differences while holding final velocity constant, Hsee et al. had to use very different starting values (stock prices) for the curves that were compared to each other. Yet at the beginning of the 3-month run, the "satisfaction" pointer was always placed for the subject at the midpoint of the scale, thereby implicitly establishing that particular stock value as corresponding to a middle value on the satisfaction scale. In reporting the findings, the authors focused on the final satisfaction rating, ignoring the differential anchor. The differential anchor, however, makes the absolute values of subjects' self-reports hard to interpret.

Of greater relevance is the profiles of satisfaction reported in the various conditions. In half the conditions a moderate rate of progress (gain or loss) shifted to a more extreme value. In these conditions, satisfaction ratings tracked the rate values quite well, consistent with a view in which velocity matters but not acceleration. In the other conditions a high rate of change (increase or decrease) moderated rather abruptly, though not reversing. Satisfaction ratings, however, reversed direction. If only velocity mattered, the ratings should have just leveled off, rather than reversing. This aspect of the findings appears to indicate a link between satisfaction and acceleration.

A second difficulty in interpreting the findings concerns the concept *satisfaction*. Thus far we've treated this quality (the outcome variable in this study, as well as the earlier Hsee & Abelson [1991] research) as though it were equivalent to positive versus negative affect. Although this may be so, it's also arguable that the two are somewhat different. It might be argued that satisfaction implies both affect and the extent to which the affect is accompanied by exhilaration/deexhilaration (surprise). Indeed, this issue points to the considerable difficulty involved in sorting out the elements of the psychological experience of events of this sort.

However one interprets these findings, this research does reinforce some important points. Although the qualities of velocity and acceleration are in principle independent, it is extraordinarily difficult to manipulate them independently (as Hsee et al. [1994] also noted). Further, it can be hard to keep clear which quality is actually under scrutiny in any given operationalization.

AFFECT AND BEHAVIOR

In the preceding section we addressed a number of issues that are suggested by the Carver–Scheier model of affect, issues that pertain to the model and its internal structure. There are also questions that arise from the fact that the origins of this model lie in a control-process approach to behavioral self-regulation. What is the relationship between the affect model and the model of behavior? There are two aspects of this relationship to which we wish to point here (further issues are discussed in Carver & Scheier, 1995).

Expectancies and Affect

Earlier in the chapter we said that we see the effects of the meta loop as manifest subjectively in two ways: as affect and as a hazy sense of expectancy. This hazy sense of expectancy is perhaps more cognitive than is the affect, but we do not mean to suggest that these expectancies are carefully thought out or that they appear in consciousness as probability estimates. Rather, they are a nonverbal sense of optimism versus pessimism pertaining to whatever content of consciousness they derive from (or are presently connected with).

There is clear evidence that these momentary situational expectancies can be overridden by more firmly established well-encoded expectancies (Carver, Blaney, & Scheier, 1979a, 1979b; Carver, Peterson, Follansbee, & Scheier, 1983). Perhaps this is one more way in which humans' elaborate cognitive capabilities can serve to remove them from the press of the situational forces of the present. Of interest at the moment, however, is not the fact that these expectancies can be overridden, but the idea that they have a link to affect.

The idea that expectancies are linked to affect is given indirect support from a variety of sources, including some work discussed elsewhere in this volume. Several authors have found that being in a bad mood causes bad events to seem more likely than they do to people in a good mood; similarly, being in a good mood can make good events seem more likely than they do to people in a bad mood (Erber, 1991; Forgas & Moylan, 1987; Johnson & Tversky, 1983; Mayer, Gaschke, Braverman, & Evans, 1992). Wegener and Petty (chap. 14, this volume; see also Wegener, Petty, & Klein, 1994) have found that this can cause people to respond differently to the content of persuasive messages.

Specifically, when presented with appeals that focus on the idea that a good outcome will result from a change in one's opinion, people in good moods see the good outcome as more likely (compared to people in bad moods) and they're more persuaded. Indeed, the more optimistic view on the outcome apparently is the reason *why* they're more persuaded. Although this finding has a boundary condition (it happens only among people who are prone to think things over), it seems consistent with the idea that the positive feeling makes people a bit more optimistic about the question they're considering, whereas the negative feeling makes people a bit more pessimistic.

Another finding that makes a similar point, but with a somewhat different twist, comes from research conducted by Martin, Ward, Achee, and Wyer (1993; see also Martin & Stoner, chap. 12 this volume). In this research, Martin et al. gave people an ambiguous task to work on, under varying instructional sets. In one experiment, some were told to continue with the task until they could come to a conclusion, others were told to continue as long as they still felt like it. In a second experiment, some subjects were told to continue until they felt that it was a good time to stop, others were told to continue as long as they still enjoyed it (subjects in both experiments were given specific questions to pose to themselves to help decide). Subjects who had been placed in positive moods stopped sooner in the first condition of each experiment than subjects placed in negative moods; those in negative moods stopped sooner in the second condition than those in positive moods.

Martin et al. argued that when people asked themselves the question that had been left with them, the tendency to answer yes or no was influenced by their mood (positive mood biasing toward yes, negative toward no). If the question is "Is it time to stop?" a yes response means stop. If the question is "Do I feel like continuing?" a yes response means continue. Thus mood caused behavior to be influenced in opposite directions under the two instructional sets, but by the same mechanism in each case. The mechanism invoked fits well with our assertion that affect and expectancies (the yes or no answer, in this case) are linked.

Negative Affect and Behavioral Disengagement

Another set of issues concerns a fundamental assumption in the Carver-Scheier (1981, 1990a, 1990b) approach to behavior that has been disregarded thus far in the chapter. This assumption concerns the role of expectancies of eventual success in the continuation of goal-directed efforts under conditions of adversity. The assumption is that if a person's expectancies of goal attainment are sufficiently unfavorable, the person may disengage from pursuit of the goal (see also Klinger, 1975; Kukla, 1972; Wortman & Brehm, 1975). Considering this disengagement response, and the emotions that often surround it, raises a variety of issues.

In considering these issues let us return to the idea that behavior is hierarchically organized, and that goals are increasingly important as one moves upward through the hierarchy. We assume that it rarely is difficult to disengage from values low in the hierarchy of control. Indeed, the nature of programs is such that disengagement from efforts at subgoals is quite common, even as the person continues to pursue the overall goal of the program (if you go to buy something and the store is closed, you often head for another store that stocks the item rather than give up altogether).

Sometimes, however, disengaging from a lower order goal has serious implications for discrepancy reduction or enlargement at a higher level. Sometimes the standards or reference values from which one is attempting to disengage have implications for higher order goals that are important, even central to one's life. One cannot withdraw from these values permanently without substantially reorganizing one's value system (Carver & Scheier, 1986; Kelly, 1955; Millar, Tesser, & Millar, 1988). Disengagement from certain goals, then, is quite difficult.

Now consider the affective consequences of being in this situation. The desire to disengage is prompted in the first place by unfavorable expectancies for discrepancy reduction, expectancies that are typically paralleled by negative affect. In this situation, then, the person is experiencing strong negative feelings (because of an inability to make adequate behavioral progress) and is unable to do anything about those feelings (because of an inability to give up the behavioral reference value). The person in this situation simply stews in the feelings that arise from irreconcilable discrepancies (see also Martin & Tesser, 1989). In our view, this bind—being unable to let go of something that is unattainable—is at the heart of depression (cf. Hyland, 1987; Klinger, 1975; Pyszczynski & Greenberg, 1987).

A second issue is also raised by the idea that effort gives way to disengagement as expectancies become more negative. Although we believe that this does occur, there is a conceptual discontinuity between this idea and the feedback ideas discussed throughout the chapter. In the affect model there is no obvious mechanism to produce disengagement. Why should the meta system not just continue endlessly to try to reduce discrepancies, however ineffectively? Why should the negative affect not simply persist or intensify? What causes the person ever to quit?

We have speculated that there may be an override mechanism of some sort that is capable of taking precedence over this feedback system and cause disengagement from the value currently being used to guide action (Carver & Scheier, 1990a). In the jargon of the computer metaphor, this would be equivalent to a *break* function, which permits processing to be suspended or abandoned altogether. Where disengagement is adaptive, it is adaptive precisely because it frees the system to take up other reference values, enables the person to turn to the pursuit of substitute or alternate goals. And we should note that disengagement is in fact very often an adaptive response, as there are many goals from which people simply must disengage, either temporarily or permanently (see Klinger, 1975, on commitment to and disengagement from incentives).

More recently, questions have been raised as to whether such an assumption is really needed. These questions derive in part from the demonstration that a separate disengagement function, assumed for some time to be an element in the process of redirected visual attention, is apparently not necessary (Cohen, Romero, Servan-Schreiber, & Farah, 1994). The shift from one focal point to another may be entirely a product of the nature of the contention for attentional resources that takes place among competing locations in the visual field. In an analogous way, it may be that disengagement from one goal occurs as a product of competition among various motivational qualities that are active simultaneously, competing for expression.

Regardless of whether there is or is not an override process, it should also be reemphasized that disengagement does not always take place, even when the desire to disengage is there. As we noted just earlier, when the goal toward which the person is unable to make progress is central to that person's implicit definition of self, the person for that reason often cannot disengage from it. Disengagement from such a goal means disengagement from oneself.

Indeed, there is evidence that the inability (or unwillingness) to disengage is a correlate of depression. Depression has been linked to behavioral indicators of failing to disengage mentally from experimentally created failures (Kuhl, 1984, 1985; Pyszczynski & Greenberg, 1985, 1987). Depression has also been linked to concurrent self-reports of a tendency to perseverate mentally on failure (Carver, La Voie, Kuhl, & Ganellen, 1988) and to ruminate on personally valued activities during forced suspension of those activities (Millar et al., 1988). Mental perseveration among depressed people is not limited to major life goals but can occur even for transient and relatively trivial intentions (Kuhl & Helle, 1986). Thus, there is evidence suggesting that depression is bound up with a general failure to disengage. It is not clear why this should be so, but in some sense this failure seems to be at the core of the dynamics of depression (see also Klinger, 1975).

AFFECT AND REPRIORITIZATION

At this point we turn to brief comparisons with other models of affect. Although there is not space here for all comparisons that might be of interest, two such comparisons are obvious enough that they beg mention (see Carver & Scheier, 1990a, 1995, for additional discussion). The first is with Simon's (1967) theory of affect as a signal for reprioritization.

Some years ago, Simon (1967) proposed a view on affect that was intended to show how affect functions within the framework of cognitive and motivational processes. He suggested that affect, particularly negative affect, causes interruption of ongoing behavior (Simon, 1967; see also Sloman, 1987). A potential consequence of this interruption, which suggests a potential function for the negative emotion, is a reconsideration and reprioritization of one's goals.

The simplest case that can be analyzed in these terms is one where a single goal for behavior is currently focal. Negative affect occurs if progress toward that goal is inadequate. If negative affect becomes sufficiently intense (or expectancies for goal attainment sufficiently unfavorable), the person disengages from the attempt to reach it. At this point the person may adopt a less exacting goal in the same domain or may simply turn to a new goal domain (cf. Schönpflug, 1983, 1985). In either case, disengagement and choice of a new goal can be construed as reflecting a reprioritization, in that attaining the previous goal is now being accorded a lower priority than it was before.

In other cases, however, emotions can induce reprioritization by a different path. It is this second path for reprioritization that Simon (1967) had in mind as a role for emotions. Simon held that many emotions cause people to interrupt their behavior and consider the possibility that an *alternative* goal (not presently focal) should have a higher priority than it currently has. The stronger the emotion, the stronger is the message that the less attended goal should be receiving high priority, in place of the goal that is currently focal.

Reprioritization and Multiple Values

Simon's analysis seems compatible with the ideas we are proposing, but his view on reprioritization makes a point that we have not yet considered here except in passing. Specifically, his analysis seems to require that discrepancies with respect to two different reference values can be monitored (and meta-monitored) simultaneously, one focally, the other less so. The emotion that serves as the call for reprioritization is being generated by what is occurring with respect to the *less focal* reference value. The call for reprioritization inevitably is a call to upgrade the priority of that second value.

The easiest illustration of this argument is what occurs when anxiety arises while the person is engaged in goal-directed effort. Consider, for example, the anxiety that arises when a snake phobic attempts to hold a snake. In such a case the rate of progress toward the focal reference value—the concrete behavioral goal that the person is trying to attain—is not itself the source of the anxiety. Rather, the anxiety is produced by something that

2. CONTROL PROCESSES AND AFFECT   41

is happening with respect to a second reference value (cf. our discussion of conflict, earlier in the chapter).

This second reference value may be the threat of physical harm (in the case of the phobic); in other cases it may be the desire to maintain a positive self-portrayal to others, or even such broader values as holistic personal integration (cf. Rogers, 1980). As the person attempts to do the intended behavior, the relation of the present state to that second value (whatever it is) is becoming other than intended (a discrepancy is being created regarding a desired goal value, or a discrepancy is being diminished regarding an undesired value). The farther the person goes in the attempted action, the greater is the problem with respect to that second value. In such a case, a discrepancy is also developing at the meta level for that second goal. The result is negative affect.

It is important to recognize that in cases such as these the threat that induces fear is occurring as a by-product of the attempt to do something else. The snake phobic is trying to hold the snake, but doing so is creating perceptions of risk of harm. The fear thus represents a signal to be devoting greater attention to the goal of harm avoidance than to the goal of holding the snake.

Simon's view on reprioritization suggests that reference values are often monitored outside awareness until discrepancy enlargement is detected, at which point the value becomes more focal. Indeed, it raises far broader questions: How often does it happen that people are monitoring multiple goals outside awareness, and how many such goals are typically being managed? This general view also suggests a way of thinking about cases in which an affect arises without a clear source. That is, it may be that the signal for reprioritization has reached awareness, but for some reason the behavioral goal itself remains outside focal awareness. Obviously there are many unanswered questions here concerning how often, and to what degree, such parallel processing concerning multiple goal values takes place in human behavior.

Although anxiety is perhaps the easiest emotion to address in terms of Simon's analysis of prioritization, other emotions can also be assimilated to his point of view. Guilt, for example, occurs when a discrepancy is created between the reference value of a moral standard and one's current behavior (behavior that may perfectly match one's action intention). Shame, or embarrassment, occurs when an action creates a discrepancy with respect to a social standard. Anger seems to result from enlarging discrepancies concerning personal control over one's experiences (cf. Averill, 1983). In each of these cases, the emotion seems not to be directly related to the reference value toward which one is trying to move. Rather, it is a by-product of that movement, occurring because the action has consequences in addition to its intended consequences. These examples thus are consistent with the idea that meta-monitoring is often occurring with respect to a second point of reference as well as the intention that is being enacted focally.

SELF-DISCREPANCY THEORY: TYPES OF GOAL AND QUALITIES OF AFFECT

Another interesting comparison is between the ideas presented here and the self-discrepancy theory proposed by Higgins and his colleagues (Higgins, 1987; Higgins, Bond, Klein, & Strauman, 1986; Strauman, 1989). Both models make considerable use of the concept of discrepancy. Higgins argued that certain emotions occur as the result of discrepancies between pairs of psychological entities that he calls self-guides. For simplicity's sake we will deal here with only two kinds of discrepancies. The first is between one's perceived actual self and one's ideal self (actual–ideal discrepancies). The second is between one's perceived actual self and one's ought self (actual–ought discrepancies).

An ideal self is a desired self, a self to which one aspires. Living up to the ideal means attaining something desired, acquiring reward. An ought self, in contrast, is a duty or obligation, a self that one feels compelled to be rather than desires to be. There is a sense in which this entity is punishment-based. Living up to an ought means doing something so as to avoid disapproval (self-disapproval, in the case we are focusing on here). Each person has ideals, and each person has oughts (which may be either interwoven or distinct), and the perceived actual self may be compared to each of these reference points.

According to self-discrepancy theory, large discrepancies between ideal and actual yield depressed affect. Pure depression thus represents an impending failure to attain rewards (see also Finlay-Jones & Brown, 1981). In contrast, large discrepancies between ought and actual are said to yield anxiety. Pure anxiety thus represents an impending failure to avoid punishment.

Three differences between self-discrepancy theory and the Carver and Scheier model deserve mention. First, self-discrepancy theory holds that depressed affect is produced by a discrepancy between an actual and an ideal representation of the self. The Carver and Scheier position is that the discrepancy that matters is one pertaining to rate of progress toward ideals. If progress is inadequate—if there is a discrepancy at the meta loop—the person experiences negative affect. Thus, from our point of view, a person who is discrepant from the ideal but is moving toward it rapidly enough should experience positive rather than negative affect.

A second difference between theories is also implicit in this last statement. The model we have described here addresses both positive affect and negative affect. Self-discrepancy theory is a theory of negative affect only. It is not apparent how to conceptualize positive affect within that framework, or at least to do so in a way that provides a conceptual basis for predicting positive, negative, and neutral affect under various circumstances. Our analysis thus goes beyond self-discrepancy theory in an important way, by suggesting a basis for the existence of positive feeling qualities, as well as a basis for the existence of negative affect.

The third point of comparison between models is in many ways the most interesting. It concerns the distinction between ideals and oughts, which is the most novel and innovative aspect of the Higgins analysis. It is this distinction that provides self-discrepancy theory a conceptual basis for differentiating anxiety from depression.

Recasting the Underlying Dynamics

Our interpretation of this distinction involves recasting slightly the dynamics behind self-regulation with respect to an ought. To do this, we return to a distinction made earlier in the chapter between two kinds of feedback systems. As indicated earlier, a negative feedback loop is a discrepancy reducing system, a system that has a positively valenced reference value, a desired goal. These loops act to create movement into conformity with the reference value. A positive feedback loop, in contrast, is a discrepancy amplifying system, a system that has a negatively valenced reference value, an undesired quality. These loops act to create movement away from the reference value. As we noted earlier in the chapter (Fig. 2.3), self-regulation with respect to positive loops is most effective when the positive loop is bounded or constrained by a negative loop—when the person tries to avoid an undesired value by moving toward a desired value.

In light of this distinction, consider the case of ideals. Ideals are simple and straightforward. They are valued for their own sake. We regard self-regulation with respect to ideals as involving primarily negative feedback processes, movement *toward*. The case of oughts, however, is more complex. Oughts are desired qualities, but they are desired largely because they help the person avoid an *un*desired quality. Oughts involve trying to escape from something, as well as trying to be something. In sum, we would suggest that the ought self-guide nicely captures the sense of a positive feedback process being overridden or bounded by a negative feedback process (Fig. 2.7). First there is a desire to create distance away from an undesired state (a state similar to what Markus & Nurius, 1986, called a *feared self*); this desire then is given form and coherence by the positive value of the ought, a value the person can move toward.

The distinction between two types of feedback loops was not heavily

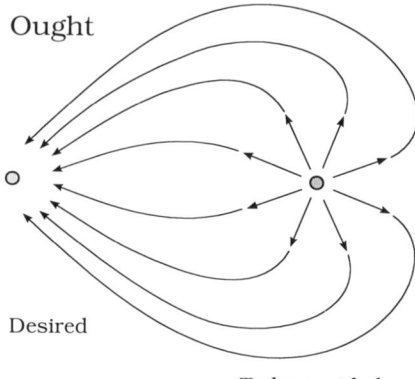

FIG. 2.7. An *ought* self-guide can be seen as involving both an explicit desire to move toward a prescribed value and an implicit desire to move away from a proscribed value, a positive feedback loop whose effects are given form by those of a negative feedback loop (from Carver & Scheier, 1995).

embedded in the Carver and Scheier (1990a) statement on affect, although they did touch on the point briefly in passing (p. 32). In first developing their ideas, they thought primarily of discrepancy reducing loops. Indeed, in describing that model earlier in this chapter we dealt solely with discrepancy reducing loops, in order to keep the principles clear. However, it's relatively easy to assimilate the distinction between types of feedback processes into the model. Specifically, if we can talk about a discrepancy *reducing* loop doing well or doing poorly at the function in which it is engaged, and about this information leading to affect via a meta-monitoring process, why shouldn't the same idea apply to a discrepancy *enlarging* loop? If it's doing well at what it's trying to do, the result should be a positive feeling; if it's doing poorly, the result should be a negative feeling. This argument has recently been made more explicitly (Carver, in press; Carver & Scheier, 1995).

The idea that positive and negative affect can arise from relevant behavior would seem to be fully comparable across the two types of systems. We believe, however, that there's one difference between the two. On this point we lean very heavily on the insights and research findings of Higgins and his collaborators. There seems to be a difference in the affective qualities that emerge from the two types of systems (see Fig. 2.8). In each case there's a positive pole and a negative pole, but the positives aren't quite the same as one another, nor are the negatives quite the same.

Following the lead of Higgins, we suggest that the affect dimension that pertains to discrepancy reducing loops is (in its purest form) the dimension that runs from depression to elation. The affect dimension that relates to discrepancy enlarging loops is (in its purest form) the dimension that runs

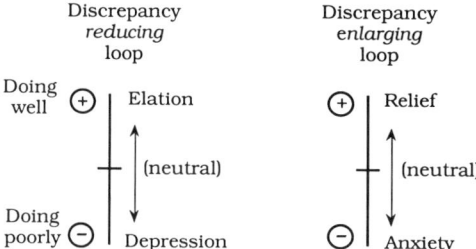

FIG. 2.8. The difference between depressed and anxious affect, postulated in self-discrepancy theory, viewed as the experiences generated by discrepancy reducing and discrepancy enlarging systems, respectively. As expressed earlier in the chapter, we believe that the affect in each case comes from a meta-level system, which is determining that the corresponding behavioral system is doing poorly in its self-regulatory efforts. Given the assumptions of the Carver–Scheier (1990a) model, we also believe that both loops can lead to positive feelings, when the behavioral system is perceived as performing its task better than needed (from Carver & Scheier, 1995).

from anxiety to relief. As Higgins and his colleagues note, dejection-related and agitation-related affect may take several forms, but these two dimensions capture the core qualities behind the various forms. The result is two dimensions of affect, one end of each being occupied by the feelings that have been the major focus of self-discrepancy theory, the other end occupied by a positive feeling. The resulting two dimensions might be characterized as elation versus depression and anxiety versus relief-tranquility-serenity.

Where Does the Affect Come From?

The line of thought shown in Fig. 2.8 begs one more question about the dynamics underlying anxiety. Self-discrepancy theory holds that the discrepancy between the actual and the ought is what determines anxiety. Higgins and his colleagues have in their recent work begun to examine more closely the fact that self-regulation with regard to oughts involves more than trying to conform to oughts. The findings reviewed by Higgins (in press) seem to confirm that ought-based self-regulation involves trying to avoid something, as well as trying to approach the oughts. However, we are led to wonder whether the avoidance tendency may still be accorded too little importance. In a sense, the avoidance tendency has motivational primacy. It's the starting point (Fig. 2.7) and thus the most fundamental part of the ought pattern. Perhaps the trying to escape is more important in some ways than the trying to approach. Perhaps it's the *avoidance* system that is more fundamental to the experience of anxiety, as suggested in Fig. 2.8, rather than the approach system.

Data we've recently collected suggest partial support for this idea, but only partial support (Carver, Lawrence, & Scheier, 1995). Subjects in this research rated how discrepant they were from their self-generated ought selves and how discrepant they were from their self-generated *feared* selves. Both kinds of discrepancies were associated with anxiety and other agitation-related affects. However, the extent to which subjects reported resembling their feared selves turned out to be a more robust predictor of these affects overall than was the extent to which they reported deviating from their ought selves. This effect was particularly pronounced among subjects who saw themselves as being relatively close to their feared selves. On the other hand, among subjects who were fairly distant from their feared selves, discrepancies from the ought self were more strongly associated with agitation-related affects.

These findings would seem to have important implications for self-discrepancy theory. It suggests that the positive feedback process (the get-away-from process) is an important contributor to the development of agitated affects. This is not to say that oughts are unimportant. As noted earlier, positive feedback processes appear, in general, to be functional only when they are constrained by negative feedback processes. This seems to be very much the case with respect to feared selves. Although there are many ways in which a person could escape from a given feared self, the mere desire to escape the feared self provides no positive direction for movement. It requires a positively valenced reference point to provide such direction. This is precisely what the ought self provides (Fig. 2.7). The ought self thus serves an important function in giving form to self-regulation that has escape and avoidance as its initial impetus.

Further Potential Integration

In closing this discussion, we note that the dimensions of affect outlined in Fig. 2.8 bear considerable resemblance to those identified by Zevon and Tellegen (1982) and Watson and Tellegen (1985), widely known as positive and negative affect. Although these labels are in widespread use, we regard them as somewhat misleading (see also Larsen & Diener, 1992, on this issue). Despite their labels, both dimensions have both positive and negative poles. To the extent that the data sets reviewed by Watson and Tellegen contained descriptors reflecting depression (and there were not many), they loaded on the *positive affect* factor. To the extent that descriptors reflecting relief were represented in the data sets (the closest were calm, carefree, and satisfied), they loaded on the *negative affect* factor. Indeed, Watson and Tellegen (1985) noted explicitly that both dimensions have markers that are both positive and negative, though it remains uncertain how this is to be reconciled with the position that the dimensions are unipolar.

We believe that the two dimensions that underlie the affective experiences labeled positive and negative affect are closely aligned with the two dimensions shown in Fig. 2.8. The core of what is termed positive affect is the bipolar dimension from elation to depression. The core of what is termed negative affect is the bipolar dimension from anxiety to relief-serenity. Each of these dimensions is related to the actions of a behavioral self-regulatory system. One of these systems involves approach, the other involving avoidance (for reviews of neuropsychological data supporting this viewpoint, see Davidson, 1992a, 1992b). This line of argument suggests that the affective dimensions discussed under the labels positive and negative affect have strong points of contact both with the Higgins (1987) self-discrepancy theory and with the Carver–Schier (1990b, 1995) model of action and affect. These points of contact, which have been little noted until now, would seem to deserve much closer scrutiny than they have yet received.

CONCLUSION

In this chapter we have presented the conceptual elements of one possible approach to affect based on the elements of control theory. In so doing, we have tried to indicate how this view might be useful as a way of thinking for others as well. We also raised a number of issues and questions concerning this approach and attempted to indicate how we think about them. We are well aware that we haven't raised all the questions that might be asked, nor have we fully answered all the questions we raised. We hope, however, that the ideas presented here are interesting enough to others that they will try them out in their own thinking about the areas in which they work.

In closing, we would like to say a word about the intended scope of this view on affect. Although most examples given here come from domains of achievement and instrumental activity, this is not a theory that is intended to be specific to achievement-related affect. Rather, the analysis was intended to be applicable to all goal-directed behavior, including behavior pertaining to goals that are amorphous and poorly specified and goals for which the idea of assessing the rate of progress toward discrepancy reduction might at first glance seem odd.

Goals such as developing and maintaining a sound relationship, being a good mother or father, dealing honorably and pleasantly with acquaintances, seeing someone you care for be happy and fulfilled, having a full life, and even becoming immersed in the fictional lives portrayed in a novel or film are all amenable to analysis in these terms. These are all qualities of experience toward which people attempt to move, goals that evolve or recur across time, as do most goals underlying human action. To the extent that progress toward goals such as these is taken by the person as important, to the extent that people are invested in experiencing these qualities in their lives sooner rather than later, positive and negative feelings will occur as progress is faster or slower than the standard of comparison.

ACKNOWLEDGMENTS

The work reported here was supported in part by NSF grants BNS 90-11653 and BNS 90-10425, by grant PBR-56 from the American Cancer Society, and by grant HL44436-A1 from the National Heart, Lung, and Blood Institute. This chapter was written while Charles S. Carver was a Visiting Scholar at the University of California, Los Angeles.

REFERENCES

Adams, J. A. (1976). Issues for a closed-loop theory of motor learning. In G. E. Stelmach (Ed.), *Motor control: Issues and trends* (pp. 87–107). New York: Academic Press.

Averill, J. A. (1983). Studies on anger and aggression. *American Psychologist, 38*, 1145–1160.

Broadbent, D. E. (1977). Levels, hierarchies, and the locus of control. *Quarterly Journal of Experimental Psychology, 29*, 181–201.

Cantor, N., & Kihlstrom, J. F. (1987). *Personality and social intelligence.* Englewood Cliffs, NJ: Prentice-Hall.

Carver, C. S. (in press). Some ways in which goals differ and some implications of those differences. In P. M. Gollwitzer & J. A. Bargh (Eds.), *The psychology of action: Linking cognition and motivation to behavior.* New York: Guilford.

Carver, C. S., Blaney, P. H., & Scheier, M. F. (1979a). Focus of attention, chronic expectancy, and responses to a feared stimulus. *Journal of Personality and Social Psychology, 37*, 1186–1195.

Carver, C. S., Blaney, P. H., & Scheier, M. F. (1979b). Reassertion and giving up: The interactive role of self-directed attention and outcome expectancy. *Journal of Personality and Social Psychology, 37*, 1859–1870.

Carver, C. S., La Voie, L., Kuhl, J., & Ganellen, R. J. (1988). Cognitive concomitants of depression: A further examination of the roles of generalization, high standards, and self-criticism. *Journal of Social and Clinical Psychology, 7*, 350–365.

Carver, C. S., Lawrence, J. W., & Scheier, M. F. (1995). *Self-discrepancies and affect: Incorporating the role of feared selves.* Unpublished manuscript.

Carver, C. S., Peterson, L. M., Follansbee, D. J., & Scheier, M. F. (1983). Effects of self-directed attention on performance and persistence among persons high and low in test anxiety. *Cognitive Therapy and Research, 7*, 333–354.

Carver, C. S., & Scheier, M. F. (1981). *Attention and self-regulation: A control-theory approach to human behavior.* New York: Springer-Verlag.

Carver, C. S., & Scheier, M. F. (1986). Functional and dysfunctional responses to anxiety: The interaction between expectancies and self-focused attention. In R. Schwarzer (Ed.), *Self-related cognitions in anxiety and motivation* (pp. 111–141). Hillsdale, NJ: Lawrence Erlbaum Associates.

Carver, C. S., & Scheier, M. F. (1990a). Origins and functions of positive and negative affect: A control-process view. *Psychological Review, 97*, 19–35.

Carver, C. S., & Scheier, M. F. (1990b). Principles of self-regulation: Action and emotion. In

R. Sorrentino & E. T. Higgins (Eds.), *Handbook of motivation and cognition* (Vol. 2, pp. 3-52). New York: Guilford.
Carver, C. S., & Scheier, M. F. (1995). *On the self-regulation of behavior.* New York: Cambridge University Press, in preparation.
Cohen, J. D., Romero, R. D., Servan-Schreiber, D., & Farah, M. J. (1994). Mechanisms of spatial attention: The relation of macrostructure to microstructure in parietal neglect. *Journal of Cognitive Neuroscience, 6*, 377-387.
Davidson, R. J. (1992a). Anterior cerebral asymmetry and the nature of emotion. *Brain and Cognition, 20*, 125-151.
Davidson, R. J. (1992b). Prolegomenon to the structure of emotion: Gleanings from neuropsychology. *Cognition and Emotion, 6*, 245-268.
Dawkins, R. (1976). Hierarchical organisation: A candidate principle for ethology. In P. P. G. Bateson & R. A. Hinde (Eds.), *Growing points in ethology* (pp. 7-54). Cambridge: Cambridge University Press.
DeAngelis, D. L., Post, W. M., & Travis, C. C. (1986). *Positive feedback in natural systems (Biomathematics, Vol. 15).* Berlin and New York: Springer-Verlag.
de Sousa, R. (1987). *The rationality of emotion.* Cambridge, MA: MIT Press.
Dweck, C. S., & Elliott, E. S. (1983). Achievement motivation. In P. H. Mussen (Ed.), *Handbook of child psychology* (4th ed., pp. 643-691). New York: Wiley.
Dweck, C. S., & Leggett, E. L. (1988). A social-cognitive approach to motivation and personality. *Psychological Review, 95*, 256-273.
Elliott, E. S., & Dweck, C. S. (1988). Goals: An approach to motivation and achievement. *Journal of Personality and Social Psychology, 54*, 5-12.
Emmons, R. A. (1986). Personal strivings: An approach to personality and subjective well being. *Journal of Personality and Social Psychology, 51*, 1058-1068.
Erber, R. (1991). Affective and semantic priming: Effects of mood on category accessibility and inference. *Journal of Experimental Social Psychology, 27*, 480-498.
Fehr, B., & Russell, J. A. (1984). Concept of emotion viewed from a prototype perspective. *Journal of Experimental Psychology: General, 113*, 464-486.
Finlay-Jones, R., & Brown, G. W. (1981). Types of stressful life event and the onset of anxiety and depressive disorders. *Psychological Medicine, 11*, 803-815.
Ford, D. H. (1987). *Humans as self-constructing living systems: A developmental perspective on behavior and personality.* Hillsdale, NJ: Lawrence Erlbaum Associates.
Forgas, J. P., & Moylan, S. (1987). After the movies: Transient mood and social judgments. *Personality and Social Psychology Bulletin, 13*, 467-477.
Frijda, N. H. (1986). *The emotions.* Cambridge: Cambridge University Press.
Frijda, N. H. (1988). The laws of emotion. *American Psychologist, 43*, 349-358.
Gallistel, C. R. (1980). *The organization of action: A new synthesis.* Hillsdale, NJ: Lawrence Erlbaum Associates.
Greenberg, L. R., Rice, L. N., & Elliott, R. (1993). *Facilitating emotional change: The moment-by-moment process.* New York: Guilford.
Higgins, E. T. (1987). Self-discrepancy: A theory relating self and affect. *Psychological Review, 94*, 319-340.
Higgins, E. T. (in press). Ideals, oughts, and outcome focus: Distinct systems for regulating pain and pleasure. In P. M. Gollwitzer & J. A. Bargh (Eds.), *The psychology of action: Linking cognition and motivation to behavior.* New York: Guilford.
Higgins, E. T., Bond, R., Klein, R., & Strauman, T. J. (1986). Self-discrepancies and emotional vulnerability: How magnitude, accessibility and type of discrepancy influence affect. *Journal of Personality and Social Psychology, 41*, 1-15.
Hsee, C. K., & Abelson, R. P. (1991). Velocity relation: Satisfaction as a function of the first derivative of outcome over time. *Journal of Personality and Social Psychology, 60*, 341-347.

Hsee, C. K., Salovey, P., & Abelson, R. P. (1994). The quasi-acceleration relation: Satisfaction as a function of the change of velocity of outcome over time. *Journal of Experimental Social Psychology, 30,* 96-111.

Hyland, M. (1987). Control theory interpretation of psychological mechanisms of depression: Comparison and integration of several theories. *Psychological Bulletin, 102,* 109-121.

Izard, C. E. (1977). *Human emotions.* New York: Plenum.

Johnson, E. J., & Tversky, A. (1983). Affect, generalization, and the perception of risk. *Journal of Personality and Social Psychology, 45,* 20-31.

Kelly, G. A. (1955). *The psychology of personal constructs.* New York: W. W. Norton.

Kelso, J. A. S. (Ed.). (1982). *Human motor behavior: An introduction.* Hillsdale, NJ: Lawrence Erlbaum Associates.

Klinger, E. (1975). Consequences of commitment to and disengagement from incentives. *Psychological Review, 82,* 1-25.

Klinger, E. (1977). *Meaning and void: Inner experience and the incentives in people's lives.* Minneapolis: University of Minnesota Press.

Kuhl, J. (1984). Volitional aspects of achievement motivation and learned helplessness: Toward a comprehensive theory of action control. In B. A. Maher (Ed.), *Progress in experimental personality research* (Vol. 13, pp. 99-170). New York: Academic Press.

Kuhl, J. (1985). Volitional mediators of cognition-behavior consistency: Self-regulatory processes and action versus state orientation. In J. Kuhl & J. Beckmann (Eds.), *Action control: From cognition to behavior* (pp. 101-128). New York: Springer-Verlag.

Kuhl, J., & Helle, P. (1986). Motivational and volitional determinants of depression: The degenerated-intention hypothesis. *Journal of Abnormal Psychology, 95,* 247-251.

Kukla, A. (1972). Foundations of an attributional theory of performance. *Psychological Review, 79,* 454-470.

Larsen, R. J., & Diener, E. (1992). Promises and problems with the circumplex model of emotion. In M. S. Clark (Ed.), *Review of personality and social psychology,* Vol. 13 (pp. 25-59). Newbury Park, CA: Sage.

Lawrence, J. W., Carver, C. S., & Scheier, M. F. (1995). *Goal-related velocity and affect.* Manuscript in preparation.

Lord, R. G., & Hanges, P. J. (1987). A control system model of organizational motivation: Theoretical development and applied implications. *Behavioral Science, 32,* 161-178.

MacKay, D. M. (1963). Mindlike behavior in artefacts. In K. M. Sayre & F. J. Crosson (Eds.), *The modeling of mind: Computers and intelligence* (pp. 225-241). Notre Dame, IN: University of Notre Dame Press.

MacKay, D. M. (1966). Cerebral organization and the conscious control of action. In J. C. Eccles (Ed.), *Brain and conscious experience* (pp. 422-445). Berlin: Springer-Verlag.

Marken, R. S. (1986). Perceptual organization of behavior: A hierarchical control model of coordinated action. *Journal of Experimental Psychology: Human Perception and Performance, 12,* 267-276.

Markus, H., & Nurius, P. (1986). Possible selves. *American Psychologist, 41,* 954-969.

Martin, L. L., & Tesser, A. (1989). Toward a motivational and structural theory of ruminative thought. In J. S. Uleman & J. A. Bargh (Eds.), *Unintended thought: The limits of awareness, intention, and control* (pp. 306-326). New York: Guilford.

Martin, L. L., Ward, D. W., Achee, J. W., & Wyer, R. S., Jr. (1993). Mood as input: People have to interpret the motivational implications of their mood. *Journal of Personality and Social Psychology, 64,* 317-326.

Maruyama, M. (1963). The second cybernetics: Deviation-amplifying mutual causal processes. *American Scientist, 51,* 164-179.

Mayer, J. D., Gaschke, Y. N., Braverman, D. L., & Evans, T. W. (1992). Mood-congruent judgment is a general effect. *Journal of Personality and Social Psychology, 63,* 119-132.

Millar, K. U., Tesser, A., & Millar, M. G. (1988). The effects of a threatening life event on

behavior sequences and intrusive thought: A self-disruption explanation. *Cognitive Therapy and Research, 12*, 441-458.
Miller, G. A., Galanter, E., & Pribram, K. H. (1960). *Plans and the structure of behavior.* New York: Holt, Rinehart, & Winston.
Norman, D. A. (1981). Categorization of action slips. *Psychological Review, 88*, 1-15.
Oatley, K. (1992). *Best laid schemes: The psychology of emotions.* Cambridge: Cambridge University Press.
Ogilvie, D. M. (1987). The undesired self: A neglected variable in personality research. *Journal of Personality and Social Psychology, 52*, 379-385.
Ortony, A., Clore, G. L., & Collins, A. (1988). *The cognitive structure of emotions.* Cambridge: Cambridge University Press.
Palys, T. S., & Little, B. R. (1983). Perceived life satisfaction and the organization of personal project systems. *Journal of Personality and Social Psychology, 44*, 1221-1230.
Pervin, L. (Ed.). (1989). *The goals concept in personality and social psychology.* Hillsdale, NJ: Lawrence Erlbaum Associates.
Powers, W. T. (1973). *Behavior: The control of perception.* Chicago: Aldine.
Pratto, F., & John, O. P. (1991). Automatic vigilance: The attention-grabbing power of negative social information. *Journal of Personality and Social Psychology, 61*, 380-391.
Pyszczynski, T., & Greenberg, J. (1985). Depression and preference for self-focusing stimuli after success and failure. *Journal of Personality and Social Psychology, 49*, 1066-1075.
Pyszczynski, T., & Greenberg, J. (1987). Self-regulatory perseveration and the depressive self-focusing style: A self-awareness theory of reactive depression. *Psychological Bulletin, 102*, 122-138.
Read, S. J., & Miller, L. C. (1989). Inter-personalism: Toward a goal-based theory of persons in relationships. In L. Pervin (Ed.), *Goal concepts in personality and social psychology* (pp. 413-472), Hillsdale, NJ: Lawrence Erlbaum Associates.
Rogers, C. R. (1980). *A way of being.* Boston: Houghton Mifflin.
Roseman, I. J. (1984). Cognitive determinants of emotions: A structural theory. In P. Shaver (Ed.), *Review of personality and social psychology* (Vol. 5, pp. 11-36). Beverly Hills, CA: Sage.
Rosenbaum, D. A. (1987). Hierarchical organization of motor programs. In S. P. Wise (Ed.), *Higher brain functions: Recent explorations of the brain's emergent properties* (pp. 45-66). New York: Wiley.
Salmoni, A. W., Schmidt, R. A., & Walter, C. B. (1984). Knowledge of results and motor learning: A review and critical reappraisal. *Psychological Bulletin, 95*, 355-386.
Schmidt, R. A. (1987). The acquisition of skill: Some modifications to the perception-action relationship through practice. In H. Heuer & A. F. Sanders (Eds.), *Perspectives on perception and action* (pp. 77-103). Hillsdale, NJ: Lawrence Erlbaum Associates.
Schmidt, R. A. (1988). *Motor control and learning: A behavioral emphasis* (2nd ed.). Champaign, IL: Human Kinetics Publishers.
Schönpflug, W. (1983). Coping efficiency and situational demands. In G. R. Hockey (Ed.), *Stress and fatigue in human performance* (pp. 299-333). Chichester, England: Wiley.
Schönpflug, W. (1985). Goal-directed behavior as a source of stress: Psychological origins and consequences of inefficiency. In M. Frese & J. Sabine (Eds.), *Goal-directed behavior: The concept of action in psychology* (pp. 172-188). Hillsdale, NJ: Lawrence Erlbaum Associates.
Shallice, T. (1978). The dominant action system: An information-processing approach to consciousness. In K. S. Pope & J. L. Singer (Eds.), *The stream of consciousness: Scientific investigations into the flow of human experience* (pp. 117-157). New York: Wiley.
Shaver, P., Schwartz, J., Kirson, D., & O'Connor, C. (1987). Emotion knowledge: Further exploration of a prototype approach. *Journal of Personality and Social Psychology, 52*, 1061-1086.

Simon, H. A. (1967). Motivational and emotional controls of cognition. *Psychological Review, 74*, 29-39.

Sloman, A. (1987). Motives, mechanisms, and emotions. *Cognition and Emotion, 1*, 217-233.

Snyder, C. R., Higgins, R. L., & Stucky, R. J. (1983). *Excuses: Masquerades in search of grace.* New York: Wiley.

Solomon, R. L. (1980). The opponent-process theory of acquired motivation: The costs of pleasure and the benefits of pain. *American Psychologist, 35*, 691-712.

Srull, T. K., & Wyer, R. S., Jr. (1986). The role of chronic and temporary goals in social information processing. In R. M. Sorrentino & E. T. Higgins (Eds.), *Handbook of motivation and cognition: Foundations of social behavior* (pp. 503-549). New York: Guilford.

Steele, C. M. (1988). The psychology of self-affirmation: Sustaining the integrity of the self. In L. Berkowitz (Ed.), *Advances in experimental social psychology* (Vol. 21, pp. 261-302). New York: Academic Press.

Strauman, T. J. (1989). Self-discrepancies in clinical depression and social phobia: Cognitive structures that underlie emotional disorders? *Journal of Abnormal Psychology, 98*, 14-22.

Taylor, S. E. (1991). Asymmetric effects of positive and negative events: The mobilization-minimization hypothesis. *Psychological Bulletin, 110*, 67-85.

Taylor, S. E., & Brown, J. D. (1988). Illusion and well-being: A social psychological perspective on mental health. *Psychological Bulletin, 103*, 193-210.

Tesser, A. (1980). Self-esteem maintenance in family dynamics. *Journal of Personality and Social Psychology, 39*, 77-91.

Tesser, A. (1986). Some effects of self-evaluation maintenance on cognition and action. In R. M. Sorrentino & E. T. Higgins (Eds.), *Handbook of motivation and cognition: Foundations of social behavior* (pp. 435-464). New York: Guilford.

Tesser, A. (1988). Toward a self-evaluation maintenance model of social behavior. In L. Berkowitz (Ed.), *Advances in experimental social psychology* (Vol. 21, pp. 181-227). New York: Academic Press.

Tesser, A. (1990). Smith and Ellsworth's appraisal model of emotion: A replication, extension, and test. *Personality and Social Psychology Bulletin, 16*, 210-223.

Tomkins, S. S. (1984). Affect theory. In K. R. Sherer & P. Ekman (Eds.), *Approaches to emotion* (pp. 163-195). Hillsdale, NJ: Lawrence Erlbaum Associates.

Vallacher, R. R., & Wegner, D. M. (1985). *A theory of action identification.* Hillsdale, NJ: Lawrence Erlbaum Associates.

Vallacher, R. R., & Wegner, D. M. (1987). Action identification theory: The representation and control of behavior. *Psychological Review, 94*, 3-15.

Van Hook, E., & Higgins, E. T. (1988). Self-related problems beyond the self-concept: Motivational consequences of discrepant self-guides. *Journal of Personality and Social Psychology, 55*, 625-633.

Watson, D., & Tellegen, A. (1985). Toward a consensual structure of mood. *Psychological Bulletin, 98*, 219-235.

Wegener, D. T., Petty, R. E., & Klein, D. J. (1994). Effects of mood on high elaboration attitude change: The mediating role of likelihood judgments. *European Journal of Social Psychology, 23*, 25-44.

Wicklund, R. A., & Gollwitzer, P. M. (1982). *Symbolic self-completion.* Hillsdale, NJ: Lawrence Erlbaum Associates.

Wortman, C. B., & Brehm, J. W. (1975). Responses to uncontrollable outcomes: An integration of reactance theory and the learned helplessness model. In L. Berkowitz (Ed.), *Advances in experimental social psychology* (Vol. 8, pp. 277-336). New York: Academic Press.

Zevon, M. A., & Tellegen, A. (1982). The structure of mood change: An idiographic/nomothetic analysis. *Journal of Personality and Social Psychology, 43*, 111-122.

3
When Does Goal Nonattainment Lead to Negative Emotional Reactions, and When Doesn't It?: The Role of Linking and Rumination

W. D. McIntosh
Georgia Southern University

A parable relates the story of a Zen monk who is chased to the edge of a cliff by tigers. The monk is cornered at a cliff face, and, scanning the cliff for some means of escape, he spies a vine and begins climbing down the cliff. After descending about halfway, he ventures a look down, and discovers that there are two tigers waiting for him at the bottom. Looking upward in hopes that the tigers above have departed, he sees that not only are the tigers still there, but the vine he is climbing is fraying as it rubs against the cliff face. Just then, he notices a big, ripe strawberry within arm's reach. He plucks it, and enjoys the last, best-tasting strawberry of his life.

The monk in this story had a very pressing, immediate goal in his life: to escape the tigers. He did everything he could to attain his goal, but it turned out in the end that his goal was out of reach. Once it became clear that his goal was unattainable, he disengaged from the goal and refocused his attention.

Although it is difficult to imagine someone confronting a painful death with such serenity, the parable raises an interesting issue. Do some people respond more strongly than others to the nonattainment of important goals? Are some people able to turn away from an important, but unattainable, goal without much distress, while others experience much negative affect if they cannot reach their goals? If so, by what process do some people become more heavily invested in goal attainment than others?

These are the issues I address in this chapter. I suggest that some people do react more strongly to goal nonattainment than others. Briefly, the model I present suggests that people will react more strongly to the nonattainment of lower order goals (e.g., buy a sports car) that they have linked to the attainment of higher order goals (e.g., be happy). Because people are more likely to ruminate about higher order as opposed to lower order goals, linking lower order goals to higher order goals will lead people to ruminate more about those goals. Ruminating about the goals will result in exacerbated negative reactions when those goals are blocked and will consequently result in lower long-term happiness among people who have a tendency to link lower order goals to higher order goals.

I begin with a general discussion of the nature of goals and goal-pursuit. Then, I discuss higher order goals specifically. Next, I examine how people react when they are having trouble attaining their goals, and the role rumination plays in goal nonattainment. I then describe why some people (*linkers*) react more strongly to goal nonattainment than other people (*nonlinkers*). I present empirical evidence for the model and consider the model's relationship to similar models that relate goals and affect. And finally, I offer some suggestion for how people might be able to avoid negative emotional reactions to goal nonattainment.

THE HIERARCHICAL NATURE OF GOALS

People spend much of their time and energy attempting to get from some current state to some desired state of affairs. Much of people's thought, emotion, and behavior surround the pursuit of goals. But what exactly is meant by a *goal*? A number of researchers have offered specific conceptualizations of what people's goal systems are like.

Klinger (1977), for example, suggested that at any given time people have a number of *current concerns*. A current concern begins when a goal is identified and ends when the goal is either attained or abandoned. In other words, current concerns are what concerns are on people's minds at the present time, such as "lose weight," "call a friend I've been meaning to speak to," "go to the park and enjoy the weather." A related concept is Little's (1983) personal project. A personal project is a "sequence of actions intended to achieve a personal goal" (Little, 1983, p. 274). Examples of personal projects are "finding a job," and "shopping for the holidays." Whereas Klinger stresses the cognitive component of having something on your mind, Little emphasizes the behavioral aspect of striving to reach the goal. Nevertheless, as identified by subjects the goals themselves are nearly identical.

The concept of a goal system is also reflected in Cantor's *life tasks* (Cantor, Norem, Brower, Niedenthal, & Langston, 1987). Life tasks are a "set of tasks that the person sees himself or herself working on and devoting energy to solving during a specified period in life" (p. 1179). Examples of life tasks are "mature beyond my high school mentality," "start a family" and "carve a career goal." The life task is not as specific and concrete as either current concerns or personal projects, but all three reflect the same underlying notion of a transition from a current life situation to a desired situation. Finally, Emmons' "personal strivings" offers a view of how people represent their goals. Personal strivings are general, abstract, enduring life goals. Some examples of personal strivings are to "appear intelligent," "lead a spiritual life," and "avoid relying on others" (Emmons, 1989).

Clearly, personal projects, personal strivings, current concerns, and life tasks all can be considered tapping into the same general concept of "goals" (Omodei & Wearing, 1990). Emmons (1989) suggested a manner in which these different concepts can be organized. He suggested that these concepts can be structured hierarchically. For example, picking up the phone with the intent of satisfying the current concern of "calling a friend" may be instrumental in fulfilling the personal striving of "developing close relationships with others." In such a hierarchy, specific, day-to-day concerns and projects are carried out in the service of more intermediate life tasks, which in turn aim to satisfy the still more general, enduring personal strivings. Personal strivings arise from the central, ultimate motivations in peoples lives, such as the desire "to be loved" or "to be happy."

This notion reflects the general assumption that people's goals are structured hierarchically. People pursue lower order goals because they are instrumental in attaining higher order goals (Carver & Scheier, 1981; Martin & Tesser, 1989). The higher order goals at the top of the hierarchy can be satisfied through the attainment of numerous, more concrete lower-order goals.

For example, a person may have a higher order goal of wanting to feel loved. He may identify a number of general goals that will facilitate the attainment of his higher order goal, such as "be more self-assured," "have a sense of humor," and "be honest and trustworthy." (This level in the hierarchy reflects Emmons' notion of the personal striving.) For each of these goals, he may identify a number of specific, concrete goals that will be instrumental in meeting these intermediate goals. For example, he may try to be more self-assured through achievements at work, taking karate classes, or dressing well.

When an important, higher order goal is identified, the hierarchy facilitates the identification of specific, concrete actions that will lead to the attainment of these higher order goals. Of course, not all actions are clearly aimed at the fulfillment of important higher order goals. A person's most pressing concern at a given moment may be to get a drink of water. But very often specific actions can be traced back to higher order goals.

Although we speak of higher order goals as if they were interchangable in terms of their influence on people, recent lines of research suggest that they are not, at least in terms of their relationship to people's well-being. When external, control-oriented goals such as power (Emmons, 1991) or material success (Kasser & Ryan, 1993) are central in people's lives, people experience poorer psychological adjustment and more negative affect than if their central goals are not control-oriented (e.g., affiliation, self-acceptance). Although all higher order goals are not equal, they do have general characteristics in common.

Characteristics of Higher Order Goals

One notable characteristic of the goal hierarchy is that the higher up the goal hierarchy that a goal is located, the more enduring that goal tends to be (Emmons, 1989). There are likely to be numerous lower order goals that are perceived as leading to the attainment of a higher order goal. So, for example, a person might satisfy the lower order goal of publishing two articles this year. Reaching this goal may be perceived as leading to the somewhat higher order goal of being productive in one's career. This goal in turn may be perceived as helping one become one's ideal self. However, publishing two articles is unlikely to be perceived as totally fulfilling the goal of becoming one's ideal self. And other lower order goals, for example "being an inspirational teacher," may also be perceived as helping one become one's ideal self (Emmons, 1989). Thus, fulfilling a higher order goal may entail satisfying an assortment of lower order goals. Some of these lower order goals may be necessary. For example, a person may believe that he *must* publish in order to attain the higher order goal of becoming his ideal self. Other lower order goals may be one of many that will satisfy the requirements of the higher order goal. For example, being a caring instructor who is always available to his students may help a person become his ideal self, even if the person's in-class performance is not inspirational.

A related feature of the goal hierarchy is that goals located higher up in the hierarchy are more abstract than goals located lower in the hierarchy. In general, lower order goals tend to be concrete, and it is easy to determine if they have been attained. If a person has a goal of getting an "A" in algebra, she can easily determine if the goal has been attained. It is more difficult, on the other hand, for her to determine if she has reached the goal of living up to her parents' expectations.

Because higher order goals tend to be abstract, it becomes difficult to determine whether or not the goal has been attained. Consequently, when linking a lower order goal to a higher order goal the higher up in the goal hierarchy that the link is made, the more "unreliable" the link will be. For example, devoting more time to exercise will lead to the higher order goal of reducing body fat. On the other hand, buying a new sports car may or may not lead to the higher order goal of being admired by one's peers. The latter link is more unreliable (in terms of the likelihood that attainment of the lower order goal will facilitate attainment of the higher order goal) than is the former. The lower order goal may contribute to the fulfillment of the higher order goal that it is linked to, but then again it may not. Almost any lower order goal that is perceived as fulfilling a highly abstract higher order goal such as "to be happy" or "to become my ideal self" may not actually lead to that goal. The abstract nature of higher order goal completion likely contributes to the enduring nature of higher order goals. It becomes difficult to determine when one is making progress toward or fulfilling the goal. In fact, Emmons (1992) found that people who identify their personal strivings at high levels (e.g., "get closer to God") report more psychological distress (although less physical illness) than people who identify their strivings at low levels (e.g., "go to church every Sunday"). Identifying strivings at high levels and linking lower order goals to higher order goals would appear to be similar processes. According to Emmons, people who identify their personal strivings at high levels are likely to have difficulty determining whether or not they are making progress toward their goals. This lack of clear feedback about goal attainment leads to higher levels of psychological distress among high-level strivers.

Goal Attainment/Nonattainment

At the center of people's pursuit of goals is the recognition of some discrepancy. People become aware that they are in one state or situation and that they want to be in another. As they go about trying to reduce the perceived discrepancy, they stop intermittently and self-focus to assess their progress. Based on this assessment, they make adjustments in behavior that are aimed at more efficiently reducing the discrepancy between the current state and the desired state, and they continue their pursuit. Theoretically, this *negative feedback cycle* ends when the goal is reached, or when people decide that it is unlikely that they will reach the goal, and therefore they disengage (Carver & Scheier, 1981).

Although we generally speak of goals as either being attained or not attained when considering people's cognitive and affective reactions to goal discrepancies, we see the central issue in goal-striving as the goal-seeker's subjective appraisal of the status of the goal when self-focusing, rather than whether or not the goal has actually been reached at any given moment. In order to predict people's reactions to goal nonattainment, one must consider whether people perceive that the goal has been reached or not, as well as people's perceived progress toward goal completion as compared to their expectations, the rate of that progress, and whether the rate of progress is accelerating or decelerating.

People may be making what they consider sufficient progress toward a goal without having actually reached the goal. If progress toward the goal exceeds expectations, they experience positive affect (Carver & Scheier, 1981). They feel good about the goal, even though they still have not reached the goal. In contrast, people may not be making what they consider sufficient progress toward a goal. If progress toward the goal falls short of expectations, they experience negative affect. They feel bad about the situation even though they may be making *some* progress toward the goal. For example, if a single man who wants to be married meets an interesting woman at a party, he has still not attained his goal. But he is likely to see his goal of marriage as closer at hand than it was before the party, and he will therefore be satisfied with his progress toward the goal. Accordingly, we consider the single man meeting a woman as goal attainment.

Another consideration is whether the rate of progress toward the goal is accelerating as people approach goal attainment or whether the rate is decelerating. If the rate of progress is increasing as people get closer to reaching a goal, they experience more positive affect than if the rate of progress is decreasing as they approach goal attainment (Hsee & Abelson, 1991).

In all cases, a perceived discrepancy (or lack thereof) is important. The discrepancy may be between what people want and what they have or between how quickly they want it and how fast they are getting it. In all cases, the reduction of a discrepancy or the lack of this reduction is related to an affective reaction. Specifically, discrepancy reduction leads to positive affect, and a lack of progress toward discrepancy reduction leads to negative affect.

Please recall, however, the monk swinging from the fraying vine, eating the strawberry. Not all people respond to goal attainment/nonattainment with equally strong affective reactions. That is, even in the face of a perceived discrepancy that they are not reducing to their satisfaction, some people will not experience much negative affect. We suggest that this is because not all people have the same subjective goal hierarchy. Specifically, we suggest that people's affective reactions to goal attainment/nonattainment will be related to the extent that they link lower order goals to higher order goals. When people link lower order goals to higher order goals, they will react more negatively to the nonattainment of those goals (i.e., experience more negative affect). Further, we suggest that people who react more negatively to goal nonattainment will subsequently be less happy overall than people who respond less negatively.

Why will linking lower order goals to higher order goals lead to more negative affect than not doing so? One reason is obvious. This link leads people to believe that they have much to gain upon attainment of the lower order goal, so frustration of the goal leads to great disappointment (Diener, Colvin, Pavot, & Allman, 1991). Of course, believing that goal attainment will result in happiness will lead to more intense (though temporary) positive affect when the goal is attained, so there is an equal tradeoff. But there is an additional reason why linking should lead to negative affect and in this case frequent negative affect, rather than simply more intense negative affect. And we know that the intensity of affect is relatively unimportant to people's overall well-being. It is the frequency, rather than the intensity, of affect that predicts overall well-being (Diener, Sandvik, & Pavot, 1991). The reason that people who link the attainment of a lower order goal to the attainment of a higher order goal should experience more frequent negative affect than people who do not is that people ruminate more about unattained higher order goals than about unattained lower order goals. Rumination is known to result in frequent negative affect.

The Nature of Rumination

> Sometimes it feels like we are locked into the prison of our mind and given a life sentence. Our punishment is to suffer under a life of sentences; the train of thought runs over our lives.
> —Wes Nisker (1990, p. 10)

A woman who desperately wants to have a child but cannot may think about the lack of children in her life all the time. She may find herself returning again and again to thoughts of the child she cannot have. It is likely that these thoughts will be distracting and unpleasant, and she may continue to have thoughts about children for months or even years. We refer to these thoughts as rumination and suggest that rumination is central in considering the affective consequences of goal nonattainment.

Although rumination has been described in different ways by different people, central in all of these descriptions is the idea that rumination is an aversive pattern of thought. Nolen-Hoeksema (1991), for example, referred to rumination as thought focused on a negative emotional state. Rumination means thinking about a dysphoric mood or thinking about the causes and consequences of that mood. In contrast, Silver and her colleagues (e.g., Silver & Wortman, 1980; Tait & Silver, 1989) described rumination as thoughts directed at making sense of an outcome. For example, a woman who thinks a great deal about why her baby died of Sudden Infant Death Syndrome is ruminating about the loss (Downey, Silver, & Wortman, 1990).

A more general description of ruminative thought was offered by Martin and Tesser (1989). According to Martin and Tesser, rumination is a repetitive, intrusive, and often aversive pattern of thought directed toward a desired state or object. In other words, to ruminate is to think repetitively about something a person wants but does not have. This description of ruminative thought is not inconsistent with Nolen-Hoeksema's or

Silver's descriptions. Looked at from a goal-seeking perspective, Nolen-Hoeksema's dysphoric people are motivated to escape the negative mood they are experiencing. In an attempt to reach this important goal, they are likely to ruminate about their dysphoric mood. Similarly, trying to make sense of a loss can be seen as thought directed at something that the person wants but does not have.

People do not ruminate about all goals, only higher order goals (or lower order goals that are seen as instrumental in attaining higher order goals), and only if their progress toward the goal is not meeting their expectations. For example, the goal of completing a crossword puzzle is seen as instrumental in attaining a higher order goal if the person judges that being good at crossword puzzles is a good measure of intelligence. In this case, the person will ruminate more if she is unable to complete the puzzle than if she were just working the crossword puzzle for entertainment. Among others, Klinger, Barta, and Maxeiner (1980) demonstrated that people are more likely to think about goals that they value highly and that are blocked by unexpected difficulties and challenges. Similarly, Emmons and King (1988) found that people spend more time thinking about ambiguous and conflicted strivings than about clear and unconflicted strivings. Certainly goals that are ambiguous and that conflict with the attainment of other goals are likely to be interpreted as blocked goals.

Rumination maps on to the negative feedback cycle discussed earlier (Carver & Scheier, 1981). The negative feedback model assumes that people pursue goals by trying to decrease the discrepancy between their current state of affairs and some desired state. People intermittently make assessments of their progress in an attempt to reduce the discrepancy between their current state and some desired state. At this point, thought directed toward a goal is likely to be a productive, problem-focused activity. But when people have difficulty reducing the discrepancy (i.e., when the goal remains out of reach) and progress toward it is unsatisfactory, people experience negative affect (Carver & Scheier, 1990; Wicklund & Gollwitzer, 1982). At this point, ruminative self-focus becomes aversive (Nolen-Hoeksema, 1991; Pyszczynski & Greenberg, 1987), and disengagement from the goal will often take place (Klinger, 1975). However, if disengagement does not occur (we later suggest when disengagement from a goal may be unlikely), rumination will persist and may even increase.

How might the negative affect associated with goal nonattainment increase rumination about a goal? When the appraisal of a situation leads to negative affect (the negative affect is typically accompanied by physiological arousal), a cognitive search (e.g., Berscheid, 1983; Mandler, 1975) for a behavior that will remove or reduce the negative affect usually ensues (Cooper & Fazio, 1984; Tesser, Pilkington, & McIntosh, 1989). The most obvious way to remove the negative affect associated with desiring some state of affairs is to attain the desired state of affairs. Therefore the cognitive search is directed toward the desired goal. If the goal remains unattainable the cognitive search will soon deteriorate into an unproductive dwelling on the unattained goal, the emotions that accompany that goal, and problems generally associated with the goal (Nolen-Hoeksema, 1991; Wood, Saltzberg, Neale, Stone, & Rachmiel, 1990). Thus, ironically, the most thought appears to be directed at a goal after it has been determined that attainment of the goal will be difficult, unlikely, or impossible (Martin & Tesser, 1989).

Notice that the negative affect experienced from a blocked goal should exacerbate thought directed toward the goal if it does not prompt disengagement. This ruminative thought tends to be unpleasant (Hsee & Abelson, 1991; Millar, Tesser, & Millar, 1988), and consequently rumination adds to the negative affect that goal blockage instigates (McIntosh & Martin, 1992; Wood et al., 1990). The result is that ruminating about goals serves to increase not only the intensity but also the duration of the negative affect related to goal nonattainment.

Goal Nonattainment and Rumination

> It intrigued the disciples that the master who lived so simply would not condemn his wealthy followers.
> "It is rare but not impossible for someone to be rich and holy," he said one day.
> "How?"
> "When money has the effect on his heart that the shadow of that bamboo has on the courtyard."
> The disciples turned to watch the bamboo's shadow sweep the courtyard without stirring a single particle of dust.
>
> —Anthony DeMello (1988, p. 83)

When pursuit of a goal begins to become an unpleasant experience, why are some people able to disengage from the goal, while others are not? Recall that when people have difficulty attaining a goal, they engage in ruminative self-focus in an attempt to reduce the perceived discrepancy. Normally, when people judge that the discrepancy is unlikely to be reduced, they disengage from the goal. They abandon the goal to avoid further ruminative self focus, because this self-focus is unpleasant when progress toward the goal has been frustrated. Indeed, recent work by Duval and her colleagues (Duval, Duval, & Mulilis, 1993) found that if a discrepancy is large, people will disengage from a goal even if it is anticipated that the discrepancy can be removed, albeit slowly. People may not be willing to endure the unpleasant self-focus for an extended period of time, even knowing that the discrepancy can be removed. Rather than stick with a blocked goal, people pursue substitute goals (Wicklund & Gollwitzer, 1982), or distract themselves from thoughts of the goal with pleasant activities (Lyubomirsky & Nolen-Hoeksema, 1993).

But, in some cases, people may be unwilling or unable to give up a goal, even if the discrepancy is large and attaining that goal is difficult or impossible. In this case, the ruminative self-focus persists. According to Pyszczynski and Greenberg, (1987), disengagement from a goal is unlikely when "what is lost or unattainable is of central importance to the person. To the extent that the object was a major source of emotional security and provided the individual with a sense of identity or self-worth" (p. 126). In other words, people may not be able to disengage from a goal when it is seen as necessary in facilitating the attainment of an enduring, higher order goal.

In sum, what I have suggested is that people who link lower order goals to higher order goals are more likely to ruminate about those goals when goal attainment is blocked. Further, it is less likely that people who link lower order goals to higher order goals will be able to disengage easily from those goals. When people ruminate about the linked goals, they will experience exacerbated negative reactions. The chronic negative affect that results from ruminating about linked goals will result in decreased happiness among people who tend to link lower order goals to higher order goals.

Two people can therefore be pursuing the same goal, but react differently to the nonattainment of that goal. We refer to people who chronically link their lower order goals to higher order goals as "linkers," and those who do not as "nonlinkers."

Linking

Theoretically, people are linking to some extent whenever they pursue some lower order goal with the belief that it will lead to the fulfillment of a goal higher up in the goal hierarchy. But there are few lower order goals that are pursued purely in and of themselves. For example, no one loses weight simply to lose weight. However, some people lose weight to feel healthier, while others lose weight to be more attractive, so that they can meet someone and consequently be happier. Accordingly, the higher up the goal hierarchy that a person links a lower order goal, the more that person is linking. As the previous example illustrates, there are changes that occur in the relationship between the higher and lower order goals as links are made higher up in the goal hierarchy. First, when links are made higher up in the hierarchy, the lower order goals to which they are linked take on added importance. There is therefore more riding on goal attainment. Second, links made higher up in the hierarchy are more likely to be unreliable. That is, the lower order goal may be perceived as instrumental in attaining the higher order goal, but it may in fact be unrelated to the higher order goal. Someone may believe that becoming the editor of a prestigious journal will make them happy, so they ruminate about becoming the editor of that journal. However, once the goal is attained, the person may discover that she is no happier now that she is the editor of the journal. By contrast, links that are made lower in the hierarchy rarely involve misperceptions. Becoming the editor of a prestigious journal will surely fulfill the goal of having more projects to work on or of learning more about current research.

Because higher order goals tend to be enduring, a lower order goal that fulfills a higher order goal once may not be enough to do so next time. In other words, links made higher up in the hierarchy may be more subject to adaptation level (Brickman, Coates, & Janoff-Bulman, 1978). According to adaptation level theory, our "usual" level of experience serves as a baseline, and new experiences are compared to this baseline to determine if they are good or bad. Experiences above this baseline are seen as positive, while experiences below this baseline are seen as negative. Outcomes that match the baseline are seen as neutral. The theory assumes that people's baselines change as new experiences are incorporated. In other words, events that at one time seemed very positive may be perceived as less positive when people get used to experiencing those kinds of events. For example, wanting to be a success may mean wanting to publish in a leading journal twice a year. But once this goal is attained and the person has gotten used to publishing often, the person may still not feel successful. Consequently, the lower order goal that is perceived as fulfilling the higher order goal of being successful may change to becoming the editor of a prestigious journal, and so on. Because the link between the lower and higher order goals is subjective, people can keep changing their evaluation of what would constitute fulfillment of the higher order goal based on their current experiences and expectations.

Happiness is one higher order goal for which these pitfalls are especially prevalent. The link between happiness and most lower order goals is not only highly subjective but often wrong. Many objective life situations that people link to happiness are actually unrelated to happiness (Andrews & Withey, 1976; Easterlin, 1974; Kammann, 1982). Happiness is also highly susceptible to adaptation level (Brickman et al., 1978). Even highly positive events, such as winning the lottery, will not significantly increase people's happiness once they get used to their good fortune. In fact, highly positive events are particularly susceptible to adaptational influences, because rarely is extreme positive affect not accompanied by some degree of negative affect as well (Diener et al., 1991). The characteristics that distinguish linking and nonlinking might best be demonstrated when focusing on the higher order goal of happiness.

We chose to focus on the higher order goal of happiness in operationalizing the concept of linking for these reasons, and also because happiness is arguably the highest higher order goal. Happiness is not strived for as a means to any loftier goal; it is desired in and of itself. On the other hand, most other goals are pursued with the ultimate intent of making one happy. Even other higher order goals, such as love, affiliation, becoming ones' ideal self, power, and so on, have as their ultimate aim the desire to be happy.

The implications of linking happiness to goal attainment might best be summarized with an example. Suppose there are two people both of whom want to go out with the same woman. One wants to go out with her because he wants some company on Friday and Saturday nights. The other wants to go out with her because he believes that going out with her will raise his self-esteem and others' opinions of him and that this will make him happier. During the time when neither has gotten a date with the woman, which one would be most distressed? Because rumination is instigated by the failure to attain higher order goals, the person who links the date to his long-term happiness would be more likely to ruminate than would the person who does not make this link. So, we have two people in objectively similar situations. Both want to date the same woman and neither has done so. Yet, the person who links the woman's favor to his happiness will be ruminating, whereas the person who does not make this link will not be ruminating. Then because of the aversive nature of rumination, the ruminator would be more likely than the nonruminator to experience frequent negative affect and, ultimately, unhappiness.

According to our model, linkers should ruminate more than nonlinkers when they have not attained a particular goal. But what about *after* a goal has been reached? Linkers tend to dwell on what they want but do not have. Once linkers have attained a goal, they should find it less compelling than goals that they have not yet attained. In fact, thoughts about other pressing unmet goals may dominate a linker's thoughts to the relative exclusion of outcomes that have already been attained. For example, a person who believes that living in a spacious, luxurious house will make her happy might ruminate about having a sunroom in her house. If she gets the sunroom, she may well sit in the sunroom and ruminate about how happy she would be if only she could have a pool in the backyard. So linkers may think very little about goals that have been attained. For nonlinkers, on the other hand, goal attainment is less pressing. For them, the attainment of any specific goal is not related to their happiness. Therefore, whether a goal has been attained or not may have less effect on the extent to which nonlinkers ruminate about the goal.

Another way to describe linkers' predicted lack of interest in goals that have already been attained is to say that linkers are outcome-oriented. When people believe that the attainment of some lower order goal will facilitate the attainment of some higher order goal, their attention should become squarely focused on attainment of the lower order goal, rather than on process of striving for the goal. Not surprisingly, people who demonstrate a heightened concern for outcomes experience less positive affect surrounding the pursuit of their goals than people who are less outcome-oriented (Cantor, Norem, Langston, Zirkel, Fleeson, & Cook-Flanagan, 1991).

The role of beliefs and rumination in producing unhappiness is depicted graphically in Fig. 3.1. Note that our model does not depict an individual

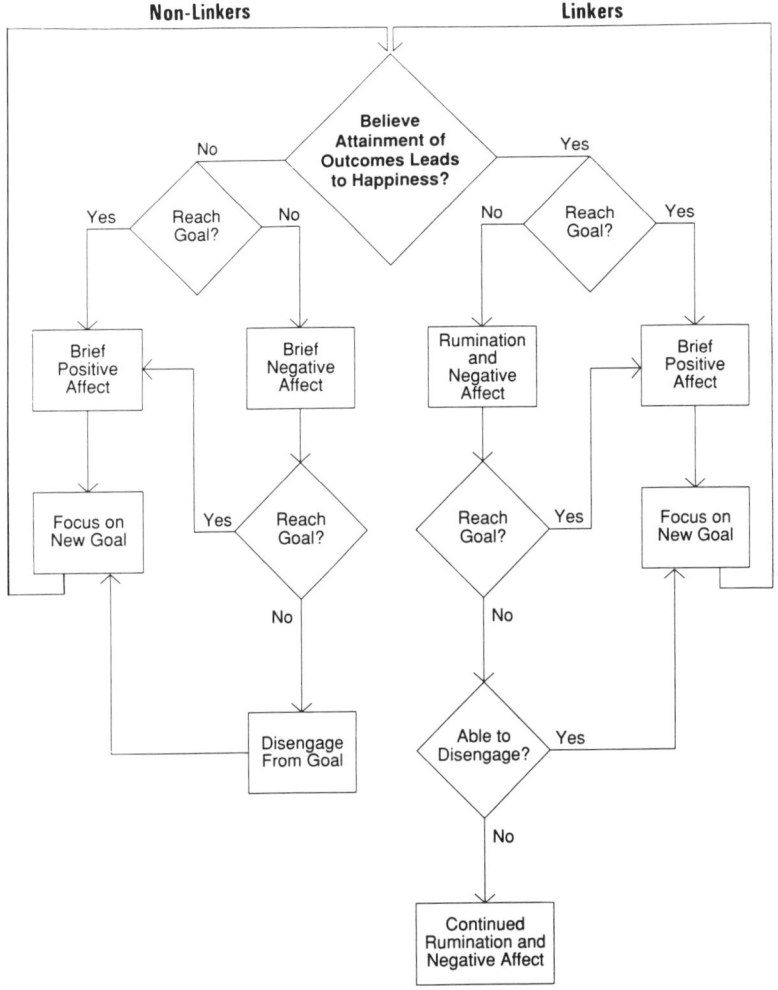

FIG 3.1. The linking model.

difference per se. It depicts a belief system that we assume would be as maleable as other belief systems (e.g., being a Christian or a Democrat). At any point, people enter the system at the "Believe this leads to happiness?" point and they may answer with either a "yes" or a "no."

On the other hand, it is likely that some people hold more linked beliefs than others, and we can use this difference to categorize people roughly as linkers and nonlinkers.

From the model, we can derive the following predictions:

1. When they have not attained the goal, people who link their goals to their happiness will ruminate more about those goals than will people who do not.
2. Rumination will be positively related to people's experience of negative affect and unhappiness.
3. People who link their goals to their happiness will report experiencing more negative affect and unhappiness than people who do not.
4. Rumination will *mediate* the relationship between linking and both negative affect and unhappiness. That is, the relationship is causal. Linking the attainment of an outcome with happiness leads to rumination when that outcome is not attained, and this, in turn, leads to chronic negative affect.

Empirical Support

Is Linking Related to Rumination? We (McIntosh & Martin, 1992) conducted a study to test whether people who link goals to their happiness do in fact ruminate more about those goals than nonlinkers. We began by blocking subjects as linkers and nonlinkers using a questionnaire that asks subjects to make judgments about how much attaining or not attaining each of 33 goals would influence their happiness (see McIntosh & Martin, 1992, for a complete description of this measure). Then, we identified a goal that some subjects wanted but did not have and other subjects already had. The goal we chose was "a romantic relationship." We then made the goal salient by having the subjects complete a computerized questionnaire about their recent love life. Finally, we determined the extent to which the subjects were ruminating about a romantic relationship.

A word recognition task was used to measure the extent to which subjects were ruminating about a romantic relationship (Martin, Tesser, & McIntosh, 1993). Subjects were presented with a series of words on a computer screen. The words were revealed one letter at a time, at 5-second intervals. The subjects' task was to recognize the word that was being presented as quickly as possible. Some words were related to romantic relationships (i.e., relationship, romance) and some were unrelated control words (i.e., military, adjective).

The assumption behind this measure is that the more subjects are ruminating about a given goal, the more accessible information related to that goal will be. Therefore, subjects ruminating about relationships should recognize words related to that topic faster than should subjects not ruminating about relationships (Martin & Tesser, 1989; Furham & Shavitt, 1990; Warren, 1972).

The results are depicted in Fig. 3.2. Linkers who wanted a romantic relationship ruminated more than did linkers who currently had a romantic relationship. However, nonlinkers did not vary in how much they ruminated about romantic relationships regardless of whether they currently were in one or not. As predicted, people who tend to link their goals to their happiness were more likely to ruminate about a current goal (i.e., a romantic relationship) than people who do not link their goals to their happiness.

For people who currently have a romantic relationship, linkers ruminated less than did nonlinkers as predicted. Once a goal is reached, it is of little interest to linkers. This is demonstrated in linkers' relatively slow reaction time in recognizing words related to a topic about which they have recently been primed.

It is important to note that there were no differences between linkers and nonlinkers in the time it took them to recognize the control words. This content-specific effect of rumination rules out the possibility that the results were due to differences in the subjects' motivation or ability to recognize

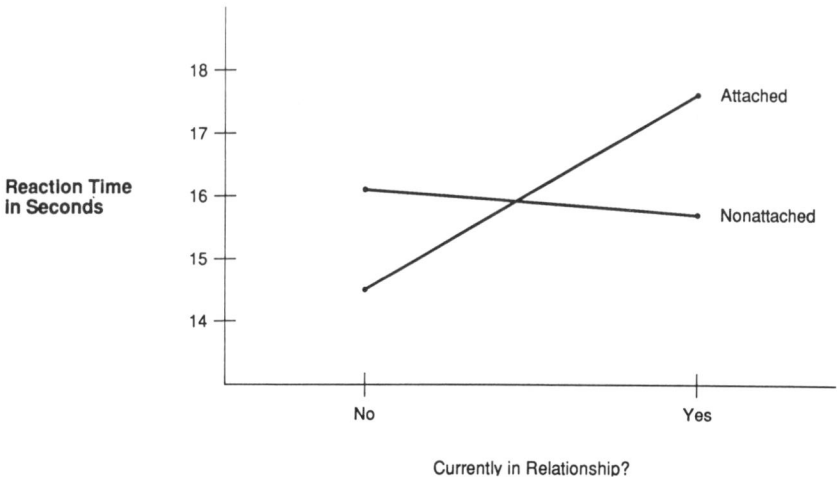

FIG 3.2. Time to recognize goal-related words as a function of status of relationship and linking score.

words in general. The differences in recognition time were specific to words about relationships.

Is Rumination Related to Negative Affect? The next question to be addressed is whether the rumination that results from linking is related to negative affect. Wood et al. (1990) found that rumination is indeed related to negative affect. In addition, Nolen-Hoeksema (e.g., Nolen-Hoeksema, 1991; Nolen-Hoeksema, Morrow, & Fredrickson, 1993) has demonstrated in a variety of settings that when people are in a dysphoric mood, ruminating about the mood will perpetuate the mood. Rumination not only results in negative affect and dysphoria, but it serves to perpetuate people's dysphoric moods.

In a questionnaire study, we tested whether people who tend to link their goals to their happiness report both more rumination and more negative affect than people who do not link. The subjects completed the linking scale, along with measures of happiness (Fordyce, 1977), affect (Watson, 1988), and rumination. The rumination measure was a 10-item questionnaire and included questions such as "When I have a problem, I tend to think about it a lot of the time" and "I often become lost in thought."

We found that linking was significantly related to unhappiness and negative mood. We also found, as expected, that the more people link the attainment of goals with happiness, the more they ruminated. The more they ruminated, the more unhappiness and negative affect they reported.

Does Rumination Mediate the Relationship Between Linking and Unhappiness? Our final prediction was that rumination would *mediate* the relationship between linking and unhappiness. Baron and Kenny (1986) described four criteria for determining if a variable is a mediator. In terms of this experiment, the criteria are (a) subjects' linking scores must be related to unhappiness, (b) rumination must be related to unhappiness, (c) the linking scores must be related to rumination, and (d) when rumination and linking are regressed simultaneously onto unhappiness, the relationship between linking and unhappiness should disappear, while the relationship between rumination and unhappiness should remain. This is precisely what was found, supporting our predictions about the causal relationship among linking, rumination, and unhappiness.

Linking and Affective Information. Our subsequent research on linking has been conducted using a different measure of linking. Whereas the previously described linking scale measures the frequency with which people link their happiness to various goals, this second scale directly asks people for their beliefs about the relationship between goals and happiness. This second linking scale is easier to administer. The measure consists of 13 forced-choice questions that tap subjects' beliefs about the relationship between goals and happiness. One question, for example, asks: How important is having money to your happiness? The response options for this item are (a) Being able to buy the things I want when I want them definitely makes me happier, and (b) Once I have enough money for the basic necessities of life, more money will not make me happier. In this example, response A represents a linking perspective, whereas response B represents a nonlinking perspective. The scale displays a reasonably high degree of internal consistency (alpha = .70), while the test-retest reliability of the scale is .78.

According to Schwarz and Bless (1992), negative moods indicate that the environment is problematic and that some action needs to be taken, whereas positive moods tell people that the environment is safe and no action needs to be taken. Because linkers tend to respond more to discrepancy than to success information, linkers should be more likely than nonlinkers to react to an induced negative state but to ignore an induced positive one.

We found this to be the case (McIntosh, Martin, Jones, & Chen, 1994). After a sad movie, linkers reported more negative affect (but not less positive affect) than did nonlinkers. After a happy movie, nonlinkers reported more happiness (but not less sadness) than did linkers. Linkers appear to be more driven by their negative moods, while nonlinkers tend to focus more on their positive moods. Perhaps this observation also has implications for long-term mood states, such as depression, as well.

Linking, Depression, and Illness. We have seen that linking can lead to chronic negative affect. Can it also lead to depression? In the area of cognitive therapy on depression we find a clear echoing of the concept of linking that suggests that linking is in fact related to depression. In working with the irrational beliefs of depressed clients, Beck pointed to beliefs about the links between lower order goals and happiness as a primary correlate of depression:

Therapist: Now what did failing mean?
Patient: That I couldn't get into law school.
Therapist: And what does that mean to you?
Patient: That I'm not smart enough.
Therapist: Anything else?
Patient: That I can never be happy.
Therapist: And how do these THOUGHTS make you feel?
Patient: Very unhappy.
Therapist: So it is the meaning of failing a test that makes you very unhappy. In fact, believing that you can never be happy is a powerful factor in producing unhappiness. So, you get yourself into a trap—by definition, failure to get into law school equals "I can never be happy."

(Beck, Goldfried, & Norcross, 1979, pp. 145-146).

Cognitive therapy points to the irrational nature of such beliefs as central to their potential depressive nature. A more specific mechanism for how linking might lead to depression hinges on the relationship of rumination and depression. We know that rumination plays a role in depression. People who ruminate show longer and more severe depression following stressful events than do nonruminators (e.g., Beck, 1982; Millar, Tesser, & Millar, 1988; Nolen-Hoeksema, 1991). Lyubomirsky and Nolen-Hoeksema (1993) found that ruminating about depression, rather than depression itself, led mildly depressed subjects to be unwilling to distract themselves from their dysphoric mood with pleasant activities. Nolen-Hoeksema and Morrow (1991) looked at the effects of a highly stressful event, the 1989 San Francisco earthquake, on ruminators and nonruminators. They found that subjects who demonstrated a ruminative response style before the quake were significantly more likely to be depressed both 10 days and 7 weeks after the earthquake, even after their initial level of depression was controlled.

But why do some people ruminate following a stressful event while others do not? It is interesting to note that relatively minor, everyday stressors can be as strongly related to depression and illness as are major negative life events (e.g., Dohrenwend & Dohrenwend, 1978; Kanner, Coyne, Shaefer, & Lazarus, 1980). In fact, while both major and minor events both predict depression, minor hassles account for more of the variance related to depression than do major life events (Dohrenwend & Dohrenwend, 1978). Recall that linkers may interpret even small everyday setbacks as threats to major life goals. To the extent that people link the goals that are frustrated by these minor stressors to higher order goals such as happiness, they will ruminate about them. And, as noted earlier, rumination is related to depression.

We should find, therefore, that the more minor stressors that linkers experience in a given time period, the more depressed they will be. Nonlinkers should be less effected by stressors. In addition, stressors usually produce not only more depression but more reports of physical illness (Pennebaker, 1989). We would therefore expect linkers under high stress to report more physical symptoms than linkers under low stress and more symptoms than nonlinkers regardless of their stress level.

McIntosh, Harlow, and Martin (1994) tested this hypothesis by measuring (a) the amount of stress subjects experienced, (b) the amount of rumination they reported, (c) their level of depression, and (d) the number of physical symptoms they reported. All of these measures were taken at two different times, 2 weeks apart. As expected, at time 1 linkers reported more rumination, more depression, and more physical symptoms than did nonlinkers. This was true even though there were no significant differences in the number of stressors reported by linkers and nonlinkers. More importantly, 2 weeks after reporting that they were under high stress, linkers were more depressed and reported more physical symptoms than if they had reported low stress 2 weeks earlier. Linkers under high stress also reported being more depressed and complained of more physical symptoms than nonlinkers, regardless of whether nonlinkers had previously reported high or low stress 2 weeks earlier. In other words, high stress was a good predictor of depression and physical complaints for linkers but not for nonlinkers. In fact, there was a strong (though nonsignificant) trend for nonlinkers to report *less* depression and illness if they had previously reported *high* stress than if they had previously reported low stress.

Linking and Mood Repair. Other research supports the contention that once in a dysphoric state, linkers will have more difficulty getting out of that state than will nonlinkers. Edelman, Ahrens, and Haaga (1994) asked dysphoric subjects whether they believed that the occurrence of various positive events would mean that they were "special in some way." One interpretation of this question is that subjects were being asked whether they linked their positive outcomes to their sense of self-worth. Dysphoria was more likely to persist in subjects who agreed that their self-worth was contingent on the occurrence of positive events than in subjects who did not hold this belief.

The picture of linkers that is coming into focus through these findings is not wholly unfamiliar. It describes a person who experiences a lot of negative affect, who worries, and who is prone to depression and stress-related illness. Does our model provide anything beyond similar constructs such as "high negative affectivity individuals," "ruminators," or "pessimists?" We believe so. We believe our model provides insight into one reason why people exhibit these negative characteristics.

Convergent and Discriminant Validity: Linking and Other Related Constructs

As noted earlier, we do not conceptualize linking as an individual difference per se, but rather as a belief system concerning the implications of goal attainment. But as we have demonstrated, it can be fruitful to categorize people as having more or less linked beliefs than other people. The profile of linkers that develops is of people who experience chronic negative affect because they ruminate about unattained goals. They are consequently more unhappy than nonlinkers, and under stress they are more likely to become depressed and ill than are nonlinkers. To some extent, this profile is similar to that of other individual difference constructs. In this section, we examine some of these constructs and consider how linking fits in.

Linkers are most notably similar to individuals who are high in negative affectivity (Watson & Clark, 1984). People high in negative affectivity experience pervasive negative affect, and they tend to have difficulty putting unpleasant experiences out of their minds. They are more introspective and self-focusing than low negative affectivity individuals, and they tend to focus on negative aspects of themselves, others, and the world in general.

Conceptually, there is a moderate degree of overlap between the characteristics of linkers and high negative affectivity individuals. Both describe people who ruminate and experience chronic negative affect.

Empirically, there is also a moderate degree of overlap. The correlation between the linking scale and neuroticism scale of the Eysenck Personality Inventory (one measure of negative affectivity; Eysenck & Eysenck, 1968) is .23 ($p < .05$). Of course, this correlation is not nearly as strong as the intercorrelations among the various constructs identified by Watson and Clark as measuring negative affectivity (the correlations ranged from $r = .44$ to $r = .88$). In addition, we have found neuroticism to be related to other adjustment-related concepts such as extraversion ($r = -.38$), agreeableness ($r = -.24$), conscientiousness ($r = -.27$), self-efficacy ($r = -.44$), and optimism ($r = -.58$), whereas linking was not significantly related to any of these concepts.

There are clear similarities between linking and negative affectivity, although they are by no means synonymous. One distinction that can clearly be made between linking and negative affectivity is that negative affectivity basically describes a state, whereas linking describes the process that leads to a state. Empirically, a high negative affectivity person is a person who consistently reports high negative affect. The conditions that lead people to become high in negative affectivity are not included in the description. We would offer that one way that people may come to experience pervasive negative emotion is through linking.

Another related concept is Nolen-Hoeksema's ruminators versus distractors. Most people engage in self-focused rumination when they experience a depressed mood. But some people are able to disengage by distracting themselves with pleasant activities, while others continue to ruminate. These ruminators experience heightened negative affect and prolonged depressed moods.

Linkers would appear to be similar to Nolen-Hoeksema's ruminators, because, after all, linkers ruminate. The finding that linkers tend to experience depression when stress is high contributes to the similarity. However, as with high negative affectivity individuals, the distinction between ruminators and distractors is descriptive. The model does not include a consideration of why some people are ruminators and others are not. In subsequent work, Nolen-Hoeksema (1991) has speculated on a number of possible explanations for why some people develop a ruminative style: (a) children may learn it from their parents (b) parents may fail to teach children other strategies for dealing with negative affect, and (c) it may be biological. Of course, these explanations address the onset of rumination from a developmental perspective. By contrast, we are addressing the present cognitive and affective processes that lead some people to ruminate about their dysphoric moods while others do not. When the onset of a negative mood is the loss or blockage of an important goal, some people (i.e., linkers) may be more likely than others to perceive the goal as necessary in facilitating the attainment of an enduring, higher-order goal and, therefore, may be more likely to ruminate and less likely to be able to disengage from the dysphoric mood through distraction. Other people, namely nonlinkers, will also experience a negative mood upon goal frustration. They will initially engage in ruminative self-focus, but because they do not perceive the goal as being necessary to their happiness, they are able to disengage when ruminative self-focus becomes too aversive.

Finally, Scheier and Carver's (1987) dispositional optimists versus pessimists bore some conceptual similarities to linkers versus nonlinkers. Optimists have the general expectancy that they will be able to attain their important life goals. They are likely to engage in problem-focused coping strategies when having difficulties with goal-attainment, whereas pessimists are likely to engage in emotion-based coping strategies, particularly denial (Carver, Scheier, & Weintraub, 1989). Are nonlinkers simply optimists? Do they refrain from ruminating about blocked goals because they believe that they will eventually attain them regardless of the setbacks they experience? We would suggest that the two concepts are unrelated for the following reasons. First, pessimists are most likely to engage in denial, whereas linkers are ruminators who self-focus and dwell rather than deny. Second, empirically linking is not correlated with the optimism scale of the Eysenck Personality Inventory ($r = -.03$).

Conclusions

Can people choose to stop ruminating, and can they become more "nonlinking" in their approach to goals? This is an empirical question that has not yet been answered. But we can offer some ideas on how these changes might be possible.

We know that trying to suppress rumination through sheer will does not help curb the unwanted thoughts and can actually make rumination worse (Wegner, Schneider, Carter, & White, 1987). Obviously a subtler approach is required to reduce rumination. One possibility is to get people to be more present-focused. Because it is not possible to ruminate and be present-focused simultaneously, the more time people spend present-focused, the less time they have to ruminate. Of course, ruminative thoughts can come unbidden and intrude on people's present experience, so this approach may be limited. But it is interesting to note that many long-time meditators report having very few intrusive thoughts. For example, Krishnamurti, a great Eastern teacher of the 20th century, reported that he would often go on 1- or 2-hour walks without having any thoughts whatsoever (Valles, 1988). Perhaps practicing a present-focus is effective in short-circuiting ruminative thoughts.

Another possibility is to get linkers to link their higher order goals to easily attainable lower order goals. If linkers believed that their self-worth was tied up in their ability to say kind things to others, or that their happiness was contingent on their ability to spend more time outdoors, they would not experience as much goal-nonattainment and would ruminate less. A question arises, however: how deeply ingrained are a person's beliefs about what goals are linked to self-worth and happiness. Can these beliefs be changed?

Finally, people might be able to break the cycle of rumination if they were more consciously aware of the process that leads people to ruminate and to the costs of that rumination. People are not very skillful at detecting covariances (Nisbett & Wilson, 1977). Detecting covariances between events in peoples lives and their affective reactions to those events is no exception (Wilson, Laser, & Stone, 1982). One striking illustration of people's lack of awareness of the affective consequences of their beliefs and behaviors is people's attitudes toward work and leisure. People are more likely to find enjoyment in work than in leisure, yet are more likely to report that they would rather be at leisure than at work (Csikszentmihalyi & LeFevre, 1989). It is likely, therefore, that linkers are not aware that their approach to goals has negative consequences. Perhaps an awareness of this connection would lead them to change their approach. Perhaps we can illustrate this suggestion with another Zen parable:

A Zen monk wandering the countryside finds a beautiful opal that is worth a year's pay to the average worker. Later in his travels he shows the opal to a farmer, who is overwhelmed by the beauty and value of the jewel and begs the monk to give it to him. The monk casually tosses the opal to the farmer and does not give the jewel another thought as he continues on his travels. A few days later the monk is surprised to see the farmer, who has been looking for him. The farmer hands the monk the opal and says, "I have decided I really don't want the opal. I want whatever it is you have that enabled you to give it to me."

REFERENCES

Andrews, F. M., & Withey, S. B. (1976). *Social indicators of well-being*. New York: Plenum.
Baron, R. A., & Kenny, D. A. (1986). The moderator-mediator variable distinction in social

psychological research: Conceptual, strategic, and statistical considerations. *Journal of Personality and Social Psychology, 51,* 1173-1182.
Beck, A. T. (1982). *Depression: Clinical, experimental, and theoretical aspects.* New York: Harper & Row.
Beck, A. T., Goldfried, M. R., & Norcross, J. C. (1979). *Cognitive therapy and depression.* New York: Guilford.
Berscheid, E. (1983). Emotion. In H. H. Kelley, E. Berscheid, A. Christensen, J. Harvey, T. L. Huston, G. Levinger, E. McClintock, A. Peplau, & D. R. Peterson (Eds.), *Close relationships* (pp. 110-168). San Francisco: W. H. Freeman.
Brickman, P., Coates, D., & Janoff-Bulman, R. (1978). Lottery winners and accident victims: Is happiness relative? *Journal of Personality and Social Psychology, 51,* 1173-1182.
Cantor, N., Norem, J. K., Brower, A. M., Niedenthal, P. M., & Langston, C. A. (1987). Life tasks, self-concept ideals, and cognitive strategies in a life transition. *Journal of Personality and Social Psychology, 53,* 1178-1191.
Cantor, N., Norem, J. K., Langston, C. A., Zirkel, S., Fleeson, W., & Cook-Flanagan, C. (1991). Life tasks and daily life experience. *Journal of Personality, 59,* 425-451.
Carver, C. S., & Scheier, M. F. (1981). *Attention and self-regulation: A control theory approach to human behavior.* New York: Springer-Verlag.
Carver, C. S., & Scheier, M. F. (1990). Origins and functions of positive and negative affect: A control-process view. *Psychological Review, 97,* 19-35.
Carver, C. S., Scheier, M. F., & Weintraub, J. K. (1989). Assessing coping strategies: A theoretically based approach. *Journal of Personality and Social Psychology, 56,* 267-283.
Cooper, J., & Fazio, R. H. (1984). A new look at dissonance theory. In L. Berkowitz (Ed.), *Advances in experimental social psychology* (Vol. 17, pp. 229-267). New York: Academic Press.
Csikszentmihalyi, M., & LeFevre, J. (1989). Optimal experience in work and leisure. *Journal of Personality and Social Psychology, 56,* 815-822.
DeMello, A. (1988). *One minute wisdom.* New York: Doubleday.
Diener, E., Colvin, C. R., Pavot, W. G., & Allman, A. (1991). The psychic costs of intense positive affect. *Journal of Personality and Social Psychology, 61,* 492-503.
Diener, E., Sandvik, E., & Pavot, W. (1991). Happiness is the frequency, not the intensity, of positive versus negative affect. In F. Strack, M. Argyle, & N. Schwarz (Eds.), *Subjective well-being* (pp. 119-140). Oxford: Pergamon.
Dohrenwend, B. S., & Dohrenwend, B. P. (1978). Some issues in research on stressful life events. *Journal of Nervous and Mental Disease, 166,* 7-15.
Downey, G., Silver, R. C., & Wortman, C. B. (1990). Reconsidering the attribution-adjustment relation following a major negative event: Coping with the loss of a child. *Journal of Personality and Social Psychology, 59,* 925-940.
Duval, T. S., Duval, V. H., & Mullis, J. (1993). *Effects of self focus, degree of discrepancy between self and standard, and outcome expectancy favorability on the tendency to match self to standard or withdraw.* Manuscript submitted for publication.
Easterlin, R. A. (1974). Does economic growth improve the human lot? Some empirical evidence. In P. A. David & M. W. Reder (Eds.), *Nations and households in economic growth.* New York: Academic Press.
Edelman, R. E., Ahrens, A. H., & Haaga, D. A. (1994). *Inferences about the self, attributions, and overgeneralization as predictors of recovery from dysphoria.* Manuscript submitted for publication.
Emmons, R. A. (1989). The personal striving approach to personality. In L. A. Pervin (Ed.), *Goal concepts in personality and social psychology.* Hillsdale, NJ: Lawrence Erlbaum Associates.
Emmons, R. A. (1991). Personal strivings, daily life events, and psychological and physical well-being. *Journal of Personality, 59,* 1058-1068.

Emmons, R. A. (1992). Abstract versus concrete goals: Personal striving level, physical illness, and psychological well-being. *Journal of Personality and Social Psychology, 62*, 292-300.

Emmons, R. A., & King, L. A. (1988). Conflict among personal strivings: Immediate and long-term implications for psychological and physical well-being. *Journal of Personality and Social Psychology, 54*, 1040-1048.

Eysenck, H. J., & Eysenck, S. B. G. (1968). *Manual of the Eysenck personality inventory*. San Diego: Educational and Industrial Testing Service.

Fordyce, M. W. (1977). Development of a program to increase personal happiness. *Journal of Counseling Psychology, 24*, 511-521.

Fuhrman, R. W., & Shavitt, S. (1990). *The effects of goal priming on speed and favorableness of attitude judgments*. Paper presented at the Midwestern Psychological Association. Chicago, IL.

Hsee, C. K., & Abelson, R. P. (1991). Velocity relation: Satisfaction as a function of the first derivative outcome over time. *Journal of Personality and Social Psychology, 60*, 341-347.

Kammann, R. (1982). *Personal circumstances and life events as poor predictors of happiness*. Paper presented at the annual convention of the American Psychological Society, Washington, DC.

Kanner, A. D., Coyne, J. C., Shaefer, C., & Lazarus, R. S. (1980). Comparison of two modes of stress measurement: Daily hassles and uplifts versus major life events. *Journal of Behavioral Medicine, 4*, 1-39.

Kasser, T., & Ryan, R. M. (1993). A dark side of the American dream: Correlates of financial success as a central life aspiration. *Journal of Personality and Social Psychology, 65*, 410-422.

Klinger, E. (1975). Consequences to commitment to and disengagement from incentives. *Psychological Review, 82*, 223-231.

Klinger, E. (1977). *Meaning and void: Inner experience and the incentives in people's lives*. Minneapolis: University of Minnesota Press.

Klinger, E., Barta, S. G., & Maxeiner, M. E. (1980). Motivational correlates of thought content frequency and commitment. *Journal of Personality and Social Psychology, 39*, 1222-1237.

Little, B. R. (1983). Personal projects: A rationale and method for investigation. *Environment and Behavior, 15*, 273-309.

Lyubomirsky, S., & Nolen-Hoeksema, S. (1993). Self-perpetuating properties of dysphoric rumination. *Journal of Personality and Social Psychology, 65*, 339-349.

Mandler, G. (1975). *Mind and emotion*. New York: Wiley.

Martin, L. L., & Tesser, A. (1989). Toward a motivational and structural theory of ruminative thought. In J. S. Uleman, & J. Bargh (Eds.), *The handbook of mental control* (pp. 552-572). New York: Guilford.

Martin, L. L., Tesser, A., & McIntosh, W. D. (1993). Wanting but not having: The effects of unattained goals on thoughts and feelings. In D. M. Wegner & J. W. Pennebaker (Eds.), *The handbook of mental control* (pp. 552-572). New York: Prentice-Hall.

McIntosh, W. D., Harlow, T. F., & Martin, L. L. (1994). *Linkers and nonlinkers: The relation between goal beliefs, rumination, and depression*. Manuscript submitted for publication.

McIntosh, W. D., & Martin, L. L. (1992). The cybernetics of happiness: The relation between goal attainment, rumination, and affect. In M. S. Clark (Ed.), *Review of Personality and Social Psychology* (pp. 222-246). Newbury Park, CA: Sage.

McIntosh, W. D., Martin, L. L., Jones, J. B., & Chen, N. (1994). *The consequences of linking goal attainment to happiness: Linkers focus on discrepancies*. Manuscript in progress.

Millar, K. U., Tesser, A., & Millar, M. (1988). The effects of a threatening life event on behavior sequences and intrusive thought: A self-disruption explanation. *Cognitive Therapy and Research, 12*, 441-457.

Nisbett, R. E., & Wilson, T. D. (1977). Telling more than we can know: Verbal reports on mental processes. *Psychological Review, 84*, 231–259.

Nisker, W. (1990). *Crazy wisdom.* Berkeley, CA: Ten Speed Press.

Nolen-Hoeksema, S. (1991). Responses to depression and their effects on the duration of depressive episodes. *Journal of Abnormal Psychology, 100*, 259–282.

Nolen-Hoeksema, S., & Morrow, J. (1991). A prospective study of depression and posttraumatic stress symptoms after a natural disaster: The 1989 Loma Prieta Earthquake. *Journal of Personality and Social Psychology, 61*, 115–121.

Nolen-Hoeksema, S., Morrow, J., & Fredrickson, B. L. (1993). Response styles and the duration of episodes of depressed mood. *Journal of Abnormal Psychology, 102*, 20–28.

Omodei, M. M., & Wearing, A. J. (1990). Need satisfaction and involvement in personal projects: Toward an integrative model of subjective well-being. *Journal of Personality and Social Psychology, 59*, 762–769.

Pennebaker, J. W. (1989). Stream of consciousness and stress: Levels of thinking. In J. S. Uleman & J. A. Bargh (Eds.), *Unintended thought.* New York: Guilford.

Pyszczynski, T. & Greenberg, J. (1987). Self-regulatory perseveration and the depressive self-focusing style: A self-awareness theory of reactive depression. *Psychological Bulletin, 102*, 122–138.

Scheier, M. F., & Carver, C. S. (1987). Dispositional optimism and physical well-being: The influence of generalized outcome expectancies on health. *Journal of Personality, 55*, 169–210.

Silver, R. L., & Wortman, C. B. (1980). Coping with undesirable life events. In J. Garber & M. E. P. Seligman (Eds.), *Human helplessness* (pp. 279–340). New York: Academic Press.

Schwarz, N., & Bless, H. (1992). Scandals and the public trust in politicians: Assimilation and contrast effects. *Personality and Social Psychology Bulletin, 18*, 574–579.

Tait, R., & Silver, R. C. (1989). Coming to terms with major negative life events. In J. S. Uleman & J. A. Bargh (Eds.), *Unintended thought* (pp. 351–382). New York: Guilford Press.

Tesser, A., Pilkington, C. J., & McIntosh, W. D. (1989). Self-evaluation maintenance and the mediational role of emotion: The perception of friends and strangers. *Journal of Personality and Social Psychology, 57*, 442–456.

Valles, C. G. (1988). *Mastering sadhana.* New York: Doubleday.

Warren, R. (1972). Stimulus encoding and memory. *Journal of Experimental Psychology, 94*, 90–100.

Watson, D. (1988). The vicissitudes of mood measurement: Effects of varying descriptors, time frames, and response formats on measures of positive and negative affect. *Journal of Personality and Social Psychology, 55*, 128–141.

Watson, D., & Clark, L. A. (1984). Negative affectivity: The disposition to experience aversive emotional states. *Psychological Bulletin, 96*, 465–490.

Wegner, D. M., Schneider, D. J., Carter, S. R. III, & White, T. L. (1987). Paradoxical effects of thought suppression. *Journal of Personality and Social Psychology, 53*, 5–13.

Wicklund, R. A., & Gollwitzer, P. M. (1982). *Symbolic self-completion.* Hillsdale, NJ: Lawrence Erlbaum Associates.

Wilson, T. D., Laser, P. S., & Stone, J. I. (1982). Judging the predictors of one's own mood: Accuracy and the use of shared theories. *Journal of Experimental Social Psychology, 18*, 537–556.

Wood, J. V., Saltzberg, J. A., Neale, J. M., Stone, A. A., & Rachmiel, T. B. (1990). Self-focused attention, coping responses, and distressed mood in everyday life. *Journal of Personality and Social Psychology, 58*, 1027–1036.

4
Goal Orientation and Emotional Well-Being: Linking Goals and Affect Through the Self

Robert A. Emmons
Heather A. Kaiser
University of California, Davis

As is evident from the contributions to this volume, affect is central to goals. At a minimum, affect plays a role in determining one's commitment to goals, energizes goal-directed behavior, and serves as feedback informing a person of the status of his or her goals. Additionally, people have goals to feel or to avoid feeling certain emotions; one may desire a happy life or a life free from strife and turmoil. Theories of emotion and of subjective well-being (SWB) are increasingly adopting the position that affective states are a function of the status of one's goal pursuits. Whether affect is examined in terms of discrete short-term states (emotions) or as long-term individual difference characteristics, there is widespread agreement that goals and related constructs, such as concerns and commitments, play an essential role in determining the quality and intensity of affective experience (Frijda, 1986; Klinger, 1977; Lazarus, 1991; Oatley, 1992; Ortony, Clore, & Collins, 1988; Pervin, 1983). Goal theories of emotion postulate that discrete emotional states are the results of appraisals regarding the significance of life circumstances for one's personally meaningful goal strivings (Lazarus, 1991; Roseman, Wiest, & Swartz, 1994). For instance, in Frijda's (1986) theory, emotions arise when external conditions either facilitate or interfere with the individual's concerns (concerns being treated by Frijda as more or less equivalent with incentives or goals).

Within the domain of SWB, characteristics of personal goal systems are being explored as precursors of life satisfaction and long-term positive and negative affective states (Emmons, 1986; Karoly, 1991; Little, 1989; Omodei & Wearing, 1990, Roseman et al., 1994). Little of the work in either the emotion or the SWB domains, however, has examined individual differences in goal orientations, and these orientations are the focus of this chapter. Individuals appraise their goals in very different ways. Some individuals identify their goals in the broadest, most expansive possible terms, whereas others rarely think about the high-level meanings of their actions. Some individuals strive primarily for positive, *approach* goals, whereas others strive to *avoid* negative, aversive outcomes from becoming reality. Some individuals strive for certain goals in a manner that simultaneously thwarts at least some of their other goals. Individuals also differ in the degree of overlap or redundancy among their various goals. These differences in orientation toward one's goals, which will be referred to as level of abstraction, approach–avoidance orientation, goal congruence, and goal complexity, respectively, are the focus of this chapter. We review evidence that demonstrates that, irrespective of the content of one's goal pursuits, individual differences in goal setting and striving have important ramifications for a person's emotional life.

PERSONAL GOALS AS UNITS OF ANALYSIS

Before considering the role of goal orientations, it is necessary to outline the approach to goals that we will be taking. Over the past several years in our laboratory we have been examining the relation between goals and SWB using the personal striving construct. In this approach, goals are conceptualized as personal strivings, defined as "what a person is typically or characteristically trying to do" (Emmons, 1989, p. 92). Personal strivings consist of all of those recurring objectives that characterize a person's behavior. For example, a person might be trying to "find that special someone," "trying to overcome shyness around strangers," or "trying to be a good Christian example." Other examples of personal strivings are listed in Table 4.1. According to the personal striving perspective, personality is organized into idiographically coherent patterns of goals strivings. More discriminating than global motives, yet more stable than specific plans or behaviors, strivings occupy a desirable yet largely unexplored position in the hierarchy of personality functioning. A personal striving is a unifying construct—it unites what may be phenotypically different goals or actions around a common quality or theme.

The personal striving approach has its theoretical roots in both control theory (Carver & Scheier, 1981, 1982, 1990; Powers, 1973) and existential theory (Yalom, 1980). According to control theory, various levels of reference values that regulate action exist in a hierarchy ranging from the narrowest, most specific actions to broadest, most abstract principles. Behavior is a discrepancy-reduction process, where individuals act to

TABLE 4.1
Examples of Personal Strivings

Find that special someone
Do as many nice things for people as I can
Avoid revealing too much of myself
Set aside time for 'emotional rest' each day
Force men to be intimate in relationships
Be a good Christian example
Avoid being dependent on my boyfriend
Make attractive women notice me
Make it appear that I am intelligent
Avoid arguments when possible
Become financially independent from others
Avoid maliciously gossiping about others
Overcome shyness around strangers
Make life easier for my parents
Do something spontaneously, once a week

minimize the discrepancy between their present condition and a desired standard or goal. Personal strivings can be thought of as one of these reference values that are used to guide action. A personal striving, defined as a class of goals that is characteristic for a particular person, describes enduring and recurring personality characteristics. Strivings are enduring goals or enduring concerns that are relatively stable over time and consistently expressed in a variety of situations.

Existentialist perspectives (e.g., Maddi, 1989; Yalom, 1980) emphasize the role of meaning and choice as the individual actively constructs his or her life circumstances. An individual creates goals amongst possibilities and arranges them so as to achieve maximum meaning and satisfaction in life. Goals are one of two broad categories of purpose—the other being fulfillments (Baumeister, 1991). At the core of the existentialist perspective is directionality and choice. Personal strivings, as personalized goals, represent choices that individuals make as they direct their lives toward certain outcomes and away from others. Strivings constitute an important source of meaning as people's lives are structured around these pursuits that they are striving to realize. Changes in goals, represented by losses, additions, and shifts in goal hierarchies, can be viewed as alterations in life meanings for that person.

The personal striving construct was initially proposed in order to offer both an additional unit of personality (to complement trait-based levels of analysis) as well as a construct that could account for individual differences in SWB. Research on personal goal strivings and well-being can be divided into three areas: goal content and SWB, goal orientation and SWB, and goal parameters and SWB. Other publications have described research on goal content and parameters (Emmons, 1986, 1989, 1992; Emmons & King, 1988, 1989). The remainder of this chapter reviews research on goal orientation and well-being.

GOAL ORIENTATION

Goal orientation refers to individual differences in the manner in which goals are represented consciously by the individual and described linguistically when communicating one's goals to others. Thus, orientation refers to individual differences in the mental representations of goals. Goal orientations have been identified with respect to both goal setting and goal striving. Ford (1992) described several dimensions along which people vary in their general orientation to goals. The first dimension, active-reactive, describes differences in the degree to which goals are self-chosen by the individual versus imposed by external circumstances. In this sense, it shares conceptual ground with Deci and Ryan's (1991) intrinsic versus extrinsic orientation. Approach-avoidance refers to whether goals are conceptualized as positive incentives to be sought after or negative consequences to be avoided. Research linking variations in this orientation with well-being are described shortly. A third dimension described by Ford is that of maintenance versus change: Does the person generally strive for change and growth in their goal system or are they more concerned with maintaining the status quo. Ford (1992) briefly reviewed other goal orientations that have appeared in the literature, including the helpless versus mastery orientation (Dweck, 1991) and the ego-involved versus task-involved orientation (Nicholls, 1990).

In our laboratory, we have been primarily interested in four orientations: level of goal abstraction (high versus low), approach versus avoidance goals, goal congruence or conflict, and goal complexity (differentiation and integration).

LEVEL OF GOAL SPECIFICATION

This orientation describes differences in *level of goal specification*. According to Little (1989), some of us dedicate our lives to *magnificent obsessions*, whereas others are content to muddle through life working on *trivial pursuits*. This distinction represents two extremes along a dimension that can be characterized as level of abstraction of one's goal strivings. In examining strivings that subjects have spontaneously generated in past studies, it became apparent that people frame their goals at various levels of generality. Some individuals describe their goals in primarily broad, abstract, and expansive ways. We refer to these individuals as *high-level strivers.* Others tend to frame their goals in concrete, specific, and more superficial terms. These individuals are referred to as low-level strivers. High- and low-level strivers may describe what are functionally equivalent goals in very different ways. Some individuals may be "trying to ward off the ravages of time," whereas others may simply be "trying to stay out of the sun." Although these are ostensibly similar goals, the goals are framed at different levels of abstraction. "Keeping my books straightened on my shelves" and "writing 10 pages a day for my new book" are low-level goals, whereas "being an organized person" and "trying to make a contribution to future generations" are examples of higher level strivings. Table 4.2 shows goals characteristic of high- and low-level strivers.

TABLE 4.2
Examples of High- and Low-Level Strivings

High-level: "Ghandi"

Treat others with dignity
Increase my understanding of the Bible
Deepen my relationship with God
Be totally honest
Express my feelings to close friends and family openly and honestly
Be humble
Discern and follow God's will for my life
Expose my faith to others without offending them or pushing it on them
Keep positive thoughts in my mind
Make new friends
Be a fun person to be around
Make others feel good about themselves
Express to people that I love them
Compete against myself rather than others
Increase my knowledge of the world

Low-level: "Coffee Bean"

Look well-groomed and clean-cut
Stand out when engaging in physical/recreational activities
Be funny and make others laugh
Speak clearly and straightforward to strangers
Look physically conditioned and physically fit
Act physically aggressive around those folks I dislike
Keep good posture/walk straight
Look attentive and not bored in class
Avoid being stereotyped
Use proper language and manners around adults and attractive girls
Make myself noticeable
Work hard (or at least make it look like it)
Keep quiet and not go talking about myself freely with others
Be organized and neat, always have a clean room and a made bed

This distinction between high- and low-level goals is reminiscent of Vallacher and Wegner's (1989) levels of action identification theory, in which actions can be identified at various levels of analysis, ranging from the molecular to the molar (see Emmons, 1989, for a detailed comparison of personal strivings approach and action identification theory). There is considerable support for the notion of levels of abstraction within many different areas of psychology, including personality, clinical, social, and cognitive psychology. Cutting across these areas, levels of abstraction can be viewed within control theory (Carver & Scheier, 1982, 1990; Hyland, 1988; Martin & Tesser, 1989; Powers, 1973). Control theory formulations posit a hierarchy of levels of control, with various levels of standards or goals arranged from the most concrete and narrow to the broadest and most abstract organizing principles. The lowest levels indicate how the action is to be carried out, while the higher levels provide information on the purposes or implications of the action. Goals or standards can be characterized at different levels within this hierarchy. People may be said to differ in terms of the level at which they tend to characterize their goals within the hierarchy. However, within the control theory literature, the interest has not been in individual differences in tendencies to phrase goals at different levels of abstraction. In a variety of different samples reported in Emmons (1992), high-level striving tended to be associated with psychological distress, particularly anxiety and depression. Table 4.3 displays correlations between striving level and well-being in a community sample of 50 married couples. Low-level striving, on the other hand, has

TABLE 4.3
Correlations Between Striving Level and Well-Being Indicators, Married Couples

	Striving Level		
	Husbands $n = 50$	Wives $n = 50$	Combined $n = 100$
Psychological WB			
Positive affect	−.22[a]	.04	−.18
Negative affect	.31[a]	.19	.21
Life satisfaction	−.29[a]	−.27[a]	−.27[a]
Physical WB			
Somatization	−.11	−.25[a]	−.13[a]
PILL	−.13	−.01[a]	.03
Spouse-rated symptoms	−.33[a]	−.16	−.20[a]
Health-care visits	−.12	−.22[a]	−.18[a]
Number of aspirins	−.08	−.23[a]	−.16[a]
Days of work missed	−.16	.01	−.04

Note. PILL = Pennebaker Inventory of Limbic Languidness.
[a]$p < .05$.

been linked to greater levels of psychological well-being but also to more physical illness. I have referred to this pattern as the "illness versus depression" tradeoff. What it really reflects, though, is a tradeoff cited by Little (1989) between having manageable versus meaningful goals. Higher level goals are rated as more difficult to accomplish and lower in clarity of means to accomplish them, thus potentially accounting for their link to negative affectivity. The logic of control theory would also predict a link between high-level goals and negative affect. Higher-order feedback systems have longer time lags for discrepancies to be reduced (Carver & Scheier, 1990). Negative affect is presumed to result from slower than desired progress from one's goals. Thus, a longer time lag would make negative affect more likely that the individual would experience emotionally distressing states, assuming they did not adjust expectations regarding goal attainment accordingly.

Low-level goals, particularly those indicating an absence of emotional self-awareness, may be linked to physical illness through mechanisms of repressive-defensiveness. Presented with the psychologically charged task of confronting one's innermost aspirations, repressors are likely to find the task threatening, engage in avoidant processing, and will produce less revealing and more superficial goals. If low-level striving is indicative of a repressive personality, then low-level strivers should also appraise their strivings more positively then high-level strivers, as repressors are prone to denying negative characteristics in themselves.

In order to test this hypothesis, Gomersall (1993) explored the relation between personal striving system variables (including level) and repressive-defensiveness. Repressors, as measured by the combination of scores on the Marlowe-Crowne and Taylor Manifest Anxiety Scale, had fewer strivings with emotional content and fewer negative, avoidant strivings (discussed later) than did nonrepressors. Repressors also rated themselves as being more satisfied with the degree of progress made toward their strivings, rated their strivings as less difficult, and reported higher levels of instrumentality among their strivings. Examples of strivings reported by repressors include "think positives about myself," "not be quick to anger because it is not a good feeling," "not show negative emotions so much," "please people," and "seek other people's approval." The theme of emotional avoidance is prevalent throughout these strivings, as is the need for social approval. The fact that repressors have insight into their mood regulation strategies suggests that avoidance is not an entirely unconscious process. It is also interesting that it is the emotionality component of the levels construct that is responsible for the links with repressive coping. There is substantial literature on avoidant coping styles, autonomic arousal, and physical health (Pennebaker & Traue, 1993), which implicates repressiveness as a risk factor for various physical illnesses.

APPROACH AND AVOIDANCE GOALS

A second goal orientation is reflected in the degree to which individuals are striving for positive, approach goals as opposed to striving to avoid negative, aversive goals. For instance, a person may be trying to "spend time with others" versus "avoid being lonely," or "trying to avoid letting anything upset me" versus "trying to stay calm even under trying circumstances." The motivation literature (e.g., fear of failure versus approaching success) has demonstrated that these differing orientations lead to very different behavioral patterns and consequences, even when similar goal content is involved (Heckhausen, 1991; Klinger, 1977).

In his work on self-defining memories, Singer (chap. 6, this volume; Singer & Salovey, 1993) found that people with primarily avoidance strivings tended to have more memories that reflected failed avoidance attempts and more distress about the outcomes of the events these memories represented. Even if they were successful in avoiding the unwanted outcome, these individuals still reported less positive emotional well-being than approach-oriented individuals. This suggested to us that individuals with primarily avoidant goal systems would be at a higher risk for emotional distress.

In order to test this hypothesis, Emmons and Kaiser (1994) investigated the relation between approach and avoidance strivings and indicators of psychological and physical well-being. They predicted that individuals whose striving lists contain a large number of avoidant strivings will experience more psychological distress, particularly anxiety, than individuals with predominantly appetitive striving systems. This prediction is based on Gray's (1987) theory of the behavioral activation and inhibition systems, and their hypothesized effect on emotional experience (see also Carver, chap. 2, this volume).

Two hundred sixty-one undergraduates in several studies on mood and goals at the University of Illinois and the University of California, Davis, and 100 community couples in Davis, California, served as subjects. After completing the Striving Assessment Packet (Emmons, 1989) subjects completed either a daily mood report for periods ranging from 3 to 6 weeks or a global measure of positive and negative affect. Subjects completed physical symptoms reports in a similar manner, by indicating whether or not they had experienced any physical symptoms (eight categories) on the daily form. Subjects in all samples completed a number of well-being questionnaires.

The open-ended lists of strivings were coded for approach–avoidance according to the guidelines in the Personal Striving Coding Manual (Emmons, 1989). Examples of two subjects with a high proportion of avoidance strivings are shown in Table 4.4. Inter-rater reliability was 100%

4. GOAL ORIENTATION AND EMOTIONAL WELL-BEING

TABLE 4.4
Subjects With a Large Percentage of Avoidant Strivings

S#10754
1. Be an honest person.
2. Do unto others as I would like to be done to me.
3. Curb my habit of telling my personal thoughts and opinions to people I just meet.
4. Share everything with my family. Not get angry at myself for being out of shape.
6. Always be prompt.
7. Want the best of life for myself and my family.
8. Not have so many expectations of my son.
9. Be a friend to my friends.
10. Avoid feeling guilt.
11. Curb my desire to spend money.
12. Avoid comparing myself to my sister.
13. Avoid the overwhelming feeling of wondering if my father approves of my decisions.
14. Want better for my son.

S#0381
1. Be understanding of others, accepting them as they are.
2. Avoid offending others by maintaining my distance.
3. Always live in the past or future, but not for today.
4. Look at matters realistically rather than accept things for what they appear to be.
5. Appear knowledgeable of any and all subjects to others.
6. Avoid taking sides in an issue even though I may feel very strongly about one side.
7. Put myself down by appearing "bumbling" as if age were causing me to slip.
8. Avoid eye contact—more with strangers than with people I know.
9. Be all things to all people, i.e., react rather than proact.
10. Give others what I think they want from me.
11. Tone down any enthusiasm I may spontaneously generate about anything I may be doing.
12. Avoid arguments or even spirited discussions.
13. Be the great mediator when thinking no one else can do the job.
14. Keep things light rather than engage in a searching, serious discussion of issues.

for this coding task. The proportion of avoidance strivings ranged from 9% to 15% in the various samples. What does it mean to be oriented toward avoiding outcomes? What are the consequences of possessing a high number of avoidance strivings? Zero-order product–moment correlations between avoidance strivings and the measures of psychological well-being are shown in Table 4.5. The correlations between avoidance strivings and physical well-being are shown in Table 4.6. Subjects with a high proportion of avoidance strivings tended to report lower well-being, across most measures and most samples. The strongest pattern of correlates was found in the community sample of adults. In that sample, adults who strive to avoid negative goals report lower positive moods, less life satisfaction, and more anxiety compared to appetitively motivated individuals. They were also higher on all five measures of physical symptomatology, as seen in Table 4.6. Thus, negative strivings appears to be a risk factor for psycho-

TABLE 4.5
Correlations Between Proportion of Avoidance Strivings
and Psychological Well-Being

Measure	Sample 1 n = 40	Sample 2 n = 105	Sample 3 n = 116	Sample 4 n = 200
PA	−.16	−.23[b]	−.18	−.47[a]
NA	.27	.12	.01	.10
SWLS	.00	−.09	−.19	−.56[a]
Depression	.34[b]	.19	.12	.13
Anxiety	.17	.29[a]	.25[a]	.28[a]
DPQ WB	−.30[b]	−.21[b]	−.24[b]	−.57[a]
Observer PA			−.30[b]	−.25[b]
Observer NA			.07	.02

Note. Samples 1–3 consisted of college students, Sample 4 consisted of 100 married community couples. PA = positive effect. NA = negative effect. DPQ WB = Differential Personality Questionnaire, Well-Being Scale.
[a]$p < .01$. [b]$p < .05$.

TABLE 4.6
Correlations Between Proportion of Avoidance Strivings
and Physical Well-Being

Measure	Sample 1 n = 40	Sample 2 n = 105	Sample 3 n = 116	Sample 4 n = 200
SOMAT	−.14	.18	.01	.31[b]
PILL		.23[b]	.08	.30[b]
Missed work			.15	.21[b]
Physician visits			.07	.24[b]
Spouse-rated symptoms				.25

SOMAT = Somatization scale. PILL = Pennebaker Inventory of Limbic Languidness.
[b]$p < .05$.

logical and physical distress. Individuals who are concerned with avoiding negative outcomes have higher levels of negative well-being, compared to persons with primarily approach orientations.

Other data that we have collected suggests that avoidant strivings may play a role in interpersonal as well as intrapersonal satisfaction. In the sample of married couples (Sample 4 in Table 4.5), we found that marital satisfaction is significantly negatively related to the proportion of the spouse's avoidant strivings. Thus, a person is likely to be less satisfied with his or her marriage if their spouse is predominantly concerned with avoiding negative outcomes. Similarly, King and Emmons (1991) found that the husband's level of avoidant strivings was a significant predictor of marital distress in their wives. Thus, avoidant strivings appear to exact an interpersonal as well as an intrapersonal toll on well-being.

POTENTIAL EXPLANATIONS FOR AVOIDANCE STRIVINGS-DISTRESS LINK

A number of mechanisms may be responsible for the association between avoidant striving and psychological distress. We briefly consider four: cognitive, biological, motivational, and existential explanations. We make no presumptions that these four are competing or mutually exclusive nor are we currently in a position to choose among them.

Norbert Schwarz' (1990) account of the *cognitive* asymmetry of approach and avoidance situations is one possible explanation. According to Schwarz, in order to obtain a certain positive outcome, there need be only a single accessible route to that goal. However, in order to avoid or prevent an undesired outcome from happening, all possible routes to that goals must be identified and blocked. For instance, the striving "to avoid offending others by maintaining my distance" requires the individual to be constantly monitoring ongoing interactions for signs of negative reactions from others and to make adjustments as necessary. On the other hand, if the striving were to "get closer to someone," theoretically there would be a number of paths that could be taken, and several of these paths would likely facilitate the goal of increasing closeness. Thus, when it comes to problem solving, avoidance goals require a very different form of analytical reasoning than approach goals.

A *biological* explanation suggests that preferences for approach versus avoidance strivings could reflect different brain processes, such as the inhibition and activation systems (Gray, 1987). Perhaps individuals preoccupied by avoidant goals have more reactive inhibition systems and are thus preoccupied with avoiding aversive outcomes. In support of this conjecture, Emmons and McAdams (1991) found that inhibition scores from a picture story exercise were significantly correlated with the individual's proportion of avoidant strivings. On the other hand, individuals whose striving system contains predominantly approach goals are more sensitive to rewards. Recently, Carver and White (1994) developed a questionnaire measure of Gray's behavioral activation and behavioral inhibition systems. We are currently exploring how scores on this measure related to approach and avoidance strivings. The present study suggests that the personal striving framework is one means of accessing these appetitive and aversive motivational systems.

The third explanation, a *motivationally* based one, suggested itself to us after examining the different patterns of appraisal for approach versus avoidance strivings. In order to determine why the avoidance strivings are so consistently related to negative outcomes, we examined the difference between how approach versus avoidance strivings are rated on the Striving Assessment Scales (SAS). The SAS consist of 18 appraisal dimensions represented parameters along which people evaluate their individual goals (see Table 4.7). Compared to approach strivings, avoidance strivings were rated as lower in desirability, less successfully consummated, engaged in for less autonomous or intrinsic reasons, and less likely to be supported by others in the person's social network. These data indicate that subjects with a high proportion of avoidance strivings tend to be more extrinsically motivated than subjects with fewer avoidance strivings. Deci and Ryan (1991) proposed that motivated behaviors vary in the degree to which they are self-determined, or autonomous, versus controlled. Ryan, Sheldon, Kasser, and Deci (in press) wrote that "the amount or level of motivation does not necessarily differ when people are autonomous versus controlled but the type or orientation of motivation does, as does the quality of functioning" (p. 5). Ryan and Connell (1989) developed a continuum of reasons for acting, ranging from extrinsic, controlling reasons to intrinsic, self-determined reasons. Acting for more autonomous reasons has been associated with more favorable outcomes in terms of academic motivation and religiosity (see Deci & Ryan, 1991, for a review). Applying this continuum to personal strivings, Sheldon and Kasser (1995) asked subjects to rate the degree to which they strove for each of their goals, either because the goal was personally interesting, important, and valued or because they felt compelled to by either interpersonal or intrapsychic reasons. Having more autonomous reasons for one's strivings was positively associated with several measures of psychological well-being, including life satisfaction, vitality, and self-actualizing tendencies. Introjected regulation (Ryan et al., in press) tends to be associated with behavior being undertaken in order to avoid an undesired outcome. Perhaps avoidant strivings are associated with

TABLE 4.7
Univariate Fs and Group Means for Approach and Avoidant Strivings

SAS Dimension	Approach	Avoidant	$F(1,244)$
Value	6.92	6.36	4.46[a]
Ambivalence	0.87	1.12	ns
Importance	3.90	3.25	19.11[c]
Attainment	6.35	5.67	6.09[a]
Success	7.18	6.26	16.55[c]
Opportunity	2.50	2.37	ns
Effort	3.25	3.15	ns
Difficulty	2.75	2.86	ns
Desirability	3.75	3.00	22.29[c]
Clarity	3.16	3.09	ns
Progress	4.43	3.95	5.82[a]
Autonomy	10.62	7.51	8.27[b]
Support	5.21	4.62	10.69[c]

[a]$p < .05.$ [b]$p < .01.$ [c]$p < .001.$

more aversive outcomes because they reflect engaging in controlled as opposed to self-determined behavior.

For a fourth and final reason why avoidant strivings are indicative of poorer emotional well-being, we return to the idea, introduced earlier, of the *existential* basis of goal striving. Meaning, achieved partly via purpose in life, is acquired through the commitment to personally relevant goals that a person has autonomously set for himself or herself. For people who are predominantly concerned with avoiding dreaded outcomes, their lives are dominated by a rejection of possible meanings. If this *meaning vacuum* (Baumeister, 1991) is not compensated for through other sources of meaning, dissatisfaction, depression, and other negative reactions are likely to be the consequence. One might argue, of course, that people engaged in avoidance goals do have purpose and meaning, albeit of a very different nature than positive strivers. It depends on one's definition of what constitutes a meaningful life. However, we contend that an orientation that involves primarily avoidance represents a turning away from and an implicit rejection of meaning that could be acquired from the active pursuit of affirmative outcomes. For instance, a person whose life is dominated by themes of avoiding closeness with others is rejecting fulfilling outcomes that could be obtained through meaningful, mutually gratifying relationships.

GOAL CONFLICT

Individuals also differ in the extent to which their goals are synergistic or compete with each other. Goal conflict stands out as an especially powerful predictor of SWB.

Intrapsychic goal conflict is an inevitable by-product of motivational life. We desire many things, but often our other desires keep us from obtaining all that we want. Conflict may be as trivial as the decision whether to have Chinese or Italian food for dinner, or it may be as monumental as the decision of whether or not to run for president. Individuals whose goals are in conflict spend more time ruminating about their goals and less time working toward achieving them (Emmons & King, 1988). This inhibitory behavior only serves to perpetuate the conflict, because the person fails to act toward resolving the conflict and is also unable to make progress toward achieving the goal. Personal goals serve as an ideal vehicle for examining intrapsychic conflict because both major and minor life decisions revolve around fundamental values, goals, desires, and other personally motivating factors.

Arising from within various theoretical perspectives, from psychodynamic to cognitive-behavioral, many terms have been offered to describe oppositional tendencies within the mind. These include *discrepancies, disregulations, disconnections, contradictions, incongruities, incompatibilities, imbalances,* and *discontinuities.* Regardless of terminological differences, these perspectives are all dealing with internal incompatibilities or the terms we have used, *conflict* and *ambivalence* (the latter being a subset of the former). The term *goal conflict* is used here to refer to two processes. First, an individual may be ambivalent about achieving a particular goal. Meehl (1964), defined intense ambivalence as "the existence of simultaneous or rapidly interchangeable positive and negative feelings toward the same object or activity, with the added proviso that both the positive and negative feelings be strong" (p. 10). Clearly, this definition conjures up a conflict situation. Ambivalence can also be thought of as an approach-avoidance conflict—wanting but at the same time not wanting the same goal object. For example, a person may be ambivalent about the goal "to express my true feelings" because of the potential negative consequences that such free expression might entail. In addition, an individual may be ambivalent about the goal "to finish my dissertation as soon as possible," not because the end is viewed as potentially negative but because the process of achieving the goal may seem unusually daunting. The second use of the term *conflict* refers to the situation in which a goal that a person wishes to accomplish interferes with the attainment of at least one other goal that the individual simultaneously wishes to accomplish. For example, the goal of trying to spend time with one's family may interfere with the goal of doing well in one's career.

The debilitating effects of conflict on self-regulatory processes has been discussed in some detail by Bargh and Gollwitzer (1994), Emmons, King, and Sheldon (1993), Gollwitzer (1993), and Karoly (1993). Emmons et al. and Gollwitzer have described how individuals may resolve conflicts between competing intentions in the service of attaining valued personal goals. The inability to resolve chronic conflicts is associated with poorer well-being. In our lab we have found that conflict between and within personal strivings is related to measures of negative affectivity and physical symptomatology, both concurrently as well as prospectively. Conflict (between goals) and ambivalence (approach-avoidance conflict) are associated with a variety of physical symptoms as well as an increase in health center visits during a 1-year follow-up (Emmons & King, 1988). Interpersonal goal conflict is also related to lower psychological well-being and to physical illness (King & Emmons, 1991).

GOAL DIFFERENTIATION

A fourth and final goal orientation that has ramifications for well-being is the differentiation or distinctiveness that exists within one's goal system.

Goal differentiation refers to the degree of interrelation that exists between individual goals in the system. A high degree of differentiation exists in systems in which goals are not highly related to each other and are thus relatively independent. Highly differentiated persons possess a variety of strivings in a variety of domains. A low degree of differentiation, on the other hand, is characteristic of systems in which the goals are highly related to each other, or are interdependent. Differentiation is one component of structural complexity, along with *integration* (Werner & Kaplan, 1956).

Emmons and King (1989) assessed the degree of differentiation both within and between strivings by having subjects assess the degree of (dis)similarity between all possible pairs of strivings. Subjects also indicated the number of distinct strategies they possessed for achieving each striving ("plan differentiation"). Using both an experience-sampling and daily diary methodology, striving differentiation was found to be positively related to affective reactivity. Individuals who possessed highly differentiated goal systems tended to experience more extreme affective states and, in general, are characterized by lower levels of psychological well-being. In another study, Sheldon and Emmons (1995) found that differentiated persons tended to appraise their strivings more negatively on a number of striving dimensions. More specifically, they reported less successful attainment and lower expectancies for future attainment and rated their strivings as more difficult than did less differentiated subjects. Donahue, Robins, Roberts, and John (1993) demonstrated that differentiation in the self-concept is negatively related to a variety of adjustment indicators, including emotional distress and interpersonal and occupational difficulties. Their work is further evidence that the "fragmentation of the self," whether conceptualized in terms of goal conflicts or discrepancies in trait attributes (see also Strauman, chap. 8, this volume), is associated with internal as well as external costs.

The problematic nature of goal differentiation may seem puzzling in the light of some past research. Differentiation has been conceptualized as one aspect of complexity, and complexity is generally considered to be desirable (Dixon & Baumeister, 1991; Linville, 1987; Niedenthal, Sutterland, & Wherry, 1992). Linville reported that highly differentiated people possess multiple selves that insulate them from negative experiences within particular roles or domains. What accounts for the discrepancy between these studies and the research we reviewed earlier?

There are both methodological and conceptual reasons for this apparent discrepancy. Measures used by Linville and others to assess complexity may assess both integration as well as differentiation. Differentiation appears to exact some mental health costs, whereas integration appears to be beneficial. Integration and differentiation are often treated as bipolar opposites on a single continuum. We believe this logic is inherently flawed. Integrated people are not those who have failed to differentiate aspects of themselves; integration is not synonymous with the lack of differentiation. Rather, integration involves coherences between everyday goals and current and future images of the self.

GOAL ORIENTATION, THE SELF, AND WELL-BEING

Having reviewed the literature on goal orientations and emotional well-being, it is now appropriate to speculate on why each style is predictive of poor emotional well-being. Although considerable differences exist among these orientations, they have at least one critical feature in common: They each are predictive of emotional distress. Avoidant strivings are linked to anxiety and depression, as are high-level, abstract strivings. Conflict among strivings is similarly associated with distress, as is possessing a highly differentiated goal system.

Why is goal orientation such a powerful predictor of affective well-being? To answer this question, it is necessary to invoke the concept of *the self*. Singer (1992) has argued that conceptual models of the self must focus on motivational elements, such as strivings, goals, and purposes, in addition to the often-emphasized cognitive constructs such as self-representations. In order to link goals with affect, an overall organizing principle that brings together and integrates separate goal strivings into a coherent structure is needed. A goals account of SWB or affect is incomplete if it does not deal with the issue of unity, coherence, and integration between goals and other aspects of personality. This is the job of identity or the self — creating an overall life purpose. This organizing principle, be it identity, or the self, or a similar structure, is that which links individual goals together and to future states and desired outcomes. It enables us to see beyond the immediate present and to interpret the present with respect to the future. It enables us to connect our current goal pursuits as relating to images of who we hope to become. Little (1993) linked personal projects with the self by identifying four self-related functions that projects serve: self-expressive (self-defining), self-enhancement (related to self-worth), self-exploration (personal growth), and self-extension (changing the self). Individual differences in goal orientations reflect differences in personality integration. Conflict and differentiation are such prepotent predictors of well-being (Emmons & King, 1988) precisely because they reflect incoherence and lack of harmony in the system. However, linking differentiated goals with future positive selves (Sheldon & Emmons, 1995) appears to circumvent the deleterious effects of differentiation on well-being. Individuals with more links between their goals and future selves, the ability to see one's current intentional action as relating to images of who they wish to become, may reclaim a sense of successful striving. Similarly, when personal projects are linked to future self-representations, rated progress toward them is higher (Yetim, 1993). King (1994) documented the importance of placing goals in the context of the individual's larger life story. She found that strivings that were most predictive of well-being were those that were linked with ultimate life goals and worst possible fears regarding future life outcomes. The research by King is a good example of the recent attempt to locate personalized goals within a broader framework of personality and identity (Singer & Salovey, 1993).

The work of Sheldon and Kasser (1995) is especially noteworthy in that they have attempted to operationalize personality integration and relate it to psychological adjustment. According to Sheldon and Kasser, integration consists of two components: coherence and congruence. Coherence represents the degree to which proximal goals contribute or are instrumental for longer-term, more distal goals and to the degree to which lower level, subordinate goals are instrumental for higher level, superordinate strivings (vertical coherence). Horizontal coherence occurs when success at particular goals contributes to success at other goals at the same level in the system (essentially the opposite of conflicting goals). Congruence in the system occurs when goals are genuinely chosen by the person and fulfill the basic needs of autonomy, relatedness (Deci & Ryan, 1991). Sheldon and Kasser (1994) found that congruence and coherence were related to questionnaire measures of health and well-being, as well as to daily measures of mood, vitality, and engagement in meaningful as opposed to distracting activities.

CONCLUSION

It is evident from a review of the literature that the general orientation that one takes in goal setting and striving and the degree to which these goals are in alignment with each other and the self-concept are essential elements of a goals theory of SWB. It is equally evident that well-being involves more than the presence of positive feelings and the absence of negative feelings. Well-being involves the search for meaningfulness in one's life. Meaning comes from involvement in personally fulfilling goals, the integration of these goals into a coherent self-system, and the integration of these goals into a broader social system. It is meaning or purpose that gives life unity and coherence, despite its paradoxes and seeming inconsistencies. Goal attainment per se will not lead to subjectively satisfying long-term states unless these goals are intrinsically meaningful and integrated within an overall structure of the individual in his or her social context. Goals capture affectively charged themes that are central to the person's life, while emerging from and determining the nature of the person's transactions with their social worlds. As such, they are ideal units for studying the contributions that motivation makes to emotion and affective well-being. The hierarchical structure of goals, with links to both higher and lower levels, the flexibility, discriminativeness, yet coherence that the concept implies, and its amenability to measurement and individual differences make it a highly desirable unit of analysis for researchers interested in motivational models of subjective well-being and, more generally, in examining the relation between motivational and emotional processes.

ACKNOWLEDGMENT

Research reported in this chapter was supported, in part, by a grant from the National Institute of Mental Health (MH47263-01).

REFERENCES

Bargh, J. A., & Gollwitzer, P. M. (1994). Environmental control of goal-directed action: Automatic and strategic contingencies between situations and behavior. *Nebraska Symposium on Motivation* (Vol. 41, pp. 71-124). Lincoln: University of Nebraska Press.

Baumeister, R. F. (1991). *Meanings of life*. New York: Guilford.

Carver, C. S., & Scheier, M. F. (1981). *Attention and self-regulation: A control theory approach to human behavior*. New York: Springer-Verlag.

Carver, C. S., & Scheier, M. F. (1982). Control theory: A useful conceptual framework for personality-social, clinical, and health psychology. *Psychological Bulletin, 92*, 111-135.

Carver, C. S., & Scheier, M. F. (1990). On the origins of positive and negative affect: A control-process view. *Psychological Review, 97*, 19-35.

Carver, C. S., & White, T. L. (1994). Behavioral inhibition, behavioral activation, and affective responses to impending reward and punishment: The BIS/BAS scales. *Journal of Personality and Social Psychology, 67*, 319-333.

Deci, E. L., & Ryan, R. M. (1991). A motivational approach to the self: Integration in personality. In R. Dienstbier (Ed.), *Nebraska symposium on motivation* (Vol. 38, pp. 237-288). Lincoln: University of Nebraska Press.

Dixon, T., & Baumeister, R. (1991). Escaping the self: The moderating effect of self-complexity. *Personality and Social Psychology Bulletin, 17*, 363-368.

Donahue, E. M., Robins, R. W., Roberts, B. W., & John, O. P. (1993). The divided self: Concurrent and longitudinal effects of psychological adjustment and social roles on self-concept differentiation. *Journal of Personality and Social Psychology, 64*, 834-846.

Dweck, C. S. (1991). Self-theories and goals: Their role in motivation, personality, and development. In R. Dienstbier (Ed.), *Nebraska symposium on motivation* (Vol. 38, pp. 199-235). Lincoln: University of Nebraska Press.

Emmons, R. A. (1986). Personal strivings: An approach to personality and subjective well-being. *Journal of Personality and Social Psychology, 51*, 1058-1068.

Emmons, R. A. (1989). The personal striving approach to personality. In L. A. Pervin (Ed.), *Goal concepts in personality and social psychology* (pp. 87-126). Hillsdale, NJ: Lawrence Erlbaum Associates.

Emmons, R. A. (1992). Abstract versus concrete goals: Personal striving level, physical illness, and psychological well-being. *Journal of Personality and Social Psychology, 62*, 292–300.

Emmons, R. A., & Kaiser, H. (1994, August). *Approach and avoidance strivings and subjective well-being.* Poster presented at the 102nd Annual Convention of the American Psychological Association, Los Angeles, CA.

Emmons, R. A., & King, L. A. (1988). Conflict among personal strivings: Immediate and long-term implications for psychological and physical well-being. *Journal of Personality and Social Psychology, 54*, 1040–1048.

Emmons, R. A., & King, L. A. (1989). Personal striving differentiation and affective reactivity. *Journal of Personality and Social Psychology, 56*, 478–484.

Emmons, R. A., King, L. A., & Sheldon, K. (1993). Goal conflict and the self-regulation of action. In D. M. Wegner & J. W. Pennebaker (Eds), *Handbook of mental control* (pp. 528–551). Englewood Cliffs, NJ: Prentice-Hall.

Emmons, R. A., & McAdams, D. P. (1991). Personal strivings and motive dispositions: Exploring the links. *Personality and Social Psychology Bulletin, 17*, 648–654.

Ford, M. E. (1992). *Motivating humans: Goals, emotions, and personal agency beliefs.* Newbury Park, CA: Sage.

Frijda, N. (1986). *The emotions.* New York: Cambridge University Press.

Gollwitzer, P. M. (1993). Goal achievement: The role of intentions. In W. Stroebe & M. Hewstone (Eds.), *European review of social psychology* (Vol. 4, pp. 141–185). Chichester, England: Wiley.

Gomersall, T. E. (1993). *Personal strivings and repression: Identifying the repressive coping style within the personal strivings framework.* Unpublished master's thesis, Humboldt State University, Arcata, CA.

Gray, J. A. (1987). *The psychology of fear and stress.* New York: Cambridge University Press.

Heckhausen, H. (1991). *Motivation and action.* Berlin: Springer-Verlag.

Hyland, M. E. (1988). Motivational control theory: An integrative framework. *Journal of Personality and Social Psychology, 55*, 642–651.

Karoly, P. (1991). Goal systems and health outcomes across the life span: A proposal. In H. E. Schroeder (Ed.), *New directions in health psychology assessment* (pp. 65–91). New York: Hemisphere.

Karoly, P. (1993). Mechanisms of self-regulation: A systems view. *Annual Review of Psychology, 44*, 23–52.

King, L. A. (1994, August). *Personal strivings and possible selves: Linking the present to the future.* Invited talk presented at the 102nd Annual Convention of the American Psychological Association, Los Angeles, CA.

King, L. A., & Emmons, R. A. (1991). Psychological, physical, and interpersonal correlates of emotional expressiveness, conflict, and control. *European Journal of Personality, 5*, 131–150.

Klinger, E. (1977). *Meaning and void: Inner experience and the incentives in people's lives.* Minneapolis: University of Minnesota Press.

Lazarus, R. (1991). *Emotion and adaptation.* New York: Oxford University Press.

Linville, P. W. (1987). Self-complexity as a cognitive buffer against stress-related illness and depression. *Journal of Personality and Social Psychology, 52*, 663–676.

Little, B. R. (1989). Personal projects analysis: Trivial pursuits, magnificent obsessions, and the search for coherence. In D. M. Buss & N. Carter (Eds.), *Personality psychology: Recent trends, and emerging directions* (pp. 15–31). New York: Springer-Verlag.

Little, B. R. (1993). Personal projects and the distributed self: Aspects of a conative psychology. In J. Suls (Ed.), *Psychological perspectives on the self* (Vol. 4., pp. 157–181). Hillsdale, NJ: Lawrence Erlbaum Associates.

Maddi, S. R. (1989). *Personality theories: A comparative analysis* (5th ed.). Homewood, IL: Dorsey.

Martin, L. L., & Tesser, A. (1989). Toward a motivational and structural theory of ruminative thought. In J. Uleman & J. A. Bargh (Eds.), *Unintended thought* (pp. 306–326). New York: Guilford.

Meehl, P. E. (1964). *Manual for use with checklist of schizotypic signs.* Minneapolis, MN: University of Minnesota Medical School.

Nichols, J. G. (1990). What is ability and why are we mindful of it? A developmental perspective. In R. J. Sternberg & J. Kolligian, Jr. (Eds.), *Competence considered* (pp. 11–40). New Haven, CT: Yale University Press.

Niedenthal, P. Sutterland, M., & Wherry, M. B. (1992). Possible self-complexity and affective reactions to goal-relevant evaluation. *Journal of Personality and Social Psychology, 63,* 5–16.

Oatley, K. (1992). *Best laid schemes: The psychology of emotions.* New York: Cambridge University Press.

Omodei, M. M., & Wearing, A. J. (1990). Need satisfaction and involvement in personal projects: Toward an integrative model of subjective well-being. *Journal of Personality and Social Psychology, 59,* 762–769.

Ortony, A., Clore, G. L., & Collins, A. (1988). *The cognitive structure of emotions.* New York: Cambridge University Press.

Pennebaker, J. W., & Traue, H. C. (Eds.). (1993). *Emotion, inhibition, and health.* Seattle, WA: Hogrefe & Huber.

Pervin, L. A. (1983). The stasis and flow of behavior: Toward a theory of goals. In M. M. Page (Ed.), *Nebraska Symposium on Motivation* (pp. 1–53). Lincoln: University of Nebraska Press.

Powers, W. T. (1973). *Behavior: The control of perception.* Chicago: Aldine.

Roseman, I. J., Wiest, C., & Swartz, T. S. (1994). Phenomenology, behaviors, and goals differentiate discrete emotions. *Journal of Personality and Social Psychology, 67,* 206–221.

Ryan, R. M., & Connell, J. P. (1989). Perceived locus of causality and internalization: Examining reasons for acting in two domains. *Journal of Personality and Social Psychology, 57,* 749–761.

Ryan, R., Sheldon, K., Kasser, T., & Deci, E. L. (in press). All goals were not created equal: The relation of goal content and regulatory styles to mental health. In J. A. Bargh & P. M. Gollwitzer (Eds.), *The psychology of action: Linking cognition to motivation and behavior.* New York: Guilford.

Schwarz, N. (1990). Feelings as information: Informational and motivational functions of affective states. In E. T. Higgins & R. Sorrentino (Eds.), *Handbook of motivation and cognition* (Vol. 2, pp. 527–561). New York: Guilford.

Sheldon, K. M., & Emmons, R. A. (1995). Comparing differentiation and integration within personal goal systems. *Personality and Individual Differences, 18,* 39–46.

Sheldon, K. M., & Kasser, T. (1995). Coherence and congruence: Two aspects of personality integration. *Journal of Personality and Social Psychology, 68,* 531–543.

Singer, J. A. (1992). Challenges to the integration of the psychoanalytic and cognitive perspectives on the self. *Psychological Inquiry, 3,* 59–61.

Singer, J. A., & Salovey, P. (1993). *The remembered self.* New York: The Free Press.

Vallacher, R. R., & Wegner, D. M. (1989). Levels of personal agency: Individual variation in action identification. *Journal of Personality and Social Psychology, 57,* 660–671.

Werner, H., & Kaplan, B. (1956). The developmental approach to cognition: Its relevance to the psychological interpretation of anthropological and ethnolinguistic data. *American Anthropologist, 58,* 866–880.

Yalom, I. (1980). *Existential psychotherapy.* New York: Basic Books.

Yetim, U. (1993). Life satisfaction: A study based on the organization of personal projects. *Social Indicators Research, 29,* 277–289.

5
The "What the Hell" Effect: Some Effects of Goal Proximity and Goal Framing on Performance

Winona Cochran
Bloomsburgh University

Abraham Tesser
University of Georgia

> Gunilla found the beautiful formal she wanted for the prom, but she needed to lose some weight. Her friend, fresh from a social psychology course, recommended that she set a specific, daily caloric goal. On the third day, after eating a serving of "lite" spaghetti, Gunilla read the package and realized that she was slightly over her daily goal. Her response was interesting: She said to herself, "What-the-hell. Since I'm already over my goal it doesn't matter what I eat." And she proceeded to consume half of her mom's apple pie.

There is a lot of research and even more in the way of common wisdom pointing to the effectiveness of goals in human accomplishment. The more concrete the goal and the more proximal the subgoals the better the performance. In spite of having a proximal, concrete goal, Gunilla's very small failure led to a highly dysfunctional abandonment of the goal system. Her "what-the-hell" response is not unusual.

This chapter is an attempt to understand the what-the-hell response. To do that, we review some of the evidence for the effectiveness of goal setting and then introduce research documenting the existence of the what-the-hell effect. Following that, we explore a variety of parameters that, while important to goal functioning, appear unable to account for the what-the-hell effect. Our own model of the effect implicates the interaction of goal proximity and goal framing. The model suggests that when the goal is framed in terms of gains, the relationship between subgoal proximity and task performance will be more positive than when the goal is framed in terms of prevention of loss/inhibition. After presenting some evidence for this model, we discuss some practical and research implications.

GOALS FACILITATE PERFORMANCE

The effectiveness of goal setting on human performance has been firmly established in numerous studies (Locke & Latham, 1984). A *goal* has been defined as an image of a future level of performance (Garland, 1985); what an individual is trying to accomplish; the object or aim of an action (Locke, Shaw, Saari, & Latham, 1981); and as the determination to perform certain activities or to attain certain future conditions (Bandura & Simon, 1977). These definitions have several factors in common:

1. A goal is *cognitive*; a goal is an image of some ideal occurrence stored in memory for comparison with the actual occurrence.
2. A goal represents a *future* consequence or outcome that influences present behavior.
3. A goal is *desirable* to the individual who seeks to obtain it; some degree of expected satisfaction or pleasure is associated with reaching the goal.
4. A goal is a *source of motivation*; it is an incentive to action.

Data show that having goals, relative to not having goals, increased performance in every area of human behavior studied (Latham & Yukl, 1975; Locke et al., 1981). Goal setting affects the amount, the perseverance, the direction, and the strategy of behavior. In a study by Locke and Bryan (1969), subjects given feedback on five different dimensions of driving performance improved only on the one dimension on which they were given a goal. Terborg (1976) found that subjects with goals spent more time looking at text material to be learned and more often used learning strategies than those with no goals. Subjects increased reaction speed (Locke, Cartledge, & Knerr, 1970); wrote shorter sentences (Rosswork, 1977); and changed standards (Sales, 1970) in response to simply being given a goal. Goals increase the amount and the duration of effort expended. Subjects work faster (Bassett, 1979; Latham & Locke, 1975); harder, as evidenced by heart rate increase and greater output (Sales, 1970); and spend more time at the task (LaPorte & Nath, 1976; Rothkopf & Billington, 1979) when provided with goals, compared to subjects without goals. Additionally, goals may serve to enhance cognitive processing of performance related information (Bandura, 1986). So, goals have been shown to be helpful. However, there is also some evidence that goal setting can have negative effects. This has been demonstrated most clearly in research on dieting.

DIETING AND THE "WHAT THE HELL" EFFECT

Goal setting is apparent in many aspects of human behavior. For example, we set career goals, budget goals, fitness goals, relationship goals, even spiritual goals. One common area in which goals are utilized is that of dieting. With at least one third of all adults in the United States 10% or more above normal weight (Taylor, 1986), the desire to be healthy and physically attractive motivates a large proportion of the population to diet. Surveys of the U. S. population indicate that at any given time, approximately two thirds of the public can be said to be dieting. In accordance with traditional goal-setting/weight-loss approaches, a *diet* generally means setting an endgoal of a specified amount of weight to be lost, as well as a daily subgoal of caloric intake. Although dieting is considered to be at least part of the proper approach to weight loss by lay people as well as the medical profession, results are notoriously bad (Polivy & Herman, 1985). Even among those who do have some success (i.e., weight loss), the pounds are usually regained rapidly (Taylor, 1986).

Restrained eaters, defined by Herman and Mack (1975) as any person who is consciously and continuously aware of their eating behavior even if normal weight, have shifted the control of eating behavior from physiological control to cognitive control. The dieter must learn to suppress normal physiological cues to eat in favor of cognitive controls that permit him or her to eat only what has been predetermined to be *proper* for the day. According to Polivy and Herman (1985), this shift in control of food intake from physiological to cognitive may result in a reaction that they termed the *what-the-hell effect*. This effect is seen in restrained eaters who are induced to eat more calories than is allowed for any one day. Because they perceive that the day is lost, so to speak, there is no longer any incentive for continued restraint, so they overindulge. This effect was seen in restrained eaters who were given milkshakes in a *taste perception* experiment (Herman & Mack, 1975); those who were led to expect a period without food (Lowe, 1982); those who observed a model overeating (Polivy, Herman, Younger, & Erskine, 1979); those who perceived alcohol intoxication (Polivy & Herman, 1976); and even in those who only thought they were taking in extra calories (Polivy, 1976; Spencer & Fremouw, 1979).

Polivy and Herman (1985) presented three aspects of this phenomenon. First, while cognitive controls allow one to eat in accordance with a caloric goal, they are also very susceptible to disruption so that when one starts to deviate from that goal, cognitive controls are usually incapable of stopping the slide. Second, when the cognitive controls are intact, the dieter tends to eat very little, essentially creating an eat/don't eat, good/bad dichotomy. Third, the dieter tends to think irrationally about his or her diet, perceiving caloric limit in diurnal units, so that if the limit is exceeded, there is no need to attempt further restraint for that subgoal (i.e., the day). Goals and related cognitive processes are usually effective in aiding performance behavior. Why do they appear to cause irrationality and the what-the-hell effect? Perhaps a closer look at what makes goals effective will aid in understanding this puzzle.

SOME CONSEQUENTIAL ASPECTS OF GOALS

Probably the most consistent and powerful attribute in goal setting is the difficulty of the goal. Goal-striving behavior occurs within a range of difficulty; this difficulty level has been termed *level of aspiration* (Lewin, Dembo, Festinger, & Sears, 1944). Harder or more difficult goals are goals that require expenditure of greater effort and attention or that require more knowledge or skill than easier goals (Locke et al., 1981). Locke (1966) found that the more difficult the goal, the higher the resulting performance level. This linear relationship held even when the goal was set so high as to be obtainable only 10% of the time. More recent studies have overwhelmingly supported these findings (Garland, 1982, 1983; Latham, Mitchell, & Dossett, 1978; Latham & Yukl, 1975; Locke, 1968). Losing weight has the reputation of being difficult, but doable. Thus, the what-the-hell effect is not likely to be due to goal difficulty.

Another goal dimension is specificity. Specific, clearly stated goals lead to higher performance than general or *do-your-best* goals. The superiority of specific goals in generating output has been shown in numerous experiments (Locke et al., 1981). A goal that is both challenging (i.e., difficult) and specific leads to higher performance levels than either type of goal alone (Locke, 1968; Latham et al., 1978). Specific and challenging goals produced better performance in dieting (Bandura & Simon, 1977), sentence construction (Rothkopf & Billington, 1979), driving (Locke & Bryan, 1969), and in many other laboratory and field studies. Locke and his colleagues (1981) reported that of 110 studies reviewed, 99 reported that specific, hard goals yielded better performance than easier goals, no goals, or vague, do-your-best goals. It is difficult to imagine a more specific goal than caloric intake. Thus, lack of goal specificity cannot account for the what-the-hell effect.

Acceptance of or commitment to a goal is expected to lead to better performance than failure to accept the goal. (Locke, 1968). Although few studies have directly addressed this issue, those that have generally fail to find significant results (Hom & Murphy, 1985; Yukl & Latham, 1978), but these negative results may be in part because of the measures of acceptance utilized (Locke et al., 1981). Closely related to the issue of goal acceptance/

commitment is the idea that goals that are set by the participant (i.e., self-determined) are more likely to be better accepted by the person than goals that are assigned by an experimenter or supervisor (see Sansone & Harackiewicz, chap. 12, this volume). However, studies show no consistent results for participative-set goals being superior to assigned goals when goal difficulty is held constant (Dossett, Latham, & Mitchell, 1979; Latham & Saari, 1979; Locke & Schweiger, 1979). However, it has been shown that participatively set goals may lead to higher performance because participation generally produces higher goals than would be assigned, and higher goals result in better performance (Latham & Saari, 1979; Latham & Yukl, 1975). Because dieting goals are generally self-imposed, acceptance does not appear to be a good candidate to explain the what-the-hell effect.

The role of incentives (i.e., money or other reinforcer) in influencing the effectiveness of goal setting is unclear. While it has been shown that monetary offers can dramatically increase worker output (Locke, Feren, McCaleb, Shaw, & Denny, 1980), these offers must be fairly substantial (Pritchard & Curtis, 1973), and the effects diminish or disappear when goal level is controlled (Latham et al., 1978; Pritchard & Curtis, 1973; Terborg & Miller, 1978). Locke et al. (1980) interpreted these data to indicate that reinforcement affects performance by increasing the likelihood of setting goals, increasing goal level, and/or increasing the value or desirability of goal attainment. (See Sansone & Harackiewicz, chap. 12, this volume, for a discussion internal vs. external goal issues.) It is possible to conceive of dieting goals as under the influence of external reinforcement, (i.e., looking good). However, the literature seems unclear that such reinforcement leads to goal success.

Self-efficacy, or what Garland (1985) referred to as performance expectancy, plays a key cognitive role in goal-setting behavior. Perceived self-efficacy strongly influences the level of future performance and, in turn, is very dependent on past performance (Bandura, 1982; Garland, 1985; Locke et al., 1984). The stronger a person's perceived self-efficacy, the more effort they will expend, and the longer they will persist at a task, resulting in better performance (Bandura & Cervone, 1986). Self-efficacy judgments also influence decisions involving choice of activities and goal level. People tend to choose situations and activities they perceive themselves capable of handling and to avoid those in which they feel incapable (Bandura, 1977).

Because self-efficacy depends heavily on the evaluative comparison process between goals and performance, Bandura (1986) proposed that frequent feedback as to goal progress is needed. Distal or long-term goals are too far off to provide accurate information about current behavior. By dividing a distant end-goal into proximal subgoals, one is able to obtain ongoing information as to accomplishments. Frequent feedback regarding subgoal successes serves to strengthen self-efficacy, thereby sustaining end-goal motivation. In short, the theory predicts that proximal goals will generally be more effective than distal goals.

Again, this does not appear to explain the effect. Indeed, the prediction from self-efficacy theory appears to be nontrivially inconsistent with the what-the-hell effect. Self-efficacy theory predicts that proximal goals will be more effective than distal goals. Yet, the what-the-hell effect appears to be a result of adopting a more proximal goal over a more distal one. For example, if an individual maintains a weekly caloric goal then exceeding one seventh of it (the daily equivalent) in a single day would not lead to overeating. It is precisely because the goal is diurnal (rather than weekly) that the effect emerges. Because the what-the-hell effect clashes so strongly with theory on this dimension, we believe that the dimension of goal proximity may be crucial to understanding the effect. But still another piece of the puzzle is missing.

In sum, we have examined a number of aspects of goals in order to better understand the what-the-hell effect. None of these dimensions seems to provide a reasonable explanation. Losing weight is admittedly difficult to do. However, difficult goals are generally more efficacious than less difficult goals. So, difficulty does not appear to be responsible. We learned that specific goals are better than general goals in promoting effective behavior. But, what can be more specific than a caloric goal? The specificity dimension is ruled out. Commitment appears to be important in maintaining goal behavior. However, most dieters are highly committed to their goals. They often spend substantial sums of money and are quite public about their intentions to lose weight. Thus, the what-the-hell effect does not seem to be based on a lack of commitment. The literature on the role of incentives is mixed so what to conclude on that dimension is unclear. We turn now to what we think are important aspects of the what-the-hell effect.

TWO CRUCIAL PARAMETERS: GOAL PROXIMITY AND GOAL DIRECTION (FRAMING)

The failure of cognitive goals as controls in dieting behavior (i.e., the what-the-hell effect) may be related to the way in which the behavior is framed. Review of the goal-setting literature reveals that goal-setting studies focus on behavior that one would like to enhance or increase (Garland, 1985; Locke et al., 1981), whereas dieting involves inhibiting or decreasing a behavior (i.e., eating). Any behavior that a person is trying to decrease or eliminate entirely can be viewed as an *inhibitional behavior*. Such behavior would include drinking, smoking, and inappropriate social behavior, as well as overeating, all refractory behavior (Bandura & Simon, 1977; Taylor,

1986). Behavior that one is attempting to increase or gain, such as skill or competency, can be conceived as *acquisitional behavior*.

A similar distinction has been drawn in a variety of other contexts. Gray (1982) for example, distinguished between appetitive behaviors (and the activation system) and avoidance behaviors (and the inhibition system). Several of the authors in this volume find the distinction useful as well. Carver, Lawrence, and Scheier (chap. 2, this volume) distinguish between approach and avoid goals. From the perspective of control systems theory approach goals are associated with a negative feedback loop (i.e., behavior is consistently moved toward a reference value). When it comes close enough to that value the system is turned off. Avoidance goals, on the other hand, are associated with positive feedback. Because the goal is to move away from the reference value, the system can never be satisfied and turned off. In assessing personal strivings, Emmons and Kaiser (chap. 4, this volume) find that most goals that persons strive for are positive (acquisitional) but that persons generally have a few avoidance (inhibitional) goals as well. Interestingly, the greater the percent of these avoidance goals the lower his subjects' general well-being (i.e., less positive affect, more anxiety, and more physical symptoms). Singer and Salovey (chap. 10, this volume) find it useful to distinguish between memories associated with approach goals and those associated with avoidance goals. The former memories tend to be associated with success and the latter with failure. And, while Strauman (chap. 8, this volume) does not stress this aspect of self-discrepancy theory in his chapter, Higgins and colleagues (e.g., Higgins, 1987) showed the generality of differences in approach-type psychological situations (associated with *ideal* discrepancies) and avoid situations (associated with *ought* discrepancies, see also Carver et al., chap. 2, this volume, for further discussion of this issue.) Even mood seems to have different effects on attitude change, depending on whether the attitude change message is framed as approach or avoid (Wegener & Petty, chap. 14, this volume.)

Because current theories of goal-setting behavior conceptualize cognitive processes as key influences in the effectiveness of goals in enhancing human performance, any perceptual differences between inhibitional and acquisitional behaviors could have considerable impact. Evidence that the perception of inhibitional and acquisitional behaviors may differ can be found in Kahneman and Tversky's (1979) presentation of prospect theory. They showed that people tend to perceive a loss as a greater negative than lack of an equivalent gain. Failure to reach an inhibitory goal (i.e., a goal that requires abstaining from a behavior) can be viewed as a loss, because by performing said behavior the person is losing what he or she did have when not performing the behavior. For example, if the goal is not drinking alcohol, then prior to taking that drink, the person has the desired goal of not drinking. Once a drink is taken, however, then the goal is lost. On the other hand, not reaching an acquisitional goal (i.e., one that requires emitting a behavior) can be seen as simply a lack of gain, because the goal was not in the possession of the individual and so cannot be *lost*. Although the results are equal in distance from the goal, the perception is that the failure to inhibit a behavior is greater than the failure to acquire a behavior.

Inhibitional failure may be seen as an all-or-none phenomenon insofar as any emission (or overemission) of the behavior in question results in loss of the immediate subgoal, regardless of behavior before or after. That is, successfully inhibiting a behavior for a portion of time followed by emitting the behavior is viewed as failure. For example, because dieting usually involves calorie counting on a daily basis such that a set limit of calories may be consumed in one day, each day of a diet becomes a goal in and of itself. The overall goal of losing weight has not changed, but the dieter's perception of the goal may have shifted so that the dieter focuses on the subgoal. Overindulgence on one day will obviously not aid weight loss, but neither does it eliminate the possibility of ever losing weight. Yet when the dieter begins to perceive a set number of calories per day as the goal, and that number is exceeded, then the goal may be perceived as lost and a failure is recorded.

Acquisitional failure may be a more graded occurrence because any period of time in which the desired behavior is emitted is seen as some progress even when followed by lack of the behavior, eventually resulting in not reaching the goal. Although failure is the result in both cases, some progress is perceived with acquisitional effort perhaps because any attempt to do something is more tangible and can more easily be cognitively represented for use as feedback information. Likewise, only failure may be perceived with imperfect inhibitional effort, inasmuch as one cannot as easily conceptualize noneffort in the cognitive comparison process. In a study on dieting behavior, restraint monitoring, noting the desire to eat without carrying out the action, did not provide enough information to be utilized as behavioral feedback (Baron & Watters, 1982).

When the focus is on decreasing or inhibiting a behavior, anything short of that may be seen as a failure. If a dieter exceeds a daily caloric quota, she may see herself as failing; it is an all-or-none perception. When persons are attempting to increase a behavior, even if they do not acquire the desired level they can still perceive some progress. It is not an all-or-none situation. If one perceives failure as anything in excess of the goal (e.g., a set number of calories per day), then frequent failures may result. Frequent failure could lead to lower perceived self-efficacy (Bandura & Simon, 1977), which, in turn, leads to lower goal commitment, lower goal level, lower performance, and in the case of the dieter, overeating (Polivy, 1976). Additionally, the closer to the goal one perceives their progress, the more personal satisfaction they report (Locke, et al., 1970). The all-or-none perception would eliminate any satisfying effect of partial progress.

Goal-setting effectiveness depends on the availability and use of feedback information regarding actual performance for comparison with a cognitive representation of ideal performance (Bandura, 1986; Garland, 1985; Locke et al., 1981). Such feedback information about ongoing performance is most often obtained through self-monitoring procedures in which one observes and evaluates their own behavior (Bandura, 1986; Kazdin, 1974). Inhibitional goal setting and acquisitional goal setting result in differential self-monitoring. Acquisitional goals direct attention toward recognizing and recording valued or desired behaviors that one is trying to increase, an orientation that is termed *positive self-monitoring*. *Negative self-monitoring*, the tracking of negative behaviors that one desires to decrease, results from inhibitional goal setting. Acquisitional goals lead one to focus on the positive and remember correct actions; inhibitional goals cause one to focus on the negative and to note one's errors.

Relative to positive self-monitoring, negative self-monitoring is detrimental to performance (Kirschenbaum & Karoly, 1977). Focusing on the negative aspects of one's behavior decreases reward, increases anxiety (Bandura, 1986; Kirschenbaum & Karoly, 1977), and reduces the frequency of self-observations (Gottman & McFall, 1972). Ultimately, these decrease overall performance level (Kirschenbaum & Karoly, 1977; Kirschenbaum, Ordman, Tomarken, & Holtzbauer, 1982). Sieck and McFall (1976) found that negative self-monitoring actually increased the incidence of smoking in those attempting to decrease. Negative feedback seems to have a more adverse effect in persons who already have low self-perceptions (Schrauger & Rosenberg, 1970), as may be the case for those individuals who are unsatisfied with their present behavior enough to attempt to decrease it. Low self-esteem plus negative focusing may result in even lower self-esteem, lower self-efficacy, and lower performance.

Moreover, recent research has shown that inhibition has an additional undesirable consequence. Wegner and his colleagues (e.g., Wegner, Schneider, Carter, & White, 1987) showed, for example, that after attempting to suppress or inhibit a thought there is a rebound effect. That is, following an attempt to suppress a thought, the suppressed thought enters consciousness more frequently than if there was no attempt to suppress the thought. This rebound may be due to associative processes. During suppression, when the unwanted thought appears people may use a variety of distractors to get rid of it. These multiple distractors may later serve to trigger the thought (Wegner, et al., 1987). Another explanation suggests that the appearance of unwanted thoughts during suppression is experienced as a failure to suppress the thought. The failure to meet the goal sets up a tension toward completion sometimes known as the *Zeigarnik effect*. The rebound may be due to reducing this motivational tension (Martin & Tesser described in Martin, Tesser, & McIntosh, 1993). Whatever the precise mediating processes, failure at inhibition has enduring consequences.

Positive self-monitoring has been shown to create more positive affect, raise self-evaluation (Kirschenbaum & Karoly, 1977), and enhance performance on mathematical problems (Kirschenbaum et al., 1982), general school performance (Gottman & McFall, 1972), and motor responses (Sieck & McFall, 1976). Kirschenbaum and Karoly (1977) suggest that positive self-monitoring may be especially beneficial at the beginning of a self-regulation attempt to provide incentive through the recognition of progress.

Inhibitional behavior and goal setting are triggered by past or present personal dissatisfaction or failure, are viewed as all-or-none with regard to success or failure, are perceived as easy, activate negative self-monitoring, and have lasting effects. These factors combined with possibility of frequent failure and little, if any, positive feedback create a negative, failure-oriented perception. Goal-setting behavior with an acquisitional direction is not as likely to begin with a negative self-perception, focuses attention on positive actions, allows for detection of some progress (i.e., positive feedback) even if failure is the final outcome, and is perceived as more difficult. Acquisitional behavior and goal setting is more likely to encourage a positive, successful orientation.

Although the perceptual differences between inhibitional and acquisitional behavior have strong impact on the cognitive mediators of goal-setting behavior, it does not mean that goal setting is detrimental in inhibitional efforts. Even in refractory behavior such as the inhibition of eating or alcohol consumption, goal setting still leads to better performance than no goal setting (Bandura & Simon, 1977; Dubbert & Wilson, 1984).

In summary, acquisitional and inhibitional goals are qualitatively different. Although goal setting is a useful strategy for both, acquisitional goals fair better than inhibitional goals. Because dieting is an inhibitional goal, this analysis provides a partial, but only a partial, explanation of the what-the-hell effect. A fuller understanding follows from integrating our observations about the proximity of goals and the direction of goals.

TOWARD SOLVING THE WHAT-THE-HELL EFFECT PUZZLE: GOAL PROXIMITY AND GOAL DIRECTION INTERACT

When one is attempting to increase the probability of a behavior occurring, frequent feedback provides a yardstick by which to evaluate progress.

When people see that they have increased the behavior, they feel self-satisfied and rewarded; when they sees that they have not increased the behavior, they feel self-dissatisfied and renew their efforts (Bandura & Cervone, 1986). In both instances, however, the emphasis is on increasing or acquiring desirable actions, and the focus of the frequent feedback is generally positive. When one is attempting to eliminate or decrease a behavior, the focus is failure-oriented and frequent feedback may serve to multiply negative aspects. By adjusting the proximity of goals through utilization of subgoals and endgoals, it may be possible to manipulate the cognitive processing of goal-related information and increase the effectiveness of inhibitory and acquisitional self-regulation.

It is proposed that an acquisitional goal is enhanced through the use of proximal subgoals that provide feedback concerning progress by encouraging positive self-monitoring. This positive feedback, cognitively multiplied by the use of frequent subgoals and positive self-monitoring, serves to increase self-efficacy and self-evaluation. Additional personal satisfaction may be gained from evidence of progress even if failure also occurs. Higher self-reactions lead to increased effort, increased goal level, and better performance.

It is proposed that task performance under an inhibitional goal is enhanced by the use of more distal subgoals or endgoals only. Because the dominant focus of inhibitional behavior is negative, the use of fewer subgoals will reduce the frequency of negative feedback concerning one's mistakes. With less negative self-knowledge, self-efficacy and self-evaluation will remain stronger and more positive. By reducing the amount of negativity contained in the information while still providing the necessary knowledge of results, it is believed that distal goals will allow for the maximum enhancement of inhibitional performance.

A fuller understanding of the what-the-hell effect begins to emerge. Rather than being an acquisitional goal, dieting is an inhibitional goal. Whereas proximal goals appear optimal for acquisitional behaviors, distal goals are more efficacious for inhibitional behaviors. It is the *combination* of adopting a proximal goal (diurnal) for an inhibitional behavior (dieting) that results in the what-the-hell effect. Daily caloric limits are only subgoals, the *actual* goal is a distal one—that of weight loss. It is not necessary to calculate caloric intake in daily units. If one were to adopt a longer unit, say weekly, then one slip may be much less likely to cause unrestrained eating, because the extra calories could be compensated for later in the same subgoal unit (Polivy & Herman, 1985). By calculating desired inhibitional goals in distal terms, even weekly or monthly units, one would not only be less likely to be thrown off by a minor transgression but, even if those transgressions occur, failures would be much less numerous.

THE STUDY

The present study was designed to examine the relationship between proximity of goal setting and type of goal setting—inhibitional or acquisitional. That is, it was designed to investigate the hypothesized interaction between goal proximity and goal direction on performance. We hypothesize that on a task in which the direction was inhibitional (not losing points), more distal subgoals should result in better performance (i.e., fewer errors) than more proximal smaller subgoals. When the direction is acquisitional (gaining points), more proximal subgoals should result in better performance (i.e., more points earned) than more distal subgoals.

Note that the use of points as a dependent variable is only an indirect reflection of the what-the-hell effect. The what-the-hell effect refers to a motivational shift where, as a result of failure on a subgoal, the individual abandons the discipline associated with attempting to meet the long-term goal. Achieving points in the experimental task is a nice behavioral measure of achievement. However, it is influenced by a variety of things, including skill and chance effects, as well as motivation. Since there is no apparent reason to expect that skill or chance factors differ across cells, we take systematic differences in points to reflect motivation.

When subjects arrived at the laboratory they were seated at a microcomputer. Software was written specifically for this experiment. The program presents a task in which a small black square (1 mm.) appears on the screen for $1\frac{1}{2}$ seconds. The subject's task is to move the mouse pointer onto the square and click the mouse before the square disappears. Ten squares appear on the screen per trial with two seconds between presentation of squares. The squares are randomly located on the screen using a 319 × 319 matrix with a total of 101,761 possible appearance locations.

Subjects were told they had an opportunity to earn points that could be traded in for extra-credit points toward their final course grade. The total number of extra-credit points earned depended on performance. The subject was then allowed one practice trial of the program. After the practice trial, the subject was asked to set a goal for the actual computer task consistent with the conditions described.

Each trial of 10 squares was presented automatically by the computer. Subjects initiated the next trial by hitting the return key. The computer recorded the number of points earned or lost on each trial for each participant. Pilot work showed that the task is difficult enough that it is virtually impossible not to make occasional misses with the mouse. However, it is not so difficult that the average person cannot perform it successfully on many attempts.

Subjects were randomly assigned to one of four behavior-goal conditions. In the two acquisitional conditions they were told that they would earn one point for each square they clicked on with the mouse before it disappeared from the screen and that they were to try to earn as many points as possible but especially to try to reach the set goal. Subjects in the two inhibitional conditions were told that they would begin the task with 100 points and that they would lose a point each time they made an error by failing to click on the square before it disappeared. They were also told that they were to lose as few points as possible but particularly not to make more errors than the set goal.

Acquisitional-Proximal: Subjects were told that they had 10 trials and that the average person earns 8 points per trial. They were then asked to set and state a per trial goal for all 10 trials.

Acquisitional-Distal: Subjects were told that they had 10 trials and that the average person earns 80 points over 10 trials. They were then asked to set and state an overall goal for the 10 trials.

Inhibitional-Proximal: Subjects were told that they had 10 trials and that the average person makes two errors per trial. They were then asked to set and state a per trial goal for all 10 trials.

Inhibitional-Distal: Subjects were told that they had 10 trials and that the average person makes 20 errors over 10 trials. They were then asked to set and state an overall goal for the trials.

When all trials were finished, the participant was asked to complete a postexperimental questionnaire. The entire procedure required approximately 20 minutes (see Fig. 5.1).

The manipulations appeared to be successful. Subjects in the acquisitional conditions (points earned for correct hits) reported greater focus on correct hits than subjects in the inhibitional conditions (points lost for errors) who reported greater attention to errors made. Subjects in the proximal goal (per trial goal) conditions reported greater focus on each trial than those in the distal goal (per session goal) conditions who reported greater attention to the session.

Task Performance

Recall that performance refers to the number of times the subject, using the mouse, covered the spot before it disappeared. It was hypothesized that acquisitional goals would be associated with better performance than inhibitional goals. Moreover, when the focus was inhibitional (not losing points), distal goals (10 trials) would result in better performance than proximal subgoals (each trial). When the focus was directed to be acquisitional (gaining points), proximal subgoals would result in better performance than distal subgoals. These hypotheses were supported by the data.

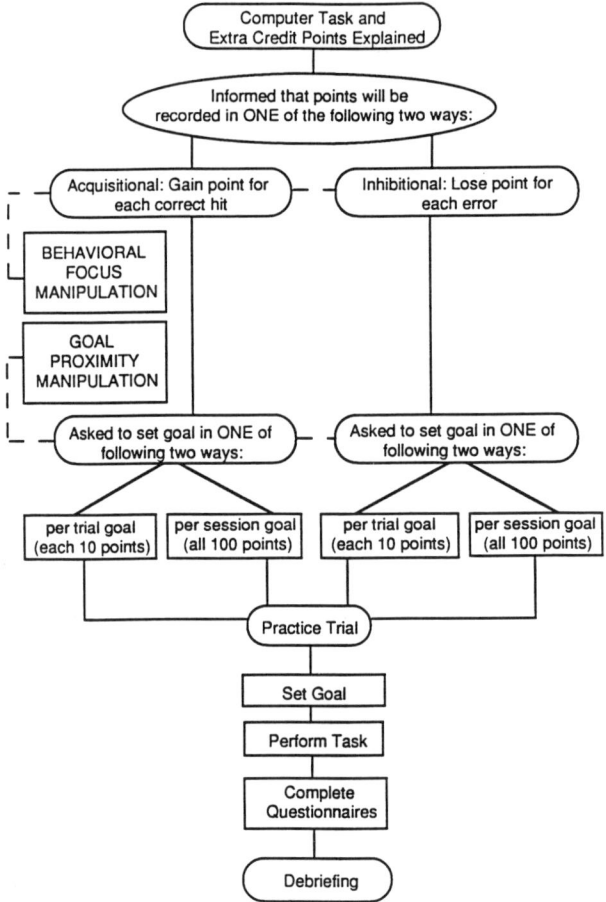

FIG. 5.1. Flowchart of experimental procedure.

Each of these predictions was realized (see Fig. 5.2). There was a significant interaction effect of behavioral focus × proximity of goal. Performance in the inhibitional proximal condition was the lowest, whereas those in the acquisitional-proximal condition performed best. Indeed, both simple effects of goal proximity was significant: When subjects performed the task with an acquisitional focus, as predicted, the *more* proximal the goal the better the performance; when subjects performed the task with an inhibitional focus, also as predicted, the *less* proximal the goal, the better the performance. There was a marginal main effect for behavioral focus with better performance in the acquisitional conditions than in the inhibitional conditions. But, as noted earlier, this was true only for the proximal goal conditions.

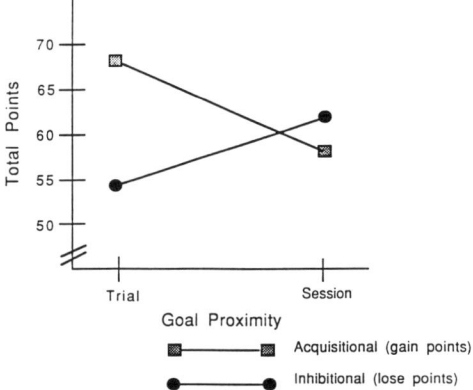

FIG. 5.2. Total points earned as a function of behavior type and goal proximity.

Subjective Goal: A Potential Mediator

The goal that participants set for themselves prior to beginning the actual computer task was affected by proximity of the assigned goal. Those in the distal goal conditions set higher goals than those in the proximal goal conditions. Also, there was a significant correlation between subjectively set goal and performance ($r = .23$).

The literature shows that the higher a person sets his or her goal, the better he or she performs (Garland, 1982, 1983; Latham, et al., 1978; Latham & Yukl, 1975; Locke, 1968). Because of the established relationship between set goal and performance, a covariance analysis of performance was done with set goal as covariate. This analysis also resulted in a significant interaction effect of behavioral focus and goal proximity with those in the acquisitional condition and setting proximal goals performing best and those in the inhibitional condition and setting proximal goals performing worst (i.e., the means were all correctly ordered). The simple main effect of proximity was significant in the acquisitional condition but not significant in the inhibitional condition. Therefore, although goal proximity had an effect on how high the participants set their goal, this set goal cannot account for the observed differences in task performance.

Perception of Performance: The Postexperimental Questionnaire

A composite index was calculated for perception of task and performance by combining items asking about distance from goal, difficulty of task, performance compared to other students, and perceived performance on task.

With this composite index as the dependent measure in a 2 × 2 ANOVA with behavioral focus and proximity of goal as between subjects' factors, a significant main effect was found for behavioral focus with subjects in the acquisitional conditions perceiving better performance than those in the inhibitional conditions. This was an accurate perception; the correlation between actual performance and perception of task and performance was substantial, $r = .70$.

Where Do We Go From Here?

This study was undertaken in an effort to understand the what-the-hell effect. Whereas more proximal subgoals are generally understood to be associated with better performance, there are circumstances under which the failure to obtain a proximal goal leads the individual to say to himself or herself "what-the-hell" and to stop trying. Herman and his colleagues have systematically observed this effect among dieters. Jefferson Singer (personal communication, 1993) reported a similar phenomenon with drug and alcohol abusers.

Our theoretical analysis of this effect led us to expect an interaction between goal proximity and goal direction (framing). As reported elsewhere in this volume, most personal goals are positive (Singer & Salovey, chap. 10, this volume; Emmons & Kaiser, chap. 4, this volume), or what we term *acquisitional*. The cognitive construal of such goals is such that even partial progress leaves the individual better off than before; failure is merely a smaller *profit*. Adequate progress on such goals leads to positive affect (Carver & Scheier, 1990). Inadequate progress is not devastating; although one does not have all that is wanted one is still better off than before. The negative emotion likely to be experienced under acquisitional goal failure is depression, an emotion that is unlikely to be associated with the energy necessary for the initiation of the decision to abandon the goal. Thus, under acquisitional goals, more frequent feedback (i.e., proximal goals) should facilitate performance.

Negative goals, or what we call inhibitional goals, are less frequent (Singer & Salovey, chap. 10, this volume; Emmons & Kaiser, chap. 4, this volume). The focus here is not on acquiring something but on holding back or preventing loss. Failure to meet this goal results in the perception of loss, and losses are regarded as more impactful than logically equivalent gains (Kahneman & Tversky, 1979). Success on such goals merely maintains the status quo and should be associated with less positive affect than success on an acquisitional goal. Failure, however, leads to the emotion of anxiety and agitation (Carver, Lawrence, & Scheier, chap. 2, this volume), a high arousal state that can supply the energy to initiate the decision to abandon the overall goal. At the same time, failure (i.e., an uncontrolled loss) may tend to be seen in all-or-none terms. Thus, with inhibitional goals more frequent (i.e., proximal) goals may be unproductive and lead to the what-the-hell effect.

The original observation of the what-the-hell effect was associated with real-world, socially consequential phenomena. However, our theoretical abstraction of what is crucial to the phenomenon led us to the laboratory to develop an experimental test. We were able to create a situation in which it was possible to orthogonally manipulate goal focus and goal proximity and to unambiguously measure performance. Our general expectations were confirmed. Overall, performance was best under a positive or acquisitional goal frame. More importantly, we also observed the predicted interaction. For acquisitional goals, more proximal goals resulted in better performance than more distal goals. For inhibitional goals, distal goals resulted in better performance than more proximal goals. The practical implications of this work seem clear and are taken up later. In spite of the fact that the results provided very nice confirmation for our hypotheses, they raise many more questions than they answer. We touch on some of these now.

Some Questions Raised By the Data

Our theoretical analysis for the interaction between goal frame and goal proximity was based on an analysis that overdetermined the outcome. That is to say, the results could have been predicted from our cognitive analysis or motivational/affective analysis alone. For example, positive goals focus on gains rather than losses, and inhibitual goals focus on losses rather than gains. Because gains and losses are differentially weighted (Kahneman & Tversky, 1979), this difference alone could account for the interaction.

It is not clear exactly how to proceed to test this possibility, but it suggests studies in which beliefs alone are free to vary while holding motives and emotions constant. Perhaps preliminary scaling studies could tell us what level of loss is equivalent to what level of reward in some domain. Then losses can be psychologically (rather than logically) matched to gains. If the predicted interaction is significantly decreased (Baron & Kenny, 1986), we would know that this aspect of the differing psychological situations is consequential.

Perhaps what is important in producing the interaction is the agitation associated with failure on an inhibitional goal. It is also difficult to manipulate emotions or motives without also manipulating concomitant beliefs. However, possibilities do suggest themselves. Products containing caffeine produce mild forms of agitation. If affective differences are crucial, then persons who have ingested coffee might be expected to perform more poorly with proximal goals than subjects who have not ingested coffee.

Even more fundamentally, we also do not know if we succeeded in producing a what-the-hell effect. Have subjects in the inhibitional-proximal condition really given up and figuratively (or literally) said what-the-hell and quit trying? How would we know? Asking them is a possibility. Trusting the answer could be risky. Subjects may not be aware of their changing state of mind, and the answer they give readily lends itself to both self- and other deception. Another possibility is refined observation. Giving up implies a qualitatively new psychological state that should be observable: There should be a discontinuity in the behavior. Performance should drop suddenly and stay consistently poorer after someone gives up compared to before giving up. If the model is correct, then trial-by-trial performance should reveal such discontinuities in the inhibitional proximal conditions more than the others. Moreover, these discontinuities should be more likely after failure to meet the subgoal than after success. Obviously, a large number of experimental variations are possible. The point is simply that more theoretical and empirical work is necessary to better understand these results.

Implications

Although more theoretical and empirical work is clearly needed in order to better understand what is going on, there do seem to be some implications from the model for practical situations concerning such behaviors as weight control and alcohol abuse. One implication is relatively straightforward. Although most goals tend to be positive (acquisitive) goals, the reduction of eating or stopping the use of alcohol or drugs are negative or inhibitional goals. If possible, a change to a positive frame would seem productive. Recall that positively framed goals are more productive than negatively framed goals.

How is it possible to frame obviously inhibitional goals positively? A baseball player concerned with batting can have an (inhibitional) goal concerning the number of strikes or an (acquisitional) goal concerning the number of hits. Similarly, instead of thinking that he must cut down on caloric intake, a dieter can reward himself or herself for each meal under a thousand calories. The drug addict can reward himself or herself for time units (e.g., days) with no drugs. In each of these reframed cases, the goal is acquisitional: The individual is trying to amass particular kinds of meals or particular kinds of days.

If reframing an inhibitional goal to an acquisitional goal is too difficult, it may be possible to operate on the proximity of the goal. Recall that goal proximity is negatively related to productivity under inhibitional goals. Thus, if the goal remains inhibitional it would be productive to make the goals more distal. Instead of having a calorie goal per day, the goal could be changed to weekly or even monthly. Less feedback, at least up to a point, seems to result in better inhibitional performance. This solution, however, is not expected to be as effective as changing the frame to acquisitional. Fewer, more distal subgoals will lead to fewer occasions for the what-the-hell effect but will also decrease the benefit associated with positive feedback (reviewed in the introduction of this chapter).

Even more speculatively, one can focus on the presumed affects associated with acquisitional and inhibitional failures. We have suggested that it is the arousal associated with the failure to obtain inhibitional goals that might provide the energy to change and give up the goal. Therefore, another tack to take with inhibitional goals is to reduce the agitation. Tranquilizers or beta blockers, for example, decrease arousal and, hence, at least theoretically, should decrease the tendency to give up the goal. Giving drugs, however, may provide the wrong example to persons trying to give up drugs or alcohol! (It is noteworthy in this context that amphetamines are often used as appetizer suppressants, and they have the effect of increasing arousal!)

Goals are a ubiquitous form of self-regulation. They facilitate performance in almost every domain. The what-the-hell effect calls our attention to the possibility that there are conditions under which goals are less productive and may even be counterproductive. The identification of such conditions is important for maximizing desirable behavior as well as controlling undesirable behavior. The understanding of such conditions will move the psychology of motivation significantly forward.

SUMMARY

Although proximal goals are often thought to be more effective than distal goals, we have seen that under certain circumstances just the opposite is true. This has been identified as the what-the-hell effect. Our theoretical analysis led us to expect to find the what-the-hell effect when individuals hold inhibitional goals *and* when their subgoals are relatively proximal. Indeed, when goals were manipulated to be either acquisitional or inhibitional, and when the subgoals were manipulated to be either proximal or distal, these variables interacted to predict performance. Subjects performed better under acquisitional than proximal goals, and goal proximity was positively related to performance under acquisitional goals and negatively related to performance under inhibitional goals. Speculation about theoretical mediators and about applications were also provided.

ACKNOWLEDGMENTS

This chapter is based on a dissertation Completed by Winona Cochran under the direction of Abraham Tesser. Work on this chapter was facilitated by NSF Grant 1021RR274100 to L. Martin and A. Tesser and NIMH Grant 1R01MH41487-01 to A. Tesser and S. Beach. We are grateful to Len Martin for helpful comments on this chapter.

REFERENCES

Bandura, A. (1977). Self-efficacy: Toward a unifying theory of behavioral change. *Psychological Review, 84*, 191-215.
Bandura, A. (1982). Self-efficacy mechanism in human agency. *American Psychologist, 37*, 122-147.
Bandura, A. (1986). *Social Foundations of Thought and Action: A Social Cognitive Theory.* Englewood Cliffs, NJ: Prentice-Hall.
Bandura, A., & Cervone, D. (1986). Differential engagement of self-reactive influences in cognitive motivation. *Organizational Behavior and Human Decision Processes, 38*, 92-113.
Bandura, A., & Simon, K. (1977). The role of proximal intentions in self-regulation of refractory behavior. *Cognitive Therapy and Research, 1*, 177-193.
Baron, P., & Watters, R. G. (1982). Effects of goal-setting and of goal levels on weight loss induced by self-monitoring. *International Review of Applied Psychology, 31*, 369-382.
Baron, R. M., & Kenny, D. A. (1986). The moderator-mediator variable distinction in social psychology research: Conceptual, strategic, and statistical considerations. *Journal of Personality and Social Psychology, 51*, 1173-1182.
Bassett, G. A. (1979). A study of the effects of task goal and schedule choice on work performance. *Organizational Behavior and Human Performance, 24*, 202-227.
Carver, C. S., & Scheier, M. F. (1990). Origins and functions of positive and negative affect: A control process view. *Psychological Review, 97*, 19-35.
Dossett, D. L., Latham, G. P., & Mitchell, T. R. (1979). The effects of assigned versus participatively set goals, KR, and individual differences when goal difficulty is held constant. *Journal of Applied Psychology, 64*, 291-298.
Dubbert, P. M., & Wilson, G. T. (1984). Goal setting and spouse involvement in the treatment of obesity. *Behavior Research and Therapy, 22*, 227-242.
Garland, H. (1982). Goal levels and task performance: A compelling replication of some compelling results. *Journal of Applied Psychology, 67*, 245-248.
Garland, H. (1983). Influence of ability, assigned goals, and normative information on personal goals and performance: A challenge to the goal attainability assumption. *Journal of Applied Psychology, 68*, 20-30.
Garland, H. (1985). A cognitive mediation theory of task goals and human performance. *Motivation and Emotion, 9*, 345-367.
Gottman, J. M., & McFall, R. M. (1972). Self-monitoring effects in a program for potential high school dropouts: A time-series analysis. *Journal of Consulting and Clinical Psychology, 39*, 273-281.
Gray, J. A. (1982). *The neuropsychology of anxiety: An enquiry into the functions of the septohippocampal system.* New York: Oxford University Press.
Herman, C. P., & Mack, D. (1975). Restrained and unrestrained eating. *Journal of Personality, 43*, 647-660.
Higgins, E. T. (1987). Self-discrepancy: A theory relating self and affect. *Psychological Review, 94*(3), 319-340.
Hom, H. L., & Murphy, M. D. (1985). Low need achiever's performance: The positive impact of a self-determined goal. *Personality Social Psychology Bulletin, 11*, 275-285.
Kahneman, D., & Tversky, A. (1979). Prospect theory: An analysis of decision under risk. *Econometrica, 47*, 263-291.
Kazdin, A. E. (1974). Reactive self-monitoring: The effects of response desirability, goal setting, and feedback. *Journal of Consulting and Clinical Psychology, 47*, 725-733.
Kirschenbaum, D. S., & Karoly, P. (1977). When self-regulation fails: Tests of some preliminary hypotheses. *Journal of Consulting and Clinical Psychology, 45*, 1116-1125.

Kirschenbaum, D. S., Ordman, A. M., Tomarken, A. J., & Holtzbauer, R. (1982). Effects of differential self-monitoring and level of mastery of sports performance: Power brain bowling. *Cognitive Therapy and Research, 6,* 335–342.

LaPorte, R. E., & Nath, R. (1976). Role of performance goals in prose learning. *Journal of Educational Psychology, 68,* 260–264.

Latham, G. P., & Locke, E. A. (1975). Increasing productivity with decreasing time limits: A field replication of Parkinson's law. *Journal of Applied Psychology, 60,* 524–526.

Latham, G. P., Mitchell, T. R., & Dossett, D. L. (1978). Importance of participative goal setting and anticipated rewards on goal difficulty and job performance. *Journal of Applied Psychology, 63,* 163–171.

Latham, G. P., & Saari, L. M. (1979). The effects of holding goal difficulty constant on assigned and participatively set goals. *Academy of Management Journal, 22,* 163–168.

Latham, G. P., & Yukl, G. A. (1975). A review of research on the application of goalsetting in organizations. *Academy of Management Journal, 18,* 824–845.

Lewin, K., Dembo, T., Festinger, L., Sears, P. S. (1944). Level of aspiration. In J. M. Hunt (Ed.), *Personality and behavior disorders* (Vol. 1, pp. 333–378). New York: Ronald Press.

Locke, E. A. (1966). The relationship of intentions to level of performance. *Journal of Applied Psychology, 50,* 60–66.

Locke, E. A. (1968). Toward a theory of task motivation and incentives. *Organizational Behavior and Human Performance, 3,* 157–189.

Locke, E. A., & Bryan, J. F. (1969). The directing function of goals in task performance. *Organizational Behavior and Human Performance, 4,* 35–42.

Locke, E. A., Cartledge, N., & Knerr, C. S. (1970). Studies of the relationship between satisfaction, goal-setting, and performance. *Organizational Behavior and Human Performance, 5,* 135–158.

Locke, E. A., Feren, D. B., McCaleb, V. M., Shaw, K. N., & Denny, A. T. (1980). The relative effectiveness of four methods of motivating employee performance. In K. Duncan, M. Gruneberg, & D. Wallis (Eds.), *Changes in working life* (pp. 301–322). New York: Wiley.

Locke, E. A., & Latham, G. P. (1984). *Goal setting: A motivational technique that works!* Englewood Cliffs, NJ: Prentice-Hall.

Locke, E. A., & Schweiger, D. M. (1979). Participation in decision making: One more look. In B. M. Staw (Ed.), *Research in organization behavior* (Vol. 1, pp. 265–339). Greenwich, CT: JAI Press.

Locke, E. A., Shaw, K. N., Saari, L. J., & Latham, G. P. (1981). Goal setting and task performance: 1969–1980. *Psychological Bulletin, 90,* 125–152.

Lowe, M. G. (1982). The role of anticipated deprivation in overeating. *Addictive Behaviors, 1,* 103–112.

Martin, L. L., Tesser, A., & McIntosh, W. D. (1993). Wanting but not having: The effects of unattained goals on thoughts and feelings. In D. M. Wegner & J. W. Pennebaker (Eds.), *The handbook of mental control* (pp. 552–572). Englewood Cliffs, NJ: Prentice-Hall.

Polivy, J. (1976). Perception of calories and regulation of intake in restrained and unrestrained subjects. *Addictive Behaviors, 1,* 237–243.

Polivy, J., & Herman, C. P. (1976). Effects of alcohol on eating behavior: Influence of mood and perceived intoxication. *Journal of Abnormal Psychology, 85,* 601–606.

Polivy, J., & Herman, C. P. (1985). Dieting as a problem in behavioral medicine. In E. Katkin & S. Manuck (Eds.), *Advances in behavioral medicine* (pp. 1–37). New York: SAI.

Polivy, J., Herman, C. P., Younger, J. C., & Erskine, B. (1979). Effects of a model on eating behavior: The induction of a restrained eating style. *Journal of Personality, 47,* 100–114.

Pritchard, R. D., & Curtis, M. I. (1973). The influence of goal setting and financial incentives on task performance. *Organizational Behavior and Human Performance, 10,* 175–183.

Rosswork, S. G. (1977). Goal setting: The effects on an academic task with varying magnitudes of incentive. *Journal of Educational Psychology, 69,* 710–715.

Rothkopf, E. Z., & Billington, M. J. (1979). Goal-guided learning from the text: Inferring a descriptive processing model from inspection times and eye movements. *Journal of Educational Psychology, 71*, 310–327.

Sales, S. M. (1970). Some effects of role overload and role underload. *Organizational Behavior and Human Performance, 5*, 592–608.

Schrauger, J. S., & Rosenberg, S. F. (1970). Self-esteem and the effects of success and failure feedback on performance. *Journal of Personality, 38*, 404–417.

Sieck, W. A., & McFall, R. M. (1976). Some determinants of self-monitoring effects. *Journal of Consulting and Clinical Psychology, 44*, 958–965.

Spencer, J. A., & Fremouw, W. J. (1979). Binge eating as a function of restraint and weight classification. *Journal of Abnormal Psychology, 88*, 262–267.

Taylor, S. (1986). *Health psychology*. New York: Random House.

Terborg, J. R. (1976). The motivational components of goal setting. *Journal of Applied Psychology, 61*, 613–621.

Terborg, J. R., & Miller, H. E. (1978). Motivation, behavior, and performance: A closer examination of goal setting and monetary incentives. *Journal of Applied Psychology, 63*, 29–39.

Wegner, D. M., Schneider, D. J., Carter, S. R., & White, T. L. (1987). Paradoxical effects of thought suppression. *Journal of Personality and Social Psychology, 47*, 237–252.

Yukl, G. A., & Latham, G. P. (1978). Interrelationships among employee participation, individual differences goal difficulty, goal acceptance, goal instrumentality and performance. *Personnel Psychology, 31*, 305–323.

11 Affective Consequences of Self-Organization and Self-Regulation

6
Cognitive Organization of Different Tenses of the Self Mediates Affect and Decision Making

Jamin B. Halberstadt
Paula M. Niedenthal
Indiana University

Marc B. Setterlund
Concordia College

At the age of 30, a man we know decided to study to become a professional architectural photographer. Before that time, he mentally, and in some cases, practically, tried on a number of different career hats: professor of medieval literature, theologian, editor, and writer, among others. Along the way, this man took quite in stride any positive or negative feedback that he received about his progress toward a particular career goal, despite a strong commitment to the career path of the moment. Ironically, what did cause him anguish was not the uncertainty of his success in various roles or their daily ups and downs, but rather the decision about what career to pursue itself. The decision gridlock also caused his parents some concern. Each time his parents raised the career dilemma, the man would pointedly share the responsibility for the dilemma and say, "But don't you see? You raised me to be able to be almost anything. How can I choose to pursue any one career goal?"

Coping with the ups and downs that reflect on one's chances for future success but not being able to choose which set of ups and downs one wants to cope with may seem at first like unrelated psychological processes. But we believe that both processes may be mediated by the organizational complexity of the future self-concept, that is, by the number of concepts of self-in-the-future an individual possesses and the extent to which they are semantically differentiated from one another. Linville (1985, 1987) demonstrated that the complexity of the present self is inversely related to the intensity of people's emotional reactions to life events. In the work presented in this chapter, we extend this notion and suggest that the complexity of the future self also mediates emotional reactivity to environmental feedback but does so only when that feedback reflects directly on the likelihood that a future self will be realized. Thus, a woman who receives news that she is unable to bear children might be less upset by the news if she has many, quite distinct, future selves of which only one is "mother" than if she has few, highly related selves. Presumably, in the latter case, the woman has fewer distinct beliefs about alternative possibilities to buffer the pain of the loss of a self-concept of "mother."

However, as the opening example suggests, there may also be difficulties associated with the development of many and diverse future selves. Some difficulties have already been demonstrated by other researchers. For instance, Emmons and King (1988) showed that multiple distinct goals are associated with feelings of goal conflict and stress (see also Donahue, Robins, Roberts, & John, 1993; Linville, 1987). Our research on the drawbacks of multiple future selves was motivated by the reasoning that having many, distinct future selves could complicate the process of selecting specific goals, such as career and lifestyle goals. This should be the case, in particular, if it is assumed that individuals tend to use a prototype matching strategy in making important decisions about future plans and directions. Niedenthal, Cantor, and Kihlstrom (1985) described prototype matching as a strategy that involves comparing the features of oneself to those of the prototypic person associated with each choice option. A number of studies indicate that decision makers tend to prefer that option associated with a prototype most like themselves; thus the strategy appears to serve self-consistency motives (Chassin, Presson, Sherman, Corty, & Olshavsky, 1981; Niedenthal et al., 1985; Setterlund & Niedenthal, 1993; see Niedenthal & Mordkoff, 1991, for variations). If people use this type of strategy when making goal choices, it may be difficult for those decision makers who possesses multiple and diverse future selves to ascertain just what single choice constitutes maximal consistency with a future self. We would expect such individuals to find a close self-prototype match to many options in a given choice domain.

In this chapter, we first review the models of self-representation and process that motivated our work. We also justify our concern with the autonomous influences of concepts of self-in-the-future, compared to self-in-the-present, in emotional reactivity and decision making. In the second half of the chapter we describe and discuss a program of research that examines the role of future self-complexity in emotional reactivity and decision making.

THE MULTIFACETED SELF AND SELF-TENSES

Currently, many theorists agree that people do not possess a single, unitary, mental representation of the "self" (Deaux, 1993; Higgins, 1987; Kihlstrom

& Cantor, 1984; Markus, 1977). Rather, people appear to represent a number of more specific conceptions of themselves in various roles, in various contexts, and possessing various traits. Thus, a woman might represent herself as a professional, a wife, a person who can cope with crises, an artist, and an empathic friend. Each of these self-conceptions is assumed to be a rich, relatively well-elaborated structure that has connections of various strengths both to other self-conceptions and to other units in the network of long-term memory (e.g., Kihlstrom & Cantor, 1984; Kihlstrom & Klein, 1993; Markus & Wurf, 1987). This entire structure is often called the self system.

Moreover, the self system seems to be organized temporally; self-concepts contain information about whether they existed in the past, exist in the present, or might exist in the future. People, that is, not only have representations of who they are, but also of who they have been, and who they could be and will be. A concern with the temporal organization of memory, and of the temporal coding of concepts of self in particular, has been around at least since William James (1890) described the *potential social me*. But since the turn of the century the attention of most self-research on temporal organization has been limited to "time orientation," the tendency for an individual to be habitually focused on the past versus the future. For example, younger people have been shown to be more future-oriented and older people more past-oriented (Nuttin, 1985). Much less research has been devoted to the content and processing of James' potential self or what Lewin called the "temporal extension of the psychological life space" (but see Gordon, 1968, and Schutz, 1964). Lewin defined this temporal extention as "the totality of the individual's views of his psychological future and his psychological past existing at a given time." (Lewin, 1951, p. 75). Of course, Freud (among others) argued that past selves—particularly unconscious aspects of them—multiply determine present behavior. However, within Lewin's field theory, the content of the future self-concept is also an important force influencing the direction and intensity of an individual's behavior.

Future self-concepts have been of particular interest to theorists and researchers again recently (e.g., Nuttin, 1984). For example, the term *possible selves* was introduced by Markus and her colleagues (Markus & Nurius, 1986; Markus & Ruvolo, 1989) to refer to people's concepts of their future possibilities. Markus depicts possible selves as specific representations of the self in particular future states that are both positive (e.g., the *full professor self* or the *wealthy and eccentric self*) and negative (e.g., the *unemployed self*, or the *terminally ill self*). In Markus' view, possible selves are not inherently motivating, but are a critical link between motivation and behavior because they *personalize* motivation and translate abstract incentives into specific behavioral paths. In this view, a person's desire for *success* is represented as a *successful self*, or, more specifically, as a *successful entrepreneur* or a *successful doctor*. These specific selves increase perseverance by making goals more detailed and tangible, and, more practically, suggest means by which those goals can be attained (Markus & Nurius, 1986; for a different interpretation, see Sherman, Zehner, Johnson, & Hirt, 1983).

Since introducing the concept of possible selves, Markus and her colleagues have implicated these structures in performance (Ruvolo & Markus, 1992), competence (Markus, Cross, & Wurf, 1990), personal growth (Wurf & Markus, 1991), and delinquency (Oyserman, 1993; Oyserman & Markus, 1990; Oyserman & Saltz, 1993). Ruvolo and Markus (1992, Study 1), for example, found that subjects who imagined an extremely successful future exerted more effort and were more persistent in performing a task that was unrelated to their future goals (i.e., circling *e's* in random letter strings) than subjects who imagined a negative future for themselves and also than subjects who simply read a story containing positive, but non-self-related, imagery. The interpretation of this result was that imagining a positive future self activated plans and scripts necessary to actualize that self. Some of the activated knowledge (e.g., a *hard work pays off* heuristic) apparently generalized to the experimental task. Conversely, negative possible selves activated failure scripts, which interfered with successful performance. This explanation is supported by a second study (Ruvolo & Markus, 1992, Study 2), in which subjects who engaged in positive self-imagery were faster than subjects who engaged in negative self-imagery to indicate that success-relevant words were *possible for me* and that failure-relevant words were *not possible for me*. The two groups did not differ in the number of success- and failure-relevant words they endorsed, but the response time data indicate that the words were differentially accessible.

Higgins' self-discrepancy theory (Higgins, 1987, 1989; Higgins, Klein, & Strauman, 1985) presents another view of the nature and relation of representations of different tenses of the self. Higgins divides the self-concept into the actual self, past self, ideal self (the self you would like to be), ought self (the self you think you ought to be), and, more recently, the can self (the self you can potentially be) and the future self (the self you expect yourself to be). These different concepts of self are collections of beliefs and expectations, representations of attributes possessed, desired, and expected. Discrepancies between the actual self and the various self-standards (particularly the ought and ideal selves) are associated with vulnerability to specific negative emotions, and it is the discrepancies, rather than the content of any particular self, that form cognitive structures. Higgins, Van Hook, and Dorfman (1988), for example, found that processing "problematic" attributes of the self (i.e., aspects for which different domains of the self give conflicting information) caused interference in a Stroop-like task, whereas nonproblematic self-attributes did not.

THE SELF-COMPLEXITY MODEL

Although the self system appears to be composed of multiple concepts, individuals differ in the number of self-concepts they possess. Some people play a number of distinct roles and have independent and well-defined conceptions of themselves in each one. Other people's entire self is wrapped up in one or two roles or contexts or in a larger number that are highly interrelated. Linville's (1985, 1987) self-complexity framework, which quantifies these individual differences, is based on an earlier literature on individual differences in cognitive complexity. We review this literature briefly before turning to the specifics of Linville's approach.

The Concept of Cognitive Complexity in Social Psychology

Barron (1953) originally used the term *complexity* to refer to the number of dimensions a person used to describe or judge a stimulus. When he examined aesthetic preferences for complex or simple drawings, Barron found that preference for complexity was positively related to verbal fluency, impulsiveness, expansiveness, originality, artistic expression, sensual effeminacy, and femininity. Preference for simplicity was related to rigidity, control of impulse, conservatism, subservience to authority, and social conformity (Barron, 1953; see also Berkowitz, 1957).

In related work, Kelly (1955) suggested that people have a system of *constructs* (a progenitor of the schema concept) for perceiving the world, which can either be relatively simple or quite complex. For example, a person may habitually describe others in terms of the constructs *good* versus *bad* (a simple system). Another person may tend to use multiple constructs such as *outgoing* versus *shy, adventurous* versus *timid*, and *nice* versus *mean* (a more complex system). Complexity was operationalized by Kelly as the number of different constructs an individual used to describe others. Greater numbers of functional constructs indicated greater cognitive complexity.

Bieri (1955) extended these notions to make sense of individuals' predictions of the behavior of others. He reasoned that cognitively simple people would fail to discriminate the differences between the motives and behaviors of themselves and others. Thus, a cognitively simple person might be prone to project her own behavior onto the target and make predictions based on her own preferences. The cognitively complex person would be better able to differentiate self and other and would not assume that her own behavior would be the same as that of the other, resulting in better prediction. Bieri's results indicated that, as expected, cognitively complex people made more accurate predictions, were less likely to believe that others would behave in the same manner as they would themselves, and were more likely to recognize differences between themselves and others, than were low complexity subjects. (See also Leventhal, 1957, and Mayo & Crockett, 1964).

The idea that constructs allow a person to understand the world, and that people differ in the number of constructs that they habitually use, also motivated investigations of the influence of cognitive complexity on the use of information (Lundy & Berkowitz, 1957; Scott, 1962, 1963). In an investigation of persuasive communication, for example, Lundy and Berkowitz (1957) reasoned that because information can only be understood if it relates to a meaningful construct, and cognitively complex people have more such constructs, then cognitively complex people would be better able to process and integrate new ideas. Consideration and integration of the ideas, it was further reasoned, would result in attitude change. Indeed, experimental participants who were cognitively complex showed greater attitude change following persuasive communication.

Despite the treatment of cognitive complexity as a personality variable, there is also evidence that complexity can vary across situations. The perceived *need for complexity* in a situation can lead people to consider information in a more complex way (Zajonc, 1960). One situation that may lead to a need for complexity is an expectation that information will have to be communicated to others. When people expect to have to communicate information they have just received, they differentiate the information more, and the information they recall is more complex and organized, than when they do not expect to have to communicate the information (Zajonc, 1960). In ongoing research in our laboratory, this finding has been exploited in an attempt to manipulate subjects' self-complexity experimentally.

More recently, the complexity with which individuals think about an attitude object has been associated with the extremity of their attitude toward, or evaluation of, the object. Tesser and colleagues (e.g., Millar & Tesser, 1986; Tesser, 1978; Tesser & Leone, 1977) have demonstrated that when subjects are induced to think about an object (or topic) about which they have extensive (presumably complex) knowledge and a publicly declared attitude, their evaluation of that object tends to polarize. This same effect of induced thinking on attitude is not observed for subjects who possess simplistic knowledge of the object. One explanation for this result is that commitment to an attitude motivates individuals to organize their beliefs in an evaluatively integrated and consistent way (Millar & Tesser, 1986). To the extent that there are many such beliefs, with conscious thought individuals become more extreme in their evaluation of the object. Interestingly, under different conditions, such as when subjects are not explicitly induced to think about the object and do not publicly commit to an attitude, more extensive and complex knowledge is associated with less extreme attitudes rather than attitude polarization (Linville, 1982). This result is typically interpreted as indicating that individuals with more complex schemas about a given object have had to integrate both positive and negative features of the object. Such an integration is associated with a more balanced, less extreme attitude—unless, of course, the attitude serves other motivational functions for the individual (Katz, 1960).

The Self-Complexity Framework

Linville (1985, 1987) argued that the organizational complexity of the self-concept mediates a number of important psychological processes. Of particular interest here is her contention that self-complexity mediates the intensity with which individuals respond emotionally to positive and negative life events. This hypothesis is based on four assumptions about self representation and the relationship between self-concept and emotional state.

First, as discussed previously, the representation of the self in memory is assumed to be comprised of multiple concepts—which Linville calls aspects—that might be represented in memory as an associative network (Cantor, Markus, Niedenthal, & Nurius, 1986; Greenwald & Pratkanis, 1984; Kihlstrom & Cantor, 1984; Kihlstrom & Klein, 1993; Linville & Carlston, 1994; Markus & Wurf, 1987). Results of recent experiments suggest that the associated propositions include both abstract generalizations about what the self is like as well as examples of specific past behaviors (Klein & Loftus, 1993, Klein, Loftus, & Sherman, 1993; Klein, Loftus, Trafton, & Fuhrman, 1992). Although we believe that there is good evidence that self-knowledge is also coded in other, nonpropositional forms of representation, such as perceptually based images of physical appearance (e.g., Mita, Dermer, & Knight, 1977; Yarmey & Johnson, 1982), most investigations of the cognitive organization of the self-concept are grounded in the proposition-based associative network model. This model has provided a useful heuristic for many studies of the influences of self-knowledge in the processing of information about the self and others.

Second, it is assumed that people vary in degree of self-complexity. As they do with objects and people in the environment (Berkowitz, 1957; Bieri, 1955; Leventhal, 1957; Scott, Osgood, & Peterson, 1979), people vary in the complexity with which they perceive and organize information about the self. In Linville's framework, self-complexity increases with the number of self-concepts and differentiation among those concepts. Specifically, high self-complexity is associated with having many, relatively distinct self-concepts, while low self-complexity is associated with having few, relatively undifferentiated self-aspects.

Third, it is assumed that individuals' evaluations of their self-concepts are contained in the corresponding self-representation (Higgins, 1987, 1989). Thus, particular self-conceptions contain features with positive, negative, or mixed evaluations (Showers, 1992). These evaluations are based on self-appraisals and other appraisals and can themselves vary across situations.

Finally, it is assumed that an individual's overall affect and self-appraisal is determined by a weighted average of the evaluation of all of the *available* self-aspects (Hammen, Marks, deMayo, & Mayol, 1985; Pelham & Swann, 1989; Showers, 1992; Tesser, 1988). The weights are determined by the importance and the salience of the concept. Note that this assumption means that even those self-concepts that are not semantically associated with the self-concept that is implicated in a given (affective) experience contribute to the overall affective state of the individual. This assumption has implicit in it the idea that following self-evaluative experiences people tend either automatically or effortfully to assess the evaluative status of all or most available self-concepts. The assumption of this assessment process makes sense in light of research showing that both positive and negative emotions induce generalized self-focused attention (e.g., Salovey, 1992; Wood, Saltzberg, & Goldsamt, 1990), as well as research showing that people often cope with threat by affirming aspects of the self that are apparently unrelated to the self-concept that has been threatened (e.g., Steele & Liu, 1983). Moreover, the assumption of this assessment process makes intuitive sense. When individuals complain to confidants, particularly about negative experiences, a typical response from the confidant is "but look at all the other things you have going for you." Often these other things are not related to the area of complaint. Thus, individuals might learn to perform the assumed weighted averaging of self-evaluations from interactions with other people.

Self-Complexity and Affective Reactivity

Linville's (1985) framework relating self-complexity to affective reactivity follows from these assumptions. She argues that self-complexity is inversely related to the intensity of people's affective reactions to positive and negative life experiences. That is, by this view, people with less complex self-concepts tend to react with strong emotion to life's ups and downs, while people with more complex self-concepts react with less extreme emotion. Why should this be the case? Recall that in the self-complexity model, individuals' emotional reactions are determined by a weighted average of the evaluation of all of the currently available self-aspects (the fourth assumption outlined earlier). If an individual with low self-complexity experiences a success or failure, the evaluation of the implicated self-concept is relevant to many other self-concepts because the other concepts are, by definition, closely semantically related to the implicated concept. In Linville's terms, there is a great deal of *affective spillage* across self-concepts; many other self-concepts are evaluated in the same way as the implicated concept. For instance, if many of Dennis' self-concepts include the features competitive, aggressive, energetic, and ambitious, then when Dennis is told that he is "obnoxiously competitive and aggressive on the tennis court," he will automatically apply the negative evaluation to most of his other self-aspects. The outcome is that Dennis temporarily views most aspects of himself as negative, and he consequently suffers a strong negative emotional reaction. On the other hand, if Dennis believes that he is only competitive and aggressive when he is on the tennis court, and no other self-concept contains these features, then his other self-aspects should remain unscathed by the critical feedback. Because less of the total self is affected by "spillage" from the negative evaluation of the tennis player concept, Dennis is far less affected by the feedback. The self-concepts that are not affected by the criticism of his tennis court behavior serve to "buffer" Dennis' emotional reaction to the criticism.

In a test of the buffering hypothesis, Linville (1985, Study 1) measured subjects' self-complexity, and then gave them an ostensible test of "analytic ability." Later, she supplied subjects with false positive or negative feedback regarding their performance on the task. The change in subjects' moods and self-evaluations following the feedback served as the dependent measure of interest. As predicted by the self-complexity model, compared to subjects with low complexity, complex subjects were less happy and less self-enhancing following success feedback and were also less sad and less self-deprecating in response to failure. This effect has been extended by Linville in several additional studies. In a conceptual replication, a new sample of subjects kept daily records of their moods for a period of two weeks. Subjects with complex self-concepts experienced less extreme mood swings relative to those with more simple self-concepts (Linville, 1985, Study 2). Linville (1987) has also found that self-complexity mediates stress-related illness and depression. Higher self-complexity is associated with less adverse effects of stress on physical symptoms and depression.

The self-complexity model takes a highly cognitive approach to the mechanisms that govern affective reactivity. However, it shares with similar positions in psychology (Steele, 1988) and sociology (Sieber, 1974; Thoits, 1983) the idea that the investment of psychological energy into many, compared to few, roles protects self-evaluation and affective reactivity. Again, this is because when individuals represent the self in multiple ways, success or failure in any one domain contributes less to the overall affective state of the individual.

COMPLEXITY OF THE FUTURE SELF

We believe that the assumptions made by the self-complexity model regarding the present self also hold for the future self. That is, the future self is assumed to be a relatively rich set of concepts corresponding to a person's ideas about herself in the future. In addition, the future self is assumed to have an internal structure whose complexity is a function of the number and distinctiveness of its component concepts. Apparently individuals can spontaneously describe multiple future self aspects and the evaluation of the aspects appears to influence individuals' affective and motivational states (Markus & Nurius, 1986; Oyserman & Markus, 1990). Moreover, investigations of daydreaming and other internally generated experiences have revealed variations in the amount of time people spend fantasizing about themselves in the future (Singer, 1975, 1984). Differences in attention to the self in the future may support individual differences in future self-complexity.

In the next section, we discuss research that testifies to the unique value of future self-complexity in accounting for affective reactivity. We provide evidence that establishes the theoretical distinction between present and future self-complexity, and report data illustrating the unique implications that future self-complexity has for feedback relevant to future performance, and for decisions relevant to future behavior. In the final section, we discuss other domains to which a future self-complexity analysis might be fruitfully applied.

EMPIRICAL STUDIES ON FUTURE SELF-COMPLEXITY

Independence of Present and Future Selves

Theoretically, the complexity of the future self does not necessarily depend on the complexity of the present self. A person could conceivably have diverse conceptions of himself in the present, yet have a very limited view of his possibilities for the future (e.g., a person on his way to prison), or vice versa (e.g., a person recovering from divorce). We assume that the content and structure of the future self can influence the psychological processes of individuals independently of the present self (Markus & Nurius, 1986; Niedenthal & Mordkoff, 1991; Strauman, 1989).

In order to establish that present and future self-complexity do, in practice, vary independently, the relationship between the two constructs was examined in two preliminary studies reported in Niedenthal, Setterlund, and Wherry (1992). In all of the studies reported in this chapter, self-complexity was measured using the card-sorting task described in Linville (1985), modeled after Scott (1969). In the task, subjects sort cards containing positive and negative personality traits into piles that represent different self-concepts. Any trait can be used in multiple piles. A subject's card sort is used to calculate *Scott's H*, a measure of differentiation among attributes, or "dimensionality" (Scott et al., 1979). H reflects both the number of groups in a sort and the degree to which groups share common traits (independence).

In the preliminary studies conducted by Niedenthal et al. (1992), the complexities of subjects' present selves and future selves were measured one day apart in the first study, (N = 39), and 10 minutes apart in the second (N = 71). The correlations between the two selves were .54 and .45, respectively. In other words, present self-complexity appears to account for only 20% to 30% of the variance in future self-complexity. Present and future self-complexity, then, appear to be related but not identical constructs.

Future Self-Complexity and Affective Reactions to Goal-Relevant Information

If the complexity of the present and future self-concepts are at least partly independent, then it is logical to ask whether the complexity of these structures mediates psychological processes under different conditions. Niedenthal et al. (1992) proposed that future self-complexity mediates affective responses to feedback but only when the feedback is specifically relevant to future goals. To the degree that present and future selves are independent, selves in the relevant tense are less likely to influence selves in the irrelevant one. Therefore, present self-complexity should primarily buffer emotional reactions to feedback related to current concerns, while future self-complexity should primarily mediate reactions to future-relevant feedback.

Present Self-Complexity Mediates Responses to Feedback About Current Concerns

Niedenthal et al. (1992) tested these predictions in three principle studies. Study 1 was a replication of the first study reported in Linville (1985). As in Linville's study, subjects took a test of their ability and then received false success or failure feedback about a current concern. There was an additional between-subject variable added to the study, however, such that half of the subjects in the study described their future self in the card-sorting procedure and the remainder described their present self before taking the ability test. Present self-complexity, but not future self-complexity, was expected to mediate affective and self-evaluative responses to the feedback.

Undergraduate premedical majors at Johns Hopkins University participated in the study. Subjects first completed a self-complexity card sort in which they described either their present or future self. All subjects then completed a mood scale. They then took an easy or difficult version of a test purported to measure achievement in science. A science test was used because it was believed that the feedback would be particularly relevant to the premed students' current goal of good performance in their science courses. The test was not linked to future concerns about medical school or the like. Regardless of their level of performance, success subjects (taking the easy test) learned that they scored in the 97th to 99th percentile of a large group of premedical majors who had taken the test, while failure subjects (taking the difficult test) received a score that corresponded to the 31st to 40th percentile. Finally, due to a bogus computer error, subjects were required to complete the mood and self-evaluation measures a second time, and this second set of measures was used to compute postmanipulation affective change.

The data were examined in hierarchical multiple regressions in which self-complexity score, tense of self described (present or future), and feedback condition (success or failure) were regressed on a score that reflected level of positive mood following feedback with the effects of initial mood partialled out. The mood scores of people in the failure condition were multiplied by -1 so that interactions due to the fact that moods generally changed in opposite directions in the two feedback conditions would not have to be interpreted. The analyses revealed only the expected Complexity × Tense of Self interaction. This indicated that self-complexity was negatively correlated with affective reactivity depending upon the self-concept on which the complexity score was based. The two-way interaction is graphed in Fig. 6.1. The complexity of the present self-concept was associated as expected with subjects' emotional reactions to their performance on the science test: Those subjects with complex present self-concepts reacted less strongly to the feedback than did those subjects with more organizationally simple self-concepts. However, future self-complexity did not explain reactions to success and failure feedback at all. That is, subjects with complex future self-concepts were no more or less likely to respond strongly to the feedback about a current concern than were subjects with more organizationally simple future self-concepts.

The results of the first study served to replicate the findings of Linville (1985). Premedical student subjects with complex present self-concepts were less affected by success or failure on a science exam than were subjects with

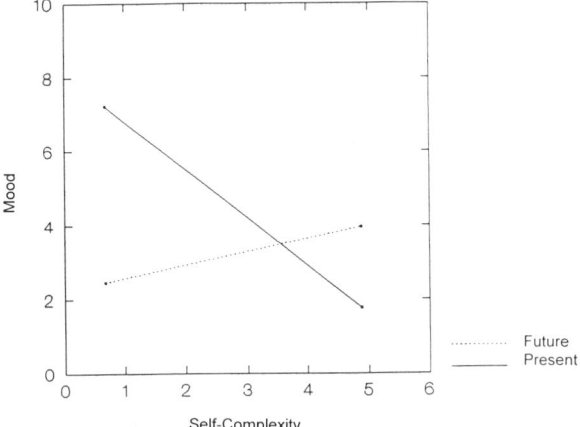

FIG. 6.1 Plot of Complexity × Tense of Self interaction (Study 1). Complexity of the present self is inversely related to the amount of mood change following success and failure feedback about a current concern. Complexity of the future self is not related to the amount of mood change. From "Possible Self-Complexity and Affective Reactions to Goal-Relevant Evaluation," by P. M. Niedenthal, M. B. Setterlund, and M. B. Wherry, 1992, *Journal of Personality and Social Psychology, 63*, p. 10. Copyright 1992 by the American Psychological Association, Inc. Reprinted with permission.

less complex present self-concepts. Moreover, the complexity of the premed students' future selves did not serve the same affect-buffering function.

Future-Self-Complexity Mediates Responses to Feedback About Future Concerns

Although the study just described replicated Linville's (1985) results with regard to the present self, the support found for the unique mediational role of future self-complexity came in the form of a null result. Thus, Niedenthal et al. (1992) undertook a second study to obtain more direct evidence that future self-complexity, but not present self-complexity, mediates responses to feedback and other evaluative experiences that are relevant to future goals. The study involved the same formal procedure as in Study 1. This time, however, subjects were students enrolled in an art school at a state university who indicated that they planned to become professional artists. Subjects again completed either a present or future self-complexity card sort, as well as a mood scale. All subjects then took a test of *creativity*, composed of drawing and computer-based verbal and creativity problems. The creativity test was described to them as a reliable predictor of future success in the art world. Success subjects learned that, based on their score on the creativity test, it was very likely they would succeed in the art world in the future. Failure subjects were informed that, based on their performance, it was very unlikely they would succeed in the art world in the future. Finally, all subjects completed a second mood scale.

Again, the data were analyzed in a multiple regression model with self-complexity score, tense of self (present or future) and feedback (success or failure) as predictor variables. Only the predicted Complexity × Tense of Self interaction, plotted in Fig. 6.2, was significant. This result complements the result observed in the first study. The organizational complexity of subjects' present self-concept appeared not to buffer their emotional reactions to the feedback regarding their future success in the art world. However, the complexity of the future self-concept was related to subjects' emotional reactivity: Those subjects with more complex future self-concepts showed less affect change in reaction to the false feedback than did those subjects who had less complex future self-concepts.

Taken together, the first two studies are important in that they provide the first solid evidence that present self-complexity and future self-complexity have analogous but distinct implications for affective response to environmental feedback relevant to the present and the future, respectively. Study 2, in particular, demonstrates that future self-complexity serves a unique role in buffering emotional reactions to future-relevant ups and downs.

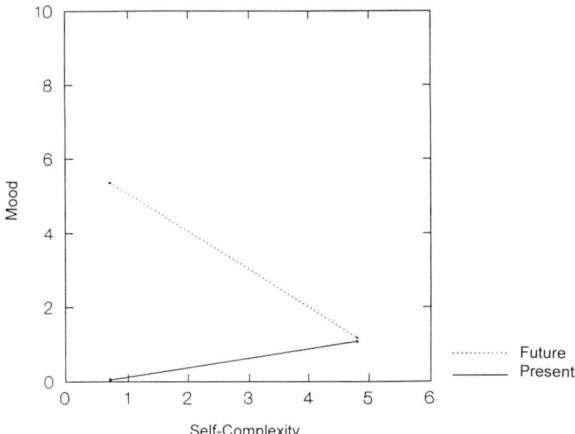

FIG. 6.2 Plot of Complexity × Tense of Self interaction (Study 2). Complexity of the future self is inversely related to the amount of mood change following success and failure feedback about a future concern. Complexity of the present self is not related to the amount of mood change. From "Possible Self-Complexity and Affective Reactions to Goal-Relevant Evaluation," by P. M. Niedenthal, M. B. Setterlund, and M. B. Wherry, 1992, *Journal of Personality and Social Psychology, 63*, p. 11. Copyright 1992 by the American Psychological Association, Inc. Reprinted with permission.

Demonstrating the Two Effects in the Same Population

Although the results reported so far provide support for the idea that the complexity of the future self exerts influences independent of the present self on psychological functioning, this conclusion is limited by the fact that the studies were conducted on different subject populations. It is possible (however unlikely) that future self-complexity, for example, buffers affective response to future feedback for art students but not for medical students, or that future self-complexity buffers all reactions of art students and present self-complexity, all reactions of medical students. In order to address this problem of interpretation, and to replicate the effects in a new domain, Niedenthal et al. (1992) undertook a third study in which the complexity of both the present and future self was measured for all subjects (thus, tense of self was a repeated measure). Also, in the context of the same study, subjects were given feedback that was relevant to either present or future concerns (tense of feedback was varied between subjects). Once again, the experimental hypothesis was that present self-complexity would be a stronger predictor of changes in the emotional states of subjects who received feedback relevant to current goals, such that individuals with complex present self-concepts would respond less strongly than would those with less complex present self-concepts. Future self-complexity was similarly expected to predict changes in subjects who received positive or negative feedback regarding their future goals.

The study was introduced to female undergraduate subjects as an investigation of men and women's beliefs about how their personality traits contribute to success in either dating or marriage (in the present and future self-feedback conditions, respectively). After completing a mood scale and several questionnaires about their beliefs and attitudes about dating or marriage, subjects performed present and future self-complexity card sorts. They then received either positive or negative feedback (a between-subject factor), a score purportedly based on their questionnaires that was said to indicate either "adjustment to and success in dating relationships at present," or "adjustment to and success in marriage in the future." To bolster the meaning of a high or low score, subjects also read a paragraph that would allegedly help them interpret their score. Interpretation of the two scores read as follows [wording for the marriage conditions appear in brackets]:

> *Excellent.* You enjoy wonderful success in dating. [You will have a wonderful marriage.] Self-assured and independent, you [you'll] only settle for a secure, honest relationship. You have the maturity, wisdom, and compassion to make

relationships [a life-long relationship] work. When problems do arise, your answers indicate that you and your mate work [will work] them out creatively — without games, name calling, or theatrics.

Poor. Being a girlfriend is not part of your personality. [Marriage may not come your way.] Relationships are [A life-long relationship is] not something you are suited for. You tend to be self-absorbed and unwilling [could be unwilling] to engage in creative problem-solving. Intimacy and relating are [Commitment is] not bad for others, but for you they are [it could be] too demanding and can [could] make you more moody than you normally are.

Finally, subjects completed another questionnaire containing the mood scale in order to assess their postmanipulation emotional state.

As in the previous studies, the data were examined using a hierarchical regression technique, in which present self-complexity, future self-complexity, feedback (success or failure), and their interactions were used as predictors of mood change. We then tested the difference between the standardized partial regression coefficient for the two tenses of self-complexity. In the present goal feedback condition, the coefficients differed at the $p < .01$ level. As seen in the top panel of Fig. 6.3, the relationship between present self-complexity and affective reactivity was negative — greater present self-complexity was associated with smaller changes in mood — but the relationship between future self-complexity and affective reactivity was slightly positive. In the future goal feedback condition, the difference between the coefficients was only marginal ($p < .10$), but, as can be seen in the bottom panel of Fig. 6.3, the relationship between future self-complexity and affective reactivity was negative (as predicted), whereas the relationship between present self-complexity and affective reactivity was slightly positive. In this study, then, we found that the complexity of the present self mediated the emotional reactions of those women who received feedback about their probable success in dating. The complexity of the same subjects' future self-concepts did not serve this function. On the other hand, the complexity of the future self mediated the emotional reactions of those women who received feedback about their likely success in marriage, but the complexity of the same subjects' present self-concepts did not.

Summary of Research

The results of the research discussed thus far provide support for a potentially valuable conception of self. To reiterate our argument, we have claimed that the self is represented by multiple concepts, some of which represent the self in specific roles, situations, and behaviors in the past, present, and future. Each *tense* of the self has an internal structure. One consequence of this structure is that the more complex the relationship

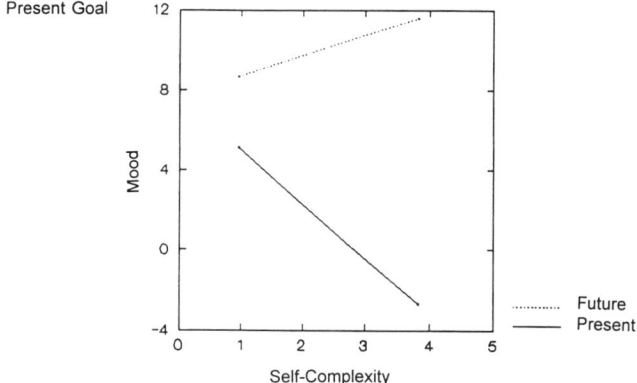

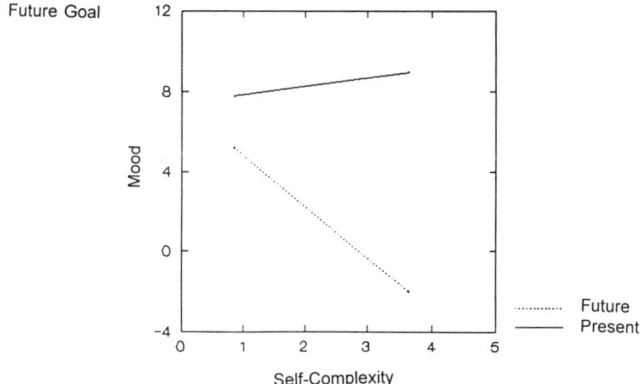

FIG. 6.3 Plots of the simple linear relationships between present self-complexity and future self-complexity and mood change for subjects in the present goal and future goal conditions (Study 3). Complexity of the self-concept that is relevant to the feedback mediates the intensity of emotional reaction to that feedback. From "Possible Self-Complexity and Affective Reactions to Goal-Relevant Evaluation," by P. M. Niedenthal, M. B. Setterlund, and M. B. Wherry, 1992, *Journal of Personality and Social Psychology, 63*, p. 14. Copyright 1992 by the American Psychological Association, Inc. Reprinted with permission.

among the various self-concepts, the less a strong evaluation of one concept will influence the evaluations of others. The reason for this affective *buffering* is that when one self-concept is evaluated, such as when a person receives positive or negative feedback relevant to that concept, the evaluation spreads to other selves as a function of the number and strength of connections in the semantic network. The more semantically differentiated self-concepts one possesses, the less likely the evaluation of one concept will spread to affect the evaluation of others. Thus, when complex individuals review the overall state of their self-concept (take a weighted average of the current evaluations of the available concepts of self), they will not find that the overall self has been influenced by the feedback. Accordingly, their affective state will shift less in the direction of the feedback, less than if they had a much more simple self-concept.

Moreover, different tenses of the self are somewhat independent. Therefore, feedback related to one tense of self affects emotional reactivity as a function of the complexity of that tense only. In support of this model, we have presented evidence that present self-complexity specifically mediates affective reactivity to success and failure in the present, while future self-complexity specifically mediates responses to future goal-relevant feedback.

IMPLICATIONS OF SELF-COMPLEXITY

It may seem implicit in the present treatment that high cognitive complexity, and self-complexity in particular, is a desired trait that affords more advantages than low complexity. But as the concept is used here, it has no absolute evaluative connotation. First, it is not at all clear that having more muted affective reactions, particularly to favorable feedback, is a good thing. Even if it can be argued that being more even-keeled is beneficial, there are other consequences of high complexity, including stress and goal conflict, that may seem more or less negative (see Emmons & King, 1988; Donahue et al., 1993, for a discussion of other drawbacks of high self-complexity).

One potential drawback to cognitive complexity was presented in our opening example and was the topic of recent research in our laboratory. The topic was decision making, in particular, the problem of making decisions about future goals (selves) and states. The rationale for the research stemmed from prior research by Niedenthal and colleagues (Niedenthal & Mordkoff, 1991; Niedenthal et al., 1985; Setterlund & Niedenthal, 1993) on the prototype matching strategy for decision making. When using this strategy, individuals compare the features of themselves with the features of the prototypic person associated with each of their choice options. In most cases, individuals tend to prefer options associated with a prototypic person who is most like themselves. This process of decision making has been shown to underlie a number of different categories of decision, including choice of college housing (Niedenthal et al., 1985), intention to become a smoker (Chassin et al., 1981), preferences for restaurants and cars (Setterlund & Niedenthal, 1993), and decisions about academic aspirations (Burke & Reitzes, 1981).

Given that individuals often employ a prototype-matching strategy for making personally relevant choices (including those related to life goals), one consequence of having a complex future self is that decisions related to the future should be more difficult, and initially postdecision regret or dissonance should be more acute. As an example, imagine a high school senior faced with choosing a college to attend. She has offers from Princeton, Oberlin, and the University of Texas, and she also possesses ideas about the prototypic student at each institution. Because she has a complex view of herself in the future, she finds it easy to imagine herself as a student at any one of these very different schools. That is, she has some, even many, features of the prototypic student of *each* of the three schools. As a result, she finds herself torn among her choices and is hard-pressed to identify a factor that distinguishes any one above the others. No one school's student is "her," because she is no one student; she is a combination of her future selves, and is *potentially* many different types of student. When the decision deadline arrives and she is forced to choose one of her alternatives, the students she could have been, but can no longer be, loom large in her mind. For a time after she sends her acceptance letter, she wonders "what if . . . ," and these thoughts cannot help but dampen her enthusiasm for her decision.

Her best friend, who, curiously, is faced with the same choice of schools, has a more simple view of himself in the future. He's a Princeton Man through and through, descended from a long line of Princeton Men, and while he has applied to Oberlin, and the University of Texas, he simply cannot imagine himself as an Oberlin or U.T. student. They just aren't "him." When he is accepted at all three schools, he accepts Princeton's offer without a moment's hesitation, nor a moment's regret. The decision is easy because there is only one good fit between the prototypic students he imagines and his future "student" self.

This example illustrates the hypothesized relation between future self-complexity and decision ease and satisfaction. Future self-complexity is, in large part, a function of the number of self-aspects composing the future self, which determine the ease with which alternative futures can be imagined. When a decision is made that commits a person, however nominally, to a future role or outcome, the immediate postdecision satisfaction experienced should be a function of the ease with which she can imagine choosing the unchosen alternatives. It is simply statistically more likely that a nonchosen alternative will be part of a future self-conception of a complex person, who should therefore find that alternative easier to imagine. Thus, we expected greater complexity to be associated with lower immediate postdecision satisfaction.

In an initial examination of this hypothesis, Setterlund (1993) conducted a correlational study relating future self-complexity and decision-making processes. After performing a card sort in which they described the complexity of their future self, female undergraduates at Indiana University were presented sets of names of jobs, hobbies, and personality traits (a within-subject variable). Initially, subjects were presented with sets of four (randomly grouped) career options and had to indicate which of the four options they *least* desired for their future. After making 14 decisions of this kind, subjects made similar decisions about 14 sets of four hobbies and, finally, about 14 sets of four traits. Examples of the career labels include marriage counselor, lawyer, stewardess, and doctor. Examples of hobbies include gardening, baking, sailing, and basketball playing. Examples of traits include fulfilled, sophisticated, loyal, and outgoing. All items were selected from among those that at least 25% of a large sample of pretest subjects from the same population of female undergraduates said they had considered for their future.

After each decision trial, subjects rated the difficulty of making that (elimination) decision and their satisfaction with the decision. Response latencies for making the decisions were collected as a third dependent variable. The decision sets were then re-presented with the options selected in the first presentations eliminated (i.e., with the option that was least preferred removed from the set) such that there were three options, one of which had to be selected as least preferred. Finally, subjects repeated the decision task a third time and chose, between the two remaining options, the one that they least preferred.

To test the hypothesis that self-complexity is positively correlated with decision difficulty, future self-complexity, set size (four, three, or two choice options), and set type (careers, hobbies, or traits) were entered into a multiple regression. For the difficulty ratings, results showed a significant main effect of complexity such that greater complexity was associated with greater decision difficulty. Predicted effects were also found for subjects' satisfaction ratings such that greater complexity was associated with lower satisfaction. On the response latency measure, future self-complexity emerged as a significant main effect: greater complexity was associated with longer latencies. There was also a set Size × Complexity interaction; as set size decreased, the strength of the relation between self-complexity and response latency increased.

Setterlund's results are consistent with the idea that people with more complex future selves have more difficulty making decisions about their future. When asked to select which option they least preferred, more complex subjects found their decisions more difficult and less satisfying relative to less complex subjects, and they took increasingly long to make their decisions as the number of options decreased.

Effect of Self-Complexity on Decision Difficulty: An Experimental Study

Because the relationship between future self-complexity and the dependent variables in the previous study was correlational, causal claims are unwarranted. It is possible, for example, that people with different levels of self-complexity use response scales differently and that the reported effects are due to these differences in scale use, rather than to decision-making difficulty. In order to draw stronger conclusions about the causal role of self-complexity in decision-making difficulty, Setterlund (1993) conducted a second study in which he manipulated future self-complexity by priming different numbers of future self-concepts in his subjects.

In the study, subjects in a low-complexity condition were instructed to sort cards that contained personality attributes into three piles representing three future selves that pilot testing had demonstrated were possessed by most undergraduate women (*as a mother, in job/career*, and *with significant other*). Subjects assigned to a high-complexity condition were instructed to sort the cards into *seven* piles (the three used in the low-complexity condition, and, in addition, *future education, volunteer/ activist, on your own*, and *physically*). This manipulation had been shown in pilot work to prime different levels of self-complexity (Setterlund, 1993). All subjects then performed the decision task described. In this study, only decisions about careers and hobbies were made; subjects did not make decisions about what traits they would like to possess in the future. Self-reports of decision difficulty and satisfaction, and response latency again served as the dependent measures of interest.

The results replicated several of the findings from the first study. There was a main effect of self-complexity on subjects' ratings of difficulty, such that subjects assigned to the high-complexity condition reported greater difficulty in their decision making. On the satisfaction measure, subjects in the high-complexity condition were also more dissatisfied with their decisions. On the response latency measures, contrary to predictions, subjects assigned to the low-complexity condition took longer to make their decisions, relative to those assigned to the high-complexity condition.

Taken together, these data provide some evidence that future self-complexity influences self-relevant decision satisfaction and difficulty. Two studies showed that, at least under certain circumstances, high self-complexity can lead to more difficult and (initially) less satisfying decisions. The response latency data from the two studies are less clear, however. Slower latencies, which presumably indicate more consideration required for decision making, were associated with high self-complexity in the correlational study, but with low self-complexity in the experimental study.

Other researchers (e.g., Anderson, 1976; Fiske & Linville, 1980; Markus, 1977; Taylor, 1981) have also found that mental structures (i.e., a schema or associative network) can sometimes facilitate processing information related to the structure and at other times interfere with processing. Although the greater degree of organization of a structure can speed judgments, the sheer amount of information associated with the structure can hinder it under some circumstances. In the correlational study, a high future self-complexity score reflected the presence of many highly accessible future selves. Greater accessibility is, in part, the result of frequent activation (Higgins & Bargh, 1987; Higgins & King, 1981; Wyer & Srull, 1981, 1986), which may be associated with greater elaboration (Baddeley, 1986; Klatzky, 1975). This additional information may slow information processing and decision making. In the experimental study, however, where self-complexity was manipulated, subjects may or may not have possessed many highly accessible future selves; they were assumed to have accessible those concepts primed by the experimental manipulation. The amount of information associated with these selves may have been smaller than in naturally occurring highly accessible selves and, in turn, may not have interfered with processing as much. Thus, the results across the two studies are not necessarily contradictory, although the factors that lead to the differential results require further investigation.

Other Implications of Self-Complexity

The research by Setterlund (1993) presented here also provides some evidence that self-complexity is malleable, suggesting that certain situations can prime more or fewer self-concepts and serve to increase or decrease self-complexity. This leaves people vulnerable not only to wily experimenters but also to those with more dubious motives, such as advertisers. Certain weight loss programs, for example, seem to reduce the self-complexity of their participants by emphasizing a single-minded, all-encompassing goal of being thin. The danger of such as narrow self-view, as we have seen, is that although dieting success will be sweeter, defeat will also be more agonizing. Religious fanaticism and cults, it could be argued, encourage the same sort of reduction in self-complexity.

Conversely, certain self-help books attempt to increase self-complexity by pointing out new roles the reader could fill. The popular book titled *What Color is Your Parachute?* (Bolles, 1990), a guide for those searching for a first job or a career change, provides worksheets on which different self-concepts can be explored by the reader. The author instructs readers to enumerate their strengths and weaknesses, likes and dislikes, and so on, and then helps them to translate their skills and goals into potential careers. Part of the therapeutic nature of this book lies in its expansion of the reader's self-complexity. The reader is encouraged to delve into less explored self-domains, thereby making it easier for him or her to imagine himself or herself inhabiting those domains. Even if the result is not finding the perfect career path, the reader may be less disappointed if a chosen path is not fruitful. We hasten to add that the research presented here suggests that this increase in self-complexity should also, in theory, make the career choice more difficult and initially less satisfying, although the pleasure in discovering what was not felt possible may be a concomitant positive experience.

Not only should changes in self-complexity influence affective reactions, but feedback may have different effects as a function of the situation. For example, by changing the framing of the feedback, one can influence the tense of self to which the feedback appears to pertain. When professors hand back exams, often they will attempt to avoid framing the feedback in terms of the future self, cautioning students that a bad grade on the exam "is not the end of the world," or "won't affect their chances of a successful career." In other words, the professor is arguing that the feedback is more relevant to students' present goals (e.g., a good grade in the course). However, the success of this strategy, which is presumably designed to downplay the emotional impact of a bad grade, depends on the relative complexity of the students' present and future selves. For a student with low present self-complexity, who has only a few self-concepts that all relate to success in school, negative feedback relevant to that goal will be devastating.

Again, this is not to imply that low self-complexity is always problematic. Although most researchers emphasize the benefits of high self-complexity, it should be clear from the research presented here that there are some advantages to low self-complexity. For one, low complexity appears to increase subjective ease and satisfaction in decision making in some circumstances. Higher complexity, on the other hand, appears to be associated with more effortful information processing. The reason, we have argued, is that decision-making difficulty and regret should be a function of the alternatives available at the time of the decision and the ease with which those alternatives can be imagined. People with high self-complexity, who have many well-used, interconnected, highly accessible selves, find it easier to imagine multiple alternatives. The facility with which one alternative can be unrepentantly selected will therefore be less for those high in complexity.

As implied earlier, another possible detrimental effect of high self-complexity suggests itself through this research. Our discussion has more often emphasized the buffering of negative affect, but high self-complexity also seems to buffer responses to positive feedback. That is, not only are people with highly complex selves less devastated in response to negative feedback but they are also less happy in response to positive feedback. Those low in self-complexity, on the other hand, though vulnerable to more extreme reactions to failure, can also look forward to more extreme joy following success. Evidence of this effect was provided in the *medical student, art student,* and *relationship* studies reported earlier. Thus, there appear to be some important, though ironic, advantages to maintaining a simple conception of your self.

CONCLUSIONS AND FUTURE DIRECTIONS

In the first section of the chapter, we provided evidence that high future self-complexity can serve as a buffer against intense affective reactions to positive and negative environmental feedback related to the future. It was argued that extremity of affective response is determined by the evaluation of all available future self-concepts. Which concepts are affected by the evaluation of the self-concept implicated in a given success or failure experience is, in turn, a function of the number and connectedness of those representations, quantified in the self-complexity measure. The less complex a person is, the more likely the evaluation of one self-concept will spread to others. This will leave the individual with the feeling that most future selves are futile, in the case of failure feedback, or possible and positive (in the case of success feedback), and he or she will thus experience strong affect. When future self-concepts are not highly integrated, the evaluation of one concept will not spread to others. Thus, the individual will react less strongly to the success or failure experience. High complexity *buffers* affective response to failure and success.

We also argued in favor of a *self-specificity* hypothesis, which proposes that people's selves are situated in the past, present, and future. We provided evidence that self-aspects are organized within each tense, and that the complexity of that organization mediates affective responses to feedback specific to that tense. Our initial studies examined the present and future selves, but the same conclusions should apply to the past self. The affect buffering hypothesis makes predictions about responses to feedback to *goals*, which by definition are desired *future* end states, so it would seem to be more difficult to test in the case of the past self. But one can imagine situations in which the past self is active and in which its complexity could mediate responses to feedback relevant to past goals. High school reunions, for example, are notoriously emotional experiences in which, despite their concerted attempts to focus on what is going on in their lives in the present, people spend much time thinking about and discussing who they were in the past (particularly, of course, in high school). Under these circumstances, people's emotional reactions may well be mediated by the complexity of the past self rather than the present self. We expect future research to reveal insights into this possibility.

ACKNOWLEDGMENTS

This chapter and the reported research were supported by a Jacob Javits predoctoral fellowship awarded to Jamin B. Halberstadt, and by NSF grants BNS-8919755 and DBS-921019 and NIMH grant MH44811 to Paula M. Niedenthal. We wish to thank Denise Beike, Jonathan Margolin, Lenny Martin, Carolin Showers, Abraham Tesser, Elissa Wurf, and the participants of the Conference on Goals and Affect for their helpful comments on these ideas.

REFERENCES

Anderson, J. R. (1976). *Language, memory, and thought.* Hillsdale, NJ: Lawrence Erlbaum Associates.

Baddeley, A. (1986). *Working memory.* Oxford: Clarendon Press.

Barron, F. (1953). Complexity-simplicity as a personality dimension. *Journal of Abnormal and Social Psychology, 48,* 163–172.

Berkowitz, L. (1957). Leveling tendencies and the complexity-simplicity dimension. *Journal of Personality, 25,* 743–751.

Bieri, J. (1955). Cognitive complexity-simplicity and predictive behavior. *Journal of Abnormal and Social Psychology, 51,* 263–268.

Bolles, R. N. (1990). *The 1990 What Color is Your Parachute?* Berkeley, CA: Ten Speed Press.

Burke, P. J., & Reitzes, D. C. (1981). The link between identity and role performance. *Social Psychology Quarterly, 44,* 83–92.

Cantor, N., Markus, H., Niedenthal, P., & Nurius, P. (1986). On motivation and the self concept. In R. M. Sorrentino & E. T. Higgins (Eds.), *Handbook of motivation and cognition: Foundations of social behavior* (pp. 96–121). New York: Guilford.

Chassin, L., Presson, C. C., Sherman, S. J., Corty, E., and Olshavsky, R. W. (1981). Self-images and cigarette smoking in adolescence. *Personality and Social Psychology Bulletin, 7,* 670–676.

Deaux, K. (1993). Reconstructing social identity. *Personality and Social Psychology Bulletin, 19,* 4–12.

Donahue, E. M., Robins, R. W., Roberts, B. W., & John O. P. (1993). The divided self: Concurrent and longitudinal effects of psychological adjustment and social roles on self-concept differentiation. *Journal of Personality and Social Psychology, 64,* 834–846.

Emmons, R. A., & King, L. A. (1988). Conflict among personal goal strivings: Immediate and long-term implications for psychological and physical well-being. *Journal of Personality and Social Psychology, 54,* 1040–1048.

Fiske, S. T., & Linville, P. W. (1980). What does the schema concept buy us? *Personality and Social Psychology Bulletin, 6,* 543–557.

Gordon, C. (1968). Self-conceptions: Configurations of content. In C. Gordon & K. J. Gergen (Eds.), *The self in social interaction* (Vol. I, pp. 115–136). New York: Wiley.

Greenwald, A. G., & Pratkanis, A. R. (1984). The self. In R. S. Wyer & T. K. Srull (Eds.), *Handbook of social cognition* (Vol. 3, pp. 129–178). Hillsdale, NJ: Lawrence Erlbaum Associates.

Hammen, C., Marks, T., deMayo, R., & Mayol, A. (1985). Self-schemas and risk for depression: A prospective study. *Journal of Personality and Social Psychology, 49,* 1147–1159.

Higgins, E. T. (1987). Self-discrepancy: A theory relating self and affect. *Psychological Review, 94*, 319-340.
Higgins, E. T. (1989). Self-discrepancy theory: What patterns of self-beliefs cause people to suffer? In L. Berkowitz (Ed.), *Advances in experimental social psychology* (Vol. 22, pp. 96-136). San Diego, CA: Academic Press.
Higgins, E. T., & Bargh, J. A. (1987). Social cognition and social perception. *Annual Review of Psychology, 38*, 369-425.
Higgins, E. T., & King, G. A. (1981). Accessibility of social constructs: Information-processing consequences of individual and contextual variability. In N. Cantor & J. F. Kihlstrom (Eds.), *Personality, cognition, and social interaction* (pp. 69-122). Hillsdale, NJ: Lawrence Erlbaum Associates.
Higgins, E. T., Klein, R., & Strauman, T. (1985). Self-concept discrepancy theory: A psychological model for distinguishing among different aspects of depression and anxiety. *Social Cognition, 3*, 51-76.
Higgins, E. T., Van Hook, E., & Dorfman, D. (1988). Do self-attributes for a cognitive structure? *Social Cognition, 6*, 177-207.
James, W. (1890). *Principles of psychology*. New York: Holt.
Katz, D. (1960). The functional approach to the study of attitudes. *Public Opinion Quarterly, 24*, 163-204.
Kelly, G. (1955). *The psychology of personal constructs*. New York: Norton.
Kihlstrom, J. F., & Cantor, N. (1984). Mental representations of the self. In L. Berkowitz (Ed.), *Advances in experimental social psychology* (Vol. 17, pp. 1-47). San Diego, CA: Academic Press.
Kihlstrom, J. F., & Klein, S. B. (1993). The self as knowledge structure. In R. S. Wyer & T. K. Srull (Eds.), *Handbook of social cognition*. Hillsdale, NJ: Lawrence Erlbaum Associates.
Klatzky, R. L. (1975). *Human memory: Structures and processes* (2nd ed.). San Francisco: W.H. Freeman.
Klein, S. B., & Loftus, J. (1993). The mental representation of trait and autobiographical knowledge about the self. In T. K. Srull & R. S. Wyer (Eds.), *Advances in social cognition* (Vol. 5, pp. 1-49). Hillsdale, NJ: Lawrence Erlbaum Associates.
Klein, S. B., Loftus, J., & Sherman, J. (1993). The role of summary and specific behavioral memories in trait judgments about the self. *Personality and Social Psychology Bulletin, 19*, 305-311.
Klein, S. B., Loftus, J., Trafton, R. G., & Fuhrman, R. W. (1992). Use of exemplars and abstractions in trait judgments: A model of trait knowledge about the self and others. *Journal of Personality and Social Psychology, 63*, 739-753.
Leventhal, H. (1957). Cognitive processes and interpersonal predictions. *Journal of Abnormal and Social Psychology, 55*, 176-180.
Lewin, K. (1951). *Field theory in social science*. New York: Harper.
Linville, P. (1982). The complexity-extremity effect and age-based stereotyping. *Journal of Personality and Social Psychology, 42*, 193-211.
Linville, P. (1985). Self-complexity and affective extremity: Don't put all your eggs into one cognitive basket. *Social Cognition, 3*, 94-120.
Linville, P. (1987). Self-complexity as a cognitive buffer against stress related illness and depression. *Journal of Personality and Social Psychology, 52*, 663-676.
Linville, P., & Carlston, D. E. (1994). Social cognition of the self. In P. G. Devine, D. L. Hamilton, & T. M. Ostrom (Eds.), *Social cognition: Its impact on social psychology*. New York: Academic Press.
Lundy, R. M., & Berkowitz, L. (1957). Cognitive complexity and assimilative projection in attitude change. *Journal of Abnormal and Social Psychology, 55*, 34-37.

Markus, H. (1977). Self-schemata and processing information about the self. *Journal of Personality and Social Psychology, 35*, 63–78.

Markus, H., Cross, S., & Wurf, E. (1990). The role of the self-system in competence. In R. J. Sternberg & J. Kolligian, Jr. (Eds.), *Competence considered* (pp. 205–225). New Haven, CT: Yale University Press.

Markus, H., & Nurius, P. (1986). Possible selves. *American Psychologist, 41*, 954–969.

Markus, H., & Wurf, E. (1987). The dynamic self-concept: A social psychological perspective. *Annual Review of Psychology, 38*, 299–337.

Markus, H., & Ruvolo, A. P. (1989). Possible selves: Personalized representations of goals. In L. A. Pervin (Ed.), *Goal concepts in personality and social psychology*. Hillsdale, NJ: Lawrence Erlbaum Associates.

Mayo, C. W., & Crockett, W. H. (1964). Cognitive complexity and primacy-recency effects in impression formation. *Journal of Abnormal and Social Psychology, 68*, 335–338.

Millar, M. D., & Tesser, A. (1986). Thought-induced attitude change: The effects of schema structure and commitment. *Journal of Personality and Social Psychology, 51*, 259–269.

Mita, T. H., Dermer, M., & Knight, J. (1977). Reversed facial images and the mere-exposure hypothesis. *Journal of Experimental Social Psychology, 35*, 597–601.

Niedenthal, P. M., Cantor, N., & Kihlstrom, J. F. (1985). Prototype matching: A strategy for social decision making. *Journal of Personality and Social Psychology, 48*, 575–584.

Niedenthal, P. M., & Mordkoff, J. T. (1991). Prototype distancing: A strategy for choosing among threatening situations. *Personality and Social Psychology Bulletin, 17*, 483–493.

Niedenthal, P. M., Setterlund, M. B., & Wherry, M. B. (1992). Possible self-complexity and affective reactions to goal-relevant evaluation. *Journal of Personality and Social Psychology, 63*, 5–16.

Nuttin, J. R. (1984). *Motivation, planning and action: A relational theory of behavior dynamics*. Hillsdale, NJ: Lawrence Erlbaum Associates.

Nuttin, J. R. (1985). *Future time perspective and motivation*. Hillsdale, NJ: Lawrence Erlbaum Associates.

Oyserman, D. (1993). Adolescent identity and delinquency in interpersonal context. *Child Psychiatry and Human Development, 23*, 201–214.

Oyserman, D., & Markus, H. (1990). Possible selves and delinquency. *Journal of Personality and Social Psychology, 59*, 112–125.

Oyserman, D., & Saltz, E. (1993). Competence, delinquency, and attempts to attain possible selves. *Journal of Personality and Social Psychology, 65*, 360–374.

Pelham, B., & Swann, W. B. (1989). From self-conceptions to self-worth: On the sources and structure of global self-esteem. *Journal of Personality and Social Psychology, 57*, 672–680.

Ruvolo, A. P., & Markus, H. R. (1992). Possible selves and performance: The power of self-relevant imagery. *Social Cognition, 10*, 95–124.

Salovey, P. (1992). Mood-induced self-focused attention. *Journal of Personality and Social Psychology, 62*, 699–707.

Schutz, A. (1964). On multiple realities. In M. Natanson (Ed.), *Collected papers of Alfred Schutz* (Vol. 1, pp. 207–259). The Hague: Martinus Niches.

Scott, W. A. (1962). Cognitive complexity and cognitive flexibility. *Sociometry, 25*, 405–414.

Scott, W. A. (1963). Cognitive complexity and cognitive balance. *Sociometry, 26*, 66–74.

Scott, W. A. (1969). Structure of natural cognitions. *Journal of Personality and Social Psychology, 12*, 261–278.

Scott, W. A., Osgood, D. W., & Peterson, C. (1979). *Cognitive structure: Theory and measurement of individual differences*. Washington, DC: Winston.

Setterlund, M. B. (1993). *The effects of possible self-complexity on self-relevant decision making*. Unpublished doctoral dissertation, Johns Hopkins University, Baltimore, MD.

Setterlund, M. B., & Niedenthal, P. M. (1993). "Who am I? Why am I here?": Self-esteem, self-clarity and prototype-matching. *Journal of Personality and Social Psychology, 65*, 769-780.

Sherman, S. J., Zehner, K. S., Johnson, J., & Hirt, E. R. (1983). Social explanation: The role of timing, set, and recall on subjective likelihood estimates. *Journal of Personality and Social Psychology, 44*, 1127-1143.

Showers, C. (1992). Evaluatively integrative thinking about characteristics of the self. *Personality and Social Psychology Bulletin, 18*, 719-729.

Sieber, S. D. (1974). Toward a theory of role accumulation. *American Sociological Review, 39*, 567-578.

Singer, J. L. (1975). Navigating the stream of consciousness: Research in daydreaming and related inner experience. *American Psychologist, 30*, 727-738.

Singer, J. L. (1984). The private personality. *Personality and Social Psychology Bulletin, 10*, 7-30.

Strauman, T. J. (1989). Self-discrepancies in clinical depression and social phobia: Cognitive structures that underlie emotional disorders. *Journal of Abnormal Psychology, 98*, 14-22.

Steele, C. M. (1988). The psychology of self-affirmation: Sustaining the integrity of the self. In L. Berkowitz (Ed.), *Advances in experimental social psychology* (Vol. 21, pp. 261-302). San Diego, CA: Academic Press.

Steele, C. M., & Liu, T. J. (1983). Dissonance processes as self-affirmation. *Journal of Personality and Social Psychology, 45*, 5-19.

Taylor, S. E. (1981). The interface of cognitive and social psychology. In J. Harvey (Ed.), *Cognition, social behavior, and the environment.* Hillsdale, NJ: Lawrence Erlbaum Associates.

Tesser, A. (1978). Self-generated attitude change. In L. Berkowitz (Ed.), *Advances in experimental social psychology* (Vol. 11, pp. 289-338). New York: Academic Press.

Tesser, A. (1988). Toward a self-evaluation maintenance model of social behavior. In L. Berkowitz (Ed.), *Advances in experimental social psychology* (Vol. 21, pp. 181-227). San Diego, CA: Academic Press.

Tesser, A., & Leone, C. (1977). Cognitive schemas and thought as determinants of attitude change. *Journal of Experimental Social Psychology, 13*, 340-356.

Thoits, P. (1983). Multiple identities and psychological well-being: A reformation and test of the social isolation hypothesis. *American Sociological Review, 48*, 174-187.

Wood, J. V., Saltzberg, J. A., & Goldsamt, L. A. (1990). Does affect induce self-focused attention? *Journal of Personality and Social Psychology, 58*, 899-908.

Wurf, E., & Markus, H. (1991). Possible selves and the psychology of personal growth. In D. Ozer, A. Stewart, & J. Healey (Eds.), *Perspectives on personality: Theory, research and interpersonal dynamics* (Vol. 3, pp. 39-62). Greenwich, CT: JAI Press.

Wyer, R. S., Jr., & Srull, T. K. (1981). Category accessibility: Some theoretical and empirical issues concerning the processing of social stimulus information. In E. T. Higgins, C. P. Herman, & M. P. Zanna (Eds.), *Social cognition: The Ontario Symposium* (Vol. 1, pp. 161-198). Hillsdale, NJ: Lawrence Erlbaum Associates.

Wyer, R. S., Jr., & Srull, T. K. (1986). Human cognition in its social context. *Psychological Review, 93*, 322-359.

Yarmey, A. D., & Johnson, J. (1982). Evidence for the self as an imaginal prototypes. *Journal of Research in Personality, 16*, 238-246.

Zajonc, R. B. (1960). The process of cognitive tuning in communication. *Journal of Abnormal and Social Psychology, 61*, 159-167.

7 The Organization of Self-Knowledge: Implications for Mood Regulation

Carolin J. Showers
Kristen C. Kling
University of Wisconsin—Madison

> Almost invariably, to see ourselves in whole or in part is to assess, evaluate, and pass judgment on what we see. We seem scarcely capable of even looking at any of our physical characteristics, dispositions, or social identity elements without immediately deploring or applauding what we observe.
>
> —Rosenberg, 1979, p. 26

Knowledge about the self is affect-laden. We care about information that is self-relevant. Not only do we tend to evaluate information about the self as positive or negative, but this information often evokes immediate, intense affect. Moreover, the accessibility of specific items of self-knowledge may be influenced by feeling states that prime affectively consistent self-beliefs (e.g., Bower, 1981).

Our goals for processing information about the self are closely related to its affective qualities. One general goal may be to regulate our affective reactions to incoming positive or negative self-knowledge. We also have goals for the use of existing self-knowledge, such as goals related to the accessibility of positive and negative self-beliefs. These two goals may coincide because our reactions to current experiences are influenced by relevant information about the self that is recalled at the time. Thus, if we want to regulate our reactions to personally relevant events, we may need to control the accessibility of positive and negative self-beliefs.

The premise of this chapter is that these two types of self-regulatory goals—the regulation of affective reactions to self-knowledge and the regulation of the accessibility of positive and negative self-beliefs — influence the organization of positive and negative self-knowledge. By organization, we mean the categorical structure of positive and negative self-beliefs and the interconnectedness (or associative links) between positive and negative items of self-knowledge. In turn, the organization of the self influences affective reactions to activated self-knowledge, the accessibility of self-beliefs, and reactions to self-relevant events. We start by outlining a theoretical framework for the relationships between specific self-regulatory goals and distinct types of self-concept organization. Then, we present some empirical evidence for the links between organization and affective states, particularly vulnerability to depressed mood and the processes of mood recovery.

THE IMPORTANCE OF ORGANIZATION

Information-processing models of the self typically focus on the relationship between the content of knowledge about the self and global self-evaluations (i.e., self-esteem). Recent literature on self-esteem emphasizes that the organization of information in the self-concept (not just its content) may influence self-evaluation. For instance, Pelham and Swann (1989) considered how specific beliefs about the self are organized according to domain, and how their positive or negative content is weighted by the perceived importance of the domain in determining its contribution to global self-esteem. Similarly, Campbell (1990) described the clarity (or confidence) of a specific belief about the self as a structural feature that may mediate the impact of a positive or negative belief on self-esteem. Generally speaking, organizational features of the self may help to compensate for the availability of negative beliefs in an individual's self-concept by making them less accessible or less central to global self-evaluations.

Literature on the self-concepts of depressed persons focuses on the accessibility of negative self-beliefs. Depressed persons are said to have negative self-schemas, evidenced by short response latencies to negative self-descriptive adjectives (Bargh & Tota, 1988; MacDonald & Kuiper, 1985). Presumably, organizational features of the depressives' self-schemas facilitate the accessibility of negative information (Segal, 1988). However, attempts to identify the underlying cognitive structures that are responsible for such accessibility have been scarce (for some exceptions, see Higgins, Van Hook, & Dorfman, 1988; Segal, Hood, Shaw, & Higgins, 1988; Spielman & Bargh, 1990).

In a series of studies, Showers (1992a, 1992b, Showers & Ryff, in press) identified different types of self-concept organization that may influence the accessibility of positive and negative beliefs about the self. In the *compartmentalized* type of organization, positive and negative beliefs are separated into distinct categories (i.e., self-aspects), so that each contains primarily positive or primarily negative information. In contrast, an *evaluatively integrative* organization has self-aspect categories that contain a mixture of positive and negative beliefs. Examples of these two types of organization are shown in Table 7.1.

Showers' model predicts that compartmentalized organization will lead to extreme affective reactions. When an event activates a self-aspect that contains primarily positive information, the individual is flooded with positive knowledge about the self, and so that person should feel extremely good. In contrast, if that self-aspect contained a combination of positive and negative beliefs (as it would in an integrative type of organization), the emotional reaction would more likely be mixed. Of course, activation of a purely negative compartment should result in an unusually negative response to the triggering event. Thus, over a range of experiences, the impact of compartmentalized organization may depend on the frequency with which purely positive or purely negative self-aspects are activated. If most experiences activate the positive self-aspects of an individual with compartmentalized organization, then that type of organization may be preferable to the integrative type. However, when the negative self-aspects are accessed more frequently (as they may be in the case of a person with important negative self-aspects), then integrative organization may be advantageous because it facilitates access to whatever positive self-knowledge does exist.

The two types of compartmentalized organization will be referred to as *positive-compartmentalized* or *negative-compartmentalized* to distinguish whether the purely positive or purely negative self-aspects are most impor-

TABLE 7.1
Examples of Compartmentalized Organization (Panel A) and Integrative Organization (Panel B) For Identical Items of Information About Self as Student

Panel A: Compartmentalized Organization		Panel B: Integrative Organization	
Renaissance Scholar (+)	Taking Tests, Grades (−)	Humanities Classes (+/−)	Science Classes (+/−)
+curious	−worrying	+creative	+disciplined
+disciplined	−tense	−insecure	+analytical
+motivated	−distracted	+motivated	−competitive
+creative	−insecure	−distracted	−worrying
+analytical	−competitive	+expressive	+curious
+expressive	−moody	−moody	−tense

Note. A positive or negative valence is indicated for each category and each item. The symbol (+/−) denotes a mixed-valence category. From Showers, C. (1992). Compartmentalization of positive and negative self-knowledge: Keeping bad apples out of the bunch. *Journal of Personality and Social Psychology, 62,* 1036–1049.

tant (i.e., most frequently accessed or most central to the self). The long-term advantages or disadvantages of these types of organization should be seen in their effects on global self-evaluations (i.e., self-esteem) or the individual's chronic predisposition toward positive or negative moods. For individuals whose positive self-aspects are important, positive-compartmentalized organization should be associated with higher self-esteem and less depressed mood than is integrative organization; conversely, for individuals whose negative self-aspects are important, negative-compartmentalization should be associated with lower self-esteem and more depressed mood than integrative organization.

The predictions of the compartmentalization model bear some resemblance to those associated with another organizational feature of the self, namely self-complexity (Linville, 1985, 1987). Self-complexity implies a self-concept with a large number of self-aspects that are independent, meaning that their attributes do not overlap. Complex individuals are expected to have less extreme affective reactions to events, presumably because having independent self-aspects means that fewer self-aspects are implicated in any one experience, reducing the "amount" of self involved. However, there is no conceptual relationship between the independence of self-aspects and degree of compartmentalization. According to the model of compartmentalization, an event's impact on the self is determined by the positive or negative content of self-knowledge activated by an event, rather than by the sheer amount of self involved.

Study 1: Empirical Evidence Relating Self-Organization and Mood

The evaluative organization of the self may be assessed by a self-descriptive sorting task (Showers, 1992a). In a typical version of this task, subjects are given a stack of 40 index cards, each containing a positive or negative trait adjective. Subjects are asked to "think of the different aspects of yourself or your life, and sort the cards into groups so that each group represents an aspect of your self or your life." Subjects are told that they may use each card in as many different groups as they like and that they should discard any cards that do not describe any aspect of themselves. After sorting the cards, subjects also rate the positivity, negativity, and importance of each self-aspect on 7-point Likert scales.

The measure of compartmentalized versus integrative organization is Cramer's phi, a coefficient based on a chi-square statistic (Everitt, 1977). Phi assesses an individual's tendency to deviate from the chance distribution of positive and negative descriptors across their complete set of self-aspects. Thus, if a person created a sort in which 60% of the cards used were positive adjectives, then one would expect each self-aspect to contain a mixture of positive and negative adjectives in the ratio of 60:40, simply due to chance. To the extent that the person's self-aspects deviate from this ratio, he or she tends to compartmentalize positive and negative characteristics. The phi coefficient ranges from 0 (if positive and negatives are distributed at chance levels) to 1 (if positives and negatives are perfectly compartmentalized). Average values of phi typically range from .65 to .75.

To distinguish positive-compartmentalized organization from negative-compartmentalized, the *differential importance* of positive and negative self-aspects is assessed (Pelham & Swann, 1989). Adopting Pelham and Swann's definition of differential importance, this index is the Pearson correlation across a person's self-aspects of their positivity and importance ratings for each self-aspect.[1] High scores on this index indicate that positive self-aspects are perceived to be more important than are negative self-aspects. Scores on this index are independent of the amount of positive or negative self-knowledge, so the index is not in itself a measure of self-esteem. However, it assesses a structural feature of the self and has been shown to explain significant variation in self-esteem, after the amount of positive or negative content is held constant (Marsh, 1993; Pelham & Swann, 1989). In the present model, individuals with positive-compartmentalized organization have high differential importance scores, whereas individuals with negative-compartmentalization have low differential importance scores.

Showers (1992a) examined the relationship between the content and organization of the self (as assessed by the self-descriptive card sorts) and subjects' current levels of self-esteem and depression. The measures of self-esteem and mood were the Rosenberg Self-Esteem Scale (RSE) (Rosenberg, 1965) and the Beck Depression Inventory (BDI) (Beck, Ward, Mendelson, Mock, & Erbaugh, 1961). First, consistent with prior studies of self-esteem, the content of the sorts (i.e., proportion of negative items used) and the differential importance index should predict substantial variance in mood and self-esteem scores. In addition, the present theoretical model predicts an interaction of phi (the measure of compartmentalization) with differential importance once content is controlled. When differential importance is high (i.e., positive self-aspects are important), compartmentalized organization should be associated with higher self-esteem and less depressed mood than integrative organization. When differential importance is low, integrative organization should be associated with higher self-esteem and less depressed mood than compartmentalized organization.

---

[1]The term *positivity ratings* refers to the difference between positivity and negative ratings made on separate 7-point Likert scales.

These hypotheses were tested by separate hierarchical regressions of RSE and BDI scores onto phi, differential importance, and their interaction, after holding constant the positive or negative content of the sorts (i.e., proportion of negative cards in the sort and the average positivity-negativity of all self-aspects). The predictions of the model were confirmed. Adjusted predicted values of BDI for high and low values of phi and differential importance are shown in Table 7.2 (line 1).

To get a clearer picture of these findings, we examined the relationship between type of organization and the positive or negative content of the sorts. Unadjusted predicted values of the proportion of negative items and of BDI are shown in lines 2 and 3 of Table 7.2. The overall main effect relationship between negative content (line 2) and unadjusted BDI scores (line 3) is clear. Looking more closely, we see that for individuals whose positive self-aspects are important, compartmentalized individuals have more negative content than integrative individuals, but their unadjusted BDI scores are the same. In other words, positive-compartmentalized organization may make it possible to have more negative self-knowledge available without a corresponding negative impact on mood or self-esteem (presumably because this type of organization limits the accessibility of negative beliefs). Among individuals whose negative self-aspects are important, compartmentalized individuals have greater negative content than their integrative counterparts, but this negative content is not sufficient to account completely for their depressed mood (as shown in line 1). Presum-

TABLE 7.2
Study 1: Predicted Values of Beck Depression Inventory (BDI) Scores and Negative Content of Card Sort as a Function of Compartmentalization and Differential Importance of Positive and Negative Self-Aspects

	High Differential Importance		Low Differential Importance	
	Compartmentalized Organization	Integrative Organization	Compartmentalized Organization	Integrative Organization
BDI (Adjusted Predicted Values)	3.6	9.0	7.8	6.3
%Negative Items in Card Sort	29.6	20.5	47.0	25.1
BDI (Unadjusted Predicted Values)	3.6	4.9	14.0	5.1

Note. High and low values of compartmentalization and differential importance correspond to 1 standard deviation above and below the mean. For compartmentalization, $M = .71$, $SD = .21$. For differential importance, $M = .46$, $SD = .42$. The adjusted predicted values in line 1 control for the proportion of negative items, the average positivity of self-aspects, and their interactions with differential importance. $N = 73$.

ably, negative-compartmentalized organization enhances the impact of negative self-beliefs.[2]

Integrative Thinking

In a related pair of studies, Showers (1992b) demonstrated a relationship between an integrative thinking process and current mood or self-esteem. Like the sorting task studies, these studies found that for individuals with important negative characteristics, integrative thinking was positively correlated with mood or self-esteem. The integrative thinking process was defined as the tendency to make mixed-valence statements when writing about a most negative characteristic (e.g., "When I'm with friends, I have no trouble speaking up, but when I'm with people I don't know very well I can hardly say a word"). Such integrative thoughts should be facilitated by the integrative organization of self-aspects assessed in the sorting task. Thus, an integrative category structure for important negative self-aspects may represent an adaptive way of thinking about one's negative characteristics (Showers, 1995).

MOTIVATIONAL MECHANISMS

As suggested earlier, organizational features of the self may serve to regulate affective reactions to self-relevant information and also to regulate the accessibility of positive and negative self-beliefs. How then do the different types of self-concept organization described above accomplish these goals? In this section, we consider the advantages and costs of each type of organization for regulating affect and/or the accessibility of valenced information. The specific advantages of each type of organization offer clues as to the specific motives that may encourage an individual to develop that type of organization.

Positive-Compartmentalization. One advantage of positive-compartmentalized organization may be a tendency *to minimize access to negative self-beliefs*. A person with a great deal of important positive knowledge about the self may have many positive experiences that tend to activate their

---

[2]It is important to note that individuals who are described as "low" in differential importance typically have scores on this index that are closer to 0 than to -1. This means that their positive and negative self-aspects tend to be similar in importance. In the study presented in Table 7.2, only 10 of 73 subjects (36 of whom were depression-prone) actually rated their negative self-aspects as more important than their positive self-aspects (i.e., differential importance scores < 0).

positive self-aspects. If the self-structure is compartmentalized, this person will rarely, if ever, encounter whatever negative characteristics they do have. The negative compartments may become so unimportant that the negative information in them is effectively "swept under the rug." Over time, this negative information may become so low in importance that it is eliminated from the self-concept. Thus, positive-compartmentalized organization may maintain a basically positive self-concept by ensuring minimal access to any negative self-beliefs.

Of course, the effectiveness of positive-compartmentalized organization depends on the successful avoidance of the negative compartments. As long as positive self-aspects are activated, the positive-compartmentalized individual should experience stable high self-esteem and positive affect. However, if a negative self-aspect were to become temporarily salient, the positive-compartmentalized person might experience a flood of negative information from that purely negative self-aspect. This could be overwhelming for the positive-compartmentalized individual who is not accustomed to activating negative self-beliefs, and who therefore may not have a well-developed set of strategies for coping with negative self-knowledge. Thus, there may be a hidden vulnerability in the positive-compartmentalized structure.

Evaluative Integration. When negative information about the self is prevalent or important, it is difficult to avoid accessing that information. In this case, an integrative type of organization has the advantage of facilitating access to some positive beliefs about the self even when a largely negative self-aspect is primed. More generally, integrative organization may serve *to minimize the impact of negative self-knowledge that cannot be avoided*. A potential cost of integrative organization is the effort and cognitive complexity required to generate integrative associations between items of opposite valence. For example, it may be difficult to integrate the perception of oneself as talented and creative with the fear and anxiety of preparing a lecture for a difficult audience. In low-stress situations, the anxious speaker may think, "I'm anxious, but also creative." However, under conditions of high stress, it may be difficult to sustain that integrative thought. The perception of oneself as anxious may become its own negative self-aspect, containing a great deal of negative self-knowledge relevant to the experience of stress. Such a shift toward a compartmentalized structure would make it difficult to keep the beliefs about one's talent and creativity accessible. Thus, the integrative category structure may sometimes be unstable for individuals who have many negative self-beliefs. Some individuals with integrative structure may tend to shift toward negative-compartmentalized organization when mood is low or stress is high.

Negative-Compartmentalization. For the most part, the negative-compartmentalized organization appears to be maladaptive. When an individual's negative self-aspects are important and frequently activated, the compartmentalized structure should minimize access to any positive self-beliefs. Thus, negative compartmentalization may facilitate and maintain negative self-evaluations and moods. As suggested earlier, negative compartmentalization may be a symptom of depression when individuals can no longer exert the effort to maintain integrative thinking. Consistent with this, Wenzlaff, Wegner, and Roper (1988) have suggested that "depression involves enhanced accessibility of interconnected negative thoughts" (p. 891), possibly because depressed persons lack the energy to divert attention to positive thoughts. Their studies of mental control show that depressed persons are unlikely to generate positive thoughts as a means of distracting themselves from an unwanted negative thought, despite their use of this strategy when positives are easily accessible.

The negative-compartmentalized structure may have a vulnerability to shifts in the relative importance of positive and negative self-aspects, as does a positive-compartmentalized structure. Any purely positive self-aspects in a negative-compartmentalized structure, even though they may not be perceived to be important, may provide a valuable resource for the depressed individual. The knowledge that some aspect of the self (whatever its perceived importance) is largely positive may help to sustain a sense of self-esteem in the face of negative mood and may even provide the route to mood recovery. A depressed person may be able to fall back on a purely positive self-aspect in order to feel somewhat better, perhaps even temporarily raising the perceived importance of that self-aspect as a way of enhancing self-esteem and mood. A similar process of mood recovery has been suggested by Pelham (1991), who found that despite the overall content differences in the self-concepts of nondepressed and severely depressed persons, the most positive self-view of severely depressed persons is as positive as that of nondepressed persons. Thus, the positive side of the negative-compartmentalized structure is that low-importance, positive self-aspects may facilitate mood recovery.

For individuals who have many important negative beliefs about the self, three alternatives seem viable: (a) A stable integrative structure may minimize the impact of accessible negative knowledge, thereby ensuring the activation of positive information along with the negative; (b) A stable negative-compartmentalized structure may make an individual vulnerable to depressed mood, but may also facilitate mood recovery via less important positive self-aspects, creating a cycle of mood depression and mood recovery; and (c) An individual with a great deal of important negative self-knowledge may be able to maintain an integrative organization when nondepressed but may fall into a negative-compartmentalized structure during depressive episodes. Note that the third alternative identifies evaluative organization as the consequence of an individual's mood, rather than as an underlying cause of affective states. Most likely, there is some reciprocity in the direction of causality.

EMPIRICAL EVIDENCE RELATING SELF-ORGANIZATION AND MOOD CHANGE

To understand the function of self-concept organization in individuals with important negative beliefs about the self, it is useful to examine the stability of self-concept organization in the same individuals across different mood states. The initial correlational studies (Showers, 1992a, 1992b; Showers & Ryff, in press) cannot speak to the question of whether self-concept organization is the cause or consequence of mood or self-esteem. Is self-concept organization a relatively stable feature of the self that creates vulnerabilities to certain moods or self-evaluations when positive or negative events occur? Or, is organization a symptom of current mood state? Moreover, are some types of organization associated with mood variability (i.e., proneness to extreme affective reactions or states)? Partial answers to these questions are provided by data from one longitudinal study and two laboratory experiments, the discussion of which will constitute the remainder of this chapter.

Study 2: Stability of Self-Organization and Mood Change (CVD Study)

Abramson and Alloy's Cognitive Vulnerability to Depression Study (CVD Study, Note 1) provided the opportunity to obtain data on the stability of self-concept organization and its relationship to mood change. In the Wisconsin sample of this study, 181 individuals were selected as being vulnerable or not vulnerable to depression based on measures of cognitive style (Abramson, 1989) and dysfunctional attitudes (Weissman & Beck, 1979). After an initial battery of assessments including the self-concept sorting task, subjects were interviewed at 6-week intervals over a 2-year period in order to assess their life experiences and mood state. For the purposes of examining self-concept organization, participants whose mood state had changed substantially from the time of the initial self-concept task were identified at the 6-week interviews. These individuals (Mood Change group) were asked to complete the sorting task a second time. A control group of individuals whose mood had not changed (Mood Stable group) was identified as well.

We predicted that individuals who had been selected for low cognitive vulnerability to depression would most likely appear in the Mood Stable group, would report positive mood, and would show positive-compartmentalized organization of the self. Individuals who were high in cognitive vulnerability to depression should be more likely to show mood change. If self-concept organization is itself a stable cognitive vulnerability factor for depression, the Mood Change group might tend to be negative-compartmentalized in both their depressed and nondepressed states. If self-concept organization changes with mood, these individuals might be able to maintain integrative organization when mood is high, yet lapse into negative-compartmentalized organization when mood is low.

To date, 107 participants have completed two sorting tasks at intervals ranging from 6 to 24 months apart. Of these, 38 experienced a mood discrepancy of 6 points or more on the BDI at the two times of their sorts, and so were classified in the Mood Change group. Forty-three participants experienced a mood discrepancy of 2 points or less and so were classified as Mood Stable. The self-concepts of these two groups were compared in their less depressed and more depressed states. (If participants' mood discrepancy was zero, their first and second sorts were randomly assigned to the less depressed or more depressed state.)

Table 7.3 shows the BDI scores, vulnerability status, and content, differential importance, and compartmentalization of the self for the Mood Stable and Mood Change groups in their less depressed and more depressed states. As predicted, the Change group contained more high vulnerability individuals than did the Stable group. Although the mean BDI score of the

TABLE 7.3
Study 2: Cognitive Vulnerability, Mood Level, and Measures of Content and Organization of the Self for Mood Change and Mood Stable Groups in Less Depressed and More Depressed States

	Mood Stable		Mood Change	
	Less Depressed	More Depressed	Less Depressed	More Depressed
% High Cognitive Vulnerability to Depression	38%		81%	
BDI	1.4	2.2	3.2	16.9
% Negative Items in Card sort	.24	.26	.30	.37
Differential Importance	.64	.54	.40	.38
Compartmentalization [raw scores]	.71	.73	.67	.75
Compartmentalization [adjusted scores]	.75	.73	.62	.62

Note. The adjusted scores for compartmentalization (line 6) are computed by dividing phi by the proportion of negative items in the sort for each subject. $n_{stable} = 37$, $n_{change} = 37$ (except for differential importance, n's = 36 and 33, respectively).

Change group when less depressed was higher than that of the Stable group, it was still in the nondepressed range.

The self-concept measures from the sorting task allowed us to evaluate the stability of organizational factors across mood states. The content of the sorts (i.e., proportion of negative items used) showed a pattern similar to the BDI scores. The negative content of the Change group was greater when they were more depressed. Most interesting was the pattern of results for phi, the measure of compartmentalization. Looking first at the raw scores (line 5), the most striking effect is the change in compartmentalization with mood state within the Change group. Organization (for these individuals with a great deal of important negative content) was more integrative when they were less depressed and more compartmentalized when they felt bad. Because compartmentalization tends to increase with negative content, adjusted means were calculated by dividing phi scores by the proportion of negative items in order to control for differences in content (line 6). These means suggest that the Stable group was highly compartmentalized, given their minimal negative content. Their high differential importance scores indicate that this was positive-compartmentalization, as was predicted for this group.

To summarize, for the Mood Stable group, positive-compartmentalized organization may contribute to a stable positive mood. The organization of the Mood Change group suggests that individuals who have a great deal of negative content may reorganize the self-concept as mood changes. For these individuals, organization was more integrative in less negative moods and more compartmentalized when these individuals felt bad.

Experiment 1: Effects of Induced Mood on Self-Descriptive Sorts

The effects of mood on organization can be tested in the laboratory by manipulating mood and observing any changes in the self-concept. Previous literature suggests that changes in mood affect the content of self-knowledge on retrieval (see Sedikides, 1990, for a review). Moreover, the negative self-schemas of depression-prone individuals may be more pronounced during depressive episodes (Brown & Taylor, 1986; Hammen, Marks, deMayo, & Mayol, 1985). However, the effects of mood on organizational factors, such as the perceived importance of positive and negative self-aspects or compartmentalization, have not been tested.

Procedure. In an initial study, 92 subjects were randomly assigned to either an elated, neutral, or sad mood condition. At the start of the session, the Velten (1968) self-statement procedure was used to induce mood. Following the mood induction, subjects completed a mood check consisting of a subset of items from the Differential Emotions Scale (Izard, 1971). Then, they performed the self-descriptive sorting task, paced so that the card sort could be completed in 15 minutes. At the 15-minute point, subjects filled out a different subset of DES items and the BDI. Finally, they rated positivity, negativity, and importance of each of the self-aspects in their sorts.

Results 1A: Effects of Mood on the Self-Concept. The first DES mood check confirmed the success of the mood induction ($M_{ela} = 3.41$, $M_{neu} = .37$, $M_{sad} = -2.62$, $F(2,89) = 63.4$, $p < .001$). However, induced mood did not affect the content of the items used by the subjects in their self-descriptive sorts (proportion of negative items $M_{ela} = .31$, $M_{neu} = .29$, $M_{sad} = .33$, $F(2,89) < 1$). Nor did induced mood affect the compartmentalization of the sorts (phi: $M_{ela} = .81$, $M_{neu} = .81$, $M_{sad} = .78$, $F(2,86) < 1$). There was a marginally significant effect of mood on the differential importance of positive and negative self-aspects, due to the lower scores of subjects in the sad condition (differential importance: $M_{ela} = .69$, $M_{neu} = .67$, $M_{sad} = .47$, $F(2,87) = 2.67$, $p < .08$). Note that these importance ratings were made after the mood check at the 15-minute point, when subjects in the sad condition reported the same mood as those in the neutral condition (second DES: $M_{ela} = 1.66$, $M_{neu} = .83$, $M_{sad} = .92$, $F(2,89) = 2.85$, $p < .07$).

These findings suggest that self-concept organization (i.e., compartmentalization or integration) is relatively impervious to short-term fluctuations in mood state. However, it cannot rule out the possibility of a causal effect of mood on compartmentalization in the CVD data. Clearly, the Velten procedure need not have the same effects on the self-concept as a naturally occuring depressed mood. Moreover, unlike the CVD study, the present study did not include a preselected group of depression-prone individuals, whose self-concepts might be especially sensitive to induced mood.

As for the failure to find differences in the content of the items used, it is important to consider the cognitive processes involved in performing the sort. During the sorting task, subjects do not need to generate the positive and negative items (a task likely to be influenced by accessibility); they simply decide whether the word is appropriate for any part of their self-description (a task likely to be influenced by availability). In this task, the perceived importance of positive and negative self-aspects appears to be the feature that is most sensitive to induced mood.

Organization as a Cognitive Diathesis for Depression. The design of this study also allowed us to examine a process suggested by the CVD Study data, namely that organization of the self may contribute to the maintenance of a mood. In the current literature, a diathesis-stress model has been used to explain negative mood (Abramson, Metalsky, & Alloy, 1989). According to this model, people differ in their cognitive vulnerabilities to negative mood. Such vulnerabilities include a depressogenic attributional style (i.e., explaining a negative event in terms of stable, global causes; Abramson, Seligman, & Teasdale, 1978) and dysfunctional attitudes (e.g., "If I do not do well all the time, people will not respect me"; Beck, Rush, Shaw, & Emery, 1979). These vulnerabilities, or diatheses, are viewed as a relatively stable feature of personality and may be observed in depression-prone individuals even when they are nondepressed. When a stressful event occurs, the cognitive diatheses come into play, contributing to a depressive interpretation of the event and resulting in a negative mood (Metalsky, Abramson, Seligman, Semmel, & Peterson, 1982). We propose that self-concept organization may be an additional cognitive diathesis for depression. The type of organization may determine what kind of information about the self is brought to bear in crafting an interpretation of a stressful event, thereby influencing affective reactions. Self-concept organization may even underlie other well-known cognitive diatheses. For example, the activation of a purely negative compartment of the self may encourage overgeneralized negative beliefs about the self (the dysfunctional attitudes) or generality of causes (the maladaptive attributional style).

Previous tests of the diathesis-stress model suggest that immediate affective reactions to an event depend largely on the valence and perceived importance of the outcome (Metalsky et al., 1982; Metalsky, Halberstadt, & Abramson, 1987). In other words, most people have the immediate reaction of feeling bad when bad things happen. However, cognitive vulnerability factors are significant predictors of delayed reactions to negative events. For example, in the studies by Metalsky and his colleagues of reactions to exam grades, the discrepancy between students' grades and their aspirations predicted mood reported immediately after receiving the grade. However, attributional style (assessed at least 1 month earlier) predicted mood 2 to 3 days after receipt of the grade. In other words, the diatheses may not prevent a negative reaction to bad events so much as they may facilitate the process of mood recovery.

Thus, any part that the organization of the self plays in maintenance or recovery from induced mood may generalize to the regulation of affective reactions to a wide range of events. Any specific negative event may create immediate bad feelings from which a person must recover. The ability to cope with a negative event may have as much to do with the ability to recover from a negative mood as with specific cognitive interpretations of the event. When the bad feelings engendered by a negative event activate negative beliefs about the self, we would expect self-concept organization to play a critical role.

Predictions: Organization Affects Mood Recovery. How might the compartmentalization or integrative organization of the self affect recovery from a sad mood? For a person with positive-compartmentalized organization, a negative mood may activate pure negative self-aspects (even though these are perceived to be of low importance). These negative compartments should perpetuate the negative mood as long as they are activated. However, the mood should start to fade when chronically accessible positive self-aspects begin to override the adverse impacts of temporarily salient negative ones.

In the case of an individual with integrative organization, the activation of negative self-aspects will bring to mind a mixture of positive and negative beliefs, suggesting that some mood recovery will begin immediately. Moreover, individuals with integrative organization should be accustomed to thinking about negative self-knowledge because it routinely comes to mind as part of most of their self-aspects. Hence, these individuals may have a great deal of experience coping with the negative thoughts that characterize their sad mood.

Like the positive-compartmentalized individuals, those with negative-compartmentalized organization should have their negative moods maintained by their purely negative self-aspects. Moreover, because these self-aspects are the important ones, persons with negative-compartmentalization may find it difficult to access any positive beliefs about the self, thereby perpetuating the negative mood. The only potential exception to this would be cases in which specific positive self-aspects are activated by features of the situation that make these otherwise low-important aspects temporarily salient.

Results 1B: Effects of Organization on Mood Recovery. To recap, the procedure for Experiment 1 consisted of the Velten mood induction followed by the self-concept sorting task. At the end of the sorting task (15 minutes after the mood induction), subjects completed the DES mood measure as an index of their recovery from the induced mood. The mediational effect of self-concept organization on mood recovery was examined by hierarchical regressions performed for each of the three mood conditions, predicting the 15-minute DES mood check. Mood immediately following the induction was held constant by entering it on the first step of the regression; thus, we were predicting mood change. Step 2 entered the measures of content (proportion of negative items) and differential importance. Steps 3 and 4 entered phi (the measure of compartmentalization) and the interaction of phi and differential importance, respectively.

Significant effects for the features of the self-concept were found only in the sad mood condition, where an interaction of phi and differential importance emerged. The predicted values shown in Table 7.4 indicate that for individuals whose positive self-aspects were important (high differential importance), compartmentalized individuals returned to a positive mood more quickly than individuals with integrative organization. For persons whose negative self-aspects were important (low differential importance), there was a trend in the opposite direction.

Thus, Experiment 1 indicates that the organization of the self-concept may mediate recovery from a sad mood. However, it also raises a number of questions about the exact nature of this process. First, is the actual performance of the sorting task necessary to obtain mood recovery effects? There are at least two potential effects of doing the sort during the mood recovery period: (a) Sorting the cards may force subjects to think explicitly about the self. This explicit focus on the self (which may not exist in more ecologically valid settings) may be necessary to obtain effects of self-concept organization on mood recovery. (b) For compartmentalized individuals, sorting the cards may enhance the natural salience of the most important self-aspects (either the positives or the negatives). The impact of these pure compartments may be insignificant without the benefit of doing the sort during the mood recovery period. A third concern about this study is the possibility that subjects are simply returning to a baseline mood that was influenced by self-concept organization. This seems unlikely, given that organization did not predict mood measured 15 minutes after the neutral mood induction. A follow-up study (Kling & Showers, 1994) was designed to address all three of these concerns.

Experiment 2: Full Mood-Recovery Paradigm

First, in order to examine whether the organization that mediates mood recovery is a relatively stable feature of the self-concept that exists prior to

TABLE 7.4
Experiment 1 (Sad Mood Condition): Adjusted Predicted Values for DES Mood at 15 Minutes as a Function of Compartmentalization and Differential Importance

	High Differential Importance		Low Differential Importance	
	Compartmentalized Organization	Integrative Organization	Compartmentalized Organization	Integrative Organization
DES Mood	1.75	−0.06	−0.32	.24

Note. High and low values of compartmentalization and differential importance correspond to 1 standard deviation above and below the mean. For compartmentalization, $M = .78$, $SD = .26$. For differential importance, $M = .54$, $SD = .41$. Predicted values are adjusted for post-induction mood and proportion of negative items in the sort. $N = 26$.

the experience of a negative mood, self-concept organization was assessed 1 week before the mood induction. Second, in order to test whether an explicit focus on self-description is necessary to obtain mood recovery effects, subjects' activities during the mood recovery period were manipulated so that they focused either on reporting beliefs about the self or on an academic performance task. Third, in order to track the course of mood recovery over time, mood was assessed at three 5-minute intervals following the mood induction.

Procedure. In the first of two sessions, 80 female subjects completed the self-descriptive sorting task and measures of current mood and self-esteem, including the BDI and the Rosenberg Self-Esteem Scale. Measures of compartmentalization and differential importance were derived from the sort. In the second session (1 week later), subjects participated in two ostensibly unrelated experiments. In the first "experiment," subjects completed the Profile of Mood States (POMS) (Lorr & McNair, 1984) for how they had been feeling that day, and a subset of 14 DES items for how they were feeling at that moment. Then, the Velten self-statement procedure was used to induce a sad mood in all subjects. The DES items were readministered immediately after the induction as a manipulation check. For the second "unrelated experiment," subjects were randomly assigned to the Who Am I or the digits task condition. In order to encourage explicit thoughts about the self, subjects in the Who Am I condition described themselves by completing 20 sentences that began with the stem "I am" (Kuhn & Partland, 1954). In the digits condition, subjects completed three digits tasks that included writing numbers backward from 1,000 by threes, a digit-symbol substitution task, and a collection of simple arithmetic problems. During these tasks, mood was assessed at three 5-minute intervals using a different subset of DES adjectives.

Procedural Checks. First, we tested the basic relationship between self-concept organization and current mood or self-esteem (replicating Study 1). Indeed, the same type of hierarchical regression revealed an interaction of phi and differential importance in predicting Rosenberg Self-Esteem scores, assessed immediately following the sorting task ($p = .03$, $N = 70$).[3] A similar pattern of results emerged for measures of mood taken 1 week later, prior to the mood induction (DES: $p < .08$; POMS-Depression: $p < .13$). After controlling for preinduction DES mood, there was no relationship between phi or differential importance and postinduction DES mood. Thus, compartmentalization did not affect the initial effectiveness of the mood induction procedure. The pre- and post-induction

---

[3] Ten subjects were dropped because of improper procedure or missing data.

DES mood measures were used to select subjects for the mood recovery analyses. Eight subjects whose mood was not lowered by the Velten procedure were excluded.

Results. The DES mood measures taken at 5, 10, and 15 minutes into the recovery period were analyzed by hierarchical regressions. Step 1 entered pre-induction mood, post-induction mood, and task; Step 2 entered the measures of content and differential importance from the sort; Steps 3 and 4 entered the two- and three-way interactions.

At all three times, there were significant main effects of preinduction and postinduction mood. No significant effects of task, differential importance, or compartmentalization were observed at the 5-minute point. At 10 minutes, a marginal triple interaction of these variables emerged, which was significant at the 15-minute point (change in $R^2 = .04, p < .04$). Significant two-way interactions of task × differential importance and task × phi were qualified by the triple interaction. Adjusted predicted values are shown in Table 7.5.

The significant interaction involving compartmentalization suggests that doing the sorting task itself was not necessary to observe a relationship between self-concept structure and mood recovery. Moreover, significant effects of compartmentalization within the digits task condition show that explicit focus on the self (in the form of a self-description task) was not necessary either. However, differences in the pattern of influence compared to that observed in Experiment 1B suggest that the nature of tasks performed during the recovery period interacted with self-structure in influencing the mood recovery process.

For the Who Am I task, the means in Table 7.5 indicate that integrative

TABLE 7.5
Experiment 2: Adjusted Predicted Values for DES Mood at 15 Minutes as a Function of Compartmentalization and Differential Importance

	High Differential Importance		Low Differential Importance	
	Compartmentalized Organization	Integrative Organization	Compartmentalized Organization	Integrative Organization
Who Am I? Task	.68	1.51	.26	1.53
Digits Task	2.14	2.77	1.93	−1.79

Note. Predicted values are adjusted for pre- and post-induction mood, proportion of negative items in sort and its interactions with task and differential importance. High and low values of compartmentalization and differential importance correspond to 1 standard deviation above and below the mean. For compartmentalization, $M = .73$, $SD = .23$. For differential importance, $M = .53$, $SD = .36$. $n_{\text{Who am I}} = 32$, $n_{\text{Digits}} = 30$.

organization tended to be associated with better mood recovery than compartmentalization. In Experiment 1B, this pattern was observed only for individuals low in differential importance. In the present study, the Who Am I task may have prolonged the activation of negative compartments primed by the Velten procedure. Both positive- and negative-compartmentalized individuals may have been stuck in activated negative compartments which then were reported during the Who Am I task. In Experiment 1B, performing the sorting task (and thereby creating important, purely positive self-aspects) may have reminded positive-compartmentalized persons of their positive self-aspects, thereby overriding the activation of negatives by the Velten procedure. Of course, negative-compartmentalized persons would not have experienced a similar benefit.

For the most part, the digits task resulted in more positive mood recovery than the Who Am I task. These tasks may have distracted subjects' attention from negative self-knowledge activated by the mood induction and, because they were fairly easy, may actually have activated positive self-aspects due to feelings of enjoyment or success at the task. The only exception to this is the low-differential importance, integrative group, who were experiencing the most negative mood 15 minutes after the induction. Success at these digit tasks may have increased the salience of pure positive self-aspects in compartmentalized individuals, regardless of their chronic differential importance. Success may also have restored the salience of positive self-aspects for the high-differential importance, integrative group. However, for the low-differential importance, integrative individuals, two explanations seem plausible. One is that their integrative thought process watered down any experience of success at the tasks, by linking incoming positive information to important negatives. Alternatively, the need to focus attention on the task (as opposed to specific self-beliefs) may have precluded the effortful process of integration that otherwise might have helped the low differential importance group cope with a negative mood.

To summarize, Experiment 2 shows that explicit focus on the self is not required to observe a relationship between self-structure and mood recovery. However, the effects of positive- versus negative-compartmentalized structures can easily be overridden by situation factors that affect the salience of positive or negative compartments. Even positive-compartmentalized individuals may get stuck in temporarily salient negative compartments, with concomitant effects on mood. Consistent with earlier results, integrative thinking seems to be advantageous when negative self-knowledge is primed. However, the poor recovery of the low-differential importance, integrative group in the digits condition suggests that the benefits of integrative organization may sometimes be limited by the available cognitive resources for carrying out the integrative process, or by a tendency for integrative thinking to neutralize positive experience.

CONCLUSIONS

In closing, we review the specific goals associated with the self-regulation of affect that we believe to be served by each type of organization, as well as the basic conclusions supported by the data described in this chapter. In general, empirical work continues to support the notion that self-concept organization plays a role in the regulation of mood and self-esteem that cannot be explained by the sheer availability of positive or negative self-knowledge.

Positive-compartmentalized organization may minimize access to negative beliefs about the self. Ironically, an organization that minimizes access to negatives may allow more negatives to be available in memory without severe impact on self-esteem or mood. In fact, individuals with positive-compartmentalization show the same positive mood and high self-esteem as integrative individuals with similarly important positive self-aspects, despite the greater amount of negative content in the compartmentalized self-concepts. For the most part, positive-compartmentalization may be associated with stable, positive mood. These individuals may be vulnerable to unusually negative reactions when situational factors increase the salience of negative self-aspects. Still, these reactions may be short-lived.

Negative-compartmentalized organization should maximize access to negative self-knowledge. For these individuals, mood is unusually negative and self-esteem is low, even when these measures are adjusted for the amount of negative content in the self-concept. This type of organization may be a symptom of negative mood, especially in individuals who are depression-prone. Although the perceived importance of pure negative self-aspects should perpetuate negative moods, these individuals seem to be able to access pure positive self-aspects when situational factors make them salient. In this way, positive self-aspects that are typically perceived to be low in importance may sometimes be used to facilitate mood recovery.

Integrative organization may minimize the impact of negative self-knowledge in persons whose negative knowledge is important. This type of organization tends to be associated with relatively positive mood states in individuals who are depression-prone. Integrative organization appears to counteract or moderate the effects of situationally induced salience of positives or negatives. When a manipulation enhances the salience of negative self-knowledge and individuals with integrative organization are given the opportunity to generate their integrative self-descriptions, they are quite resilient and recover well. However, the benefits of integration may be limited by a tendency to water down positive experience or by constraints on time, effort, and attention.

To summarize, positive-compartmentalized organization may be advantageous in maintaining a stable positive mood and high self-esteem for most individuals (who likely have a great deal of important positive content). Still, one limitation of positive-compartmentalization may be that by protecting individuals from their negative self-beliefs, this type of organization leaves them ill-prepared to cope with extreme stressors. Integrative organization may be advantageous for individuals with a great deal of important negative self-knowledge, especially when they have the opportunity to engage in the effortful integrative process. In contrast, negative-compartmentalized organization may typically contribute to negative moods and low self-esteem, although low-importance (but pure) positive self-aspects may sometimes provide a route to mood recovery.

ACKNOWLEDGMENTS

This research was supported in part by NIMH National Research Service Award MH10058. We thank Lenny Martin, Abe Tesser, and the participants in the Goals and Affect Conference, Athens, GA, 1994, for their insightful comments on this work.

REFERENCES

Abramson, L. Y. (1989). *Revision of the Attributional Styles Questionnaire*. Manuscript in preparation.

Abramson, L. Y., Metalsky, G. I., & Alloy, L. B. (1989). Hopelessness depression: A theory-based subtype of depression. *Psychological Review, 96*, 358-372.

Abramson, L. Y., Seligman, M. E. P., & Teasdale, J. (1978). Learned helplessness in humans: Critique and reformulation. *Journal of Abnormal Psychology, 87*, 49-74.

Bargh, J. A., & Tota, M. E. (1988). Context-dependent automatic processing in depression: Accessibility of negative constructs with regard to self but not others. *Journal of Personality and Social Psychology, 54*, 925-939.

Beck, A. T., Rush, A. J., Shaw, B. F., & Emery, G. (1979). *Cognitive therapy of depression*. New York: Guilford.

Beck, A. T., Ward, C. H., Mendelson, M., Mock, J., & Erbaugh, J. (1961). An inventory for measuring depression. *Archives of General Psychiatry, 4*, 561-571.

Bower, G. H. (1981). Mood and memory. *American Psychologist, 36*, 129-148.

Brown, J. D., & Taylor, S. E. (1986). Affect and the processing of personal information: Evidence for mood-activated self-schemata. *Journal of Experimental Social Psychology, 22*, 436-452.

Campbell, J. D. (1990). Self-esteem and clarity of the self-concept. *Journal of Personality and Social Psychology, 59*, 538-549.

Everitt, B. S. (1977). *The analysis of contingency tables*. London: Chapman and Hall.

Hammen, C., Marks, T., de Mayo, R., & Mayol, A. (1985). Depressive self-schemas, life stress, and vulnerability to depression. *Journal of Personality and Social Psychology, 49*, 1147-1159.

Higgins, E. T., Van Hook, E., & Dorfman, D. (1988). Do self-attributes form a cognitive structure? *Social Cognition, 6*, 177-206.

Izard, C. E. (1971). *The face of emotion*. New York: Appelton-Century-Crofts.

Kling, K. C., & Showers, C. (1994, May). *Self-concept mediates mood recovery*. Paper presented at the annual meeting of the Midwestern Psychological Association, Chicago.

Kuhn, M. H., & Partland, T. (1954). An empirical investigation of self-attitudes. *American Sociological Review, 19*, 551-562.

Linville, P. W. (1985). Self-complexity and affective extremity: Don't put all of your eggs in one cognitive basket. *Social Cognition, 3*, 94-120.

Linville, P. W. (1987). Self-complexity as a cognitive buffer against stress-related illness and depression. *Journal of Personality and Social Psychology, 52*, 663-676.

Lorr, M., & McNair, D. M. (1984). *Manual for the Profile of Mood States*. San Diego: EDITS.

MacDonald, M. R., & Kuiper, N. A. (1985). Efficiency and automaticity of self-schema processing in clinical depressives. *Motivation and Emotion, 9*, 171-184.

Marsh, H. W. (1993). Relations between global and specific domains of self: The importance of individual importance, certainty, and ideals. *Journal of Personality and Social Psychology, 65*, 975-992.

Metalsky, G. I., Abramson, L. Y., Seligman, M. E. P., Semmel, A., & Peterson, C. (1982). Attributional styles and life events in the classroom: Vulnerability and invulnerability to depressive mood reactions. *Journal of Personality and Social Psychology, 43*, 612-617.

Metalsky, G. I., Halberstadt, L. J., & Abramson, L. Y. (1987). Vulnerability to depressive mood reactions: Toward a more powerful test of the diathesis-stress and causal mediation components of the reformulated theory of depression. *Journal of Personality and Social Psychology, 52*, 386-393.

Pelham, B. W. (1991). On the benefits of misery: Self-serving bias in the depressive self-concept. *Journal of Personality and Social Psychology, 61*, 670-681.

Pelham, B. W., & Swann, W. B., Jr. (1989). From self-conceptions to self-worth: On the sources and structure of global self-esteem. *Journal of Personality and Social Psychology, 57*, 672-680.

Rosenberg, M. (1965). *Society and the adolescent self-image*. Princeton, NJ: Princeton University Press.

Rosenberg, M. (1979). *Conceiving the self*. New York: Basic Books.

Sedikides, C. (1990). Changes in the valence of the self as a function of mood. In M. S. Clark (Ed.), *Review of personality and social psychology* (Vol. 14, pp. 271-311). Newbury Park, CA: Sage.

Segal, Z. V. (1988). Appraisal of the self-schema construct in cognitive models of depression. *Psychological Bulletin, 103*, 147-162.

Segal, Z. V., Hood, J. E., Shaw, B. F., & Higgins, E. T. (1988). A structural analysis of the self-schema construct in major depression. *Cognitive Therapy and Research, 12*, 471-485.

Showers, C. (1992a). Compartmentalization of positive and negative self-knowledge: Keeping bad apples out of the bunch. *Journal of Personality and Social Psychology, 62*, 1036-1049.

Showers, C. (1992b). Evaluatively integrative thinking about characteristics of the self. *Personality and Social Psychology Bulletin, 18*, 719-729.

Showers, C. J. (1995). The evaluative organization of self-knowledge. In M. Kernis (Ed.), *Efficacy, agency, and self-esteem* (pp. 101-120). New York: Plenum.

Showers, C. J., & Ryff, C. D. (in press). Self-differentiation and well-being in a life transition. *Personality and Social Psychology Bulletin*.

Spielman, L. A., & Bargh, J. A. (1990). Does the depressive self-schema really exist? In C. D. McCann & N. S. Endler (Eds.), *Depression: New directions in theory, research, and practice* (pp. 111–126). Toronto: Wall & Emerson, Inc.

Velten, E., Jr. (1968). A laboratory task for induction of mood states. *Behavior Research and Therapy, 6*, 473–482.

Weissman, A., & Beck, A. T. (1979, August). *The dysfunctional attitude scale.* Paper presented at the annual meeting of the American Psychological Association, New York, NY.

Wenzlaff, R. M., Wegner, D. M., & Roper, D. W. (1988). Depression and mental control: The resurgence of unwanted negative thoughts. *Journal of Personality and Social Psychology, 55*, 882–892.

8
Self-Beliefs, Self-Evaluation, and Depression: A Perspective on Emotional Vulnerability

Timothy J. Strauman
University of Wisconsin-Madison

Depression poses an enormous health problem, with incalculable economic and psychological costs. The NIMH Epidemiological Catchment Area study indicated that major depression has a lifetime prevalence of approximately 6% in American adults (Regier, Hirschfeld, Goodwin et al., 1988). Other studies estimate the lifetime prevalence to be as high as 26% for women and 12% for men (APA Work Group on Major Depressive Disorder, 1993). A problem of this magnitude deserves the fullest possible commitment of scientific resources to remediate, and ultimately prevent, such a devastating disorder.

In some respects, we know a great deal about depression. Statistically speaking, the probability of suffering a major depressive episode is influenced by a number of risk factors, including gender, parental loss, pathogenic rearing practices, personality, history of traumatic experiences, previous episodes of depression, low social support, recent stressful events, and genetic influences (Kendler, Kessler, Neale, Heath, & Eaves, 1993). But much less is known about predicting who will become depressed and why a depressive episode begins and remits.

This chapter addresses the relation between self-evaluation and vulnerability to negative mood states potentially leading to a depressive syndrome. As a recent volume (Segal & Blatt, 1993) illustrates, an extensive literature exists relating aspects of the self and self-evaluation to emotional distress. Nonetheless, to my knowledge there are no theories of depression based specifically on the psychology of self-evaluation. This chapter offers such a model, utilizing theory and research in social, personality, and developmental psychology as well as studies of emotion and psychopathology. In keeping with the theme of this book, self-evaluation is conceptualized as a process in which a person's self-regulatory goals and standards for behavior can influence her or his emotional state. My purpose is twofold: first, to demonstrate the conceptual power of a psychological perspective informed by developmental and social-cognitive theory, and second, to push our understanding of self-evaluation to the limit and identify questions meriting further study.

The complexity and heterogeneity of affective disorders have belied efforts to formulate universal theories of depressive vulnerability (Akiskal & McKinney, 1975; Karasu, 1990a, 1990b). Thus, I begin with the qualifier (perhaps obvious) that not all depression results from negative self-evaluation and its emotional sequelae. There is also a long-standing belief among some investigators that more severe, so-called *endogenous* depression is primarily a result of biological (as opposed to psychological) sources of vulnerability (Coryell, Winokur, Shea, Maser, Endicott, & Akiskal, 1994). Still, considerable evidence suggests that self-evaluation may play a role in the development of at least a subset of affective syndromes. And even if the most severe depressions are unlikely to have resulted primarily from a self-evaluative cognitive diathesis, psychological contributory causal factors still should not be underestimated (Abramson, Metalsky, & Alloy, 1989). Recent prevalence data for so-called *mild* or nonendogenous depression and anxiety (Kessler, Kendler, Heath, Neale, & Eaves, 1992) indicate that almost half of all adults will experience an episode during their lifetime. If even a small percentage suffer as a result of a breakdown in self-regulation, then the potential contribution of a self-evaluation perspective on depression is great indeed.

Note that the model is not meant to imply the existence of a discrete subtype of depression. Rather, I hope to depict a general *pathway* to a final dysregulated state, borrowing the terminology of Akiskal and McKinney (1975). The likelihood of becoming depressed via such a cognitively mediated pathway would not depend primarily on genetic or temperamental predisposition, although they are probably involved distally. This is not a perspective in which biological factors are sufficient causal agents. As I argue, the relative contributions of neurobiological and cognitive processes to the etiology of depression are more clearly understood if each is viewed in the context of the other.

GENERAL ASSUMPTIONS

The model involves four fundamental assumptions about self-evaluation and its links with affect. None of them is particularly radical, but together they emphasize the interdependence of psychological and biological processes and the adaptive significance of self-evaluation. That is, self-evaluation is understood as in the service of psychological adaptation and well-being, and its links with emotion and motivation are inherent (Carver & Scheier, 1990). I briefly discuss their implications for the study of depression and then present the model itself.

1. *Early in development, people rapidly and efficiently learn the emotional consequences for their behavior and the internal and external stimuli related to those consequences.* The process of self-evaluation involves three domains of psychological activity: cognition, emotion, and motivation (Sorrentino & Higgins, 1986). These domains are concerned with detecting, interpreting, and responding to adaptively significant stimuli (Derryberry & Reed, in press) – a functional view sometimes overlooked in biological critiques of cognitive theories of depression. With others (e.g., Harter, 1986), I assume that self-evaluation develops within the context of the individual's overall cognitive-emotional maturation. Infancy and childhood are periods in which the individual's emotional response tendencies become increasingly shaped by a combination of several forces. Temperament determines the intensity of inborn emotional responses and in addition functions to elicit certain types of environmental events that in turn further influence emotion. The child's motivated behavior has obvious influences on the environment and serves to selectively expose her or his developing nervous system to particular affectively charged information. The environment presents the child with a complex array of innate as well as conditioned signals for emotional responding. Thus, psychological development involves the continuing acquisition of information about the adaptive significance of events (in terms of both the characteristics of the events themselves and response options) and constructing representations of self, others, and environment.

2. *Early in development, people are predisposed to perceive, interpret, and represent the behaviors of caregivers toward them.* This postulate asserts that the general *emotional learning* process takes place predominantly within the context of parent–child interactions. There is a wealth of data supporting the assertion that early relations with caregivers are critical for establishing the individual's basic social knowledge structures and interpersonal response styles. In the language of Higgins' (1989) model for the acquisition of self-evaluative standards, children are keenly aware of, and likely to internalize (i.e., develop representations of), interpersonal outcome contingencies in which they experienced positive or negative emotions. Following the Lewinian tradition, we refer to these experiences as *psychological situations*. In its strongest form, this assumption implies that each person's emotional repertoire develops almost exclusively through the experience of psychological situations involving the child and parent(s).

3. *Representations of self that are acquired on the basis of psychological*

situations involving the child and her/his caregiver(s) will possess inherent emotional and motivational significance. As Sroufe (1990) and others suggest, representations of self originate within an affective matrix formed by significant relationships. As children experience psychological situations in the context of interactions with parents, they acquire beliefs about who they are and about who they may (and may not) be. These self-beliefs will include dispositional and behavioral information (what I do, what I am like, what I may/may not do or be like) as well as emotional information (how it feels when I behave that way). Further, because such beliefs will have been associated with repeated experiences of positive or negative affect, their representations will be *high priority* elements within the individual's developing information processing system, which itself will become increasingly attuned to the self-evaluation process (Dweck, 1991). In other words, self-beliefs come to matter more and more to the individual, as a result of their associations with pleasant or unpleasant feelings.

4. *Self-evaluation is a continuous cognitive-regulatory process that can, via its developmental basis in fundamental aspects of emotion and cognition, render the individual vulnerable to chronic negative affect.* The question of whether the *self* is distinct from other social constructs has been hotly debated (Higgins & Bargh, 1987; Linville & Carlston, in press). My assertion here is that self-evaluative cognition, although sharing many features of social cognition in general, is not *just* another form of social cognition. Although in many respects the self can be construed using the same principles of information processing as other social constructs and categories (Kihlstrom & Cantor, 1984), it is unique in terms of the circumstances under which it is acquired and, therefore, in its emotional and adaptive significance (Strauman & Higgins, 1993). Furthermore, because a child's emotional state depends largely on whether her or his behavior is sufficiently congruent with situationally relevant standards, over time children develop the capacity for continuous, largely unintended self-evaluation. In short, self-evaluation constitutes a locus for the interface of biological systems subserving emotion with cognitive processes embodying the individual's emotionally significant goals and standards.

These assumptions are intended as a basis upon which to consider self-evaluation as a source of vulnerability to dysphoric affect. The perspective on depression presented herein that self-evaluation is *inherently* linked with emotion, including facial-efferent, neuroendocrine, and autonomic systems. Cognitive models of depression have been criticized for failing to address how abstract/symbolic information processing (e.g., semantic knowledge, declarative memory) becomes functionally associated with brainstem, limbic, and cortical systems controlling emotional responses. My view is that this criticism reflects a misunderstanding regarding the nature of cognition. Cognitive processes are never entirely independent of other adaptational processes (such as emotion) within the organism (Panksepp, 1992). In some respects, *information processing* is a misnomer; more accurately, *cognition* involves the processing of information about stimuli per se, and *emotion* involves the processing of information about the adaptive significance of stimuli (LeDoux, 1989). Whereas it is certainly the case that the specifics of such a functional link remain to be delineated, there is little reason to doubt that the link exists.

A second implication of these assumptions is that psychological processes underlying depressive vulnerability are likely to be habitual and highly efficient and thus need not be accessible to awareness. It is a truism that people cannot always identify the reasons why they feel or behave in certain ways or the means by which they draw conclusions (e.g., Nisbett & Wilson, 1977). A number of investigators have reported unconscious, unintended influences on self-concept, self-evaluation, and affect (for a review, see Higgins & Bargh, 1987). In this respect, self-evaluation is very much like other forms of cognitive activity. Therefore, I presume that the process of self-regulation involves the interplay of conscious and unconscious factors (Higgins, 1990).

Both research and theory suggest that certain types of self-beliefs are particularly likely to be associated with emotional vulnerability (Higgins, 1990). Such beliefs are emotionally significant because they embody goals for behavior, formed within the context of parent–child interactions and representing desirable and undesirable attributions and actions. They are presumed to take the form of cognitive structures (Strauman & Higgins, 1993). These self-evaluative cognitive structures are referred to as *self-guides*. I argue that self-guides are distinctive in several respects. Because they possess certain characteristics of cognitive structures (or representations within a larger memory structure), they can be studied using cognitive-experimental techniques. And more importantly, self-guides are utilized continuously, with or without awareness, to perceive, interpret, and respond to events in the ongoing stream of social interactions. It is this continuing role in self-evaluation that makes self-guides potential determinants of affective vulnerability.

OUTLINE OF THE MODEL

I now describe a hypothetical self-evaluative *pathway* to depression. The outline, shown as Table 8.1, is comprised of four segments, which are ordered chronologically (or more properly, developmentally). I prefer to think of the model as an approximate sequence of psychological events occurring over a period of many years rather than as a formal progression of stages. Although the model is meant to incorporate both social-cognitive

TABLE 14.1
Self-Evaluation-Based Vulnerability to Depression

A. *Predisposing factors*

   1. Individual differences in the intensity or regulation of emotional states
   2. Individual differences in emotional learning, i.e., construing and representing information about adaptively significant stimuli
   3. Traumatic early life events

B. *Factors influencing the development of self-representations and self-evaluation*
   1. Personality structure and maturation
   2. Parenting styles

C. *Factors triggering negative self-evaluation*
   1. Within-self discrepancy
   2. Current life events or difficulties
   3. Negative mood

D. *Final common pathways to depression*

---

and neurobiological viewpoints, in keeping with the theme of this volume I emphasize the former. The presentation is at a rather abstract level, but periodically I refer to particular studies or findings.

Predisposing Factors

Let me begin the presentation by considering briefly the role of biology in a theory of depression. Much of the polarization between biological and psychological perspectives on depression arises from an inadequate appreciation for the complex relations between psychosocial and neurophysiological factors in the etiology and pathogenesis of emotional disorders (Gabbard, 1992). As with most dichotomous classifications, the distinction between psychological and biological causation is oversimplified and artificial. Depression is best construed as an organism-wide failure of regulation originating within response systems most closely linked with cognition and adaptation (Whybrow, Akiskal, & McKinney, 1984). It is a profound inability to *cope with life*, one in which the individual's capacity to pursue positive states and modulate negative ones becomes impaired. It should be noted that there are some people for whom a biological propensity to dysregulation is so dominant that psychological factors play a minor role. As suggested by Post (1992) in a provocative discussion of how psychological stresses are *transduced* into neurochemical abnormalities, this is particularly likely for individuals who already have experienced multiple episodes of depression.

Conversely, psychological models of depression sometimes neglect biological considerations. As stated above, some cognitive theories oversimplify (and even overlook) the critical interface between high-level information processing and biological systems. How does a negative self-schema (presuming that such a hypothetical cognitive structure is causally related to depression) come to be associated with changes in appetite, sleep architecture, sexual desire, and neuroendocrine activity? How do the kinds of representations typically studied in cognitive laboratories ultimately influence biological response systems? In brief, my approach to this issue is to argue as follows:

- Both cognition and emotion operate in the service of adaptation.
- Cognition involves the representation and processing of information about the environment, whereas emotion involves the representation and processing of information about the significance of the environment for the individual.
- Cognition and emotion are interdependent processes, both neuroanatomically and psychologically.
- This functional interdependence ensures that information with adaptive significance is directed in the most efficient way possible to all of the organism's available response systems.
- Because of the social nature of human existence, cognitive and emotional development are inevitably linked with socialization, and in particular, relations between a child and her or his parents or caretakers.
- Specialized cognitive processes involving attention, categorization, and memory develop to construe and represent interpersonal response contingencies.
- Specialized emotional and motivational response systems, involving inborn and acquired facets, develop to regulate behaviors associated with high probabilities of positive or negative interpersonal outcomes.

What I am suggesting is that humans are prepared to organize emotional responses primarily around certain categories of personal knowledge and come to do so with increasing efficiency (Oatley, 1985). The child's emerging understanding of who he or she is, may be, and may not be *becomes* organized, in part, by means of the emotional states with which self-beliefs are associated. Even in their earliest forms, self-evaluative beliefs evolve from experiences in which salient interceptive states and conspicuous behaviors of significant others feature prominently. So it is no mystery that cognitive processes become associated with emotional response tendencies. Cognition and emotion, particularly in the realm of self-evaluation, are simply two sides of the same adaptive coin. Rather, the question is how did psychologists come to view cognition and emotion as essentially nonoverlapping domains?

Individual Differences in the Intensity or Regulation of Emotional States. A great deal has been written about temperament and its influence on emotion and behavior. Still, we know comparatively little about how much variability in behavior in general, and emotional vulnerability in particular, is accounted for by inherited or inborn factors and how much by the influence of learning and memory processes (even at the earliest stages of life) on those factors (Bates, 1989). Such a dichotomy is itself misleading. This state of affairs is exacerbated by the fact that many of the behaviors regarded as indicators of temperament (or of emotion) are influenced substantially by learning and memory processes (Steinmetz, in press). Although there undoubtedly are inherited differences in the intensity and/or regulation of emotional states, those differences rarely operate in isolation and are immediately modified by the initiation of social experience (Derryberry & Tucker, 1992). Accordingly, I focus on how temperament interacts with learning to influence the acquisition and content of self-evaluative standards and related self-regulatory goals. Temperament here is understood as individual differences in predispositions toward particular kinds of emotional states in the presence or absence of certain triggers (Gray, 1991).

Is it meaningful to suggest that certain individuals are born to depression? Aside from recent discoveries regarding specific genetic vulnerabilities to bipolar illness in certain groups, there remains as much speculation as solid evidence concerning genetic vulnerability to affective disorder. The greatest difficulty in specifying genetic influences on emotional vulnerability is to delineate the pathway(s) from genotype to phenotype (Kendler et al., 1993), either for particular subtypes of depression or for affective dysregulation in general. The developmental histories of self-representation and self-evaluation are closely interconnected with affect regulation (Westen, 1994). Thus, can we identify pathways by which inborn variability in the intensity and modulation of affect might influence subsequent self-evaluation (goals)?

Recent research suggests several possible links between temperament and self-evaluation. Studies of the neurobiology of impulsivity and neuroticism, utilizing Gray's model of the neuropsychology of temperament (Gray, 1991), have demonstrated that individuals at extremes of particular temperament dimensions are likely to manifest involuntary patterns of attention allocation and memory, both of which play important roles in monitoring and regulating social behavior (Derryberry & Tucker, 1991). For instance, highly impulsive individuals appear to be unusually sensitive to cues for *reward* and unusually *in*sensitive to cues for danger or *punishment*. Gray's model postulates that individual differences in dimensions of personality are produced by differences in the activity and interactions among fundamental *emotion systems* controlling approach and withdrawal tendencies in response to appetitive and aversive stimuli. Inborn divergences in such basic mechanisms as attending to (or away from) signals for impending reward or punishment, thresholds for registration and encoding of visceral sensations, and efficiency of learning via classical or operant conditioning in which emotional states are involved all influence affective responses to social situations and experiences.

Temperament thus shapes the outcome of the development of self-evaluation through its effect on the *hardware* of cognition and emotion (Zuckerman, 1991). For example, two infants might differ in the intensity with which they experience, and react to, positive or negative reinforcers within their social environments. These differences would likely be associated with different learning curves for representation of environmental contingencies associated with pain and its cessation and avoidance (Depue & Iacono, 1989). Over time, one child learns that her or his world is an emotionally potent one in which he or she is continuously experiencing intense emotions. The infant constructs a working model of the environment in which he or she is likely to have such intense reactions to significant others and a working model of self as emotionally labile and therefore greatly influenced by the actions of significant others. Another pair of children might vary in their patterns of attending to signals for reward versus frustrative nonreward; such a contrast would tend to be associated with differences in how the children responded to their parents' efforts to supply and withhold affection and approval as a motivator (Zuckerman, 1991).

Higgins (in press) has presented a model of the development of self-regulation that postulates two distinct systems for self-evaluation, distinguishable in terms of outcome focus: a *positive outcome focus* regulatory system that involves maximizing positive outcomes (pleasure) and a *negative outcome focus* regulatory system that involves minimizing negative outcomes (pain). The two systems function semiautonomously, and individual differences would be expected in relative dominance between the systems based on inborn factors, socialization, and their interaction. This sort of model has the important advantage of serving as a conceptual bridge between the heretofore unrelated domains of infant temperament and adult self-evaluation.

The notion that a bidirectional path of influence exists between neurobiological and psychological influences on behavior also has implications for the link between temperament and self-evaluation (Derryberry & Reed, in press). For example, Kagan and his colleagues observed that a substantial proportion of infants characterized as extreme on certain temperament dimensions at 3 months of age appeared progressively less extreme at successive points of development (Kagan, Reznick, & Snidman, 1988). Kagan et al. attributed much of that change to parents' adapting their socialization practices to the unique temperaments of their young children. In turn, adaptations of child-parent interactions facilitate neurobiological changes leading to less extreme emotional responses and help provide the children with psychological mechanisms for tolerating and modulating affect (Dodge, 1986). Children whose parents successfully modified their rearing styles to the child's temperament should be less likely to have evolved extreme, harsh, or frightening beliefs about themselves in relation to their parents than children whose families were not as effective in accommodating to their inborn emotional reaction patterns (Derryberry & Reed, in press). The latter group of children will be at greater risk for the emergence of chronic negative self-evaluation and affective disorders.

Individual Differences in Emotional Learning. In addition to variability in how people attend and respond to their environments, there is great diversity in people's learning of emotional consequences for behavior and the circumstances related to those consequences—that is, the self-evaluative goals individuals acquire and the contingencies linking those goals with positive or negative affect. Although cognitive theories of emotional disorders necessarily presuppose that people learn to associate certain aspects of themselves or their environments with the probability of positive or negative outcomes, in general they have not made explicit what influences the strength of association.

Evidence for the relevance of individual differences in emotional learning is plentiful. Lang's cognitive-psychophysiological approach to fear and anxiety (e.g., Lang, 1984) is an effort to conceptualize how organisms comprehend and represent associations between stimuli and emotional responses. Studies of emotional processing demonstrate the importance of individual differences in the capacity to tolerate anxiety sufficiently to permit extinction of conditioned fear responses (Leventhal & Tomarken, 1986). Mineka's investigations of the acquisition and extinction of fears and phobias (Mineka, 1985, 1987) provide compelling testimony that in domains for which species are prepared to learn associations between particular classes of stimuli and emotional responses, learning is both efficient and highly resistant to change. Likewise, studies of individual differences in electrodermal conditioning to emotional facial configurations (e.g., Dimberg & Ohman, 1983; Lanzetta & Orr, 1980) suggest a mechanism for associating interpersonal stimuli and affective responses.

Acquisition of conditioned or symbolic associations between interpersonal stimuli and emotional response patterns is a necessary condition for the emergence of self-guides. The self-beliefs of individuals predisposed to more intense emotional responses (i.e., who internalize beliefs about themselves on the basis of fewer-than-average trials, or who develop more extensive, immediately accessible, and/or polarized representations) will differ substantially from self-beliefs of individuals who are not as emotionally reactive. The former would be more profoundly influenced by single experiences, or psychological situations occurring infrequently, than the latter. In addition, the former may be more vulnerable to affective disorders, anxiety, and other forms of psychopathology.

Traumatic Early Life Events. Within the scope of this perspective on depression, traumatic events occurring early in life are particularly deleterious to the individual's well-being, both during childhood and in subsequent years (Brown & Harris, 1978). Increasing attention is being paid to this risk factor, but as yet little empirical research has emerged concerning the influence of childhood trauma on adult self-evaluation. Given our discussion concerning how emotional patterns in childhood influence the acquisition of self-beliefs, however, such a contributory causal link is a compelling possibility.

There are at least two mechanisms by which exposure to childhood trauma could increase self-evaluation-based emotional vulnerability. From a neurobiological standpoint, such experiences can be intense enough to cause potentially permanent changes in the neural substrates of emotion, particularly with regard to modulatory mechanisms that permit the individual to process and ultimately resolve emotion-inducing events (Tucker, 1992). Victims of childhood abuse frequently report periods of intrusive memories and feelings related to remote abuse events. These intrusions are accompanied by high levels of sympathetic arousal, as if the nervous system were stuck in an acute reaction to the trauma (Litz & Keane, 1989). This route of influence would be essentially content-free, that is, there would be no necessary relation between the meaning of the traumatic event itself and subsequent patterns of negative self-evaluation.

In addition, ideas or images related to the original trauma could act as internally generated priming stimuli eliciting negative affect, even in the absence of an objective loss or stressor. This route is congruent with psychodynamic observations that chronic stress or loss early in life can render people vulnerable to depression as adults (Bibring, 1953). It is also supported by the results of a series of priming studies based on self-discrepancy theory (for a review, see Strauman & Higgins, 1993). In those studies, normal as well as depressed subjects were covertly exposed to stimuli related to their own problematic self-beliefs (which, in some cases, were associated with memories of negative experiences). We observed that such priming consistently led to increased negative affect. Thus, encounters with situations bearing literal or symbolic resemblance to previous stress or loss would be expected to activate the same pattern of emotional reaction as the original stresses.

Several recent studies have examined affective vulnerability in individuals with histories of sexual abuse or other childhood traumatic experiences. Women who experienced childhood sexual abuse but were relatively asymptomatic prior to the onset of depression in adulthood frequently manifest posttraumatic symptoms, such as intrusive memories, exaggerated startle response, and sympathetic hyperarousal (Kuyken & Brewin, 1994). Although the depression is probably not a direct result of childhood trauma, individuals with such a history may report more severe neurovegetative symptoms, greater suicidal ideation, and greater associated anxiety, all of which suggest the impact of some additional mechanism of vulnerability as compared with depressed patients not having trauma histories (Friedman, 1988). The increased accessibility of unpleasant memories experienced by such depressed individuals is likely to affect self-concept and self-evaluation and in so doing contribute to the maintenance of the depressed state.

Factors Influencing the Development of Self-Representations and Self-Evaluation

Perhaps the most significant interpersonal task for children is the challenge of learning who they are, who they might or must be, and who they must not be, usually within the context of their family. In many respects this knowledge is constructed, rather than passively acquired, as children attempt to make sense of their experiences. Social and personality psychology has learned a great deal regarding the ways in which meaning is construed, represented, and utilized. In this section I present two developmentally based theories of self-knowledge: one a social-cognitive approach to the acquisition of self-beliefs, and the other addressing individual differences in the maturity of self-representations.

Cognitive and Personality Maturation. The literature on the development of the self-system describes dramatic changes in children's self-beliefs and self-evaluation from infancy through adolescence (Harter, 1983). Higgins (1989) examined how developmentally induced changes in children's representational capacities bring about changes in aspects of the self-system relevant to the emergence of affective vulnerability. Summarized next are a series of changes in children's capacity to form representations of self and others and their implications for the nature and emotional consequences of self-beliefs.

By the end of the first year of life, children are capable of representing the relation between two events, such as the relation between a behavior produced by them and their mother's response. This ability permits children to generate and interpret interpersonal (and intrapersonal) signals and to experience emotions that involve anticipating the occurrence of some event. Even at this early stage, children can experience basic psychological situations: the presence or absence of positive outcomes, and the presence or absence of negative outcomes. Thus, from the time that children begin to form representations of interpersonal experiences, those representations will be associated with emotional states if the events themselves elicited affect. These representations, although relatively primitive, nonetheless embody the child's psychological situation.

A dramatic shift in children's ability to represent events occurs between 18 months and 2 years of age (Werner & Kaplan, 1963): Children become capable of recognizing a higher order relation that exists between two other relations. As a consequence, children can now comprehend a reciprocal relationship between themselves and another person (Harter, 1983). For instance, they can grasp the relation between a self-feature (e.g., throwing a tantrum) and a particular response by a parent (e.g., being ignored). Thus, children can now represent *self-other contingencies*, which are precursors of mature self-evaluative standards. Such contingencies can be used to self-regulate so as to avoid or approach different psychological situations. This capacity allows children to deal more successfully with social demands, leading to feelings of pride and joy; conversely, the possibility of failure introduces feelings of abandonment and rejection by others.

Between the ages of 4 and 6, children's representational capacity shifts from egocentric to nonegocentric thought (Piaget, 1965). The intellectual changes at this stage are reflected in children's increased ability to infer the thoughts, expectations, motives, and intentions of others (Shantz, 1983), as well as increased ability to use sources of information beyond the immediate situation when evaluating self or others (Ruble & Rholes, 1981). Children can now regulate and evaluate their behavior in terms of a standard that involves another person's viewpoint. Such standards have the important benefit of increasing the range of circumstances under which children can assert self-control and experience positive emotions. However, this new capacity to self-evaluate in terms of a set of standards contributes to new emotional vulnerabilities, such as guilt, apprehension, and embarrassment.

Between 9 and 11 years of age children become capable of making dispositional judgments about self and others, so that children's self-concepts can now contain dispositional attributes (friendly, honest, intelligent, etc.). Therefore, a psychological situation (and the emotions that result) can be induced not only from evaluation of one's current performance but also by activating the representation of a trait belief ("I am intelligent"; "I am not popular"). In addition, the self-evaluation process for a single self-feature could activate evaluation along other trait dimensions because of spreading activation among interconnected self-beliefs. At this point, the possibility of a structural source of vulnerability such as a *depressive self-schema* begins to emerge.

Finally, between 13 and 16 years of age children become capable of interrelating different perspectives on the self (Fischer, 1980). Adolescents can now integrate information about distinct traits into higher order abstractions. This development could further increase the structural interconnectedness among adolescents' self-attributes, with concomitant implications for increased emotional vulnerability. In the case of within-self discrepancies, this is likely to increase vulnerability to new global negative psychological situations, such as the overgeneralizations and negative views of self, world, and future (Beck's [1976] "negative cognitive triad") described in the depression literature.

The Piagetian approach to changes in the structure and differentiation of knowledge upon which Higgins' model is based can be extended to changes in personality as a whole. Although cognitive theories of the self typically do not emphasize qualitative stages in the development of knowledge and information processing, they are compatible with such a focus. For instance, it is logical to postulate that if individuals at varying stages of development manifest systematic differences in how they think, then such differences should also be evident in how they evaluate themselves (Lane & Schwartz, 1987). Thus, the relative immaturity versus maturity of self-representations should influence the likelihood of their association with emotional outcomes (Strauman, Sisco, & Keehn, 1994).

One promising framework to integrating developmental perspectives on personality with the study of self-representation is Loevinger's theory of ego development (Loevinger, 1976). The theory conceptualizes ego as an organized unity of impulse control, character, style of interpersonal relations, and self-conception. Ego level reflects successive degrees of complexity and synthesis in organizing cognition, emotion, and behavior. Loevinger's approach implies that a person's behavior and conscious experience will vary in important respects as a function of the perceiver's maturity. As such, there should be significant variability in the structure and content of self-representations cross-sectionally and in the same subjects over time, and, more specifically, in the quality and magnitude of associations between self-guides and affective states.

Consider a few general predictions concerning the possible role of personality in self-evaluation-based vulnerability to depression. Self-beliefs acquired at earlier points in development should tend to be more simplistic, extreme, and absolute than self-beliefs acquired at a subsequent level of maturation (Shapiro, 1963). If such beliefs persist and remain highly accessible, then they are likely to play an inappropriately dominant role in self-evaluation, with potentially problematic consequences (Strauman, 1989b). Relatively little is known about the fate of early self-representations—whether and how they are modified in the course of cognitive and personality maturation. Individuals who remain at less mature levels of ego development into adulthood would be likely to possess less complex, abstract, and flexible self-guides. And even among more mature individuals, early self-representations might persist because they were associated with unusually intense or prolonged emotional states (e.g., extremes of temperament or experiences of abuse).

Similarly, self-beliefs should reflect the dominant motivational orientations of individuals at different points in development. Representations of self and others acquired at the so-called anaclitic stage, a relatively immature point in development, would be likely to reflect concerns about dependency, nurturance, support, approval, and loss. Representations acquired at the introjective stage, a more mature point in development, would tend to reflect concerns about achievement, recognition, social comparison, and guilt (Blatt, 1974). As such, different self-representations would be expected to contribute to different types of emotional vulnerability (in Blatt's model, dependency vs. self-criticism) and to be activated in response to different life circumstances (Zuroff & Mongrain, 1987).

Parenting Styles. I already have implied that the formation of the self-concept is significantly influenced by the individual's socialization history, which in turn is dominated by parent–child relations. Researchers have identified several aspects of parent–child interactions that may contribute to self-evaluation-based depressive vulnerability: (a) characteristic patterns of rewards and punishments, including how parents express and withhold love and affection and how they administer or withhold sanctions and discipline; (b) psychological situations that children experience within their modal patterns of interactions with parents; (c) the representations that children construct on the basis of interactions with parents and resulting psychological situations; and (d) emotional response patterns derived from children's expanding base of self-representations.

According to this framework, different types of parent–child interactions will involve the child experiencing different types of psychological situations. Such patterns, in turn, are associated with the acquisition of particular representations involving self–other contingencies: "When I do this, my parents respond like that, which makes me feel sad (angry, frightened, etc.)". With sufficient cognitive maturation, the representations begin to take the form of what was labeled *self-guides*: representations of behaviors or attributes that constitute standards against which the child learns to compare his or her behavior (Strauman, 1992). And finally, different types of self-guides come to be associated with different emotional predispositions, as is elaborated on in the next section. *Whenever a self-guide is activated for use in self-evaluation (intentionally or unintentionally), the potential exists for the specific positive or negative emotional state associated with that self-guide.*

Reviews of the parenting styles in literature (e.g., Maccoby & Martin, 1983) have identified parental behaviors that are especially likely to be associated with vulnerability to negative emotions in children, including over-permissiveness, excessive control, authoritarianism, and lack of warmth. Two basic dimensions have been proposed to link socialization patterns with emotional vulnerabilities (Higgins, 1989). Rearing patterns that would be expected to produce the psychological situation of an absence of positive outcomes in children (such as minimal attention to a child's needs, disengagement or withdrawal from the child) are associated with children feeling dejection-related emotions like sadness, lethargy, and lack of enthusiasm. Conversely, socialization patterns that would be expected to result in the psychological situation of the presence of negative outcomes in children (such as yelling, being intrusive, or overstimulating) are associated with children experiencing agitation-related emotions such as wariness, restlessness, or panic. These two dimensions are hypothesized to relate to different classes of self-guides, and, in turn, different kinds of affective states. A recent investigation (Manian, Denney, & Strauman, 1995) found support for this two-dimensional scheme in a retrospective study of parenting style.

This model of self and depression emphasizes the combined cognitive/affective nature of self-representations, which embody both the self-regulatory goals derived from the individual's socialization history and the emotional contingencies associated with those goals. Whatever influences a child's learning who they are, must be, and must not be will have an effect on whether that child will become vulnerable to emotional distress as a function of self-evaluation. It is from this perspective that the confluence of psychological and biological processes underlying self-evaluation is most clearly seen. Successful adaptation during childhood is determined largely by how well the child can fulfill the expectations of her or his parents. Thus, it is no surprise that the psychological and biological mechanisms most relevant for adaptation would come to be focused on the evaluation and regulation of one's behavior within the context of socialization.

Factors Triggering Negative Self-Evaluation

The first two parts of the proposed model pertain to the developmental history of self-evaluation. The remaining sections consider proximal and concurrent influences of self-evaluation on affect. Most theories of the self assign a central role to self-beliefs in the ongoing process of self-regulation. Among contemporary investigators, the control-theory perspective on self-regulation proposed by Carver and Scheier has been particularly influential. Carver and Scheier (1981, 1983) characterized human behavior as a process of moving toward various kinds of goal representations, guided by a feedback control system. Their cybernetic model stipulates that people continuously monitor their behavior and attributes and compare them to salient standards, usually reflecting some predefined hierarchy of goals that the individual is motivated to achieve (or avoid). Social psychologists have identified numerous influences on the emotional outcomes of this self-regulation process (Linville & Carlston, in press), of which several are of particular relevance for vulnerability to depression.

Within-Self Inconsistency. The notion that people who hold incompatible or conflicting beliefs about themselves are likely to experience discomfort has a long and well-established history in psychology. Classic theories relating self and affect held that self-inconsistencies produced emotional problems (e.g., Freud, 1923/1961; Rogers, 1961). Most of these theories focused on the process of self-evaluation, which was viewed as a continuous influence of the person's emotional state that did not require her or his direct awareness to operate. However, many of these theories were limited by not predicting which kinds of negative emotional states will be associated with particular kinds of incompatibilities.

Self-discrepancy theory (Higgins, 1987, 1989) is a model of self and affect that offers some advantages over preceding theories upon which it is based. The theory distinguishes among domains of self-representations, including (a) the *actual* self, a person's representation of the attributes that he or she or a significant other believe he or she actually possesses; (b) the *ideal* self, a representation of the attributes that he or she or another would ideally like him or her to possess; and (c) the *ought* self, a representation of the attributes that he or she or another believes he or she should or ought to possess. The actual self constitutes what is typically meant by a person's self-concept; the ideal and ought self-representations are self-directive standards or self-guides.

Different types of discrepancy between the actual self and specific self-guides reflect particular negative psychological situations and hence are associated with particular motivational and emotional states. A discrepancy between the actual self-state and an ideal self-guide signifies an absence of positive outcomes and so is associated with dejection-related emotions like sadness, disappointment, and dissatisfaction. A discrepancy between the actual self-state and an ought self-guide signifies the presence of negative outcomes and so is associated with agitation-related emotions, such as feeling fearful, apprehensive, guilty, or anxious. Both correlational (Higgins, Klein, & Strauman, 1985; Strauman & Higgins, 1988) and experimental (Higgins, Bond, Klein, Strauman, 1986; Strauman & Higgins, 1987; Strauman, 1989a) studies have confirmed the hypothesized links between self-discrepancies and specific kinds of negative affect.

Within the present model, self-discrepancies (as cognitive structures that induce negative emotional states when activated) can be contributory vulnerability factors in the onset and maintenance of emotional disorders. Self-discrepancy theory proposes that it is the relation among self-beliefs (e.g., actual self, ideal and ought self-guides) that produces emotional vulnerabilities, rather than the content of self-beliefs per se. Chronic actual:ideal discrepancy (AI) is postulated to represent a specific vulnerability factor for depression, and chronic actual: ought discrepancy (AO) is postulated to represent a specific vulnerability factor for anxiety states (Strauman, 1989a). Higgins, Bond, et al. (1986) demonstrated that the magnitude, type, and accessibility of self-discrepancies predict the type and intensity of emotional vulnerability that individuals experience when discrepancies are activated.

Research in unselected, analogue, and clinical samples supports the prediction that AO discrepancy is specifically related to anxiety, whereas AI discrepancy is specifically related to depressive symptoms. Strauman and Higgins (1988) observed that AO discriminantly predicted vulnerability to psychological (e.g., fear of negative evaluation) and physiological (restlessness, agitation) manifestations of anxiety 2 months later, whereas AI predicted subsequent vulnerability to depressive affect as well as to physiological symptoms such as anhedonia and decreased energy. Experimental studies have demonstrated a causal relation between activation of particular self-discrepancies and induction of different types of negative affect. Activating a self-discrepancy (by experimentally manipulating features of the immediate context) induces the negative psychological situation the discrepancy represents, thereby producing the associated emotional state with or without the awareness of the individual.

Strauman and Higgins (1987) used a covert, idiographic priming technique to test several aspects of self-discrepancy theory relevant to the present model. Two studies examined the role of matching (synonymous), nonmatching (unrelated), and mismatching (antonymous) pairs of self-state attributes in inducing emotional states through contextual priming. Activation of a self-guide attribute that was a mismatch with an actual-self attribute induced the predicted negative emotional responses. Strauman (1989a) replicated these findings in an experimental study comparing diagnosed depressives with social phobics and age-matched controls.

The presence of chronically accessible self-discrepancies increases the likelihood that the individual will experience repeated bouts of negative affect, which in combination with other risk factors creates the risk of a more serious emotional problem (Strauman, 1989a, 1992). To the extent that the individual's accessible self-guides are associated with other emotionally potent representations, activating a self-discrepancy could create a chain reaction of negative self-evaluation and resultant negative affect—all without the conscious participation of the individual being necessary. Other research has linked the self-guides and self-discrepancies of adults with memories of childhood experiences involving the kinds of psychological situations that would be expected to contribute to the formation of such guides (Strauman, 1990, 1992). These memories become more highly accessible when self-discrepancies are activated, creating a greater tendency for the negative thought patterns characteristic of depression. Follow-up data indicate that self-discrepancies are stable, as are their associations with memories for negative childhood events and with chronic negative affect (Strauman, 1994a). In our most recent study, we observed that clinically depressed and anxious individuals, who characterized by relatively higher levels of AI versus AO discrepancy respectively, manifested reduced levels of discrepancy and emotional sensitivity to covert self-guide priming following cognitive-behavioral psychotherapy (Strauman, 1994b). Repeated activation of self-discrepancies, regardless of its source, may bring the individual closer to the final common pathway in which dysphoric states culminate in depression.

Current Life Events or Difficulties. Perhaps the best-documented psychosocial risk factor for depression is the presence of one or more recent stressful life events (Lewinsohn, Hoberman, & Rosenbaum, 1988). Risk for depression and other forms of psychopathology increases in proportion to the number and severity of life events experienced within the past year (Lin, Dean, & Ensel, 1986). Many possible explanations, from neuroendocrine to sociological, have been proposed to account for the influence of life events on vulnerability to depression (Cohen & Wills, 1985), and it is unlikely that the various causal factors hypothesized are completely independent. I now focus briefly on how life events might relate to *self-evaluative* vulnerability to depression.

At least two possible associations between self-evaluation and life events or hassles have been suggested (e.g., Thoits, 1983). First, exposure to a stressful life event might reactivate memories of earlier unpleasant or traumatic experiences via the event's intensity and corresponding demand on emotion and memory systems (Kuyken & Brewin, 1994). That is, the quality or overall negativity of the individual's reaction to a current life experience might be sufficient to trigger memories of other unpleasant experiences, which, in turn, could influence the accessibility of self-representations and the outcome of self-evaluation. In essence, this pattern would constitute a mood-as-retrieval-cue phenomenon (see following), similar to the aforementioned finding that depressed adults with histories of childhood trauma often suddenly experience intrusive memories of the traumatic events, even if they have not recalled those events in years. From this logic it follows that the experience of negative psychological situations, however induced, may activate other representations embodying the same affective state.

An alternative link between life events and self-evaluation would be via the individual's interpretation of the current situation, which could activate self-referential cognitive structures (self-guides, self-discrepancies, self-schemas, etc.) through category resemblance. For instance, having one's applications to graduate school rejected might activate previously acquired representations of self as failure (Segal, 1988). One may recognize in this description the phenomenon of depressive cognitive bias. The presence of a highly accessible AI discrepancy means that the individual is ready to construe situations to which the particular self-guide might be relevant as "another example of (for instance) me as a failure." With this type of association, the life event itself need not be a negatively valenced one; indeed, a wedding or graduation would serve just as well as context for construing failure or rejection as a divorce or bad report card.

Negative Mood. The chapters in this volume offer state-of-the-art reviews of the ways in which mood states and cognitive processes interact. Rather than attempting to summarize them here, I will just point out that there is ample evidence that negative affective states can increase self-critical thinking, pessimism, and the accessibility of negative self-beliefs and autobiographical memories. The current controversies in the mood-and-cognition literature involve the conditions qualifying the effects of mood on information processing. Nonetheless, whether a main-effect or interactive model is more appropriate for any particular case, negative mood is a probable contributor to increased accessibility of negative self-evaluation.

The Final Common Pathway

For individuals whose development and current self-evaluation have predisposed them to the experience of chronic periods of dysphoric affect, the possibility of depression is substantial. Whereas there is an enormous diversity of views concerning distal and proximal contributory factors in depression, there is little dispute that separate causal influences converge upon a final common pathway—the depressive episode. As such, depression linked to chronic negative self-evaluation is not likely to be distinguishable on the basis of symptomatology from depression resulting primarily from other influences. Also, it is not clear whether so-called cognitive depressions respond more favorably to cognitive-behavioral or other psychotherapy than so-called biological depressions (Elkin, 1994).

Neurobiologically, episodes of depression begin when dysregulation occurs in synaptic mechanisms in specific areas of the brain responsible for uptake and/or blockage of critical neurotransmitters (Whybrow et al., 1984). The dysregulation is presumed to occur as a result of continued intense negative emotional states causing pre- and post-synaptic regulatory mechanisms to exceed some threshold, beyond which recovery of normal emotional balance is not possible for months or years (Post, Ballenger, Uhde, Putnum, & Bunney, 1982). The neurobiological changes coincide with the appearance of *vegetative* symptoms (e.g., decreased appetite, changes in sleep patterns, decreased energy, loss of interest in sex) as well as the cognitive changes accompanying depression (Beck, Rush, Shaw, & Emery, 1979). It should be noted that this view of biological dysfunction applies as well to self-evaluation-based depression as it does to other hypothesized types of affective disorder.

Regardless of the etiological sequence leading to a particular individual's depression, once the episode is under way predictable changes in thinking will occur (Kovacs & Beck, 1978). It is here that cognitive approaches to depression have had their clearest application. Not only are preexisting patterns of negative self-evaluation likely to be exacerbated, but new sources of cognitively mediated vulnerability to negative affect also may arise. Generalized hopelessness, global negative self-evaluation, pessimism, and other negative thought patterns characteristic of depression increase the likelihood that everyday experiences will be interpreted in ways that intensify suffering and delay or prevent recovery (Teasdale, 1988). The common observation that some depressed individuals appear to seek out negative experiences is a manifestation of the profound cognitive changes brought on by the episode itself, as though the person's goals for self-evaluation and social perception have become distorted.

In addition, the experience of depression may have a more lasting influence on self-evaluation. Teasdale and Dent (1987) and others found that people who have ostensibly recovered from a depressive episode manifest self-evaluative tendencies significantly more negative than people who have never been depressed. Thus, an episode of depression is likely to bring about lasting alterations in social cognition, changing the rules under which goals and affective states interact as well as the goals themselves. The extent (if any) to which neurobiological changes are responsible for such alterations is still unclear. Post (1992) hypothesized that initial episodes of depression (which in his view are more likely to be the result of psychological factors) modify critical neurotransmitter thresholds, increasing vulnerability to further episodes and transforming the disorder into a progressively more biological phenomenon. Post's hypothesis underscores the urgency of intervening with vulnerable individuals (in this context, people manifesting chronic negative self-evaluation) to prevent the initial depressive episode.

CONCLUSION

I am hardly the first to emphasize the significance of self-evaluation as a potential locus for vulnerability to depression. Both biologically oriented and psychologically oriented theorists have identified self-evaluation as a route by which other risk factors may operate to create and maintain depressive episodes. These authors have noted the role of self-evaluation in determining the individual's ongoing emotional status, as well as its origins in critical developmental sequences for emotional response and regulatory systems. My purpose in this chapter has been to organize existing findings into a conceptual framework for generating testable predictions regarding how self-evaluation (as a fundamental goal process) might lead to chronic negative affect culminating in clinical depression.

It must be stressed that this model is a preliminary one, yet to be tested as such. Our own research has examined particular aspects of the model, such as the immediate emotional changes following covert activation of self-discrepancies, but there remains a great deal to be explored. It is also important to recognize that testing any theory of depression is a daunting task, given the likelihood that developmental factors (biological and psychological) are involved and the logistic challenges inherent in prospective research. Finally, the model is probably on firmer ground in some respects (its social-cognitive aspects) than in others (e.g., developmental neurobiology).

Although at this stage in the evolution of the model caveats might seem obvious, let me list two important ones. First, not all self-beliefs are acquired in the way that my developmental hypotheses suggest. Certainly each of us holds many beliefs or bits of knowledge about ourselves that were not constructed early in life or that carry little self-evaluative significance but nonetheless are frequently utilized in ongoing social and self-perception. The model should not be seen as implying that self-guides (as defined earlier) are the only type of self-beliefs potentially associated with chronic negative affect. There are numerous kinds of self-evaluative standards (see Higgins, Strauman, & Klein, 1986, for one taxonomy) that are utilized under particular circumstances. Second, the model presumes that self-guides are stable over periods of years or decades. Although it is reasonable to suggest that people's views of themselves do not change substantially across a lifetime, this permanence needs to be more carefully considered and documented. In several recent studies of self-guides and autobiographical memory (Strauman, 1994), my colleagues and I have observed that self-guides and their association with memories of emotionally congruent childhood experiences are stable across periods of several years. Further research should clarify this issue.

As the different fields represented within this chapter continue to advance, the notion of a self-evaluative pathway to depression (as well as other problems such as anxiety and eating disorders) will become, I believe, more familiar. The ultimate goal of self-evaluation amounts to nothing less than the well-being of the individual within her or his life circumstances. The emotional consequences of meeting or not meeting that superordinate goal are momentous. Depression can indeed be understood as a disorder in which the individual's strivings and feelings become dysregulated. Our knowledge of the psychological and biological processes underlying such regulation will serve well to pursue better treatment and prevention strategies for this immense problem.

REFERENCES

Abramson, L. Y., Metalsky, G. I., & Alloy, L. B. (1989). Hopelessness depression: A theory-based subtype of depression. *Psychological Review, 96*, 358-372.

Akiskal, H. S., & McKinney, W. T. (1975). Overview of recent research in depression: Integration of ten conceptual models into a comprehensive clinical framework. *Archives of General Psychiatry, 32*, 285-305.

Bates, J. E. (1989). Concepts and measurements of temperament. In G. Kohnstamm, J. Bates, & M. Rothbart (Eds.), *Temperament in childhood* (pp. 3-26). New York: Wiley.

Beck, A. T. (1976). *Cognitive therapy and the emotional disorders*. New York: Basic Books.

Beck, A. T., Rush, A. J., Shaw, B. F., & Emery, G. (1979). *Cognitive therapy of depression*. New York: Guilford.

Bibring, E. (1953). The mechanism of depression. In P. Greenacre (Ed.), *Affective disorders* (pp. 202-248). New York: International Universities Press.

Blatt, S. J. (1974). Levels of object representation in anaclitic and introjective depression. *Psychoanalytic Study of the Child, 29*, 107-157.

Brown, G. W., & Harris, T. (1978). *Social origins of depression*. London: Tavistock.

Carver, C. S., & Scheier, M. F. (1981). *Attention and self-regulation: A control-theory approach to human behavior*. New York: Springer-Verlag.

Carver, C. S., & Scheier, M. F. (1983). A control-theory model of normal behavior, and implications for problems in self-management. In P. C. Kendall (Ed.), *Advances in cognitive-behavioral research and therapy* (Vol. 2, pp. 27-194). New York: Academic Press.

Carver, C. S., & Scheier, M. F. (1990). Principles of self-regulation: Action and emotion. In E. T. Higgins & R. M. Sorrentino (Eds.), *Handbook of motivation and cognition: Foundations of social behavior* (Vol. 2, pp. 3-52). New York: Guilford.

Cohen, S., & Wills, T. A. (1985). Stress, social support, and the buffering hypothesis. *Psychological Bulletin, 1985*, 310-337.

Coryell, W., Winokur, G., Shea, T., Maser, J. D., Endicott, J., & Akiskal, H. (1994). The long-term stability of depressive subtypes. *American Journal of Psychiatry, 151*, 199-204.

Depue, R. A., & Iacono, W. G. (1989). Neurobehavioral aspects of affective disorders. *Annual

Review of Psychology, 40, 457-492.

Derryberry, D., & Reed, M. A. (in press). Temperament and the self-organization of personality. *Development and Psychopathology.*

Derryberry, D., & Tucker, D. M. (1991). The adaptive base of the neural hierarchy: Elementary motivational controls on network function. In R. Dienstbier (Ed.), *Nebraska Symposium on Motivation, Vol. 38: Perspectives on motivation* (pp. 289-342). Lincoln: University of Nebraska Press.

Derryberry, D., & Tucker, D. M. (1992). Neural mechanisms of emotion. *Journal of Consulting and Clinical Psychology, 60,* 329-338.

Dimberg, U., & Ohman, A. (1983). The effects of directional facial cues on electrodermal conditioning to facial stimuli. *Psychophysiology, 20,* 160-167.

Dodge, K. A. (1986). A social information processing model of social competence in children. In M. Perlmutter (Ed.), *Minnesota Symposium on Child Psychology* (Vol. 18, pp. 77-90). Hillsdale, NJ: Lawrence Erlbaum Associates.

Dweck, C. S. (1991). Self-theories and goals: Their role in motivation, personality, and development. In R. Dienstbier (Ed.), *Nebraska Symposium on Motivation, Vol. 38: Perspectives on motivation* (pp. 198-235). Lincoln: University of Nebraska Press.

Elkin, I. (1994). The NIMH Treatment of Depression Collaborative Research Program: Where we began and where we are. In Bergin, A., & Garfield, S. (Eds.), *Handbook of psychotherapy (2nd edition)* (pp. 114-139). New York: Guilford.

Fischer, K. W. (1980). A theory of cognitive development: The control and construction of hierarchies of skills. *Psychological Review, 87,* 477-531.

Freud, S. (1961). The ego and the id. In J. Strachey (Ed. and Trans.), *The standard edition of the complete psychological works of Sigmund Freud* (Vol. 19, pp. 3-66). London: Hogarth Press. (Original work published 1923)

Friedman, M. J. (1988). Toward rational pharmacotherapy for post-traumatic stress disorder: An interim report. *American Journal of Psychiatry, 145*(3), 281-285.

Gabbard, G. O. (1992). Psychodynamic psychiatry in the "decade of the brain." *American Journal of Psychiatry, 149,* 991-998.

Gray, J. A. (1991). The neuropsychology of temperament. In J. Strelau & A. Angeleitner (Eds.), *Explorations in temperament: International perspectives on theory and measurement* (pp. 105-128). New York: Plenum.

Harter, S. (1983). Developmental perspectives on the self-system. In P. H. Mussen (Ed.), *Handbook of child psychology: Vol. 4. Socialization, personality, and social development* (pp. 275-385). New York: Wiley.

Harter, S. (1986). Cognitive-developmental processes in the integration of concepts about emotions and the self. *Social Cognition, 4,* 119-151.

Higgins, E. T. (1987). Self-discrepancy: A theory relating self and affect. *Psychological Review, 94,* 319-340.

Higgins, E. T. (1989). Continuities and discontinuities in self-regulatory and self-evaluative processes: A developmental theory relating self and affect. *Journal of Personality, 57,* 407-444.

Higgins, E. T. (1990). Personality, social psychology, and person-situation relations: Standards and knowledge activation as a common language. In L. Pervin (Ed.), *Handbook of personality: Theory and research* (pp. 301-338). New York: Guilford.

Higgins, E. T. (in press). Ideals, oughts, and regulatory outcome focus: Relating affect and motivation to distinct pains and pleasures. In P. Gollwitzer & J. Bargh (Eds.), *Action science: Linking cognition and motivation to behavior.* Mahwah, NJ: Lawrence Erlbaum Associates.

Higgins, E. T., & Bargh, J. A. (1987). Social cognition and social perception. *Annual Review of Psychology, 38,* 369-425.

Higgins, E. T., Bond, R. N., Klein, R., & Strauman, T. (1986). Self-discrepancies and emotional vulnerability: How magnitude, accessibility and type of discrepancy influence affect. *Journal of Personality and Social Psychology, 51*, 1–15.

Higgins, E. T., Klein, R., & Strauman, T. J. (1985). Self-concept discrepancy theory: A psychological model for distinguishing among different aspects of depression and anxiety. *Social Cognition, 3,*(1), 51–76.

Higgins, E. T., Strauman, T. J., & Klein, R. (1986). Standards and the process of self-evaluation: Multiple affects from multiple stages. In R. Sorrentino & E. T. Higgins (Eds.), *Handbook of motivation and cognition: Foundations of social behavior* (pp. 3–47). New York: Guilford.

Kagan, J. Reznick, J. S., & Snidman, N. (1988). Biological bases of childhood shyness. *Science, 240*, 167–173.

Karasu, T. B. (1990a). Toward a clinical model of psychotherapy for depression, I: Systematic comparison of three psychotherapies. *American Journal of Psychiatry, 147*, 133–147.

Karasu, T. B. (1990b). Toward a clinical model of psychotherapy for depression, II: An integrative and selective treatment approach. *American Journal of Psychiatry, 147*, 269–278.

Kendler, K. S., Kessler, R. D., Neale, M. C., Heath, A. C., & Eaves, L. J. (1993). The prediction of major depression in women: Toward an integrated etiologic model. *Archives of General Psychiatry, 150*, 1139–1148.

Kessler, R. C., Kendler, K. S., Heath, A. C., Neale, M. C., & Eaves, L. J. (1992). Social support, depressed mood, and adjustment to stress: A genetic epistemological investigation. *Journal of Personality and Social Psychology, 62*, 257–272.

Kihlstrom, J. F., & Cantor, N. (1984). Mental representations of the self. *Advances in Experimental Social Psychology, 17*, 1–47.

Kovacs, M., & Beck, A. T. (1978). Maladaptive cognitive structure in depression. *American Journal of Psychiatry, 135*, 525–533.

Kuyken, W., & Brewin, C. R. (1994). Intrusive memories of childhood abuse during depressive episodes. *Behaviour Research and Therapy, 32*, 525–533.

Lane, R. D., & Schwartz, G. E. (1987). Levels of emotional awareness: A cognitive-developmental theory and its application to psychopathology. *American Journal of Psychiatry, 144*, 133–143.

Lang, P. J. (1984). Cognition in emotion: Concept and action. In C. Izard, J. Kagan, & R. Zajonc (Eds.), *Cognition, emotion, and behavior* (pp. 192–226). New York: Cambridge University Press.

Lanzetta, J. T., & Orr, S. P. (1980). Influence of facial expressions on the classical conditioning of fear. *Journal of Personality and Social Psychology, 39*, 1081–1087.

LeDoux, J. E. (1989). Cognitive–emotional interactions in the brain. *Cognition and Emotion, 3*, 267–289.

Leventhal, H., & Tomarken, A. J. (1986). Emotion: Today's problems. In M. Rosenzweig & L. Porter (Eds.), *Annual review of psychology* (pp. 118–150). Palo Alto, CA: Annual Reviews.

Lewinsohn, P. M., Hoberman, H. M., & Rosenbaum, M. (1988). A prospective study of risk factors for unipolar depression. *Journal of Abnormal Psychology, 97*, 251–264.

Lin, N., Dean, A., & Ensel, W. (1986). *Social support, life events, and depression*. New York: Academic Press.

Linville, P. W., & Carlston, D. E. (in press). Social cognition of the self. In P. G. Devine, D. L. Hamilton, & T. M. Ostrom (Eds.), *Social cognition: Its impact on social psychology*. New York: Academic Press.

Litz, B. T., & Keane, T. M. (1989). Information processing in anxiety disorders: Application to the understanding of post-traumatic stress disorder. *Clinical Psychology Review, 9*(2), 243–257.

Loevinger, J. (1976). *Ego development: Conceptions and theories*. San Francisco: Jossey-Bass.

Maccoby, E. E., & Martin, J. A. (1983). Socialization in the context of the family: Parent–child interaction. In P. H. Mussen (Ed.), *Handbook of child psychology, Vol. 4: Socialization, personality, and social development* (pp. 643–691). New York: Wiley.

Manian, N., Denney, N., & Strauman, T. J. (1995). *Self-discrepancy and parenting style, and their influence on emotional distress.* Manuscript submitted for publication.

Mineka, S. (1985). Animal models of anxiety-based disorders: Their usefulness and limitations. In A. Tuma & J. Maser (Eds.), *Anxiety and the anxiety disorders* (pp. 199–244). Hillsdale, NJ: Lawrence Erlbaum Associates.

Mineka, S. (1987). A primate model of phobic fears. In H. Eysenck & I. Martin (Eds.), *Theoretical foundations of behavior therapy* (pp. 81–111). New York: Plenum.

Nisbett, R. E., & Wilson, T. D. (1977). Telling more than we can know: Verbal reports on mental processes. *Psychological Review, 84*, 231–259.

Oatley, K. (1985). Representations of the physical and social world. In D. Oakley (Ed.), *Brain and mind* (pp. 32–58). New York: Methuen.

Panksepp, J. (1992). A critical role for "affective neuroscience" in resolving what is basic about basic emotions. *Psychological Review, 99*, 554–560.

Piaget, J. (1965). *The moral judgment of the child.* New York: Free Press. (Original work published 1932)

Post, R. M. (1992). Transduction of psychosocial stress into the neurobiology of recurrent affective disorder. *American Journal of Psychiatry, 149*, 999–1010.

Post, R. M., Ballenger, J. C., Uhde, T. W. Putnum, F. W., & Bunney, W. E. (1982). Kindling and drug sensitization: Implications for the progressive development of psychopathology and treatment with carbamazepine. In M. Sandler (Ed.), *Psychopharmacology of anticonvulsants* (pp. 97–124). Oxford: Oxford University Press.

Regier, D. A., Hirschfeld, R. M. A., Goodwin, F. K., et al. (1988). The NIMH Depression Awareness, Recognition, and Treatment Program: Structure, aims and scientific basis. *American Journal of Psychiatry, 145*, 1351–1357.

Rogers, C. R. (1961). *On becoming a person.* Boston: Houghton Mifflin.

Ruble, D. N., & Rholes, W. S. (1981). The development of children's perceptions and attributions about their social world. In J. D. Harvey, W. Ickes, & R. F. Kidd (Eds.), *New directions in attribution research* (Vol. 3, pp. 3–36). Hillsdale, NJ: Lawrence Erlbaum Associates.

Segal, Z. V. (1988). Appraisal of the self-schema construct in cognitive models of depression. *Psychological Bulletin, 103*, 147–162.

Segal, Z. V., & Blatt, S. J. (Eds.). (1993). *Self representation in emotional disorders: Cognitive and psychodynamic perspectives.* New York: Guilford.

Shantz, C. U. (1983). Social cognition. In P. H. Mussen (Series Ed.), J. H. Flavell & E. M. Markman (Vol. Eds.), *Carmichael's manual of child psychology: Vol. 3. Cognitive development* (4th ed., pp. 495–555). New York: Wiley.

Shapiro, D. (1963). *Neurotic styles.* New York: Norton.

Sorrentino, R. M., & Higgins, E. T. (1986). Motivation and cognition: Warming up to synergism. In R. M. Sorrentino & E. T. Higgins (Eds.), *Handbook of motivation and cognition: Foundations of social behavior* (pp. 3–19). New York: Guilford.

Sroufe, L. A. (1990). An organizational perspective on the self. In D. Cicchetti & M. Beeghly (Eds.), *The self in transition: Infancy to childhood* (pp. 281–308). Chicago: University of Chicago Press.

Steinmetz, J. E. (in press). Brain substrates of emotion and temperament. In J. Bates & T. Wachs (Eds.), *Temperament: Individual differences at the interface of biology and behavior.*

Strauman, T. J. (1989a). Self-discrepancies in clinical depression and social phobia: Cognitive structures that underlie emotional disorders? *Journal of Abnormal Psychology, 98*, 5–14.

Strauman, T. J. (1989b). The paradox of the self: A psychodynamic/social-cognitive integration. In R. C. Curtis (Ed.), *Self-defeating behaviors: Experimental findings, clinical impressions, and practical implications* (pp. 311-339). New York: Plenum.

Strauman, T. J. (1990). Self-guides and emotionally significant childhood memories: A study of retrieval efficiency and incidental negative emotional content. *Journal of Personality and Social Psychology, 59*, 869-880.

Strauman, T. J. (1992). Self-guides, autobiographical memory, and anxiety and dysphoria: Toward a cognitive model of vulnerability to emotional distress. *Journal of Abnormal Psychology, 101*, 87-95.

Strauman, T. J. (1994a). *Self-guides, childhood memories, and the stability of self-representations over time*. Manuscript submitted for publication.

Strauman, T. J. (1994b). Self-representations and the nature of cognitive change in psychotherapy. In B. E. Wolfe (Ed.), The cognitive sciences and psychotherapy [Special issue]. *Journal of Psychotherapy Integration, 4*, 291-316.

Strauman, T. J., & Higgins, E. T. (1987). Automatic activation of self-discrepancies and emotional syndromes: When cognitive structures influence affect. *Journal of Personality and Social Psychology, 53*, 1004-1014.

Strauman, T. J., & Higgins, E. T. (1988). Self-discrepancies as predictors of vulnerability to distinct syndromes of chronic emotional distress. *Journal of Personality, 56*, 685-707.

Strauman, T. J., & Higgins, E. T. (1993). The self construct in social cognition: Past, present, and future. In Z. Siegel & S. Blatt (Eds.), *Self in emotional distress* (pp. 3-40). New York: Guilford.

Strauman, T. J., Sisco, C., Keehn, D. (1995). *The personality of the self: How the nature and processing of self-beliefs vary according to level of ego development*. Manuscript submitted for publication.

Teasdale, J. D. (1988). Cognitive vulnerability to persistent depression. *Cognition and Emotion, 2*, 247-274.

Teasdale, J. D., & Dent, J. (1987). Cognitive vulnerability to depression: An investigation of two hypotheses. *British Journal of Clinical Psychology, 26*, 113-126.

Thoits, P. A. (1983). Dimensions of life events that influence psychological distress: An evaluation and synthesis of the literature. In H. B. Kaplan (Ed.), *Psychosocial stress: Trends in theory and research* (pp. 210-239). New York: Academic Press.

Tucker, D. M. (1992). Developing emotions and cortical networks. In M. Gunnar & C. A. Nelson (Eds.), *Minnesota Symposium on Child Psychology: Vol. 24. Developmental behavioral neuroscience* (pp. 75-128). Hillsdale, NJ: Lawrence Erlbaum Associates.

Werner, H., & Kaplan, B. (1963). *Symbol formation*. New York: Wiley.

Westen, D. (1994). Toward an integrated model of affect regulation: Applications to social-psychological research. *Journal of Personality, 62*, 641-667.

APA Work Group on Major Depressive Disorder (1993). Practice guideline for major depressive disorder in adults. *American Journal of Psychiatry, 150*(4), Supplement.

Whybrow, P. C., Akiskal, H. S., & McKinney, W. T. Jr. (1984). Toward a psychobiological integration: Affective illness as a final common path to adaptive failure. In P. Whybrow (Ed.), *Mood disorders: Toward a new psychobiology* (pp. 242-280). New York: Plenum.

Zuckerman, M. (1991). *Psychobiology of personality*. Cambridge: Cambridge University Press.

Zuroff, D. C., & Mongrain, M. (1987). Dependency and self-criticism: Vulnerability factors for depressive affective states. *Journal of Abnormal Psychology, 96*, 14-22.

9 "I Don't Feel Like It": The Function of Interest in Self-Regulation

Carol Sansone
University of Utah

Judith M. Harackiewicz
University of Wisconsin-Madison

Individuals often give "I don't feel like it" as their justification for declining to start or continue some action. Is this a poor excuse or a legitimate explanation? Does affective experience play a role in the regulation of behavior? In the present chapter, we consider the possibility that the "I don't feel like it" defense may in fact have some merit. That is, we consider the role played by feelings of intrinsic interest in regulating motivation and behavior.

The regulation of behavior is typically defined in terms of movement toward some goal. With the goal in mind, regulation can involve planning in advance of a situation, adopting specific strategies during an activity, evaluating progress toward the goal, and subsequently revising or maintaining the present course of action. Researchers have focused on various aspects of this process, such as whether or not individuals plan (e.g., Miller, Galanter, & Pribram, 1960; Scholnick & Friedman, 1993), the types of strategies used (e.g., Berg, 1989; Mischel, 1973; Schunk, 1991), and different aspects of the self-evaluation process, including the types of standards employed and the corresponding reactions once the standards are used to evaluate performance (e.g., Bandura, 1986; Higgins, 1987; Ruble & Frey, 1992). Other researchers have focused on the types and levels of goals individuals may have, both chronically and in terms of a particular situation or life stage (e.g., Ames, 1992; Butler, 1987; Cantor & Kihlstrom, 1987; Dweck & Leggett, 1988; Emmons, 1989; Harackiewicz & Elliot, in press; Harackiewicz & Sansone, 1991; Nicholls, 1984; Sansone & Berg, 1993).

Research and theory has primarily emphasized the cognitive and behavioral determinants of goal-driven regulation, with less attention given to the underlying motivational dynamics. When it is mentioned, *motivation* can refer to a wide variety of constructs. For example, for some theorists motivation in self-regulation is defined in terms of the importance or value of a goal to an individual (Cantor, Norem, Niedenthal, Langston, & Brower, 1987; Emmons, 1989). Others discuss the role of the intensity of the push or pull toward action, defined in terms of distance to the goal (e.g., Lewin, 1951) or probability of reaching the goal (e.g., Atkinson, 1964; Bandura, 1982; Carver & Scheier, 1990). For still others, motivation is discussed in terms of affective states (e.g., satisfaction, pride, shame) resulting from reaching or failing to reach a goal (e.g., Atkinson, 1964; Baumeister, Tice, & Heatherton, 1994; Higgins, 1987; Pervin, 1983; Strauman & Higgins, 1987).

Although the approaches vary, they have at least two things in common. The first is an assumption that individuals may hold similar goals but differ in their motivation to reach them (as evidenced in differences in task selection, persistence, and reactions to failure or success). Secondly, these approaches share a teleological emphasis. That is, the motivation as discussed depends on and is defined in terms of potential outcomes.

Although outcome-derived motivation may be sufficient to energize behavior when the goal is specific and short-term (e.g., getting at least a "B" on tomorrow's math exam), what happens when goals are higher level, longer term, or require making choices among multiple options (e.g., having a successful career as an engineer)? We argue that, in these cases, what an individual "feels like" doing at a given moment in time may be the more vivid and compelling determinant of present action than motivation evoked by the thought of achieving or avoiding a particular hypothetical and future outcome. Figure 9.1 illustrates the addition of "feeling like it" (indicated by dashed paths) to an idealized representation of the self-regulation process (indicated by solid paths).

We are thus suggesting a bridge between the work on self-regulation of behavior and the work on intrinsic motivation. As typically operationalized, studies on intrinsic motivation reflect the ideal of self-regulation. Individuals initially perform an activity in response to a request from an external source, and then researchers measure whether these individuals are subsequently likely to perform the activity when it is no longer required by the external source.

Although in terms of outcomes the study of intrinsic motivation appears similar to the study of self-regulation, intrinsic motivation tends to be discussed in terms of a particular class of activities, restricted to optimal conditions that are relatively rare in daily life. We propose, however, that if we think about intrinsic motivation not only as an outcome but also as a process, we may see that it is a process embedded in our day-to-day regulation of behavior. That is, motivation to perform goal-directed action at a given moment in time may be determined by the experience of the positive phenomenal state of intrinsic interest (the epitome of which Csikszentmihalyi (1975) has termed *flow*).

In addition to negative motivational forces (such as anxiety) preventing goal-directed action (e.g., Bandura, 1982), therefore, we propose that it is critical to understand the potential mediating role of this positive phenomenal experience that occurs during the process of performance (Murray, Sujan, Hirt, & Sujan, 1990; Saavedra & Earley, 1991; Sansone & Morgan, 1992). In fact, coordinating and regulating both process-derived and outcome-derived motivation may be an essential task of self-regulation.

This distinction between outcome and process resembles that made between teleologic and autotelic goals (Csikszentmihalyi, 1975), instrumental and consummatory behaviors (Millar & Tesser, 1992), and exogenous and endogenous behaviors (Kruglanski, 1975), among others. Millar and Tesser (1992) further suggested that cognition may guide instrumental behaviors, whereas affect guides consummatory behaviors. We argue that there may be different kinds of motivation associated with each, and that over time both may be necessary in the process of self-regulation. We next present a model that attempts to place these different kinds of motivation within a self-regulatory system.

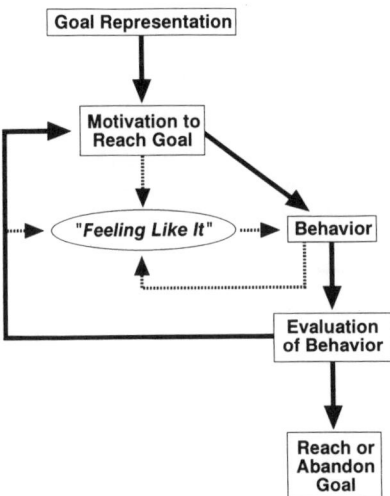

Fig. 9.1 An idealized representation of the process of self-regulation. Solid paths indicate the relationships between components in the idealized version; dashed paths indicate the relationships added when "feeling like it" is included in the process.

MODEL OF SELF-REGULATION AND INTRINSIC INTEREST

The model illustrated in Fig. 9.2 attempts to combine our previous theorizing about goals and intrinsic motivation (Harackiewicz & Sansone, 1991) with our conceptions of the self-regulation process. As an individual initially approaches an activity, characteristics of the individual and the situation combine to determine the goals held by the individual at that point in time. Included as an individual characteristic is the extent to which the individual "feels like" performing the activity initially, along with other, more stable individual differences (e.g., achievement orientation). Although for the sake of clarity we have illustrated paths from individual and

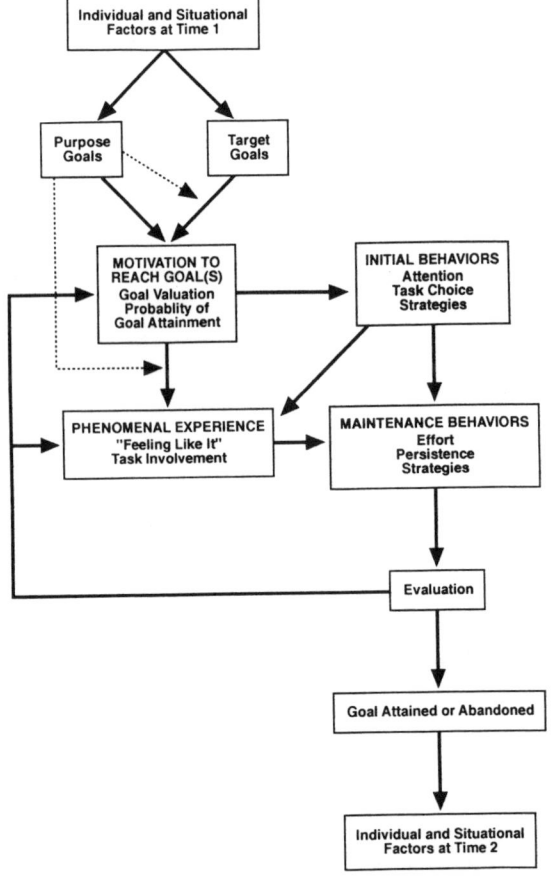

9.2 Model of self-regulation and intrinsic interest. Solid paths indicate direct effects; dashed paths indicate potential moderating effects of purpose goals.

situational factors solely to goals, as we discuss the model we note the impact of these factors at other points in the process.

We have previously suggested (Harackiewicz & Sansone, 1991) that two levels of goals are most relevant to an individual's performance of an activity at a particular point in time: task-specific target goals and higher level purpose goals. *Purpose goals* provide the reason for performing an activity and may be relevant to multiple tasks. They represent what an individual is trying to accomplish in a situation (e.g., to develop reading skills, to satisfy curiosity). *Target goals*, in contrast, provide more concrete guidelines as to what to do at a particular point in time. They are specific to the activity at hand and have behavioral referents (e.g., learn five new vocabulary words, finish the mystery story).

Individual and situational factors may influence both levels of goals held at a particular point in time. For example, classroom contexts and educational interventions might lead students to adopt the purpose goal of developing reading skills and the specific target goal of learning new vocabulary words. Alternatively, an achievement-oriented student may hold the same competence-related purpose and target goals whether home alone, at school, or on summer vacation.

These goals are cognitive representations of desired end states.[1] As noted in the introduction, individuals' motivation to reach these goals determine their subsequent actions. Researchers in self-regulation have tended to focus on two aspects of this outcome-derived motivation: the degree to which the individual values the goal and the degree to which he or she expects to attain the goal. In many formulations these two aspects are proposed to work multiplicatively, such that if either one is missing there will be insufficient motivation for behavior (e.g., Atkinson, 1964; Eccles, 1983; Lewin, 1951).

In research on intrinsic motivation, these expectancy and goal valuation processes are also important and take on a specific appearance. Many theorists assume that individuals' striving to achieve competence underlies intrinsically motivated behavior (Bandura, 1982; DeCharms, 1968; Deci & Ryan, 1985; Harackiewicz, 1989; White, 1959). They have thus suggested competence-related processes as mediators of the effects of external events on intrinsic motivation. Specifically, theorists have emphasized the individual's expectation of attaining competence-relevant goals (perceived competence) and the importance or value of competence-relevant goals to the individual (competence valuation). These specific manifestations of the components of motivation to reach the goal are included in our present model in their more general form.

---

[1] They might also be cognitive representations of negative end states to be avoided (c.f. Higgins, Roney, Crowe, & Hymes, 1994; Elliot, 1994).

As Fig. 9.2 shows, the resultant motivation to reach a particular goal guides initial behaviors. This outcome-derived motivation serves to focus attention, influence task choice, and direct strategy selection. For example, a child who is reading a novel to discover what happens to a fictional character may skip over an unknown word unless it is central to the plot. In contrast, a child reading to develop reading skills may stop and look up the word despite the interruption of the story.

It is at this point in the process that our model differs most from other conceptualizations of self-regulation. In addition to motivation to reach the goal, we propose that motivation also derives from the individual's phenomenal experience while working toward his or her goal. Thus, once an individual begins an activity, the extent to which he or she feels like continuing may exert a greater influence on subsequent behaviors (such as persistence, degree of effort, attention, and so on) than the initial motivation to reach the goal. In other words, outcome-derived motivation may be necessary and sufficient to draw individuals into an activity, but process-derived motivation may be necessary to maintain performance over time. For example, a child may begin reading because he or she is motivated by the goal of developing reading skills. However, whether he or she continues to read over the long term may depend on the degree of enjoyment experienced in the process of building those skills.

In our work, "feeling like it" is captured by the variable we termed *task involvement*. Task involvement reflects the degree of cognitive and affective absorption in the task. As such, it can be considered the positive phenomenal experience of intrinsic interest (Csikszentmihalyi, 1975). By focusing on the phenomenal experience while performing the task and by including a motivational process that captures this ongoing experience, our model reflects a dimension frequently missing in discussions of self-regulation.

As can be seen in Fig. 9.2, whenever individuals evaluate their progress with respect to their goals, they may adjust their behavior or their goals. The outcome of this evaluation will influence both the motivation to reach the goal and the phenomenal experience in a feedback function loop. Our model thus suggests that the relative importance of these two types of motivation in determining behavior may fluctuate over time, with the necessity of one decreasing as the other becomes stronger. This cycle should continue until the individual either reaches the goal or decides to abandon the goal. This cyclic process leads to the set of individual and situational characteristics operating at Time 2, and this set again includes whether the individual "feels like" continuing or resuming the activity.

Our distinction between outcome-derived motivation and process-derived motivation is important for several reasons. First, it suggests that they may influence each other but are not identical. The determinants of each and the nature of their relationship thus becomes important. Second, this distinction allows the possibility that sometimes these motivations may pull in different directions. External interventions aimed at increasing an individual's motivation to reach a goal, for example, may have the opposite effect on the phenomenal experience while working toward the goal. Self-regulation of behavior therefore involves the regulation of both types of motivation.

Determinants of Motivation to Reach Goal

As Fig. 9.2 illustrates, the primary determinants of the degree of motivation to reach a goal are the nature of the purpose and target goals themselves, with individual and situational factors moderating the degree of motivation associated with a particular goal at a particular point in time. For example, two students may hold the same goal of winning a reading contest at school. However, the achievement-oriented student may possess greater motivation to reach this goal because he or she cares more about winning (i.e., higher competence valuation) or feels that winning is more likely (i.e., higher perceived competence).

Valuation and expectancy processes may be associated with each level of goal (represented in Fig. 9.2 by solid paths from the purpose goal and from the target goal to motivation to reach the goal). Furthermore, purpose goals can serve to moderate the effect of a specific target goal on these processes (represented in Fig. 9.2 by a dashed path from the purpose goal to the path between the target goal and motivation to reach the goal). For example, a child may care most about reaching a target goal of finishing a story when his or her purpose in reading is to satisfy curiosity about the main character.

The potential direct and interactive effects of both purpose and target goals suggest that individuals should have the greatest resultant motivation to reach a goal when target goals are congruent with purpose goals. In these cases, the expectancy and valuation processes operating at both levels are oriented toward compatible outcomes, and may work in an additive or complementary fashion. However, as purpose and target goals diverge and result in ambivalent or conflicting orientations towards the task (Dodge, Asher, & Parkhurst, 1989; Morgan, 1993; Sansone & Berg, 1993), individuals may decrease the importance or the expectation of reaching either type of goal.

We have suggested elsewhere (Harackiewicz & Sansone, 1991) that motivational processes might also be differentially related to purpose and target goals. For example, in our present model, valuation processes might be more relevant to the motivation to reach a purpose goal, because individuals are more likely to represent the importance or value of a goal at the level of the perceived reason for behavior. In contrast, expectations about goal attainment may be more relevant to the motivation to reach a target goal, because individuals are more likely to represent expectations at the level of specific behaviors. This analysis suggests that greater resultant motivation to reach the goal occurs when purpose and target goals are congruent because the impact of both the valuation and expectancy components is maximized. It further suggests that when purpose and target goals are dissimilar, pursuing one goal at the expense of the other will diminish the motivation to reach the goal primarily by decreasing the impact of one of the components. For example, the valuation component may weaken if the individual pursues the target goal at the expense of the purpose goal; yet the expectancy component may diminish if the individual pursues the purpose goal at the expense of the target goal. We do not discuss or pursue these possibilities further in the present chapter, however, because our primary focus is on the role of the phenomenal experience in self-regulation.

Determinants of Phenomenal Experience

The nature and degree of motivation to reach a particular goal is in turn one determinant of the phenomenal experience while performing a task. Motivation to reach a goal may influence task involvement directly (e.g., a child may become more involved in a story when he or she cares about completing it) or indirectly through its effects on initial behaviors (e.g., once a child has begun reading, he or she may find something of interest in the story). Moreover, individuals' purpose goals may moderate the relationship between their motivation to reach the goal and their phenomenal experience (illustrated in Fig. 9.2 by a dashed path from the purpose goal to the path between the motivation to reach the goal and the phenomenal experience). For example, a student may expect to successfully learn five new vocabulary words, but this expectation may only result in a positive phenomenal experience when his or her purpose in reading is to develop reading skills.

The moderating function of purpose goals suggests that the match between purpose and target goals is critical to the self-regulatory process. In fact, we suggest that a key determinant of task involvement is the correspondence between individuals' purpose goals and target goals and between these goals and subsequent information and feedback from the environment. For example, when given a homework assignment (or target goal) to complete two chapters of a novel, a student whose purpose in reading is to demonstrate reading prowess may have a more positive subjective experience than a student whose purpose is to find out what happens to a fictional 19th-century orphan. Furthermore, feedback that they had done well by completing the two chapters may only enhance the first student's experience. Thus, in addition to facilitating performance (cf. Cantor, 1994; Vallacher & Wegner, 1987), we suggest that congruence among individuals' goals and between these goals and the environment has important motivational consequences.

Figure 9.2 illustrates determinants of task involvement that are a function of goals, their match, or the motivation to reach them. However, the phenomenal experience may be determined by non-goal-related factors such as fatigue, idiosyncratic likes or dislikes, or activity characteristics that limit how interesting and involving the task can be. Individual and situational factors may also affect the phenomenal experience by determining initial behaviors (e.g., the physical environment may constrain certain movements).

Over time, then, the phenomenal experience may or may not be congruent with the motivation to reach the goal, depending on the congruence among goals and the environment and on the diversity in factors affecting the phenomenal experience. At the same time, the phenomenal experience may acquire a primary role in motivating subsequent behavior, as the motivation to reach the goal becomes more diffuse and distant from the immediate behavior.

We next turn to examples from our recent research to illustrate the role that phenomenal experience plays in the regulation of behavior. We first show that the effects of goals on individuals' long-term likelihood of performing an activity depends on their phenomenal experience while performing. Specifically, we show that different goals for the same activity can have similar outcomes if the phenomenal experience while performing the activity was similar. We also show that similar goals can result in different outcomes if the previous phenomenal experience differed.

Secondly, we show that when individuals are not interested in performing an activity, changing the phenomenal experience can also change the subsequent likelihood of performance. External intervention may be able to change the phenomenal experience from neutral or negative to a more positive state by addressing the factors that lead to the less positive experience. Perhaps more important for self-regulation, individuals may themselves *intervene* and transform the activity into something more positive to perform. By making the experience more positive, these interventions should make individuals more likely to subsequently perform the activity.

MEDIATING ROLE OF PHENOMENAL EXPERIENCE

Sansone, Sachau, and Weir (1989) examined the effects of different purpose goals for a fantasy-based computer activity. In this activity, points are accumulated as the player moves through a fantasy "world." Individuals were told that the purpose of the activity was either to score as many points as possible while navigating the fantasy world (competence purpose goal) or to become involved in the fantasy adventure (fantasy purpose goal). Half of the individuals were next provided instruction on how to improve their scoring. The receipt of instruction would be consistent with a competence purpose goal, as it should ostensibly help individuals achieve their goal. However, the same instruction might prove disruptive or irrelevant in fantasy purpose goal conditions, where the emphasis on competence would be incongruent with the purpose. At the end of the session, we assessed individuals' subsequent interest in performing the activity through their attitudes about the task and whether they took home a brochure about the software.

We examined whether the match between purpose goals and the environment affected individuals' subsequent likelihood of performance, and if so, whether this effect was mediated by the phenomenal experience while doing the activity. To demonstrate mediation, three criteria must be met (Judd & Kenny, 1981). First, the independent variables must affect the outcome variable(s). Second, the independent variables must affect the potential mediator. Third, the potential mediator must affect the outcome variable when controlling for the effects of the independent variables. The effects of the independent variables should be reduced in the last case.

We found that the congruence between the purpose goal and subsequent environmental cues was a better predictor of subsequent interest in performing the activity than was the purpose goal itself. In the fantasy purpose goal condition, subsequent interest was greatest in the absence of instruction. In the competence goal condition, in contrast, subsequent interest was greater when instruction was received. This significant interactive effect of goal type and instruction indicated that there were significant effects to be mediated, satisfying the first criterion for establishing mediation.

Satisfying the second criterion, we also found a significant interaction between goal type and instruction on the degree of positive affect (e.g., excited, energetic) reported at the midpoint of performing the activity. Individuals in the fantasy goal condition who did not receive instruction and individuals in the competence goal condition who did receive instruction reported similarly higher levels of positive affect relative to the asynchronous conditions (i.e., fantasy goal paired with instruction, and competence goal paired with no instruction).

Finally, increased positive affect was associated with greater subsequent interest in performing the task (as measured by task attitudes), controlling for goal type and instruction. Furthermore, the previously significant interactive effect was no longer significant in this analysis. Thus, when subsequent environmental cues were congruent with the purpose goal adopted at the outset, dissimilar purpose goals resulted in similar levels of task involvement. In turn, task involvement was associated with greater subsequent interest in performing the task.

Harackiewicz and Elliot (1995) varied the synchrony between competence-related purpose and target goals in the context of a skill-based pinball game. Some individuals were told that the purpose of their involvement was to demonstrate their ability and outperform other college students (performance purpose goal). Other individuals were told that their purpose was to become experienced with the pinball machine (neutral purpose goal). Individuals were then given specific pinball scores to aim for (a competence-based target goal). However, for half of the subjects, this standard ostensibly represented improvement in their own performance (mastery target goal); for the other half, this standard ostensibly represented surpassing 65% of other college students' past performances (performance target goal). Performance was under unobtrusive control so that virtually all participants met these goals. We measured students' subsequent interest in performing the activity in terms of the amount of time spent playing the game during a free-choice period, their self-reported intentions to play similar games in the future, and their self-reported attitudes about pinball enjoyment.

The type of purpose goal was less important in predicting subsequent interest than was the match between the purpose and target goals. Specifically, individuals with performance purpose goals showed the highest levels of interest when they were given performance target goals, whereas individuals in the neutral purpose goal condition showed the highest levels of interest when given mastery target goals. Moreover, these two synchronous groups showed comparably high levels of interest relative to the two asynchronous groups (performance purpose goals coupled with mastery target goals, and neutral purpose goals coupled with performance target goals). That is, relative to the asynchronous conditions, these individuals performed the activity longer during the free-choice period, rated the task more positively, and indicated greater intention to play pinball in the future. Subjects in a no-goal control condition demonstrated levels of interest comparable to asynchronous conditions, suggesting that the synchronous goals actually enhanced interest.

Furthermore, as in the Sansone et al. study, this interactive effect was mediated by the phenomenal experience while playing pinball. Specifically, when goals were synchronous, subjects indicated higher levels of competence valuation at the outset of the pinball games and higher levels of task involvement during the game, as measured by frequency of on-task thoughts while playing (reported at the midpoint of engagement). Thus, congruence between purpose and target goals resulted in greater valuing of the goal, which was associated with greater task involvement.

Moreover, task involvement significantly predicted subsequent interest in performance (measured behaviorally and attitudinally), controlling for both the goal conditions and competence valuation. Thus, the degree of cognitive absorption while playing the game mediated both the effects due to matching purpose and target goals and the effects due to the valuation of these goals.

In two different contexts with different activities and different types of purpose goals, therefore, we found similar results. Purpose goals did not affect behavior in isolation, but rather interacted with target goals and other cues present in the environment. The degree of match among the goals and between the goals and the environment affected the individual's experience while performing the task. When purpose goals were consistent with target goals and with environmental cues, the phenomenal experience (as indexed by both affective and cognitive measures) was more positive. In turn, this positive phenomenal experience promoted continued interest, as documented in mediation analyses.

The converse should also hold true. That is, individuals holding similar goals but having different experiences should also show different outcomes. We illustrate this pattern using the case of competence goals. Competence goals direct attention to individual performance and may lead to better performance (e.g., Bandura & Schunk, 1981; Locke & Bryan, 1967; Locke & Latham, 1990). Will individuals pursuing similar competence goals and receiving similarly positive evaluative outcomes be equally likely to subsequently perform the task? We suggest that this would occur primarily if the intervening phenomenal experience was also similar. We thus illustrate how characteristics of the individual and of the activity might moderate the phenomenal experience and thereby change subsequent interest in performance.

First we examine what happens when individuals who characteristically differ in achievement orientation hold similar competence goals in a particular situation. Achievement-oriented individuals typically seek diagnostic ability assessment and feedback, place a high value on competent performance, and are motivated to attain high levels of skill in competition with a standard of excellence (Heckhausen, 1968; McClelland, Atkinson, Clark, & Lowell, 1953; Murray, 1938; Trope, 1975). These individuals would be expected to respond most positively when pursuing goals that emphasize competence. In contrast, those low in achievement orientation typically attempt to avoid ability assessment and achievement settings and are more likely to experience performance anxiety in such contexts (Atkinson, 1974; Geen, 1980; Trope, 1975). They would be expected to have a more negative experience pursuing the exact same goals, even when the outcomes are positive.

In several different studies we asked individuals who differed in achievement orientation to perform a skill-based activity (e.g., word puzzles, pinball). We then varied the focus of potential competence goals through environmental cues. Across studies we found similar results: Individuals with the same performance focus and achieving comparable positive performance levels differed in their subsequent interest in performing the activity as a function of achievement orientation. For example, Epstein and Harackiewicz (1992) found that interpersonal competition raised subsequent interest in an interesting word game for achievement-oriented subjects but undermined interest for individuals low in achievement orientation. Harackiewicz and Elliot (1993) manipulated the focus of competence purpose goals for a game of pinball by emphasizing normative comparisons (performance purpose goal) or personal improvement (mastery purpose goal). They found that the performance goal enhanced interest in performing the game for achievement-oriented individuals, whereas only the mastery goal raised subsequent interest for low-achievement-oriented subjects. In a study of target goals, Elliot and Harackiewicz (1994) found that performance goals for pinball (specific normative scores to aim for) reduced interest for individuals low in achievement orientation but raised interest for achievement-oriented individuals. Thus, relative to individuals low in achievement orientation, achievement-oriented individuals pursuing competence goals that emphasized competition and doing better than others showed greater subsequent interest in performing the activity. This pattern was obtained even though feedback indicated similarly positive performance levels for both groups (Sansone & Voisard, 1994).

According to our present thesis, this difference in subsequent interest should be due to different experiences while pursuing the similar goals. In fact, measures of competence valuation, perceived competence, and task involvement (typically measured by the reported frequency of on-task thoughts) were collected in many of these studies, and achievement-orientation differences on these processes reflected the results for subsequent interest. In general, individuals high in achievement orientation valued competence more and had higher levels of task involvement when pursuing goals that emphasized performance relative to others. In the same situation, individuals low in achievement orientation valued competence less, had lower perceptions of competence, and had lower levels of task involvement. Mediation analyses suggested that the differences in subsequent interest were due to these different experiences during the course of performing the activities.

Clearly, individual differences may have a major impact on the phenomenal experience during goal-directed behavior. Another critical factor is the nature of the task. Specifically, similar performance goals may result in different phenomenal experiences because of task characteristics. For example, Sansone and Voisard (1994) gave high school students comparable target goals (specific standards for performance representing the 80th percentile of other students) for two different tasks: an interesting hidden words activity and an uninteresting copying activity. These goals enhanced subsequent likelihood of performing the hidden words task but not of performing the copying task. Process analyses revealed that the goal reduced attention to performance-irrelevant aspects of the boring task, but it was these aspects of task involvement that proved most likely to enhance subsequent interest. Thus, the performance goal reduced the potential for involvement and interest by directing attention to performance.

Together, these results show that a competence goal may serve to direct attention to performance but only promote subsequent interest in performing the activity when working toward the goal promotes a positive phenomenal experience. If individuals characteristically or situationally do not value performing well, have doubts about their ability to perform, or find performance boring, a different phenomenal experience results, with corresponding effects on subsequent actions.

More generally, the results reviewed in this section suggest that a particular goal serves to orient an individual's approach to and interaction with the activity. The environment may serve to facilitate, interfere with, or be irrelevant to goal attainment, and each possibility influences the individual's phenomenal experience. The phenomenal experience may also be partially determined by non-goal-related factors (such as we found for achievement orientation and activity characteristics). Together, then, these data suggest that simply knowing the particular content of a goal may not be sufficient in understanding or predicting an individual's behavior in a given situation. Rather, it may be necessary to know the nature of the individual's experience while pursuing the goal.

CHANGING PHENOMENAL EXPERIENCE

When people possess some motivation to reach a goal but find the experience working toward the goal to be neutral or unpleasant, the impact of their motivation to reach the goal may suffer. As a consequence, individuals may devote less time and effort to pursuing their goal and may even decide that the goal is not worth pursuing and abandon it altogether. An alternative and possibly more adaptive response is to address the problematic affective experience. This is an approach that has been gaining adherents as recent research continues to emphasize the importance of interest in facilitating and maintaining performance in both educational and organizational domains (e.g., Csikszentmihalyi, 1978; Kohn, 1993; Lepper & Cordova, 1992; Renninger, Hidi, & Krapp, 1992).

For example, the results reviewed in the previous section suggest that, when pursuing performance goals, individuals high and low in achievement orientation differ in their subsequent motivation to perform the task, and often in their competence valuation, perceived competence and task involvement. According to our model, these differences in subsequent motivation result from different phenomenal experiences while working toward the performance goal, and differences in competence valuation and perceived competence will contribute to different phenomenal experiences. In terms of intervention, then, factors that attenuate differences in the phenomenal experience should also attenuate achievement orientation differences in subsequent behavior.

Although not examined directly, several studies supply indirect support for this hypothesis. By definition individuals low in achievement orientation do not spontaneously generate performance goals. When provided a performance goal either at the purpose or target level, therefore, they should be less likely to have a matching goal, and according to our model, correspondingly less likely to have a positive phenomenal experience while working toward the goal. In fact, individuals low in achievement orientation have shown negative responses when receiving either performance purpose goals (Harackiewicz & Elliot, 1993) or performance target goals (Elliot & Harackiewicz, 1994). On the other hand, if individuals low in achievement orientation can be induced to adopt both performance purpose and performance target goals, they should look similar to achievement-oriented individuals. Harackiewicz & Elliot (1995) found that when this congruence was experimentally induced, both high- and low-achievement-oriented individuals responded positively. Other studies indicate that individuals low in achievement orientation show greater levels of subsequent interest when they are provided a performance target goal early in the process of engagement, the timing of which allows them to evaluate their own progress from the beginning (e.g., Harackiewicz, Sansone, & Manderlink, 1985; Sansone, 1989). In this circumstance, individuals low in achievement orientation report higher levels of perceived competence and competence valuation and, ultimately, greater subsequent interest.

These results illustrate that outside intervention can change the individual's phenomenal experience and subsequent action if it is targeted correctly for that individual in a particular situation. Unfortunately, much of our behavior takes place outside the purview of others who may intervene to make our experience better, or takes place in situations where the individualized attention required for this type of intervention is either impossible or improbable.

Given the difficulties of effective external interventions, researchers have focused on promoting *self*-regulation, and discussed how motivation may be initiated and maintained despite a negative or neutral affective experience. In essence they focus on ways to increase the motivation to reach the goal. For example, socialization may lead to an internalized *other* who continues to exert pressure in terms of perceived duty, guilt, and responsibility (e.g., Deci, 1992; Higgins, 1987). This increases the negativity of the experience but sufficiently compels individuals to perform the behaviors when others are not physically present to ensure compliance. Ryan, Deci, and colleagues recently suggested that by emphasizing the rationale behind and value of continued performance, social influence can instead lead to internalization in which the individual feels more self-directed than other-directed. In this instance, performance of an activity continues to be boring or unpleasant, but motivation is maintained through positive feelings of self-determination (Deci, 1992; Ryan, Koestner, & Deci, 1991; Ryan & Stiller, 1991).

In a recent series of studies (Sansone, Weir, Harpster & Morgan, 1992), we have suggested another possibility. We proposed that if the phenomenal experience is critical to self-regulation of behavior over the long term, then a process should exist through which individuals actively regulate their phenomenal experience. In other words, individuals may strategically initiate behaviors with the intention of making the activity more positive to perform. Moreover, persistence at the activity should vary as a function of the use of these strategies.

Results reviewed previously suggested that there may be a variety of routes to interest, depending on individuals' purpose goals in a particular situation. In the process of self-regulation, individuals may actively pursue a variety of these routes through strategies that create or maintain a more positive phenomenal experience. In so doing, individuals may psychologically or physically change the activity into something more positive or interesting to perform. In this way individuals may develop *intrinsic* interest. However, the activity may not be identical to the one with which they began.

Several hypotheses follow from the existence of this self-regulatory process. In line with research on self-regulated learning, individuals should have implicit theories about how to regulate their own motivation, which should include knowledge about specific strategies (declarative knowledge) and about how and when they will be most effective (procedural knowledge) (Paris & Byrnes, 1989; Zimmerman, 1989). In addition, the actual use of these strategies should occur primarily in situations in which there is an evident need for self-regulation. That is, individuals should be most likely to engage in these interest-enhancing actions when they find the activity currently uninteresting *and* have a sufficient reason to persist at the uninteresting activity.

In a first study, we examined college students' beliefs about effective interest-enhancing strategies. They gained experience with one of two novel tasks: a hidden words task (finding words embedded in a letter matrix) or a copying task (copying a letter matrix). They were then asked to list what they would do to make performance of the task more interesting if performed on a regular basis. Individuals suggested strategies keyed to their perception of each task. For example, individuals defined the hidden words task as an interesting verbal skill activity. These individuals were more likely to suggest interest-enhancing strategies that increased the skill or challenge component of the activity (e.g., find longer words). In contrast, individuals defined the copying task as an uninteresting manual dexterity task. In this case, individuals were more likely to suggest strategies that involved interesting aspects of the surrounding context (e.g., listening to music while performing) (Suedfeld, 1981). For both activities, individuals suggested varying the procedure used in performing the activity (Liu & Gollwitzer, 1990).

In a second study, we examined the conditions under which individuals would be most likely to actually use these types of strategies. We therefore experimentally created conditions that varied in the need to self-regulate motivation. We again compared the hidden words task and the copying task. The need to enhance the phenomenal experience while performing should be greater when individuals repetitively copied letters than when they searched for words formed by those letters.

Within copying task conditions, we then also varied an ostensible reason to wish to persist at the copying task. Half of the individuals performing the copying task were told that there were health benefits from performing the task on a regular basis. If there is indeed a motivational self-regulatory process, then individuals should be most likely to engage in interest-enhancing strategies when they performed the copying task, with the knowledge of health benefits from regular performance, and least likely when they performed the hidden words task. Individuals performing the copying task without knowledge of health benefits should fall between these two. These individuals would have a greater *need* to regulate their phenomenal experience than individuals performing the hidden words task but less *reason* to regulate their experience then individuals performing the copying task with knowledge of health benefits.

We used the information from the first study to operationalize the available interest-enhancing strategies. To vary features of the context, for half the participants we provided interesting text that was incidental to performance demands. This incidental text conveyed historical and other information about the different styles of type font displayed in the letter matrices. To permit individuals to vary their procedure, in the second half of the task session we informed students that they could record their responses using whatever writing or script they wished. We then assessed whether students attempted to vary how they recorded the letters during the task session (e.g., whether they attempted to reproduce the style of type displayed in the matrix), as well as students' degree of recognition of the incidental text after the task session was completed. Neither reading the incidental text nor varying how responses were recorded were actions required by task demands.

We found that students were most likely to engage in these interest-enhancing strategies in conditions signifying self-regulation. That is, when students performed the uninteresting task in the context of ostensible health benefits from regular performance, they recognized more words from the incidental text and were more likely to vary how they recorded their responses. Students were least likely to use these strategies when performing the hidden words task, with strategy use by individuals performing the copying task without knowledge of health benefits falling between the other two conditions. Equally important for a self-regulation interpretation, we further found that strategy use by individuals performing the copying task was associated with greater likelihood of subsequently performing the task. Strategy use was also associated with a relatively more positive definition of the activity.

The combination of these two studies are important because they show that by engaging in certain behaviors, individuals became more likely to subsequently perform an uninteresting activity. These behaviors were incidental to performance of the assigned task. However, they were not incidental to the phenomenal experience while performing.

The results also suggest that the reason to value persistence (the ostensible health benefit) did not directly affect the likelihood of subsequently performing the task. Rather, it provided the context in which individuals were most likely to use interest-enhancing strategies. This suggests that when the phenomenal experience of performing a task is sufficiently negative, emphasizing the reason for performance may be a necessary but not sufficient condition of continued performance. In these cases, valuing persistence may lead to continued performance primarily if this valuation motivates regulation of the phenomenal experience. Together, these results strongly support a model of the self-regulatory process in which the phenomenal experience plays a critical role.

A CRITICAL TASK OF SELF-REGULATION

Our review suggests that the experience of interest is important not only in its own right but also because it may function as a proximal motivator for moment-to-moment action. Self-regulation thus involves coordinating outcome-derived motivation with motivation resulting from the phenomenal experience while performing intermediate actions. The individual must decide whether it is worth pursuing activities that result in neutral or negative experiences. This decision may depend on the importance of the goal initially, the perceived costs and benefits of achieving or not achieving the goal, and the perceived costs and benefits of changing or not changing the phenomenal experience.

It is the last parameter that becomes clear only by combining work on self-regulation and intrinsic motivation. It is also the parameter that has received the least attention in the study of self-regulation. Therefore, we turn next to a few results from recently conducted studies that illustrate the perceived costs associated with regulating the phenomenal experience.

In the study described previously (Sansone et al., 1992), varying how one recorded the letters was associated with increased likelihood of subsequently performing the copying task. However, use of this strategy was also associated with fewer letters being copied in the time allowed, suggesting that the benefit to motivation came at the cost to performance. The results from a subsequent study suggested that this trade-off may appear primarily in the short term (Sansone, Wiebe, Morgan, Palmer, & Rich, 1992). We used basically the same paradigm, with the exception that individuals themselves decided when to stop copying. In this case, individuals who varied how they recorded the letters also copied more letters, persisting longer at the task. In combination, these results illustrate that at least in the short term the strategy to enhance the experience came at a cost to productivity. However, this was reversed over the longer term. Moreover, there may be costs to continuing tasks without changing the phenomenal experience for the better. For example, the same type of physical and psychological effects may result in this instance as results with prolonged exposure to other stressors (e.g., Leventhal & Tomarken, 1987; Selye, 1956).

As with other components of self-regulation, we would expect the parameters of this self-regulatory process to change across individuals, other situational contingencies, and time. For example, individuals may differ in what is important to them initially, in what they find interesting, and in how easily they are bored. Individuals may also differ in terms of how long they can persist when the phenomenal experience is not positive, in their sensitivity to changing contingencies in the environment, and in their ability and willingness to exploit opportunities to change the phenomenal experience. We might thus expect to see differences in whether and how individuals regulate their motivation in a particular situation as a function of age, gender, or culture (Asher, 1979; Cantor, 1994; Deaux, 1984; Markus & Kitayama, 1991; Meece & Courtney, 1992; Spence, 1985); as a function of individual differences in values, abilities, and strategies within a particular age group, sex, or culture (Costa & McCrae, 1988; Kihlstrom & Cantor, 1984; Kruglanski, 1989; Murray, 1938; Rosenbaum, 1988); and as a function of situational contingencies that may change over time, cultures, or subgroups within a culture (Cantor & Kihlstrom, 1987; Higgins & Eccles-Parsons, 1983; Sansone & Berg, 1993).

We recently conducted several studies in which we measured a number of individual differences that conceptually should be related to this self-regulatory process, and used the paradigm described in Sansone, Weir, et al. (1992). We expected that to the extent that the individual difference changes a parameter in the self-regulatory process, we should see corresponding differences in the appearance of self-regulation of the phenomenal experience.

We found, for example, that the effect of being given a reason to value performance of the boring task did not exert the same effect on the self-regulatory process for all individuals (Sansone, Wiebe, et al., 1992). The reason for performance was less important for individuals high in conscientiousness, who persisted longer than individuals low in conscientiousness whether or not there was a reason to value the task. Moreover, although rating the task equally boring, individuals high in conscientiousness persisted longer without being correspondingly more likely to engage in the strategy to enhance the phenomenal experience.

Individuals high in hardiness, in contrast, appeared very sensitive as to whether there was a reason to value performance of the task. That is, individuals high in hardiness showed the previously found relationship between regulating the phenomenal experience and persistence at the task. However, high hardy individuals only engaged in these strategies when they were provided a reason to value the task. In the absence of this reason, they were least likely to attempt to regulate their experience, and they quit copying sooner. This pattern again illustrates the self-regulatory nature of this process. That is, in the absence of a good reason to prolong exposure to an unpleasant experience, individuals who are typically good at coping with stressors (Wiebe & Williams, 1992) were the first to withdraw from the task.

CONCLUSION

Rather than being an annoying whine, the phrase "I don't feel like it" appears to be a legitimate explanation in terms of how we function. This suggests that feelings of interest in what we do may be inherent to our ability to maintain sufficient motivation to reach the goals that are important to us.

Perhaps the phenomenal experience of interest functions initially to get us to attempt to learn and master all the novel things we must learn to survive (Woodworth, 1921; White, 1959). However, it appears that, at least with adolescents and adults, the motivational capacity of this experience is not limited to learning new things. Rather, this experience can be critical to maintaining as well as initiating behaviors. This subjective experience appears to become a function of goals, which in turn may be due to characteristics of the task, person, and surrounding context, and which may change over time.

To be effective in a changing world, self-regulation must be fluid. Thinking of motivation as operating in the fluid manner we described is thus consistent with the aim of self-regulation. This is also consistent with other recent work on the function of affect, which suggests that the same affect may serve different functions depending on the larger context and individuals' goals within that context (e.g., Forgas, 1992; Martin, Ward, Achee, & Wyer, 1993). Ultimately, motivation is critical to navigating our world. Our work suggests that we must be able to "feel like" doing the things that are critical for us to do if we are to continue to do them over the long term. Fortunately, our work also suggests that we are flexible in what makes us "feel like it," and that we possess the capacity to regulate whether we do "feel like it."

ACKNOWLEDGMENTS

We thank Lenny Martin and Abraham Tesser in their role as hosts of the Goals and Affect conference held in Athens, Georgia, January, 1994. Their comments and the comments by Carolyn Morgan and Andy Elliot on earlier versions of this chapter were very helpful, as was Kenn Baron's assistance in graphically depicting the models presented. We also thank the participants at the Goals and Affect conference as well as the participants at the 1994 Social Psychology Winter Conference in Park City, Utah, for their stimulating feedback on the ideas presented in this chapter. Much of the research reported was supported by grants from NIH Biomedical Research Support Program (BRSG S07 RR07092) and from the Spencer Foundation to Carol Sansone, a grant from the National Institute of Child and Human Development and the National Institute on Aging (HD 25728) awarded to Carol Sansone and Cynthia Berg, and grants from the Vilas Foundation and the Spencer Foundation awarded to Judith Harackiewicz. Finally, preparation of the chapter was facilitated by the generous resources and opportunities for intellectual discussion placed at the disposal of the first author while on sabbatical at the University of Maryland–College Park.

REFERENCES

Ames, C. (1992). Achievement goals and the classroom motivational climate. In D. H. Schunk & J. L. Meece (Eds.), *Student perceptions in the classroom* (pp. 327–348) Hillsdale, NJ: Lawrence Erlbaum Associates.

Asher, S. R. (1979). Influence of topic interest on Black children's and White children's reading comprehension. *Child Development, 50,* 686-690.
Atkinson, J. W. (1964). *An introduction to motivation.* Princeton, NJ: Van Nostrand.
Atkinson, J. W. (1974). The mainsprings of achievement oriented activity. In J. W. Atkinson & J. O. Raynor (Eds.), *Motivation and achievement* (pp. 11-39). Washington, DC: Winston.
Bandura, A. (1982). Self-efficacy mechanism in human agency. *American Psychologist, 37,* 122-147.
Bandura, A., (1986). *Social foundations of thought and action: A social cognitive theory.* Englewood Cliffs, NJ: Prentice-Hall.
Bandura, A., & Schunk, D. H. (1981). Cultivating competence, self-efficacy, and intrinsic interest through proximal self-motivation. *Journal of Personality and Social Psychology, 41,* 586-598.
Baumeister, R. F., Tice, D. M., & Heatherton, T. (1994). *Losing control: How and why people fail at self-regulation.* New York: Academic Press.
Berg, C. A. (1989). Knowledge of strategies for dealing with everyday problems from childhood through adolescence. *Developmental Psychology, 25,* 607-618.
Butler, R. (1987). Task-involving and ego-involving properties of evaluation: Effects of different feedback conditions on motivational perceptions, interest and performance. *Journal of Educational Psychology, 79,* 474-482.
Cantor, N. (1994). Life task problem solving: Situational affordances and personal needs. *Personality and Social Psychology Bulletin, 20,* 235-243.
Cantor, N., & Kihlstrom, J. F. (1987). *Personality and social intelligence.* Englewood Cliffs, NJ: Prentice-Hall.
Cantor, N., Norem, J. K., Niedenthal, P. M., Langston, C. A., & Brower, A. M. (1987). Life tasks, self-concept ideals, and cognitive strategies in life transition. *Journal of Personality and Social Psychology, 53,* 1178-1191.
Carver, C. S., & Scheier, M. F. (1990). Origins and functions of positive and negative affect: A control-process view. *Psychological Review, 97,* 19-35.
Costa, P. T., Jr., & McCrae, R. R. (1988). From catalog to classification: Murray's needs and the five-factor model. *Journal of Personality and Social Psychology, 55,* 258-265.
Csikszentmihalyi, M. (1975). *Beyond boredom and anxiety.* San Francisco: Jossey-Bass.
Csikszentmihalyi, M. (1978). Intrinsic rewards and emergent motivation. In M. R. Lepper & D. Greene (Eds.), *The hidden costs of reward* (pp. 205-216). Hillsdale, NJ: Lawrence Erlbaum Associates.
Deaux, K. (1984). From individual differences to social categories: Analysis of a decade's research on gender. *American Psychologist, 39,* 105-116.
Deci, E. L. (1992). Interest and the intrinsic motivation of behavior. In K. A. Renninger, S. Hidi, & A. Krapp (Eds.), *The role of interest in learning and development* (pp. 43-70). Hillsdale, NJ: Lawrence Erlbaum Associates.
Deci, E. L., & Ryan, R. M. (1985). *Intrinsic motivation and self-determination in human behavior.* New York: Plenum.
DeCharms, R. (1968). *Personal causation: The internal affective determinants of behavior.* New York: Academic Press.
Dodge, K. A., Asher, S. R., & Parkhurst, J. T. (1989). Social life as a goal-coordination task. In C. Ames & R. Ames (Eds.), *Research on motivation and education: Goals and cognitions* (Vol. 3, pp. 107-135). New York: Academic Press.
Dweck, C. S., & Leggett, E. L. (1988). A social-cognitive approach to motivation and personality. *Psychological Review, 95,* 256-273.
Eccles, J. (1983). Expectancies, values and academic behaviors. In J. T. Spence (Ed.)., *Achievement and achievement motives: Psychological and sociological approaches* (pp. 75-146). San Francisco: W. H. Freeman.

Elliot, A. J., (1994). *Approach and avoidance achievement goals: An intrinsic motivation analysis.* Unpublished doctoral dissertation, University of Wisconsin-Madison.

Elliot, A. J., & Harackiewicz, J. M. (1994). Goal setting, achievement orientation, and intrinsic motivation: A mediational analysis. *Journal of Personality and Social Psychology, 66,* 968-980.

Emmons, R. A. (1989). The personal striving approach to personality. In L. A. Pervin (Ed.), *Goal concepts in personality and social psychology* (pp. 87-126). Hillsdale, NJ: Lawrence Erlbaum Associates.

Epstein, J. A., & Harackiewicz, J. M. (1992). Winning is not enough: The effects of competition and achievement orientation on intrinsic interest. *Personality and Social Psychology Bulletin, 18,* 128-138.

Forgas, J. P. (1992). Affect in social judgments and decisions: A multiprocess model. In M. Zanna (Ed.), *Advances in experimental social psychology* (Vol. 25, pp. 227-275). New York: Academic Press.

Geen, R. B. (1980). Test anxiety and cue utilization. In I. G. Sarason (Ed.), *Test anxiety: Theory, research, and applications* (pp. 253-259). Hillsdale, NJ: Lawrence Erlbaum Associates.

Harackiewicz, J. M. (1989). Performance evaluation and intrinsic motivation processes: The effects of achievement orientation and rewards. In D. Buss & N. Cantor (Eds.), *Personality psychology: Recent trends and emerging directions* (pp. 128-137). New York: Springer.

Harackiewicz, J. M., & Elliot, A. J. (1993). Achievement goals and intrinsic motivation. *Journal of Personality and Social Psychology, 65,* 904-915.

Harackiewicz, J. M., & Elliot, A. J. (1995). *Hierarchical goals and intrinsic motivation: A mediational analysis.* Unpublished manuscript.

Harackiewicz, J. M., & Elliot, A. J. (in press). Life is a roller coaster when you view the world through entity glasses. *Psychological Inquiry.*

Harackiewicz, J. M., & Sansone, C. (1991). Goals and intrinsic motivation: You *can* get there from here. In M. L. Maehr & P. R. Pintrich (Eds.), *Advances in motivation and achievement* (Vol. 7, pp. 21-49). Greenwich, CT: JAI Press.

Harackiewicz, J. M., Sansone, C., & Manderlink, G. (1985). Competence, achievement orientation, and intrinsic motivation: A process analysis. *Journal of Personality and Social Psychology, 48,* 493-508.

Heckhausen, H. (1968). Achievement motive research: Current problems and some contributions towards a general theory of motivation. In W. J. Arnold (Ed.), *Nebraska Symposium on Motivation* (pp. 103-174). Lincoln: University of Nebraska Press.

Higgins, E. T. (1987). Self-discrepancy: A theory relating self and affect. *Psychological Review, 94,* 319-340.

Higgins, E. T., & Eccles-Parsons, J. (1983). Social cognition and the social life of the child: Stages as subcultures. In E. T. Higgins, D. N. Ruble, & W. Hartup (Eds.), *Social cognition and social development* (pp. 15-62). Cambridge, England: Cambridge University Press.

Higgins, E. T., Roney, C. J. R., Crowe, E., & Hymes, C. (1994). Ideal versus ought predilections for approach and avoidance: Distinct self-regulatory systems. *Journal of Personality and Social Psychology, 66,* 276-286.

Judd, C. M., & Kenny, D. A. (1981). Process analysis: Estimating mediation in treatment evaluations. *Evaluation Review, 5,* 602-619.

Kihlstrom, J. F., & Cantor, N. (1984). Mental representations of the self. In L. Berkowitz (Ed.), *Advances in experimental social psychology* (Vol. 17, pp. 1-47). Orlando, FL: Academic Press.

Kohn, A. (1993). *Punished by rewards: The trouble with gold stars, incentive plans, A's, praise, and other bribes.* Boston: Houghton Mifflin.

Kruglanski, A. W. (1975). The endogenous-exogenous partition in attribution theory. *Psychological Review, 82,* 387-406.

Kruglanski, A. W. (1989). *Lay epistemics and human knowledge: Cognitive and motivational bases.* New York: Plenum.

Lepper, M. R., & Cordova, D. I. (1992). A desire to be taught: Instructional consequences of intrinsic motivation. *Motivation and Emotion, 16,* 187–208.

Leventhal, H., & Tomarken, A. J. (1987). Stress and illness: Perspectives from health psychology. In V. Kasl & C. L. Cooper (Eds.), *Stress and health: Issues in research methodology* (pp. 27–55). Sussex, England: Wiley.

Lewin, K. (1951). *Field theory in social science: Selected theoretical papers* (D. Cartwright, Ed.). New York: Harper & Row.

Liu, C., & Gollwitzer, P. M. (1990, August). *Stopping: People's thoughts involved in ending task persistence.* Paper presented at the 98th annual meeting of the American Psychological Association, Boston, MA.

Locke, E. A., & Bryan, J. F. (1967). Performance goals as determinants of level of performance and boredom. *Journal of Applied Psychology, 51,* 120–130.

Locke, E. A., & Latham, G. P. (1990). *A theory of goal setting and task performance.* Englewood Cliffs, NJ: Prentice-Hall.

Markus, H. R., & Kitayama, S. (1991). Culture and the self: Implications for cognition. *Psychological Review, 98,* 224–253.

Martin, L. L., Ward, D. W., Achee, J. W., & Wyer, R. S. (1993). Mood as input: People have to interpret the motivational implications of their moods. *Journal of Personality and Social Psychology, 64,* 317–326.

McClelland, D. C., Atkinson, J. W., Clark, R. A., & Lowell, E. (1953). *The achievement motive.* New York: Appleton-Century-Crofts.

Meece, J. L., & Courtney, D. P. (1992). Gender differences in students' perceptions: Consequences for achievement-related choices. In D. H. Schunk & J. L. Meece (Eds.), *Student perceptions in the classroom* (pp. 209–228). Hillsdale, NJ: Lawrence Erlbaum Associates.

Millar, M. G., & Tesser, A. (1992). The role of beliefs and feelings in guiding behavior: The mismatch model. In L. L. Martin & A. Tesser (Eds.), *The construction of social judgments* (pp. 277–300). Hillsdale, NJ: Lawrence Erlbaum Associates.

Miller, G. A., Galanter, E., & Pribram, K. (1960). *Plans and the structure of behavior.* New York: Holt, Rinehart & Winston.

Mischel, W. (1973). Toward a cognitive social learning reconceptualization of personality. *Psychological Review, 80,* 252–283.

Morgan, C. L. (1993). *Examining gender differences in attributions: The roles of problem domain and goal type.* Unpublished master's thesis, University of Utah, Salt Lake City, UT.

Murray, H. A. (1938). *Explorations in personality.* New York: Oxford University Press.

Murray, N., Sujan, H., Hirt, E. R., & Sujan, M. (1990). The influence of mood on categorization: A cognitive flexibility interpretation. *Journal of Personality and Social Psychology, 59,* 411–425.

Nicholls, J. G. (1984). Achievement motivation: Conceptions of ability, subjective experience, task choice and performance. *Psychological Review, 91,* 328–346.

Paris, S. G., & Byrnes, J. P. (1989). The constructivist approach to self-regulation and learning in the classroom. In B. J. Zimmerman & D. H. Schunk (Eds.), *Self-regulated learning and academic achievement: Theory research and practice* (pp. 169–200). New York: Springer-Verlag.

Pervin, L. A. (1983). The stasis and flow of behavior: Toward a theory of goals. In M. M. Page (Ed.), *Personality: Current theory and research* (pp. 1–53). Lincoln: University of Nebraska Press.

Renninger, K. A., Hidi, S., & Krapp, A. (1992). *The role of interest in learning and development.* Hillsdale, NJ: Lawrence Erlbaum Associates.

Rosenbaum, M. (1988). Learned resourcefulness, stress, and self-regulation. In S. Fisher & J.

Reason (Eds.), *Handbook of life stress, cognition, and health* (pp. 483-496). New York: Wiley.
Ruble, D. N., & Frey, K. (1992). Changing patterns of comparative behavior as skills are acquired: A functional model of self-evaluation. In J. Suls & T. A. Wills (Eds.), *Social comparison: Contemporary theory and research* (pp. 79-113). Hillsdale, NJ: Lawrence Erlbaum Associates.
Ryan, R. M., Koestner, R., & Deci, E. L. (1991). Varied forms of persistence: When free-choice behavior is not intrinsically motivated. *Motivation and Emotion, 15*, 185-205.
Ryan, R. M., & Stiller, J. (1991). The social contexts of internalization: Parent and teacher influences on autonomy, motivation and learning. In M. L. Maehr & P. R. Pintrich (Eds.), *Advances in motivation and achievement* (Vol. 7, pp. 115-149). Greenwich, CT: JAI Press.
Saavedra, R., & Earley, P. C. (1991). Choice of task and goal under conditions of general and specific affective inducement. *Motivation and Emotion, 15*, 45-65.
Sansone, C. (1989). Competence feedback, task feedback, and intrinsic interest: An examination of process and context. *Journal of Experimental Social Psychology, 25*, 33-361.
Sansone, C., & Berg, C. A. (1993). Adapting to the environment across the life span: Different process or different inputs? *International Journal of Behavioral Development, 16*, 215-241.
Sansone, C., & Morgan, C. (1992). Intrinsic motivation and education: Competence in context. *Motivation and Emotion, 16*, 249-270.
Sansone, C., Sachau, D. A., & Weir, C. (1989). The effects of instruction on intrinsic interest: The importance of context. *Journal of Personality and Social Psychology, 57*, 819-829.
Sansone, C., & Voisard, B. (1994). *Effects of performance goals on subsequent motivation as a function of task and achievement orientation.* Unpublished manuscript.
Sansone, C., Weir, C., Harpster, L., & Morgan, C. (1992). Once a boring task always a boring task?: Interest as a self-regulatory mechanism. *Journal of Personality and Social Psychology, 63*, 379-390.
Sansone, C., Wiebe, D. J., Morgan, C., Palmer, S., & Rich, T. (1992, August). *Making aversive tasks better: An individual differences approach.* Paper presented at the 100th annual meeting of the American Psychological Association, Washington, DC.
Scholnick, E. K., & Friedman, S. L. (1993). Planning in context: Developmental and situational considerations. *International Journal of Behavioral Development, 16*, 145-167.
Schunk, D. (1991). Goal setting and self-evaluation: A social cognitive perspective on self-regulation. In M. L. Maehr & P. R. Pintrich (Eds.), *Advances in motivation and achievement* (Vol. 7, pp. 85-113). Greenwich, CT: JAI Press.
Selye, H. (1956). *The stress of life.* New York: McGraw-Hill.
Spence, J. T. (1985). Achievement American style: The rewards and costs of individualism. *American Psychologist, 40*, 1285-1295.
Strauman, T. J., & Higgins, E. T. (1987). Automatic activation of self-discrepancies and emotional syndromes: When cognitive structures influence affect. *Journal of Personality and Social Psychology, 53*, 1004-1014.
Suedfeld, P. (1981). Environmental restriction and "stimulus hunger": Theories and applications. In H. I. Day (Ed.), *Advances in intrinsic motivation and aesthetics* (pp. 71-86). New York: Plenum.
Trope, Y. (1975). Seeking information about one's own ability as a determinant of choice among tasks. *Journal of Personality and Social Psychology, 32*, 1004-1013.
Vallacher, R. R., & Wegner, D. M. (1987). What do people think they're doing: Action identification and human behavior. *Psychological Review, 94*, 3-15.
White, R. W. (1959). Motivation reconsidered: The concept of competence. *Psychological Review, 66*, 297-333.
Wiebe, D. J., & Williams, P. G. (1992). Hardiness and health: A social psychophysiological perspective on stress and adaptation. *Journal of Social and Clinical Psychology, 11*, 238-262.

Woodworth, R. S. (1921). *Psychology: A study of mental life*. New York: Henry Holt.
Zimmerman, B. J. (1989). Models of self-regulated learning and academic achievement. In B. J. Zimmerman & D. H. Schunk (Eds.), *Self-regulated learning and academic achievement: Theory, research and practice* (pp. 1-25). New York: Springer-Verlag.

10 Motivated Memory: Self-Defining Memories, Goals, and Affect Regulation

Jefferson A. Singer
Connecticut College

Peter Salovey
Yale University

In 1981, at the virtual peak of the information processing revolution, Gordon Bower published his famous paper on mood and memory (Bower, 1981). Ironically, nearly 15 years later, it now seems that this article, so confident in its extension of semantic network theory to affective memory, actually defined the limitations of purely cognitive theories as applied to emotion and personality. Although many studies have supported an associational congruency between mood state and remembered material (e.g., Madigan & Bollenbach, 1982; Natale & Hantas, 1982; Snyder & White, 1982; Teasdale, Taylor, & Fogarty, 1980; Wright & Mischel, 1982), other researchers have found congruency between positive mood and positively toned material but not between negative affect and negatively toned memories or cognitions (e.g., Clark & Waddell, 1983; Macht, Spear, & Levis, 1977; Mischel, Ebbesen, & Zeiss, 1976; Teasdale & Fogarty, 1979). Bower himself (Bower & Mayer, 1989) was able to demonstrate reliable effects for the learning of mood congruent material but not for mood dependent retrieval.

More recently, Parrott and Sabini (1990) and Wegner, Erber, and Zanakos (1993) demonstrated the emergence of mood *incongruent* memories—cognitions that are in direct opposition to the individuals' desired mood. Isen (1985), Blaney (1986), Singer and Salovey (1988), and Matt, Vasquez, and Campbell (1992) reviewed studies relevant to Bower's network model of affect and suggested its explanatory power is insufficient to account for the range of empirical findings. More specifically, Isen (1985) and Singer and Salovey (1988, 1993; Salovey & Singer, 1991) argued that an associational model of mood and memory is silent concerning the role of motivation in memory recall. Difficulties in finding negative mood congruency may be due to individuals' motivation to repair negative mood states by summoning more positive memories. In a related vein, Parrott and Sabini (1990) suggested that individuals may recall incongruent memories in positive moods to protect themselves from a reckless euphoria. Feeling too good may be the prelude to a let-down or disappointment, so it is better to modulate even our happiest moments. Results by Wegner et al. (1993) suggested that individuals interested in controlling their mood states may automatically test themselves to see if the desired mood has been reached and maintained. Under situations of heavy cognitive load, this checking process may ironically lead to the emergence of thoughts relevant to the opposite of the desired mood. For example, negative memories or associations that might be raised fleetingly, only to be contrasted with the current positive frame of mind, may fail to be filtered out and assume a more prominent role in conscious thought.

The earlier findings of asymmetries in mood congruencies combined with these recent demonstrations of mood incongruent processes may all be encompassed by the broad rubric of motivated cognition (Showers & Cantor, 1985). That is, cognitive processes do not operate in a vacuum separate from the personal needs and self-regulatory tendencies of each individual. Memories may be one of the many components of thought (fantasies, self-statements, focus of attention, etc.) individuals use to control mood (Erber & Tesser, 1992; Salovey, Hsee, & Mayer, 1993; Wenzlaff, 1993). For example, in the Wegner et al. (1993) study described earlier, subjects who were asked to create certain mood states did so by "retrieving memories and expressing feelings consciously that helped to substantiate the mood they were intending to create" (p. 1102).

Conscious recruitment of memories may provide vital cognitive and affective information about the status of future events and desired goals. Memories may help us to estimate the difficulty of achieving a desired goal; they may inform us about what conditions or preparations are necessary for the goal to be accomplished. Memories may provide a picture of what the experience of success or failure in goal attainment would be like. For example, if the memory refers to a moment from a past romantic relationship, it may provide information about how much work it took to find this partner, how relaxed and confident one needed to be, and how pleasing it was to share time with another person. In building the courage to call a potential partner for a date, one may focus consciously on this memory or set of memories to gain reassurance and commitment to go through with the telephone call.

Memories also provide affective information directly by causing a set of emotions to be experienced as they are played out in the mind's eye. In the example of the prospective suitor poised by the telephone, the memory of a positive encounter from the old relationship creates the immediate affects of happiness, warmth, and yearning. It is the real-time experience of these emotions that reinforces the individual's desire to find a new partner. Each time the memory is recalled, the emotion generated by the recollection lets the individual feel the relative value of experiencing this event. This is the power of memory in motivating action—it does not offer simply an abstract expectancy-value calculation of the goal's desirability, it provides an affective *virtual reality* that makes meaningful the effect of goal success or failure.

The picture of memory offered by researchers studying its role in self-regulatory and mental control processes is very different from the associational model described by Bower (1981). Since Bower sketched his brilliant skeleton of the mind's linkage between affect and memory, researchers have added flesh and blood to the model. Affect theorists based in cognitive perspectives, such as our teacher, Robert Abelson, talk about "hot ·cognitions" and more complex personological affective responses (Smith, Haynes, Lazarus, & Pope, 1993). Far from being static nodes in a passive network waiting to be activated by congruent stimuli in the environment, affective memories are part of a dynamic personality, filled with wishes, needs, desires, and goals, a personality that actively links past, present, and future in an evolving narrative of the self (McAdams, 1988).

This view of the role of memory in social cognition and personality fits well with new perspectives on memory emerging from clinical psychology. Although repressed memories continue to be an area of vigorous debate and research (Herman, 1992; Loftus, 1993; Ross, 1991; Spence, 1982), clinical psychologists have placed a renewed emphasis on the importance of consciously recalled memories in the lives of their patients (Bruhn, 1991; Singer & Salovey, 1993). Far from attributing screenlike properties to memories recalled in therapy, as psychoanalytic therapists have persistently done, this research suggests that important life goals and affective concerns may be identified from analysis of the content of these memories. Individuals may come to know themselves and be known by others through the repetition of certain vivid, affectively laden, and personally meaningful memories, what we have called "self-defining memories" (Singer & Moffitt, 1991–1992; Moffitt & Singer, 1994; Singer & Salovey, 1993).

In the sections that follow, we illustrate how motivated memory can play an important role in affect and personality. In particular, we argue that emotion-memory relationships are best understood through their intermediary relationship to the self and the self's most desired goals. Drawing upon our research programs and clinical work, we present data that demonstrate how the affective intensity of memories is strongly linked to the memories' self- and goal-relevance. Finally, we present recent findings that return to the original puzzle of asymmetries in mood congruency research. These data suggest that individuals do indeed employ conscious strategies to repair negative mood states. Individuals may vary in their strategies and effectiveness at mood repair. Proneness to depression may play a mediating role in this effectiveness.

MEMORY'S ROLE IN THE LIFE STORY OF THE PERSON

In contrast to the 1980s vision of an associational, static memory, we have proposed an exploration of more active and motivation-based memories. To make this inquiry more concrete, we shall draw upon an example from clinical work. One of us consults to a drug and alcohol agency that offers a residential program for chronic drug addicts and alcoholics. In this capacity, I was asked to see a client whose mother had died in the past year (we shall give him the fictitious name of Roger). In the evaluation meeting, Roger began to describe his life's course, which consisted of much early promise and then a series of subsequent disappointments and failures, always precipitated by alcohol and drug abuse. As he presented his life history, he continually returned to his relationship with his mother, who had been an important administrator in his hometown's school system. Roger described her powerful personality and her strong influence over him and his father, who was also an alcoholic. He talked about how she had tried to guide his life for the better and repeatedly saved him from scrapes and problems due to his drinking. As he discussed her, he emphasized his own shortcomings and "laziness," how he had exploited her strength, and his refusal to take responsibility for himself.

At one moment in the interview, Roger described the following memory:

> I think a lot of this time when I was 12 or so. I had just gotten a paper route through a friend of my mom's. I was supposed to be out of the house early in the morning to deliver the papers. I remember waking up early one Sunday and looking out my window; I could see the front porch of our house from my bed. There was my mom, in her bathrobe, on her hands and knees, putting the inserts into each Sunday paper. I watched her for a bit and then I remember thinking (I can still remember this exact thought), thinking she's got this taken care of, so I rolled over and shut my eyes and went back to sleep. There she was, bare knees on that stone porch.

In subsequent meetings with Roger, he discussed his mother's last days before her death. With great self-hatred, he described stealing money from her pocketbook to go to the bars, as she lay an invalid in her bedroom. In our work on memory, we would indeed identify Roger's memory of the newspapers as a *self-defining memory*. As we have described in *The Remembered Self* (Singer & Salovey, 1993, pp. 27-46), the memory meets the criteria of affective intensity, vividness, repetition, linkage to similar memories (the more recent *stealing money* memories), and a focus on an unresolved conflict in his life (his ambivalent relationship with his mother). Given the painful nature of this memory, one must wonder, why does Roger choose to recall it and, as he indicates, think of it often? What function does this memory serve in his personality? Clearly, he has tried to escape this and other painful memories and thoughts by the use of mind-altering substances. Still, when sobriety returns, so do these autobiographical memories with the affectively laden information they provide about the status of his self-image and his desired goals. This memory and others like it may be a way of telling Roger what to avoid, what he does not want to be, showing him an *undesired self* (Ogilvie, 1987) that with sufficient strength and recovery he could learn to renounce. (It is an interesting historical note that Freud's development of the *death instinct* in *Beyond the Pleasure Principle* (1920/1973) grew out of the same question—why are people compelled to have recurring nightmares or to recall traumatic memories?)

To begin to make sense of why we recall self-defining memories, whether positive or negative in content, it would be helpful to place these memories in a larger context of personality. A leading theorist and researcher in the field of personality, McAdams (1988, 1990, 1993) presented a theory of identity grounded in the idea that individuals create continuity and purpose in their lives by forging a narrative life story. Each individual is a playwright who draws on the raw material of life experience to fashion a narrative; this narrative changes with developmental stages of the life course, offering the possibility of comedy, drama, or tragedy. There are four major components to this life story model of the person: *nuclear episodes, imagoes, ideological settings*, and *generativity scripts*. There are also two underlying dimensions that cross through each component—*thematic lines* and *narrative complexity*. Let us take a look at these two dimensions first. McAdams argues that running through all our lives is a tension between our desire to be intimate with and close to others (communion) and our desire to separate from others and establish our autonomy, competence, and independence (agency). These two themes exist in different levels within each individual and may rise and fall in importance over the life span. An individual's important life goals and autobiographical memories may be scored for motives related to agency (n-power and n-achievement) and communion (n-intimacy) (Emmons & McAdams, 1991; McAdams, 1982). In our brief case study of Roger, it is clear that both his sense of communion and agency are markedly flawed; he sees himself as uncomfortably dependent upon his mother;

intimacy is thus highly ambivalent for him. At the same time, this dependency has led him to be irresponsible and insufficiently autonomous in his adult life.

The second underlying dimension is narrative complexity, which refers to the degree of ambiguity and nuance present in one's life story. Some individuals describe the major narratives of their lives in straightforward linear terms. Others see each page as filled with twists and turns, ironies and paradoxes. By positing narrative complexity as a basic unit of identity, McAdams argues that the structure of the life story is as significant as its specific content. Several lines of investigation have demonstrated that memory narrative structure, in particular the specificity or generality of memory narratives, can be tied to personality differences in proneness to depression (McAdams, Lensky, Daple, & Allen, 1988; Moffitt, Singer, Nelligan, Carlson, & Vyse, 1994; Moore, Watts, & Williams, 1988; Singer & Moffitt, 1991–1992; Williams & Dritschel, 1988; Williams & Scott, 1988). These studies have variously found that depressed individuals have greater difficulty retrieving specific positive memories (Moffitt et al., 1994; Moore et al., 1988; Williams & Dritschel, 1988; Williams & Scott, 1988) and form more nuanced categories of negative as opposed to positive information (McAdams et al., 1988). The concept of complexity also applies to how individuals view their long-term goals. Emmons and King (1988, 1989) demonstrated that individuals feel ambivalence about the attainment of a particular personal striving as well as conflict among different personal strivings, each of which they desire. As McAdams suggests, individuals' variation in the complexity of these striving hierarchies is a basic dimension of a person's life story. Once again, one could explore goal conflicts and ambivalences for Roger. Although he professes love and respect for his mother, he also conveys themes of resentment and hostility toward her efforts at control and domination of his life course.

Along with these two dimensions of theme and complexity, there are the four basic components of the life story model. The first, nuclear episodes, is the most relevant to our discussion of motivated memory and we address it in some detail. For this chapter, we can give a brief mention of the other three. *Imagoes* refer to the reoccurring archetypal characters of our life story narrative. These characters often embody different aspects of the themes of agency and communion—they return in our memories as nurturing mother figures, heroic fathers, romantic lovers who remain elusive, challenging teachers, loyal friends, and so on. In Roger's memories, his mother emerges as an archetypal imago, an all-powerful maternal figure somewhat larger than life. *Ideological setting* encompasses the beliefs and values that form the backdrop to the occupational and personal choices we make in our lives. At what price do we cherish communion versus agency? How much of our social and intimacy needs would we sacrifice to reach fulfillment in our work or in our self-exploration? In regard to Roger's newspaper memory, it draws in ironic fashion upon a strong work ethic ideology and ingrained expectations about what constitutes a successful individual in the society.

Finally, *generativity scripts* are the most future-oriented. Generativity, a term coined by Erikson, refers to individuals' investment in the legacy of their lives' narratives. Will a life rich in communion yield an ending based in family and community connectedness where service and respect prevail? Will a life focused on agency demonstrate the power of the individual spirit to render beauty, model courage, or enhance the material lives of others? The long-term goals or personal strivings we set for ourselves are really the abbreviated versions of generativity scripts. Our personal strivings are brief statements about how we want the world to turn out, how we want our life story to end. In Roger's case, he stands at a crossroads regarding his future. Having reached his late 30s, he still holds the possibility of living a meaningful and productive life, as well as marrying and raising a family. However, he feels a gathering sense of despair that he will not be capable of ever *getting straight*, of joining the functioning world. There are too many moments in recent years in which he looks to the future and sees nothing, only rehabs, "detoxes," and the blacked-out world of addiction.

In describing the various components of McAdams' life story model, we have alluded to how autobiographical memories are linked in meaningful ways to these components. All of these aspects of the life story find their way into the individuals' nuclear episodes. *Nuclear episodes* are the critical sequences from our past that influence the rest of our lives.

> As we construct our identities through narrative, we confer upon certain experiences in our lives a salience or centrality which denotes that they are very, very special. These incidents may be highly positive or negative. They may mark perceived transformations of self—identity turning points—or they may affirm perceived continuity and sameness. They may involve things we did or things that were done to us. They may entail private moments or a shared experience with an entire community. (McAdams, 1988, p. 133)

From this description, it is clear that Roger's self-defining memory would constitute a nuclear episode in the life story theory of identity. It should then be expected to have the capacity to play a critical role in self-regulation and mood control in his life. By the nature of its centrality to the self, it should be densely connected to a range of affective responses. It is also rich in association to other components of thought-related recollections, fantasies, and strivings. By summoning up his particular nuclear episode from memory, Roger gains immediate access to a vast array of information about himself and his desires. Both thematically (in terms of agency and communion) and structurally (in terms of the complexity of the narrative), his memory can tell him what kind of person he has been and has the potential to be (if he does not make changes in his life).

McAdams' theory offers us a fully realized vision of the role of narrative memory in identity. It helps us to see how memories function for the person as expressions of motivational trends across the life span. However, the theory is silent on how these nuclear episodes influence the moment-to-moment responses individuals make when affected by transitory mood states and situational demands. The research described in the next section of this chapter describes how we can operationalize these nuclear episodes in terms of long-term goals and current affective states experienced by the individual. By working with measures created to tap *self-defining memories* and *personal strivings*, we can demonstrate the relationship among memories, goals, and affect in our daily lives.

SELF-DEFINING MEMORIES AND LONG-TERM GOALS

In developing a measure to study individuals' self-defining memories, it is important to examine their resemblance to similar constructs. As we have seen, self-defining memories might include the kind of turning point memories defined by McAdams' nuclear episodes. However, both self-defining memories and nuclear episodes may be traced to Tomkins' script theory of personality and its emphasis on the *nuclear scene* (Tomkins, 1979, 1987, 1991). Script theory argues that individuals often respond to situations through the lens of influential prior affective episodes in their lives. These affective episodes or "scenes" are repetitive cognitive-affective sequences that contain linked characters, settings, and plots. When individuals have experienced a critical number of highly similar affective scenes, these scenes blend into a schema or *script*, which then imposes itself upon new interactions. Individuals respond to and shape these interactions according to the predetermined script. Many interpersonal misunderstandings and, in a more extreme form, neurotic repetitions stem from the overly rigid application of certain personal scripts to interactions in relationships.

"Nuclear scenes" are scenes in script theory that are particularly intense affectively and center on wishes or conflicts that loom as unresolvable (e.g., fear of death, competition with siblings, early abandonment by a parent). Within the nuclear scene, there is usually a sharp shift from one affective state to another (joy to despair, anger to shame, embarrassment to anger). Investigators have explored nuclear scenes through experimental research (Carlson & Carlson, 1984; Demorest & Alexander, 1992; McAdams, 1988), nonclinical case material (Carlson, 1981), historical material (Carlson,

1982), and clinical case studies (Singer & Salovey, 1993; J. A. Singer & J. L. Singer, 1992).

It would seem that self-defining memories meet all the criteria of "scenes" in Tomkins' theory, but they are not necessarily bound to the more primal and unresolvable quality contained within the nuclear scene. Another difference is that individuals are aware of and in fact continue to critique and revise their self-defining memories. On the other hand, a nuclear scene is not necessarily immediately apparent or even accessible to many individuals. Access to the events articulated in one of these affective scenes is a critical question in considering a relationship to goals. If we assume that the kind of goals we are proposing to study are conscious goals individuals set for themselves to guide their desires and behaviors, then are there corresponding scenes that fall squarely within the awareness of these individuals? If so, is it possible that these conscious memories have a strong affective hold over individuals and continue to influence their lives?

To explore whether or not consciously recalled important episodes from individuals' lives continue to have some bearing on their desired goals, we generated the hypothesis that individuals' current affective responses to their memories would be linked to the relevance of these memories to the attainment or nonattainment of their most desired goals. This hypothesis is derived directly out of goal-based theories of affect, which argue that how we feel about an event, whether past or present, may be a function of that event's contribution to attainment of desired goals (Ortony, Clore, & Collins, 1988; Roseman, Spindel, & Jose, 1990; Weiner, 1985). Two additional qualifications on this hypothesis should be noted. First, the relationship of memories and goals should be considered reciprocal—not only might affective responses of the memory be linked to goal status, but the desirability of one's current goals may be predicted from and in fact shaped by one's affect about past attainment or nonattainment of these goals. Second, we feel strongly that the memories individuals recall are not veridical but are active reconstructions. In fact, due to life circumstances and shifting goal priorities, we might actually experience not only shifts in affective responses to the memories but subtle shifts in the content of the memories as well.

To test our hypotheses regarding memories and goals, we created a methodology that would allow us to collect autobiographical memories and long-term goals. In a first set of experiments (Singer, 1990), subjects received a list of 15 life goal sentences, each paraphrasing sentences written by Murray (1938) and, later, Edwards (1959) to convey Murray's psychogenic needs (e.g., "I would like to create a lasting and notable accomplishment"). These needs included, among others, achievement, nurturance, affiliation, harm avoidance, order, autonomy, and play. To elicit autobiographical memories, we drew upon a commonly used method that dates back to Galton's (1911) association experiments and has been used more recently by Robinson (1976, 1980) and Rubin (Rubin, Wetzler, & Nebes, 1986). This technique consists of providing subjects with a verbal cue (usually a single word) that serves to spark an autobiographical memory of diverse content and temporal distance. In our first experiment, we used life goal sentences as cues for memories, and in our second experiment, we used general categories of experience (family, friends and relationships, school, and activities). Once subjects located a memory and wrote it down, they rated it for their current affective responses in recalling them.

To ascertain the relationship of these autobiographical memories to the life goals they had rated, we requested that subjects make an additional rating of how relevant each memory was to the attainment of the life goal that cued it (or in the second experiment, to each of the 15 life goals). We looked first at subjects' affective responses to their memories and their ratings of goal attainment. Our hypothesis was confirmed: the more relevant participants' memories were to goal attainment, the more positively they felt about their memories. For example, subjects who rated the goal *loving relationships* as very important in their lives tended to have memories about powerful turning points in their relationships with lovers or family members; these memories were given affective response scores of great intensity (whether strongly positive if relevant to goal attainment and strongly negative if relevant to goal nonattainment). This connection between goal relevance and affective intensity of the memories was especially true for the goals they most desired (loving relationships, notable accomplishments, helping others). In general, these goals cued happy memories about times in which subjects had attained aspects of *communion* (relationships with friends, lovers, or family) or *agency* (academic or athletic triumphs).

However, when we looked at how subjects' memories were linked to avoidance goals (avoid pain, avoid failure, accept fate), which as a group tended to be less desired, we found a fascinating divergence. The more participants actually desired these goals, the more unpleasant their memories cued by these goals tended to be. On the other hand, when participants disliked these goals, they tended to retrieve more positive memories.

Table 10.1 divides the subjects into those who endorsed the goal "Avoid pain or danger" and those who did not. Participants who preferred to avoid pain or danger recalled distressing incidents in which they had failed to do so. Participants who disliked this harm avoidance goal remembered positive experiences in which they had risked pain or danger and thrived. It is still an open question as to whether subjects recall these events to justify their current stance or whether these memories have helped to create their stance. If we translate this finding into an analysis of Roger's memory, we might

TABLE 10.1
Memories Cued by the Goal "Avoid Pain or Danger"

Subjects Who Desired the Goal	Subjects Who Rejected the Goal
1. Getting lost in Kennedy Airport	1. Backpacking in the Grand Canyon
2. Breaking an elbow in camp	2. After a football game, the pain and bruises were like trophies
3. A stress fracture from running. Not able to compete	3. Riding a horse, jumping fences without reins or stirrups, hands over eyes
4. Taught to box; never again	4. Rock climbing at Tahoe; got hurt, but had lots of fun
5. Being chased by police	5. When Mom didn't let me go hang gliding
6. Did not jump off a very high wall into a very small pool of water	6. How good I felt after I crossed a dangerous river in Outward Bound
7. Afraid to ride horse	7. Hurting my back in fourth grade
8. A car accident when I cracked my head	8. Having my wisdom teeth out
9. Getting asthma at desert camp in Kenya	
10. Afraid to go parasailing	
11. Walking backward and hitting my head on hydrant	
12. Injuring an ankle and producing hemophiliac bleeding	
13. A boy beat me up when I was seventeen and left a lot of scars	
14. Climbing Debbie's tree to read	

Note. Five subjects gave a neutral rating to this goal: three had memories that were uninterpretable. Adapted from "Affective Responses to Autobiographical Memories and Their Relationship to Long Term Goals," by J. A. Singer, 1990, *Journal of Personality, 58,* p. 549.

suggest that one of Roger's strongly desired goals is to avoid a sense of self-hatred and humiliation regarding his mother. He then strongly draws upon the newspaper memory to invoke in himself the feelings of self-reproach and disgust that caution him against further behavior in this regard. In drawing this parallel to Roger, we also emphasize that it is the current affective response to the memory with which we are concerned. At the time of the incident, Roger rolling over in bed may have felt only a twinge of remorse about his behavior. It is clear that the memory has gained in its affective intensity over time due to its connection to what has become a dominating goal of Roger's life.

Although we were gratified with the results of this experiment and of our second experiment that no longer used the life goals as cues for the memories, we were not satisfied with the way we had operationalized the memories and the goals. We had no assurances that the memories we collected were particularly self-defining or that the life goals subjects rated were the goals they found personally important. To improve our measures, we conducted another study that collected memories and goals in a more sophisticated way (Moffitt & Singer, 1994). Drawing upon our theoretical description of self-defining memories, we created a self-defining memory request that would encourage subjects to retrieve more affective and consequential memories. Singer and Moffitt (1991-1992) reviewed a series of experiments that examine the self-defining memory request in comparison to other methods of eliciting autobiographical memories. We have included an excerpted version of this request in Table 10.2.

As Table 10.2 indicates, we elicit memories that are at least one year old, especially vivid, affectively intense, repetitive, and that convey crucial information about one's personal identity. As Singer and Moffitt (1991-1992) demonstrated, the self-defining memory request, compared to other requests matched for detail and complexity, evokes memories that subjects describe as more important to them; raters have also found more themes of self-discovery in these memories.

In addition to the self-defining memory request, we also asked subjects to generate a list of 15 personal strivings (Emmons, 1986, 1989, 1990). Personal strivings are "idiographically coherent patterns of goal strivings and represent what an individual is typically trying to do" (Emmons, 1989, p. 92). Emmons has described successful applications of his personal striving method in the areas of subjective well-being, physical health, and goal conflict (Emmons, 1986; Emmons & King, 1988, 1989). Participants are presented with the stem, "I typically try to [??]" and after filling in their striving, they rate it on a variety of dimensions, including happiness upon

TABLE 10.2
Instructions for the Self-Defining Memory Request (Excerpted)

A self-defining memory has the following attributes:

1. It is at least one year old.
2. It is a memory from your life that you remember very clearly and still feels important to you even as you think about it.
3. It is a memory that helps you to understand who you are as an individual and might be the memory you would tell someone else if you wanted that person to understand you in a more profound way.
4. It may be a memory that is positive or negative, or both, in how it makes you feel. The only important aspect is that it leads to strong feelings.
5. It is a memory that you have thought about many times. It should be familiar to you like a picture you have studied or a song (happy or sad) you have learned by heart.

To understand best what a self-defining memory is, imagine you have just met someone you like very much and are going for a long walk together. Each of you is very committed to helping the other get to know the "Real You." . . . In the course of conversation, you describe a memory that you feel conveys powerfully how you have come to be the person you currently are. It is precisely this memory that constitutes a self-defining memory.

Note. Adapted from "An Experimental Investigation of Specificity and Generality in Memory Narratives," by J. A. Singer and K. H. Moffitt, 1991-1992, *Imagination, Cognition, and Personality, 11*, p. 242. Copyright by the Baywood Publishing Co., Inc. Adapted by permission.

attainment, difficulty of attainment, and ambivalence about attainment. Daily positive affect is linked to a tendency to have valued and important strivings, but ambivalence about strivings is linked to more negative affect and higher rates of physical symptoms (Emmons & King, 1988).

In the Moffitt and Singer (1994) study, subjects recalled 10 self-defining memories, and then a week later, listed 15 personal strivings. After completing the personal striving task, subjects were asked to review their memories from the week before and rate their relevance to the attainment of each of the 15 personal strivings. Our results in this experiment replicated the earlier two experiments. The more positive subjects felt about their memories, the more relevant their memories were to the attainment of their strivings. The more embarrassed, sad, and angry they felt about their memories, the more their memories reflected nonattainment of their strivings. These findings were strong and significant even though subjects had rated their affective responses to their memories a week before they rated the relevance of these memories to their strivings.

Of equal importance, we again looked at the goals that were organized around a desire to avoid rather than gain an outcome. This time, as we had now predicted, the more subjects desired avoidance strivings, the more their memories conveyed themes of failed avoidance and the less happy they felt about the outcomes of these memories. Table 10.3 provides an example from one such subject.

The results of this study and the previous experiments we described on memories and life goals help to articulate memory's possible role in motivation and personality. Individuals may retrieve memories selectively relevant to the attainment of desired goals as a means of self-encouragement in the pursuit of these goals. On the other hand, individuals may learn to desire certain goals more as they accumulate examples of successful attainment of these goals. In this mutually reinforcing relationship, memories may become one aspect of the *self-talk* that individuals engage in when confronted with challenges or performance demands related to self-efficacy (Bandura & Cervone, 1983).

In contrast, individuals who favor higher percentages of avoidance goals (e.g., avoidance of pain or failure) may recall and ruminate about their memories in a very different way. Instead of retrieving memories about the successful avoidance of risky or disappointing situations, they tend to recall accidents, injuries, or failures. The negative affect generated by these memories may actually reinforce their choice to avoid risk or challenge. Repetitive recall of these negative incidents could be part of the problem in phobic behavior. From a clinical standpoint, phobic or excessive anxiety might involve an individual's cyclic return to affective memories that are relevant to the nonattainment of avoidance goals. Phobic individuals, who highly esteem the avoidance of certain fear-provoking situations, habitually

TABLE 10.3
Strivings and Memories

Personal Strivings:

I typically try to:
Avoid taking my anger out on people who don't deserve it.
Get eight hours of sleep a night
Avoid public speaking.[a]
Avoid caring about people too much.
Avoid most physical activity.[b]
Avoid being overly competitive.
Avoid being a complete cynic.
Make my family proud of me.
Avoid giving advice unless its asked for.
Avoid trusting people until they've proven many times that they deserve it.
Be loyal to my friends and especially my family.
Avoid going somewhere where I won't know anyone else.[c]
Help friends who are in trouble.
Not to be argumentative and stubborn.

Self-Defining Memories of Failure in Avoidance Strivings:

[a]"I remember having to give a demonstration speech in tenth-grade English. I absolutely hated giving speeches. We had done several others but this was absolutely the worst because it was the longest—ten minutes. I was demonstrating how to make brownies; I was very nervous and was shaking badly. When I was trying to put the tablespoon of water in the bowl it ended up taking two tries because I shook so much half the water spilled out."

[b]"The summer after my freshman year I went to a sports camp for one week. I wasn't in great shape and this was the type of place where you did your sport (gymnastics) for eight hours a day. The whole week was a huge exercise in will power trying to convince myself that I could get out of bed and my body would make it through another day. I lasted through the week and fell asleep for fourteen hours when I got home."

[c]"I remember driving to Florida for spring break last year. As soon as I got there I missed my family terribly and called them every night. I was happy to be there, but whenever it was right around dinner time I would wish I had stayed home."

Note. Adapted from *"Linking Personal Past, Present, and Future: Self-Defining Memories, Affect, and Strivings,"* by K. H. Moffitt, 1991, unpublished master's thesis, Connecticut College, New London, CT.

may revive memories relevant to their failure to avoid these situations. The resultant negative affect, caused by these memories, reinforces the phobics' need to avoid these fear-provoking situations. Imagery or desensitization treatments often attempt to break the phobics' cycle and to replace negative memories or images with more pleasant ones.

In a related fashion, individuals prone to depression may engage in a similar replaying of nonattainment memories. However, for the depressive, their memories would concern the nonattainment of approach rather than avoidance goals. As Carver and Scheier (1982) have emphasized, a sustained mismatch between desired goals and perceived outcomes often results in persisting negative affect. It may be that individuals caught in depression ruminate over failed attainment of goals and find a reduced accessibility of memories related to goal attainment. Although some brooding over disappointments or failures can be valuable, because it allows for problem solving about what went wrong and reminds us of how aversive it is to fail, excessive absorption can make us vulnerable to despair and hopelessness. Certainly, Roger could use his memories of letting down his mother as a spur to build a strong recovery, but unfortunately he has more often used these memories as a trigger to engage in addictive and self-destructive behavior.

In raising these questions about the function of memories, we are anticipating the next section of this chapter concerning memory and mood regulation. We have demonstrated the self-defining aspect of personal memories, as well as their relationship to affect and goals in personality. If memories are one source of affective responses and feedback in the person, they could be enlisted when individuals seek to address and alter undesired mood states. Motivated memory may not refer simply to the role of memory in goal attainment, but also to memory's capacity to modulate and change aversive mood states. In contrast to the depressed individual, nondepressed individuals may indeed recruit positive memories to repair negative moods. We alluded to such theories of mood maintenance and repair at the beginning of this chapter; now let us turn to empirical work that addresses the possibility that more positive memories may be recollected to diffuse negative mood states.

MEMORY AND MOOD REGULATION

We often hear the homilies, "put on a happy face" or "whistle in the dark." These sayings encourage individuals to take positive actions or think positive thoughts to counteract negative moods. Empirically, there is some indirect evidence that individuals do engage in recruitment of positive memories to regulate negative moods. Singer and Salovey (1988) reviewed the mood and memory literature and found that subjects temporarily made sad by mood manipulations often showed a dearth of positive memories rather than an increase in negative memories.

Researchers have speculated about what factors may lead to a deficit in positive memories for depressed individuals. Williams and his colleagues have demonstrated that individuals suffering from clinical depression have difficulty retrieving specific positive memories (Moore et al., 1988; Williams & Broadbent, 1986; Williams & Dritschel, 1988; Williams & Scott, 1988). Williams has suggested that depressed individuals may be less attentive to specific event cues both when they are encoding and retrieving information. By operating at a more general and abstract level of information processing, they have more difficulty retrieving specific information that is not salient in their immediate situation. For the depressed individual, negative cues are much more salient and therefore more easily encoded and retrieved. Lacking specific positive cues, the depressed individual has difficulty going beyond a general level of representation for positive events.

Building on this theoretical and empirical work, Singer and Salovey (1993) suggested the following model. First, as the Williams' research indicates, depressed individuals may possess an overgeneralizing style during both the encoding and the recall of information. Second, as a depressive episode develops, their physical resources, attention, and concentration may become impaired. Third, as the depression deepens, it becomes a primary focus of thought, siphoning away increasing attentional resources (Ellis, 1990; Conway & Giannopoulus, 1991).

The combination of an overly abstract processing style with a depletion of effortful attentional resources may result in a deficit in the ability to repair negative moods. Nondepressed individuals who enter a bad mood may begin to search their memories for positive experiences that will oppose their negative ideation. In contrast, depressed individuals face obstacles to this strategy. Because of their overly general approach to encoding events, they may have fewer specific memories of positive events stored in long-term memory. In addition, the positive events they have stored may be more vague and less densely associated to other aspects of memory. To make matters worse, their attentional resources may be depleted due to their physical condition. Finally, the attentional resources remaining may be diverted to the self-absorbing demands of the painful depression. The outcome, as Williams found, is that depressed individuals function at a more general level of autobiographical memory and in particular are slower to find specific positive memories.

Although Williams' work illustrates a deficit in mood repair for a clinically depressed population, there have not been any studies that demonstrate that a nondepressed sample actually recalls positive memories to repair a negative mood. To examine this question, Josephson, Singer, and Salovey (1994) conducted the following study. In a first session, subjects filled out a series of self-report measures including the Beck Depression Inventory. A week later, subjects viewed either a negative mood video (a clip of the more tearful scenes from the film *Terms of Endearment*) or a neutral mood video (a segment about making end tables from the *Yankee Workshop*). After taking a mood check that established significant differences in their mood state depending on the video viewed, subjects were asked to recall and write down a personal memory. There were no stipulations about the content or kind of memory; the request indicated that the valence (positive or negative) of the memory was completely up to the subject. When subjects completed the recording of this memory, they were then requested to write down a second memory according to the same guidelines as the first memory.

Once subjects finished writing down their memories, they rated each memory on a list of emotion adjectives for how it had made them feel in recalling it. They also made a global judgment as to whether each memory was positive or negative. They then rated their overall mood state again. Finally, subjects were asked to provide an explanation for why they recalled their two memories in the order that they chose.

As an operationalization of the mood repair hypothesis, we proposed that subjects would display mood congruence initially; subjects who watched the sad video would be more likely to recall first memories that were negative compared to subjects who viewed the neutral video. However, by the second memory, subjects in the negative mood condition would begin to engage in repair strategies and start to recall more positive memories.

To examine these hypotheses, we looked at subjects' ratings of their affective responses to each memory. Subjects in the negative mood condition did indeed rate their first memories as more sad and less happy than subjects in the neutral mood condition. However, by the second memory, there is a changing pattern. As Table 10.4 shows, the neutral subjects stay virtually the same from the first memory to the next regarding their ratings of happiness and sadness. In contrast, the subjects in the negative mood condition report increases in happy ratings and decreases in sad ratings of their memories. They do appear to be repairing the negative mood evidenced by the first memory ratings.

Before we jump on the mood repair bandwagon, we must address the objection that all we are seeing is the wearing-off of a transitory mood

TABLE 10.4
Affective Responses to Memories in Negative vs. Neutral Mood Conditions

	Ratings of Happiness		
Mood	1st Memory	2nd Memory	
Negative	1.55	2.65	($n = 49$)
Neutral	3.73	3.40	($n = 57$)
	Ratings of Sadness		
Mood	1st Memory	2nd Memory	
Negative	3.88	2.51	($n = 49$)
Neutral	1.88	2.14	($n = 57$)

Note. Subjects rated their affective responses to the memories on a 0–6 scale where 6 indicated "extremely" happy or sad.

induced by the viewing of the video clip. That is, the mood induction stirred up some negative feelings and cognitive associations, but over the time of the experiment, even without active mood repair, it ceased to influence the subjects strongly. There are no direct data that can counter this argument, but we did build into the study a final question regarding why subjects recalled the memories in the order that they did.

To examine these data, we first looked at the breakdown of subjects in the negative mood condition. Of the 49 subjects who viewed the sad video, 36 subjects (73%) recalled a negative first memory. Of these 36 subjects, 19 recalled a second positive memory. Two questions are worth examining. First, how many of these 19 report an explicit, conscious effort at "mood repair" when asked to account for why they recalled the memories in the order that they did? The answer is 68%, and some sample responses are listed in Table 10.5. Second, given that there were 17 subjects who recalled two negative memories in a row, it would be important to compare these subjects' scores on a depression inventory to the 19 subjects who recalled a negative followed by a positive memory. If subjects with a second positive memory compared to a second negative memory were to show lower depression scores, it might suggest that these subjects were more effective at practicing mood repair strategies.

The results indicated that subjects who recalled two negative memories had a mean BDI of 11.00, whereas those subjects who recalled a negative followed by a positive had a significantly lower mean BDI of 6.63. This is a promising finding when one considers that subjects with two negative memories in a row are scoring in the range Beck would characterize as mildly clinically depressed. It might also be valuable to show that if a happy mood were induced, subjects would be more likely to recall more positive

TABLE 10.5
Sample Responses of Subjects' Open-Ended Responses in the Sad Mood Induction with a Negative First Memory and Positive Second Memory (NP)

I am in a negative mood today so it was easier to come up with something negative for the first time. The second time, I decided to choose something positive to try to make myself feel better.

The first memory was negative because the video we saw was about cancer, which brought back negative memories for me. The second memory was positive because I wanted to do something that would lift my mood.

The first memory was negative because the film we had just watched was sad, therefore all the memories I thought of were sad. The second memory was positive because I wanted to think of happier things.

I chose to make my first memory negative because the scene in the video reminded me of the memory. My second memory was positive so that I could try to feel a little less sad.

first *and* second memories in an effort to maintain the good feeling achieved. If this were the case, we should expect to see a sustained difference in positive affect over the second memory when comparing happy mood subjects to neutral mood subjects. This result would argue against a simple mood attenuation explanation.

CONCLUSION

The work discussed in this chapter suggests that researchers benefited greatly from Bower's model of mood and memory but that we have since expanded and enriched this model. When one places the relationship of mood and memory in the context of personality and motivation, it allows us to see autobiographical memory from a dynamic, but not necessarily psychodynamic, standpoint. By examining the connection of memory to current affect and future strivings, we can see how memories may be recruited for cognitive and affective information about the status of desired goals. We can also see how memory can play a role in life story narratives that comprise identity. Through the sensorial imagery and affective immediacy memory can generate, individuals can re-experience episodes from their life as a means of communicating to the self and others who they are. In this sense, memory is truly self-defining.

These memories are hardly finished creations that wait in storage to be viewed at an opportune time. Rather, memories are part of an active, constructive consciousness that works continuously to regulate the cognitive and affective systems of the personality. As the study we presented on mood regulation suggests, individuals may draw upon memories to respond to changes in mood and ongoing mental concerns. When experimental participants were subjected to a sad mood induction, certain memorial associations became more prominent. However, just as important, countervailing positive memories were recruited, and in several cases, with clear conscious intent by the subject. Memories, along with fantasies, daydreams, current concerns, logical abstractions, and generalizations, all contribute to the "stream of consciousness" that psychologists like James, J. L. Singer, and Klinger and writers like Proust, Joyce, and Faulkner have all studied and described. In this chapter, we have attempted to demonstrate how memories do not simply float in this stream but are directed and guided by the motivational and affective concerns of the individual.

REFERENCES

Bandura, A., & Cervone, D. (1983). Self-evaluative and self-efficacy mechanisms governing the motivational effects of goal systems. *Journal of Personality and Social Psychology, 45*, 1017–1028.

Blaney, P. H. (1986). Affect and memory: A review. *Psychological Bulletin, 99,* 229-246.
Bower, G. H. (1981). Mood and memory. *American Psychologist, 36,* 129-148.
Bower, G. H., & Mayer, J. D. (1989). In search of mood-dependent retrieval. *Journal of Social Behavior and Personality, 4,* 133-168.
Bruhn, A. R. (1991). *Earliest childhood memories: Vol. 1. Theory and application to clinical practice.* New York: Praeger.
Carlson, L., & Carlson, R. (1984). Affect and psychological magnification: Derivations from Tomkins' script theory. *Journal of Personality, 52,* 36-45.
Carlson, R. (1981). Studies in script theory: I. Adult analogues of a childhood nuclear scene. *Journal of Personality and Social Psychology, 40,* 501-510.
Carlson, R. (1982). Studies in script theory: II. Altruistic nuclear scripts. *Perceptual and Motor Skills, 55,* 595-610.
Carver, C. S., & Scheier, M. F. (1982). Control theory: A useful conceptual framework in personality-social, clinical, and health psychology. *Psychological Bulletin, 92,* 111-135.
Clark, M. S., & Waddell, B. A. (1983). Effects of moods on thoughts about helping, attraction, and information acquisition. *Social Psychology Quarterly, 46,* 31-35.
Conway, M. A., & Giannopoulus, C. (1991). *Dysphoria and decision making: Restricted information use for judgments of multi-attribute targets.* Unpublished manuscript, Concordia University, Montreal, Canada.
Demorest, A. P., & Alexander, I. E. (1992). Affective scripts as organizers of personal experience. *Journal of Personality, 60,* 645-663.
Edwards, A. L. (1959). *Edwards personal preference schedule manual.* New York: Psychological Corporation.
Ellis, H. C. (1990). Depressive deficits in memory: Processing initiative and resource allocation. *Journal of Experimental Psychology: General, 119,* 60-62.
Emmons, R. A. (1986). Personal strivings: An approach to personality and subjective well-being. *Journal of Personality and Social Psychology, 51,* 1058-1068.
Emmons, R. A. (1989). The personal striving approach to personality. In L. A. Pervin (Ed.), *Goal concepts in personality and social psychology* (pp. 87-126). Hillsdale, NJ: Lawrence Erlbaum Associates.
Emmons, R. A. (1990). Motives and life goals. In S. Briggs, R. Hogan, & W. Jones (Eds.), *Handbook of personality psychology.* Orlando, FL: Academic Press.
Emmons, R. A., & King, L. A. (1988). Conflict among personal strivings: Immediate and long-term implications for psychological and physical well-being. *Journal of Personality and Social Psychology, 54,* 1040-1048.
Emmons, R. A., & King, L. A. (1989). Personal striving differentiation and affective reactivity. *Journal of Personality and Social Psychology, 56,* 478-484.
Emmons, R. A., & McAdams, D. P. (1991). Personal strivings and motive dispositions: Exploring the links. *Personality and Social Psychology Bulletin, 17,* 648-654.
Erber, R., & Tesser, A. (1992). Task effort and mood regulation: The absorption hypothesis. *Journal of Experimental Social Psychology, 28,* 339-359.
Freud, S. (1920/1973). Beyond the pleasure principle. In J. Strachey (Ed.), *The complete works of Sigmund Freud, standard edition* (Vol. 18, pp. 93-136). London: Hogarth.
Galton, F. (1911). *Inquiries into human faculty and its development.* (2nd ed) New York: E. P. Dutton.
Herman, J. L. (1992). *Trauma and recovery.* New York: Basic Books.
Isen, A. M. (1985). The asymmetry of happiness and sadness in effects on memory in normal college students. *Journal of Experimental Psychology: General, 114,* 388-391.
Josephson, B. R., Singer, J. A., & Salovey, P. (1994, August). *Memory and the regulation of negative mood.* Poster presented at the annual meeting of the American Psychological Association, Los Angeles, CA.
Loftus, E. F. (1993). The reality of repressed memories. *American Psychologist, 48,* 518-537.

Macht, M. L., Spear, N. E., & Levis, D. J. (1977). State-dependent retention in humans induced by alternatives in affective state. *Bulletin of the Psychonomic Society, 10,* 415–418.

Madigan, R. J., & Bollenbach, A. K. (1982). Effects of induced mood on retrieval of personal episodic and semantic memories. *Psychological Reports, 50,* 147–157.

Matt, G. E., Vasquez, C., & Campbell, W. K. (1992). Mood-congruent recall of affectively toned stimuli: A meta-analytic review. *Clinical Psychology Review, 12,* 227–255.

McAdams, D. P. (1982). Experiences of intimacy and power: Relationships among social motives and autobiographical memory. *Journal of Personality and Social Psychology, 42,* 292–302.

McAdams, D. P. (1988). *Power, intimacy, and the life story: Personological inquiries into identity.* New York: Guilford.

McAdams, D. P. (1990). Unity and purpose in human lives: The emergence of identity as the life story. In A. I. Rabin, R. A. Zucker, R. A. Emmons, & S. Frank (Eds.), *Studying persons and lives* (pp. 148–200). New York: Springer.

McAdams, D. P. (1993). *The stories we live by.* New York: William Morrow.

McAdams, D. P., Lensky, D. B., Daple, S. A., & Allen, J. (1988). Depression and the organization of autobiographical memory. *Journal of Social and Clinical Psychology, 7,* 332–349.

Mischel, W., Ebbesen, E. E., & Zeiss, A. (1976). Determinants of selective memory about the self. *Journal of Consulting and Clinical Psychology, 44,* 92–103.

Moffitt, K. H., & Singer, J. A. (1994). Continuity in the life story: Self-defining memories, affect, and approach/avoidance personal strivings. *Journal of Personality, 62,* 21–43.

Moffitt, K. H., Singer, J. A., Nelligan, D. W., Carlson, M. A., & Vyse, S. A. (1994). Depression and memory narrative type. *Journal of Abnormal Psychology, 103,* 581–583.

Moore, R. G., Watts, F. N., & Williams, J. M. G. (1988). The specificity of personal memories in depression. *British Journal of Clinical Psychology, 27,* 275–276.

Murray, H. A. (1938). *Explorations in personality.* New York: Oxford University Press.

Natale, M., & Hantas, M. (1982). Effect of temporary mood states on selective memory about the self. *Journal of Personality and Social Psychology, 42,* 927–934.

Ogilvie, D. (1987). The undesired self: A neglected variable in personality research. *Journal of Personality and Social Psychology, 52,* 379–385.

Ortony, A., Clore, G. L., & Collins, A. (1988). *The cognitive structure of emotion.* New York: Cambridge University Press.

Parrott, W. G., & Sabini, J. (1990). Mood and memory under natural conditions: Evidence for mood incongruent recall. *Journal of Personality and Social Psychology, 59,* 321–336.

Robinson, J. A. (1976). Sampling autobiographical memory. *Cognitive Psychology, 8,* 578–595.

Robinson, J. A. (1980). Affect and retrieval of personal memories. *Motivation and Emotion, 4,* 149–174.

Roseman, I. J., Spindel, M. S., & Jose, P. E. (1990). Appraisals of emotion-soliciting events: Testing a theory of discrete emotions. *Journal of Personality and Social Psychology, 59,* 899–915.

Ross, B. M. (1991). *Remembering the personal past.* New York: Oxford University Press.

Rubin, D. C., Wetzler, S. E., & Nebes, R. D. (1986). Autobiographical memory across the life span. In D. C. Rubin (Ed.), *Autobiographical memory.* New York: Cambridge University Press.

Salovey, P., Hsee, C., & Mayer, J. D. (1993). Emotional intelligence and the self-regulation of affect. In D. M. Wegner & J. W. Pennebaker (Eds.), *Handbook of mental control* (pp. 258–277). Englewood Cliffs, NJ: Prentice-Hall.

Salovey, P., & Singer, J. A. (1991). Cognitive behavior modification. In F. H. Kanfer & A. P. Goldstein (Eds.), *Helping people change: A textbook of methods* (4th ed., pp. 361–395). New York: Pergamon.

Showers, C., & Cantor, N. (1985). Social cognition: A look at motivated strategies. *Annual Review of Psychology, 36*, 275-305.

Singer, J. A. (1990). Affective responses to autobiographical memories and their relationship to long-term goals. *Journal of Personality, 58*, 535-563.

Singer, J. A., & Moffitt, K. H. (1991-1992). An experimental investigation of specificity and generality in memory narratives. *Imagination, Cognition, and Personality, 11*, 233-257.

Singer, J. A., & Salovey, P. (1988). Mood and memory: Evaluating the network theory of affect. *Clinical Psychology Review, 8*, 211-251.

Singer, J. A., & Salovey, P. (1993). *The remembered self: Emotion and memory in personality*. New York: Free Press.

Singer, J. A., & Singer, J. L. (1992). Transference in psychotherapy and daily life: Implications of current memory and social cognition research. In J. W. Barron, M. N. Eagle, & D. L. Wolitzky (Eds.) *Interface of psychoanalysis and psychology* (pp. 516-538). Washington, DC: American Psychological Association.

Smith, C. A., Haynes, K. N., Lazarus, R. S., & Pope, L. K. (1993). In search of the "hot" cognitions: Attributions, appraisals, and their relation to emotion. *Journal of Personality and Social Psychology, 65*, 916-929.

Snyder, M., & White, P. (1982). Moods and memories: Elation, depression, and the remembering of events in one's life. *Journal of Personality, 50*, 149-167.

Spence, D. P. (1982). *Narrative truth and historical truth: Meaning and interpretation in psychoanalysis*. New York: Norton.

Teasdale, J. D., & Fogarty, S. J. (1979). Differential effects of induced mood on retrieval of pleasant and unpleasant memories from episodic memory. *Journal of Abnormal Psychology, 88*, 248-257.

Teasdale, J. D., Taylor, R., & Fogarty, S. J. (1980). Effects of induced elation-depression on the accessibility of memories of happy and unhappy experiences. *Behavior Research and Therapy, 18*, 339-346.

Tomkins, S. S. (1979). Script theory: Differential magnification of affects. In H. E. Howe and R. A. Dienstbier (Eds.), *Nebraska symposium on motivation* (Vol. 26, pp. 201-236). Lincoln: University of Nebraska Press.

Tomkins, S. S. (1987). Script theory. In J. Aranoff, A. I. Rabin, & R. A. Zucker (Eds.), *The emergence of personality* (pp. 147-216). New York: Springer.

Tomkins, S. S. (1991). *Affect, imagery, consciousness* (Vol. 3). New York: Springer.

Wegner, D. M., Erber, R., & Zanakos, S. (1993). Ironic processes in the mental control of mood and mood-related thought. *Journal of Personality and Social Psychology, 65*, 1093-1104.

Weiner, B. (1985). An attributional theory of achievement motivation and emotion. *Psychological Review, 92*, 548-573.

Wenzlaff, R. (1993). The mental control of depression: Psychological obstacles to emotional well-being. In D. M. Wegner & J. W. Pennebaker (Eds.), *Handbook of mental control* (pp. 239-257). Englewood Cliffs, NJ: Prentice-Hall.

Williams, J. M. G., & Broadbent, K. (1986). Autobiographical memory in suicide attempters. *Journal of Abnormal Psychology, 95*, 144-149.

Williams, J. M. G., & Dritschel, B. H. (1988). Emotional disturbance and the specificity of autobiographical memory. *Cognition and Emotion, 2*, 221-234.

Williams, J. M. G., & Scott, J. (1988). Autobiographical memory in depression. *Psychological Medicine, 18*, 689-695.

Wright, J., & Mischel, W. (1982). Influence of affect on cognitive social learning person variables. *Journal of Personality and Social Psychology, 43*, 901-914.

11 The Self-Regulation of Moods

Ralph Erber
DePaul University

The experience of moods is a common and pervasive one for most people, and the range of moods that we experience may include happiness, sadness, irritation, and anxiety to name only a few. Frequently, the events that trigger our moods are beyond our immediate control. Good news and bad, for example, can often propel us instantaneously into temporary feelings of elation and depression as well. By and large, few people would mind being subjected to these types of affective states, perhaps because, as one observer put it, our changing moods "give our experienced world its liveliness and color" (Wessman & Ricks, 1966, p. vii). There may be times, however, when our moods may be unwanted. When this is the case, we may feel compelled to initiate attempts toward controlling or regulating them.

This chapter has two interrelated foci. First, it provides a theoretical and empirical account of the conditions that are likely to elicit attempts toward mood regulation. Second, it discusses the processes that are likely to be effective toward that end and present a theoretical framework for understanding them. In both cases, the discussion is specific to unwanted feelings of sadness and happiness, primarily because these states have received the bulk of attention in psychological research. Because a full understanding of the processes inherent in the self-regulation of moods can hardly be accomplished without understanding what moods are, I take a brief detour to clarify the nature of moods.

The Nature of Moods

The terms *mood, affect, feeling,* and *feeling state* are generally used in reference to transient yet global and pervasive affective states, such as temporary states of happiness or sadness (e.g., Isen, 1984). As such they are considered to be different from "emotions," despite dictionary-type definitions that tend to emphasize different levels of intensity as the distinguishing mark. Based on such definitions, moods are often considered to be "little emotions." However, there is good reason to consider moods as affective states that are qualitatively different from emotions (Isen, 1984; Nowlis, 1963). Along these lines, Clark and Isen (1982) provided a more sophisticated analysis of the differences between moods and emotions. Specifically, moods differ from emotions primarily in terms of their target-directedness. In other words, whereas emotions such as love, jealousy, anger, and envy usually have a specific target such as a loved one, a rival, a provoker, or a more famous colleague, moods are more diffuse. It is possible to be happy, sad, irritated, or anxious in the absence of a specific internal or external event.

This is not to say that moods come out of nowhere. Rather, it means that moods constitute experiences that are qualitatively different from the experience of emotions. For example, I can be happy about a pay raise or a kind word. Over time, my happiness may become disconnected from the eliciting event and be replaced by a feeling of happiness that is more global than the one I initially experienced. However, because my happiness is now without an immediate target, it is considered to be a mood rather than an emotion. Thus, moods can result as carry-over from a specific emotional experience that has lost its target. In other cases, our moods can have multiple targets to the point where no single one can explain their onset by itself. This is common in the experience of irritation and anxiety, which are often brought on by a multitude of internal and external events.

The extent to which moods depend on memory for their maintenance and intensity is another dimension on which they differ from emotions. Moods and emotions can both be brought on by specific memories, such as flashbulb memory in the case of emotions (Neisser, 1982) or the reminiscing about past events in the case of moods (Strack, Schwarz, & Gschneidinger, 1985). However, whereas emotions tend to dissipate once the emotion-eliciting conditions are terminated, moods usually sustain themselves for a nontrivial amount of time (Klinger, 1993; Nowlis, 1963), in part because they tend to trigger memories that are congruent with one's mood.

The phenomenon of mood congruent memory is by now well-established and has been the subject of several reviews (e.g., Blaney, 1986). It has important implications for the self-regulation of moods in that it suggests that moods are a little like credit card debts: they can be easily incurred but at the same time it can be extremely hard to get rid of them. For example, fairly innocuous events like changes in the weather can lead to improvements or deteriorations in our moods (Cunningham, 1979; Schwarz & Clore, 1983). The resulting recollection of mood congruent memories inherent in the experience of moods then helps to maintain the mood much in the same way that high interest on a credit card helps to maintain a debt.

What this suggests is that trying to rid oneself of a burdensome debt or an unwanted mood may be a nontrivial enterprise. Neither one goes away by itself, instead, as we will see, the regulation of both requires two things. First, one needs to instantiate a goal such as resolving to settle one's financial matters or to stop feeling sad. Second, because the elimination of an unwanted debt or mood is somewhat subverted by the process of mood congruent thinking, it can take considerable effort and resources to reach the desired state.

The credit card debt analogy is useful in the understanding of how we look at the processes by which people regulate their moods in that it illustrates the importance of examining the specific goals and processes that operate in the self-regulation of moods. The perspective taken here is somewhat at odds with previous treatments of mood regulation, which paid little attention to the issue of goals and processes. I next examine how the issue of mood regulation has been treated historically in order to clarify why and how the present perspective differs from previous approaches.

THE HEDONIC VIEW

Prior research has largely failed to take the importance of goals for the self-regulation of moods into account. There is a simple reason for this. Up to this point social psychologists have considered the mood itself to be a primary motivator for self-regulation. The conventional wisdom holds that we would always seek out good moods and do everything to preserve them because it is pleasant and rewarding to feel good. At the same time we avoid or "repair" bad moods with a vengeance because their experience is aversive (e.g., Isen, 1984; Taylor, 1991). Of course, this hedonic view on mood regulation stems from social psychology's longstanding tradition of conceptualizing human motivation in terms of seeking pleasure and avoiding pain (Allport, 1984). Thus it is not surprising that some have argued that people would mobilize all available resources to fend off the emotional consequences of aversive events (Taylor, 1991), unless they are in a state of resource depletion brought on by being too tired or overworked (Clark & Isen, 1982).

It is hard, if not impossible, to reject the hedonic view out of hand. Everything else being equal, people probably prefer pleasant emotional states over unpleasant ones. On the other hand, the hedonic view may paint an oversimplified picture of people's mood regulation tendencies. In fact, a closer inspection of its propositions reveals that it has some shortcomings in accounting for several phenomena related to the self-regulation of mood.

PROBLEMS WITH THE HEDONIC VIEW

Seeking out Happy Moods

In order to achieve a happy mood, people need access to an internal or external event that produces happiness in the first place. The problem is that we have limited control over such external events. For example, we can be pretty sure that Chicago winters will not become more tolerable simply because we wish it or because the mayor issues a proclamation to that effect. Our ability to produce happiness through retrieving happy memories may also be more tricky than one might think. For example, reminiscing about the glory days of our youth appears to be limited by the existence or availability of such memories. Even if they do exist, they may be difficult to retrieve for people who are feeling sad because they are incongruent with one's mood (Erber & Erber, 1994).

Maintaining Happy Moods

If people are as motivated to maintain a happy mood as the hedonic view advocates, the question is "Why are they not better at it?" As it turns out, people are notoriously bad about savoring positive experiences. They have difficulties reminiscing about past positive experiences, savoring the joy of the moment, and anticipating upcoming events (Bryant, 1989). Moreover, these difficulties are reflected in people's beliefs about their ability to savor positive experiences from the past, present, or future (Bryant, 1993). In other words, people are seriously deficient in employing strategies that are appropriate to maintain a happy mood. The moment we hear that a paper was accepted for publication, we sit down at our computers and try to crank out another one. Of course, what we have in hand at the end of the day is several thousand light-years away from being a publishable manuscript, and rather than patting ourselves on our backs, we end up trying to cope with the emotional fallout of having only written a few incoherent pages of material. Similarly, when we reminisce about the past our thoughts often take a disturbing turn in which we soon find ourselves reminded that we were much younger, trimmer, and carefree then. Of course, this can become a new source of unhappiness, which likely will foil our attempts at maintaining our good mood. Finally, we often subvert our attempts to maintain a happy mood through looking forward to a positive event by engaging our suspicions that something will probably go wrong.

Avoiding Sad Moods

Perhaps the most sweeping evidence against the hedonic idea of trying to avoid sad moods at all cost comes from the observation that people frequently engage in activities that make them feel sad. They watch heartrending movies, listen to plaintive music, and read stories with tragic endings. Is this the result of latent masochistic tendencies? Probably not. Instead, feelings of sadness have been shown to be associated with greater self-focus (e.g., Wood, Saltzberg, & Goldsamt, 1990). It may be that people have developed beliefs about their ability to gain self-insight through sadness, and their attempts to put themselves into a bad mood can perhaps be understood as a means toward that end. In a similar vein, the work of many artists and poets was born out of the misery of failed love and abject poverty.

Repairing Negative Moods

People's ability to repair an existing sad mood may often be limited, at least in part, by a lack of motivation as well as shortcomings in their ability to execute effective strategies (e.g., Wenzlaff, Wegner, & Roper, 1988). The fact that people encounter persistent negative moods, such as unhappiness and even depression, suggests that such impediments to what the hedonic view would consider "normal" mood regulation do in fact exist. Even if people are motivated to repair a negative mood, they still may fail to accomplish it because they may simply not have access to mood relevant stimuli to be implemented in their quest (Erber & Tesser, 1992; Zillmann, 1988). After all, negative moods make negative material more accessible in memory than positive material (e.g., Erber, 1991), and thus it may be hard to bring to mind thoughts that would help generate neutral or even happy moods.

ALTERNATIVES TO THE HEDONIC VIEW: A SOCIAL CONSTRAINTS MODEL

It is clear that the hedonic approach to mood regulation is in need of substantial modifications to account for the previously mentioned problems and others as well.

One sweeping way to modify it to account for a wide variety of exceptions is to suggest that people elect to modify their moods not just in response to what is positive but in response to perceptions of what is appropriate or fitting given the social constraints on our behavior, thoughts, and emotions. Although this suggestions still falls short of explaining wildly deviant moods, such as mania or depression, it helps to account for the many cases in which people seem to act in defiance of hedonistic principles. Furthermore, it is consistent with a long-standing tradition to conceptualize the experience of affect in terms of the situational context in which it takes place (Schachter & Singer, 1962). Seeking and maintaining an appropriate mood means hedonism when the goal is to be and stay happy. When feeling happy is not appropriate, however, the present framework predicts that people would direct their mood regulation attempts toward attaining a neutral or even a negative mood.

The appropriateness of a given mood is, according to the present perspective, defined by the social situation. Different settings can contain cues about *feeling rules* (Hochschild, 1983), prescriptions as to how one ought to feel. Good moods are appropriate in some settings, such as a party or a friendly game of horse. Neutral moods may be the goal while standing in line in the cafeteria or upon hearing that our flight has been canceled. Finally, negative moods, may be perfectly appropriate when talking to a friend who has experienced misfortune, at home after a bad day, or when we get stuck with a grumpy confederate while waiting for the experiment to begin.

There is evidence for some of the propositions of the social constraints model of mood regulation. Sometimes people seem to want to attain a sad mood. This is the case, for example, when they have to convey bad news to another. The idea behind this MUM effect (Tesser & Rosen, 1975) is that it can be quite awkward to have a smile on one's face while informing the neighbors that their house has burned down. It appears that in such instances people attempt to get into the mood they expect the target of the bad news to take on upon hearing it (Tesser, Rosen, & Waranch, 1973). Further, there are circumstances under which people may be motivated to maintain feelings of anger. It appears that anger can come in handy for people who have the opportunity to retaliate against an aggressor. In one study (O'Neal & Taylor, 1989), subjects who had been angered by the experimenter and knew that they would be able to retaliate against the provoker preferred to watch videos with more aggressive, violent content than angered subjects who did not have an opportunity to retaliate.

The present modifications of the hedonic theory do a fairly decent job explaining why people would sometimes want to feel sad or remain angry. However, to say that people, rather than trying to feel good all the time, will try to feel whatever fits the situation, is problematic in its own way. There are simply too many different situations demanding too many different moods to enable general predictions about people's tendencies to regulate them.

To increase the predictive power of the social constraints model it is necessary to recognize that the most general social constraint on mood is aimed at the eradication of inappropriate moods. In the absence of specific information that would allow a person to distinguish what mood should be attained in a given situation, the best choice is to avoid any mood, positive or negative, that might be inappropriate for whatever reason. This line of reasoning then suggests that, as a default, people would seek neutral moods. This appears to be the safest bet among the many different demands placed on our moods by the complexities of the social settings.

Admittedly, the suggestion that people will seek neutral moods rather than happy ones is likely to raise a considerable number of eyebrows. After all, it is the pursuit of happiness, not the pursuit of emotional neutrality that is guaranteed by the constitution. However, neutrality for social reasons is not all that inconsistent with a general goal to be happy. If nothing else, it may simply be easier to change a neutral mood to a happy or sad one once the particular situational demands have been discerned rather than switch directly to depression from elation or vice versa. From this perspective, emotional neutrality is also not to be equated with indifference. Instead it is a form of readiness that people bring to the task at hand.

To some extent, people in this state of affective neutrality may be best characterized as having a deliberative mindset (Gollwitzer, Heckhausen, & Steller, 1990) in which they process happy and sad information in an unbiased fashion. When the demands of the social setting change so as to require a happy or sad mood, people may shift their preferences accordingly in order to implement the appropriate affective state.

Anticipatory mood regulation of this kind has an interesting parallel in the study of attitude change. People tend to moderate their attitudes prior to engaging in a discussion about the attitude object with another person (Cialdini, Levy, Herman, & Levenbeck, 1973). Interestingly, such anticipatory attitude change is generally in the direction of the center of the opinion scale (i.e., the neutral points) rather than toward the actual or presumed position of the other.

Finally, cybernetic approaches to self-regulation (Carver & Scheier, 1981) also predict that people may be motivated to seek out neutral moods. Within this framework, negative affect usually signals a discrepancy between the desired goal state and the actual state leading people to increase their efforts at reducing the discrepancy. Positive affect may indicate a different type of discrepancy, namely that the goal has been overshot. Of course, it is possible that this realization may sometimes lead to discrepancy enlargement. However, under some circumstances people may reduce their efforts toward goal attainment and as a result their affective state may become more neutral.

EVIDENCE FOR THE SOCIAL CONSTRAINTS MODEL

Anticipating Social Interaction

The theoretical speculation up to this point, along with the findings on anticipatory attitude change, suggests that people might be particularly likely to regulate their moods prior to interacting with a stranger. The direction of their regulatory attempts should be toward a neutral mood, and this should happen regardless of the presumed mood of the other person.

To test these hypotheses, we (Erber, Wegner, & Therriault, in press) surreptitiously exposed subjects to either uplifting or depressing music to induce a happy or sad mood. Selections from David Byrne's "Beleze Tropical, Brazil Classics 1" and Hubert Laws' jazz version of Bach's "Brandenburg Concierto No. 3" were used to induce a happy mood. The music used to induce a sad mood included "Russia under the Mongolian Yoke" and "Field of the Dead," both from Prokofiev's "Alexander Nevsky, Op. 78." Following the mood manipulations, subjects were asked to choose from among a number of newspaper headlines those stories they would most like to read by putting them in the order of their choice. Some of the headlines suggested cheerful stories, such as "Woman Sues City, County After Being Hit by Toilet," or "Adventurer Aborts Attempt to Cross Bering Strait in a Tub." Other headlines conveyed depressing stories, such as "9 Men, Woman Rape Pregnant Woman," or "Officials, Witnesses Say 62 People Killed." A third set of headlines conveyed stories that were affectively neutral such as "Shuttle Workers Load Galileo on Atlantis," or "Crack for Bush Gotten in Federal Sting." Prior to rank-ordering the stories all subjects had been informed that there would be an unspecified second task following the main experiment. Half were told that they would be doing the task with another subject, whereas the remainder were told that they would be doing it by themselves.

Figure 11.1 shows the valence of subject's story preferences in the experimental conditions. The numbers represent a positivity index that we obtained by multiplying the ranks of the positive stories by 3, the neutral stories by 2, and the negative stories by 1. By this method, higher scores indicate a relative preference for more depressing stories, and lower scores indicate a preference for cheerful stories. As expected, both happy and sad subjects preferred to read stories that were congruent with their moods as long as they knew they would be by themselves. This finding replicates the familiar mood congruency effect. Quite a different picture emerges, however, for subjects who expected to interact with a stranger. They preferred mood incongruent stories, presumably in an attempt to neutralize their mood prior to the anticipated interaction.

Note that subjects in this study had no information about the emotional state of the other. Thus it is possible that subjects' tendencies to seek out mood incongruent information prior to the anticipated interaction reflected a desire to match the presumably neutral mood of the other. However, when we informed subjects that the other was feeling happy, depressed, or somewhere in between (Erber et al., in press, Study 2), the pattern of results did not change very much at all. Specifically, there was no indication

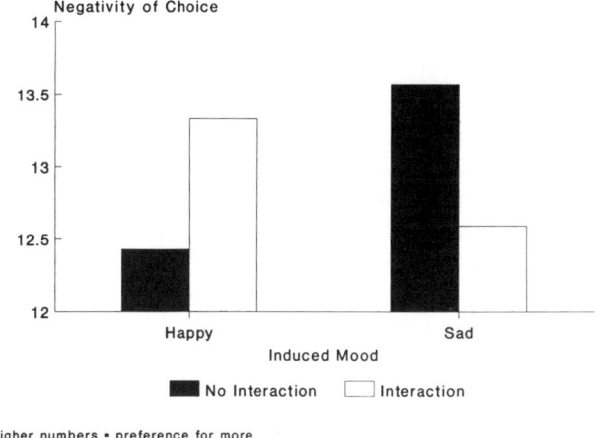

Fig. 11.1 Valence of subjects' story preferences as a function of induced mood and anticipated interaction. Higher numbers = preference for more depressing stories.

that subjects were trying to feel sad themselves when they knew they would be meeting a depressed other. If anything, there was a tendency on the part of happy subjects to bolster their happy mood, presumably because they knew that having to interact with someone who is depressed would eventually get them down.

The findings of the studies on mood regulation in anticipation of social interaction provide support for the social constraints model, and they have recently been replicated (Nelson & Baumgardner, 1993). They also make a great deal of sense. To enter into an interaction with an unwanted happy or sad mood can interfere with the goals of the interaction, as Goffman (1963) pointed out some time ago. At the very least, they can interfere with the smoothness or efficiency of the interaction, and thus people may be inclined to first achieve a state of readiness by neutralizing their moods.

Anticipating a Cognitively Complex Task

Interacting with others probably constitutes a considerable chunk of our daily chores. Unwanted moods may interfere with more solitary activities as well. Everyone who has ever tried to do an ounce of serious thinking while in a state of deep depression or utter elation has probably experienced first-hand the futility of such an effort. Remember that the experience of happy and sad moods is marked by a preoccupation with mood-congruent thoughts. These thoughts may interfere with tasks that place heavy demands on our capacity to process information, and it may be that people attempt to neutralize their moods prior to undertaking a mentally challenging task.

We (Erber & Erber, 1994) tested this hypothesis in a quasi-experimental setting. Our subjects were students enrolled in an introductory psychology course. Once a week the class was split into discussion sections that required students to actively participate in class, if for no other reason than getting a good participation grade. We reasoned that these students might be most likely to attenuate a sad and perhaps even a happy mood at the beginning of class when it could possibly interfere with the cognitive processing required for answering questions, raising issues, and so forth. On the other hand, these same demands on students' cognitive resources should be greatly reduced at the end of class. At that time there is little with which an unwanted mood might interfere, and other opportunities for mood regulation may become available (such as meeting friends in the cafeteria or having a smoke).

To test this idea, we asked students to recall an event from their recent past that made them feel either very happy or very sad. Half of the subjects (i.e., the students in two out of four sections) did this at the beginning of class, the remainder did it at the end of class. Additionally, following this initial recall, all subjects were asked to remember another event with the instructions that they could remember anything they wanted. We then coded the emotional content of what subjects recalled the second time around. Figure 11.2 depicts the outcome of this experiment. As expected, when the task was completed at the end of class, that is, in the absence of a specific goal to regulate one's mood, subjects' recollections were once again largely mood congruent. However, at the beginning of class, sad

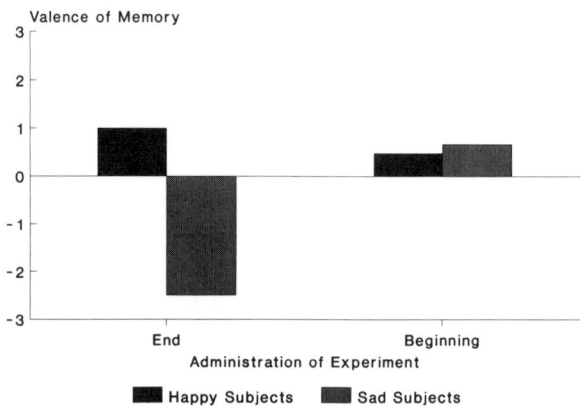

Fig. 11.2 Emotional content of subjects's recollections as a function of induced mood and anticipation of a cognitively demanding task. Negative scores = sad memories; positive stories = happy memories.

subjects recalled happy memories the second time around, presumably in an attempt to regulate their mood. Happy subjects showed a nonsignificant tendency to recall less happy memories.

Self-Deception in the Service of Happiness

A final piece of evidence comes from an ongoing research project on the motivational underpinnings of self-deception (Erber & Case, 1993). As alluded to earlier, some situations, such as parties and other social gatherings, often require people to be downright happy. Imagine that prior to attending the wedding of a friend you find out that you were nearly left off the invitation list because of your generally depressive and morose demeanor. It is too late to send your regrets, but, at the same time, the newly acquired knowledge about yourself may induce negative feelings that might be at odds with the positive ones required for attending the wedding. One way to take care of this discrepancy between actual and desired affective state might be to deceive yourself about the extent of your depression and moroseness by downplaying the veracity of the feedback. For example, convincing yourself of a proposition like "I'm a little morose sometimes, but they just happen to see me when I'm feeling down" may induce enough good feelings to save the day. This type of finding is exactly what we (Erber & Case, 1993) obtained when we gave subjects negatively discrepant feedback on a bogus personality test. Subjects who had previously been told that they would have to appear happy in a subsequent videotaping session distorted feedback indicative of their self-presentational abilities in their favor. In the absence of an explicit goal to be happy, this same effect was not observed.

The studies reviewed so far provide support for the social constraints model of mood regulation. They provide a basis for redrawing the picture of people as mainly hedonistic creatures determined to seek positive moods and avoid negative moods. Instead, the picture that emerges is one of people as active mood regulators who are sensitive to the demands that the social setting places on the appropriateness of their emotional states. What is still missing is insight into the actual processes that aid in attaining the desired moods. This is the focus of the next section.

STRATEGIES FOR THE SELF-REGULATION OF MOODS

When people have a goal to regulate their moods, what strategies are they likely to use and which of these strategies will yield the desired results? We know a little about the home remedies people seem to use in their everyday lives (Larsen, 1993; Morris & Reilly, 1987). Most of these naive strategies are designed to alleviate bad moods, which could be due to either one of two things. It could be that people develop better strategies to cope with bad moods (Bryant, 1993; Taylor, 1991) or it could be because no self-respecting hedonistically oriented social psychologist would bother to ask people what they do to alleviate happiness or maintain sadness (Parrott, 1993). Either way, simply asking people about their mood regulation strategies or providing them with a particular one they could use in an experiment does not necessarily provide information about their effectiveness. In other words, we do not really know if the mood of subjects in the Erber et al. (in press) experiments would have changed in the desired direction if they had actually read the newspaper stories they chose. Similarly, we do not know if the sad subjects in the Erber and Erber (1994) study felt better after reminiscing about a happy event.

Some Strategies That Do Not Work

The issue of what works and what does not is not entirely frivolous. Consistent with the present conceptualization of moods as processes that carry a predilection toward mood congruent thought, some mood regulation strategies may be inherently worse than others in achieving the desired effects. This appears to be true for two strategies in particular (a) the deliberate attempt to convince oneself not to feel sad or happy in the presence of a sadness- or happiness-inducing event and (b) the attempt to distract oneself from one's sadness by thinking about something happy.

Evidence for the first contention comes from a study in which subjects were asked not to get into a sad mood as they were reminiscing about a sad event from their life or not to get into a happy mood as they were reminiscing about a happy event (Wegner, Erber, & Zanakos, 1993). Half of the subjects did this while at the same time trying to remember the number 741296835; the remainder of the subjects did the task without this burden. As it turns out, in the absence of the cognitive load imposed by trying to remember a nine-digit number, subjects were fairly successful in controlling the onset of both sad and happy moods. More importantly, subjects who attempted to control their moods while under cognitive load failed miserably, experiencing the very moods they were trying to control in the first place. This effect has a perfectly reasonable explanation (Wegner, 1994; Wegner & Erber, 1992) and it makes perfectly good sense (those readers who might be inclined to take this contention with a grain of salt are invited to read the remainder of this chapter while trying to remember a nine-digit number). Moreover, most social situations that stipulate the control of moods carry some load, which is perhaps one of the reasons bearers of bad news often ask us to sit down before proceeding to say "Try not to get upset, but . . . ." As it turns out, even subjects who succeed at controlling their moods in the short run can suffer from a massive return of these moods, primarily because thoughts about moods were bonded to distracting thoughts (Wenzlaff, Wegner, & Klein, 1991).

If the goal of controlling the onset of good and bad moods cannot be met through sheer willpower, perhaps it is possible to alleviate the invoked mood by distracting oneself through focusing attention to something that is incongruent with one's mood, as some have suggested (e.g., Clark & Isen, 1982; Isen, 1984)? Again, this strategy, while entirely plausible, has its pitfalls. Wenzlaff, Wegner, and Roper (1988) induced sad moods in mildly dysphoric college students and then asked them to distract themselves from their mood. An analysis of the types of distractors subjects used showed that they employed thoughts about other distressing events. Even when subjects were provided with a positive distractor, they eventually returned to entertaining distressing thoughts.

From the theoretical perspective of this chapter, the findings of Wenzlaff et al. (1988) are hardly surprising. Moods have the propensity to trigger a continuing stream of mood-congruent thought. The problem is further complicated by the fact that moods tend to affect our evaluations of ourselves and the world around us (e.g., Clark & Isen, 1982; Clark, Milberg, & Ross, 1983). When we are in a sad mood, for example, we often find it hard to cheer ourselves up with things that would ordinarily make us laugh, such as a funny movie.

STRATEGIES THAT DO WORK: THE ABSORPTION HYPOTHESIS

In light of the difficulties of regulating one's mood through willpower, suppression, or simple distraction, it becomes necessary to formulate a viable alternative. After all, by and large, most people do manage their moods fairly well most of the time. One promising way to gain insight into the processes that lead to the successful regulation of moods is to first identify one underlying mechanism that can then be applied to making predictions about the usefulness of a variety of singular strategies.

The key to such an attempt lies in recognizing why the depressed subjects in the Wenzlaff et al. (1988) study were unable to maintain their attention on happy thoughts. Mood congruent thoughts are said to come to mind automatically upon encountering a happy or sad mood (Clark & Isen, 1982; Wenzlaff, 1993). Thus by imposing a task that is (a) taxing working memory and (b) unrelated to one's mood it may be possible to curb the automatic generation of mood congruent thoughts, and as a consequence previously induced moods should be attenuated. In essence, the demands placed on working memory by this type of task should *absorb* moods.

It is worth pointing out that the prediction that cognitive load would absorb moods is nonobvious for a couple of reasons. First, cognitive load may facilitate automatic responses because its arousing properties may further constrain our ability to process information (Easterbrook, 1959) or make the dominant automatic response even more likely (Hull, 1943; Spence, 1956). Additionally, cognitive load may stand in the way of any attempt to "correct" one's mood simply because to do so requires additional capacity (cf. Gilbert, Pelham, & Krull, 1988).

However, there are several theoretical notions in the literature that speak to the veracity of the absorption hypothesis as well as its boundary conditions. For instance, Csikszentmihalyi (1975) described the experience of being cognitively and physically immersed in a task as the *flow*, a state in which people are relatively free of affect as well as conscious awareness of self-referent and task-irrelevant thought. This type of experience is best achieved when both the task demands as well as people's abilities to meet these demands are high. Mismatches can lead to either boredom or anxiety. In a similar vein, Wicklund (1986) described situations marked by a *dynamic fit* between the task demands and people's abilities. Under these circumstances people are likely to focus the bulk of their attention on the task rather than aspects of themselves that are peripheral to the execution of the task, such as thoughts about one's emotional state. Thus there is reason to believe that putting effort into a cognitively demanding task will attenuate both happy and sad moods, as long as the task demands do not fall below or above people's ability.

Empirical evidence for the absorption hypothesis comes from a study in which we induced a happy or sad mood through exposure to either a cheerful video (comedy routines by Robin Williams and Billy Crystal) or a depressing video (scenes from the movie *Sophie's Choice*). Subsequently, subjects were asked to solve simple or difficult algebra problems (additions and subtractions or multiplications and divisions) or to solve no problems, waiting instead for the experimenter to return. (Erber & Tesser, 1992; Study 3). In line with the previously mentioned reasoning, we predicted that subjects completing the difficult, cognitively demanding problems would experience an attenuation of their moods, whereas the moods of subjects who worked on the simple problems or worked on no problems should be relatively unaffected. Figure 11.3 shows the results of this experiment. Consistent with our predictions, the self-reported mood of subjects who watched the cheerful video was still good after the 10-minute waiting period, and the mood of subjects who watched the depressing video was still bad. This finding in and of itself is noteworthy because it suggests that subjects made no attempt to regulate their happiness and sadness in the absence of a specific goal or the presence of suitable mood regulation strategies. Interestingly, subjects who solved the simple algebra problems

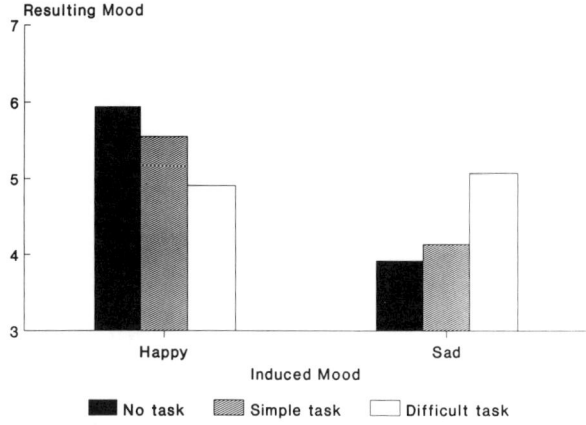

Fig. 11.3 Self-reported mood as a function of induced mood and task difficulty. Higher numbers indicate happier mood.

showed no significant attenuation of their mood as a result of completing the task. It is likely that this happened because the simplicity of the task did not infringe upon their ability to think about the movie and entertain other mood-related thoughts. On the other hand, subjects who completed the cognitively demanding task experienced an attenuation in both their happy and sad moods.

Of course, looking at self-reported mood alone does not allow any inferences about the processes by which completing the difficult problems attenuated subjects' moods. However, in support of our contention that subjects' moods were attenuated because of a reduction in mood-related thought, we found that subjects who worked on the cognitively demanding task recalled fewer details about the mood-inducing video they had seen compared to subjects who completed the simple task or no task at all.

Similar findings were obtained when we held the task demands constant by giving happy and sad subjects a novel task while manipulating their motivation to work on it (Erber & Tesser, 1992; Studies 1 and 2). Specifically, we asked subjects to prepare themselves to compete against the computer in marketing a new laundry detergent. Subjects prepared themselves by accessing marketing-relevant information prior to the competition. Half the subjects were told that the amount of effort expended in the preparation would likely help them to succeed. The other half were told that success at the task was largely a matter of innate ability.

As it turns out, subjects who believed that effort was instrumental for success worked much harder at preparing themselves for the task. They accessed more relevant items and looked at them for a longer amount of time than subjects who did not believe in the instrumentality of the preparation. This finding in itself is hardly surprising given the nature of the instructions. More importantly, there was a marked difference in the moods of initially happy and sad subjects depending on the type and amount of effort they expended. Subjects who had been led to believe that their effort was instrumental for success at the task experienced more attenuated moods than subjects who worked on it believing that their effort would not make a difference. This was true for happy and sad subjects as well. In other words, expending meaningful, instrumental effort did not appear to have a unidirectional effect upon subjects' mood as there was no further improvement in the mood of happy subjects as a result of their effort. Instead it appears that subjects' happy and sad moods were absorbed by the increased commitment of cognitive resources to the task when they believed their effort to be instrumental for their success.

The findings of the studies on the absorption hypothesis suggest that a goal of controlling one's mood may be best met by engaging in a cognitively demanding task. The constraints placed on working memory by such tasks prevent us from dwelling on our sad moods or savoring our happy moods. There is simply not enough capacity left to engage in the kind of mood congruent thinking that would be sufficient to maintain one's mood. This renders task involvement, which requires a great deal of cognitive effort, a highly useful strategy for neutralizing undesired moods regardless of whether they are positive or negative. Even in the absence of tasks that are challenging because of their nature, it may be possible to turn an otherwise mundane task into an absorbing one by inducing a strong orientation toward the task. Of course, the flipside is that it is highly unsuitable should the goal be to maintain a happy mood. Note that task involvement of this sort is very different from simple distractions, such as watching *Ernest Goes to Camp* or solving simple algebra problems while in a bad mood, which require little or no cognitive effort. These types of strategies are less effective because they allow mood congruent thinking to persist. Furthermore, distractors may bond to mood congruent thoughts and thus lead to a massive return of the mood that was to be controlled in the first place (Wenzlaff et al., 1991).

The finding that task involvement, which is taxing of one's cognitive resources, would successfully attenuate both happy and sad moods (Erber & Tesser, 1992) seems to be at odds with the previously discussed research showing that cognitive load can undermine attempts to regulate one's mood (Wegner et al., 1993). However, there is one important difference in the two paradigms that may account for the different effects of task effort. In the Wegner et al. studies, subjects performed two tasks simultaneously — attempting to achieve a desired mood along with remembering a nine-digit number. What happened was that performing the secondary task of recalling the number interfered with the successful execution of the primary task of achieving or avoiding a sad or happy mood. In the Erber and Tesser studies, on the other hand, subjects were not provided with an explicit mood regulation goal, and thus the effort expended on the task absorbed the previously induced moods somewhat incidentally.

FURTHER APPLICATIONS OF THE ABSORPTION HYPOTHESIS

The absorption hypothesis provides a basis for understanding the processes that underlie the self-regulation of moods once a goal toward that end has been instantiated. If nothing else, it points to the role that effort, especially cognitive effort, plays in the attenuation of both happy and sad moods. Additionally, it provides a basis for explaining the effects of various strategies people use in regulating their emotional life. Research to date specifically allows for a consideration of mood incongruent recall and physical exercise.

The Mood Absorbing Qualities of Mood Incongruent Recall

To think of something happy is a popular and intuitively plausible strategy to rid oneself of a sad mood. Maria, the nanny in Rogers and Hammerstein's *Sound of Music*, recognized its value when she advised the children in her care to think of their favorite things when they felt sad. Parrott and Sabini (1990), finding that students remembered happy events when they were asked to recall an autobiographical memory from high school, proposed that a desire toward mood regulation was operating. Subjects were attempting to alleviate the blues brought on by the bad weather. Further, recall that the sad subjects in the Erber and Erber (1994) study chose to recall happy events in the presence of a specific goal to alleviate a sad mood. Neither of these studies bothered to measure subjects mood following the mood incongruent recall, and thus the question remains, does it really work?

There are at least two reasons why recalling something that is incongruent with one's mood should alter feelings of happiness and sadness. The first one is fairly obvious and is related to the difference in the valence of such memories compared to the current mood. In other words, if remembering something sad makes people feel sad, then remembering something happy should lead to happiness or at least less sadness and vice versa. The second reason has to do with the amount of effort it may take to recall mood incongruent memories. Remember that mood congruent thoughts are more easily accessible than mood incongruent thoughts. Because of their decreased accessibility, it may take more effort, concentration, and cognitive capacity, in general, to bring mood incongruent memories into consciousness. This raises the possibility that mood incongruent recall may absorb previously induced moods in part because of the effort involved in retrieving suitable mood incongruent memories.

We (Erber & Erber, 1994; Study 1) examined this possibility in an experiment in which we attempted to manipulate the valence of mood incongruent memories and the effort involved in retrieving them separately. Subjects first recalled a happy or sad event from their lives in great and vivid detail. Following this initial manipulation of their mood, one group of subjects was instructed to recall a mood incongruent event at the same level of vividness and detail. A second group of subjects recalled a mood incongruent memory using a form that prompted them to fill in the mundane aspects of their memory, such as the time and place the event happened. A third group did not recall a mood incongruent memory. All subjects then reported their mood on a self-report inventory. The outcomes of this study are depicted in Fig. 11.4. As it turns out, the difference in the valence of the mood incongruent memory and the effort with which it was recalled had additive effects on subjects' moods. Relative to subjects in the control condition, sad subjects felt better and happy subjects felt worse simply by recalling a mood incongruent memory. Moreover, when subjects recalled the mood incongruent event with a great deal of effort, their moods improved or deteriorated even further, thus lending credence to the assertion that effort is at least partially responsible for the mood altering consequences of mood incongruent recall.

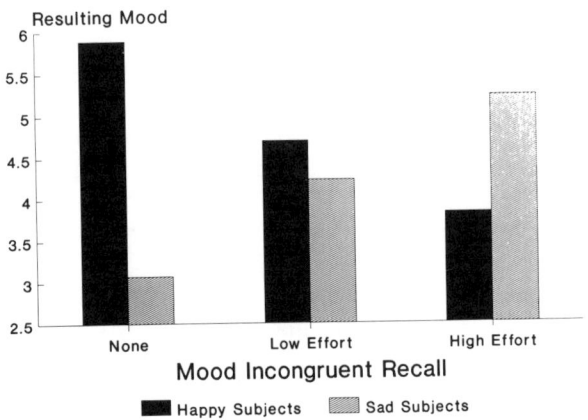

Fig. 11.4 Observer rated mood as a function of mood induction and difficulty of mood incongruent recall. Higher numbers indicate happier mood.

The Mood Absorbing Qualities of Exercise

To hop on a treadmill, run around the block, or engage in other forms of physical exercise have long been suspected to alleviate negative moods, although the evidence in the literature is somewhat mixed (e.g., Nagy & Frazier, 1988; Otto, 1990; Watson, 1988). In general, exercise is presumed to have a unidirectional effect on people's moods, although this seems to depend on the nature and intensity of the exercise (Steptoe & Cox, 1988). Currently the processes by which this occurs are poorly understood. The absorption hypothesis provides a somewhat novel framework for understanding how exercise affects moods. Specifically, it predicts that exercise would attenuate rather than improve people's moods, primarily because it may reduce the amount of mood related thought and increase the amount of thoughts that are irrelevant to one's mood.

To test this hypothesis, we (Erber & Therriault, 1993) first exposed subjects to the sad or happy videos previously used by Erber and Tesser (1992). Following this manipulation of their mood, half the subjects engaged in a 5-minute step exercise while the other half did not exercise. Subjects then reported on their stream-of-consciousness. Two independent raters who were blind to conditions coded subjects' reports and provided an overall assessment of their mood.

The effects of the manipulations of mood and exercise on subjects' moods are depicted in Fig. 11.5. They indicate that subjects who exercised following the sad mood induction felt better and made fewer references to negative emotional states than subjects who did not exercise. Consistent with predictions from the absorption hypothesis, these subjects also re-

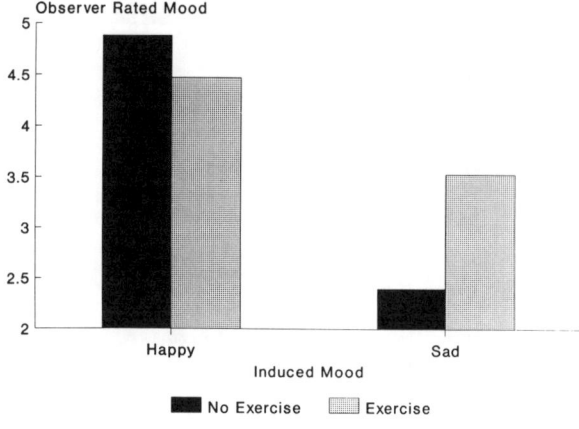

Fig. 11.5 Observer rated mood as a function of mood induction and level of physical exercise. Higher numbers indicate happier mood.

ported fewer affectively negative thoughts (e.g., "Life sucks") and more affectively neutral thoughts (e.g., "I have to stop at the dry cleaner's on the way home"). At the same time, exercise had no significant effect on subjects in whom a happy mood had been induced.

Despite the failure to obtain symmetrical effects of exercise on sad and happy moods, the pattern of results is supportive of the absorption hypothesis, primarily because there was no unidirectional effect. Happy subjects who exercised did not feel any better than happy subjects who did not exercise.

At the same time, our failure to find symmetrical effects for happy and sad moods was troublesome enough to warrant further probing. One thing that struck us in this process was the low-tech approach we had taken in operationalizing the exercise condition: subjects performed their stepping on a rather unappealing gray cinder block. Reasoning that this perhaps limited the extent to which subjects immersed themselves in the step exercise, we decided to replicate the study using a shiny, commercially available, aerobic stepper. We also added a couple of conditions in which subjects watched a video about step exercise, fittingly called "Buns of Steel." This set of conditions essentially took the place of the simple math problems in the Erber and Tesser (1992) study and allowed us to once again see whether doing anything at all may have mood-attenuating effects in itself. The results of this study are depicted in Fig. 11.6. As expected, engaging in the step exercise absorbed previously induced sad moods and happy moods as well, presumably because subjects were more involved with the task than was the case in the first study. Also as expected, simply watching a tape of other people exercising did not attenuate either kind of mood.

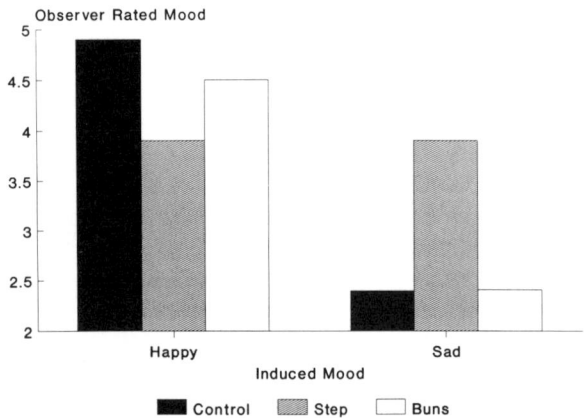

Fig. 11.6 Observer rated mood as a function of mood induction and exercise condition. Higher numbers indicate happier mood.

SUMMARY AND CONCLUSIONS

This chapter has presented theory and research as it pertains to the self-regulation of moods. It has suggested that the prevailing hedonic view, which proposes that people's mood regulation tendencies are best described as maintaining positive moods and repairing negative moods, is in need of a major overhaul. There is reason to believe that people are sensitive to the constraints that social settings place on their liberty to experience negative moods and positive moods as well. As a result, people's striving toward happiness may be less prevalent than commonly thought. Furthermore, this chapter has shed light on the nature of the processes by which people regulate their moods. Whereas moods can be triggered by relatively trivial and innocuous events, it appears that it takes effort to get rid of them once the situation signals that they may have overstayed their welcome.

In fairness to the hedonic view it must be said that the conclusions of this chapter may be limited to mild forms of sadness (as well as happiness). It may well be that more severe negative emotional states may in fact command a mobilization of resources to fend off their impact, as Taylor (1991) suggested. However, the bulk of the moods we experience in our daily lives are probably less than severe. Thus the mobilization-minimization hypothesis may be an exception to the idea that our emotional experience is somewhat constrained by the situation in which we find ourselves.

The conclusions of this chapter may also be limited to the particular moods that we have studied so far, namely sadness and happiness. For example, it seems fairly obvious that people would be likely to make attempts to alleviate such moods as anxiety and irritation for social reasons. It is less clear, however, if this could be achieved through the same methods that alleviate sadness. It is conceivable that facing a cognitively challenging task could increase anxiety and thus wipe out the effects of the otherwise absorbing task. Of course, whether this is in fact the case is a question that remains for future research.

To the extent that the research reported in this chapter informs us about the self-regulation of sad moods, the present theoretical models may have implications for the understanding of various aspects of depression. In general, it appears that chronic experiences of sadness may stem from two sources. First, it may be that people are insensitive to the demands the social setting places on the appropriateness of a sad mood. From this point of view, failure to regulate feelings of sadness may be due to a lack of motivation. More likely, it may be that chronically depressed people lack appropriate strategies to alleviate their feelings of sadness. With regard to the latter, the present framework could be informative for the understanding of sex differences in depression. The higher incidence of depression among women (Nolen-Hoeksema, 1990) may be due to differences between women and men with regard to the strategies available for the regulation of moods. It may be that men acquire the ability to immerse themselves in mood absorbing activities, such as playing basketball, to fend off a bout of depression to a greater extent than women who tend to ruminate instead. Note that this explanation is different from an account based on socialization differences between men and women in the appropriateness of expressing sadness. Naturally, its usefulness in accounting for the sex differences in depression still needs to be examined through empirical research.

Finally, the work presented in this chapter may have larger implications for how social psychology should treat the interplay between emotion and motivation. To conceptualize motivation in terms of seeking pleasure and avoiding pain, as is commonly done, may be more than just an oversimplification. It is decidedly contrary to social psychological thinking because, for one thing, it deemphasizes the importance of the social context. Moreover, simple hedonistic theorizing may be plain wrong to the extent that it does not predict people's actions most of the time. This shortcoming is exacerbated by the pervasiveness with which hedonistic assumptions have influenced social psychological theorizing to the present day. Perhaps it is time to finally discard the notion of humans as primarily hedonistically motivated creatures and replace it with something more complex. Who knows what we might discover in the process?

ACKNOWLEDGMENTS

I wish to thank Maureen Wang Erber for all of her help with this chapter. Thanks also to the attendees of the conference on Goals and Affect and the students in my Mental Control course for their insightful feedback.

REFERENCES

Allport, G. W. (1984). The historical background of social psychology. In G. Lindzey & E. Aronson (Eds.), *The handbook of social psychology*, Vol. I (3rd ed.). New York: Random House.
Blaney, P. H. (1986). Affect and memory: A review. *Psychological Bulletin, 99*, 229-246.
Bryant, F. B. (1989). A four-factor model of perceived control: Avoiding, coping, obtaining, and savoring. *Journal of Personality, 57*, 773-797.
Bryant, F. B. (1993, May). *Coping and savoring: Just because you're not down doesn't mean you're up*. Paper presented at the annual meeting of the Midwestern Psychological Association. Chicago, IL.
Carver, C. S., & Scheier, M. F. (1981). *Attention and self-regulation: A control-theory approach to human behavior*. New York: Springer-Verlag.

Cialdini, R., Levy, A., Herman, C. P., & Levenbeck, S. (1973). Attitudinal politics: The strategy of moderation. *Journal of Personality and Social Psychology, 25*, 100-108.

Clark, M. S., & Isen, A. M. (1982). Toward understanding the relationship between feeling states and social behavior. In A. Hastorf & A. M. Isen (Eds.), *Cognitive social psychology*. New York: Elsevier North-Holland.

Clark, M. S., Milberg, S., & Ross, J. (1983). Arousal cues arousal-related material in memory: Implications for understanding effects of mood on memory. *Journal of Verbal Learning and Verbal Behavior, 22*, 633-649.

Csikszentmihalyi, M. (1975). *Between boredom and anxiety*. San Francisco: Jossey-Bass.

Cunningham, M. R., (1979). Weather, mood, and helping behavior. *Journal of Personality and Social Psychology, 37*, 1947-1956.

Easterbrook, J. A. (1959). The effect of emotion on the utilization of cues and organization of behavior. *Psychological Review, 66*, 183-201.

Erber, R. (1991). Affective and semantic priming: Effects of mood on category accessibility and inference. *Journal of Experimental Social Psychology, 27*, 480-498.

Erber, R., & Case, D. E. (1993, August). *Self-deception in the service of mood regulation.* Paper presented at the 101st annual meeting of the American Psychological Association. Toronto, Ontario.

Erber, R., & Erber, M. W. (1994). Beyond mood and social judgment: Mood incongruent recall and mood regulation. *European Journal of Social Psychology, 24*, 79-88.

Erber, R., & Tesser, A. (1992). Task effort and the regulation of mood: The absorption hypothesis. *Journal of Experimental Social Psychology, 28*, 339-359.

Erber, R., & Therriault, N. (1993, October). *Sweating to the oldies: The mood-absorbing qualities of exercise*. Paper presented at the annual meeting of the Society for Experimental Social Psychology, Santa Barbara, CA.

Erber, R., Wegner, D. M., & Therriault, N. (in press). On being cool and collected: Mood regulation in anticipation of social interaction. *Journal of Personality and Social Psychology*.

Gilbert, D. T., Pelham, B. W., & Krull, D. S. (1988). On cognitive business: When person perceivers meet persons perceived. *Journal of Personality and Social Psychology, 54*, 733-739.

Goffman, E. (1963). *Behavior in public places*. New York: The Free Press.

Gollwitzer, P. M., Heckhausen, H., & Steller, B. (1990). Deliberative and implemental mind-sets: Cognitive tuning toward congruous thoughts and information. *Journal of Personality and Social Psychology, 59*, 1119-1127.

Hochschild, A. R. (1983). *The managed heart*. Berkeley: University of California Press.

Hull, C. L. (1943). *Principles of behavior*. New York: Appleton-Century-Crofts.

Isen, A. M. (1984). Toward understanding the role of affect in cognition. In R. S. Wyer, Jr., & T. K. Srull (Eds.), *Handbook of social cognition* (pp. 179-236). Hillsdale, NJ: Lawrence Erlbaum Associates.

Klinger, E. (1993). Clinical approaches to mood control. In D. M. Wegner & J. W. Pennebaker (Eds.), *Handbook of mental control* (pp. 344-369). Englewood Cliffs, NJ: Prentice-Hall.

Larsen, R. (1993, August). *Mood regulation in everyday life*. Paper presented at the 101st annual meeting of the American Psychological Association, Toronto, Ontario.

Morris, W. N., & Reilly, N. P. (1987). Toward the self-regulation of mood: Theory and research. *Motivation and Emotion, 11*, 215-249.

Nagy, S., & Frazier, S. (1988). The impact of exercise on locus of control, self-esteem, and mood states. *Journal of Social Behavior and Personality, 3*, 263-268.

Neisser, U. (1982). *Memory observed: Remembering in natural contexts*. San Francisco: W. H. Freeman.

Nelson, T. D., & Baumgardner, A. H. (1993). *Affect distancing and mood regulation*. Manuscript submitted for publication.

Nolen-Hoeksema, S. (1990). *Sex differences in depression*. Stanford, CA: Stanford University Press.
Nowlis, V. (1963). The concept of mood. In S. M. Farber & R. H. L. Wilson (Eds.), *Conflict and creativity* (pp. 73-88). New York: McGraw-Hill.
O'Neal, E. C., & Taylor, S. L. (1989). Status of the provoker, opportunity to retaliate, and interest in video violence. *Aggressive Behavior, 15*, 171-180.
Otto, J. (1990). The effects of physical exercise on psychophysiological reactions under stress. *Cognition and Emotion, 4*, 341-357.
Parrott, W. G. (1993). Beyond hedonism: Motives for inhibiting good moods and maintaining bad moods. In D. M. Wegner & J. W. Pennebaker (Eds.), *Handbook of mental control* (pp. 278-305). Englewood Cliffs, NJ: Prentice-Hall.
Parrott, W. G., & Sabini, J. (1990). Mood and memory under natural conditions: Evidence for mood incongruent recall. *Journal of Personality and Social Psychology, 59*, 321-336.
Schachter, S. & Singer, J. E. (1962). Cognitive, social, and physiological determinants of emotional state. *Psychological Review, 69*, 379-399.
Schwarz, N., & Clore, G. L. (1983). Mood, misattribution, and judgments of well-being: Informative and directive functions of affective states. *Journal of Personality and Social Psychology, 45*, 513-523.
Spence, K. W. (1956). *Behavior theory and conditioning*. New Haven, CT: Yale University Press.
Steptoe, A., & Cox, S. (1988). Acute effects of aerobic exercise on mood. *Health Psychology, 7*, 329-340.
Strack, F., Schwarz, N., & Gschneidinger, E. (1985). Happiness and reminiscing: The role of time perspective, affect, and mode of thinking. *Journal of Personality and Social Psychology, 49*, 1460-1469.
Taylor, S. E. (1991). The asymmetrical effects of positive and negative events: The mobilization-minimization hypothesis. *Psychological Bulletin, 110*, 67-85.
Tesser, A., & Rosen, S. (1975). The reluctance to transmit bad news. In L. Berkowitz (Ed.), *Advances in experimental social psychology* (Vol. 8, pp. 193-232), New York: Academic Press.
Tesser, A., Rosen, S., & Waranch, E. (1973). Communicator mood and the reluctance to transmit bad news. *Journal of Communication, 23*, 619-628.
Watson, D. (1988). Intraindividual and interindividual analyses of positive and negative affect: Their relation to health complaints, perceived stress, and daily activities. *Journal of Personality and Social Psychology, 54*, 1020-1030.
Wegner, D. M. (1994). Ironic processes in mental control. *Psychological Review, 101*, 34-52.
Wegner, D. M., & Erber, R. (1992). The hyperaccessibility of suppressed thoughts. *Journal of Personality and Social Psychology, 63*, 903-912.
Wegner, D. M., Erber, R., & Zanakos, S. (1993). Ironic processes in the mental control of mood and mood-related thought. *Journal of Personality and Social Psychology, 65*, 1093-1104.
Wenzlaff, R. M. (1993). The mental control of depression: Psychological obstacles to emotional well-being. In D. M. Wegner & J. W. Pennebaker (Eds.), *Handbook of mental control* (pp. 239-257). Englewood Cliffs, NJ: Prentice-Hall.
Wenzlaff, R. M., Wegner, D. M., & Klein, S. B. (1991). The role of thought suppression in the bonding of thought and mood. *Journal of Personality and Social Psychology, 60*, 500-508.
Wenzlaff, R. M., Wegner, D. M., & Roper, D. W. (1988). Depression and mental control: The resurgence of unwanted negative thoughts. *Journal of Personality and Social Psychology, 55*, 882-892.
Wessman, A. E., & Ricks, D. F. (1966). *Mood and personality*. New York: Holt, Rinehart, and Winston.
Wicklund, R. A. (1986). Orientation to the environment versus perception with human

potential. In R. M. Sorrentino & E. T. Higgins (Eds.), *Handbook of motivation and cognition*. New York: Guilford.

Wood, J. V. Saltzberg, J. A., & Goldsamt, L. A. (1990). Does affect induce self-focused attention? *Journal of Personality and Social Psychology, 58*, 899–908.

Zillmann, D. (1988). Mood management: Using entertainment to full advantage. In L. Donohew, H. E. Sypher, & E. T. Higgins (Eds.), *Communication, social cognition, and affect* (pp. 147–171). Hillsdale, NJ: Lawrence Erlbaum Associates.

III How Goals and Affect Influence Other Processes

12 Mood as Input: What We Think About How We Feel Determines How We Think

Leonard L. Martin
Peggy Stoner
University of Georgia

We begin this chapter on mood effects with the paradoxical statement that there are no such things as mood effects. What we mean by this is that there are few, if any, effects that follow directly from the mere fact that one is experiencing a certain mood. We argue instead that the effects of any given mood depend upon the context within which the mood is experienced. In making this point, we discuss the mood as input model (Martin, Achee, Ward, & Harlow, 1993; Martin, Ward, Achee, & Wyer, 1993) and then present some data that tested implications of this model. Prior to doing this, however, we discuss three alternate accounts of mood effects: the syndrome view, the cognitive tuning model, and the capacity model.

The Syndrome View

In medical terminology, a *syndrome* is a collection of symptoms that tend to co-occur. When people are suffering from hay fever, for example, they experience not only a stuffy nose but also sneezing as well as itchy, watery eyes. These symptoms form a unit such that when you see one, you tend to see the others.

The suggestion that emotions exist as part of a syndrome was first explicitly put forth by Averill (1982). This characterization, however, is consistent with the more general view that emotions can be represented in an associative network in which specific types of feelings, physiological reactions, motor responses, thoughts, and memories are interconnected (e.g., Berkowitz, 1993; Bower, 1981; Lang, 1979; Leventhal, 1980). These interconnections make it likely that activation of any one component of the network would activate the others. Thus, recalling a sad event can elicit feelings of sadness (Strack, Schwarz, & Gschneidinger, 1985), whereas experiencing feelings of sadness can foster the recall of sad events (Bower, 1981).

Theorists taking a syndrome view further assume that emotion networks contain more than just feelings and event memories. They also contain response information. In other words, when people experience the feelings associated with a specific emotion, they also experience an activation of the motivations, muscles, glands, and organ systems associated with that emotion. Stated more simply, the experience of an emotion not only makes people feel a certain way, it also predisposes them to respond in certain ways.

The view that feelings are inherently associated with specific kinds of thoughts and actions has been laid out succinctly by Berkowitz (1993) in his description of the link between negative feelings and aggression. He wrote, "People who are feeling bad, whatever the reason . . . are theoretically apt to feel angry, have hostile thoughts, and be predisposed to attack a suitable available target" (Berkowitz, 1993, p. 10). The activation of these emotion-related thoughts and action tendencies is assumed to be automatic and not mediated by higher order cognitive processes, such as attributions. The higher processes are not needed because the response information is inherent in the syndrome. In other words, activation of the feelings directly activates the thoughts and behavioral predispositions.

It is important to note, however, that although the syndrome view suggests a strong connection between feelings and action tendencies, it does not suggest that the feelings will inevitably lead to the actual expression of those tendencies. By exerting sufficient effort, people can, at times, inhibit the overt expression of their emotion-induced predispositions. As Berkowitz (1993) described it, when people become "highly conscious of what they [are] feeling and what they [are] tempted to do, these people presumably [engage] in 'higher order' thinking so that they [consider] the possible appropriateness of their emotions and urges in the given circumstances and then [decide] to restrain themselves" (p. 35).

In short, the syndrome view suggests that the experience of an emotion automatically and directly predisposes people toward certain thoughts and actions but the overt expression of these predispositions can be inhibited with effortful thinking. Note that, in this view, the connection between the feeling state and the predisposition is not moderated by contextual factors because this connection is inherent in the syndrome. The context plays a role only in determining whether or not the predisposition is actually expressed.

The Cognitive Tuning Model

In contrast to the syndrome view, the cognitive tuning model (Schwarz & Bless, 1991) does not assume direct connections between feelings and predispositions. It assumes, instead, that people's subjective experiences provide them with information and that this information, rather than any automatically activated syndrome, is what guides their subsequent thoughts, motivations, and actions (Schwarz & Clore, 1983, 1988; Wyer & Carlston, 1979).

What kind of information do feeling states provide? Basically, information about one's goals (Carver & Scheier, 1990; Hsee & Abelson, 1991; Ortony, Clore, & Collins, 1988). It appears that approach to a goal elicits positive affect, whereas retreat from a goal elicits negative affect (Carver, Lawrence, & Scheier, chap. 9, this volume; Hsee & Abelson, 1991). It also appears that people in positive moods report feeling closer to attaining their goals than do people in negative moods (Cervone, Kopp, Schaumann, & Scott, 1994). Together, these findings suggest, for example, that people who feel threatened may experience fear and that people who experience fear may infer that they have been threatened (even if they are unaware of any actual threat). According to the cognitive tuning model, it is through such goal-relevant information that feelings influence motivation, and, in turn, cognitive processing. As Schwarz (1990) put it, "individuals' thought processes are tuned to meet the requirements of the psychological situation that is reflected in their feelings" (p. 544).

What psychological situations are reflected in positive and negative moods? According to the cognitive tuning model, negative moods inform people that their current situation is problematic, whereas positive moods inform people that their current situation is safe and satisfactory (see also Frijda, 1988). Because of this, negative moods motivate people to change their situations, whereas positive moods do not.

It is not always easy to change a negative situation, however. Attempts to do so often require a careful assessment of the features of the situation, an analysis of their causal links, detailed explorations of possible mechanisms of change, and anticipation of the potential outcomes of any action that might be initiated (Schwarz, 1990). So, if people hope to change their negative situations, then they may have to engage in careful, systematic processing. When they have done this often enough, the relation between being in a negative mood and engaging in systematic processing will become automatic. This means that merely being in a negative mood will be enough to foster in people a motivation to process systematically.

It is further assumed that negative moods prime procedural knowledge relevant to detail-oriented, effortful problem solving. To the extent that these procedures are general, then people may apply them to any processing that they do while in a negative mood. Thus, negative moods may lead people to process almost any information in an effortful, systematic, detail-oriented way even when this processing is not directly relevant to rectifying their presumed negative situation. So, for example, we might see people in negative moods expending more effort on tasks as trivial as estimating the degree of relationship depicted in scatterplots (Sinclair & Mark, 1992).

Positive moods, in contrast, inform people that their current situation is satisfactory and not in need of change. So, people in positive moods are unlikely to experience a motivation to engage in systematic, effortful processing. To the extent that they do process in the service of other goals, however, then the inferred safety of their situation may allow them to take risks, use simple heuristics, try out new procedures, and explore unusual, creative associations.

In sum, the cognitive tuning model suggests that different moods provide people with different conclusions about the safety of their environment and in this way do or do not motivate a systematic processing style. It is important to note, however, that while the cognitive tuning model implies a strong connection between different moods and specific motivations, it does not imply an inevitable connection between moods and the actual expression of these motivations. Other currently active goals or task requirements can override the default motivational effects. To use Schwarz's (1990, p. 552) example, "an author who is trying to meet the deadline for a chapter revision may attempt to remain in an analytic processing mode, despite being in a good mood as a result of other events."

The model suggests, however, that there may be an asymmetry in the likelihood that people will override their mood-induced motivations. Because positive moods inform people that their situation is safe, ignoring this signal in favor of other action requirements is not likely to pose a problem. Negative moods, on the other hand, inform people that their situation is not safe. Ignoring this signal, therefore, could be problematic. It could lead people to overlook a real danger. Accordingly, the cognitive tuning model suggests that the impact of negative moods on processing style will be more immune to the influence of other variables than will the impact of positive moods.

In sum, the cognitive tuning model differs from the syndrome view in that it does not assume a direct, structural connection between feelings and specific predispositions. Mood-induced predispositions are a function of the information provided by people's feelings. Negative moods inform people that their situation is unsatisfactory and, therefore, tunes their cognitive system toward effortful processing, whereas positive moods inform people that their situation is satisfactory and, therefore, tunes their cognitive system toward creative, heuristic processing. However, like the syndrome model, the cognitive tuning model suggests that the default motivations can be overridden with effort.

The Capacity Model

The capacity model (e.g., Mackie & Worth, 1989, 1991; Worth & Mackie, 1987) begins with the assumption that positive moods cause people to organize information in memory differently than do negative moods. This is, in part, because people are more likely to think about positive as compared to negative information. As a result, people may be likely to form more and stronger associations between positive information and other information. People in positive moods have also been shown to use broader categories and make looser associations than have people in neutral moods. In other words, many stimuli that might seem unrelated when people are in neutral moods may seem related when people are in positive moods.

These differences in memory organization are particularly important when one considers that moods can cue information from memory. When positive moods operate as cues, they bring more information—and more diverse information—to mind than do negative or neutral moods. The presence of all this positively cued information provides a cognitive environment that is both complex and distracting. So, according to the capacity model, people in positive moods find their attention broadened and diffused. They experience a continual allocation and reallocation of their processing capacity and have a difficult time keeping their attention focused on the central task. As a result, they show performance deficits on tasks that require sequential or analytic processing. Realizing their inability to process in an extensive or systematic way, people in positive moods may intentionally employ heuristics to simplify their processing.

In summary, the capacity model assumes that positive moods are more likely than negative or neutral moods to prime a great deal of diverse information in memory. This diverse collection of information diffuses attention and causes people to adopt simple processing strategies. Because of this, people's performance on cognitively demanding tasks tends to suffer. These mood-induced performance deficits can be overcome, however, if people are given sufficient time or motivation. In other words, the capacity model, like the syndrome view and the cognitive tuning model, depicts a strong mood-to-processing link the effects of which can be overcome under the right conditions (e.g., extra time and motivation). As Mackie, Asuncion, and Rosselli (1992) described it, "We assume that mood always has the same effects on a particular subprocess but that these subprocess may play a more or less dominant role in persuasion at any given time" (p. 263).

The Mood as Input Model

We have seen that despite their differences, the syndrome view, the cognitive tuning model, and the capacity model all suggest that affective states give rise to specific sorts of predispositions that can then be overridden by contextual influences. The mood as input model (Martin, Achee, Ward, & Harlow, 1993; Martin, Ward, Achee, & Wyer, 1993) differs from these models in not assuming such initial predispositions. Rather, the model suggests that even the connection between the mood and the initial predisposition is context-dependent.

This flexible view of moods follows directly from the assumption that moods operate as sources of information (Schwarz & Clore, 1988). If this assumption is correct, then the implications of moods, like the implications of other types of information, should be context-dependent (cf. Bransford & Johnson, 1972). A clear example of the context-dependent nature of information was provided by Anderson and Ortony (1975). Consider what comes to mind when you think of a container in each of the following sentences:

1. The container held the cola.
2. The container held the fruit.

In both cases, the term *container* suggests a vessel that holds other items or substances. In the first case, however, specific instantiations of container might include bottle, can, or cup. In the second case, specific instantiations might include bowl, basket, or box. In other words, although some aspects of the term's meaning stayed the same across the two contexts (i.e., a container holds other things), the specific implications of this meaning were context-dependent (i.e., bottle vs. basket). Our argument is that moods operate the same way. They carry context-specific implications.

This view of mood might be made clearer by means of an analogy. Research within the cognitive dissonance framework has shown that when people engage in a behavior that is inconsistent with their attitudes, they often change their attitudes so that these are consistent with the implications of their behavior. The explanation for this effect is that the attitude–behavior inconsistency gives rise to negative feelings that then motivate the attitude change. This interpretation is supported by findings that the attitude change does not occur when people interpret their negative feelings as a reaction to something irrelevant to the inconsistency (e.g., a pill).

If we explain this dissonance effect in terms of the kind of override process inherent in the syndrome, cognitive tuning, and capacity models, then we would assume that the negative drive state would give rise to a motivation to change one's attitude but that this motivation would be overridden by the attribution to the pill. Phenomenologically, this would mean that the person would feel a desire to change his or her attitude but think better of it and effortfully restrain him or herself from doing so. This seems implausible to us.

It seems more likely that the attribution completely bypassed any motivation to change one's attitude, and that the most immediate effect of attributing the negative feelings to the pill would be to make subjects avoid taking those kinds of pills in the future. Under these conditions, there would be no attitude change predisposition to override because the negative mood was never seen as relevant to the attitude-behavior inconsistency. To use a cliché from old Western movies, the predisposition was headed off at the pass.

This is the essence of the mood as input model. Moods do not have default motivational or processing effects that are automatically put into place and then have to be effortfully inhibited. Rather, moods suggest different motivations in different contexts. In one context, feeling good might motivate a person to process heuristically, whereas in another context, it might motivate the person to process systematically.

EVIDENCE FOR THE MOOD AS INPUT MODEL

Mood as Input to Motivational Decisions

As noted earlier, both the cognitive tuning model and the capacity model assume that positive moods are inherently associated with heuristic processing, whereas negative moods are inherently associated with systematic processing. The mood as input model does not make such as assumption. It assumes instead that either positive or negative moods can motivate systematic or heuristic processing depending on the context. How does this work?

We begin with the assumption that there are two types of cues that tell people when they have finished a task: objective and subjective. A person may stop eating when their plate is empty, for example, or they may stop when they feel full. In many cognitive tasks, however, there are no objective stop cues. When one is forming an impression, for example, or responding to a persuasive communication, how much processing is enough? Following Chaiken, Liberman, and Eagly (1989), we assume that in the absence of objective stop rules, people often rely upon a rough sense of confidence. If they feel confident with heuristic processing then they stop there. If they do not feel confident, then they continue with more systematic processing.

The mood as input model makes the further assumption that one factor that can influence confidence is one's mood. If, in the course of processing, people implicitly ask themselves "Have I processed enough?" then one's positive moods may lead him or her to answer favorably, whereas one's negative moods may lead him or her to answer unfavorably. If so, then those in positive moods would cease processing, whereas those in negative moods would continue processing. The end result would reflect the typical finding in the literature: people in positive moods would process less systematically than would people in negative moods.

Suppose, however, that in the course of processing, people ask themselves a different question. Suppose they ask, "Am I enjoying this task?" Again, one's positive mood may lead him or her to answer favorably, whereas one's negative mood may lead him or her to answer unfavorably. This time, though, the implications of these answers would be different. The positive answer would lead people to continue processing, whereas the negative answer would lead people to cease processing. The result would be a reversal of the typical finding in the literature: people in positive moods would process more systematically than would people in negative moods.

Evidence of this kind of reversal has been obtained by Martin, Ward, et al., (1993, Experiment 1). They placed subjects in either positive or negative moods by having them watch a series of positive or negative video clips. After this, the subjects were asked to read a series of behaviors with the goal of forming an impression of the person described by these behaviors. Subjects were told that they did not have to read all of the behaviors. The number they read was up to them. There was no right or wrong time to stop.

Half of the subjects were instructed more specifically to ask themselves as they were reading the behaviors, "Do I have enough information to form my impression? If the answer is yes, then stop. If the answer is no, then continue." The remaining subjects were instructed to ask themselves, "Am I enjoying this task? If the answer is yes, then continue. If the answer is no, then stop." The dependent measure was the amount of time subjects spent looking at the cards and the number of cards the subjects looked at before moving on the make their ratings of the target.

As can be seen in Fig. 12.1, the results were consistent with the mood as input predictions. When given the "Enough?" question, subjects in positive moods stopped sooner than did those in negative moods. When given the "Enjoy?" question, subjects in negative moods stopped sooner than did those in positive moods. These results suggest that the motivational implications of people's moods are mutable. All subjects performed the same impression-formation task, and (within the positive and negative conditions) subjects were in equivalent moods. Yet, the amount of time subjects spent on the task and the number of behaviors they considered differed as a function of their stop rules and their moods.

It is important to note that the results are not easily interpreted in terms of the kind of inhibition or override model depicted in the syndrome view,

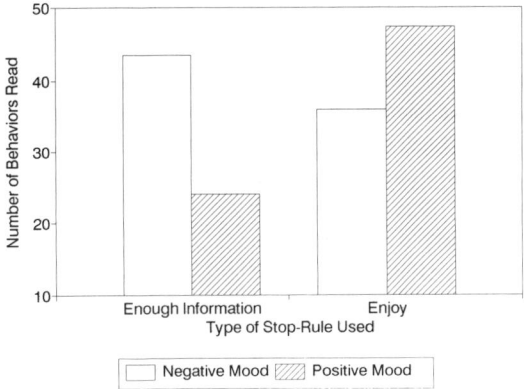

Fig. 12.1 Number of behaviors read as a function of mood and stop-rule.

the cognitive tuning model, and the capacity model. This is because the stop rules did not explicitly direct the subjects toward a type of processing. In other words, the rules did not induce a demand to inhibit or override any natural processing tendencies. In fact, the subjects were explicitly told that there was no right or wrong time to stop. It was up to them to decide how much to process. It is unclear, therefore, why they would continue or cease processing if they did not want to. What the stop rules did was direct the subjects toward an interpretation of their moods, and this, in turn, directed them toward different types of processing. In other words, the positive mood subjects given the enjoy stop rule continued processing because their moods told them to, not because the experimenter told them to. This can be contrasted with the Bless, Bohner, Schwarz, and Strack (1990) procedure in which positive mood subjects processed systematically because they were instructed to pay attention to the quality of the messages they were receiving.

Mood as Input During Group Behavior

Additional evidence that goals (i.e., stop rules) can influence the motivational implications of moods was obtained by Sanna, Turley, and Mark (1995). Research on social loafing has shown that when people work on a group project and their individual input to the project cannot be evaluated, people work at a level below their maximum output (see Geen, 1991, for a review). It appears, however, that self-evaluation can eliminate this effect even when evaluation from an external source is not possible (Sanna & Pusecker, 1994). Sanna et al. (1995) tested the hypothesis that self-evaluation could interact with the subjects' moods to determine the likelihood that the subjects would socially loaf.

They placed subjects in either positive, negative, or neutral moods by having them view video clips. Then they asked the subjects to generate uses for a knife. For half of the subjects, these uses were collected individually, whereas for half, the uses were ostensibly pooled with those generated by other subjects. For half of the subjects in each of these conditions, the instructions for the generation task included having the subjects ask themselves, "Have I generated as many uses as I can?" These instructions parallel those typically used in social loafing experiments. The remaining subjects were instructed to ask themselves, "Do I feel like continuing with this task?"

If the typical social loafing effect were to occur, then we would see subjects generating more uses when their individual inputs were identified then when they ostensibly were not. What would happen, however, when subjects in negative moods ask themselves, "Have I done enough?" The negative mood might cause the subjects to evaluate their progress negatively. If so, then they would continue to generate uses for a knife, and the social loafing effect would be eliminated, even in the absence of external evaluation. Similarly, when subjects in positive moods ask themselves "Do I feel like continuing with this task?" their moods might cause them to evaluate the task as enjoyable. Hence, they would continue generating uses, and, again, the social loafing effect would be eliminated, even in the absence of external evaluation. In no other condition would the combination of mood and stop rule motivate the subjects to continue processing. So, in all the other conditions in which the subjects' output was not externally evaluated, we should see social loafing. As can be seen in Fig. 12.2, these were precisely the results obtained. Thus, the results conceptually replicate those of Martin, Ward, et al. (1993) and further suggest that the motivational implications of moods are mutable.

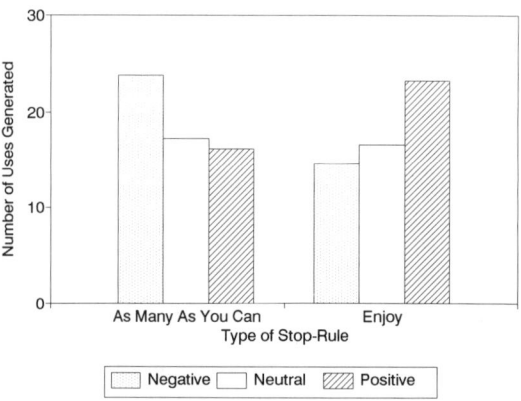

Fig. 12.2 Number of uses generated as a function of mood and stop-rule.

Mood as Input to Categorization Processes

The experiments just described showed that moods can interact with the subjects' processing objectives to influence the *amount* of effort they exert on tasks. Can mood and processing objectives interact to influence the *quality* of the processing as well? Previous research has shown that people in positive moods categorize more broadly than do people in negative moods (see Sinclair & Mark, 1992). Is this type of processing inherent to positive moods or can people in positive moods categorize like those in negative moods and vice versa? This hypothesis was tested by Martin and Ward (1994). They showed subjects some video clips to place the subjects in positive or negative moods. Then, the subjects were presented with a stack of cards, each of which had the name of a bird printed on it. The subjects were told to place these birds into as many or as few categories as they wanted. The number was up to them. There was no right or wrong answer.

Half of the subjects were instructed that, while performing this task, they should ask themselves, "Does this bird belong in the large pile? If so, leave it there. If not, place it in one of the smaller piles." The remaining subjects were instructed to ask themselves, "Does this bird belong in one of the smaller piles? If so, put it there. If not, leave it in the large pile." Under these conditions, subjects' positive moods might make them answer their question more favorably than might their negative mood. Thus, we would expect that when subjects are given the "large pile?" question, those in positive moods would place more birds in the large pile than would subjects in negative moods. This result would replicate the typical finding that people in positive moods categorize more broadly than do people in negative moods.

When given the "smaller pile?" question, however, subjects in positive moods would place more birds in the smaller piles than would subjects in negative moods. This would reverse the typical finding. As can be seen in Fig. 12.3, the predicted crossover interaction was obtained. The results extend our earlier findings by showing that the effects of moods are mutable not only in how much processing they foster but also in the kind of processing they foster. The results show that either positive or negative moods can foster broad categorization and that this kind of thinking is not the exclusive domain of people in positive moods.

Mood as Input to Creativity Decisions

Previous research has shown that people in positive moods are more likely than those in negative or neutral moods to generate unusual associations (Isen, Johnson, Mertz, & Robinson, 1985). From a mood as input perspective, however, this need not always be the case. A number of studies

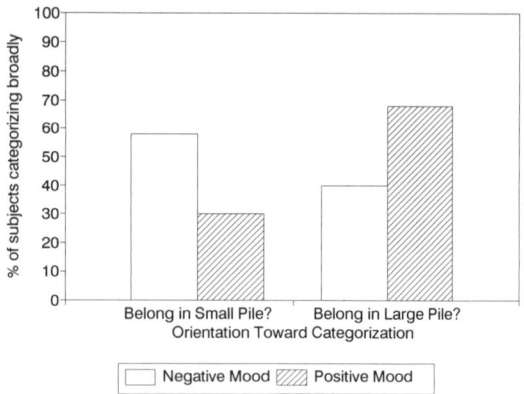

Fig. 12.3 Breadth of categorization as a function of mood and orientation.

have suggested that people are more likely to generate unusual or creative responses if they think about their response than if they respond with the first idea that comes to mind (Amabile, 1972). To say it oddly, but correctly, the first thing that comes to most people's minds is the first thing that comes to most people's mind. I say "cat"; you say "dog," the same response most people would give as their first response. With a little extra thinking, however, you might have responded with something like "Tennessee Williams," making the connection to *Cat on a Hot Tin Roof*. In other words, when people respond with the first thing on their mind, they are likely to produce fewer uncommon responses than if they take their time to think before they generate a response. If moods can cause people to continue or cease processing, then they should be able to increase or decrease the number of uncommon responses people generate.

Martin and Stoner (1994) tested this hypothesis by placing subjects in either positive or negative moods and asking the subjects to perform a word-association task. In this task, subjects were presented with a sequence of common words (e.g., dog, light, city) and were given three seconds to generate the first word they thought of in response to the presented word. After each first response, the subjects were given the opportunity to generate a different response if they wanted. In making this second decision, half of the subjects were instructed to ask themselves "Can I come up with a better response?", whereas half were instructed to ask themselves "Is my initial response a good one?" The main dependent measures were the number of uncommon associates in the subjects' first responses, the number of times the subjects chose to generate a second response, and the number of these second responses that were uncommon.

The mood as input model predicts that, regardless of their moods, subjects would generate common responses when they are given only three seconds to respond. This is because with such a short amount of time, the subjects would not be able to explore responses beyond the most common ones (e.g., cat-dog). With the "Can I come up with a more creative response?" question, however, subjects in positive moods should be more likely than those in negative moods to switch to a new response. The positive mood would make the subjects evaluate their chances of coming up with a creative second response more favorably than would a negative mood. Then, because second responses tend to be more unusual than initial responses, we should obtain the typical finding from the literature: subjects in positive moods would generate more unusual associates than would subjects in negative moods.

This pattern is expected to be reversed, however, when subjects ask themselves "Is my initial response a creative one?" With this question, subjects in positive moods will evaluate their initial responses more favorably than will subjects in negative moods. So, they will be less likely to switch to a second response, and we get the reverse of the typical finding: subjects in negative moods will generate more unusual responses than will subjects in positive moods. All three predictions were supported (see Fig. 12.4).

When subjects were given only three seconds to respond with the first thought on their mind, there was no effect of mood. With the "Can I come up with a more creative response?" instructions, subjects in positive moods generated more unusual responses than did subjects in negative moods. With the "Is my initial response a creative one?" instructions, subjects in positive moods generated fewer unusual responses than did subjects in negative moods. In short, in this one experiment, we found all possible outcomes: no effects of moods on processing, people in positive moods outperforming people in negative moods, and people in negative moods

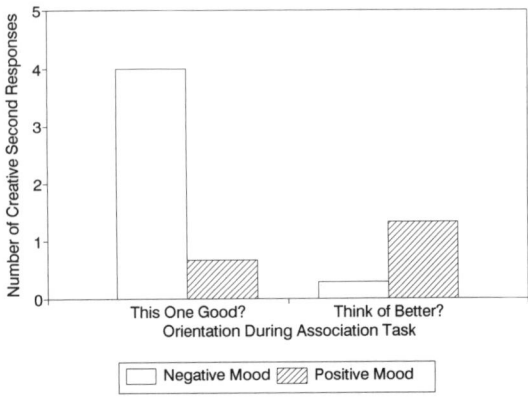

Fig. 12.4 Number of creative second responses by mood and stop-rule.

outperforming people in positive moods. And all three outcomes are interpretable in terms of the mood as input model.

Is Positive Always Good and Negative Always Bad?

Each of the experiments we have discussed has been based on the assumption that positive moods lead people to make more favorable evaluations than do negative moods. When subjects asked themselves "Do I have enough information?," for example, it was assumed that those in positive moods answered "yes," whereas those in negative moods answered "no." The same was true with the "Am I enjoying this task?" question. People in positive moods were assumed to answer "yes," whereas those in negative moods were assumed to answer "no." Does this mean that the mood as input model, despite its claims to the contrary, is still based on an assumption of a default difference between positive and negative moods? In other words, do positive moods always imply "yes" and "good," whereas negative moods always imply "no" and "bad"? We do not believe so.

First of all, it is easy to think of conditions under which a positive mood will lead people to a "no" and a negative mood will lead them to a "yes." For example, suppose we had reversed our enjoyment question to "Is this task boring?" In this case, the positive mood subjects would have answered "no" and continued with the task, whereas the negative mood subjects would have answered "yes" and stopped working. Similarly, what if the question had been relative to aggression? Suppose the subjects had asked themselves "Should I deliver more shocks to this person?" We suspect that in this case, those in positive moods would have been more likely than those in negative moods to answer "no" (for a more complete discussion of this issue, see Martin, Achee, et al., 1993). This is because aggression can be motivated by negative affect (Berkowitz, 1993). So, we do not interpret our results as a general tendency for people in positive moods to say "yes" and to acquiesce and for people in negative moods to say "no" and to become obstinate. We suggest instead that people attend to the information provided by their moods and that this information is different in different contexts.

The only inherent difference we assume is that positive moods feel better than do negative moods. This does not imply, however, the being in a positive mood is invariably evaluated more favorably than is being in a negative mood. There are times when a negative mood is seen as the more favorable outcome (cf. Erber, chap. 11, this volume). Suppose, for example, we have just learned of the tragic death of a loved one. Would our positive mood be acceptable here? Not necessarily. In fact, if people were feeling positive in such a situation, they might begin to wonder what kind of person they are. Why are they feeling so glib immediately after receiving such sad news?

As another example, consider going to see a movie. If you see a funny movie, then you would expect to feel good. If you see a "tearjerker," then you would expect to feel sad. What would happen if you came out of a comedy feeling sad or came out of a tearjerker feeling happy? In this case, something is wrong. The movies did not do what they were made to do. A movie that was designed to induce sadness and does would be considered a better movie than one that was designed to induce sadness but does not. Under these conditions, people in negative moods would make a more favorable evaluation than would people in positive moods.

Evidence consistent with this hypothesis was obtained by Martin and Abend (1995). They showed subjects a series of video clips that induced in subjects either a happy mood or a sad mood. Then, they presented the subjects with a story that was either happy or sad. The subjects were asked to indicate how effective they thought the story was in inducing the expected mood, how much they liked the story, and what grade (i.e., A+ to F) they would give the story.

If mere conditioning or mood as information were operating, then we would expect a main effect of mood. Subjects would render less favorable ratings when they were in negative as compared to positive moods. If the moods primed mood-congruent information, then we might expect that the least favorable ratings would be rendered by sad subjects rating sad stories and the most favorable ratings would be rendered by happy subjects reading the happy stories. This is because, in these conditions, the valence of the movie and the valence of the story would summate to elicit even more polarized thoughts.

From a mood as input perspective, however, we have to ask what information the moods would carry in the different contexts. Specifically, what represents attainment of the goal when a person is reading a story that is supposed to be uplifting? The attainment of positive feelings. What represents attainment of the goal when a person is reading a story that is supposed to be depressing? The attainment of sad feelings. Thus, the mood as input model predicts that the most favorable ratings (i.e., most effective, most liking, highest grade) will come from subjects in positive moods reading positive stories and from subjects in negative moods reading negative stories. These are the conditions in which the subjects' moods tell them that the story has attained its goal. When subjects feel positive after reading a sad story or sad after reading a positive story, then the story must not have been very effective. So, the ratings should be unfavorable.

As can be seen in Fig. 12.5, these predictions were supported. The most positive ratings occurred when the subjects' moods matched the intended tone of the story, whereas the least positive ratings occurred when there was

Fig 12.5 Liking for stories as a function of mood and valence of story.

a mismatch. These results do not fit easily with the cognitive tuning assumption that positive moods inform people that their situation is safe and negative moods inform them that their situation is unsafe. If this were occurring, then we would have found that people in positive moods would have rendered more favorable evaluations than did people in negative moods. The data raise the possibility, therefore, that positive moods inform people that their situation is satisfactory only when people are in pursuit of positively valenced goals. If they are pursuing negatively valenced goals (e.g., lowering one's mood to empathize with a sad friend, psyching oneself up for anger or revenge), then a negative mood would indicate progress. The converse would be true for positive goals. For evidence that people pursue negatively valenced goals, see Erber (chap. 11, this volume).

THEORETICAL IMPLICATIONS

How to Explain Mood Main Effects

A number of studies have been conducted showing reliable processing differences between people in positive and negative moods. Together, these data suggest that people in positive moods tend to process more flexibly, more creatively, and less systematically than do people in negative moods (for a summary see Sinclair & Mark, 1992). How can we reconcile these consistent main effect findings with the mood as input assumption that there are no default mood effects? There are at least two answers.

The first is that most of the experiments reporting main effects did not include variables that would allow for interactions (e.g., stop rules). Although this answer allows us to reconcile most of the findings, it does not seem sufficient to explain the data obtained by Hirt, McDonald, and Melton (chap. 13, this volume). They did include variables shown to change the impact of moods on processing. Namely, they used the "Enough?" and "Enjoy?" stop rules used by Martin, Ward, et al. (1993). They even found the same kind of crossover interactions on the amount of time their subjects spent on the task and on the number of similarities and differences their subjects generated. However, Hirt et al. did not find an interaction when they examined the creativity of the subjects' responses. On this measure, the typical main effect was observed: Subjects in positive moods generated more creative responses than did subjects in negative moods, regardless of the stop rule.

Hirt, McDonald, and Melton concluded that the mood as input model operates for time and number of responses, but that some other model (e.g., mood-induced task interest) operates for creativity. Recall, however, that Martin and Stoner (1994) obtained a crossover interaction in the number of uncommon responses shown by their subjects. How can we reconcile these results with the main effects obtained by Hirt and McDonald? One possibility deals with the way in which moods are brought into play in a judgment. As we stated in the beginning, we do not believe in "mood effects." That is, we do not believe that moods produce any effects merely because a person is experiencing a mood. Like any other kind of information, affective information has to be accessed in order for it to play a role in processing. Consider how this works.

Strack, Martin, and Stepper (1987) asked subjects to read cartoons while holding a pen either lightly between their teeth or loosely between their protruding lips. The former position fosters positive affect, whereas the latter fosters negative affect. When subjects were asked to rate how amused they felt while reading the cartoons, subjects experiencing positive affect rated the cartoons as funnier than did subjects experiencing negative affect. When subjects were asked to rate the cartoon relative to an objective standard, however, there was no difference in the ratings of subjects experiencing positive or negative affect. These results suggest that merely experiencing the state is insufficient for it to influence judgments. Affect, like any other piece of information, must be accessed before it comes into play. In other words, the effect of people's affective states on their judgments is not direct and passive. It is a function of what people do with their moods.

Our synthesis, therefore, is simply that the affect was not accessed in a way that was relevant to creativity in the Hirt et al. study but was in the Martin and Stoner study. What reason is there to believe this? In the Martin and Stoner study, the questions subjects asked themselves were directly relevant to the quality of their answers (Is this a good one? vs. Can I come up with a better one?). In the Hirt et al. study, this was not the case. In that study, subjects were instructed to ask themselves, "Am I enjoying the task?" or "Have I generated enough?" These questions reflect on the quantity rather than the quality of their output. Because of these different questions, Martin and Stoner observed a crossover interaction on the quality of subjects' responses, whereas Hirt, McDonald, and Melton observed a crossover on quantity but not quality.

More generally, we hypothesize that moods will have quantitative effects when the processing objectives lead people to consider their moods in relation to the quantity of their output, but they will have qualitative effects when the processing objectives lead people to consider their moods in relation to the quality of their output. Of course, processing objectives relevant to both considerations will produce effects that differ in both quantity and quality, whereas processing objectives relevant to neither consideration will lead to null effects for moods.

RELATION TO OTHER, MORE FLEXIBLE MODELS

Throughout the chapter we have contrasted the mood as input model with the syndrome view, the cognitive tuning model, and the capacity model. We did this, in part, because these "override models" made a good background against which to highlight certain aspects of the mood as input model. In this section, we discuss two other theoretical positions that come closer to the mood as input model in hypothesizing that the effects of moods are mutable. One is the positive priming model developed by Isen (1993) and the other is the hedonic contingency model developed by Wegener and Petty (1994; chap. 14, this volume).

The Positive Priming Model

The positive priming model (Isen, 1993) is concerned primarily with the effects of positive affect. It begins with the assumption that the influence of positive affect on cognitive processes will be different in different situations. Moreover, when the effects are different, this does not represent an inhibition of some more fundamental tendency. It is in the nature of positive affect to allow for such differences.

In order to understand how positive affect leads naturally to this flexibility, it is necessary to understand what being in a positive affective state does to a person. According to Isen (1993), positive affect produces two major classes of effects. First, it creates a cognitive environment that is richer and more complex than that experienced while people are in neutral or negative moods. This is because positive affect cues positive material from memory, material that is thought to be more extensive and diverse than other material. People in positive affective states also perform extensive elaboration on material they think about (as long as this material is neutral or positive in tone), and they see more things as relating together than do people in neutral or negative moods. In short, the first effect of positive affect is that it brings to mind a great deal of highly interrelated information.

The second effect is motivational. Relative to neutral and negative affect, positive affective states promote greater enjoyment and interest in neutral and positive tasks, and it gives rise to a strong motive to maintain the positive state.

Together, these two effects imply that as long as people are working on a task that they think will not diminish their positive state, they will operate in an efficient, and complex way. The exact performance seen, however, will depend on the specific task. Because positive affect brings a great deal of interrelated information to mind, people in positive states have a lot of options from which to draw. So, if they are asked to find similarities between two stimuli, for example, then they will be able to do so. If they are asked to find differences, then they will be able to do that as well. This flexibility will occur, however, only if the task allows for it and only if people are motivated to process (e.g., the task is not unpleasant).

The positive priming model differs from the mood as input model in several ways. First, it focuses primarily on positive affect. The mood as input model addresses both positive and negative affect. Second, the positive priming model assumes that positive affect creates a more complex cognitive environment than does neutral or negative affect. The mood as input model does not assume that moods are inherently associated with differences in cognitive organization. Such differences can be obtained, but they are a function of subjects' processing objectives (e.g., Martin & Ward, 1994). Third, the positive priming model does not explicitly assume that the experienced affect provides any information. Rather, affect influences judgments and decision making through its cueing effect on memory. The mood as input model, on the other hand, is based on the assumption that the most proximate influence of affective states on judgments and decisions is in the form of the meaning people derive from their subjective experiences (in the context in which these experiences occur).

The Hedonic Contingency Model

The hedonic contingency model (Wegener & Petty, 1994; chap. 14, this volume) is similar to the positive priming model in assuming that positive moods foster a strong motive to maintain the positive mood, and people in positive moods will exert considerable cognitive effort in tasks they think will be enjoyable but not in tasks they think will be unenjoyable. The hedonic contingency model differs from the positive priming model, however, in being more specific about the relationship between people's moods and people's tendencies to process on different tasks.

Generally speaking, if people wish to avoid getting in a worse mood, then they should process only information that is at least as positive if not more positive than their current mood. This means that people in moderately positive moods are restricted to engaging in tasks that are moderately to extremely positive, whereas, people in moderately negative moods can engage in tasks ranging from slightly negative to neutral to highly positive. Stated another way, there is a greater chance that engagement in any given task will lower the mood of people in positive as compared to negative moods.

Because of this asymmetry, people in positive moods are assumed to be more sensitive than are people in negative moods to the hedonic qualities of the tasks they are about to perform. People in positive moods are more likely than those in negative moods to consider carefully the consequences of their performance and to choose to exert effort only on tasks that they think will not lower their moods. In the words of Wegener and Petty (chap. 14, this volume), "one might consider a person's current mood as a discriminative stimulus that signals what kind of hedonic reinforcement contingencies are operating" (p. 344).

The hedonic contingency model is similar to the mood as input model in considering people's subjective experience to be informative (i.e., it is a discriminative stimulus). Unlike that model, however, the hedonic contingency model assumes that the information carried by a mood is always relevant to the same question: Is this task likely to decrease my current mood? The answer to this question will depend on the specific task in which people are engaged, but the actual meaning of the mood does not change with the context as it is assumed to do in the mood as input model. Also, the hedonic contingency model assumes that people are driven to maintain positive states and avoid negative ones. The mood as input model does not include such an assumption, and, in fact, speculates that there are times when just the opposite is true (see Erber, chap. 11, this volume). From this perspective, whether people seek out positive or negative feelings depends on the meaning of those feelings in the situation (e.g., people prefer feeling sad rather than happy when attempting to empathize with a friend who is sad).

CONCLUSIONS

We have presented the results of several studies that are supportive of the mood as input model. The results of these studies suggest that there are no judgment, processing, or motivational effects that follow from the mere fact that one is experiencing a certain mood. Rather, moods operate as input to other processes and these processes determine the effects that the moods will have.

We should point out, however, that while the studies we have presented are supportive of the mood as input model, they do not definitively rule out other models either as alternative explanations (given certain assumptions) or as possibilities in their own right alongside the processes specified in the mood as input model. The take-home message of the chapter, therefore, is more in the spirit of the mood as input model than in its details. For example, the general approach would suggest that we should be careful to include in our designs variables that could allow for interactions, especially interactions reflecting reversals of the usual main effects. Such interactions may or may not be observed. But if we do not include variables in our designs that allow for such interactions, then they will never be observed. Without these variables in our studies, what we might see in the literature is a series of separate and contradictory findings.

The type of designs we use also influences the type of theories we create. Do we want to theorize about main effects and then try to account for the exceptions to these hypothesized general rules or do we want theories that, from the start, allow for multiple possibilities within their basic assumptions? Arguments can be made for either approach. It is our belief that the latter approach not only more closely approximates the complexity of human beings but also that it is more fun. It is for these reasons that we have pursued and will continue to pursue work derived from the mood as input model.

REFERENCES

Amabile, D. (1972). The social psychology of creativity: A componential conceptualization. *Journal of Personality and Social Psychology, 45*, 357–376.

Anderson, R. C., & Ortony, A. (1975). On putting apples into bottles: A problem of polysemy. *Cognitive Psychology, 7*, 167–180.

Averill, J. (1982). *Anger and aggression: An essay on emotion.* New York: Springer-Verlag.

Berkowitz, L. (1993). Towards a general theory of anger and emotional aggression: Implications of the cognitive-neoassociationistic perspective for the analysis of anger and other emotions. In R. S. Wyer & T. K. Srull (Eds.), *Advances in social cognition* (Vol. 6, pp. 1–46). Hillsdale, NJ: Lawrence Erlbaum Associates.

Bless, H., Bohner, G., Schwarz, N., & Strack, F. (1990). Mood and persuasion: A cognitive response analysis. *Personality and Social Psychology Bulletin, 16*, 331–345.

Bower, G., (1981). Mood and Memory. *American Psychologist, 36*, 129–148.

Bransford, J. D., & Johnson, M. K. (1972). Contextual prerequisites for understanding: Some investigations of comprehension and recall. *Journal of Verbal Learning and Verbal Behavior, 11*, 717–726.

Carver, C. S., & Scheier, M. F. (1990). Origins and functions of positive and negative affect: A control process view. *Psychological Review, 97*, 19-35.

Cervone, D., Kopp, D. A., Schaumann, L., & Scott, W. D. (1994). Mood, self-efficacy, and performance standards: Lower moods induce higher standers for performance. *Journal of Personality and Social Psychology, 67*, 499-512.

Chaiken, S., Liberman, A., & Eagly, A. H. (1989). Heuristic and systematic processing within and beyond the persuasion context. In J. S. Uleman & J. A. Bargh (Eds.), *Unintended thoughts* (pp. 21-252). New York: Guilford.

Frijda, N. H. (1988). The laws of emotion. *American Psychologist, 43*, 349-358.

Geen, R. G. (1991). Social motivation. *Annual Review of Psychology, 42*, 377-399.

Hsee, C. K., & Abelson, R. P. (1991). Velocity relations: Satisfaction as a function of the first derivative of outcome over time. *Journal of Personality and Social Psychology, 60*, 341-347.

Isen, A. M. (1993). Positive mood and decision making. In M. Lewis & J. Haviland (Eds.), *Handbook of emotion* (pp. 63-85). New York: Guilford.

Isen, A. M., Johnson, M., Mertz, E., & Robinson, G. (1985). Positive affect and the uniqueness of word association. *Journal of Personality and Social Psychology, 48*, 1414-1426.

Lang, P. J. (1979). Cognition in emotion: Concept and action. In C. E. Izard, J. Kagan, & R. B. Zajonc (Eds.), *Emotions, cognitions, and behavior* (pp. 192-228). New York: Cambridge University Press.

Leventhal, H. (1980). Toward a comprehensive theory of emotion. In L. Berkowitz (Ed.), *Advances in experimental social psychology* (Vol. 13, pp. 139-207). New York: Academic Press.

Mackie, D. M., & Worth, L. T. (1989). Processing deficits and the mediation of positive affect in persuasion. *Journal of Personality and Social Psychology, 57*, 27-40.

Mackie, D. M., & Worth, L. T. (1991). Feeling good, but not thinking straight: The impact of positive moods on persuasion. In J. Forgas (Ed.), *Emotion and social judgments* (pp. 201-219). New York: Pergamon.

Mackie, D. M., Asuncion, A. G., & Rosselli, F. (1992). The impact of positive affect on persuasion processes. M. S. Clark (Ed.), *Emotion and social behavior* (Vol. 14, pp. 247-270). Newbury Park, CA: Sage.

Martin, L. L., & Abend, T. (1995). *When it's good to feel bad: Mood as input to a configural evaluative process.* Manuscript under review.

Martin, L. L., Achee, J. W., Ward, D. W., & Harlow, T. F. (1993). The role of cognition and effort in the use of emotions to guide behavior. In R. S. Wyer & T. K. Srull (Eds.), *Advances in social cognition* (Vol. 6, pp. 147-157). Hillsdale, NJ: Lawrence Erlbaum Associates.

Martin, L. L., & Stoner, P. (1994). *Mood as input to the creativity process.* Manuscript in preparation.

Martin, L. L., & Ward, D. W. (1994). *Mood as input to the categorization process.* Manuscript in preparation.

Martin, L. L., Ward, D. W., Achee, J. W., & Wyer, R. S. (1993). Mood as input: People have to interpret the motivational implications of their moods. *Journal of Personality and Social Psychology, 64*, 317-326.

Ortony, A., Clore, G. L., & Collins, A. (1988). *The cognitive structure of emotions.* Cambridge: Cambridge University Press.

Sanna, L. J., & Pusecker, P. A. (1994). Self-efficacy, valence of self-evaluation, and performance. *Personality and Social Psychology Bulletin, 20*, 82-92.

Sanna, L. J., Turley, K. J., & Mark, M. M. (1995). Expected evaluation, goals, and performance: Mood as input. *Personality and Social Psychology Bulletin.*

Schwarz, N. (1990). Feelings as information: Informational and motivational functions of affective states. In E. T. Higgins & R. M. Sorrentino (Eds.), *Handbook of motivation and cognition: Foundations of social behavior* (Vol. 2, pp. 527-561). New York: Guilford.

Schwarz, N., & Bless, H. (1991). Happy and mindless, but sad and smart? The impact of affective states on analytic reasoning. In J. P. Forgas (Ed.), *Emotion and social judgment* (pp. 55-72). New York: Pergamon.

Schwarz, N., & Clore, G. L. (1983). Mood, misattribution, and judgements of well-being: Informative and directive functions of affective states. *Journal of Personality and Social Psychology, 45*, 513-523.

Schwarz, N., & Clore, G. L. (1988). How do I feel about it? The information function of affective states. In K. Fiedler & J. Forgas (Eds.), *Affect, cognition and social behavior.* (pp. 44-62). Lewinston, NY: C. J. Hogrefe.

Sinclair, R. C., & Mark, M. M. (1992). The influence of mood state on judgment and action: Effects on persuasion, categorization, social justice, person perception, and judgmental accuracy. In L. L. Martin & A. Tesser (Eds.), *The construction of social judgments* (pp. 165-193). Hillsdale, NJ: Lawrence Erlbaum Associates.

Strack, F., Martin, L. L., & Stepper, S. (1987). Inhibiting and facilitating conditions of the human smile: A nonobtrusive test of the facial feedback hypothesis. *Journal of Personality and Social Psychology, 54*, 768-777.

Strack, F., Schwarz, N., & Gschneidinger, E. (1985). Happiness and reminiscing: The role of time perspective, mood, and mode of thinking. *Journal of Personality and Social Psychology, 49*, 1460-1469.

Wegener, D. T., & Petty, R. E. (1994). Mood management across affective states: The hedonic contingency hypothesis. *Journal of Personality and Social Psychology, 66*, 1034-1048.

Worth, A. M., & Mackie, D. M. (1987). Cognitive mediation of positive affect in persuasion. *Social Cognition, 5*, 76-94.

Wyer, R. S., & Carlston, D. E. (1979). *Social cognition, inference and attribution.* Hillsdale, NJ: Lawrence Erlbaum Associates.

13 Processing Goals and The Affect–Performance Link: Mood as Main Effect or Mood as Input?

Edward R. Hirt
Hugh E. McDonald
R. Jeffrey Melton
Indiana University

In recent years, the relationship among mood states, information processing strategies, and task performance has been the subject of intense interest within social psychology. Certainly, the assertion that mood can affect both cognition and action is beyond debate; the questions to be explored involve the manner in which mood influences information processing and performance. A perusal of the literature exploring such mood effects, however, reveals a somewhat confusing collection of findings; furthermore, an examination of the major theoretical frameworks proposed in this area reveals that individually they are unable to account for the full pattern of data. We note two general positions about the effects of mood on processing and performance. One position argues that mood typically has stable and predictable effects on processing and thus on performance; a competing view argues that mood has no such stable processing implications and that the effects of mood on performance are dependent on subjects' current processing goals. In this chapter, we discuss the research supporting each of these views and present some new data suggesting a possible bridge between the two.

REVIEW OF THE LITERATURE ON MOOD, PROCESSING STRATEGIES, AND PERFORMANCE

There has been considerable research demonstrating that happy mood is associated with particular performance consequences. It has consistently been found, for example, that individuals in happy moods exhibit greater originality of thought and perform better on tasks requiring creativity than individuals in unmanipulated moods. Isen, Daubman, and Nowicki (1987), for instance, found that subjects in an induced happy mood performed better on Duncker's (1945) candle problem and Mednick's (Mednick, Mednick, & Mednick, 1964) Remote Associates Test than subjects in unmanipulated moods. Similarly, Isen, Johnson, Mertz, and Robinson (1985) found that subjects in happy moods gave more unusual associations than control subjects in a word association task, and Sinnett and Larsen (1989) found that subjects in happy moods generated more words using the letters contained in a longer word than did control subjects.

In addition, happy mood has been shown to affect categorization. Isen and Daubman (1984) showed that happy subjects categorized stimuli in a broader, more inclusive fashion than controls. For instance, happy subjects were more likely than neutral mood subjects to include *camel* and *feet* in the category *vehicle*. Further research (Murray, Sujan, Hirt, & Sujan, 1990; Showers & Cantor, 1985) has demonstrated, however, that happy mood is associated with more *flexible* categorization; that is, subjects in a happy mood not only can categorize stimuli in a broader, more inclusive fashion than subjects in other moods but are also more adept than others at making narrower, more specific categorizations if asked to do so.

In stark contrast to the studies illustrating the benefits of happy mood for performance on these tasks, several lines of work suggest that being in a happy mood is often detrimental to performance on tasks requiring systematic, analytic processing. For instance, subjects in happy moods have been observed to perform worse than others on physics problems (Isen, Means, Patrick, & Nowicki, 1982), frequency judgments (Isen et al., 1982), estimating correlations from scatterplots (Sinclair & Mark, in press), syllogisms (Melton, 1995), group variability judgments (Stroessner, Hamilton, & Mackie, 1992; Stroessner & Mackie, 1992), and performance appraisals (Sinclair, 1988).

Interestingly, many of these same studies have demonstrated that sad mood is associated with improved task performance. Sinclair and his colleagues (Mark & Sinclair, 1994; Sinclair, 1988; Sinclair & Mark, in press) found that sad subjects made more accurate contingency judgments of correlation coefficients from scatterplots (even using more significant digits) and were less prone to judgmental biases (e.g., primacy effects) in impression formation tasks than neutral mood subjects.

Researchers have argued that these findings are understandable in terms of differences in processing style between individuals in different moods. There is, in fact, considerable evidence for the existence of such processing style differences. On one hand, observation of individuals in happy moods suggests that they are often more flexible and efficient in their information processing than those in other moods. In observing subjects as they solved the Duncker candle task, for instance, Isen and her colleagues noted that happy mood subjects "got many ideas, rapidly tried them, and rejected inadequate hypotheses, until they came up with the correct solution," whereas controls "tended to stare at the display without trying any solutions, or to perseverate in one mode even after they saw that it did not seem to be working" (Isen et al., 1982, p. 253). Similarly, Isen and Means (1983) found that subjects in a happy mood who were asked to decide which of several cars they would purchase if they had the opportunity made their decisions more efficiently than control subjects. For instance, although they made similar decisions, they took significantly less time to do so and were significantly less likely to review previously considered information.

On the other hand, researchers have also observed a fairly consistent tendency for happy moods to be associated with superficial, unsystematic processing and for sad moods to be associated with thoughtful and systematic (albeit not necessarily imaginative) processing. For instance, happy subjects have been found to be more likely than subjects in neutral moods to resort to the availability heuristic in making frequency judgments (Isen et al., 1982), to rely more on stereotypes in forming impressions of others (Bodenhausen & Kramer, 1990, 1991), and to use less of the available information in forming impressions of others (Mark & Sinclair, 1994). In contrast, individuals in sad moods use more of the available information (Mark & Sinclair, 1994) and use more individuating (as opposed to category-based) information (Bodenhausen, 1993) in impression formation tasks than do neutral mood subjects. A similar pattern of results has been obtained in studies examining the effects of mood on persuasion. Specifically, happy subjects engage in less systematic processing of the arguments contained in persuasive messages than subjects in unmanipulated or negative moods (Batra & Stayman, 1990; Bless, Bohner, Schwarz, & Strack, 1990; Kuykendall & Keating, 1990; Mackie & Worth, 1989; Worth & Mackie, 1987) and are more likely to base their attitudes on simple heuristics, such as source expertise (Mackie & Worth, 1989; Worth & Mackie, 1987). As a result, their attitudes are significantly less affected by the quality of the arguments the message contains.

It should be noted that, although sad mood has typically been found to be associated with systematic processing, there are several studies that demonstrate that sad mood is sometimes associated with decrements in processing or performance. For example, Stroessner and Mackie (1992) and Stroessner et al. (1992) found that sad subjects, like happy subjects, made less accurate group variability judgments than did neutral mood subjects. Furthermore, Bodenhausen (1993; Bodenhausen & Kramer, 1990, 1991) has found that moods associated with high arousal, whether positive or negative in valence, are associated with greater use of stereotypes.

This review highlights the difficulty of making definitive statements regarding the effects of mood states on performance. Some of the previously mentioned research implies that happy subjects will outperform sad subjects, whereas other research implies the opposite. Despite these inconsistencies, however, recent reviews of this literature (Schwarz & Bless, 1991; Sinclair & Mark, 1992) have concluded that there is a common thread to most if not all of the observed effects; namely, it appears that, in general, mood states predispose subjects toward particular styles of information processing. This general position proposes that positive moods are likely to promote a more casual style of processing, a style characterized by reduced processing effort and a greater willingness to use simplifying heuristics or other potentially risky processing strategies. Negative moods, on the other hand, are likely to promote a more careful, systematic, and risk-averse style of processing. According to this view, the effect of a given mood on later performance depends on the adaptiveness of the particular processing strategy associated with that mood for the task being performed. For some tasks, the more casual processing style characteristic of positive moods may lead to better task performance because such a style promotes flexibility and creativity in problem solving. However, for other tasks, more deliberate, systematic processing is required. For these types of tasks, we would expect that negative moods would improve task performance, whereas positive moods would lead to poorer task performance (relative to neutral mood). The general implication of this position, therefore, is that moods have predictable effects on performance through their promotion of specific styles of information processing.

Two major theoretical frameworks have been offered to explain the observed differences in processing styles associated with different mood states. Although each view does a reasonable job of accounting for a good portion of the available data, we feel that there are important limitations of both positions. In the next section, we discuss these two views, highlighting the strengths and weaknesses of each view for understanding the role of mood in performance.

THE MOOD-CONGRUENT RETRIEVAL VIEW

Isen (1984, 1987) argued that the facilitative effect of positive mood on creative problem solving could be explained in terms of mood-congruent retrieval. Specifically, Isen argues that positive mood states increase the accessibility of positive material in memory (Bower, 1981; Isen, Shalker, Clark, & Karp, 1978; Laird, Wagener, Halal, & Szegda, 1982; Nasby & Yando, 1982; Teasdale & Russell, 1983). Because this positive material "is more extensive and at the same time better integrated (than, for example, negative material), positive affect is able to cue a wide range of thoughts" (1987, p. 217). Thus, the individual in a positive mood is able to forge links between disparate sets of material. Although this explanation of the effect of mood on creativity is plausible, no direct evidence that the effect of positive mood on creativity is mediated by mood-congruent retrieval has been reported to date. Thus, at present, it is unclear whether the effect of positive mood on creativity is attributable to mood-congruent retrieval.

Mackie and Worth (1989, 1991; Worth & Mackie, 1987) apply Isen's hypothesis to other types of tasks, arguing that mood influences systematicity of processing by changing the amount of cognitive resources available for processing information. Specifically, because positive mood states increase the accessibility of positive material in memory, and because this positive material is assumed to be quite extensive, positive moods result in a condition of relative cognitive *overload* in which deeper analytic processing is abandoned in favor of simpler heuristic processing. Mackie and Worth (1989) found that, in comparison to control subjects, happy subjects presented with persuasive communications were more influenced by peripheral cues and less by the quality of arguments. However, this was only true if they were under time pressure; the opinions of happy subjects who were given as much time as they needed to read over the message were just as influenced by argument strength as those of subjects whose mood was not manipulated. This finding suggests that happy subjects can process the information contained in the message just as systematically as neutral mood subjects when given unlimited time. These data were interpreted as ruling out the motivational view that happy subjects are not motivated to systematically process the message and supporting the view that happy moods automatically activate task-irrelevant material in memory, thus reducing the cognitive resources available for task-relevant processing.

More recently, Mackie and Worth (1991) provided further evidence that the effect of happy mood on systematicity of processing cannot be explained purely in motivational terms. In their experiment, subjects in happy or unmanipulated moods read and evaluated a persuasive communication under one of two incentive conditions. Subjects in the high-incentive condition were told that it was quite important for them to do a thorough, accurate, and complete job of evaluating the communication and that they would be paid according to how well they did so. Subjects in the low-incentive condition were given no such instructions. Mackie and Worth found that even though the incentive had a significant impact on the amount of motivation and effort subjects reported expending, happy subjects given that incentive still did not exhibit any evidence of systematic message processing. That is, despite being highly motivated to process the persuasive communication thoroughly, happy subjects in the high-incentive condition were, like their counterparts in the low-incentive condition, no more persuaded by strong persuasive arguments than by weak ones. Thus, these results imply that the induction of a happy mood produces a strong preference for a processing style that, although quite adaptive for performing creativity tasks, is not conducive to evaluating persuasive communications on their merits and cannot be changed by simply motivating subjects to try harder.

It should be noted, however, that other evidence is inconsistent with the mood-congruent retrieval hypothesis. Several researchers (e.g., Parrott & Sabini, 1990) have demonstrated that mood-congruent retrieval only occurs under certain conditions, and to date no direct evidence exists that the effect of positive mood on systematicity of processing is mediated by mood-congruent retrieval. Thus, in our opinion, the hypothesis that positive affect restricts cognitive capacity by cueing retrieval of positive material is at best only a partial explanation of the effects of mood on processing strategy. In addition, the mood-congruent retrieval hypothesis cannot explain the tendency for sad mood to increase systematic processing. An extension of the hypothesis to sad mood would generate the prediction that, due to its tendency to cue retrieval of negatively valenced material, the induction of sad mood would reduce the capacity for systematic processing. Yet, although some research has found that sad as well as happy mood reduced systematic processing of group variability information (Stroessner & Mackie, 1992; Stroessner et al., 1992), other research finds that sad subjects process information more systematically than neutral mood controls (Mark & Sinclair, 1994) or happy subjects (Bless et al., 1990; Mark & Sinclair, 1994), findings not easily reconciled with such an extension of the mood-congruent retrieval view.

THE COGNITIVE TUNING VIEW

An alternative to the mood-congruent retrieval view is the *cognitive tuning* view proposed by Schwarz and Bless (Schwarz, 1990; Schwarz & Bless, 1991). Their formulation, which is an extension of Schwarz and Clore's (1983) affect-as-information hypothesis, draws on earlier work in emotion theory (e.g., Frijda, 1988) arguing that the function of emotional states is to inform the individual whether conditions warrant action. This position makes the point that negative mood states generally indicate trouble, and thus induce a motivation to examine the situation carefully and find solutions. Positive mood states, on the other hand, generally indicate that all is well, and thus induce no such processing motivation. These motivations result in a tendency for subjects in a positive mood to process superficially and for subjects in a negative mood to process systematically.

Moreover, individuals in a positive mood may be more willing than individuals in a negative mood to explore novel procedures and possibilities in creative problem-solving situations because as they contemplate such procedures or possibilities they are less likely to "feel" that they are risky (cf. Johnson & Tversky, 1983). Additionally, Schwarz and Bless (1991) propose that negative affective states increase the accessibility of specific procedural knowledge that is functional in situations typically associated with negative affect; on the other hand, positive affective states, which are not generally associated with situations requiring any particular action, do not do so. This latter aspect of the cognitive tuning formulation in a sense stands the mood-congruent retrieval view on its head, arguing that it is negative (rather than positive) mood that cues retrieval of information that under some circumstances facilitates and under some circumstances inhibits processing and performance. For tasks on which the specific procedures cued by negative mood are useful for performing the task at hand, being in a negative mood facilitates performance; on the other hand, for some tasks, such procedural knowledge is irrelevant and only serves to restrict the amount of cognitive capacity that can be devoted to the task.

It is important to note a major conceptual difference between the cognitive tuning and mood-congruent retrieval views in terms of the role of mood in performance. The cognitive tuning formulation explains the effects of mood on processing strategy (and subsequent performance) largely in terms of motivational factors; in contrast, the mood-congruent retrieval view argues that cognitive capacity limitations underlie the effects of mood on processing strategy.[1]

The cognitive tuning perspective does an excellent job of explaining the enhanced performance of sad mood subjects and the impaired performance of happy mood subjects (as well as the associated differences in systematicity of processing) found in much of the previously discussed research. Moreover, this view plausibly explains the enhanced creativity of individuals in a happy mood by asserting that performance on such tasks is facilitated by a certain degree of fearlessness about exploring novel procedures and possibilities that is promoted by being in a happy mood. The notion that being in a happy mood would promote such a confident approach to problem solving is certainly plausible in light of findings that individuals in a happy mood feel significantly more confident about their proficiency in a wide variety of tasks than individuals in a neutral mood

---

[1]Clearly, however, these two views are not necessarily mutually exclusive. Indeed, recent evidence (cf. Mackie, Asuncion, & Rosselli, 1992) suggests that motivational considerations can sometimes override capacity constraints. Thus, in both views, a consideration of subjects' motivations is essential to understanding and predicting performance.

(Kavanagh & Bower, 1985). However, to date there is no evidence bearing on Schwarz and Bless' hypothesis that particular procedures are primed by negative moods.

THE MOOD-AS-INPUT VIEW

Although they postulate different mechanisms by which moods influence processing and performance, the mood-congruent retrieval and cognitive tuning formulations both predict that specific processing strategies will be associated with happy and sad moods. Because the use of a particular processing style is argued to be a direct outcome of a given mood state, these views both predict that moods will typically have "main effects" on processing strategy and performance. Recent research by Martin and his colleagues (Martin, Ward, Achee, & Wyer, 1993), however, provides evidence that suggests a different interpretation of the effects of mood on processing and performance. Martin et al. (1993) found that particular mood states can have very different effects on later performance depending on subjects' processing goals. These results strongly imply that particular mood states will not have consistent effects on performance; instead, mood states interact with subjects' goals and task conceptions to determine performance. Indeed, Martin et al. stated that "we do not believe that moods have stable motivational implications. Rather, moods have different implications depending on people's interpretations of their moods" (1993, p. 318).

In Martin et al.'s formulation, which, like Schwarz and Bless' (1991) position, is an extension of the affect-as-information explanation of mood-congruent evaluation (Schwarz & Clore, 1983), mood serves as an input into other processes that ultimately determine performance. Martin and his colleagues found that happy subjects in an impression-formation task spent more time and examined more behaviors than did sad subjects when they were using an experimenter-provided *stop rule* indicating that they should stop examining behaviors when they no longer enjoyed the task. Conversely, happy subjects spent less time and examined fewer behaviors when using a rule indicating that they should stop when they had enough information to complete the task. Similar results were obtained in a subsequent experiment requiring subjects to generate items from memory rather than reading lists of behaviors (Martin et al., 1993). Martin et al. argued that results of this type were incompatible with a formulation assigning global *main effects* to mood states because the effects of mood in these studies depended upon the goals and task conceptions of the subjects.

In Martin et al.'s alternative, *mood as input* conceptualization, mood serves as a cue providing input into evaluative and judgmental processes that then determine the effects of mood on performance. For example, mood could serve as input in the judgment about whether one has obtained sufficient information to render a final decision. Happy mood might lead one to answer "yes" to this query because happy mood may be interpreted as indicating that enough information has been gathered, and this may result in a cessation of information-gathering efforts. In contrast, sad mood might lead one to answer "no" to this query (because sad mood may be interpreted as indicating that more information is required), and this may result in the gathering of additional information before rendering a final decision. However, if the judgment is to determine whether one is enjoying the task and wants to continue, mood may have quite different implications for performance: Happy subjects would perceive their mood as reflecting greater task enjoyment and continue performing the task, whereas sad subjects would perceive little task enjoyment and stop performing the task. Thus, depending on the processing goal of the individual, a given mood can lead one to stop a task prematurely or to persist at a task longer than usual. In other words, the *mood as input* view argues that mood will have *interactive* effects rather than *main effects* on subsequent performance. According to Martin et al. (1993), mood affects performance only indirectly, by serving as an *answer* to questions regarding, for example, one's progress on, or enjoyment of, the task at hand.

The work of Martin et al. (1993) clearly challenges the view that mood states directly influence performance through a promotion of specific processing strategies. It is difficult to reconcile the interaction of mood state and stop rule in Martin et al.'s (1993) work with a formulation proposing that mood states have direct effects on processing style.[2] The primary goal of this chapter is to present a basic framework that incorporates both the *main effect* accounts of mood's effects on processing and performance and the more recently proposed *mood as input* formulation of Martin et al. (1993). We present data indicating that both of the above positions represent a part of the total picture; certain elements of processing and task

---

[2]It is important to note that both the mood-congruent retrieval and cognitive tuning views have mechanisms for explaining Martin et al.'s (1993) effects. Mackie et al. (1992) report that "we assume that mood always has the same effects on a particular subprocess but that subprocess may play a more or less dominant role in persuasion at any given time" (p. 263). Thus, the presence of strong motivations or experimenter-provided stop rules may override the main effects of mood. Similarly, Schwarz, Bless, and Bohner (1991) discuss how external goals can override default main effects of mood on processing. However, both of these positions require the invocation of overrides to the typical main effects of mood on processing.

It is important to acknowledge that Mackie et al. and Schwarz et al. do not predict main effects of mood on *performance*; rather, they argue that mood has main effects on *processing* that may or may not translate into main effects on performance depending on goals, contextual factors, and so on. However, these two positions differ from the mood as input view in that they maintain that moods invariantly have certain effects on processing.

performance may indeed be directly and predictably affected by mood states, whereas mood may also interact with subjects' goals or task perceptions and thus indirectly affect other aspects of processing and task performance. In other words, we propose that mood may have both main effects and interactive effects upon processing and, as a result, performance. We also discuss how mood may operate at several different stages of the processing sequence to ultimately affect task performance. Indeed, we believe a consideration of the multiple levels at which mood could influence information processing is essential if we are to achieve a more complete understanding of the complex relationship between mood and performance.

The Present Research

The present research uses as a point of departure the results obtained by Murray et al. (1990, Studies 2 and 3). In the following section, we review this work, highlighting the relevant questions that serve as the focus of the present research.

The paradigm used by Murray et al. (1990) was similar to that employed in many mood studies. Using a two-experiment ploy, subjects' moods were manipulated in the "first" study. Two different mood inductions were used in this research; one study used the Velten mood induction procedure (cf. Sinclair, 1988), the other used film clips (cf. Worth & Mackie, 1987). However, in both studies, only happy and neutral mood conditions were included. In a second, ostensibly unrelated study, subjects were told that they were participating in "an experiment looking at how consumers perceive television programs." In the experiment, subjects were given two different pairs of TV shows ("The Cosby Show" and "Cheers," "M*A*S*H" and "Moonlighting") and were asked to think about the characters portrayed in those shows. Subjects were then asked to list both similarities and differences between the characters in each of the two pairs of shows. Specifically, subjects did four separate listing tasks (similarities for pair 1, differences for pair 1, etc.), and order of task (similarities first vs. differences first) was counterbalanced.

Three critical dependent measures were assessed. First, the number of similarities and differences generated was tallied. However, because we were interested in assessing qualitative as well as quantitative measures of performance, two additional indices of performance were calculated. One measure consisted of the number of distinct types of similarities and differences generated. That is, some subjects might simply focus on several similarities and differences of a single type (e.g., similar or different demographic features of the characters), whereas other subjects might identify several different types of similarities and/or differences (e.g., personality characteristics, behavioral characteristics, characteristics of the relationships between the characters, time- or location-based references, etc.). An additional qualitative index of performance was the creativity of subjects' responses. Responses were coded as creative if they were both novel (i.e., infrequent) and insightful. An example of a creative response for "Cheers" and "The Cosby Show" might be "more sophisticated and modern versus more traditional value systems." We then computed the proportion of creative responses generated by the subject as a final index of performance.

The findings of these experiments were intriguing. In Murray et al. (1990), Study 2, subjects were given a fixed amount of time (2.5 minutes) per listing task. The results indicated that happy subjects were able to generate a greater number of both similarities and differences than neutral mood subjects. This finding was particularly interesting in that it suggested that happy subjects could categorize stimuli not only at a broader, more inclusive level (cf. Isen & Daubman, 1984) but also at a narrower, more specific level. In addition, happy subjects generated more distinct types and more creative similarities and differences than did neutral mood subjects. Thus, on both qualitative and quantitative indices, happy subjects showed better performance than did neutral mood subjects.

A later experiment (Murray et al., 1990, Study 3) allowed subjects to determine the amount of time spent on the listing tasks. Thus, an additional measure of interest was time spent on the task. Happy subjects spent significantly less time at the task than did neutral mood subjects, yet generated just as many similarities and differences. This finding suggested that task persistence could not account for these effects. Moreover, in addition to demonstrating greater efficiency (cf. Isen & Means, 1983), happy subjects generated qualitatively better responses, in terms of both the number of distinct types and the creativity of their responses. In addition, these same effects were observed for both positively valenced (i.e., comedies) and neutrally valenced (i.e., documentaries, news shows) stimuli, arguing against mood congruence explanations for the observed effects.

This last experiment also included an additional measure that suggested a possible mechanism underlying the effects of mood on performance. Happy subjects reported greater task interest than subjects in neutral mood. Furthermore, for happy subjects, task interest was significantly correlated with both qualitative indices of performance (number of distinct types and creativity), suggesting that task interest might mediate the effects of mood on performance.

However, there were a number of unanswered questions with the Murray et al. findings. First and foremost was the question of the role of task interest in the relationship between mood and performance. Two possibilities seemed plausible. Murray et al. suggested that happy mood may lead subjects to perceive greater task interest and that this enhanced task interest leads them to use strategies during the task that result in better task performance. Alternatively, it could be the case that happy mood leads directly to better task performance (perhaps through increasing subjects' use of particularly effective strategies) and that better task performance leads subjects to perceive greater task interest. This sequence is more akin to the directionality of the relationship between performance feedback and subsequent task interest discussed by intrinsic motivation researchers (cf. Sansone & Harackiewicz, chap. 12, this volume). Given that Murray et al. assessed task interest only after subjects performed the task, either of these causal pathways could underlie the observed correlations between interest and performance.

A related issue concerns the generality of the relationships among mood state, task interest, and task performance. Although Murray et al. could not clearly specify the relationships among these variables, these results suggest that mood has main effects on both task interest and task performance. However, one could imagine how these relationships might vary as a function of features of the particular task employed (e.g., one might find different results for a more analytic or algorithmic task), the particular stimuli used (e.g., one might expect happy subjects to be less interested in a task involving negatively valenced—and potentially mood-threatening—stimuli), and the processing goals operative as subjects perform the task. Thus, the present research represents an initial exploration of the interactive relationship among several variables—mood, task interest, processing goals, and performance.

THE MARTIN ET AL. (1993) PROCESSING GOAL MANIPULATIONS

As we noted earlier, recent work by Martin et al. (1993) challenges the notion that mood has direct, *main effect* implications for performance. Instead, these researchers argued that one's mood state has different implications for performance depending on the subjects' interpretation of their mood. That is, building on the *affect as information* idea proposed by Schwarz and Clore (1983; see also Schwarz, 1990), Martin et al. believe that mood serves as input to evaluative and judgmental processes that determine the effects that mood will have on performance.

In order to demonstrate these notions, Martin et al. varied the processing goals (or stop rules) that subjects were given as they performed the experimental task. In one study (Martin et al., 1993, Study 2), subjects performed a generation task (generating names of as many birds as they could think of) under one of three different stop rules. One group of subjects (the TIME TO STOP condition) were told that "as you are making your list, keep asking yourself 'Do I think this is a good time to stop?' If the answer is yes, then stop. If the answer is no, then keep listing. There is no right or wrong time to stop. Stop when you feel it is a good time to stop." In this condition, Martin et al. argued that happy subjects would stop earlier than sad subjects, because research (Heady & Veenhoven, 1989; Johnson & Tversky, 1983; Kavanagh & Bower, 1985) has shown that happy mood leads subjects to perceive that they have attained or made progress toward their goals, whereas sad mood leads subjects to perceive that they have not attained or made progress toward their goals.

A second group of subjects (the ENJOY condition) were told that "as you are making your list, keep asking yourself 'Do I feel like continuing with this task?' As long as the answer is yes, then continue making your list. When the answer becomes no, then stop. There is no right or wrong time to stop. List the items until you no longer enjoy it. We are interested in people's enjoyment of different tasks." In this condition, it was expected that happy subjects would persist longer at the task than would sad subjects, because happy mood leads subjects to perceive themselves as having greater interest in the task, whereas sad mood leads subjects to perceive themselves as not enjoying the task (cf. Murray et al., 1990; Pretty & Seligman, 1984).

A third group (the STOP WHEN YOU FEEL LIKE STOPPING condition) was told that "there are no right or wrong answers and we are not concerned with how many of these things you can come up with. We just want to see which ones come to your mind. You can stop listing whenever you feel like stopping." This condition was designed to represent a control or baseline condition, illustrating subjects' default stop rule, against which the other two stop rules could be compared.

Martin et al.'s (1993) results provide strong support for the mood as input position. In the TIME TO STOP processing goal condition, happy subjects spent significantly less time on the generation task and generated significantly fewer items than did sad subjects. Conversely, in the ENJOY processing goal condition, happy subjects spent significantly more time on the generation task and generated significantly more items than did sad subjects. Subjects in the control (STOP WHEN YOU FEEL LIKE STOPPING) condition did not differ from the TIME TO STOP condition on either the time spent or number generated measures, suggesting that, for this task, subjects' default stop rule may be "stop when you feel it is a good time to stop."

These results have important implications for the pattern of findings observed in Murray et al. (1990). We might expect that these processing goal manipulations could affect the amount of time spent on the task as well as the number of similarities and differences generated by subjects in happy or sad mood conditions. However, it is unclear whether these effects of processing goal would extend to more qualitative measures of performance, in particular creativity. Thus, one goal of the present research is to investigate the effects of these stop rule manipulations on both the quantity and quality of subjects' responses in the Murray et al. paradigm.

As we mentioned earlier, a second goal of the present work was to assess the causal role of task interest in the mood–performance relationship. In order to do this, we included a measure of perceived task interest *prior* to performing the experimental task to assess whether happy mood reliably leads to the perception of greater task interest. Indeed, an assumption inherent in Martin et al.'s (1993) predictions regarding the effect of the ENJOY stop rule is that happy mood serves as input in judgments of task enjoyment. Thus, the present research allows us to validate this assumption by demonstrating that happy subjects tend to report greater interest in the task. Furthermore, we could then examine whether changes in task interest mediated the effects of mood on task performance.

A final goal of the present research was to assess subjects' perceptions of their task performance. That is, we were interested in whether happy subjects perceive their performance as qualitatively better than do sad or neutral mood subjects. Again, an assumption inherent in the Martin et al. (1993) TIME TO STOP stop rule is that happy subjects perceive that they have made greater progress toward their goals than do sad subjects. Thus, we wanted to test this assumption in our paradigm and see whether happy subjects actually think that they have performed the task better. In addition, we wanted to correlate these perceptions of performance with actual performance to examine whether these perceptions are strongly correlated with actual differences in performance or are a direct consequence of mood state (and are uncorrelated with performance).

Procedure

The present research followed the general Murray et al. (1990) procedure with some notable changes. First, we manipulated subjects' mood using the Velten mood induction technique. However, in the present study, we included a sad mood condition in addition to the happy and neutral mood conditions used in Murray et al. Thus, unlike Murray et al., we are able to look for the crossover pattern of effects of mood on performance that were found by Martin et al. (1993). In addition, we could examine the performance of neutral mood subjects (a group not included in Martin et al.) to establish a baseline of comparison for the effects of mood state on performance.

After the generation task was introduced, subjects were given one of three processing goals: the TIME TO STOP processing goal, the ENJOY processing goal, or a no goal condition (in which no mention was made of stop rule at all). After the processing goal manipulation, subjects completed an initial measure of task interest. These items (adapted from Harackiewicz, Abrahams, & Wageman, 1987) assessed the degree to which subjects thought the task would be fun, interesting, and enjoyable.[3]

Again, the domain of interest was television shows; however, the pairs of TV shows chosen for the present study were "The Cosby Show" and "Cheers" (as in Murray et al., 1990) and "The Simpsons" and "Married . . . with Children." We chose these particular shows on the basis of pretesting that indicated that our subjects were all very familiar with these shows. Subjects listed both similarities and differences between the characters in each of these two pairs of shows. As in Murray et al., Study 3, time spent on the listing task was assessed for each subject.

Following the listing task, subjects completed a second interest measure. This Time 2 interest measure used the same five questions as the Time 1 measure; however, in the Time 2 measure, these questions were phrased in the past tense (e.g., How enjoyable did you find the task?) as opposed to the future tense (e.g., How enjoyable do you think the task will be?). We also included a question asking subjects about their desire to perform a similar task again (FUTURE PARTICIPATION) as an additional measure of subsequent task interest.[4] In addition, we asked subjects to report how well they thought they did at the task (ESTIMATED PERFORMANCE), their level of satisfaction with their performance (SATISFACTION), and the level of effort they put into the task (EFFORT). These three indices constituted our measures of perceived task performance.

Results

3 (Mood: happy, neutral, sad) × 3 (Stop Rule: time to stop, enjoy, control) analyses of variance (ANOVAs) were performed on the main dependent

---

[3]In our control condition, there was no mention of any stop rule. We acknowledge that this condition is a departure from the control (i.e., STOP WHEN YOU FEEL LIKE STOPPING) condition used in Martin et al. (1993). However, we chose to do this primarily because we wanted this condition to serve as a replication condition for the results of Murray et al. (1990), Studies 2 and 3.

[4]Given that our focus in this chapter is on the mood-performance link, we chose not to discuss the results on these measures of subsequent task interest in any detail. For interested readers, these results are detailed elsewhere (see Hirt, Melton, McDonald, & Harackiewicz, 1995). However, we believe that a full understanding of the relationship between mood, interest, and performance requires the consideration of the role of mood and performance on subsequent task interest. Indeed, our results suggest that task performance is a critical component in perceptions of subsequent task interest, demonstrating that both causal sequences (i.e., mood → interest → performance, and mood → performance → interest) are occurring.

variables. We found that subjects' mood state did reliably affect Time 1 interest, with happy subjects reporting greater interest than either neutral or sad subjects. Thus, even before they had any experience with the task, happy subjects perceived the task as likely to be more interesting and enjoyable than did subjects in the other mood conditions. Mood state exerted similar effects on the measures of perceived task performance. Happy subjects' estimates of their own performance, feelings of satisfaction with their performance, and reported effort exerted all exceeded those of neutral and sad subjects. Moreover, when we examined the correlations between subjects' estimates of their own performance and their actual performance (in terms of both number of items generated and proportion of creative responses), we found no relationship between estimated and actual performance for either happy or sad subjects (rs ranged from $-.08$ to .15, ns), whereas subjects in neutral mood conditions showed significant correlations between these measures (rs ranging from .37 to .39, $ps < .01$). These results imply that subjects' judgments of their own performance are more affected by their mood state than by their actual performance. Thus, our results are consistent with the assumptions underlying the Martin et al. processing goals; namely, that happy subjects use their mood state as input in determining their level of task enjoyment and in judging the quality of their performance.

On objective measures of performance, we found, consistent with Martin et al. (1993), that the processing goal manipulation interacted with induced mood to affect both time spent on the generation task and number of items generated. In the TIME TO STOP processing goal condition, happy subjects spent significantly less time at the task than did either neutral or sad subjects. In the ENJOY processing goal condition, happy subjects spent significantly more time at the task than did either neutral or sad subjects. This result perfectly replicates the crossover pattern found by Martin et al. on their measure of time spent. Consistent with Murray et al. (1990, Study 3), however, happy subjects in the control (no stop rule) condition spent significantly less time at the task than did either neutral or sad subjects. These results are illustrated in Fig. 13.1.

The pattern of results obtained on the number of items generated measure was similar to the previously cited results on the measure of time spent; however, on this measure, we obtained a significant main effect of mood condition as well as a significant mood by processing goal interaction. As a result, there were no differences in number of items generated between happy, sad, and neutral subjects in the TIME TO STOP condition. However, in the ENJOY condition, happy subjects generated significantly more items than did either sad or neutral subjects. These results are again consistent with Martin et al. However, unlike in Murray et al. (Study 3),

13. PROCESSING GOALS AND THE AFFECT-PERFORMANCE LINK   319

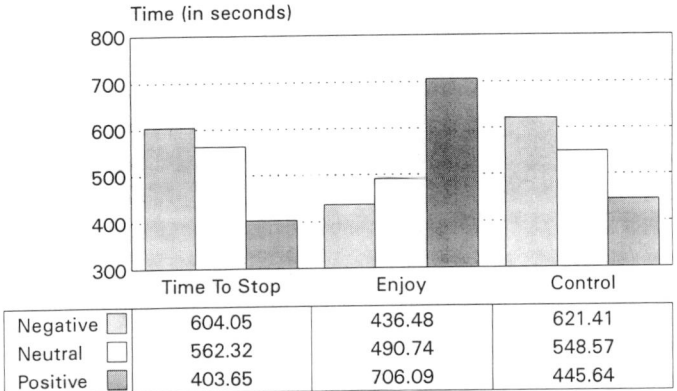

Fig. 13.1 Time spent at the generation task as a function of mood and processing goal.

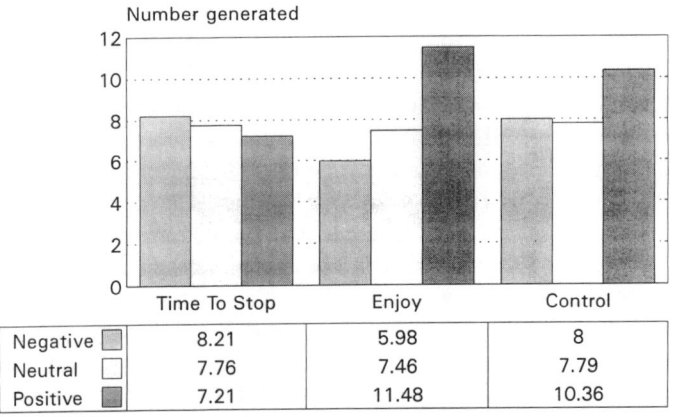

Fig. 13.2 Number of items generated as a function of mood and processing goal.

happy subjects in the control condition of the present study actually generated more items despite spending less time at the task. These results are displayed in Fig. 13.2.

Taken together, these results provide strong support for Martin et al.'s argument that the implications of mood for performance vary as a function of processing goal. However, when we turn from the quantitative to the qualitative measures of performance, a different pattern emerges.[5] On our

---

[5]In the present discussion, we focus only on one qualitative measure of performance — creativity. The other qualitative measure of performance, the number of distinct types of similarities and differences generated, was so highly correlated with the total number measure

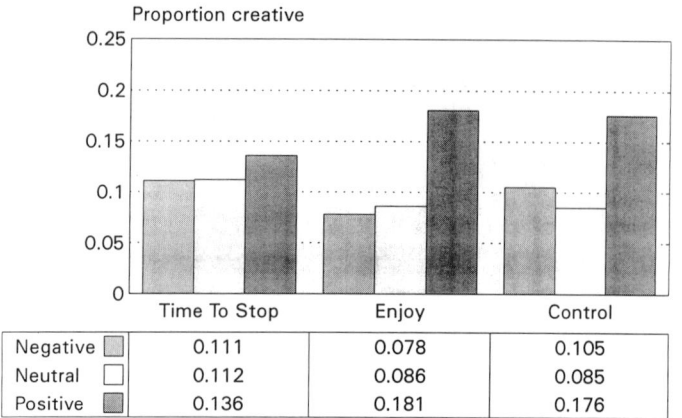

Fig. 13.3 Proportion of creative responses as a function of mood and processing goal.

measure of creativity, we obtained only a main effect of mood condition, with happy subjects producing more creative responses than either sad or neutral subjects; importantly, we found that mood condition and processing goal did not interact to affect creativity. These results are shown in Fig. 13.3. Thus, it appears that this qualitative aspect of task performance may be unaffected by the processing goal manipulation.

Given that mood reliably affected both task interest and task performance, we next sought to clarify the possible mediating role of task interest in the mood–performance relationship. To do this, we performed path analyses following the procedures outlined by Judd and Kenny (1981a, 1981b). They proposed that data are congruent with a mediational model when (a) the independent variables significantly predict the final outcome measure, (b) these variables also significantly predict the hypothesized mediating variable, and (c) the mediator significantly predicts the outcome measure when the independent variables are controlled.

In the regression model, mood was represented as two orthogonal contrasts: a *valence* contrast (in which happy mood was coded +1, sad mood −1, and neutral mood 0) and a *neutral* contrast (in which both happy and sad moods were coded +1 and neutral mood was coded −2). In other words, the valence contrast examined differences between subjects in happy and sad moods, whereas the neutral contrast examined differences between subjects experiencing happy or sad moods versus subjects in

---

that the results for these two measures were nearly identical. The creativity measure (given that it was the *proportion* of creative responses) was only weakly correlated with the number measure and thus provided the only independent qualitative measure of performance.

neutral mood conditions. Additionally, processing goal condition was also represented in these analyses, with both a *goal* contrast (in which the ENJOY condition was coded +1, the TIME TO STOP condition was coded −1, and the control condition was coded 0) and a *control* contrast (in which both ENJOY and TIME TO STOP conditions were coded +1 and the control condition was coded −2). We also computed the four multiplicative two-way interaction terms among the independent variables. Thus, a total of eight terms were computed for each subject and entered simultaneously into each regression.

In our initial series of analyses, we regressed our two major outcome measures (NUMBER and CREATIVITY) on the full independent variables model. In this model, we found both a significant effect of valence contrast as well as a valence contrast by goal contrast interaction on the number of items generated; consistent with the ANOVA results reported earlier, these results show that the effects of mood differed as a function of processing goal. Subjects in the ENJOY processing goal condition showed strong effects of mood on the number of items measure (b = .66), whereas subjects in the TIME TO STOP condition showed no effects of mood on this measure (b = −.02). For creativity, we found significant effects of both valence contrast and neutral contrast, with no interaction with processing goal. Both of these effects result from the fact that happy subjects displayed significantly greater creativity than did either sad or neutral subjects. Thus, we have evidence that our independent variables model predicts each of our outcome measures.

Next, we regressed our hypothesized mediator (Time 1 interest) on the full independent variables model. In this model, the valence contrast was the only individually significant term. Again, consistent with the ANOVA results, happy subjects reported greater task interest than did sad subjects.

Given that we had shown that our independent variables model significantly predicted both the outcome measures and the hypothesized mediator, we could then test for mediation in a final set of analyses. In these analyses, we regressed the full independent variables model, along with Time 1 interest and all possible interaction terms (between Time 1 interest and any of the terms from the independent variables model), on each of the outcome variables. For the number of items generated, we found that the effects of mood on performance were partially mediated by Time 1 interest (see Fig. 13.4). That is, the path from Time 1 interest to number generated was significant with the independent variables controlled. However, the valence contrast and valence contrast by goal contrast interaction terms remained significant even after Time 1 interest was entered into the regression model, indicating that interest is only playing a *partially* mediating role. Nonetheless, on this measure, we have evidence that Time 1 interest is playing a mediating role in the mood–performance relationship.

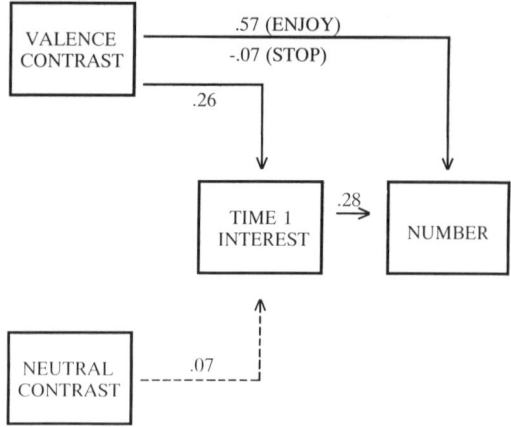

Fig. 13.4 Path mediational model for the number of items generated.

A similar set of analyses performed on the creativity measure revealed a very different pattern (see Fig. 13.5). When controlling for the independent variables, the path from Time 1 interest to creativity disappeared, indicating Time 1 interest did not significantly affect the mood–performance relationship; that is, the link between mood and creativity appears to be direct and unmediated by either subjects' interest prior to actual performance or by processing goal.

Thus, it appears that we have obtained evidence for both the mood as main effect and mood as input positions within the same data set. On quantitative measures of time spent on the task and number of items generated, the pattern of interactions between mood and processing goal

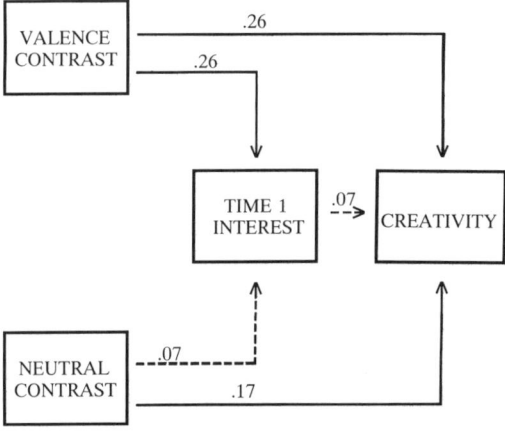

Fig. 13.5 Path mediational model for the proportion of creative responses.

provide strong support for Martin et al.'s (1993) mood as input position. On these measures, the effect of mood on performance differed as a function of the processing goal associated with the task. However, no interactions with processing goal were obtained on our measure of creativity, nor were such interactions present on subjects' estimates of their own performance. It thus appears that the effect of mood on these measures is a direct one, a finding supportive of the mood as main effect position.

Implications and Future Directions

Given the results for our creativity measure, it is tempting to conclude that mood may have general and direct effects on performance that occur regardless of processing goal. However, we acknowledge the fact that these effects may be a function of the particular kind of task used. The present task certainly allowed for creative responding to a much greater degree than other tasks. That is, subjects were not constrained by rules specifying acceptable solutions. Moreover, it appeared from pretests that the vast majority of our subjects were relatively familiar with the television shows we used in the experiment; thus, the opportunity for positive mood to stimulate creative associations was maximized by the existence of an extensive knowledge base. The degree to which these results would generalize to more structured, constraining, or novel tasks is an empirical question. Indeed, we feel that this research calls for the development of a taxonomy of different kinds of tasks and the features associated with tasks that engender creative responding.

In addition to the issue of what dimensions of tasks allow opportunities for creativity, another important issue for future theory and research is that of what dimensions of tasks make them interesting. It may be that some tasks are simply too boring for them to ever be misperceived as interesting no matter how good a mood someone is in; thus, under such circumstances, the effects of processing goals might be limited. An attempt to address this issue may also have relevance for work in the area of intrinsic motivation. Work in this area has tended to use tasks that subjects find intrinsically interesting (e.g., pinball, SOMA puzzles, video games), but the features that discriminate these tasks from other (less interesting) tasks remain unclear.

In addition to being specific to a certain type of task, our results might also be specific to certain types of stimuli. Comedies in particular (and perhaps television programs in general) are inherently positive stimuli, and thus it may not be surprising that effects of the sort we obtained occurred for these stimuli. However, negatively valenced stimuli, particularly those that might be construed as threatening one's positive mood, might lead to a very different pattern of results. Recent work by Wegener and Petty (1994;

chap. 14, this volume) addresses this issue within their hedonic contingency hypothesis, which is based on the standard assumption that people are motivated to maintain positive moods and to repair negative moods. However, whereas previous researchers (e.g., Cialdini, Baumann, & Kenrick, 1981; Cunningham, Shaffer, Barbee, Wolff, & Kelley, 1990) have argued that individuals in negative moods engage in relatively stronger efforts at mood management than do people in positive moods, Wegener and Petty argue that the opposite is true. Their reasoning is that, for individuals in a sad mood, almost any task they might choose to do will make them feel better than they currently do. Individuals in positive moods, however, are confronted with the opposite situation: Although many activities may attenuate a positive mood, relatively few activities might be expected to maintain or enhance this mood state. Given this assymetry, Wegener and Petty (1994) argued that individuals in positive moods should base their choices of future activities on the perceived hedonic consequences of those activities to a greater extent than those in neutral or negative moods. This prediction was supported in several experiments.

These findings indicating that subjects in positive moods pay greater attention to affect-related task elements imply that the nature of the task may be more critical for subjects in positive moods than for those in negative moods. Because happy subjects are presumably motivated to maintain their positive moods, these subjects may be unwilling to continue processing negative stimuli, resulting in poorer task performance relative to sad subjects under these conditions.

Moreover, one could expect that there might be interactive effects of task and stimuli. For example, perceptions of interest in some tasks may depend upon the nature of the stimuli used (e.g., "I only like trivia games if they involve sports"), whereas for other tasks interest may be independent of the stimuli used (e.g., "I just like all crossword puzzles"). Thus, a profitable avenue for future research involves the exploration of the mood-performance relationship across different tasks and different stimuli.

Our data suggest that task interest plays a mediating role in the relationship between mood and quantitative measures of performance (e.g., number of items generated). However, we entertained the possibility that task performance might also mediate the effects of mood on subsequent task interest. That is, subjects might perceive greater task interest as a result of good performance. In this chapter, we have focused on the mood-performance link, but our data also suggest that better task performance (in terms of both number of items generated and the creativity of subjects' responses) led to greater subsequent task interest. These results are detailed elsewhere (see Hirt, Melton, McDonald, & Harackiewicz, 1995) and demonstrate evidence for both causal pathways: Mood affects task interest that then affects task performance, but task performance provides feedback that in turn affects subsequent task interest. Thus, the present research serves to forge a link between work on mood and performance and work on intrinsic motivation.

Finally, our results provide strong support for the mood as input position argued by Martin et al. (1993). Indeed, our data provided empirical support for the assumptions underlying the ENJOY and TIME TO STOP processing goal manipulations in that happy mood led subjects to perceive greater task interest and to report higher estimates of perceived task performance than subjects in other moods. Thus, it appears that people do use their moods as information in making judgments of task interest and performance. However, such a position assumes that subjects are unaware of the true source of their mood and misinterpret their moods as indicative of greater interest and performance. Research within the mood as information tradition (e.g., Schwarz & Clore, 1983) has demonstrated that making subjects aware of the source of their mood (e.g., the weather) eliminates the effect of mood on judgments of well being. Similarly, we might predict that making subjects aware of the source of their current mood might reduce or eliminate the interaction between mood and processing goals. Such a study would provide the most straightforward evidence in support of the mood as input effect. We are currently conducting research along these lines in our lab.

GENERAL CONCLUSIONS

A central theme of this chapter has been to show how the mood as main effect and mood as input positions can peacefully coexist; that is, mood can simultaneously have both direct and indirect effects on performance. Indeed, our results demonstrate that mood can affect performance in many ways. However, perhaps the most important conclusion that can be drawn from the present work is that we need to consider how mood can affect performance at a number of different points in the information-processing sequence. Within the present data set, we have presented evidence indicating that mood can exert a direct effect on initial perceptions of task interest, which may affect subsequent task engagement and performance. Much research has been conducted illustrating how mood may affect the manner in which task information is processed, leading to the use of heuristic or systematic processing styles. Our research adds to the literature demonstrating that happy mood tends to lead to more creative processing; furthermore, we have provided evidence that creativity appears to be a direct effect of mood, independent of subjects' current processing goals. In addition, consistent with the work of Martin et al. (1993), our results indicate that mood may serve as input into decisions regarding the continuation of the activity. Finally, we have shown that mood may affect judgments of effort and performance made after cessation of the task, which could affect subsequent interest in performing the task at a later time. Certainly this does not even begin to exhaust all the points in the information processing sequence at which mood could impact on task performance. For instance, one could imagine how mood could affect subjects' decisions as to whether to engage in a particular activity, or subjects' choices of which of several activities to engage in (cf. Wegener & Petty, 1994). The implication of this discussion is not merely that mood *can* have effects at any of these points; it is that mood is most likely exerting effects on performance at multiple points. This realization implies that a true understanding of the effects of mood on performance requires consideration of how mood may be operating at each of these points.

REFERENCES

Batra, R., & Stayman, D. M. (1990). The role of mood in advertising effectiveness. *Journal of Consumer Research, 12,* 432–445.

Bless, H., Bohner, G., Schwarz, N., & Strack, F. (1990). Mood and persuasion: A cognitive response analysis. *Personality and Social Psychology Bulletin, 16,* 331–345.

Bodenhausen, G. V. (1993). Emotions, arousal, and stereotypic judgments: A heuristic model of affect and stereotyping. In D. M. Mackie & D. L. Hamilton (Eds.), *Affect, cognition, and stereotyping: Interactive processes in group perception* (pp. 13–37). San Diego, CA: Academic Press.

Bodenhausen, G. V., & Kramer, G. P. (1990, June). Affective states trigger stereotypic judgments. Paper presented at the annual convention of the American Psychological Society, Dallas, TX.

Bodenhausen, G. V., & Kramer, G. P. (1991, May). Smiling and stereotyping: Does happiness trigger stereotypic judgments? Paper presented at the annual meeting of the Midwestern Psychological Association, Chicago, IL.

Bower, G. H. (1981). Mood and memory. *American Psychologist, 36,* 129–148.

Cialdini, R. B., Baumann, D. J., & Kenrick, D. T. (1981). Insights from sadness: A three step model of the development of altruism as hedonism. *Developmental Review, 1,* 207–223.

Cunningham, M. R., Shaffer, D. R., Barbee, A. P., Wolff, P. L., & Kelley, D. J. (1990). Separate processes in the relation of elation and depression to altruism: Social and personal concerns. *Journal of Experimental Social Psychology, 26,* 13–33.

Duncker, K. (1945). On problem-solving. *Psychological Monographs, 58* (Whole No. 5).

Frijda, N. H. (1988). The laws of emotion. *American Psychologist, 43,* 349–358.

Harackiewicz, J. M., Abrahams, S., & Wageman, R. (1987). Performance evaluation and intrinsic motivation: The effects of evaluative focus, rewards, and achievement orientation. *Journal of Personality and Social Psychology, 53,* 1015–1023.

Heady, B., & Veenhoven, R. (1989). Does happiness induce a rosy outlook? In R. Veenhoven (Ed.), *How harmful is happiness? Consequences of enjoying life or not* (pp. 106–127). Rotterdam, The Netherlands: Universitaire Pers.

Hirt, E. R., Melton, R. J., McDonald, H. E., & Harackiewicz, J. M. (1995). *Processing goals, task interest, and the mood–performance relationship: A mediational analysis.* Manuscript under review.

Isen, A. M. (1984). Toward understanding the role of affect in cognition. In R. S. Wyer & T.

K. Srull (Eds.), *Handbook of social cognition* (Vol. 3, pp. 179-236). Hillsdale, NJ: Lawrence Erlbaum Associates.

Isen, A. M. (1987). Positive affect, cognitive processes, and social behavior. In L. Berkowitz (Ed.), *Advances in experimental social psychology* (Vol. 20, pp. 203-253). New York: Academic Press.

Isen, A. M., & Daubman, K. A. (1984). The influence of affect on categorization. *Journal of Personality and Social Psychology, 47,* 1206-1217.

Isen, A. M., Daubman, K. A., & Nowicki, G. P. (1987). Positive affect facilitates creative problem solving. *Journal of Personality and Social Psychology, 52,* 1122-1131.

Isen, A. M., Johnson, M. M. S., Mertz, E., & Robinson, G. F. (1985). The influence of positive affect on the unusualness of word associations. *Journal of Personality and Social Psychology, 48,* 1413-1426.

Isen, A. M., & Means, B. (1983). The influence of positive affect on decision making strategy. *Social Cognition, 2,* 18-31.

Isen, A. M., Means, B., Patrick, R., & Nowicki, G. (1982). Some factors influencing decision making and risk taking. In M. S. Clark & S. T. Fiske (Eds.), *Affect and cognition: The seventeenth annual Carnegie symposium on cognition* (pp. 241-261). Hillsdale, NJ: Lawrence Erlbaum Associates.

Isen, A. M., Shalker, T. E., Clark, M. S., & Karp, L. (1978). Positive affect, accessibility of material in memory, and behavior: A cognitive loop? *Journal of Personality and Social Psychology, 36,* 1-12.

Johnson, E., & Tversky, A. (1983). Affect, generalization, and the perception of risk. *Journal of Personality and Social Psychology, 45,* 20-31.

Judd, C. M., & Kenny, D. A. (1981a). *Estimating the effects of social interventions.* Cambridge, England: Cambridge University Press.

Judd, C. M., & Kenny, D. A. (1981b). Process analysis: Estimating mediation in treatment evaluations. *Evaluation Review, 5,* 602-619.

Kavanagh, D. J., & Bower, G. H. (1985). Mood and self-efficacy: Impact of joy and sadness on perceived capabilities. *Cognitive Therapy and Research, 9,* 507-525.

Kuykendall, D., & Keating, J. P. (1990). Mood and persuasion. *Psychology and Marketing, 7,* 1-9.

Laird, J. D., Wagener, J., Halal, M., & Szegda, M. (1982). Remembering what you feel: Effects of emotion on memory. *Journal of Personality and Social Psychology, 42,* 646-657.

Mackie, D. M., Asuncion, A. G., & Rosselli, F. (1992). The impact of positive affect on persuasion processes. In M. S. Clark (Ed.), *Review of personality and social psychology* (Vol. 14, pp. 247-270). Beverly Hills, CA: Sage.

Mackie, D. M., & Worth, L. T. (1989). Processing deficits and the mediation of positive affect in persuasion. *Journal of Personality and Social Psychology, 57,* 27-40.

Mackie, D. M., & Worth, L. T. (1991). Feeling good, but not thinking straight: The impact of positive mood on persuasion. In J. Forgas (Ed.), *Emotion and social judgements* (pp. 201-219). London: Pergamon.

Mark, M. M., & Sinclair, R. C. (1994). *The effects of mood state on impression formation: Implications for processing strategy perspectives on mood.* Unpublished manuscript, The Pennsylvania State University, University Park, PA.

Martin, L. L., Ward, D. W., Achee, J. W., & Wyer, R. S., Jr. (1993). Mood as input: People have to interpret the motivational implications of their moods. *Journal of Personality and Social Psychology, 64,* 317-326.

Mednick, M. T., Mednick, S. A., & Mednick, E. V. (1964). Incubation of creative performance and specific associative priming. *Journal of Abnormal and Social Psychology, 69,* 84-88.

Melton, R. J. (1995). The role of positive affect in syllogism performance. *Personality and Social Psychology Bulletin, 21,* 788-794.

Murray, N., Sujan, H., Hirt, E. R., & Sujan, M. (1990). The influence of mood on categorization: A cognitive flexibility interpretation. *Journal of Personality and Social Psychology, 59*, 411-425.

Nasby, W., & Yando, R. (1982). Selective encoding and retrieval of affectively valenced information. *Journal of Personality and Social Psychology, 43*, 1244-1255.

Parrott, W. G., & Sabini, J. (1990). Mood and memory under natural conditions: Evidence for mood incongruent recall. *Journal of Personality and Social Psychology, 59*, 321-336.

Pretty, G. H., & Seligman, C. (1984). Affect and the overjustification effect. *Journal of Personality and Social Psychology, 46*, 1241-1253.

Schwarz, N. (1990). Feelings as information: Informational and motivational functions of affective states. In E. T. Higgins & R. M. Sorrentino (Eds.), *Handbook of motivation and cognition: Foundations of social behavior* (Vol. 2, pp. 527-561). New York: Guilford.

Schwarz, N., & Bless, H. (1991). Happy and mindless, but sad and smart? The impact of affective states on analytic reasoning. In J. Forgas (Ed.), *Emotion and social judgements* (pp. 55-71). London: Pergamon.

Schwarz, N., Bless, H., & Bohner, G. (1991). Mood and persuasion: Affective states influence the processing of persuasive communications. In M. Zanna (Ed.), *Advances in experimental social psychology* (Vol. 24, pp. 161-199). New York: Academic Press.

Schwarz, N., & Clore, G. L. (1983). Mood, misattribution, and judgments of well-being: Informative and directive functions of affective states. *Journal of Personality and Social Psychology, 45*, 513-523.

Showers, C., & Cantor, N. (1985). Social cognition: A look at motivated strategies. *Annual Review of Psychology, 36*, 275-305.

Sinclair, R. C. (1988). Mood, categorization breadth, and performance appraisal: The effects of order of information acquisition and affective state on halo, accuracy, information retrieval, and evaluations. *Organizational Behavior and Human Decision Processes, 42*, 22-46.

Sinclair, R. C., & Mark, M. M. (in press). The effects of mood state on judgmental accuracy: Processing strategy as a mechanism. *Cognition and Emotion*.

Sinclair, R. C., & Mark, M. M. (1992). The influence of mood state on judgment and action: Effects on persuasion, categorization, social justice, person perception, and judgmental accuracy. In L. L. Martin & A. Tesser (Eds.), *The construction of social judgments* (pp. 165-193). Hillsdale, NJ: Lawrence Erlbaum Associates.

Sinnett, L. M., & Larsen, R. J. (1989, May). *An affect and memory theory of creativity*. Paper presented at the annual meeting of the Midwestern Psychological Association, Chicago, IL.

Stroessner, S. J., Hamilton, D. L., & Mackie, D. M. (1992). Affect and stereotyping: The effect of induced mood on distinctiveness-based illusory correlations. *Journal of Personality and Social Psychology, 62*, 564-576.

Stroessner, S. J., & Mackie, D. M. (1992). The impact of induced affect on the perception of variability in social groups. *Personality and Social Psychology Bulletin, 18*, 546-554.

Teasdale, J. D., & Russell, M. (1983). Differential effects of induced mood on the recall of positive, negative, and neutral words. *British Journal of Clinical Psychology, 22*, 163-171.

Wegener, D. T., & Petty, R. E. (1994). Mood management across affective states: The hedonic contingency hypothesis. *Journal of Personality and Social Psychology, 66*, 1034-1048.

Worth, L. T., & Mackie, D. M. (1987). Cognitive mediation of positive affect in persuasion. *Social Cognition, 5*, 76-94.

14
Effects of Mood on Persuasion Processes: Enhancing, Reducing, and Biasing Scrutiny of Attitude-Relevant Information

Duane T. Wegener
Yale University

Richard E. Petty
Ohio State University

How do moods influence attitude change? The initial investigations of this question searched for the "one true process" by which mood and other affective states influenced attitudes. For many years, the most researched mood process was classical conditioning. In this view, affective states were hypothesized to influence attitudes by being directly associated with the attitude object. That is, pairing the attitude object with stimuli that brought about positive feeling states (e.g., a free lunch or snacks) was found to lead to more positive attitudes than pairing the attitude object with stimuli that brought about negative feeling states (e.g., unpleasant odors) (Razran, 1940; see also Griffitt, 1970; Janis, Kaye, & Kirshner, 1965; Zanna, Kiesler, & Pilkonis, 1970).

More recently, researchers have identified additional processes by which feeling states can influence attitudes. For example, one's mood could be consulted in order to answer a "How do I feel about it?" heuristic when people encounter an attitude object. This would lead to more positive attitudes toward the object when in a positive rather than negative mood (e.g., Schwarz, 1990). Alternatively, mood can influence the extent to which information of a similar valence comes to mind (Bower, 1981; Isen, Shalker, Clark, & Karp, 1978), which could influence the extent to which particular persuasive arguments are viewed as compelling (Petty & Wegener, 1991). Rather than affecting the overall persuasiveness of the communication or the arguments per se, some research suggests that mood can influence how much the message recipient carefully scrutinizes the information presented in a communication (see Mackie, Asuncion, & Rosselli, 1992; Mackie & Worth, 1991; Schwarz, Bless, & Bohner, 1991, for reviews). To the extent that each of these processes occurs, there would appear to be no "one true process" by which mood influences attitudes. Instead, a variety of processes appear to operate, and thus it becomes critical to understand when and why each of the various mechanisms influences attitudes.

One way of organizing the literature on mood effects in persuasion is to consider the goals that message recipients have when they encounter persuasive appeals. For example, if a message recipient has the goal of forming an opinion toward the attitude object without expending any more effort than absolutely necessary, mood is likely to impact persuasion differently than if the message recipient has a goal of forming the most highly informed opinion possible regardless of the amount of effort that is required. In this chapter and in our research, we use the elaboration likelihood model (ELM) of persuasion (Petty & Cacioppo, 1981, 1986) as a guide to understanding the situations in which mood would influence attitudes by different means. The ELM is a model of attitude-change processes that considers people's ability to think about a persuasive message as well as their information-processing goals. Within this framework, different attitude-change processes are most likely to determine persuasion at different specifiable levels of elaboration likelihood. For example, when message recipients have a goal of effortfully scrutinizing attitude-relevant information and are also able to do so, the ELM posits that variables are most likely to influence persuasion to the extent that they can influence the thoughts that people have in response to the attitude-relevant information. When message recipients have a goal of forming an opinion with minimum effort (or when ability is compromised), however, mood is more likely to influence attitudes by influencing direct associations between feelings and the attitude object or by being incorporated into low-effort inferences (e.g., the "How do I feel about it?" heuristic, Schwarz, 1990) with little scrutiny of the substantive issue-relevant information provided (see Petty, Gleicher, & Baker, 1991).

Although the ELM can organize the general literature on mood and social judgment, in this chapter we use the ELM to understand how a person's goals can determine the process by which mood influences attitudes in response to persuasive communications. First, we examine how a person's goals to avoid cognitive effort or to form an accurate opinion regardless of effort can influence the role of mood in persuasion. That is, we examine how mood influences attitudes when people are either very low or very high in their motivation to think about a persuasive message. Following our discussion of mood effects on low- and high-elaboration attitude change, we examine how mood management goals can influence the extent to which a person thinks about a persuasive message when the likelihood of thinking about the message is not particularly high or low as a result of the operation of other goals. Before beginning our discussion of these processes, it is useful to review the guiding assumptions of our work within the ELM.

ELM FRAMEWORK: MULTIPLE ROLES FOR PERSUASION VARIABLES

In brief, within the ELM, persuasion variables are postulated to take on different roles at different levels of elaboration likelihood (Petty & Cacioppo, 1986; Petty, Wegener, Fabrigar, Priester, & Cacioppo, 1993). Specifically, when the elaboration likelihood is low (i.e., when people are unwilling or unable to scrutinize attitude-relevant information), variables such as a person's mood state have an impact on attitudes by the operation of relatively low effort peripheral processes such as forming a direct association between the feeling and the attitude object (Zanna et al., 1970), or serving as part of a mood-based heuristic (Chaiken, 1987). When the elaboration likelihood is high (i.e., when people are both willing and able to scrutinize attitude-relevant information), variables have an impact by influencing the type of reactions that people have to attitude-relevant information or by acting as items of attitude-relevant information (i.e., providing information central to the merits of the attitudinal position). Finally, when elaboration likelihood is neither so high that people are already thinking extensively about attitude-relevant information nor so low that people are avoiding extensive attitude-relevant thought, moods like other variables can influence the amount of scrutiny that people give to attitude-relevant information (Petty, Cacioppo, & Kasmer, 1988; Petty et al., 1991). With this framework in mind, we turn to the impact of mood on attitudes across the elaboration continuum.

LOW-ELABORATION EFFECTS OF MOOD ON PERSUASION

As just noted, if people are either unmotivated or unable to think carefully about the substantive information in a persuasive communication, mood should act primarily as a simple persuasion cue. That is, when people are not effortfully scrutinizing the central merits of the attitude object, if mood is to have an impact, it should do so primarily through relatively low-effort peripheral processes that do not depend on scrutiny of attitude-relevant information.

Studies linking mood to attitude objects via classical conditioning processes (e.g., Griffitt, 1970; Janis et al., 1965; Razran, 1940; Zanna et al., 1970) provide an example of mood influencing attitudes by a peripheral mechanism in that classical conditioning does not depend on people considering the central merits of the attitudinal position. In fact, conditioning should impact attitudes most when people are relatively unmotivated and/or unable to consider the merits of the attitude object. Consistent with this notion, Cacioppo, Marshall-Goodell, Tassinary, and Petty (1992) showed that classical conditioning using electric shock was more effective for nonwords (i.e., items for which no knowledge existed on which to form an elaborated attitude) than for words (i.e., items for which knowledge did exist on which to form an elaborated attitude; see also Shimp, Stuart, & Engle, 1991).

Another process by which mood can act as a peripheral cue is by misattribution of one's mood to the attitude object (e.g., I must feel bad because I dislike or oppose the position in the message; see Cacioppo & Petty, 1982a; Petty & Cacioppo, 1983). Consistent with the notion that mood would be more likely to affect attitudes by this process when the likelihood of elaboration of the attitude object is low, Schwarz (1990) argued that use of mood as an answer to a "How do I feel about it?" heuristic is most likely when knowledge about the judgment target is low rather than high (pp. 538–539; see also Schwarz & Clore, 1983; Srull, 1983).

Finally, additional evidence of the relatively direct impact of mood on attitudes under low-elaboration conditions comes from studies in which the level of elaboration has been either manipulated by varying subjects' involvement with the communication (Petty, Cacioppo, & Schumann, 1983) or identified by assessing subjects' level of Need for Cognition (i.e., the extent to which message recipients enjoy engaging in effortful thought; Cacioppo & Petty, 1982b). In one pertinent study, Petty, Schumann, Richman, and Strathman (1993; Experiment 2) exposed subjects to a commercial advertisement for a pen and several other products in the context of either a happy television program (i.e., a situation comedy) or a neutral program (i.e., a documentary). Also, half of the subjects were told that they would be allowed to select a free pen as a gift at the end of the experiment, whereas half of the subjects were told that they would be allowed to select a free gift from an unrelated product category. When subjects would be selecting a pen as a free gift, they should be highly likely to think about the pen advertisement that appeared in the program, but when they would be selecting a different gift, thinking about the pen advertisement would be much less likely (Petty et al., 1983). After viewing the pen ad in the context of the happy or neutral program, subjects reported their moods, rated their attitudes toward the target pen, and listed their thoughts in response to the information in the ad. In an analysis that controlled for effects of mood on attitudes via differential positivity of thoughts, positivity of mood was found to have a direct effect on attitudes under low- but not high-elaboration conditions (see top panel of Fig. 14.1).

14. EFFECTS OF MOOD ON PERSUASION PROCESSES

Low Involvement

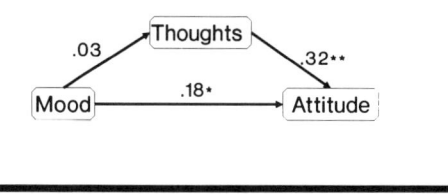

High Involvement

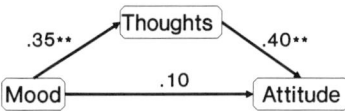

Fig. 14.1 Direct (top panel) and indirect (bottom) effects of mood on attitudes (data from Petty, Schumann, Richman, & Strathman, 1993, Experiment 2).

Similar direct effects of mood have been found in low-elaboration conditions when elaboration likelihood was identified through a measure of individuals' Need for Cognition (Batra & Stayman, 1990; Petty et al., 1993; Experiment 1).

HIGH-ELABORATION EFFECTS OF MOOD ON PERSUASION

At very high levels of elaboration likelihood, when people are paying a great deal of attention to the central merits of attitude-relevant information (e.g., when people care deeply about the issue in the message; Petty & Cacioppo, 1979b), there are two possibilities for how mood can influence attitudes. If the mood is relevant to the central merits of the attitudinal position, mood can act as an argument (i.e., as a piece of attitude-relevant information). For example, when one is considering the merits of a person as a potential spouse, feelings elicited by that person would likely serve as an important piece of central information about that person. Similarly, the feelings of excitement produced by a roller coaster are likely to be a critical ingredient in a thoughtful evaluation of the merits of the coaster (Petty & Cacioppo, 1986; Petty et al., 1991).

In addition to serving as a piece of issue-relevant information, mood can also affect the valence of material that is brought to mind when the merits of an attitude-object are being considered. For example, a variety of research is consistent with the view that positive moods activate positive material in memory, whereas negative moods activate negative material (e.g., Bower, 1981; Clark & Isen, 1982; Isen et al., 1978). Thus, when active processing of attitude-relevant information is taking place (i.e., under conditions of high elaboration), positive moods might encourage positive interpretations of the information more than negative moods (see Breckler & Wiggins, 1991; Mathur & Chattophadyay, 1991). This bias in information processing should be most likely when the information is relatively ambiguous and other biasing factors are not operating (e.g., the person does not possess a highly accessible attitude or set of knowledge that is opposite in valence to the feeling state; Chaiken & Maheswaran, 1994; Petty et al., 1991; Petty et al., 1993).

Mood and Positivity of Thoughts

Evidence of positive mood-biasing processing of message arguments is found in the high-elaboration conditions of the Petty et al. (1993) experiment described earlier. Recall that subjects were exposed to an ad for a pen in the context of a happy or neutral television program. In the high-elaboration conditions, subjects were led to believe that they would choose a free gift at the end of the experiment that came from the same product class as the product in the focal advertisement. In addition, recall that subjects reported their mood, attitudes toward the focal product, and thoughts in response to the advertising information after viewing the ad. Although mood had no impact on thoughts in the low-elaboration conditions (see top panel of Fig. 14.1), mood was found to influence thoughts, which in turn influenced attitudes under high-elaboration conditions (see bottom panel of Fig. 14.1). That is, in high-elaboration conditions, the more positive the mood induced by the television program, the more positive were subjects' thoughts in response to the advertisement. Also, the more positive the thoughts in response to the ad, the more favorable were attitudes toward the advertised product. Thus, the Petty et al. (1993) experiment shows that mood can influence attitudes by different processes under high- and low-elaboration conditions. When the likelihood of elaboration is low, the impact of mood on attitudes is relatively direct and unmediated by thoughts, but when the likelihood of elaboration is high, mood influences attitudes by biasing the cognitive activity taking place.

Mood-Based Biases in Elaboration: Mood-Congruent Versus Mood-Incongruent Outcomes

The fact that positive mood led to more positive thoughts in the Petty et al. (1993) high-elaboration conditions might make it appear as if positive mood invariably leads to favorable persuasion outcomes under high-elaboration conditions. This is not the case, however, when one considers the underlying processes by which mood can influence the evaluation of message arguments (Petty & Wegener, 1991). In order to appreciate how positive mood can produce either mood-incongruent or mood-congruent persuasion outcomes when argument processing is high, it is useful to consider the typical form of a persuasive argument and the demonstrated effects of mood on the components of a typical argument.

Likelihood, Desirability, and the Persuasive Argument. The typical persuasive argument asserts that a desirable consequence is likely to follow if the advocated proposal is adopted. For example, in Petty et al. (1993; Experiment 1), one of the arguments was that "foster care will improve if foster children are required to stay with their foster parents until 18 years of age rather than the customary 16 years." For a message recipient processing this argument, the persuasiveness of the argument depends on the extent to which the recipient believes that the consequence of foster care improving is likely and desirable (Fishbein & Ajzen, 1975). Thus, mood could influence the persuasiveness of this argument by making the consequence seem more or less desirable and/or likely (see Petty & Wegener, 1991).

The importance of likelihood and desirability factors are evident in expectancy-value models of attitudes. In Fishbein and Ajzen's (1975) model, for example, an attitude toward an object is a sum over all attributes of the likelihood that the object possesses each attribute (b_i) multiplied by the desirability of that attribute (e_i). A large body of research supports the notion that attitudes are more favorable toward objects for which desirable attributes are likely and for which undesirable attributes are unlikely (see Ajzen & Fishbein, 1980, and Pieters, 1988, for reviews).

Mood and Likelihood Judgments. In an early study of mood and judgment, Johnson and Tversky (1983) induced either positive or negative mood in subjects and then asked them to provide frequency estimates of a number of negative events (e.g., fatalities due to heart disease, floods). People in a negative mood viewed the negative events as more frequent than people in a positive mood. A number of recent studies have extended these findings by showing that people in positive states also give higher likelihood estimates of positive events than people in neutral or negative states (e.g., Erber, 1991; Forgas & Moylan, 1987; Mayer, Gaschke, Braverman, & Evans, 1992). Thus, positive mood could make the positive consequence in an argument (e.g., improving foster care) seem more likely than negative mood. Positive mood would make any negative consequences in an argument seem less likely.

Mood and Desirability Judgments. Because moods are directly experienced and might be classified by the person as desirable or undesirable, the desirability of a mood state might be used as a judgmental anchor against which to evaluate the desirability of other events (just as one's attitude can be used as an anchor for judging the favorability of other attitude statements; Sherif, Sherif, & Nebergall, 1965). If mood can be used as an anchor in this way, then social judgment theory (Sherif & Hovland, 1961) provides insight into when assimilation versus contrast is expected. People should generally assimilate events that are affectively similar to their moods (just as statements that are evaluatively similar are assimilated to one's own opinion), but should contrast those that are dissimilar (just as evaluatively dissimilar statements are contrasted). That is, very happy people might view slightly positive events as more positive than usual (assimilation) but might view slightly negative events as more negative than usual (contrast). Similarly, very sad people could view slightly negative events as more negative than usual (assimilation) but view slightly positive events as more positive than usual (contrast). Evidence for these notions was found by Gleicher, Baker, and Petty (1989; see discussion in Petty & Wegener, 1991), at least among subjects who were high in Need for Cognition. Thus, in high-elaboration conditions, both positive and negative moods might make a positive consequence in an argument seem more desirable (assimilation and contrast, respectively). In addition, negative consequences in an argument would seem less desirable when in a positive mood (contrast) and a negative mood (assimilation) than when mood is neutral.[1]

Combining Mood Effects on Likelihood and Desirability. By considering the combined effects of mood on likelihood and desirability judgments, one can make specific predictions about the persuasive impact of the typical argument that argues that adoption of the advocacy makes a desirable consequence likely. Specifically, positive mood should lead to greater persuasion than negative mood, because positive mood increases both the desirability and the likelihood of the consequence, whereas negative mood increases the desirability but *decreases* the likelihood of the consequence (see Petty & Wegener, 1991). Thus, for high-elaboration conditions, this analysis suggests that the mechanism by which happy mood would lead to greater persuasion than sad mood is that of making the positive consequences outlined in the message arguments seem more likely. However, if a message consisted of arguments that indicated that a negative consequence would occur if an advocacy is *not* adopted (i.e., a negatively framed argument, Meyerowitz & Chaiken, 1987), the impact of mood

---

[1] Of course, the mood-based assimilation and contrast effects found by Gleicher et al. (1989) would be most likely when the mood state is more extreme than the event(s) to be judged.

would be different. For a negatively framed argument, both positive and negative moods would make the undesirable consequence seem worse than usual, but negative moods would make the negative consequence seem *more likely* than positive moods. If a bad consequence of rejecting the advocacy would seem more likely, then the argument would constitute a more compelling reason to adopt the advocacy. Thus, the negatively framed arguments should be more persuasive to sad than to happy people—a mood-incongruent persuasion outcome opposite to those found in past studies of mood and biased elaboration.

An Empirical Test of Mood-Based Biases in Elaboration. In order to examine the notion that mood can lead to mood-congruent or mood-incongruent persuasion outcomes depending on message framing, Wegener, Petty, and Klein (1994, Experiment 2) randomly assigned students at Ohio State University (OSU) to read or watch either happy or sad material. That is, participants viewed either a segment from a television comedy/variety show or a segment from a movie about a child with cancer, or they read a happy or sad article that had been used in past research to manipulate mood (e.g., Kuykendall & Keating, 1990; Wegener & Petty, 1994). Following the mood induction, participants read a message advocating that OSU students be allowed to work part-time for the university in exchange for tuition cuts.

The arguments in support of the message position were framed in either a positive or negative manner. For example, the positively framed arguments began with the statement "If OSU *does* have a University Service program, then compared to schools *without* the program . . . ." This lead was followed by five statements that had been used in past research as strong arguments (see Baker & Petty, 1994). One of the statements was "More students would obtain valuable work experience." In the negative frame condition, the lead was "If OSU *does not* have a University Service program, then compared to schools *with* such a program . . . ." One of the statements was "More students would fail to obtain valuable work experience." Following the message, subjects responded to attitude, likelihood, and desirability questions. Finally, subjects responded to the Need for Cognition scale.

According to our likelihood-desirability analysis, we expected an interaction between mood and argument framing for subjects high in Need for Cognition. That is, for the positively framed arguments, positive mood should be more effective than negative mood (replicating past research using the typical positively framed message; e.g., Petty et al., 1993). Demonstrating the flexibility of mood-based biases, however, for the negatively framed arguments, negative mood should produce greater persuasive influence than positive mood. Because the Mood × Frame interaction for high Need for Cognition subjects was expected to result from mood-based differences in likelihood assessments, we expected the same interaction pattern to be present on the likelihood questions for these subjects. No interaction should occur on the attitude or likelihood questions for subjects low in Need for Cognition, nor should any differences exist on the desirability questions for any subjects. These patterns would result in three-way interactions (Mood × Frame × Need for Cognition) for the attitude and likelihood questions. In addition, path analyses should indicate that the mood effects on attitudes for high Need for Cognition individuals are plausibly mediated by likelihood judgments. Only a main effect of framing was expected for the desirability judgments (i.e., positively framed arguments should have consequences that are more desirable than negatively framed arguments).

Results showed our expected Mood × Frame × Need for Cognition interaction on attitudes toward university service. This three-way interaction reflected a significant Mood × Frame interaction when Need for Cognition was high, such that positively framed arguments were more persuasive in positive than negative mood, but negatively framed arguments were more persuasive in negative than positive mood (see Fig. 14.2). There were no effects of mood or frame when Need for Cognition was low.

In addition, our expected Mood × Frame × Need for Cognition interaction appeared on ratings of consequence likelihood. This three-way interaction reflected a significant Mood × Frame interaction when Need for Cognition was high such that consequences in positively framed arguments were viewed as more likely in positive than negative mood, but consequences in negatively framed arguments were viewed as more likely in negative than positive mood. As expected, no Mood × Frame interaction existed when Need for Cognition was low. In order to examine the possible mediational role of likelihood judgments for individuals high in Need for Cognition, a path analysis was conducted that included the dichotomous

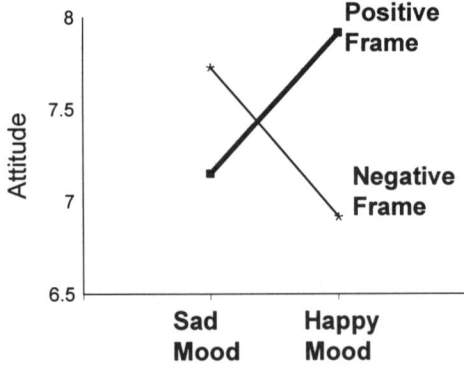

Fig. 14.2 Attitude as a function of mood and argument frame for subjects high in need for cognition (data from Wegener, Petty, & Klein, 1994, Experiment 2).

mood manipulation, the attitude index, and the overall likelihood measure. This analysis revealed that there was no direct effect of mood on attitudes. Mood had a significant effect on likelihood judgments, and the likelihood judgments in turn influenced attitudes, however.[2] Thus, Wegener et al. (1994, Experiment 2) provided additional support for the ELM notion that under high-elaboration likelihood conditions, mood should not have a direct impact on attitudes but should instead influence attitudes by modifying cognition.

Furthermore, this study provided support for the specific mediational role of likelihood judgments in mood effects on attitude change for individuals who engage in argument elaboration. In the critical high-elaboration (i.e., high need for cognition) conditions, positive moods led to more favorable attitudes than negative moods when the arguments were framed positively (as in past research), but negative moods led to more favorable attitudes than positive moods when the arguments were framed negatively. In addition, path analyses supported the view that assessments of consequence likelihood mediated the effect of mood on attitudes.

Thus, it appears that the mood-based biases in persuasive message processing are more flexible than has been portrayed in past empirical research. As predicted by our likelihood/desirability analysis of the impact of persuasive arguments, mood has now been shown to foster mood-congruent and mood-incongruent persuasion outcomes, depending on the framing of the arguments in the persuasive appeal. This framework might help to account for previous studies in which negative affects such as fear enhanced persuasion (e.g., Schwarz, Servay, & Kumpf, 1985). Specifically, when fear is combined with a negatively framed message (e.g., if you don't stop smoking you'll get lung cancer), the negative consequence might seem more likely, thereby increasing the effectiveness of the message (Petty et al., 1991; Petty & Wegener, 1991).

MODERATE-ELABORATION EFFECTS OF MOOD ON PERSUASION

Now that we have covered the processes by which mood influences attitudes when the likelihood of elaboration is quite high or very low, we turn to

---

[2]The path analysis tested the hypothesized relationships among mood, likelihood, and attitude across the message frame conditions. Because mood was postulated to have different effects depending upon the message frame condition (i.e., positive mood would increase the likelihood of the events in the positive message but decrease the likelihood of the events in the negative message), the mood variable was reverse scored when the framing condition was negative. Likelihood and attitude ratings were each scaled to a mean of zero within levels of need for cognition and frame without changing the original standard deviations associated with each group. Correlations among the resultant mood, likelihood, and attitude measures were then submitted to the path analysis.

perhaps the more common case in which nothing salient in the persuasion situation has predetermined the likelihood of message elaboration. According to the ELM, when elaboration likelihood is neither extremely high nor low based on nonmood factors, mood itself can determine the extent of message processing. Mood-based influences on the extent of message elaboration have important implications for the ultimate impact of the persuasive attempt. For example, if positive mood reduces argument scrutiny and the arguments are weak (i.e., specious or uncompelling), attitudes might be more favorable than if the person was not in the positive mood because the flaws in weak arguments would be less likely to be noted. On the other hand, if arguments are strong, then reduction of processing in positive moods might lead attitudes to be less favorable than if the person was not in the positive state, because the compelling nature of the strong arguments would not be as likely to be noted (Petty, Wells, & Brock, 1976).

In one of the first studies designed to examine effects of mood on the processing of persuasive communications, Worth and Mackie (1987) induced either positive or neutral mood states and then presented subjects with a message either supporting or opposing their pretested views on the topic of acid rain. The message was presented to subjects only long enough to read the communication once, and the message was composed of either strong or weak arguments.[3] For subjects receiving the counter-attitudinal message, those in a neutral mood were more persuaded by strong than weak arguments, whereas people in a positive mood were equally persuaded by strong and weak arguments. That is, positive mood appeared to reduce message processing. Similar positive-mood processing deficits using counter-attitudinal topics have been found when happy mood is compared with either sad (e.g., Bless, Bohner, Schwarz, & Strack, 1990; Kuykendall & Keating, 1990) or neutral mood (e.g., Kuykendall & Keating, 1990; Mackie & Worth, 1989; see Mackie et al., 1992; Mackie & Worth, 1991; Schwarz et al., 1991, for reviews).[4]

Why would positive mood lead to less message processing than sad or neutral mood? Two theoretical positions have been advocated to account

---

[3]In the ELM, the extent to which strong arguments are associated with more favorable attitudes toward the advocacy than weak arguments is taken as an index of the amount of message processing (see Petty & Cacioppo, 1986, for discussions).

[4]For subjects receiving the proattitudinal message in the Worth and Mackie (1987) study, there was little change in attitudes for either happy or neutral people, and the pattern of means revealed that neither happy nor neutral people were persuaded more by strong than weak arguments (although no three-way interaction between mood, argument quality, and message position was reported). The lack of persuasion for any of these groups might have been due to a ceiling effect in which people in the proattitudinal condition already supported the position so extremely that little room was left for persuading people in the direction of the message advocacy. Because of this ceiling effect, the proattitudinal condition in Worth and Mackie (1987) might not constitute a very strong test of the effects of positive mood on message processing.

for reductions in message processing on the part of happy people. The "cognitive capacity" view contends that positive affective states render people less able to process incoming information (Mackie & Worth, 1989). This is because positive moods activate many positive thoughts in memory, and these thoughts then occupy the person's attentional capacity and make the message recipient less able to process incoming information (see Mackie & Worth, 1989; Mackie & Worth, 1991). Alternatively, the "feelings-as-information" framework (Schwarz, 1990) views positive moods as informing people that the environment is safe, thereby reducing their motivation to scrutinize the information in that environment.

After reviewing representative studies within the contexts of these currently accepted theoretical frameworks, we present an alternative theoretical position based on differential mood-management across affective states (i.e., the hedonic contingency view). In addition to discussing how this mood-management perspective can organize past work, we note that this mood-management perspective differs from the accepted frameworks in that it also posits that positive moods can enhance rather than reduce message processing. Finally, we present new research exploring the differences between past views (i.e., cognitive capacity and feelings-as-information) and our mood-management alternative. But first, what are the prevailing models of the impact of mood on message processing?

Positive Mood and Cognitive Capacity

Mackie and Worth (1989) conducted two studies that expanded on their 1987 efforts in an attempt to provide additional support for the cognitive capacity view. In each study, positive and neutral subjects were presented with a counter-attitudinal strong or weak version of a persuasive message for either a limited or unlimited amount of time. In the limited time condition, subjects were told that the message would only appear for long enough to be read once, but in the unlimited time condition, subjects were explicitly told that they could take as long as they wished to read (and reread) the message. In the limited time condition, people in a neutral mood were more persuaded by strong than weak arguments, whereas people in a positive mood were equally persuaded by strong and weak arguments. That is, attitudes were based less on message scrutiny in positive than neutral mood. In unlimited time conditions, however, people in both positive and neutral moods were more persuaded by strong than weak arguments. In addition, in the unlimited time conditions, people in a positive mood took approximately 10 seconds longer to read the communication than did people in a neutral mood.[5]

---

[5]In the second Mackie and Worth (1989) study, although the predicted three-way interaction among mood, argument quality, and time limit was not significant ($F < 1$), a planned contrast

Taken together, these studies were interpreted by Mackie and Worth (1989) as supporting a cognitive capacity view of mood effects on message processing. They argued:

> A positive mood state appears to activate positive material stored in memory, which in turn activates other material to which it is linked (Bower, 1981; Isen et al., 1978). . . . The easy accessibility of this material, or its presence in working memory, could reduce cognitive capacity. . . . From this perspective, then, people in a positive mood may wish to process incoming information systematically, but because their capacity and attention are being used elsewhere, they cannot (Mackie & Worth, 1989, p. 28)

Thus, Mackie and Worth (1989) believed that in limited time situations, positive-mood subjects were less able to effortfully process the communication. Yet, when given unlimited time, positive-mood subjects were just as motivated to process the message and did so to the same extent as neutral subjects; it just took them a little longer to process the message in order to overcome their ability deficit.

Feelings-as-Information

As noted previously, the feelings-as-information framework views positive mood as leading to motivational deficits rather than capacity deficits. According to Schwarz et al. (1991):

> Negative feelings may inform individuals that their current situation is problematic. They may therefore trigger processing styles that are adequate for analyzing the problematic situation in order to determine adequate reactions. . . . Positive states, on the other hand, inform individuals that their current environment is a safe place. . . . (this) may inhibit the spontaneous use of effortful analytic processing strategies unless they are required by other active goals. (p. 166)

Thus, positive states lead to less processing than negative states, unless some external goal motivates processing on the part of happy people.

In order to test this notion, Bless et al. (1990) asked subjects to relive either happy or sad experiences from their lives and then presented them with a message announcing a fee increase at the subjects' university. The message justified this fee increase with either strong or weak arguments. In

---

was significant comparing argument differentiation in positive-mood/limited-time conditions with argument differentiation in the other three cells of the mood × time limit design. That is, the contrast showed that the average argument differentiation across the three cells was greater than in the positive-mood/limited-time condition.

addition, subjects were told either that the study was concerned primarily with forms of language (so that any message processing would be relatively spontaneous) or that the study was concerned with the ability of people to evaluate message content (providing an external goal that would presumably motivate all people to process the message).

When the study was presented to subjects as a study of language use, sad subjects were more persuaded by strong than weak arguments, whereas happy subjects were not. That is, positive mood reduced argument scrutiny as in the prior work by Mackie and colleagues. When subjects in the study were asked to focus their attention on scrutinizing the quality of the arguments presented, however, subjects in both positive and negative moods were more persuaded by strong than weak arguments. Thus, in spontaneous processing conditions, the predicted processing deficit in positive states was evident; when an external goal was motivating subjects to pay attention to message content, however, both happy and sad people processed the message to the same extent.

Cognitive Capacity Versus Feelings-as-Information

Based on the evidence to date, there is relatively little conclusive evidence to favor one of the prevalent views over the other. Given that theorists supporting the capacity view allow that motivation can overcome at least some capacity differences (e.g., Mackie et al., 1992), evidence in support of the feelings-as-information view can largely be interpreted as external motivation overriding mood-based capacity differences, rather than external motivation overriding mood-based motivational differences. Similarly, however, instructions stressing to subjects that they can use as much time as they want to view a message (see Mackie & Worth, 1989) have been noted as possibly providing an external goal to scrutinize the message that overrides default motivational differences—consistent with the feelings-as-information view (see Schwarz et al., 1991). Thus, supporters of each view have noted that the current evidence can be interpreted as consistent with their proposed framework.

A Mood-Management Alternative: The Hedonic Contingency Hypothesis

A third explanation is possible for these studies, however. Rather than positive mood informing people that the environment is safe or taking up processing capacity, positive mood might be leading to especially high levels of mood management. In mood-management terms, reduction of message processing might be in service of maintaining a happy mood or relieving a sad one (see Isen, 1993; Clark & Isen, 1982; Sinclair & Mark, 1992; Wegener

& Petty, 1994). This is because the messages that have been used have generally been counter-attitudinal or on potentially depressing topics (e.g., acid rain, gun control, etc.). If this is so, however, what mood-management basis might one have for predicting the observed processing differences between people in happy versus neutral or sad moods?

One possible basis for predicting differences comes from our *hedonic contingency hypothesis* (Wegener & Petty, 1994). This hypothesis considers the fact that one outcome that would reward or punish people for their choices of behavior is the effect of those behaviors on people's moods. When rewards and punishments are viewed in this way, mood management becomes more likely in happy as opposed to sad moods. This is because of the hedonic relationship between one's current feeling state and the distribution of feelings that result from alternative behaviors. That is, for a very sad person, the range of affective outcomes from alternative behaviors is almost entirely more positive than the current affective state. So, engagement in almost any activity would tend to make the person feel better and thus, would be rewarded. This would be the case regardless of whether the person carefully considers the hedonic qualities of the available behaviors or not. That is, reinforcement would be relatively *noncontingent* on scrutiny of the hedonic consequences of action. When in a positive state, however, only a limited set of behaviors will lead to hedonic rewards. In fact, most activities would tend to make the person feel worse—resulting in hedonic punishment. Thus, hedonic rewards would be *highly contingent* on scrutinizing the hedonic consequences of behavior when in positive states. Because contingency of reward is an important factor in operant learning of behavior (e.g., Hammond, 1980; Rachlin, 1976), this set of circumstances over time would lead to greater attention to the hedonic consequences of action in positive as opposed to negative states (i.e., greater use of mood-management strategies when happy than sad).

Thus, one might consider a person's current mood as a discriminative stimulus that signals what kind of hedonic reinforcement contingencies are operating (cf. Miller, 1975; Norborg, Osborne, & Fanting, 1983). When current mood is positive, scrutinizing the hedonic consequences of action is rewarded and ignoring the consequences is punished; when current mood is negative, however, both scrutinizing and ignoring the hedonic consequences of action are rewarded. To the extent that this is so, happy people should manage mood by paying attention to the hedonic consequences of future action to a greater extent than sad people.

Neutral moods might relate to mood-management in one of two ways. Based only on the relationship between neutral mood and the distribution of hedonic outcomes from action alternatives, neutral mood might foster mood-management at a level between that of positive and negative mood. It could also be, however, that the value of mood as a discriminative stimulus depends on the mood being different from a *normal* state. That is, for a mood to act as a salient signal of reinforcement contingencies, it might be necessary for the feeling state to differ from neutral or normal. Thus, because hedonic rewards are noncontingent in sad moods and current feelings (as well as motives to manage the feelings) might not be salient in neutral moods, there might be little difference in the level of mood-management activity found in neutral and sad moods.

In fact, in empirical research driven by the hedonic contingency framework, results have shown similar levels of mood-management for neutral and sad subjects (with higher levels of mood-management found for happy than for sad or neutral subjects). Specifically, Wegener and Petty (1994) performed three experiments testing the hedonic contingency notion. In three experiments using different mood manipulations, subjects who were assigned to either happy, sad, or neutral conditions were asked to choose videotapes to watch later in the session. These choices were to be made based on information about various qualities of the tapes as purportedly rated by previous college students. The information about the tapes included information about how each tape made people feel. Across the experiments, happy people based their choices of tapes on differences in the affective qualities of the tapes to a greater extent than neutral or sad people. Use of the affective information did not differ between the neutral and sad people.[6]

Mood-Management and Message Processing

As noted earlier, although positive-mood processing deficits have been shown using a variety of topics (e.g., student fee increases, acid rain, gun control, institution of senior comprehensive exams), the messages on these topics have been largely counter-attitudinal and/or depressing in nature. To the extent that thinking about any of these topics would be likely to strip happy people of their mood, happy people might avoid scrutinizing messages on these topics in order to remain happy (see Isen, 1987; Sinclair & Mark, 1992; Wegener & Petty, 1994).[7] Thus, it seems possible that the

---

[6]In addition, although not guided by the hedonic contingency idea, evidence from other areas of social psychology supports the hedonic contingency analysis (Carlson, Charlin, & Miller, 1988; Carlson & Miller, 1987; Miller & Carlson, 1990). It is also important to note that ours is not the only possible mood-management framework. For example, Cialdini and his colleagues developed the negative state relief (NSR) model in the area of mood and helping (e.g., Cialdini, Darby, & Vincent, 1973; Cialdini, Baumann, & Kenrick, 1981), and have also discussed mood-management motives in positive states (e.g., Schaller & Cialdini, 1990; see Wegener & Petty, 1994, for discussion of additional support for the hedonic contingency hypothesis and the relative merits of it versus the NSR framework).

[7]Recall that in the one study using a proattitudinal appeal (albeit on a potentially depressing

positive-mood processing deficits found in past research could be the result of mood-management on the part of happy people rather than being the result of reduced capacity or of mood informing people that scrutiny is unnecessary. In addition, across these studies, similar processing results have been found for subjects in neutral and sad moods. Also, those studies that explicitly compared processing by neutral and sad subjects found no differences in processing across sad and neutral mood (e.g., Kuykendall & Keating, 1990).

When compared with other frameworks, perhaps the most important distinguishing characteristic of our mood-management alternative is that our view does not limit positive mood to inhibiting processing. The processes hypothesized within the cognitive capacity and feelings-as-information views both hold that positive mood will either decrease processing or have no effect compared to neutral or negative moods. In stark contrast, our mood-management view predicts that positive moods only lead to processing deficits when avoiding thought about the message allows one to feel better than thinking about the message. Positive moods could, in fact, lead to increased processing if a message recipient believes that processing the message will allow him or her to feel better than not processing the message. This prediction is not derivable from the cognitive capacity or feelings-as-information views.[8]

Consistent with our mood-management perspective, there is some evi-

---

topic—acid rain; Worth & Mackie, 1987) the pattern of means suggested no difference in processing between neutral and happy subjects (although the lack of overall attitude change in both groups weakens these data as a test of any of the theoretical models).

[8]Some nonpersuasion research has also suggested that positive moods can sometimes be associated with increased information processing activity. For example, using the *feelings-as-information* view (Schwarz et al., 1991) as a starting point, Martin, Ward, Achee, and Wyer (1993) theorized that either positive or negative moods could lead to either increased or decreased motivation to engage in effortful cognitive processes, depending on the question or *stop-rule* that mood served to answer. Consistent with this notion, Martin et al. (1993) found that instructing people to work on a task until they thought it was a "good time to stop" led to greater effort from sad than happy people, but instructing people to work on the task as long as they "feel like continuing" led to greater effort from happy than sad people. In a control condition when no particular processing goals were made salient, sad mood led to greater effort than happy mood. Since it is not clear what question people spontaneously ask themselves (if any) in persuasion settings, the applicability of this framework to the current research is not clear. However, if the typical persuasion study is most comparable to the Martin et al. control group, then the stop-rule framework would predict that sad moods are associated with greater information processing activity than happy moods—the same prediction as the feelings-as-information and the cognitive capacity views. If we were to translate the hedonic contingency analysis into a stop-rule framework, this view would hold that people in a positive mood would be more likely to ask themselves if they are enjoying the task than sad or neutral subjects. Thus, if the task is perceived as pleasant, happy people would continue processing, but if the task is not perceived as pleasant, they would stop (see Wegener, Petty, & Smith, 1995, for additional discussion).

dence that increases in effortful thought in positive as opposed to neutral moods might depend on the subjects' enjoyment of the activity involved. For instance, Murray, Sujan, Hirt, and Sujan (1990, experiments 2 and 3) induced positive or neutral moods in subjects and then asked them to generate similarities and differences between pairs of target stimuli (i.e., television programs). In both experiments, Murray et al. found that happy subjects generated a larger number of distinct types of similarities and differences when compared with neutral subjects, suggesting greater cognitive engagement in the task in happy as opposed to neutral moods. In addition, Murray et al. measured the extent to which subjects found the task to be interesting or enjoyable. Importantly, there was a significant correlation between interest in the task (i.e., task enjoyment) and the number of distinct types of similarities and differences generated, but only for happy people. There was no relationship between task interest measures and thought generation for neutral subjects. Thus, to the extent that people believe that thinking might be enjoyable, it appears that people in a positive mood might actually think more than people in a neutral mood. This result is very consistent with the hedonic contingency view that people in happy moods should be more sensitive to the mood-altering qualities of activities than people in neutral or sad moods (see Carlson et al., 1988; Miller & Carlson, 1990; Wegener & Petty, 1994).

Testing Mood-Management in Message Processing: Two Initial Experiments

In two initial experiments (Wegener, Petty, & Richman, 1991; Wegener et al., 1995, Experiment 1), we attempted to demonstrate message processing effects of elevated mood-management in positive as opposed to neutral mood. The experiments shared the same design. In each experiment, either neutral or positive mood was induced (in Wegener et al., 1991, by means of neutral or happy instrumental music, and in Wegener et al., 1995, by means of neutral or happy imagination tasks). Then, subjects listened to excerpts from an editorial on the topic of improving foster care (see Petty et al., 1993) that was introduced in such a way as to make it appear that the editorial would either include rather depressing or rather uplifting information. This was done by presenting subjects with a description of a person who had supposedly grown up in either a bad or good foster care program. Supposedly as a result of his foster care experience, the person was either homeless, unemployed and unhappy, or rich and happy. The editorial presented either strong or weak reasons to make changes in the foster care program of the subjects' home state to be more like a fictitious foster care program in a distant state. Following the editorial, subjects reported their attitudes toward the fictitious foster care program and listed any thoughts that they could recall coming to mind while listening to the editorial. The editorial was presented by audiotape so that the pace of the message was not under the control of the subjects (cf. Mackie & Worth, 1989).

According to our hedonic contingency mood-management perspective, to the extent that the message content is expected to be unpleasant, reduced processing of the message would be the best mood-management strategy for people in a happy mood. However, to the extent that message recipients believe that message content might in fact be pleasant, this should encourage processing of the message as a way to feel good. Thus, positive-mood enhancement of processing should be most likely when message recipients expect the content of the message to be uplifting, whereas positive-mood processing reduction would be most likely when the content of the message is expected to be depressing.

The comparison of processing in happy versus neutral mood is especially important for the cognitive capacity view. This is because the processes proposed as responsible for the attentional capacity differences should create the largest differences between happy and neutral moods. Although negative moods might also activate negative material that would occupy attentional capacity (Ellis & Ashbrook, 1988), the associative links among negative items might be weaker than those among positive elements because people are more likely to attempt to distract themselves from negative than from positive states (Mackie & Worth, 1991). Thus, attentional capacity would be occupied most by positive, followed by negative, and then neutral moods. Therefore, if only the processes postulated by the cognitive capacity view were operating, subjects in a neutral mood would always engage in greater message processing than subjects in a happy mood. Of course, if the current message is not as cognitively demanding as the messages used by Mackie and Worth, then happy and neutral subjects might both have sufficient capacity and, as a result, might process the message equally, but in no case would the cognitive capacity view predict positive mood enhancing message scrutiny over neutral mood. In addition, because the *same* arguments were used for both the uplifting and depressing conditions, differences in processing across uplifting and depressing conditions could not be due to differences in ability to process the information in the arguments.

Similarly, if the motives postulated by the Schwarz (1990) feelings-as-information view were the only motives invoked by mood, then happy people, informed that the environment is safe and that careful scrutiny of the environment is unnecessary, would always process less than neutral people. To the extent that neutral moods might also include the absence of problems in the environment, however, it is possible that the informative functions of mood would create little difference in processing between neutral and happy moods (see Petty et al., 1993), but default informative functions would not predict enhanced message scrutiny in positive as opposed to neutral mood.

Surprisingly, the results of both studies showed Mood × Argument Quality interactions that reflected only enhancement of processing in positive as opposed to neutral mood (see Fig. 14.3). That is, in both studies, happy people were more persuaded by strong than weak arguments, but neutral people were not. Thus, contrary to the cognitive capacity and feelings-as-information predictions that happy moods decrease message processing, the results of these experiments show that happy mood can increase message processing over neutral states. Because of this, it would appear that some theoretical framework other than cognitive capacity limitations or informative functions of feeling states should be brought to bear on the data. Of the theoretical frameworks suggested in the persuasion literature, only our mood-management framework predicts that positive moods could enhance message processing over neutral or negative states. According to that mood-management position, however, happy people should not be likely to effortfully process information expected to remove that positive state. Thus, the current results suggest either that the mood-management position does not fully account for the data or that the

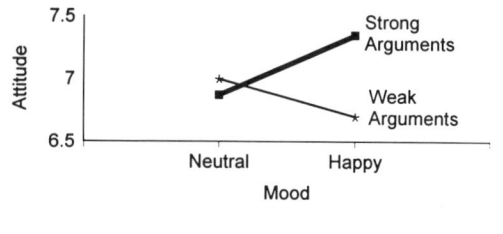

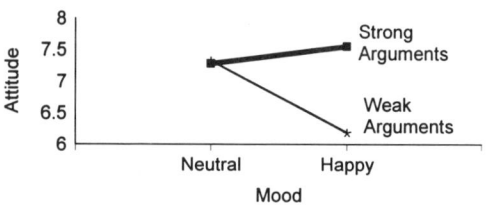

Fig. 14.3 Attitude as a function of mood and argument quality (data in top panel from Wegener, Petty, & Richman, 1991; data in bottom panel from Wegener et al., 1995, Experiment 1).

depressing expectation manipulation we attempted was unsuccessful at making the message seem depressing enough to threaten happy moods.

When one inspects the data from the experiments, there are indications that the "improve foster care" message might have been generally too positive to appear sufficiently mood-threatening to decrease processing in a happy mood (especially compared to past messages on tuition increases, acid rain, etc.). For example, the attitude data show that the message was quite proattitudinal with even the weak version of the message under high-processing conditions (i.e., happy mood) leading to attitudes significantly *above* the midpoint of the attitude scale. In addition, although a number of subjects noted in cognitive responses that the information in the message was uplifting under uplifting expectation conditions, no subjects noted that the "depressing" message was upsetting or sad. Instead, a number of subjects stated that the message was not depressing (and some noted that it was certainly not as depressing as the source seemed to think that it would be). In addition, in ratings of the actual content of the messages, subjects rated the content of even "depressing" messages above the midpoint of the scale.

It appears, then, that problems in the induction of depressing hedonic expectations might have been responsible for the lack of a replication of past positive-mood processing deficits in "depressing expectation" conditions. At a minimum, however, this research clearly suggests that positive mood need not disrupt message processing in persuasion paradigms. Because we apparently failed to induce strong expectations of both pleasant and unpleasant message content, we conducted another study.

Testing Mood-Management in Message Processing: A Stronger Test

If the mood-management explanation is correct, then using a message that subjects truly believe will be depressing should produce processing deficits in happy moods. Thus, in a second experiment (Wegener et al., 1995, Experiment 2), we used a message for which the same arguments supported either a clearly proattitudinal (and mood-enhancing) position or a clearly counterattitudinal (and mood-disrupting) position in order to form a stronger test of the mood-management position. In addition, this experiment manipulated expectation information more strongly by providing prior experience with materials for which expectations were given and confirmed. Finally, this experiment used sad rather than neutral mood in order to investigate whether happy-mood processing enhancement over sad mood could be demonstrated. This comparison is of special interest within the feelings-as-information framework, which predicts the largest differences in processing to occur between positive and negative moods.

In order to create stronger manipulations of hedonic expectations and content, it was necessary to create a situation in which the information provided to subjects about the affective content of the message was credible and sensible to provide. Therefore, the following study began by engaging subjects in the selective exposure paradigm used by Wegener and Petty (1994) to study mood effects on activity choices. In this paradigm, subjects are told that they will be choosing activities in which to be engaged later in the period, and that they will engage in those activities based on their individual rankings of a number of options. Prior to making their rankings, subjects are provided with ratings of the activities—in this case, articles to be read—provided by past subjects. The prior subjects have purportedly read the articles and rated the qualities of the articles on a number of dimensions. Subjects were told that tabulating their rankings would take some time and that the experimenter wished to verify the qualities of two separate articles during that tabulation. The experimenter was said to already know the basic qualities of the articles but wanted to verify those qualities.

Therefore, subjects received two articles to read and rate. The first was the mood-induction article (either the happy or sad article used in Wegener et al., 1994), and the second was the persuasive message (either pro- or counter-attitudinal and either strong or weak, adapted from Baker & Petty, 1994). In order to provide expectations about the affective content of articles, a brief statement preceded each article. For the mood-induction article, subjects were instructed that "the primary quality of the following article is that it makes people feel sad (happy)." For the persuasion article, a similar statement was used. That is, subjects were instructed that "the primary quality of the following article is that it makes people feel sad (happy) if they think carefully about the information presented." Thus, because the mood-induction article did have the hedonic qualities predicted by the statement preceding the article, the statement creating the expectation of hedonic content of the persuasive message should be of high credibility.

Also, in order to ensure that subjects' initial perceptions of whether message processing would be uplifting or depressing were confirmed in the first part of the message, the arguments provided in the message were presented on behalf of either a proattitudinal position (in the uplifting condition) or a counter-attitudinal position (in the depressing condition). That is, in the uplifting condition, the advocacy was that students have the opportunity to work as part-time university staff in exchange for drastic tuition cuts, and the title of the article was "Students Pleased With Tuition Plan That Gives Them a Break." In the depressing condition, however, the advocacy was that students be required to work as part-time secretarial and maintenance staff or else pay out-of-state tuition, and the title of the article was "Students Upset With Tuition Plan That Places New Burdens on Them." This differential framing of the same issue allows the same arguments to be used in support of the advocacy regardless of the proattitudinal (uplifting) or counter-attitudinal (depressing) position of the overall message (see Baker & Petty, 1994; Petty & Brock, 1976). Thus, differences in processing across hedonic content conditions cannot be due to differential ability to process the information in the arguments.

If our hedonic contingency mood-management perspective is correct, then happy people should process the proattitudinal (uplifting) message more than sad people. This would provide a conceptual replication of the enhanced message processing by subjects in a positive mood found in our initial research using the foster care message (see Fig. 14.3). In addition, happy people should process the counter-attitudinal (depressing) message less than sad people. This would provide a conceptual replication of past work on mood and message processing (e.g., Bless et al., 1990; Kuykendall & Keating, 1990; Mackie & Worth, 1989).

Results showed the predicted three-way interaction among mood, hedonic content, and argument quality (see Fig. 14.4). Happy subjects engaged in greater scrutiny of the message than sad individuals when the content was uplifting, but sad subjects engaged in greater scrutiny of the message than happy individuals when the content was depressing. Viewed differently, the three-way interaction also shows that processing of happy people was more contingent on the expected hedonic qualities of the message than was that of sad individuals. Happy people processed the message when it was uplifting but not when it was depressing. The message scrutiny of sad individuals was not influenced significantly by the hedonic content of the message. Interestingly the trend in processing for sad subjects was actually toward processing counter-attitudinal (depressing/threatening) information more than proattitudinal (uplifting) information (see Apaniesk & Ditto, 1994; Cacioppo & Petty, 1979, for conceptually similar results for subjects in nonmanipulated mood states). Thus, these data are compatible with the hedonic contingency mood-management view of mood and message processing.

Importantly, the hedonic contingency view appears capable of organizing the past literature on mood and message processing. That is, as predicted by the hedonic contingency analysis, reduction of processing in happy as opposed to sad moods occurs when the hedonic content of the message is negative. This conceptually replicates past demonstrations of positive-mood processing deficits. Also, as predicted by the hedonic contingency analysis, enhancement of processing in happy as opposed to sad moods occurs when the hedonic content of the message is positive. This conceptually replicates the positive-mood processing enhancement found in our past research when a proattitudinal message was used (Wegener et al., 1995, Experiment 1).

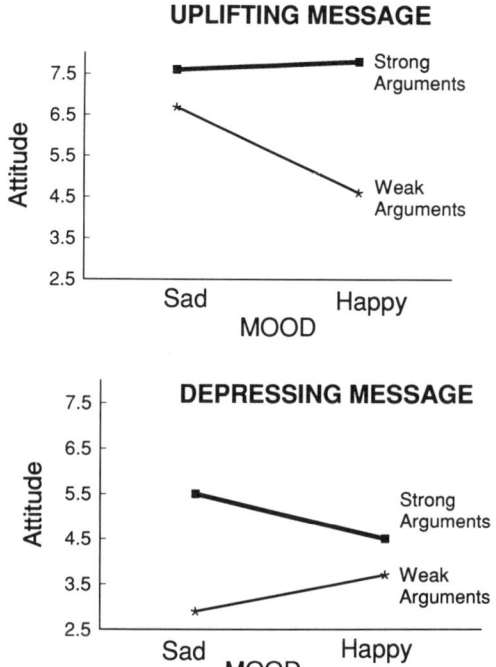

Fig. 14.4 Attitude as a Function of Mood, Hedonic Content, and Argument Quality (data from Wegener et al., 1995, Experiment 2).

In addition, these data provide a substantial challenge to "cognitive capacity" and "feelings-as-information" views as general explanations of the mood and processing literature. This is because both the "cognitive capacity" and "feelings-as-information" views predict that mood-based differences in processing will be such that happy people process less than people in neutral or negative states. This is clearly not always the case.

FUTURE DIRECTIONS

In this chapter we have emphasized how the primary impact of mood on persuasion can take place by different processes depending upon the level of elaboration likelihood. We have seen that mood can influence attitudes by relatively simple and low-effort peripheral processes when the elaboration likelihood is low. However, mood can bias the processing of message arguments when the elaboration likelihood is high, and mood can influence the extent of message processing when the elaboration likelihood is neither particularly high nor low. Next, we offer some suggestions for future research on mood and persuasion across the elaboration likelihood continuum.

Mood and Peripheral Processes Under Low Elaboration Likelihood

Although relatively low-effort peripheral processes were the first to be examined in studies of mood and persuasion, there is still much to learn about the role of mood in low-elaboration persuasion. Perhaps one of the most fundamental questions to be addressed concerns the process by which mood has a peripheral impact when the elaboration likelihood is low. For example, does mood have an impact by classical conditioning (Cacioppo, Marshall-Goodell, Tassinary, & Petty, 1992; Zanna et al., 1970), or by serving to invoke a decision heuristic (e.g., "I feel good so I must like it;" Cacioppo & Petty, 1982a; Chaiken, 1987), or is each possible under different circumstances?

It is important to consider that a person's mood is only one of many peripheral cues that might be present in any persuasion situation. The presence of competing cues can influence the likelihood of mood having a peripheral effect. Consider a person in a given mood state (Petty et al., 1993) who encounters a persuasive message with a given number of arguments (Petty & Cacioppo, 1984) presented by a source with identifiable levels of likability (Chaiken, 1980; Petty et al., 1983) and expertise (Petty, Cacioppo, & Goldman, 1981; Rhine & Severance, 1970) under distraction conditions that discourage effortful scrutiny of the central merits of the attitude-relevant information (Petty et al., 1976). Which of the potential peripheral cues will have an impact on the person's attitude? Although each of these factors has been shown to affect attitudes under low-elaboration conditions, little is known about which peripheral cues are most likely to be used under which circumstances.

A number of factors might influence when a potential peripheral cue will impact persuasion. For example, some cues in the persuasion setting might be more salient to the message recipient than the other cues in the setting. A variable would generally be more likely to have a cue impact when it is noticed rather than unnoticed. For example, a message recipient might be more likely to base his or her opinion toward the issue on the number of arguments presented when the arguments are numbered or otherwise segmented in order to highlight the number of separate points supporting the conclusion. Similarly, attractiveness of the source might be more likely to impact attitudes when the source is prominently pictured with the attitude-relevant information than when the appearance of the source is less prominent (e.g., if the appearance of the source is noted but only in a brief verbal description). As a result, one might imagine that mood would be most likely to have an impact on persuasion under low-elaboration likelihood conditions when mood is salient (e.g., when the person is high rather than low in mood awareness, Giuliano & Swinkels, 1992) and plausibly tied to the message, and when peripheral cues other than mood are not particularly salient within the persuasion setting.

Another factor that might influence the extent to which variables such as mood serve as peripheral cues is the presence or absence of an existing attitude toward the issue or object. That is, if a person has a goal of arriving at an attitude using the least amount of effort necessary, perhaps the easiest way to assess the merits of a position toward the object is to consult an existing evaluation. Therefore, when an accessible attitude toward the object already exists, peripheral cues that require additional inferences might be less likely to have an impact than when no accessible attitude toward the object exists (Petty, Cacioppo, & Haugtvedt, 1992). Thus, to the extent that one assumes that using mood to answer a "How do I feel about it?" heuristic requires more effort than accessing an existing attitude, mood might have less impact as a peripheral cue when an accessible attitude exists than when no such attitude exists.

Mood and Biased Message Processing Under High Elaboration Likelihood

What future research might expand on our initial steps to investigate mechanisms responsible for mood-based biases in elaboration of attitude-relevant information? A number of directions seem plausible. First, although we have provided some evidence that mood can influence the evaluation of a message argument by influencing the likelihood that the consequence specified in the argument occurs, mood should also be capable of influencing the desirability of the consequence specified (Petty & Wegener, 1991). In order to maximize the probability of finding mood effects on desirability in persuasion situations, it might be necessary to use consequences that include both positive and negative implications (i.e., ambivalent consequences). The desirability of ambivalent consequences might be more influenced by mood states than the univalent consequences used in the current research.

One of the intriguing recent perspectives on judgments of likelihood and desirability is the thought-systems approach developed by McGuire and McGuire (1991). A portion of this perspective postulates that desirability components are more tightly linked than likelihood components. Because of this, McGuire and McGuire (1991) hypothesize that persuasive appeals will have differential difficulty in changing perceptions of likelihood versus desirability, depending on whether the attempt at attitude change is undertaken by introducing new external information or by making salient information already in the person's thought system. If the persuasive attempt is externally provided (as in our research), the thought-systems approach predicts that changes in perceptions of likelihood are easier than changes in perceptions of desirability, but if the persuasive attempt is self-generated, changes in desirabilities become more likely. Thus, the role of mood in both self-generated versus externally initiated changes might be explored. Finally, it is worth noting that just as other more salient peripheral cues could attenuate the impact of mood as a cue when the elaboration likelihood is low, so too can other motivated biases attenuate the impact of mood on message processing when the elaboration likelihood is high. For example, if people were forewarned of the persuasive intent of the speaker on a highly involving topic, the reactance and resistance processes provoked (see Petty & Cacioppo, 1979a) would likely attenuate any positivity bias induced by a pleasant mood.

Mood Management Motives Under Moderate Elaboration Likelihood

The mood-management perspective that we introduced to account for mood effects on the extent of message processing and the research that supports this framework suggest a variety of directions for future research that would not necessarily follow from other theoretical perspectives. For example, our studies have shown that positive mood can enhance rather than reduce message processing when compared with neutral or negative mood. In our experiments, this occurred when message content was relatively proattitudinal or non-mood-threatening. There might be times, however, when mood-management strategies also direct happy people to effortfully process information that is at least temporarily mood-threatening. For example, consider a situation in which a person finds out that a negative consequence might take place, but that he or she can do something to avert that occurrence. In such a case, a happy person might effortfully process information about that event in order to find out what can be done to make sure that the negative consequence does not take place. That is, in order to avoid feeling worse in the future, a happy person might temporarily give up feeling good (see Parrott, 1993). In effect, happy states might not only produce greater short-term mood-management than neutral or sad states, but also produce greater attention to long-term mood-management concerns (see Salovey, Mayer, & Rosenhan, 1991; Wegener & Petty, 1994). Of course, a happy person's willingness to defer short-term mood-management to long-term goals might depend on the expected magnitude of the impending negative event. For example, if the negative event would produce severe effects, it might be well worth the happy person's time to take action to avert the event. If the negative outcome is not so severe, however, then the happy person might be more likely to put off thinking about the negative occurrence in an attempt to maintain the current positive state. A number of possibilities exist, depending on such factors as how unpleasant thinking about the event would be, how controllable the event appears, and how undesirable the eventual outcome of the event would be.

In addition, even within a short-term mood-management perspective, both situational and personal factors that increase or decrease the salience of mood-management goals are likely to influence the impact of mood-management strategies on levels of message processing. Take, for instance, individual differences in people's awareness of their mood states (Giuliano & Swinkels, 1992). It could be that our hedonic contingency results especially hold for people who are highly aware of their moods (e.g., because for these people, mood is a more powerful signal of hedonic reward contingencies) than for people who are relatively unaware of their moods. It could also be, however, that people who are chronically aware of their mood states are also quite aware of what they can do to manage mood, regardless of what that mood is. In fact, some evidence exists (for negative states) that mood awareness precedes expectations of whether anything can be done to manage the state (Giuliano & Swinkels, 1993).

CONCLUSIONS

A central theme of this chapter is that the influence of mood on persuasion can be through different primary mechanisms in different persuasion situations. This chapter has highlighted research showing that mood can serve in multiple roles and that the effects of mood appear to be more flexible than previously described and demonstrated. That is, mood can serve as an argument, a cue, bias message processing, and determine the extent of message scrutiny. Furthermore, under high-elaboration conditions, mood not only can encourage mood-congruent persuasion outcomes (e.g., Breckler & Wiggins, 1991; Petty et al., 1993) but also can encourage mood-incongruent persuasion outcomes (Wegener et al., 1994). Similarly, under relatively moderate elaboration conditions, positive moods not only can encourage reductions of message processing when compared with neutral and negative moods (e.g., Bless et al., 1990; Mackie & Worth, 1989) but also can foster increases in message processing (Wegener et al., 1995). In addition, in each case, conceptual moderators have been introduced to account for past findings as well as current results. Thus, the flexibilities in mood-based effects on persuasion that have been presented in this chapter help to more fully explain the psychological processes underlying the various effects of mood. It is our hope that demonstration of these flexibilities of mood and the conceptual factors that appear to underlie them will initiate further studies of the processes by which mood can influence the way we think about and organize our world.

ACKNOWLEDGMENTS

The authors thank the Ohio State Group for Attitudes and Persuasion for comments on the research reviewed in this chapter. The research conducted by the authors and the preparation of this chapter were supported by an NIMH predoctoral traineeship (T32 MH19728) to Duane T. Wegener and an NSF grant (BNS 9021647) to Richard E. Petty.

REFERENCES

Ajzen, I., & Fishbein, M. (1980). *Understanding attitudes and predicting social behavior.* Englewood Cliffs, NJ: Prentice-Hall.

Apaniesk, A. M., & Ditto, P. H. (1994, May). *Motivated sensitivity to argument quality in the processing of preference-relevant information.* Paper presented at the annual meeting of the Midwestern Psychological Association, Chicago, IL.

Baker, S. M., & Petty, R. E. (1994). Majority and minority influence: Source-position incongruency as a determinant of message scrutiny. *Journal of Personality and Social Psychology, 67,* 5-19.

Batra, R., & Stayman, D. M. (1990). The role of mood in advertising effectiveness. *Journal of Consumer Research, 17,* 203-214.

Bless, H., Bohner, G., Schwarz, N., & Strack, F. (1990). Mood and persuasion: A cognitive response analysis. *Personality and Social Psychology Bulletin, 16,* 331-345.

Bower, G. (1981). Mood and memory. *American Psychologist, 36,* 129-148.

Breckler, S. J., & Wiggins, E. C. (1991). Cognitive responses in persuasion: Affective and evaluative determinants. *Journal of Experimental Social Psychology, 27,* 180-200.

Cacioppo, J. T., Marshall-Goodell, B. S., Tassinary, L. G., & Petty, R. E. (1992). Rudimentary determinants of attitudes: Classical conditioning is more effective when prior knowledge about the attitude stimulus is low than high. *Journal of Experimental Social Psychology, 28,* 207-233.

Cacioppo, J. T., & Petty, R. E. (1979). Effects of message repetition and position on cognitive responses, recall, and persuasion. *Journal of Personality and Social Psychology, 37,* 97-109.

Cacioppo, J. T., & Petty, R. E. (1982a). A biosocial model of attitude change. In J. T. Cacioppo & R. E. Petty (Eds.), *Perspectives in cardiovascular psychophysiology* (pp. 151-188). New York: Guilford.

Cacioppo, J. T., & Petty, R. E. (1982b). The need for cognition. *Journal of Personality and Social Psychology, 42,* 116-131.

Carlson, M., & Miller, N. (1987). Explanation of the relationship between negative mood and helping. *Psychological Bulletin, 102,* 91-108.

Carlson, M., Charlin, V., & Miller, N. (1988). Positive mood and helping behavior: A test of six hypotheses. *Journal of Personality and Social Psychology, 55,* 211-229.

Chaiken, S. (1980). Heuristic versus systematic information processing and the use of source versus message cues in persuasion. *Journal of Personality and Social Psychology, 39*, 752-756.

Chaiken, S. (1987). The heuristic model of persuasion. In M. P. Zanna, J. M. Olson, & C. P. Herman (Eds.), *Social influence: The Ontario Symposium* (Vol. 5, pp. 3-39). Hillsdale, NJ: Lawrence Erlbaum Associates.

Chaiken, S., & Maheswaran, D. (1994). Heuristic processing can bias systematic processing: Effects of source credibility, argument ambiguity, and task importance on attitude judgment. *Journal of Personality and Social Psychology, 66*, 460-473.

Cialdini, R. B., Baumann, D. J., & Kenrick, D. T. (1981). Insights from sadness: A three step model of the development of altruism as hedonism. *Developmental Review, 1*, 207-223.

Cialdini, R. B., Darby, B., & Vincent, J. (1973). Transgression and altruism: A case for hedonism. *Journal of Experimental Social Psychology, 9*, 502-516.

Clark, M. S., & Isen, A. M. (1982). Toward understanding the relationship between feeling states and social behavior. In A. Hastorf & A. Isen (Eds.), *Cognitive social psychology* (pp. 93-108). New York: Elsevier-North Holland.

Ellis, H. C., & Ashbrook, P. W. (1988). Resource allocation model of the effects of depressed mood states on memory. In K. Fiedler & J. Forgas (Eds.), *Affect, cognition, and social behavior* (pp. 25-43). Toronto: Hogrefe.

Erber, R. (1991). Affective and semantic priming: Effects of mood on category accessibility and inference. *Journal of Experimental Social Psychology, 27*, 480-498.

Fishbein, M., & Ajzen, I. (1975). *Belief, attitude, intention, and behavior: An introduction to theory and research*. Reading, MA: Addison-Wesley.

Forgas, J. P., & Moylan, S. (1987). After the movies: The effects of mood on social judgments. *Personality and Social Psychology Bulletin, 13*, 467-477.

Giuliano, T. A., & Swinkels, A. (1992, August). *Development and validation of the mood-awareness scale*. Paper presented at the 100th meeting of the American Psychological Association, Washington, DC.

Giuliano, T. A., & Swinkels, A. (1993, August). *Exploring the role of mood awareness in mood regulation*. Paper presented at the 101st meeting of the American Psychological Association, Toronto, Canada.

Gleicher, F., Baker, S. M., & Petty, R. E. (1989, May). *The influence of affect on judgments of life events*. Paper presented at the annual meeting of the Midwestern Psychological Association, Chicago, IL.

Griffitt, W. B. (1970). Environmental effects on interpersonal affective behavior: Ambient effective temperature and attraction. *Journal of Personality and Social Psychology, 15*, 240-244.

Hammond, L. J. (1980). The effect of contingency upon the appetitive conditioning of free operant behavior. *Journal of the Experimental Analysis of Behavior, 34*, 297-304.

Isen, A. M. (1987). Positive affect, cognitive processes, and social behavior. In L. Berkowitz (Ed.), *Advances in experimental social psychology* (Vol. 20, pp. 203-253). New York: Academic Press.

Isen, A. (1993). Positive mood and decision making. In M. Lewis & J. Haviland (Eds.), *Handbook of emotion* (pp. 261-277). New York: Guilford.

Isen, A., Shalker, T., Clark, M., & Karp, L. (1978). Affect, accessibility of material in memory, and behavior: A cognitive loop? *Journal of Personality and Social Psychology, 36*, 1-12.

Janis, I., Kaye, D., & Kirschner, P. (1965). Facilitating effects of "eating while reading" on responsiveness to persuasive communications. *Journal of Personality and Social Psychology, 1*, 181-186.

Johnson, E., & Tversky, A. (1983). Affect, generalization, and the perception of risk. *Journal of Personality and Social Psychology, 45*, 20-31.

Kuykendall, D., & Keating, J. (1990). Mood and persuasion: Evidence for the differential influence of positive and negative states. *Psychology and Marketing, 7,* 1-9.

Mackie, D. M., Asuncion, A. G., & Rosselli, F. (1992). The impact of positive affect on persuasion processes. In M. S. Clark (Ed.), *Review of Personality and Social Psychology* (Vol. 14, pp. 247-270).

Mackie, D. M., & Worth, L. T. (1989). Processing deficits and the mediation of positive affect in persuasion. *Journal of Personality and Social Psychology, 57,* 27-40.

Mackie, D. M., & Worth, L. T. (1991). Feeling good, but not thinking straight: The impact of positive mood on persuasion. In J. Forgas (Ed.), *Emotion and social judgments* (pp. 201-219). Oxford, England: Pergamon.

Martin, L. L., Ward, D. W., Achee, J. W., & Wyer, R. S. (1993). Mood as input: People have to interpret the motivational implications of their moods. *Journal of Personality and Social Psychology, 64,* 317-326.

Mathur, M., & Chattopadhyay, A. (1991). The impact of moods generated by television programs on responses to advertising. *Psychology and Marketing, 8,* 59-77.

Mayer, J., Gaschke, Y., Braverman, D., & Evans, T. (1992). Mood-congruent judgment is a general effect. *Journal of Personality and Social Psychology, 63,* 119-132.

McGuire, W. J., & McGuire, C. V. (1991). The content, structure, and operation of thought systems. In R. S. Wyer, Jr., & T. Srull (Ed.), *Advances in social cognition* (Vol. 4, pp. 1-78). Hillsdale, NJ: Lawrence Erlbaum Associates.

Meyerowitz, B. E., & Chaiken, S. (1987). The effect of message framing on breast self-examination attitudes, intentions, and behavior. *Journal of Personality and Social Psychology, 52,* 500-510.

Miller, L. (1975). Compounding of discriminative stimuli correlated with chained and multiple schedules. *Journal of Experimental Analysis of Behavior, 23,* 95-102.

Miller, N., & Carlson, M. (1990). Valid theory-testing meta-analyses further question negative state relief model of helping. *Psychological Bulletin, 107,* 215-225.

Murray, M., Sujan, M., Hirt, E., & Sujan (1990). The influence of mood on categorization: A cognitive flexibility interpretation. *Journal of Personality and Social Psychology, 59,* 411-425.

Norborg, J., Osborne, S., & Fanting, E. (1983). Duration of components and response rates on multiple fixed-ratio schedules. *Animal Learning and Behavior, 11,* 51-59.

Parrott, W. G. (1993). Beyond hedonism: Motives for inhibiting good moods and for maintaining bad moods. In D. M. Wegner & J. W. Pennebaker (Eds.), *Handbook of mental control* (pp. 278-305). Englewood Cliffs, NJ: Prentice-Hall.

Petty, R. E., & Brock, T. C. (1976). Effects of responding or not responding to hecklers on audience agreement with a speaker. *Journal of Applied Social Psychology, 6,* 1-17.

Petty, R. E., & Cacioppo, J. T. (1979a). Effects of forewarning of persuasive intent and involvement on cognitive responses and persuasion. *Personality and Social Psychology Bulletin, 5,* 173-176.

Petty, R. E., & Cacioppo, J. T. (1979b). Issue-involvement can increase or decrease persuasion by enhancing message-relevant cognitive responses. *Journal of Personality and Social Psychology, 37,* 1915-1926.

Petty, R. E., & Cacioppo, J. T. (1981). *Attitudes and persuasion: Classic and contemporary approaches.* Dubuque, IA: Wm. C. Brown.

Petty, R. E., & Cacioppo, J. T. (1983). The role of bodily responses in attitude measurement and change. In J. T. Cacioppo & R. E. Petty (Eds.), *Social psychophysiology: A sourcebook* (pp. 51-101). New York: Guilford.

Petty, R. E., & Cacioppo, J. T. (1984). The effects of involvement on responses to argument quantity and quality: Central and peripheral routes to persuasion. *Journal of Personality and Social Psychology, 46,* 69-81.

Petty, R. E., & Cacioppo, J. T. (1986). *Communication and persuasion: Central and peripheral routes to attitude change.* New York: Springer-Verlag.

Petty, R. E., Cacioppo, J. T., & Goldman, R. (1981). Personal involvement as a determinant of argument-based persuasion. *Journal of Personality and Social Psychology, 41,* 847–855.

Petty, R. E., Cacioppo, J. T., & Haugtvedt, C. (1992). Involvement and persuasion: An appreciative look at the Sherifs' contribution to the study of self-relevance and attitude change. In D. Granberg & G. Sarup (Eds.), *Social judgment and intergroup relations: Essays in honor of Muzafer Sherif* (pp. 147–174). New York: Springer/Verlag.

Petty, R. E., Cacioppo, J. T., & Kasmer, J. (1988). The role of affect in the Elaboration Likelihood Model. In L. Donohew, H. Sypher, & E. T. Higgins, (Eds.), *Communication, social cognition, and affect* (pp. 117–146). Hillsdale, NJ: Lawrence Erlbaum Associates.

Petty, R. E., Cacioppo, J. T., & Schumann, D. (1983). Central and peripheral routes to advertising effectiveness: The moderating role of involvement. *Journal of Consumer Research, 10,* 134–148.

Petty, R. E., Gleicher, F., & Baker, S. M. (1991). Multiple roles for affect in persuasion. In J. Forgas (Ed.), *Emotion and social judgments* (pp. 181–200). Oxford, England: Pergamon.

Petty, R. E., Schumann, D., Richman, S., & Strathman, A. J. (1993). Positive mood and persuasion: Different roles for affect under high and low elaboration conditions. *Journal of Personality and Social Psychology, 64,* 5–20.

Petty, R. E., & Wegener, D. T. (1991). Thought systems, argument quality, and persuasion. In R. S. Wyer & T. K. Srull (Eds.), *Advances in social cognition* (Vol. 4, pp. 143–161). Hillsdale, NJ: Lawrence Erlbaum Associates.

Petty, R. E., Wegener, D. T., Fabrigar, L., Priester, J. R., & Cacioppo, J. T. (1993). Conceptual and methodological issues in the Elaboration Likelihood Model of persuasion: A reply to the Michigan State critics. *Communication Theory, 3,* 336–363.

Petty, R. E., Wells, G. L., & Brock, T. C. (1976). Distraction can enhance or reduce yielding to propaganda: Thought disruption versus effort justification. *Journal of Personality and Social Psychology, 34,* 874–884.

Pieters, R. G. M. (1988). Attitude-behavior relationships. In W. F. V. Raaij, G. M. V. Veldhoven, & K. Warneryd (Eds.), *Handbook of economic psychology* (pp. 147–204). Dordrecht, The Netherlands: Kluwer Academic.

Rachlin, H. (1976). *Behavior and learning.* San Francisco: W. H. Freeman.

Razran, G. H. S. (1940). Conditioned response changes in rating and appraising sociopolitical slogans. *Psychological Bulletin, 37,* 481.

Rhine, R., & Severance, L. (1970). Ego-involvement, discrepancy, source credibility, and attitude change. *Journal of Personality and Social Psychology, 16,* 175–190.

Salovey, P., Mayer, J. D., & Rosenhan, D. L. (1991). Mood and helping: Mood as a motivator of helping and helping as a regulator of mood. In M. S. Clark (Ed.), *Review of personality and social psychology: Vol. 12. Prosocial behavior* (pp. 215–237). Newbury Park, CA: Sage.

Schaller, M., & Cialdini, R. B. (1990). Happiness, sadness, and helping: A motivational integration. In R. Sorrentino & E. T. Higgins (Eds.), *Handbook of motivation and cognition: Foundations of social behavior* (Vol. 2, pp. 265–296). New York: Guilford Press.

Schwarz, N. (1990). Feelings as information: Informational and motivational functions of affective states. In R. M. Sorrentino & E. T. Higgins (Eds.), *Handbook of motivation and cognition: Foundations of social behavior* (Vol. 2, pp. 527–561). New York: Guilford.

Schwarz, N., Bless, H., & Bohner, G. (1991). Mood and persuasion: Affective states influence the processing of persuasive communications. In M. P. Zanna (Ed.), *Advances in experimental social psychology* (Vol. 24, pp. 161–201). San Diego: Academic Press.

Schwarz, N., & Clore, G. L. (1983). Mood, misattribution, and judgments of well-being: Informative and directive functions of affective states. *Journal of Personality and Social*

Psychology, 45, 513-523.
Schwarz, N., Servay, W., & Kumpf, M. (1985). Attribution of arousal as a mediator of the effectiveness of fear-arousing communications. *Journal of Applied Social Psychology, 15,* 74-84.
Sherif, C., Sherif, M., & Nebergall, R. (1965). *Attitude and attitude change: The social judgment-involvement approach.* Philadelphia: Saunders.
Sherif, M., & Hovland, C. (1961). *Social judgment: Assimilation and contrast effects in communication and attitude change.* New Haven, CT: Yale University Press.
Shimp, T. A., Stuart, E. W., & Engle, R. W. (1991). A program of classical conditioning experiments testing variations in the conditioned stimulus and context. *Journal of Consumer Research, 18,* 1-22.
Sinclair, R. C., & Mark, M. (1992). The influence of mood state on judgment and action: Effects on persuasion, categorization, social justice, person perception, and judgmental accuracy. In L. L. Martin & A. Tesser (Eds.), *The construction of social judgments* (pp. 165-193). Hillsdale, NJ: Lawrence Erlbaum Associates.
Srull, T. K. (1983). The role of prior knowledge in the acquisition, retention, and use of new information. *Advances in Consumer Research, 10,* 572-576.
Wegener, D. T., & Petty, R. E. (1994). Mood management across affective states: The hedonic contingency hypothesis. *Journal of Personality and Social Psychology, 66,* 1034-1048.
Wegener, D. T., Petty, R. E., & Klein, D. J. (1994). Effects of mood on high elaboration attitude change: The mediating role of likelihood judgments. *European Journal of Social Psychology, 24,* 25-44.
Wegener, D. T., Petty, R. E., & Richman, S. A. (1991, May). *Positive mood and processing of persuasive communications.* Paper presented at the annual meeting of the Midwestern Psychological Association, Chicago, IL.
Wegener, D. T., Petty, R. E., & Smith, S. M. (1995). Positive mood can increase or decrease message scrutiny: The hedonic contingency view of mood and message processing. *Journal of Personality and Social Psychology, 69,* 5-15.
Worth, L. T., & Mackie, D. M. (1987). Cognitive mediation of positive mood in persuasion. *Social Cognition, 5,* 76-94.
Zanna, M. P., Kiesler, C. A., & Pilkonis, P. A. (1970). Positive and negative attitudinal affect established by classical conditioning. *Journal of Personality and Social Psychology, 14,* 321-328.

15
The Communicative Theory of Emotions: Empirical Tests, Mental Models, and Implications for Social Interaction

Keith Oatley
Ontario Institute for Studies in Education
University of Toronto

Philip N. Johnson-Laird
Princeton University

Emotions are at the center of human mental and social life. They integrate subjective experience, bodily changes, planned action, and social relating. We have proposed a theory (Oatley & Johnson-Laird, 1987) in which we integrated the biological approach to emotions deriving from Darwin (1872) and the cognitive science approach applied to emotions by Simon (1967). We proposed that emotions are communicative: They are based on signals within the brain that set it into distinct modes that reflect priorities of goals and that predispose toward appropriate classes of action. Such action includes expressive behavior that communicates emotions to other people.

Our theory has led to empirical studies and has provoked controversy; certain tenets have been shown to be wrong, so it needs revision. Our aim here is to present a revised version of the theory, to show how it accords with new evidence, and to draw out consequences for aspects of human emotional life that we did not originally consider. First, we briefly restate the original theory and its account of the semantics of emotion words. Next, we consider criticisms and tests of the theory, and then its relations with other theories. A revised version of the theory follows. Finally, we frame some conjectures to deal with attachment, psychopathology, emotions in reaction to entertainment, and the interaction between emotions and intellectual performance.

EMOTIONS AS MANAGING GOALS: THE COMMUNICATIVE THEORY

Emotions are typically caused by cognitive evaluations that may be conscious or unconscious. According to the communicative theory, each kind of evaluation gives rise to a distinct signal that propagates through the multiple processors of cognitive architecture to produce a basic emotion. This signal is evolutionarily old and simple. It has no internal structure, and in this sense it is not propositional: it does not carry semantic information. Its function is to control the organization of the brain, to make ready mechanisms of action and bodily resources, to direct attention, to set up biases of cognitive processing, and to make the issue that caused the emotion salient in consciousness. The phenomenological experience of this signal is a distinctive feeling of happiness, sadness, anger, or some other emotional state.

In a typical emotional experience, people are aware of an emotion and of some aspects of the evaluation that gave rise to it. Thus the experience depends on two separate signals: the emotion signal and a propositional signal of the evaluation that caused it. The theory allows for dissociations between these two kinds of signal. On the one hand, people may be unaware of the emotion signal, and hence unaware of their emotional state. On the other hand, a person may experience an emotion but without realizing its cause, or why it is so intense.

There is good evidence that emotions can sometimes be caused by purely bodily changes. For instance, Strack, Martin, and Stepper (1988) showed that subjects asked to hold a pencil between their teeth were made mildly happy—the manipulation unobtrusively provided facial feedback like that of smiling. Moreover, Schiff and Lamon (1989) showed that contracting the left side of the face causes sadness, and contracting the right side causes more positive emotions; these manipulations work without conscious mediation, probably by differentially affecting (respectively) right or left hemispheric activation. We believe that physiological changes can be highly ambiguous to their experiencers. Such changes can occur for many reasons: a nonpropositional signal of emotion can occur although the subject does not know its cause, autonomic effects can occur because the subject has drunk too much coffee, feedback of expressions of emotion can be mimicked, differential activation of right and left hemispheres can occur, physical activity can cause changes that the subject feels but does not understand. Where there is ambiguity about any inner perturbation, experimental manipulation of the outer environment can suggest causes for it. It has been shown in many experiments that interpretations of inner states can be labile, and that people can misattribute their causes—a bodily state can be interpreted as a mood and it is affected by the context Clore & Parrott, 1991).

Although experimentally demonstrated effects point to important processes, they need to be balanced by other kinds of investigation of how episodes of emotion are caused in everyday life. Later in this chapter we present some evidence on everyday emotions. To anticipate: in ordinary life most episodes of emotion are caused in obvious ways by evaluations of events in relation to goals—e.g., something we are working on goes well and we feel happy, someone slights us and we feel angry. In the usual course of events emotions have objects, and we know what caused them. Usually, according to our theory, the emotion signal and the information about its object and/or what caused it are tied together.

For our original theory (Oatley & Johnson-Laird, 1987) we derived a small number of basic emotions from our analysis of the evolutionary origins of emotions in the ontology of social mammals. We proposed that the social life of mammals revolves around a small number of significant individuals: parents and offspring, mates, predators and prey, cooperators in food acquisition, rivals. Important events arise as actions occur to achieve goals concerning such individuals.

This idea led us to postulate five basic emotions that arise at the junctures of such action sequences, corresponding to significant changes in relation to goals. They corresponded to states referred to in English, approximately, as happiness, sadness, anger, fear, and disgust. Thus achievement of subgoals elicits happiness, which prompts the person to continue the current activity until the goal is reached when he or she can stop; loss of a goal elicits sadness, which prompts disengagement from the goal; frustration elicits anger and aggressive striving to reach the goal or to avenge a wrong; threats, dangers, and conflicts of goals elicit fear (or the corresponding mood of anxiety) and hence freezing, flight, or fight; contaminating or toxic substances elicit disgust leading to repulsion and withdrawal. Our line of thinking converged with that of Ekman (1989), which was based on his discovery of pan-culturally recognized facial expressions for these same five emotions, along with a sixth, surprise, that we did not regard as separate because it can occur with any event in relation to a goal. For us the precise number of basic emotions is less important than the hypothesis that each kind of emotion has specific functions and that mechanisms that evolved to serve these functions map diverse events into a small set of emotional modes.

According to our original theory, when an event occurs that is important in relation to a goal, its cognitive evaluation either maintains (as a mood) the brain's present activities, or switches them (in a discrete emotion) into a new emotional mode appropriate to the event. We agree with Carver and Scheier (1990; Carver, Lawrence, & Scheier, chap. 9, this volume) that emotions are based on a system that monitors progress toward goals. Our version is depicted in Fig. 15.1. We disagree with Carver and Scheier's idea that affect derives continuously from rates of change of such progress. We believe that elicitation of emotions is more discrete; we think an emotion arises when an event indicates that the probability of attaining a goal has become discriminably better or worse than expected. So when some line of action is going well, when events are being dealt with successfully, when

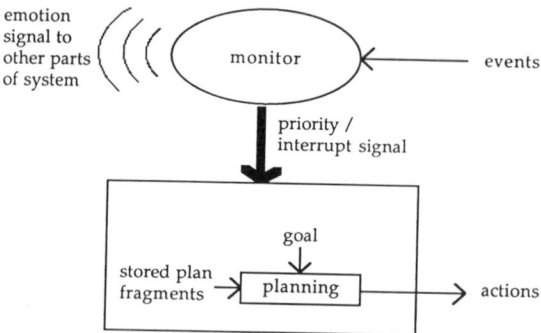

Fig. 15.1 Diagram of the emotion system that monitors the status of goal-plan complexes. When an event occurs that indicates that the probability of reaching the goal has changed substantially, the monitoring system sends out a nonpropositional signal that changes the priority of the current plan (indicated by the thicker arrow), and modulates other parts of the brain.

problems are being solved with resources that are at hand, when subgoals are being attained, the emotion signal produces a mood of happiness that encourages us to continue what we are doing. When the goal is achieved the person stops that activity. As Chaiken, Liberman, and Eagly (1989) concluded, people stop what they are doing when they reach "a sufficient degree of confidence that they have accomplished their processing goals." The process is not entirely straightforward, however, because, as Martin, Ward, Achee, and Wyer (1993) have shown, under some circumstances the pleasantness of a mood can itself be a goal, the feeling of happiness can itself be interpreted and used to determine whether or not to continue with an activity.

Carver and Scheier propose a positive–negative dimension, as in a servo-regulator, with a positive affective signal stopping activity because a goal state has been achieved and a negative one generating movement to reduce the error. By contrast we propose that happiness is usually the mood of active engagement in what one is doing (cf. Csikszentmihalyi, 1990; also see later for our own evidence) and encourages one to continue until the goal is reached, or in non-goal-directed activities while the activity lasts. According to our formulation people usually stop not because of a happy emotion but because a goal is reached or an interruption occurs. Moreover, in contrast to Carver and Scheier, we postulate distinct kinds of negative emotion, because during evolution it has been possible to discriminate among negative events and because appropriate responses to different classes of negative event are very different. For instance disengagement from a goal that is sadly lost is quite different from the striving of anger.

Concepts of Emotions and a Theory of Semantics

According to our theory human beings usually know what events cause emotions. We believe that the findings of Nisbett and Ross (1980) have been overgeneralized. Nisbett and Ross argued that because behavior and mental states can be manipulated in ways of which subjects are unaware in social psychological experiments, then in general people do not know the causes of their behavior or mental states. This conclusion has been extended to emotions. Thus Wilson, Laser, and Stone (1982) asked one group of 50 students to predict their mood on the basis of variables such as the weather, physical health, amount of physical exercise, and so on and found that these subjects were no better at predicting their own moods than a second group of subjects who made predictions of the moods of first group without any direct personal knowledge of them. The authors said it would be unparsimonious to conclude that people in the first group had access to their own inner states or to the causes of such states; instead both groups were consulting their folk theories about what affects mood. We believe that this and all the studies done by Nisbett, Wilson, and their colleagues so far are irrelevant to most emotions; in such studies changes of behavior or judgment are measured in relation to causes that are not obvious, remote in time, and/or probablistic. It is indeed true that people are very bad at judging causality in such cases. But in everyday life the majority of emotions have a cause that is salient, temporally contiguous, and seemingly direct. In other words the relation of events to emotions they cause comes close to the conditions in which humans learn well and make good predictions. Although sometimes people do not know what has caused an emotion or mood, for the most part they do, and their personal knowledge converges with scientific knowledge (see Oatley & Duncan, 1992, for a more extended discussion of this issue).

Folk knowledge of emotions and their causes is reflected in folk theories on which language is based and from which derive the vocabularies of emotion in different cultures. We therefore proposed a semantic theory of English emotion terms in which we brought together basic emotions and propositional knowledge (Johnson-Laird & Oatley, 1989). The theory motivated semantic analyses of 590 words — all the emotion terms in English that we could then find — in which we indicated for each word its underlying basic emotion and a propositional component, where necessary, that indicated the intensity of the emotion, its cause, or its object. Thus, we proposed that embarrassment is based on fear, plus the propositional knowledge that this fear is of being the center of unwelcome attention. This semantic theory is an empirically distinct alternative to appraisal theories (Ellsworth, 1991; Scherer, 1988) in which the meaning of an emotion is a profile of values on 5 to 15 appraisal features, such as whether an event was novel, whether it was pleasant, whether it was controllable, and so on.

CHALLENGES AND DIRECT TESTS OF COMMUNICATIVE THEORY

Three Kinds of Criticism

Criticisms of the communicative theory fall into three main categories. First, some theorists have attacked the idea of basic emotions (Ortony & Turner, 1990; Russell, 1991). All theories of emotion reduce the heterogeneous phenomena of emotional life to more manageable principles, and as Reisenzein (1992) pointed out, the reduction is either to a set of irreducible states that are themselves emotions or to a set of irreducible states that are not emotions, such as dimensions (Russell, 1991) or components of cognitive appraisal (Ortony & Turner, 1990). Our view (Johnson-Laird & Oatley, 1989) is that theories that eschew basic emotions neglect psychological functions in favor of the dimensions or components of appraisal that they postulate. Their theoretical elements do not map well onto brain mechanisms or functional principles of social life.

A second kind of criticism concerns our claim that emotional terms are not based on prototypes. Prototypes have their attractions. Everyone is familiar with prototypical sequences of emotional events, for example, one person insults another who then loses his or her temper and in anger threatens the transgressor. In our view the meaning of an emotional term, such as the word *anger* as it occurs in this vignette, neither refers to nor depends on the prototypical sequence of events. Instead, we argue that *anger* refers to a mental state that arises in the person who was insulted. Anger can be understood perfectly well in an assertion such as: For no good reason, Joseph K. woke up feeling angry. Here is no prototypical sequence, and the mental state may or may not be accompanied by somatic and bodily changes, may or may not lead to prototypical behaviors. Instead we claim that people know that a state of mind called "anger" can occur with varying intensity. But unless one has experienced it one cannot understand the meaning of the word *anger*. It cannot be analyzed into smaller nonemotional components. Although we do not deny that people have useful prototypical knowledge of angry sequences we do argue that the semantics of terms like anger are not themselves prototypical (Oatley & Johnson-Laird, 1992).

The third kind of criticism is based on empirical studies, and in the next subsection we review these briefly.

Empirical Tests of the Communicative Theory

Oatley and his colleagues have tested four predictions of the communicative theory in studies in which subjects completed structured diaries of incidents of emotion in everyday life (Oatley & Duncan, 1992, 1994). In these studies we are beginning to delineate what we think of as an epidemiology of emotions by asking to whom emotions occur, how they are caused, and what their accompaniments and consequences are. Our first prediction was that the sort of emotion that individuals experience would depend on the kind of goal-relevant event that they perceived as causing the emotion. This has also been tested in a study in which subjects recorded emotions experienced while reading short stories (Biason, 1993). Both in this study, and in those by Oatley and Duncan, the communicative theory correctly predicted about 69% of the basic emotions arising from goal-relevant events: achievements of subgoals cause happiness, losses cause sadness, frustrations cause anger, and threats cause fear. In comparison, consider the leading appraisal theory of Scherer. Chwelos and Oatley (1994) showed that the expert system in which Scherer (1993) expressed his theory does not instantiate sequences of stimulus evaluation checks as Scherer (1988; 1993) proposed. When Scherer's verbal postulates are instantiated computationally, some patterns of evaluation are intuitively implausible. We believe difficulties of this kind apply generally to feature-appraisal theories. Chwelos (1992) compared Oatley and Duncan's goal-relevance criteria with Scherer's appraisal features on emotion incidents newly collected to meet requirements of both systems, with emotions predicted in terms of Oatley and Johnson-Laird's five basic emotions. Chwelos found the communicative theory correctly predicted 72% of emotions. He wrote a version of Scherer's program. When allowed one guess this version predicted 41% of emotions. Scherer has suggested (personal communication, 1995) that this unexpected low value may have occurred in part because Chwelos did not normalize values in his version of the program. So an accurate comparison has yet to be achieved. The proper value for Scherer's system is no doubt around 60% correct with one guess or 71% with two guesses, calculated from totals in Scherer's (1993) Table 4. Ideally the two systems probably achieve similar results. Because eliciting of emotions needs to be simple, our simpler goal relevance criteria might be preferred to the more complex appraisal system with 15 dimensions.

A second prediction of the communicative theory tested in Oatley and Duncan's diary studies is that basic emotions can be experienced without awareness of their causes. As we explained earlier, the communicative theory allows for dissociations between propositional or semantic cause of an emotion and the nonpropositional emotion mode. When people are conscious only of an emotional mode, or if it occurs without clear connection to any propositional element, they experience an emotion without knowing why. This gives a principled explanation of moods as long-lasting states based on emotion modes sustained by a basic nonpropositional signal: we postulate that the only true moods are those of basic emotions that can occur acausally.

Appraisal theories implicitly (Ellsworth, 1991) or explicitly (Ortony, Clore, & Collins, 1988) propose that elicitation of an emotion is always based on a cognitive appraisal. By contrast, our theory is unique among cognitive theories in proposing that emotions are based on a signal that has no semantic meaning as such, and which can sometimes be triggered by means other than an evaluation. Although it is usually caused by an evaluation and attached to a signal indicating this cause, the emotion signal need not be attached to any conscious understanding of causation. Our evidence (Oatley & Duncan, 1992) is that in about 6% of 645 incidents of emotion subjects did not know the cause of the emotion; there were cases of acausal happiness, sadness, anger, and fear. Emotions that we said always contained some propositional content — shame, embarrassment, and jealousy — were never (in 55 incidents) experienced as free floating. Contrary to the communicative theory, however, we have found no cases of acausal disgust.

A third prediction of the original communicative theory was that mixtures of basic emotions should be rare. An emotion makes ready a repertoire of actions in response to a recurring kind of goal-relevant event, so we thought each emotion mode should inhibit others, as reflected in experiences such as the difficulty of feeling happily amorous when anxious. Oatley and Duncan's (1992, 1994) diary studies showed this hypothesis about mixtures was quite wrong. Subjects reported that about one third of their incidents of emotion were mixtures. Table 15.1 shows mixtures of four basic emotions, derived from 57 students each collecting five incidents (Oatley & Duncan, 1992), plus Carson's sample of 58 physically disabled and able-bodied people each collecting five incidents (reported in Oatley & Duncan, 1992) plus 47 employed people each collecting four incidents

TABLE 15.1.
Numbers of Incidents of Emotion in Which There Were Mixtures of Basic Emotions (Happiness, Sadness, Anger and Fear) Derived From Several Diary Studies

	Emotions in the Mixture		
	Happiness	*Sadness*	*Anger*
Emotions in the mixture			
Sadness	15		
Anger	4	31	
Fear	18	13	27

(Oatley & Duncan, 1994). Mixtures that included disgust were omitted because they were very rare; mixtures that included a nonbasic emotion, and incidents reported as mixed without naming the emotions, were also omitted. The most common mixture of basic emotions was anger and sadness, but all possible combinations of happiness, sadness, anger, and fear occurred; although there were only a few of happiness and anger. Typically a mixture of emotions occurred when people reacted with different emotions to different aspects of a situation.

Finally, Oatley and Duncan (1994) found a significant corroboration of our theory's prediction that positive emotions prompt continuation of the current plan—of 20 emotion episodes rated as helping a current plan, 19 were of happiness. Negative emotions functioned to change the course of action—of 69 episodes rated as hindering the ongoing plan, 61 were of negative emotions. There was also, however, a fair number of episodes (82) rated as neither helping nor hindering the current plan.

Other relevant empirical studies have addressed our semantic analysis of emotion terms. The communicative theory led us to argue that certain English words imply a disjunction of basic emotions, for example, "fed up" means either angry or sad. But, as Jones and Martin (1992) showed, such terms can convey a mixture of emotions; *fed up* can mean feeling both angry and sad. A long paper with several studies of our semantic theory was written by Reisenzein (1995). He assumed, as do we, that the folk theories underlying European languages are similar. He translated our terms into German and investigated subjects' intuitions about the relations between basic emotions in terms that implied semantic content as well as a basic emotion. Reisenzein asked subjects to rate on six-point scales such propositions as the following (the scale is in parentheses): "If one feels glad, then one (never, rarely, occasionally, often, in most cases, always) feels happy." From our perspective, his main finding was that disgust was not judged to underlie hatred and its cognates and that it did not appear to be objectless. The other results of Reisenzein's first study provide modest support for the communicative theory's postulates about the semantics of happiness, sadness, anger, and fear, for example, when a person feels glad, they do typically feel happy. In his second study, Reisenzein changed the form of questions to his subjects. He asked, for instance, "Can one feel remorse about something *without* simultaneously also feeling sad about that same thing?" The results were less supportive of our theory than his first study, and he took this to count against our semantic analyses. We disagree with his interpretation and think a basic emotion that one experiences need not have the same object as the related complex emotion; for example, remorse is sadness from evaluating one's past performance as morally wrong. The cause was a past action, but the sadness is different and is currently felt toward oneself. The very form of Reisenzein's second study invites subjects to search for episodes in which they might be remorseful about something without feeling sad about the same thing. We believe it asks subjects to think not about the semantic properties of words but to search for incidents in which they might discover this kind of dissociation. This same problem is probably exacerbated in Reisenzein's third study in which the subjects rated the emotions that they would experience in hypothetical scenarios. We regard Reisenzein's studies as an important contribution to the study of emotional concepts, particularly of the question of whether such concepts are hierarchically organized. Studies of the semantics of words, however, may need not just direct judgments about relations between words—a task that taxes linguists (Bendix, 1966)—but also indirect methods, such as examining release from proactive inhibition in conceptual judgments as one moves from one category to another or studies in which a basic emotion is used to prime retrieval from memory of terms related to this word; Conway and Bekerian (1987) found results favorable to our kind of hypothesis using this method.

CONVERGING THEORIES AND EVIDENCE

Cognitive Theories

Considering alternative theories, our communicative theory is most similar to the theory of Stein, Trabasso, and Liwag (1993) and is also close to the theories of Frijda (1986) and Lazarus (1991). All these are based on the postulate that emotions primarily concern evaluation of events in relation to goals. Along with Ekman (1992) and Stein et al. (1993), we believe that the phenomena are best explained by a set of basic emotions, whereas Lazarus, Frijda, and most appraisal theorists are sceptical about the existence of basic emotions. We claim that an evaluation of an event in relation to a goal is the usual cause of an emotion. But, as Stein et al. and Lazarus point out, when emotional experiences unfold, secondary evaluations are made to assess what, if anything, can be done in response to events causing the experience. Some appraisal theorists (Roseman, 1991) and attribution theorists (Wiener & Graham, 1989) have made excellent proposals about secondary evaluation, and Smith, Haynes, Lazarus, and Pope (1993) did a study that implies that attributions are more closely related to secondary appraisals than to elicitation. Our original theory was weak in respect of secondary appraisal.

Biological Theories and Evidence

The communicative theory derives from the design of cognitive agents that could operate with multiple goals, which are often achieved in cooperation or competition with other people, in a world of which the agents' knowledge is incomplete and their mental models often incorrect. Yet, remarkably, it has converged with theories drawing on quite independent literatures. One of these is due to Tooby and Cosmides (1990). They proposed a theory similar to ours, though specified in less detail, from considerations of evolutionary biology. Another is LeDoux's (1990, 1993) neurophysiological account. He argued on the basis of conditioning experiments that the amygdala is an emotional computer that evaluates the emotional significance of stimuli. These stimuli may either be very simple percepts (aspects of a sound or sight) or they may depend on conscious recognition of meaning and significance. In either case, the amygdala transmits to other parts of the brain a signal that is not verbal but that functions to alter attention and to initiate physiological responses to the emotionally significant event.

Advances in understanding neurochemical systems have indicated that peptides can have effects that the communicative theory postulated for nonpropositional emotion signals (Panksepp, 1993). The signals for fear are the clearest: Bradwejn (1993) showed that if the peptide cholecystokinin (CCK) is injected into people in small quantities, it can cause free-floating fear. Patients describe resulting feelings as identical to panic attacks. Further evidence shows that CCK modulates some neural systems, and that its emotional effects are based on physiological (not artifactual) mechanisms.

Still other recent discoveries bear out the communicative theory's prediction that emotions can be induced without any conscious, informational content. In a study of the psychopathology of epilepsy, MacLean (1993) concluded that a small number of basic emotions can exist independently of semantic content in the auras of temporal lobe epilepsy. He writes that six kinds of emotions occur in these auras: desire, fear, anger, dejection (sadness), gratulant feelings (feelings of happiness, insight, or achievement), and feelings of affection. Often there is a sense of great conviction, and: *"Significantly, these feelings are free-floating, being completely unattached to any particular thing, situation, or idea"* (p. 79, emphasis in original).

An Evaluation of the Original Communicative Theory

The original communicate theory of emotions had some virtues. It is a member of a family of theories expressing views that are plausible to others. It survived, with some knocks, a first round of empirical tests, and it has made successful predictions: about emotions being caused by goal-relevant events, about emotions occurring without conscious cause, and about the effects of emotions on the current plan. The evidence has shown the theory was wrong in two substantial respects: its treatment of the emotions of disgust and hatred was mistaken and its prediction that mixtures of emotions would be rare was incorrect. It also neglected the secondary evaluation of emotional experiences. We therefore propose a revision.

THE REVISED COMMUNICATIVE THEORY OF EMOTIONS: FOUNDATIONAL ISSUES

What Emotions Are Basic?

In our revised theory we still accept the functional role of emotions as both internal and external communications and believe that the four most common basic emotions (the *big four* as we are tempted to call them) correspond approximately to the English terms: happiness, sadness, anger, and fear. They are basic emotions in the sense that we described earlier. People can experience them without knowing their cause and without their having any apparent object. They also occur as free-floating emotions in epileptic auras. These four emotions are the foundation of moods and even perhaps of certain personality types. Their existence is acknowledged at a conceptual level by most people in most cultures. In ordinary life these four emotions can be, and usually are, experienced with a knowledge of their cause, so one usually knows why one feels happy, sad, angry, or afraid. The majority of terms in European languages and we believe in other languages combine reference to a basic emotion and to an indication that the person knows its cause. Thus glad means that one is happy and knows why, disappointment is sadness about a known event, and so forth. We have considered English terms. Our analysis also translates well into Italian (Johnson-Laird & Oatley, 1988), and our interpretation is moderately consistent, we believe, with the results of Reisenzein (1995), using German translations.

In the revised theory, we propose that in addition to these four, there are five further emotions that are basic in the sense of being founded on innate, biological substrates: attachment, parental love, sexual attraction, disgust, and interpersonal rejection. What distinguishes them from the first set of four emotions is that they necessarily have objects. They can only be experienced in relation to someone or something. Attachment occurs between offspring and parent; parental love occurs toward offspring, and erotic attraction occurs between sexual partners (Shaver, Hazan, & Bradshaw, 1988). The emotions of disgust and personal rejection likewise must have objects. We were wrong to postulate that disgust can be free floating; one can only feel disgust at something or someone. In the emotion of personal rejection, with its cognates of disdain and contempt, one always rejects someone. Frijda (personal communication, 1994) has said that our revised theory would be more elegant if we had added to the emotions that can be acausal (happiness, sadness, anger, and fear) just two types of emotion that are object-related—an emotion of attraction or desire (that would include the various kinds of love) and an emotion of repulsion or withdrawal (that would include both disgust and interpersonal rejection). We are very tempted by this idea. We had suggested it previously (Johnson-Laird & Oatley, 1992), and it would make our set of basic emotions correspond exactly to those suggested by MacLean (1983). We regard the classification of object-related emotions as tentative. Our (slight) preference for thinking that there may be several kinds of object-related emotions of desire is due to the persuasion of Shaver et al.'s (1988) argument that three quite different systems underlie love of intimates, and our preference for more than one emotion of rejection is due to persuasion by Rozin, Haidt, and McCauley's (1993) account of disgust in comparison with the emotions of inter-individual rejection described by Goodall (1986) in her study of chimpanzees at Gombe, who began systematically killing a subgroup of chimpanzees, formerly companions, who had separated from the main group. The subgroup began to be treated as a different species, somewhat like prey, quite differently from how ingroup members were treated in angry fights for dominance.

It may be that there is no single term in English for the emotion of personal rejection. Cognates include contempt, disdain, and hatred (as in *race-hatred*). But although *hatred* seems in some ways a good name for this mode, in English the term is used more widely—this may have contributed to the results on this term that Reisenzein (1995) found which were so discrepant with our theory. Larocque (personal communication, 1994) collected an example from each of 25 English speakers of an experience of hatred; in her corpus the common attribute of hatred was an intense negative emotion (there were examples of anger, fear, disgust, and interpersonal rejection) with no way of doing anything about the eliciting situation. On the basis of this we should regard the ordinary usage of the English term *hatred* as a superordinate for intense negative emotions where lack of control is salient.

Mental Models as Mediating Emotions

If happiness, sadness, anger, and fear usually have objects, and emotions such as love and rejection necessarily have objects, then what is the psychological nature of these objects, which we become aware of via perception? Perceptual processes occur unconsciously; what they yield are mental models of the world (Marr, 1982; Oatley, Sullivan, & Hogg, 1988).

Craik (1943) speculated that thinking is a process of manipulating such models; there is now considerable evidence in favor of this hypothesis and of the hypothesis that verbal comprehension yields analogous models (Johnson-Laird, 1983, 1993).

The essential characteristic of a model, as opposed to other proposed forms of mental representation, is that it has a structure that corresponds to the structure of what it represents. But it always represents only some aspects. It is necessarily incomplete, so it is compatible with more than one possibility. This fact is brought home perceptually by the existence of visual illusions. As far as emotions are concerned this means that as well as the phenomena of the emotions of happiness, sadness, anger, and fear, being able to occur (although rarely) without the subject knowing the cause, the necessarily object-related emotions can be detached from one object and reattached to another that has some attributes of the model. If a Jane falls in love with John then she falls in love with her idea of him, or if Jack rejects people of a different skin color than his own, anyone fitting this minimal description will serve as object.

Self-awareness depends also depends on a model: on a model of the self (Johnson-Laird, 1993) and on the ability to embed one model within another, as when one becomes aware of oneself as perceiving the world. Models of the self are essential to meta-cognition, and indeed for the maintenance of the sense that one has a coherence and integrity over time. Yet, these models of the self are also always incomplete and sometimes erroneous (Oatley, 1992; Singer & Salovey, 1993).

Attachment, Parental Love, and Sexual Attraction. The role of models is central not only to the experience of object-directed emotions but also to their development. Infant attachment requires a model of the caregiver. Bowlby (1971) wrote of "internal working models" of relationships with attachment figures, and this concept has become central to understanding attachment (Bretherton, 1985; Main, 1991). Bowlby believed that a healthy child should develop a single coherent model of an attachment figure. To account for incoherence in the thought of emotionally disturbed people, Bowlby (1973) argued that they suffer from "multiple models" Psychoanalytic thinkers of the school of object relations (Fairbairn, 1952) hold a similar theory. People with partly unconscious disjunctive models can behave unpredictably to themselves and others, as first one model and its interpretations are invoked and then, in a different emotional situation, another and quite different model. The difficulty of reasoning coherently in disjunctive situations is manifest in laboratory studies of deductive reasoning (Bauer & Johnson-Laird, 1993; Johnson-Laird, Byrne, & Schaeken, 1992) and in judgment and decision making (Shafir & Tversky, 1992).

Tesser and Cornell (1991) showed how self-esteem may work through a hierarchical system, the components of which all affect a single high-level variable that a person tries to maintain. Adults must maintain hierarchies of models in order to cope with the representation of propositional attitudes, such as one person's beliefs about another's beliefs, meta-cognitive abilities, self-awareness, as well as self-esteem. The development of such representations is being actively explored (Halford, 1993; Stern, 1985).

There are several important aspects of mental models for the revised communicative theory of emotions. Infants' models of caregivers are likely to be formed early in life. To start with they need merely recognize caregivers and detect presence or absence. As a result of interactions, an initial model becomes a model of the relationship between the self and the caregiver. The model of the relationship comes to accommodate emotions other than the feeling of attachment, for instance temporary losses of the caregiver give rise to sadness, anger of the caregiver give rise to feelings of fear which can then become represented in the model. The model becomes the means by which the individual predicts the behavior of significant people and influences interactions with them. Comparably, parents must become emotionally attached to, and preoccupied with, their offspring. Every parent knows the problems of children not conforming to a model he or she has of them. Sexual attraction, too, is mediated by models; their role can be seen not only in initial idealizations that occur in romantic love but in the emotions of disappointment that occur when the actual other does not fulfill expectations. In idealization, a person uses a model that is closer to his or her object of desire than to any real person. Recently Hazan and Shaver (1987) and others proposed that adult love is based on infant models of attachment.

Disgust and Personal Rejection. The other basic emotions that have objects are disgust and personal rejection. In our original theory we had assumed that disgust could be free floating and also the basis of interpersonal rejection. We now accept that there are no feelings of free-floating disgust: Disgust always has an object (Rozin et al., 1993). We had confused it with the physiological state of nausea, as brought on by, say, seasickness. Disgust is undoubtedly an emotion with a biological base. Rozin et al. reported many ingenious studies that demonstrate the importance of an individual's models in eliciting disgust. Thus their subjects felt disgusted by a plastic fly in their drink, even knowing that it was clean and not a real fly. One of the most potent elicitors of disgust is the idea of wearing a sweater that belonged to Hitler, even though subjects are assured that it has been thoroughly cleaned.

A further modification is to distinguish between disgust and the emotion of interpersonal rejection. Disgust is rooted in gustatory aversion (as Rozin et al. proposed), whereas interpersonal rejection is a reaction to someone shunned who can be treated as less than human. Although, as Darwin (1872) pointed out, the two emotions are very close, a distinction between them is borne out by the existence of distinct facial expressions for disgust and contempt (Ekman & Friesen, 1986).

Goals of Basic Object-Directed Emotions. All five object-related emotions serve clear goals in the life of the species: attachment, parental love, and sexual attraction are the bases of rearing young and reproduction; disgust protects the body from infection and other kinds of contamination. Interpersonal rejection (contempt or hatred) seems perhaps more questionable, but several human paleontologists have seen lethal intergroup conflict as an important part of hominid evolution (Stringer & Gamble, 1993).

Mixtures of Emotions

In our original theory we allowed that mixed emotions could occur but thought that one emotion mode would tend to inhibit others. Hence, mixtures should be ephemeral. The evidence shows this was wrong. A plausible revision of the theory is that individuals can react to events by making more than one cognitive evaluation, and such evaluations can create distinct emotions in parallel or in rapid alternation. With loss of a loved one, one may feel both sad at the loss and angry at what was responsible for it. Threats from a hostile person may induce both anger and anxiety—a combination that may be quite stable if it induces conflict between approach and avoidance (Dollard & Miller, 1950). Happiness on achieving subgoals can be accompanied by anxiety about what follows when the goal is achieved.

One consequence of mixtures of emotions is that they make ready for disparate courses of action. Individuals who feel both angry and fearful tend both to advance aggressively and to flee. Such conflicts may be apparent in conflicting facial expressions, a phenomenon that Ekman and O'Sullivan (1991) reported in terms of "impure" emotions, such as smiling while lying but letting small facial signs of anxiety leak out. Mixtures occur often in relation to aggression (Lorenz, 1967). Aggressive actions occur when a predator kills prey. Goodall (1986) observed some prey-killing actions (e.g., biting and tearing flesh) among the chimpanzees that started killing out-group members. Anger relates to within-group aggression, whereas the emotions of personal rejection relate to aggression against outsiders and to treating them as nonmembers of the species. But with aggression sharing parts of the action repertoire, mixtures of anger and interpersonal rejection are not surprising.

The hypothesis that separate evaluations lead to dual emotions has empirical implications. First, in children it indicates increasing cognitive ability to entertain distinct cognitive evaluations of different aspects of the same state of affairs. Harris (1989) reported a study in which children were told a story about a dog that gets lost and later returns with a wounded ear. Older children say they feel happy at the dog's return and sad about its injury; younger children report just one emotion. Second, the complexity of contemporaneous but distinct cognitive evaluations calls for processing at a relatively high level in mental architecture. We can postulate that mixed feelings would not occur without knowing something about their cause. An interesting special case would be mixed feelings with awareness of the cause of only one of the emotions.

Mixtures can also arise from secondary evaluations. A primary evaluation evokes an emotion, then secondary evaluations of what to do about the situation can include new emotions about the original one. Oatley and Duncan (1992) found examples such as guilt about being angry and anger with the self about being fearful. Emotions need not just follow one another like beads on a string; they can overlay one another like strata.

One final thought about mixed feelings: Granted the existence of stable mixtures, it is perhaps surprising how few words in English denote mixed emotions. In the everyday conception of emotions we have a natural grasp of distinct emotions and generally refer to mixtures by indicating the emotions that occur in them.

A Summary of the Revised Theory

We have now outlined a new version of our communicative theory. We will here restate the main functions of emotions in relation to goals.

Evaluation of Goal-Relevant Events. Emotions typically arise from evaluations of events relevant to goals. These evaluations occur within a hierarchy of parallel processors, and they may be conscious or unconscious. They give rise to nonpropositional signals within the brain that induce and maintain emotion modes.

Emotions Have Signal Functions, to Ourselves and to Others. An emotion usually implies the existence of a goal, which may be unconscious, and of an event evaluated as relevant to a goal.

Readiness and the Management of Goals. Emotions function to manage plans and goals: maintaining readiness of ongoing activity in happy moods, interrupting such activity and changing readiness to act in a different plan where a negative emotion occurs. Just as within the individual cognitive system, emotions and moods maintain goal-plan complexes that involve other people. Happiness, attachment emotions, and love induce and maintain cooperation. Sadness is the emotion of disengagement from a relationship. Anger sets up a script for competition, aggression, and perhaps renegotiation of the relationship. Interpersonal fear signals deference. Contempt and disdain signal withdrawal from relationship.

Cognitive Organization. Each kind of emotion produces a distinctive mode of brain organization that includes distinctive attentional characteristics, biases of memory, and characteristics of problem solving.

Emotions Inject the Problem That Prompted Them Into Consciousness. They induce conscious rumination. That such preoccupation can lasts a long time indicates the importance of the cognitive changes that must occur with serious emotions, such as falling in love or coping with death or separation from someone who was close.

The principal changes to our original theory are as follows:

1. Four basic emotions, although their causes are usually known, can be experienced acausally: happiness, sadness, anger, and fear.
2. Five other basic emotions are necessarily object-related, each requires a known object (although they can be experienced toward objects without knowing why): attachment, parental love, sexual attraction, disgust, and personal rejection.
3. The object of an emotion is experienced via a mental model, a schematic, partial, and sometimes erroneous, representation that corresponds in structure to what it represents, a person or object in the world.
4. Secondary evaluations of events occur. These can give rise to sequences of changing emotions as people review what they can do about a situation. Some emotions may depend on secondary evaluation. For some closely held goals, it may take a long time to understand that a goal is lost and must be relinquished.
5. Mixtures of emotions occur. Although one emotion mode may inhibit others, different interpretative evaluations of the same situation, or secondary evaluations of an emotional experience as it unfolds, can lead to stable mixtures of emotions, and these can elicit conflicting kinds of readiness to act.

CONSEQUENCES AND CONJECTURES

We now turn to conjectures based on the revised theory. We deal with attachment, psychopathology, experience of real emotions in unreal circumstances, and the interaction between emotions and intellectual performance.

Mental Models in Attachment

One of Bowlby's (1971) proposals was that love in infancy has consequences for later life and is the foundation of emotional development. Though he was too pessimistic about ill effects of early maternal deprivation (Rutter, 1972) his idea that children form working mental models of their attachment relationships has been influential. Brown and Harris (1978) found that losing a parent before the age of 11 made women vulnerable to depression when faced with a severe adversity in adulthood. One can hypothesize that the model of self-with-other of such people includes a tendency toward hopelessness because of the impossibility of restoring a loved one lost early in life.

Ainsworth et al. (1978) constructed a test of putting infants in an unfamiliar room and having their mothers leave briefly and then return. On the basis of this *strange situation* test, they described three styles of attachment. The first is secure attachment, characterized by distress at separation but with the infant allowing himself or herself to be comforted when the mother returns. Then there are two kinds of insecure attachment: In one, the child avoids the mother when she returns, and in the other the child is angry.

Main (1991) has developed the adult attachment interview, in which people are asked to recall aspects of their own attachment relationships in infancy. Mothers whose children show secure attachment in the strange situation tend to give coherent accounts of their own attachment history; they construct a single mental model and the implication is that they had a single coherent model of their own attachment. In contrast, mothers of insecure children give incoherent accounts of their own attachment history. In another kind of study of the effects of early models on later life, Hazan and Shaver (1987) showed that the style of relating to a love partner in adulthood is predicted by the style of attachment that people remembered in their own childhood. As well as being based on emotions, models of our earliest intimate relationships also carry scriptlike instructions about interacting with any other person who will be the object of love.

The contribution of our theory to this kind of work is in the argument that where emotions have an object this object is mediated by a model. The relation of infant models to those inferred to be operating in parenting, and in adult sexual relationships, indicates both the persistence through time of such internal models for love relationships and the way in which they can be detached from one love object and attached to another.

Predictions for Psychopathology

Although the idea of internal working models, as operationalized in styles of attachment derived from the strange situation test, is currently a popular object of research, children make other kinds of models. For instance, Jenkins, Franco, Dolins, and Sewell (in press) showed that children exposed to an enacted scenario in which two adults spoke to each other in angry voices form a representation of this interaction. When the same people return and speak in nonangry voices the children are again fearful and interrupt their play. The implication is that children form models of the interactions between people that need not include themselves. One of the strong predictors of childhood psychiatric disorder is having parents in a very conflictual marriage. Jenkins and Smith (1991) showed that the active factor is the frequency of the parents' angry quarrels. Their children form models of this kind of interaction, and a history of being exposed to frequent interpersonal anger between parents is a better predictor of childhood psychopathology than are any measures derived from the strange situation test. Moreover, as Dodge, Bates, and Pettit (1990) showed, patterns of aggressive interaction learned at home are compiled into scripts for dealing with problematic situations and become the basis of angry, defiant behavior, which often then develops into delinquency. According to Jenkins and Oatley (1995), children with a emotional disorder of the oppositional/defiant kind have formed a model, an emotion schema, to which very many kinds of event are assimilated; all of them give rise to anger with its accompanying interpersonal consequences. Children with more normal emotion schemata evaluate some events as frustrations, others as losses, and others as dangers, and hence interact with other people across the whole emotional range.

A second implication of our theory of predictions for psychopathology concerns the relations of emotions to adult emotional disorders. Emotions are clearly part of emotional disorders, but it is not fully understood how. It is an empirical question as to how incidents of emotion are affected during a psychiatric syndrome. At least five different variables may be affected: the intensity, duration, and frequency of episodes of emotion, whether the emotions are comprehensible to the sufferer, and the extent to which they bring to mind previous episodes of the same kind. We believe that emotional disorders are not just prolonged moods. They have other attributes, but like normal emotions the majority of emotional breakdowns occur because some event has happened with a clear relation to the person's goals. Thus Brown and Harris (1978) showed that 89% of depressive breakdowns (by far the most common kind of psychiatric syndrome) occurred in response to a severe life event (such as a marital separation, a bereavement, loss of employment) or a chronic difficulty. Oatley and Bolton (1985) proposed that such events and difficulties could be understood in terms of the loss of an important role, without alternative ways of experiencing oneself as worthwhile (cf. Straubman, chap. 8, this volume). Oatley (1988) proposed the schema of Fig. 15.2 to explain the relation

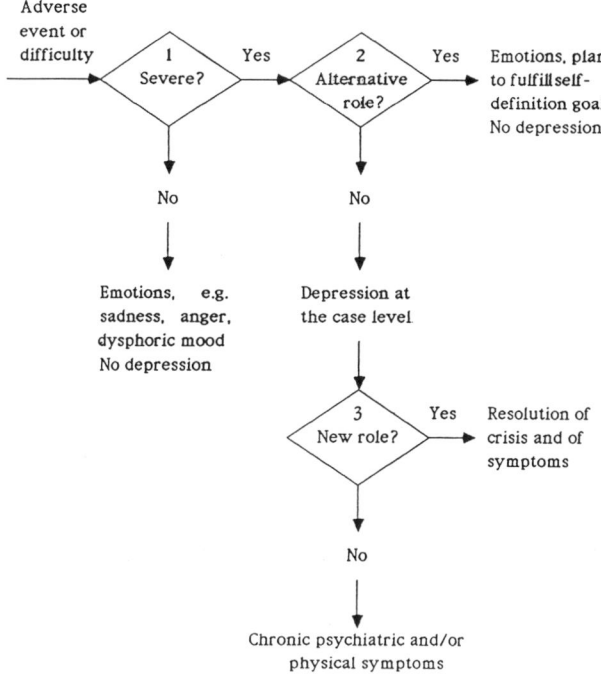

Fig. 15.2 Schematic diagram to show how an event can cause emotions, or an emotional breakdown, depending on its severity and on whether it damages or removes a role that is central to a person's life. If it does remove such a role, clinical depression results if the person has no current alternative role that allows him or her to maintain a sense of self (Oatley, 1988).

between emotions and emotional disorders. Not just emotions but most emotional disorders occur in relation to goals in people's life projects (see Emmons & Kaiser, chap. 4, this volume). Oatley and Perring (1991) showed that recovery from a psychiatric breakdown is affected by how well new plans are going.

A third kind of relation of emotions to psychopathology is the idea that dysphoric moods of depression and anxiety states are based on emotion modes of the kind postulated in the communicative theory. If in depression a mode of sadness is set up, it changes cognitive processing biases. One effect is to bring to mind memories of previous losses and failures. These in turn tend to prolong the sad mood. Similarly, when an anxious mood is set up, this directs attention to danger. The consequence of a monopolized attention to danger and its consequences can completely drain people of self-confidence: since dangers can lurk anywhere and thoughts about them make one feel yet more anxious. So here again is a self-sustaining cycle, which may contribute to chronic anxiety states. The hypothesis that these states are based on emotion modes that have identifiable cognitive properties is a distinct alternative to the hypothesis of Bower (1981). According to Bower, emotions can be nodes in semantic networks. An emotion can then act as a retrieval cue: thus if I was happy on a holiday by a lake then activation of the happiness node can cue recall of this holiday as well as the word *lake*. But this hypothesis, which predicts emotion-state dependent learning, has not fared well empirically (Bower, 1987). Our hypothesis — that an emotion mode sets up processing and attentional biases as well as access to memories of previous events in which the same emotion has occurred — gives an easier explanation of mood-congruent recall. Our hypothesis (of modes rather than nodes) is preferred by some researchers in experimental psychopathology (Mathews, 1993; Power, 1990).

A fourth issue related to psychopathology is whether our theory of emotions might help to understand the processes of psychotherapy. Emotions are the central issue in most systems of psychotherapy, and it is surprising that their role has not been more prominent in writings on the subject. This discrepancy is being remedied (Greenberg & Safran, 1989; Singer & Salovey, 1993). Although one of us has written about the implication of our theory for psychotherapy (Oatley, 1992), a much more extensive development would be possible. Let us briefly indicate just two directions.

First, people in psychotherapy often say there are things they do not understand about their emotions. Oatley and Duncan (1992) found that 27% of incidents of emotion recorded by psychiatric patients had something about them that the patient said he or she could not understand. By contrast only 5% of incidents recorded by patients with an organic disorder of the gut had anything about them they could not understand. The possibility of strong and even disabling emotional states detached from information about what caused them, or what they mean, derives directly from our theory, and such feelings are indeed the frequent object of psychotherapy.

Second, if emotions deriving from intimate relationships have objects mediated by mental models, then again there flows from our theory a conception of how such models can be incomplete, fragmented, contradictory, or even downright false (Power & Champion, 1986), when projected onto spouses, lovers, and children. We believe that our revised theory may be a useful means to think about such issues.

Real Emotions in Unreal Circumstances

One surprising feature of human life is that people value emotions so much that they read novels, watch television, go to the theater, listen to music, and take part in hobbies and sports, all in an effort to experience emotions. Why do people enjoy vicarious emotions? Why should anyone pay money to view the final scene of Hamlet and feel profound sadness, yet know that the scene is a fiction played by professional actors? The reality of situations eliciting emotions in waking life varies considerably: Oatley and Duncan (1992) found that 20% of emotion incidents were caused not by immediate events but by events at one remove (e.g., by something seen on television, something read in a book, something remembered, or something imagined).

Music may move listeners profoundly, yet it has no significance beyond itself. It is wholly unreal. In the movies the situation is typically unreal; as spectators we can feel angry about an injustice and identify with the protagonist who acts with ferocity to put it right, although the incidents are fictional. In sports the situation is perhaps a little more real. As spectators we are happy when our team is succeeding, anxious when it is at risk of failing, angered by opponents who cheat, appalled by injuries, and depressed when our team finally loses. But we know it is just a game. Some leisure activities depend on situations that are wholly real: In mountaineering you really may be killed, and in a casino you may lose your money, but their fascination rests in part on the strong emotional arousal they produce (Anderson & Brown, 1984).

So it seems that most of the people, most of the time, like to experience emotions, and not just positive ones. Experiencing emotions becomes a goal in itself. Why? The communicative theory provides the beginning of an answer: provided that readers', spectators', or participants' mental models yield evaluations on which emotions are based, they will experience the corresponding emotions. Oatley (1994) proposed a taxonomy and a theory of emotional response to narrative literature and the theater, concentrating on emotions of identification. But material that can elicit emotions can be content-free, for instance, music, dance, and abstract pictures. It seems possible that relatively abstract—though possibly simple—aspects of an event, perhaps of a relation between shapes in a painting or tones in a melody, can elicit an emotion, and then of course we find the object that elicited the emotion *moving*. It seems that it is not so much that positive emotions are pleasant and negative ones unpleasant but that people like being in an emotional state, perhaps because of the single-mindedness and sense of conviction it affords.

The limbic system is an evolutionarily ancient part of the brain, and according to LeDoux (1993) the amygdala, which is part of this region, is the mechanism in which the evaluations occur that create emotions. It seems that the epistemic status of the events that it evaluates—whether or not they are real—is of less importance than one might think. It is as though only a minimal cognitive effort is needed to generate an emotion. Whether there

Emotions and Intellect

If emotions are so central to mental life, then what are their effects on thinking of the kind that is deliberative or involves problem solving? There is already a substantial body of work on effects of mood on various aspects of problem solving (e.g., Isen, Daubman, & Nowicki, 1987) and on social judgments (Forgas, 1992). Other contributors to this volume (e.g., Hirt, McDonald, & Melton; Martin & Stoner; Wegener & Petty) review this work.

There is another extensive body of work that overlaps slightly with this one, based on the characteristics and nature of human reasoning (Johnson-Laird, 1993). In this, it has been found that beliefs bias reasoning in a way that is relevant to understanding emotions. In a study of conclusions that reasoners drew when given syllogisms (Oakhill, Johnson-Laird, & Garnham, 1989), the majority of subjects (72%) who were given the set of premises

> All the Frenchmen are gourmets.
>
> Some of the gourmets are wine-drinkers.

drew the conclusion:

> Some of the Frenchmen are wine-drinkers.

But given the following set of premises,

> All the Frenchmen are gourmets.
>
> Some of the gourmets are Italians.

only a few subjects (8%) drew the logically equivalent conclusion

> Some of the Frenchmen are Italians.

This pattern of results is predicted by the theory that reasoning is based on mental models of the premises. In the first case, the subjects construct an initial model of the premises

15. COMMUNICATIVE THEORY OF EMOTIONS   387

[Frenchman]	gourmet	wine-drinker
[Frenchman]	gourmet	wine-drinker
...		

where each line represents a separate sort of individual, the three dots allow that there may be other sorts of individual or entity in the domain of discourse, and the square brackets indicate that the set of Frenchmen has been exhaustively represented, that is, no member of the set can be found among other individuals in the domain of discourse. From this model the conclusion can be drawn: "Some of the Frenchmen are wine-drinkers," which is highly plausible—a fact that the experimenters had established from the ratings of a separate panel of subjects from the same population.

In the second case, the equivalent model

[Frenchman]	gourmet	Italian
[Frenchman]	gourmet	Italian
...		

yields the conclusion: "Some of the Frenchmen are Italians," which, as the independent ratings showed, is highly unbelievable. Subjects in this condition were accordingly more motivated to search for an alternative model of the premises. Such a model could take the form

[Frenchman]	gourmet	
[Frenchman]	gourmet	
	gourmet	Italian
	gourmet	Italian
...		

The two models together establish that there is no valid conclusion relating Frenchmen to Italians. The initial conclusion is invalid in both inferences, plausible only in the first.

In summary, reasoners tend to accept as valid the conclusions that they find congenial. Putting the matter in the terms of Martin and Stoner (chap. 12, this volume) when reasoners reach a conclusion they like—a goal—they apply their stop rule. They only continue to search for alternative mental models if they dislike the conclusion. This pattern of performance is common in daily life. People "satisfice"; they tend to consider only their initial models of situations and stop there. Unless their initial models yield unacceptable conclusions, they tend to overlook alternative possibilities.

The effect of emotions on other aspects of intellectual performance is likely to be comparable. When people feel strongly about some matter, particularly if its refutation is damaging to their self-model and might cause regret or loss of self-esteem, they can hold to their model, despite mere facts. There are many examples. In a study of 20 widows of men killed in traffic accidents in Tokyo (Yanomoto, Okonogi, Iwasaki, & Yoshimura, 1969), 6 weeks after the accidents 12 of the widows had difficulty believing that their husbands were dead and carried out actions predicated on their being alive. In a yet more striking example, the team of electrical engineers who were testing new safety equipment at Chernobyl and the operating staff of the reactor persisted in carrying out their experiments even when it was easy to infer that these experiments were impossible to complete. The result was the death of many people and the release of a quantity of radiation many times greater than released by the Hiroshima bomb. The engineers and plant operators were not prepared to admit a model of failure (Reason, 1987). Things got worse: Even after the explosion of the reactor, the electrical engineers refused to believe it had been destroyed. There was much evidence to the contrary, including the reports of two young engineers whom they had sent to examine it and who paid with their lives for their observations. Both the electrical engineers and the staff of the power plant had mental models of the plant and of the situation that allowed them to maintain their view of themselves as competent persons. They were not prepared to admit alternative models.

The purpose of emotion, according to the communicative theory, is to prepare body and mind for an course of action appropriate to a general class of goals. It is an effective way to mobilize actions. It has immediate causal consequences on body and behavior, whereas deliberative thinking is a costly and relatively slow way to develop plans to deal with the exigencies of life. In conflicts between emotion and reasoning, there is no simple way to determine which to choose. Often, however, where reasoning suggests one course of action people may find themselves under the control of emotions and may do something quite different. Thought may say "stay," fear makes one run.

We do not suggest that emotions are irrational in contrast to thinking which is rational. There is ample evidence that people make mistakes in thinking when no emotions are involved. Our position is that emotions function to induce certain kinds of readiness, to change brain organization, to prompt certain kinds of conclusion when there is no fully rational solution to a problem that has arisen. As Dyer (1987) put it, emotions are locally rational, they prompt conclusions relevant to a small set of goals and organize the brain to meet just one kind of contingency. Sometimes thinking, or consultation with others whose goals are not affected in the same way, might provide answers that widen the scope of rational choice. But sometimes it is maybe best to rely directly on an emotion: in our society falling in love is generally thought to be the reason to commit oneself to someone whom one does not know, to face a lifetime of unforeseeable events with that person. Maybe, in Western society there is no better heuristic; certainly there is no algorithm for correct choice.

ACKNOWLEDGMENTS

Preparation of this chapter was supported in part by a grant to Keith Oatley from the Social Science and Humanities Research Council of Canada and by a grant to Philip Johnson-Laird from the John S. McDonnell Foundation. We are most grateful to the editors of this volume (Lenny Martin and Abe Tesser) and to Laurette Larocque and Ilaria Grazanni for helpful comments on a draft of this chapter.

REFERENCES

Ainsworth, M. D. S., Blehar, M. C., Walters, E., & Wall, S. (1978). *Patterns of attachment: A psychological study of the strange situation.* Hillsdale, NJ: Erlbaum.

Anderson, G., & Brown, R. I. D. (1984). Real and laboratory gambling. *British Journal of Psychology, 75,* 401–410.

Bauer, M. I., & Johnson-Laird, P. N. (1993). How diagrams can improve reasoning. *Psychological Science, 4,* 372–378.

Bendix, E. H. (1966). *Componential analysis of general vocabulary: The semantic structure of a set of verbs in English, Hindi, and Japanese.* The Hague: Mouton.

Biason, A. (1993). *Emotional responses of high-school students to short stories.* Unpublished doctoral dissertation, University of Toronto.

Bower, G. H. (1981). Mood and memory. *American Psychologist, 36,* 129–148.

Bower, G. H. (1987). Commentary on mood and memory. *Behavior Research and Therapy, 25,* 443–455.

Bowlby, J. (1971). *Attachment and loss: Vol. 1. Attachment.* London: Hogarth Press (reprinted by Penguin, 1978).

Bowlby, J. (1973). *Attachment and loss: Vol. 2. Separation: Anxiety and anger.* London: Hogarth Press (reprinted by Penguin, 1978).

Bradwejn, J. (1993). Neurobiological investigations into the role of cholecystokinin in panic disorder. *Journal of Psychiatry and Neuroscience, 18,* 178–188.

Bretherton, I. (1985). Attachment theory: Retrospect and prospect. In I. Bretherton & E. Waters (Eds.), *Growing points in attachment: Theory and research. Monographs of the Society for Research in Child Development, 50* (1–2, serial No. 209).

Brown, G. W., & Harris, T. O. (1978). *Social origins of depression: A study of psychiatric disorder in women.* London: Tavistock.

Carver, C. S., & Scheier, M. F. (1990). Origins and functions of positive and negative affect: A control process view. *Psychological Review, 97,* 19–35.

Chaiken, S., Lieberman, A., & Eagly, A. H. (1989). Heuristic and systematic information processing within and beyond the persuasion context. In J. S. Uleman & J. A. Bargh (Eds.), *Unintended thought: Limits of awareness, intention and control* (pp. 212-252). New York: Guilford.

Chwelos, G. (1992). *Emotion elicitation models: A comparative study.* Unpublished master's thesis, University of Toronto.

Chwelos, G., & Oatley, K. (1994). Appraisal, computational models, and Scherer's expert system. *Cognition and Emotion, 8,* 245-257.

Clore, G. L., & Parrott, W. G. (1991). Moods and the vicissitudes: Thoughts and feelings as information. In J. P. Forgas (Ed.), *Emotion and social judgements* (pp. 107-123). Oxford: Pergamon.

Conway, M. A., & Bekerian, D. A. (1987). Situational knowledge and emotions. *Cognition and Emotion, 1,* 145-191.

Craik, K. J. W. (1943). *The nature of explanation.* Cambridge: Cambridge University Press.

Csikszentmihalyi, M. (1990). *Flow: The psychology of optimal experience.* New York: HarperCollins.

Darwin, C. (1872). *The expression of the emotions in man and the animals.* Chicago: University of Chicago Press. (Reprinted 1965).

Dodge, K. A., Bates, J. E., & Pettit, G. S. (1990). Mechanisms in the cycle of violence. *Science, 250,* 1678-1683.

Dollard, J., & Miller, N. E. (1950). *Personality and psychotherapy.* New York: McGraw-Hill.

Dyer, M. G. (1987). Emotions and their computations: Three computer models. *Cognition and Emotion, 1,* 323-347.

Ekman, P. (1989). The argument and evidence about universals in facial expressions of emotion. In H. Wagner & A. Manstead (Eds.), *Handbook of social psychophysiology* (pp. 143-164). Chichester: Wiley.

Ekman, P. (1992). An argument for basic emotions. *Cognition and Emotion, 6,* 169-200.

Ekman, P., & Friesen, W. V. (1986). A new pan-cultural facial expression of emotion. *Motivation and Emotion, 10,* 159-168.

Ekman, P., & O'Sullivan, M. (1991). Who can catch a liar? *American Psychologist, 46,* 913-920.

Ellsworth, P. (1991). Some implications of cognitive appraisal theories of emotion. In K. T. Strongman (Ed.), *International Review of Studies on Emotion* (pp. 143-161). Chichester: Wiley.

Fairbairn, W. R. D. (1952). *Psychoanalytic studies of the personality.* London: Routledge & Kegan Paul.

Forgas, J. P. (1992). Affect in social judgement and decisions: A multi process model. In M. Zanna (Ed.), *Advances in experimental social psychology.* New York: Academic Press.

Frijda, N. H. (1986). *The emotions.* Cambridge: Cambridge University Press.

Goodall, J. (1986). *The chimpanzees of Gombe: Patterns of behavior.* Cambridge, MA: Harvard University Press.

Greenberg, L. S., & Safran, J. D. (1989). Emotion in psychotherapy. *American Psychologist, 44,* 19-29.

Halford, G. S. (1993). *Children's understanding: The development of mental models.* Hillsdale, NJ: Lawrence Erlbaum Associates.

Harris, P. L. (1989). *Children and emotion: The development of psychological understanding.* Oxford: Blackwell.

Hazan, C., & Shaver, P. (1987). Romantic love conceptualized as an attachment process. *Journal of Personality and Social Psychology, 52,* 511-524.

Isen, A. M., Daubman, K. A., & Nowicki, G. P. (1987). Positive affect facilitates creative problem solving. *Journal of Personality and Social Psychology, 52,* 1122-1131.

Jenkins, J. M., Franco, F., Dolins, F., & Sewell, A. (in press). Toddlers' reactions to negative

emotion displays. *Infant Behavior and Development.*
Jenkins, J. M., & Oatley, K. (1995). The development of emotion schemas in children: the processes underlying psychopathology. In W. Flack & J. Laird (Eds.), *Emotions and psychopathology.* New York: Oxford University Press.
Jenkins, J. M., & Smith, M. A. (1991). Marital disharmony and children's behaviour problems: Aspects of a poor marriage which affect children adversely. *Journal of Child Psychology and Psychiatry, 32,* 793-810.
Johnson-Laird, P. N. (1983). *Mental models: Towards a cognitive science of language, inference, and consciousness.* Cambridge: Cambridge University Press.
Johnson-Laird, P. N. (1993). *Human and machine thinking.* Hillsdale, NJ: Lawrence Erlbaum Associates.
Johnson-Laird, P. N., Byrne, R. M. J., & Schaeken, W. (1992). Propositional reasoning by model. *Psychological Review, 99,* 418-439.
Johnson-Laird, P. N., & Oatley, K. (1988). Il significato delle emozioni: una teoria e un' analisi semantica. In V. D'Urso & R. Trentin (Eds.), *Psicologia delle emozioni* (pp. 119-158). Bologna: Il Mulino.
Johnson-Laird, P. N., & Oatley, K. (1989). The language of emotions: An analysis of a semantic field. *Cognition and Emotion, 3,* 81-123.
Johnson-Laird, P. N., & Oatley, K. (1992). Basic emotions, rationality, and folk theory. *Cognition and Emotion, 6,* 201-223.
Jones, G. V., & Martin, M. (1992). Conjunction in the language of emotions. *Cognition and Emotion, 6,* 369-386.
Lazarus, R. S. (1991). *Emotion and adaptation.* New York: Oxford University Press.
LeDoux, J. E. (1993). Emotional networks in the brain. In M. Lewis & J. M. Haviland (Eds.), *Handbook of emotions* (pp. 109-118). New York: Guilford.
LeDoux, J., Ciccetti, P., Xagoraris, A., & Romanski, L. R. (1990). The lateral amygdaloid nucleus: Sensory interface pf the amgydala in fear conditioning. *Journal of Neuroscience, 10,* 1062-1069.
Lorenz, K. Z. (1967). *On aggression.* (M. Latzke, Trans.). London: Methuen.
MacLean, P. D. (1993). Cerebral evolution of emotion. In M. Lewis & J. M. Haviland (Eds.), *Handbook of emotions* (pp. 67-83). New York: Guilford.
Main, M. (1991). Metacognitive knowledge, metacognitive monitoring, and singular (coherent) vs. multiple (incoherent) models of attachment: Findings and directions for future research. In C. Parkes, J. Stevenson-Hinde, & P. Marris (Eds.), *Attachment across the life cycle* (pp. 127-159). New York: Routledge.
Marr, D. (1982). *Vision.* San Francisco: W. H. Freeman.
Martin, L. L., Ward, D. W., Achee, J. W., & Wyer, R. S. (1993). Mood as input: People have to interpret the motivational implications of their moods. *Journal of Personality and Social Psychology, 64,* 317-326.
Mathews, A. (1993). Biases in emotional processing. *The Psychologist: Bulletin of the British Psychological Society, 6,* 493-499.
Nisbett, R., & Ross, L. (1980). *Human inference: Strategies and shortcomings of of social judgement.* Englewood Cliffs, NJ: Prentice-Hall.
Oakhill, J. V., Johnson-Laird, P. N., & Garnham, A. (1989). Believability and syllogistic reasoning. *Cognition, 31,* 117-140.
Oatley, K. (1988). Life events, social cognition and depression. In S. Fisher & J. Reason (Eds.), *Handbook of life stress, cognition and health* (pp. 543-557). Chichester: Wiley.
Oatley, K. (1992). *Best laid schemes: The psychology of emotions.* New York: Cambridge University Press.
Oatley, K. (1994). A taxonomy of the emotions of literary response and a theory of identification in fictional narrative. *Poetics, 23,* 53-74.
Oatley, K., & Bolton, W. (1985). A social-cognitive theory of depression in reaction to life

events. *Psychological Review, 92,* 372-388.

Oatley, K., & Duncan, E. (1992). Incidents of emotion in daily life. In K. T. Strongman (Ed.), *International Review of Studies on Emotion* (pp. 250-293). Chichester: Wiley.

Oatley, K., & Duncan, E. (1994). The experience of emotions in everyday life. *Cognition and Emotion, 8,* 369-381.

Oatley, K., & Johnson-Laird, P. N. (1987). Towards a cognitive theory of emotions. *Cognition and Emotion, 1,* 29-50.

Oatley, K., & Johnson-Laird, P. N. (1992). Terms of emotion: The inferences that can be drawn. *Revista de Psicologia Social, 7,* 97-104.

Oatley, K., & Perring, C. (1991). A longitudinal study of psychological and social factors affecting recovery from psychiatric breakdown. *British Journal of Psychiatry, 158,* 28-32.

Oatley, K., Sullivan, G. D., & Hogg, D. (1988). Drawing visual conclusions from analogy: A theory of preprocessing, cues and schemata in the perception of three dimensional objects. *Journal of Intelligent Systems, 1,* 97-133.

Ortony, A., Clore, G. L., & Collins, A. (1988). *The cognitive structure of emotions.* New York: Cambridge University Press.

Ortony, A., & Turner, T. J. (1990). What's basic about basic emotions? *Psychological Review, 97,* 431-461.

Panksepp, J. (1993). Neurochemical control of moods and emotions: Amino acids to neuropeptides. In M. Lewis & J. M. Haviland (Eds.), *Handbook of emotions* (pp. 87-107). New York: Guilford.

Power, M. J. (1990). A prime time for emotion: Cognitive vulnerability and the emotional disorders. In K. J. Gilhooly, M. T. G. Keene, R. H. Logie, & G. Erdos (Eds.), *Lines of thinking: Reflections on the psychology of thought: Vol. 2. Skills, emotion, creative processes, individual differences and teaching thinking* (pp. 157-165). Chichester: Wiley.

Power, M. J., & Champion, L. A. (1986). Cognitive approaches to depression: A theoretical critique. *British Journal of Clinical Psychology, 25,* 201-212.

Reason, J. (1987). The Chernobyl errors. *Bulletin of the British Psychological Society, 40,* 201-206.

Reisenzein, R. (1992). Stumpf's cognitive-evaluative theory of emotion. *American Psychologist, 47,* 34-45.

Reisenzein, R. (1995). On Oatley and Johnson-Laird's theory of emotions and hierarchical structures. *Cognition and Emotion, 9,* 383-416.

Roseman, I. J. (1991). Appraisal determinants of discrete emotions. *Cognition and Emotion, 5,* 161-200.

Rozin, P., Haidt, J., & McCauley, C. R. (1993). Disgust. In M. Lewis & J. M. Haviland (Eds.), *Handbook of emotions* (pp. 575-594). New York: Guilford.

Russell, J. A. (1991). In defense of a prototype approach to emotion concepts. *Journal of Personality and Social Psychology, 60,* 37-47.

Rutter, M. (1972). *Maternal deprivation reassessed.* Harmondsworth: Penguin.

Scherer, K. R. (1988). Criteria for emotion antecedent appraisal: A review. In V. Hamilton, G. H. Bower, & N. H. Frijda (Eds.), *Cognitive perspectives on emotion and motivation* (pp. 89-126). Kluwer: Dordrecht.

Scherer, K. R. (1993). Studying the emotion-antecedent appraisal process: An expert system approach. *Cognition and Emotion, 7,* 325-355.

Schiff, B. B., & Lamon, M. (1989). Inducing emotion by unilateral contraction of facial muscles: A new look at hemispheric specialization and the experience of emotion. *Neuropsychologia, 27,* 923-935.

Shafir, E., & Tversky, A. (1992). Thinking through uncertainty: Nonconsequential reasoning and choice. *Cognitive Psychology, 24,* 449-474.

Shaver, P., Hazan, C., & Bradshaw, D. (1988). Love as attachment: The integration of three behavioral systems. In R. J. Sternberg & M. L. Barnes (Eds.), *The psychology of love* (pp.

68-99). New Haven, CT: Yale University Press.

Simon, H. A. (1967). Motivational and emotional controls of cognition. *Psychological Review, 74*, 29-39.

Singer, J. A., & Salovey, P. (1993). *The remembered self: Emotion and memory in personality*. New York: Free Press.

Smith, C. A., Haynes, K. N., Lazarus, R. S., & Pope, L. K. (1993). In search of "hot" cognitions: Attributions, appraisals and their relation to emotion. *Journal of Personality and Social Psychology, 65*, 916-929.

Stein, N. L., Trabasso, T., & Liwag, M. (1993). The representation and organization of emotional experience: unfolding the emotion episode. In M. Lewis & J. M. Haviland (Eds.), *Handbook of emotions* (pp. 279-300). New York: Guilford.

Stern, D. (1985). *The interpersonal world of the infant*. New York: Basic Books.

Strack, F., Martin, L. L., & Stepper, S. (1988). Inhibiting and facilitating conditions of the human smile: A nonobtrusive test of the facial feedback hypothesis. *Journal of Personality and Social Psychology, 54*, 768-777.

Stringer, C., & Gamble, C. (1993). *In search of the Neanderthals*. New York: Thames and Hudson.

Tesser, A., & Cornell, D. P. (1991). On the confluence of self processes. *Journal of Experimental Social Psychology, 27*, 501-526.

Tooby, J., & Cosmides, L. (1990). The past explains the present: Emotional adaptations and the structure of ancestral environments. *Ethology and Sociobiology, 11*, 375-424.

Wiener, B., & Graham, S. (1989). Understanding the motivational role of affect: Lifespan research from an attributional perspective. *Cognition and Emotion, 3*, 401-419.

Wilson, T. D., Laser, P. S., & Stone, J. I. (1982). Judging the predictors of one's own mood: Accuracy and the use of shared theories. *Journal of Experimental Social Psychology, 18*, 537-556.

Yanomoto, J., Okonogi, K., Iwasaki, T., & Yoshimura, S. (1969). Mourning in Japan. *American Journal of Psychiatry, 125*, 1660-1665.

Author Index

A

Abelson, R. P., 24, 25, 34, 35, 49, 50, 58, 61, 76, 281, 300
Abend, T., 293, 300
Abrahams, S., 317, 326
Abramson, L. Y., 160, 164, 171, 172, 176, 197
Achee, J. W., 37, 50, 223, 226, 279, 284, 286, 288, 292, 295, 300, 310, 311, 314, 315, 316, 317, 318, 319, 323, 325, 327, 346, 360, 366, 391
Adams, J. A., 13, 48
Ahrens, A. H., 71, 75
Ainsworth, M. D. S., 381, 389
Ajzen, I., 335, 358, 359
Akiskal, H. S., 176, 180, 195, 197, 201
Alexander, I. E., 236, 248
Allen, J., 234, 249
Allman, A., 58, 75
Alloy, L. B., 164, 171, 176, 197
Allport, G. W., 1, 7, 253, 272
Amabile, D., 290, 299
Ames, C., 203, 223
Anderson, G., 385, 389
Anderson, J. R., 144, 147
Anderson, R. C., 284, 299
Andrews, F. M., 63, 74
APA Work Group on Major Depressive Disorder, 175, 201

Apaniesk, A. M., 352, 358
Ashbrook, P. W., 348, 359
Asher, S. R., 209, 221, 224
Asuncion, A. G., 283, 300, 309, 311, 327, 329, 340, 343, 360
Atkinson, J. W., 204, 207, 214, 224, 226
Averill, J. A., 41, 48, 279, 299

B

Baddeley, A., 144, 147
Baker, S. M., 330, 331, 333, 334, 336, 337, 339, 351, 352, 358, 359, 361
Ballenger, J. C., 195, 200
Bandura, A., 100, 102, 103, 104, 106, 107, 108, 118, 203, 204, 205, 207, 214, 224, 241, 247
Barbee, A. P., 324, 326
Bargh, J. A., 92, 96, 144, 148, 152, 171, 173, 178, 179, 198
Baron, P., 106, 118
Baron, R. A., 68, 74
Baron, R. M., 115, 118
Barron, F., 127, 147
Barta, S. G., 60, 76
Bassett, G. A., 100, 118
Bates, J. E., 182, 197, 382, 390
Batra, R., 305, 326, 333, 358
Bauer, M. I., 376, 389
Baumann, D. J., 324, 326, 345, 359

Baumeister, R. F., 81, 91, 93, 96, 204, 224
Baumgardner, A. H., 259, 273
Beck, A. T., 69, 70, 75, 155, 160, 164, 171, 173, 188, 195, 197, 199
Bekerian, D. A., 372, 390
Bendix, E. H., 372, 389
Berg, C. A., 203, 209, 222, 224, 227
Berkowitz, L., 127, 128, 129, 147, 148, 280, 292, 299
Berscheid, E., 60, 75
Biason, A., 369, 389
Bibring, E., 185, 197
Bieri, J., 127, 129, 147
Billington, M. J., 100, 102, 120
Blaney, P. H., 36, 48, 229, 248, 252, 272
Blatt, S. J., 175, 189, 197, 200
Blehar, M. C., 381, 389
Bless, H., 69, 77, 287, 299, 301, 305, 306, 308, 309, 310, 311, 326, 328, 329, 340, 342, 343, 346, 352, 357, 358, 361, 381
Bodenhausen, G. V., 305, 326
Bohner, G., 287, 299, 305, 308, 311, 326, 328, 329, 340, 342, 343, 346, 352, 357, 358, 361
Bollenbach, A. K., 229, 249
Bolles, R. N., 144, 147
Bolton, W., 382, 391
Bond, R. N., 42, 49, 192, 198
Bower, G. H., 151, 171, 229, 231, 248, 280, 299, 306, 310, 315, 326, 327, 329, 334, 342, 358, 384, 389
Bowlby, J., 376, 381, 389
Bradshaw, D., 374, 375, 392
Bradwejn, J., 373, 389
Bransford, J. D., 284, 299
Braverman, D. L., 36, 50, 335, 360
Breckler, S. J., 334, 357, 358
Brehm, J. W., 37, 52
Bretherton, I., 376, 389
Brewin, C. R., 186, 193, 199
Brickman, P., 63, 75
Broadbent, D. E., 14, 48
Broadbent, K., 243, 250
Brock, T. C., 340, 352, 354, 360, 361
Brower, A. M., 54, 75, 204, 224
Brown, G. W., 42, 49, 185, 197, 381, 382, 389
Brown, J. D., 16, 52, 162, 171
Brown, R. I. D., 385, 389
Brown, J. D., 16, 52, 162, 171
Bruhn, A. R., 231, 248
Bryan, J. F., 100, 102, 119, 214, 226

Bryant, F. B., 254, 262, 272
Bunney, W. E., 195, 200
Burke, P. J., 140, 147
Butler, R., 203, 224
Byrne, R. M. J., 376, 391
Byrnes, J. P., 218, 226

C

Cacioppo, J. T., 330, 331, 332, 333, 340, 352, 354, 355, 356, 358, 360, 361
Campbell, J. D., 152, 171
Campbell, W. K., 229, 249
Cantor, N., 13, 48, 54, 65, 75, 124-125, 129, 140, 147, 148, 149, 178, 199, 203, 204, 210, 221, 222, 224, 225, 230, 250, 304, 328,
Carlson, R., 236-237, 248
Carlson, L., 236, 248
Carlson, M., 345, 347, 358, 360
Carlson, M. A., 234, 249
Carlston, D. E., 129, 148, 178, 191, 199, 281, 301
Carter, S. R. III, 73, 77, 107, 120
Cartledge, N., 100, 107, 119
Carver, C. S., 11, 12, 16, 19, 20, 25, 27, 28, 31, 34, 36, 37, 38, 39, 44, 45, 46, 47, 48, 49, 50, 55, 57, 58, 60, 73, 75, 77, 80, 84, 85, 89, 96, 114, 118, 177, 191, 197, 204, 224, 242, 248, 257, 272, 281, 300, 365, 389
Case, D. E., 261, 273
Cervone, D., 103, 108, 118, 241, 247, 281, 300
Chaiken, S., 285, 300, 331, 334, 336, 354, 359, 360, 366, 390
Champion, L. A., 384, 392
Charlin, V., 345, 347, 358
Chassin, L., 124, 140, 147
Chattopadhyay, A., 334, 360
Chen, N., 69, 76
Chwelos, G., 369, 390
Cialdini, R. B., 257, 273, 324, 326, 345, 359, 361
Ciccetti, P., 373, 391
Clark, R. A., 214, 226
Clark, M. S., 229, 248, 252, 253, 263, 273, 306, 329, 327, 334, 342, 343, 359
Clark, L. A., 72, 77
Clore, G. L., 12, 34, 51, 79, 98, 237, 249, 252, 274, 281, 284, 300, 301, 308, 310,

314, 325, 328, 332, 361, 364, 370, 390, 392
Coates, D., 63, 75
Cohen, S., 193, 197
Cohen, J. D., 39, 49
Collins, A., 12, 34, 51, 79, 98, 237, 249, 281, 300, 370, 392
Colvin, C. R., 58, 75
Connell, J. P., 90, 98
Conway, M. A., 244, 248, 372, 390
Cook-Flanagan, 65, 75
Cooper, J., 60, 75
Cordova, D. I., 216, 226
Cornell, D. P., 376, 393
Corty, E., 124, 140, 147
Coryell, W., 176, 197
Cosmides, L., 373, 393
Costa, P. T., Jr., 221, 224
Courtney, D. P., 221, 226
Cox, S., 269, 274
Coyne, J. C., 70, 76
Craik, K. J. W., 376, 390
Crockett, W. H., 128, 149
Cross, S., 126, 149
Crowe, E., 207, 225
Csikszentmihalyi, M., 74, 75, 205, 208, 216, 224, 264, 273, 366, 390
Cunningham, M. R., 252, 273, 324, 326
Curtis, M. I., 103, 119
Daple, S. A., 234, 249
Darby, B., 345, 359
Darwin, C., 363, 378, 390
Daubman, K. A., 304, 313, 327, 386, 390
Davidson, R. J., 47, 49
Dawkins, R., 14, 49
de Mayo, R., 162, 172
de Sousa, R., 11, 49
Dean, A., 193, 199
DeAngelis, D. L., 19, 49
Deaux, K., 124, 147, 221, 224
DeCharms, R., 207, 224
Deci, E. L., 82, 90, 95, 96, 98, 207, 218, 224, 227
deMayo, R., 130, 147, 162
Dembo, T., 102, 119
DeMello, A., 61, 75
Demorest, A. P., 236, 248
Denney, N., 190, 200
Denny, A. T., 103, 119
Dent, J., 195, 201
Depue, R. A., 183, 197
Dermer, M., 129, 149

Derryberry, D., 177, 182, 183, 184, 198
Diener, E., 46, 50, 58, 59, 63, 75
Dimberg, U., 184, 198
Ditto, P. H., 352, 358
Dixon, T., 93, 96
Dodge, K. A., 184, 198, 209, 224, 382, 390
Dohrenwend, B. P., 70, 75
Dohrenwend, B. S., 70, 75
Dolins, F., 382, 390
Dollard, J., 378, 390
Donahue, E. M., 93, 96, 140, 147
Dorfman, D., 126, 148, 152, 172
Dossett, D. L., 102, 103, 113, 118, 119
Downey, G., 59, 75
Dritschel, B. H., 234, 243, 250
Dubbert, P. M., 108, 118
Duncan, E., 367, 369, 370, 371, 379, 384, 385, 392
Duncker, K., 304, 326
Duval, T. S., 61, 75
Duval, V. H., 61, 75
Dweck, C. S., 13, 24, 49, 82, 96, 178, 198, 203, 224
Dyer, M. G., 388, 390

E

Eagly, A. H., 285, 300, 366, 390
Earley, P. C., 205, 227
Easterbrook, J. A., 264, 273
Easterlin, R. A., 63, 75
Eaves, L. J., 175, 176, 182, 199
Ebbesen, E. E., 229, 249
Eccles, J., 207, 224
Eccles-Parsons, J., 222, 225
Edelman, R. E., 71, 75
Edwards, A. L., 237, 248
Ekman, P., 365, 372, 378, 390
Elkin, I., 195, 198
Elliot, A. J., 11, 203, 207, 213, 215, 217, 225
Elliott, E. S., 13, 24, 49
Elliott, R., 11, 49
Ellis, H. C., 244, 248, 348, 359
Ellsworth, P., 367, 370, 390
Emery, G., 164, 171, 195, 197
Emmons, R. A., 13, 18, 32, 49, 55, 56, 57, 60, 76, 79, 80, 82, 84, 86, 88, 89, 91, 92, 93, 94, 96, 97, 98, 124, 140, 147, 203, 204, 225, 233, 234, 240, 241, 248
Endicott, J., 176, 197
Engle, R. W., 332, 362

AUTHOR INDEX

Ensel, W., 193, 199
Epstein, J. A., 215, 225
Erbaugh, J., 155, 171
Erber, M. W., 267, 268, 273
Erber, R., 36, 49, 229, 230, 248, 250, 254, 255, 258, 259, 260, 261, 262, 264, 265, 266, 267, 268, 269, 270, 273, 274, 335
Erskine, B., 101, 119
Evans, T. W., 36, 50, 335, 360
Everitt, B. S., 154, 172
Eysenck, H. J., 72, 76
Eysenck, S. B. G., 72, 76

F

Fabrigar, L., 331, 361
Fairbairn, W. R. D., 376, 390
Fanting, E., 344, 360
Farah, M. J., 39, 49
Fazio, R. H., 60, 75
Fehr, B., 34, 49
Feren, D. B., 103, 119
Festinger, L., 102, 119
Finlay-Jones, R., 42, 49
Fischer, K. W., 188, 198
Fishbein, M., 335, 358, 359
Fiske, S. T., 144, 147
Fleeson, 65, 75
Fogarty, S. J., 229, 250
Follansbee, D. J., 36, 48
Ford, D. H., 19, 49
Ford, M. E., 82, 97
Fordyce, M. W., 68, 76
Forgas, J. P., 36, 49, 223, 225, 335, 359, 386, 390
Franco, F., 382, 390
Frazier, S., 273, 269
Fredrickson, B. L., 68, 77
Fremouw, W. J., 101, 120
Freud, S., 191, 198, 233, 248
Frey, K., 203, 227
Friedman, M. J., 186, 198
Friedman, S. L., 203, 227
Friesen, W. V., 378, 390
Frijda, N. H., 11, 22, 24, 33, 49, 79, 97, 281, 300, 308, 326, 372, 375, 390
Fuhrman, R. W., 67, 76, 129, 148

G

Gabbard, G. O., 180, 198
Galanter, E., 13, 51, 203, 226
Gallistel, C. R., 14, 49
Galton, F., 238, 248
Gamble, C., 378, 393
Ganellen, R. J., 39, 48
Garland, H., 100, 102, 103, 104, 107, 113, 118
Garnham, A., 386, 391
Gaschke, Y. N., 36, 50, 335, 360
Geen, R. B., 214, 225
Geen, R. G., 287, 300
Giannopoulus, C., 244, 248
Gilbert, D. T., 264, 273
Giuliano, T. A., 355, 357, 359
Gleicher, F., 330, 331, 333, 334, 336, 339, 359, 361
Goffman, E., 259, 273
Goldfried, M. R., 69, 75
Goldman, R., 354, 361
Goldsamt, L. A., 130, 150, 255, 275
Gollwitzer, P. M., 18, 52, 60, 62, 77, 92, 96, 97, 219, 226, 257, 273
Gomersall, T. E., 85, 97
Goodall, J., 375, 378, 390
Goodwin, F. K., 175, 200
Gordon, C., 125, 147
Gottman, J. M., 107, 108, 118
Graham, S., 372, 393
Gray, J. A., 86, 89, 97, 105, 118, 182, 198
Greenberg, J., 38, 39, 51, 60, 62, 77
Greenberg, L. R., 384, 390
Greenberg, L. S., 11, 49
Greenwald, A. G., 129, 147
Griffitt, W. B., 329, 331, 359
Gschneidinger, E., 274, 252, 280, 301

H

Haaga, D. A., 71, 75
Haidt, J., 375, 377, 392
Halal, M., 306, 327
Halberstadt, L. J., 164, 172
Halford, G. S., 377, 390
Hamilton, D. L., 304, 308, 328
Hammen, C., 130, 147, 162, 172
Hammond, L. J., 344, 359
Hanges, P. J., 30, 50
Hantas, M., 229, 249
Harackiewicz, J. M., 203, 206, 207, 209, 213, 215, 217, 225, 217, 225, 317, 324, 326
Harlow, T. F., 70, 76, 279, 284, 292, 300
Harpster, L., 218, 221, 222, 227

Harris, P. L., 379, 390
Harris, T. O., 185, 197, 381, 382, 389
Harter, S., 177, 186, 187, 198
Haugtvedt, C., 355, 361
Haynes, K. N., 231, 250, 372, 393
Hazan, C., 374, 375, 377, 381, 390, 392
Heady, B., 315, 326
Heath, A. C., 175, 176, 182, 199
Heatherton, T., 204, 224
Heckhausen, H., 86, 97, 214, 225, 257, 273
Helle, P., 39, 50
Herman, C. P., 101, 108, 118, 119, 257, 273
Herman, J. L., 231, 248
Hidi, S., 216, 226
Higgins, E. T., 13, 18, 32, 42, 45, 47, 49, 52, 105, 118, 124, 126, 130, 144, 148, 152, 172, 177, 178, 179, 183, 185, 186, 190, 191-192, 196, 198, 199, 200, 201, 203, 204, 207, 218, 222, 225, 227
Higgins, R. L., 16, 52
Hirschfeld, R. M. A., 175, 200
Hirt, E. R., 126, 150, 205, 226, 304, 312, 313, 315, 316, 317, 318, 324, 326, 328, 347, 360
Hoberman, H. M., 193, 199
Hochschild, A. R., 256, 273
Hogg, D., 375, 392
Holtzbauer, R., 107, 108, 119
Hom, H. L., 102, 118
Hood, J. E., 152, 172
Hovland, C., 336, 362
Hsee, C. K., 24, 25, 34, 35, 49, 50, 58, 61, 76, 230, 249, 281, 300
Hull, C. L., 264, 273
Hyland, M. E., 24, 38, 50, 84, 97
Hymes, C., 207, 225

I

Iacono, W. G., 183, 197
Isen, A. M., 229, 248, 253, 263, 273, 289, 296, 300, 304, 305, 306, 313, 326, 327, 329, 334, 342, 343, 345, 352, 359, 386, 390
Iwasaki, T., 388, 393
Izard, C. E., 34, 50, 163, 172

J

James, W., 125, 148
Janis, I., 329, 331, 359

Janoff-Bulman, R., 63, 75
Jenkins, J. M., 382, 390, 391
John, O. P., 28, 51, 93, 96, 140, 147
Johnson, E. J., 36, 50, 309, 315, 327, 335, 359
Johnson, J., 129, 150
Johnson, J., 126, 150
Johnson, M. K., 284, 299
Johnson, M. M. S., 289, 300, 304, 327
Johnson-Laird, P. N., 363, 365, 367, 368, 374, 375, 376, 386, 389, 391, 392
Jones, G. V., 371, 391
Jones, J. B., 69, 76
Jose, P. E., 237, 249
Josephson, B. R., 244, 248
Judd, C. M., 212, 225, 320, 327

K

Kagan, J., 184, 199
Kahneman, D., 105, 114, 115, 118
Kaiser, H., 86, 97
Kammann, R., 63, 76
Kanner, A. D., 70, 76
Kaplan, B., 93, 98, 187, 201
Karasu, T. B., 176, 199
Karoly, P., 79, 92, 97, 107, 108, 118
Karp, L., 306, 327, 329, 334, 342, 359
Kasmer, J., 331, 361
Kasser, T., 56, 76, 90, 95, 98
Katz, D., 129, 148
Kavanagh, D. J., 310, 315, 327
Kaye, D., 329, 331, 359
Kazdin, A. E., 107, 118
Keane, T. M., 185, 199
Keating, J. P., 305, 327, 337, 340, 346, 352, 360
Keehn, D., 188, 201
Kelley, D. J., 324, 326
Kelly, G. A., 38, 50, 127, 148
Kelso, J. A. S., 13, 50
Kendler, K. S., 175, 176, 182, 199
Kenny, D. A., 68, 74, 115, 118, 212, 225, 320, 327
Kenrick, D. T., 324, 326, 345, 359
Kessler, R. C., 176, 199
Kessler, R. D., 175, 182, 199
Kiesler, C. A., 331, 329, 354, 362
Kihlstrom, J. F., 13, 48, 124-125, 129, 140, 148, 149, 178, 199, 203, 221, 222, 224, 225
King, G. A., 144, 148

King, L. A., 60, 76, 82, 88, 91, 92, 93, 94, 95, 97, 124, 140, 147, 234, 240, 241, 248
Kirschenaum, D. S., 107, 108, 118, 119
Kirschner, P., 329, 331, 359
Kirson, D., 34, 51
Kitayama, S., 221, 226
Klatzky, R. L., 144, 148
Klein, D. J., 36, 52, 337, 338, 339, 351, 357, 362
Klein, R., 42, 49, 126, 148, 192, 196, 198, 199
Klein, S. B., 125, 129, 148, 263, 274
Kling, K. C., 166, 172
Klinger, E., 13, 17, 37, 38, 39, 50, 54, 60, 76, 79, 86, 97, 252, 273
Knerr, C. S., 100, 107, 119
Knight, J., 129, 149
Koestner, R., 218, 227
Kohn, A., 216, 225
Kopp, D. A., 281, 300
Kovacs, M., 195, 199
Kramer, G. P., 305, 326
Krapp, A., 216, 226
Kruglanski, A. W., 205, 221, 225, 226
Krull, D. S., 264, 273
Kuhl, J., 39, 48, 50
Kuhn, M. H., 167, 172
Kuiper, N. A., 152, 172
Kukla, A., 37, 50
Kumpf, M., 339, 362
Kuyken, W., 186, 193, 199
Kuykendall, D., 305, 327, 337, 340, 346, 352, 360

L

La Voie, L., 39, 48
LaFevre, J., 74, 75
Laird, J. D., 306, 327
Lamon, M., 364, 392
Lang, P. J., 184, 199, 280, 300
Lane, R. D., 188, 199
Langston, C. A., 54, 65, 75, 204, 224
Lanzetta, J. T., 184, 199
LaPorte, R. E., 100, 119
Larocque, 375
Larsen, R. J., 46, 50, 261, 273, 304, 328
Laser, P. S., 74, 77, 367, 393
Latham, G. P., 100, 102, 103, 104, 107, 113, 118, 119, 120, 214, 226
Lawrence, J. W., 25, 46, 48, 50
Lazarus, R. S., 70, 76, 79, 97, 231, 250, 372, 391, 393
LeDoux, J. E., 179, 199, 373, 385, 391
LeFevre, J., 74, 75
Leggett, E. L., 24, 49, 203, 224
Lensky, D. B., 234, 249
Leone, C., 128, 150
Lepper, M. R., 216, 226
Levenbeck, S., 257, 273
Leventhal, H., 128, 129, 148, 184, 199, 221, 226, 280, 300
Levis, D. J., 229, 249
Levy, A., 257, 273
Lewin, K., 102, 119, 125, 148, 204, 207, 226
Lewinsohn, P. M., 193, 199
Liberman, A., 285, 300, 366, 390
Lin, N., 193, 199
Linville, P. W., 93, 97, 123, 124, 127, 129, 130, 131, 133, 134, 135, 144, 147, 148, 154, 172, 178, 191, 199
Little, B. R., 13, 51, 54, 76, 79, 82, 85, 94, 97
Litz, B. T., 185, 199
Liu, C., 219, 226
Liu, T. J., 130, 150
Liwag, M., 372, 393
Locke, E. A., 100, 102, 103, 104, 107, 113, 119, 214, 226
Loevinger, J., 188, 199
Loftus, E. F., 231, 248
Loftus, J., 129, 148
Lord, R. G., 30, 50
Lorenz, K. Z., 378, 391
Lorr, M., 167, 172
Lowe, M. G., 101, 119
Lowell, E., 214, 226
Lundy, R. M., 128, 148
Lyubomirsky, S., 62, 70, 76

M

Maccoby, E. E., 190, 200
MacDonald, M. R., 152, 172
Macht, M. L., 229, 249
Mack, D., 101, 118
MacKay, D. M., 13, 50
Mackie, D. M., 283, 300, 301, 304, 305, 307, 308, 309, 311, 312, 327, 328, 329, 340, 341, 342, 343, 346, 348, 352, 357, 360, 362
MacLean, P. D., 373, 375, 391
Maddi, S. R., 81, 97

AUTHOR INDEX   401

Madigan, R. J., 229, 249
Maffitt, K. H., 242
Maheswaran, D., 334, 359
Main, M., 376, 381, 391
Manderlink, G., 217, 225
Mandler, G., 60, 76
Manian, N., 190, 200
Mark, M. M., 282, 287, 289, 294, 300, 301, 304, 305, 306, 308, 327, 328, 343, 345, 362
Marken, R. S., 15, 50
Marks, T., 130, 147, 162, 172
Markus, H., 13, 43, 50, 125, 126, 129, 132, 144, 147, 149, 150
Markus, H. R., 126, 149, 221, 226
Marr, D., 375, 391
Marsh, H. W., 155, 172
Marshall-Goodell, B. S., 332, 354, 358
Martin, J. A., 190, 200
Martin, L. L., 37, 38, 50, 55, 59, 61, 66, 67, 69, 70, 76, 84, 98, 108, 119, 223, 226, 279, 284, 286, 288, 289, 290, 292, 293, 295, 297, 300, 301, 310, 311, 314, 315, 316, 317, 318, 319, 323, 325, 327, 346, 360, 364, 366, 391, 393
Martin, M., 371, 391
Maruyama, M., 19, 50
Maser, J. D., 176, 197
Mathews, A., 384, 391
Mathur, M., 334, 360
Matt, G. E., 229, 249
Maxeiner, M. E., 60, 76
Mayer, J. D., 36, 50, 229, 230, 248, 249, 335, 356, 360, 361
Mayo, C. W., 128, 149
Mayol, A., 130, 147, 162, 172
McAdams, D. P., 89, 97, 231, 233, 234, 235, 236, 248, 249
McCaleb, V. M., 103, 119
McCauley, C. R., 375, 377, 392
McClelland, D. C., 214, 226
McCrae, R. R., 221, 224
McDonald, H. E., 317, 324, 326
McFall, R. M., 107, 108, 118, 120
McGuire, C. V., 355, 360
McGuire, W. J., 355, 360
McIntosh, W. D., 60, 61, 66, 69, 70, 76, 77, 108, 119
McKinney, W. T., 176, 197
McKinney, W. T. Jr., 180, 195, 201
McNair, D. M., 167, 172
Means, B., 304, 305, 313, 327

Mednick, E. V., 304, 327
Mednick, M. T., 304, 327
Mednick, S. A., 304, 327
Meece, J. L., 221, 226
Meehl, P. E., 92, 98
Melton, R. J., 304, 317, 324, 326, 327
Mendelson, M., 155, 171
Mertz, E., 289, 300, 304, 327
Metalsky, G. I., 164, 171, 172, 176, 197
Meyerowitz, B. E., 336, 360
Milberg, S., 263, 273
Millar, K. U., 38, 39, 50, 61, 70, 76
Millar, M. D., 128, 149
Millar, M. G., 38, 39, 50, 61, 70, 76, 205, 226
Miller, C. C., 15, 51
Miller, G. A., 13, 51, 203, 226
Miller, H. E., 103, 120
Miller, L., 344, 360
Miller, N. E., 345, 347, 358, 360, 378, 390
Mineka, S., 184, 200
Mischel, W., 203, 226, 229, 249, 250
Mita, T. H., 129, 149
Mitchell, T. R., 102, 103, 113, 118, 119
Mock, J., 155, 171
Moffitt, K. H., 231, 234, 239, 240, 241, 249, 250
Mongrain, M., 189, 201
Moore, R. G., 234, 243, 249
Mordkoff, J. T., 124, 132, 140, 149
Morgan, C., 205, 209, 218, 221, 222, 226, 227
Morris, W. N., 261, 273
Morrow, J., 68, 70, 77
Moylan, S., 36, 49, 335, 359
Mullis, J., 61, 75
Murphy, M. D., 102, 118
Murray, H. A., 214, 221, 226, 237, 249
Murray, M., 347, 360
Murray, N., 205, 226, 304, 312, 313, 315, 316, 317, 318, 328

N

Nagy, S., 269, 273
Nasby, W., 306, 328
Natale, M., 229, 249
Nath, R., 100, 119
Neale, J. M., 61, 68, 77
Neale, M. C., 175, 176, 182, 199
Nebergall, R., 336, 362
Nebes, R. D., 238, 249

Neisser, U., 252, 273
Nelligan, D. W., 234, 249
Nelson, T. D., 259, 273
Nicholls, J. G., 82, 98, 203, 226
Niedenthal, P. M., 54, 75, 93, 98, 124, 129, 132, 133, 135, 136, 137, 139, 140, 147, 149, 204, 224
Nisbett, R. E., 74, 77, 179, 200, 367, 391
Nisker, W., 59, 77
Nolen-Hoeksema, S., 59, 60, 61, 62, 68, 70, 72, 76, 77, 272, 274
Norborg, J., 344, 360
Norcross, J. C., 69, 75
Norem, J. K., 54, 65, 75, 204, 224
Norman, D. A., 14, 17, 51
Nowicki, G. P., 304, 305, 327, 386, 390
Nowlis, V., 252, 274
Nurius, P., 13, 43, 50, 125, 126, 129, 132, 147, 149
Nuttin, J. R., 125, 149

O

O'Connor, C., 34, 51
O'Neal, E. C., 256, 274
O'Sullivan, M., 378, 390
Oakhill, J. V., 386, 391
Oatley, K., 12, 51, 79, 98, 181, 200, 363, 365, 367, 368, 369, 370, 371, 374, 375, 376, 379, 382, 383, 384, 385, 390, 391, 392
Ogilvie, D. M., 19, 51, 233, 249
Ohman, A., 184, 198
Okonogi, K., 388, 393
Olshavsky, R. W., 124, 140, 147
Omodei, M. M., 55, 77, 79, 98
Ordman, A. M., 107, 108, 119
Orr, S. P., 184, 199
Ortony, A., 12, 34, 51, 79, 98, 237, 249, 281, 284, 299, 300, 368, 370, 392
Osborne, S., 344, 360
Osgood, D. W., 129, 133, 149
Otto, J., 269, 274
Oyserman, D., 126, 132, 149

P

Palmer, S., 221, 222, 227
Palys, T. S., 13, 51
Panksepp, J., 200, 373, 392
Paris, S. G., 218, 226
Parkhurst, J. T., 209, 224

Parrott, W. G., 229, 230, 249, 262, 267, 274, 308, 328, 356, 360, 364, 390
Partland, T., 167, 172
Patrick, R., 304, 305, 327
Pavot, W. G., 58, 59, 63, 75
Pelham, B. W., 130, 149, 152, 155, 159, 172, 264, 273
Penksepp, J., 179, 200
Pennebaker, J. W., 70, 77, 85, 98
Perring, C., 383, 392
Pervin, L. A., 13, 51, 79, 98, 204, 226
Peterson, C., 129, 133, 149, 164, 172
Peterson, L. M., 36, 48
Pettit, G. S., 382, 390
Petty, R. E., 36, 52, 232, 301, 324, 326, 328, 329, 330, 331, 332, 336, 332, 333, 334, 335, 336, 337, 338, 339, 340, 343-344, 345, 346, 347, 349, 350, 351, 352, 353, 354, 355, 356, 357, 358, 359, 360, 361, 362
Piaget, J., 187, 200
Pieters, R. G. M., 335, 361
Pilkington, C. J., 60, 77
Pilkonis, P. A., 329, 331, 354, 362
Polivy, J., 101, 106, 108, 119
Pope, L. K., 231, 250, 372, 393
Post, R. M., 180, 195, 200
Power, M. J., 384, 392
Powers, W. T., 13, 14, 15, 16, 51, 80, 84, 98
Pratkanis, A. R., 129, 147
Pratto, F., 28, 51
Presson, C. C., 124, 140, 147
Pretty, G. H., 315, 328
Pribram, K. H., 13, 51, 203, 226
Priester, J. R., 331, 361
Pritchard, R. D., 103, 119
Pusecker, P. A., 287, 300
Putnam, F. W., 195, 200
Pyszczynski, T., 38, 39, 51, 60, 62, 77

R

Rachlin, H., 344, 361
Rachmiel, T. B., 61, 68, 77
Razran, G. H. S., 329, 331, 361
Read, S. J., 15, 51
Reason, J., 388, 392
Reed, M. A., 177, 184, 198
Regier, D. A., 175, 200
Reilly, N. P., 261, 273
Reisenzein, R., 368, 371, 374, 375, 392

AUTHOR INDEX 403

Reitzes, D. C., 140, 147
Renninger, K. A., 216, 226
Reznick, J. S., 184, 199
Rhine, R., 354, 361
Rholes, W. S., 187, 200
Rice, L. N., 11, 49
Rich, T., 221, 222, 227
Richman, S. A., 332, 333, 334, 335, 337, 347, 349, 354, 357, 361, 362
Ricks, D. F., 251, 274
Roberts, B. W., 93, 96, 140, 147
Robins, R. W., 93, 96, 140, 147
Robinson, J. A., 238, 249
Robinson, G. F., 289, 300, 304, 327
Rogers, C. R., 41, 51, 191, 200
Romanski, L. R., 373, 391
Romero, R. D., 39, 49
Roney, C. J. R., 207, 225
Roper, D. W., 159, 173, 255, 263, 266, 274
Roseman, I. J., 34, 51, 79, 98, 237, 249, 372, 392
Rosen, S., 256, 274
Rosenbaum, D. A., 13, 15, 51
Rosenbaum, M., 193, 199, 221, 226
Rosenberg, M., 151, 155, 172
Rosenberg, S. F., 107, 120
Rosenhan, D. L., 356, 361
Ross, B. M., 231, 249
Ross, J., 263, 273
Ross, L., 367, 391
Rosselli, F., 283, 300, 309, 311, 327, 329, 340, 343, 360
Rosswork, S. G., 100, 119
Rothkopf, E. Z., 100, 102, 120
Rozin, P., 375, 377, 392
Rubin, D. C., 238, 249
Ruble, D. N., 187, 200, 203, 227
Rush, A. J., 164, 171, 195, 197
Russell, M., 306, 328
Russell, J. A., 34, 49, 368, 392
Rutter, M., 381, 392
Ruvolo, A. P., 125, 126, 149
Ryan, R. M., 56, 76, 82, 90, 95, 96, 98, 207, 218, 224, 227
Ryff, C. D., 152, 160, 172

S

Saari, L. M., 103, 119
Saari, L. J., 100, 102, 104, 107, 119
Saavedra, R., 205, 227
Sabini, J., 229, 230, 249, 267, 274, 308, 328

Sachau, D. A., 211, 227
Safran, J. D., 384, 390
Sales, S. M., 100, 120
Salmoni, A. W., 13, 51
Salovey, P., 34, 35, 50, 86, 95, 98, 130, 149, 229, 230, 231, 233, 237, 243, 244, 248, 249, 250, 356, 361, 376, 384, 393
Saltz, E., 126, 149
Saltzberg, J. A., 61, 68, 77, 130, 150, 255, 275
Sandvik, E., 59, 63, 75
Sanna, L. J., 287, 300
Sansone, C., 203, 205, 206, 207, 209, 211, 215, 217, 218, 221, 222, 225, 227
Schoenpflug, W., 40, 51
Schachter, S., 256, 274
Schaeken, W., 376, 391
Schaller, M., 345, 361
Schaumann, L., 281, 300
Scheier, M. F., 11, 12, 16, 19, 20, 25, 27, 28, 31, 34, 36, 37, 38, 39, 44, 45, 46, 47, 48, 49, 50, 55, 57, 58, 60, 73, 75, 77, 80, 84, 85, 96, 114, 118, 177, 191, 197, 204, 224, 242, 248, 257, 272, 281, 300, 365, 389
Scherer, K. R., 367, 369, 392
Schiff, B. B., 364, 392
Schmidt, R. A., 13, 51
Schneider, D. J., 73, 77, 107, 120
Scholnick, E. K., 203, 227
Schrauger, J. S., 107, 120
Schumann, D., 332, 333, 334, 335, 337, 347, 349, 354, 357, 361
Schunk, D. H., 203, 214, 224, 227
Schutz, A., 125, 149
Schwartz, G. E., 188, 199
Schwartz, J., 34, 51
Schwarz, N., 69, 77, 89, 98, 252, 274, 280, 281, 282, 284, 287, 299, 300, 301, 305, 306, 308, 309, 310, 311, 314, 325, 326, 328, 329, 330, 332, 339, 340, 341, 342, 343, 346, 348, 352, 357, 358, 361, 362
Schweiger, D. M., 103, 119
Scott, W. A., 128, 129, 133, 149
Scott, J., 234, 243, 250
Scott, W. D., 281, 300
Sears, P. S., 102, 119
Sedikides, C., 162, 172
Segal, Z. V., 152, 172, 175, 194, 200
Seligman, C., 315, 328
Seligman, M. E. P., 164, 171, 172
Selye, H., 221, 227

Semmel, A., 164, 172
Servan-Schreiber, D., 39, 49
Servay, W., 339, 362
Setterlund, M. B., 124, 133, 135, 136, 137, 139, 140, 141, 142, 143, 144, 149
Severance, L., 354, 361
Sewell, A., 382, 390
Shaefer, C., 70, 76
Shaffer, D. R., 324, 326
Shafir, E., 376, 392
Shalker, T. E., 306, 327, 329, 334, 342, 359
Shallice, T., 17, 51
Shantz, C. U., 187, 200
Shapiro, D., 189, 200
Shaver, P., 34, 51, 374, 375, 377, 381, 390, 392
Shavitt, S., 67, 76
Shaw, B. F., 152, 164, 171, 172, 195, 197
Shaw, K. N., 100, 102, 103, 104, 107, 119
Shea, T., 176, 197
Sheldon, K. M., 90, 92, 93, 94, 95, 97, 98
Sherif, C., 336, 362
Sherif, M., 336, 362
Sherman, J., 129, 148
Sherman, S. J., 124, 126, 140, 147, 150
Shimp, T. A., 332, 362
Showers, C., 130, 150, 152, 153, 154, 155, 157, 160, 166, 172, 230, 250, 304, 328
Sieber, S. D., 131, 150
Sieck, W. A., 107, 108, 120
Silver, R. C., 59, 75, 77
Silver, R. L., 59, 77
Simon, H. A., 39, 40, 52, 363, 393
Simon, K., 100, 102, 104, 106, 108, 118
Sinclair, R. C., 282, 289, 294, 301, 304, 305, 306, 308, 312, 327, 328, 343, 345, 362
Singer, J. A., 86, 94, 95, 98, 114, 229, 231, 233, 234, 237, 239, 240, 241, 243, 244, 248, 249, 250, 376, 384, 393
Singer, J. E., 256, 274
Singer, J. L., 132, 150
Sinnett, L. M., 304, 328
Sisco, C., 188, 201
Sloman, A., 40, 52
Smith, C. A., 231, 250, 372, 393
Smith, M. A., 382, 391
Smith, S. M., 346, 347, 349, 350, 352, 353, 357, 362
Snidman, N., 184, 199
Snyder, C. R., 16, 52
Snyder, M., 229, 250

Solomon, R. L., 30, 31, 52
Sorrentino, R. M., 177, 200
Spear, N. E., 229, 249
Spence, D. P., 231, 250
Spence, J. T., 221, 227
Spence, K. W., 264, 274
Spencer, J. A., 101, 120
Spielman, L. A., 152, 173
Spindel, M. S., 237, 249
Sroufe, L. A., 178, 200
Srull, T. K., 24, 52, 144, 150, 332, 362
Stayman, D. M., 305, 326, 333, 358
Steele, C. M., 16, 52, 130, 131, 150
Stein, N. L., 372, 393
Steinmetz, J. E., 182, 200
Steller, B., 257, 273
Stepper, S., 295, 301, 364, 393
Steptoe, A., 269, 274
Stern, D., 377, 393
Stiller, J. 218, 227
Stone, A. A., 61, 68, 77
Stone, J. I., 74, 77, 367, 393
Stoner, P., 290, 295, 300
Strack, F., 252, 274, 280, 287, 295, 299, 301, 305, 308, 326, 340, 342, 352, 357, 358, 364, 393
Strathman, A. J., 332, 333, 334, 335, 337, 347, 349, 354, 357, 361
Strauman, T., 42, 49, 52, 126, 132, 148, 178, 179, 185, 188, 189, 150, 190, 192, 193, 196, 197, 198, 199, 200, 201, 204, 227
Stringer, C., 378, 393
Stroessner, S. J., 304, 305, 308, 328
Stuart, E. W., 332, 362
Stucky, R. J., 16, 52
Suedfeld, P., 219, 227
Sujan, H., 205, 226, 304, 312, 313, 315, 316, 317, 318, 328
Sujan, M., 205, 226, 304, 312, 313, 315, 316, 317, 318, 328, 347, 360
Sullivan, G. D., 375, 392
Sutterland, M., 93, 98
Swann, W. B., Jr., 130, 149, 152, 155, 172
Swartz, T. S., 79, 98
Swinkels, A., 355, 357, 359
Szegda, M., 306, 327

T

Tait, R., 59, 77
Tassinary, L. G., 332, 354, 358

AUTHOR INDEX   405

Taylor, R., 229, 250
Taylor, S. E., 16, 28, 52, 101, 104-105, 120, 144, 150, 162, 171, 253, 262, 271, 274
Taylor, S. L., 256, 274
Teasdale, J. D., 164, 171, 195, 201, 229, 250, 306, 328
Tellegen, A., 46, 52
Terborg, J. R., 100, 103, 120
Tesser, A., 16, 34, 38, 39, 50, 52, 55, 59, 60, 61, 66, 67, 70, 76, 77, 84, 98, 108, 119, 128, 130, 149, 150, 205, 226, 230, 248, 255, 256, 264, 265, 269, 270, 273, 274, 376, 393
Therriault, N., 269, 273
Thoits, P. A., 131, 150, 193, 201
Tice, D. M., 204, 224
Tomarken, A. J., 107, 108, 119, 184, 199, 221, 226
Tomkins, S. S., 34, 52, 236, 250
Tooby, J., 373, 393
Tota, M. E., 152, 171
Trabasso, T., 372, 393
Trafton, R. G., 129, 148
Traue, H. C., 85, 98
Travis, C. C., 19, 49
Trope, Y., 214, 227
Tucker, D. M., 182, 183, 185, 198, 201
Turley, K. J., 287, 300
Turner, T. J., 368, 392
Tversky, A., 36, 50, 105, 114, 115, 118, 309, 315, 327, 335, 359, 376, 392

U

Uhde, T. W., 195, 200

V

Vallacher, R. R., 13, 14, 16, 17, 52, 84, 98, 210, 227
Valles, C. G., 74, 77
Van Hook, E., 18, 32, 52, 126, 148, 152, 172
Vasquez, C., 229, 249
Veenhoven, R., 315, 326
Velten, E., Jr., 162, 173
Vincent, J., 345, 359
Voisard, B., 215, 227
Vyse, S. A., 234, 249

W

Waddell, B. A., 229, 248
Wageman, R., 317, 326
Wagener, J., 306, 327
Wall, S., 381, 389
Walter, C. B., 13, 51
Walters, E., 381, 389
Waranch, E., 256, 274
Ward, C. H., 155, 171
Ward, D. W., 37, 50, 223, 226, 279, 284, 286, 288, 289, 292, 297, 295, 300, 310, 311, 314, 315, 316, 317, 318, 319, 323, 325, 327, 346, 360, 366, 391
Warren, R., 67, 77
Watson, D., 46, 52, 68, 72, 77
Watson, E., 269, 274
Watters, R. G., 106, 118
Watts, F. N., 234, 243, 249
Wearing, A. J., 55, 77, 79, 98
Wegener, D. T., 36, 52, 232, 301, 324, 326, 328, 329, 331, 335, 336, 337, 338, 339, 343-344, 345, 346, 347, 349, 350, 351, 352, 353, 355, 356, 357, 361, 362
Wegner, D. M., 13, 14, 16, 17, 52, 73, 77, 84, 98, 107, 120, 159, 173, 210, 227, 229, 230, 255, 258, 262, 263, 266, 273, 274
Weiner, B., 237, 250
Weintraub, J. K., 73, 75
Weir, C., 211, 218, 221, 222, 227
Weissman, A., 160, 173
Wells, G. L., 340, 354, 361
Wenzlaff, R. M., 159, 173, 230, 250, 274, 255, 263, 266, 274
Werner, H., 93, 98, 187, 201
Wessman, A. E., 251, 274
Westen, D., 182, 201
Wetzler, S. E., 238, 249
Wherry, M. B., 93, 98, 133, 135, 136, 137, 139, 149
White, P., 229, 250
White, R. W., 207, 222, 227
White, T. L., 73, 77, 89, 96, 107, 120
Whybrow, P. C., 180, 195, 201
Wicklund, R. A., 18, 52, 60, 62, 77, 264, 274
Wiebe, D. J., 221, 222, 227
Wiener, B., 372, 393
Wiest, C., 79, 98
Wiggins, E. C., 334, 357, 358
Williams, J. M. G., 234, 243, 249, 250
Williams, P. G., 222, 227

Wills, T. A., 193, 197
Wilson, T. D., 74, 77, 179, 200, 367, 393
Wilson, G. T., 108, 118
Winokur, G., 176, 197
Withey, S. B., 63, 74
Wolff, P. L., 324, 326
Wood, J. V., 61, 68, 77, 130, 150, 255, 275
Woodworth, R. S., 222, 228
Worth, A. M., 283, 301
Worth, L. T., 283, 300, 305, 307, 312, 327, 328, 329, 340, 341, 342, 343, 346, 348, 352, 357, 360, 362
Wortman, C. B., 37, 52, 59, 75, 77
Wright, J., 229, 250
Wurf, E., 125, 126, 129, 149, 150
Wyer, R. S., Jr., 24, 37, 50, 52, 144, 150, 223, 226, 279, 281, 284, 286, 288, 295, 300, 301, 310, 311, 314, 315, 316, 317, 318, 319, 323, 325, 327, 346, 360, 366, 391

X

Xagoraris, A., 373, 391

Y

Yalom, I., 80, 81, 98
Yando, R., 306, 328
Yanomoto, J., 388, 393
Yarmey, A. D., 129, 150
Yetim, U., 95, 98
Yoshimura, S., 388, 393
Younger, J. C., 101, 119
Yukl, G. A., 100, 102, 103, 113, 119, 120

Z

Zajonc, R. B., 128, 150
Zanakos, S., 229, 230, 250, 262, 266, 274
Zanna, M. P., 329, 331, 354, 362
Zehner, K. S., 126, 150
Zeiss, A., 229, 249
Zevon, M. A., 46, 52
Zillmann, D., 255, 275
Zimmerman, B. J., 218, 228
Zirkel, 65, 75
Zuckerman, M., 183, 201
Zuroff, D. C., 189, 201

Subject Index

A

Affect
  definition of, 252
  and disengagement from goals, 37-39
  as a motivator of goal-direct effort, 28-29, 211-217
  and reprioritization of goals, 39-42, 363
Affect and performance
  amount of processing, 285-288
  categorization, 289
  context dependent, 284-285, 310-312
  context invariant, 294-296, 303-306
  creativity, 289-292
  effects of, on persuasion
    low elaboration effects, 331-333, 354-355
    moderate elaboration effects, 344-353, 356-357
    high elaboration effects, 333-339
  evaluation, 292-294
  matching goal and task, 211-217
  models
    capacity, 283, 341-343, 348
    cognitive tuning, 281-283, 308-310, 342-343, 348
    hedonic contingency, 297-298, 344-345
    mood as input, 284-294, 310-312
    priming, 296-297, 306-308
    syndrome, 279-280
  task interest, 211-217, 320-321
Awareness
  of causes of emotions, 367, 369-370, 373
  emotion as a nonpropositional brain signal, 364-373
  irrationality, 388

C

Control systems, 13-14, 18-20, 57-58
  and affect, 21-24, 33-35, 59-61

E

Emotions (*see also* Affect, Affect and performance)
  basic emotions, 365, 369, 374-375
  and goal progress, 365-366
  and mental models, 376-378, 381
  and psychopathology, 381-384
  vicarious emotions, 384-386
  vs. intellect, 86-388

G

Goals
  approach vs. avoidance, 43-45, 86-91, 104-108, 238-247
  avoidance and distress, 89-91
  conflict and emotion, 32, 91-92, 370-372,

378–379
    hierarchies, 14–18, 55–58, 62–68
    purpose vs. target, 207
Goals and performance
    persuasion and framing, 337–339
    proximity and framing, 110–114
    "what the hell" effect, 101–102

H

Happiness (*see* Subjective well-being)
Hedonism (*see* Mood regulation)

I

Individual differences
    achievement orientation, 214–217
    goal orientations, 82
    linking, 58–73
    optimism, 36–37
    personal strivings, 80

M

Memory
    and avoidance goals, 238–247
    life stories, 233–236
    self-defining, 233
        as information about goals, 233
        role in producing affect, 237–239
    and self-regulation motivation, 230–231, 243–247
Mood effects (*see* Affect and performance)
Mood regulation (*see also* Self-regulation)
    and hedonism,
        alternative to, 255–256
        problems with, 254–255
    and interaction goals, 257–259
    and memory, 243–247
    and message processing, 344–353, 356–357
    strategies of, 262–260
    and task performance, 259–261
Motivations to attain goals
    determinants of, 209–210
    process-derived vs. outcome-derived, 204–205

role of affect, 205, 211–217, 320–321
task involvement, 208, 221–222, 320–321

R

Rumination
    goal nonattainment, 54, 61–62
    negative affect, 59–61, 68
    unhappiness, 64, 68

S

Self-complexity
    and affective reactivity, 130–132
    comparmentalization
        affective consequences, 153
        positive vs. negative, 153–154
        vs. evaluatively integrated, 153
    and decision making, 140–144
    and depression, 154–157
    and feedback about current concerns, 132–133
    and feedback about future concerns, 135–138
    malleability of, 144–146
    and self-esteem, 154–157
    tenses of the self, 125–126
Self-evaluation
    and affect
        self-discrepancies, 191–193
        stressful life events, 193–194
    connection to emotion, 178–179
    and depression, 194–196
    development of, 177–178
    and pathways to depression, 180–186
Self-regulation
    and affective state, 218–220
    and intrinsic motivation, 221–222
    and mood repair, 163–170
    and self-organization, 157–163
Self-representations
    development of, 186–189
    and parenting styles, 189–190
Subjective well-being
    goal conflict, 91–92
    goal differentiation, 93–94
    goal hierarchies, 62–71
    level of goal specification, 82–85